W9-BLP-593

Adult Literacy Perspectives

Adult
Literacy
Perspectives

Maurice C. Taylor
James A. Draper
Editors

Krieger Publishing Company
Malabar, Florida
1994

Original Edition 1989
First U.S. Printing 1994

Printed and Published by
KRIEGER PUBLISHING COMPANY
KRIEGER DRIVE
MALABAR, FLORIDA 32950

FROM A DECLARATION OF PRINCIPLES JOINTLY ADOPTED BY A COMMITTEE
OF THE AMERICAN BAR ASSOCIATION AND A COMMITTEE OF PUBLISHERS:

This publication is designed to provide accurate and authoritative information in regard to the
subject matter covered. It is sold with the understanding that the publisher is not engaged in
rendering legal, accounting, or other professional service. If legal advice or other expert
assistance is required, the services of a competent professional person should be sought.

Library of Congress Cataloging-In-Publication Data
Adult literacy perspectives / edited by Maurice C. Taylor and James A.
  Draper.
      p.   cm.
    Includes bibliographical references (p.   ) and index.
    ISBN 0-89464-858-6 (U.S.)   ISBN 0-921472-04-8 (Canada)
    1. Adult education--Canada. 2. Literacy--Canada. 3. Basic
education--Canada. 4. Adult education. I. Taylor, Maurice C.
(Maurice Charles), 1952-   . II. Draper, James A., 1930-
LC5254.A38 1994
374'.012'0971--dc20   93-31840
                                                 CIP

10   9   8   7   6   5   4   3   2

TABLE OF CONTENTS

Maurice C. Taylor
James A. Draper
editors

I

Page

Page

INTRODUCTION

As a field of practice and disciplined inquiry, adult basic education (ABE) has a rich and varied tradition. Over the past twenty-five years it has emerged as a distinct area within education providing important innovations and substantial resources. However, the parameters of both theory and practice are often unclear for those working in ABE.

There is difficulty in defining literacy or adult basic education, and this may speak more to the diversities of theory and practice and their many interpretations – often specific to the locale or the individual involved – than to any lack of knowledge or skill. In this book, the editors have tried to capture something of the richness of this diversity, the divergence of theories and practices, as well as their political and economic contexts in daily life. To accomplish this, they invited a wide range of scholars, practitioners and analysts to share their expertise. Their writing styles are as diverse as their specialities, and the editors have sought to preserve their distinct voices rather than opt for some kind of conformity in style and presentation. This makes for rich and varied reading, the kind of reading that one will return to again and again. The difficulty in defining and the expressed diversity of expertise and style must be seen as a positive expression of the individuality and the dynamism of the field and the people working within it.

ADULT LITERACY PERSPECTIVES does not purport to represent all current views or practices, but does seek to capture a 'moment in time' of this field of literacy and adult basic skills, to be used as a stepping stone for future directions. The reader may well be mulling over some questions like: What seems to be working best in what situations? Are there some practices that should be discarded? Can we assemble some universal essential characteristics of this work – or should we be more concerned with localizing and individualizing the practices?

The reader's attention should be drawn to the two broadly-drawn viewpoints that are expressed in varying ways by both practitioners and researchers: the quantitative, accountable and technological approach to teaching literacy and basic skills education, versus the qualitative, learner-evaluated humanistic approach. These are also referred to as 'teacher-centred approaches' and 'learner-centred approaches'. These two approaches are frequently juxtaposed within the same section, sometimes contradicting each other, although the writers may never have met – or known what the other was submitting for this book. Like the field itself, controversy, viewpoints and discussions are vibrant and provocative. But the fact that the authors present strong arguments provides the reader with anything but passively acceptable viewpoints!

Given that the individual contributors have grounded their writing in day-to-day experience as well as (frequently) a survey of related litera-ture, we have here, then, a fine distillation of expertise across most of the aspects of literacy. The contributors are known in this field and related fields in education, and their intensity and committment shines through this work.

If each of us, as careful readers examining what is particularly relevant for ourselves, closely examine these 'distillations of experience', we may discover that what emerges may be important indicators for practical and effective directions for the future in literacy and basic skills education both in research and in teaching as well as in policy.

This book is particularly addressed to three groups. First, it can provide an introductory statement and resource for graduate students in adult education, especially those in adult basic education. Secondly, it can provide an overview of the field for professionals in related areas such as teachers, administrators, counsellors, facilitators, tutors and volunteers in school boards, community colleges, CGEPS (Quebec), universities, and research institutes as well as small learning centres. Finally, it can provide a source of information for those who value being informed generally about a variety of topics and issues in adult basic education.

This book proposes to define the field, at least in its evolution, its contribution to professional education and the principle problems and issues. It is an attempt to delineate the parameters of inquiry and practice and is intended to serve as a professional reference work. It does not attempt to describe the scores of agencies in detail involved in the delivery of programs as they are covered in other publications.

ACKNOWLEDGEMENTS

Our acknowledgements and thanks go to the superior work of the individual authors who laboured so diligently and patiently (often through many re-writes) to turn out this volume. We also express gratitude to Jamie Riddell, director of the Adult Basic Education Department and Bill Conrod, vice president of Continuing Education, Algonquin College of Applied Arts and Technology (Ottawa, Canada) for their support and encouragment in the pursuit of knowledge to improve adult instruction.

Special appreciation and acknowledgement to the National Literacy Secretariat, Department of the Secretary of State of Canada for their encouragement and their generous financial assistance for the publication of this book and to the Ontario Ministry of Skills Development for their support and assistance.

In keeping with its tradition since incorporation in 1955, to facilitate literacy work in many developing countries as well as in Canada, World Literacy of Canada has been a staunch and continual supporter of the publication and distribution of this book and we are most grateful.

Our sincerest thanks as well to the Department of Adult Education, Ontario Institute for Studies in Education.

Maurice C. Taylor
James A. Draper

THE CONTRIBUTORS

THE EDITORS
Maurice C. Taylor is a Teaching Master at Algonquin College in the Adult Basic Education Department, and a Lecturer in adult education at the University of Ottawa, Educational Studies, Graduate Section. He received his B.A. degree (1974) from St. Patrick's College, Carleton University in psychology and sociology, his B.ED. degree (1977) from Queen's University, his M.ED. degree (1980) from the University of Ottawa in educational administration and his Ph.D. degree (1984) from the Ontario Institute for Studies in Education, University of Toronto in adult education. He also holds a diplôme de langue et lettres françaises (1975) from the Université d'Aix-en-Provence.

Taylor's main research activities have been in the fields of occupational literacy, locus of control, young adult identity formation and readability assessment. He has taught adults in basic orientation and college preparatory programs both in English and French and co-ordinated community and institutional literacy programs. He also has supervised teachers of adults and served as a consultant to literacy and basic education groups in both Canada and the United Kingdom. Taylor has initiated and managed several government grants and applied research projects in the area of basic skills training. Through committee membership he has provided policy development advice to national and provincial governments on adult learning and competency-based curriculum.

James A. Draper, Ph.D., since 1967, has been a faculty member in the department of adult education, Ontario Institute for Studies in Education (University of Toronto) and was recently cross-appointed to the University of Toronto Centre for South Asian Studies. It was in 1964, while a faculty member for two years at the University of Rajasthan, India, that he began to work in the area of adult literacy education. After undertaking a survey for the university, he co-authored a book *A Plan for the University of Rajasthan* which, among other things, outlined ways in which universities can support the work of literacy education. While in India, he became acquainted with various rural and urban adult literacy programs and agencies.

Since 1969 he has been associated with World Literacy of Canada, was president from 1973-78 and continues as a member of the Board of Directors of WLC. It was while he was president that WLC undertook the first national study of adult literacy/basic education in Canada. From activities following the release of this report at a national conference in 1976, arose the Movement for Canadian Literacy of which he is a founding member.

He chaired the Ministry of Labour (Government of Ontario) Task Force on Literacy and Occupational Health and Safety. The final report of the task force, *Policies and Priorities for Dealing with Literacy and Occupational Health and Safety,* was published in 1985. Under contract with the Ministry of Education he undertook a review of literature relating to adult literacy. This was later published as a book *Re-Thinking Adult Literacy* (published by World Literacy of Canada, 1986).

James has spoken on literacy in Canada, India, the Caribbean, Thailand, the United Kingdom and was a key speaker at a national literacy conference in Australia in 1985 as well as a resource person and speaker at a conference on literacy and community development organized by the University of New England in Australia. In 1987, he was on the planning committee for the international conference on Literacy in Industrialized Countries, held in Toronto. As a member of the graduate school, at the University of Toronto, he has supervised many masters and doctoral theses relating to adult literacy. He also teaches graduate courses relating to literacy and ABE. In 1986, on behalf of WLC, he presented a brief on literacy and international communication and national development to the Government of Canada's Special Joint Committee on Canada's International Relations. In 1972, he was nominated by UNESCO, Paris, for the position of director of the International Institute for Adult Literacy Methods in Iran.

Other publications relating to the topic which he has authored or co-authored include:

Towards an Adult Basic Education Model for Ontario Boards of Education, Toronto: Department of Adult Education, OISE, 1982.

"Preface", *Three Decades for Literacy and Development* (A History of World Literacy of Canada), Toronto: WLC, 1988.

"World Literacy of Canada", in *The Canadian Encyclopedia,* 1988.

"Literacy and Development: A Case Study of World Literacy of Canada", in *World Perspective on Adult Education: A Collection of Country Case Studies,* edited by Alan B. Knox, Madison, Wisconsin: University of Wisconsin, 1988.

Literacy Experience-Reflection by Canadian Educationists, a special issue of *Literacy Discussion,* Vol. V, No. 2, Summer, 1974.

"Universities and the Challenge of Illiteracy", *Indian Journal of Adult Education,* Vol. 48, No. 11, 1987.

Adult Basic and Literacy Education: Teaching and Support Programs Within Selected Colleges and Universities in Canada, Toronto: Department of Adult Education, OISE, 1980.

AND THE AUTHORS

Ethel Anderson is a Curriculum Co-ordinator at the Ontario Ministry of Education's Independent Learning Centre where she is responsible for developing distance education courses for adults who have limited formal schooling. Prior to joining the Ministry of Education, she was head of an adult basic education program in Toronto.

Eunice N. Askov, Ph.D., is a Professor of Education and Director of the Institute for the Study of Adult Literacy at Pennsylvania State University. The thrust of the Institute's efforts fall into: applications of technology to adult literacy, workplace literacy, inter-generational literacy, teacher training and special needs populations. She was the recipient of the Fulbright Senior Scholar's Award to the University of Western Australia to study the development of computer-based adult literacy courseware.

Thelma Barer-Stein, Ph.D., founder and president of Culture Concepts Inc. is an independent scholar and consultant specializing in cross-cultural understanding, learning and phenomenology. She has taught courses at the University of Western Ontario, University of Saskatchewan and the University of New Brunswick and lectured nationally and internationally including in India, Thailand, Hong Kong, United Kingdom and Australia. She was co-editor of *The Craft of Teaching Adults* and author of *You Eat What You Are: A Study of Ethnic Food Traditions.*

Paul Bélanger is the present director of the Institut de recherche appliquée sur le travail (IRAT) in Montréal. He was the director of the Institut canadien d'éducation des adultes (ICEA) from 1972 to 1984 and has been the North American vice-president of the International Council for Adult Education. Mr. Bélanger has published articles and books on adult education and life-long learning and has been active in the Canadian Commission for UNESCO.

Jill Bell is currently working on a Ph.D. in the Modern Language Centre, Ontario Institute for Studies in Education, Toronto. Her thesis research focuses on basic literacy learning and teaching for non-English speaking immigrants. Jill has formerly been involved in teaching and materials development in English as a Second Language in the workplace settings both in Canada and in Singapore.

Harlans Bhola, Ph.D., is Professor of Education, Indiana University at Bloomington, Indiana, where he holds joint appointments in the departments of instructional systems technology and educational leadership and policy studies in education. His research interests include international literacy and nonformal education, educational planning and policy analysis, and design and renewal of instructional systems at various levels.

Jenny Brown was formerly Hampshire County Co-ordinator for Adult Basic Education. She is now Organizing Tutor, Adult Basic Education for the County of Avon.

Barbara Burnaby, Ph.D., is currently working in the field of Adult Basic Education in the Department of Adult Education, Ontario Institute for Studies in Education, Toronto. Her work has been divided between research and materials development in English as a Second Language (ESL) for adult immigrants as well as ESL and Native language learning for Native people. She is the Past-President of TESL Canada, the national English as Second Language Association.

Lynn Burton is currently Senior Advisor to the Prime Minister's National Advisory Board on Science and Technology and is completing her doctorate in adult education at Columbia University. Lynn directed the major sector skill development leave work that produced *Learning a Living in Canada* and *Learning for Life* for the federal Minister of Employment and Immigration in 1984. She has served on the Boards of the Canadian Association for Adult Education, the Canadian Association for the Study of Adult Education, the Education Sub-Committee for the Canadian Commission for UNESCO, Countdown 2001, and the Centre for Human Resource Development and Assessment Centres in Shanghai, China.

Sharon E. Cameron is a Teaching Master and Life Skills Coach in the Adult Basic Education Department of Algonquin College. Target populations she has taught include job readiness training for employment disadvantaged adults and youth, groups for physically and developmentally delayed handicapped adults and psychiatrically disabled clients. She has served as Department Co-ordinator and President of the Association of Life Skills Coaches of Ontario. Sharon holds a Master's degree in Psychiatric Rehabilitation Counselling from Boston University.

Kathryn Chang is currently the Assistant Director of Community Education at Medicine Hat College in Medicine Hat, Alberta. She is also President of the Alberta Association for Adult Literacy. Kathryn has several year's experience in the field of adult literacy and basic education and is pursuing a doctoral degree in educational administration at the University of Alberta.

Elaine Chapline, Ph.D., is a licensed psychologist in New York and a Professor of Education at Queens College of the City University of New York. She is currently Chair of the Department of Elementary and Early Childhood Education. Elaine continues to be interested in the role of affective factors in learning.

Alan Clarke is an Ottawa based community development specialist serving as an Advisor to the International Joint Commission. He has held senior administrative positions with the Canadian Citizenship Council, The Centre for Community Development, The Futures

Secretariat and also served as an Advisor to the Canadian Emergency Co-ordinator for the African Famine. Alan is a founding member of the Movement for Canadian Literacy and a member of the Board of Governors of Frontier College.

D. Stuart Conger is an Ottawa consultant, specializing in the area of counselling and guidance. He has served in the Canada Employment and Immigration Commission as Director General of employment support services. He has acted as Chairman and Executive Director of Saskatchewan NewStart and Director of the Training Research and Development Station in Prince Albert, Saskatchewan. Now retired, he is exploring the application of artificial intelligence and difficult counselling situations.

Gary Conti, Ph.D., is Associate Professor of Adult Education Research Conference, Montana State University, and is co-editor of *Adult Literacy and Basic Education*. Gary is a member of the Executive Board of the Commission on Adult Basic Education and has served on various research and award committees of national, regional and local adult education associations. His major research interests include teaching style and evaluation.

Richard Darville is a sociologist and adult educator who has worked in adult literacy and plain language for a dozen years — teaching, writing materials for learners and organizing within the movement for Canadian Literacy and the Vancouver Eastside Educational Enrichment Society. He is currently at the Centre for Policy Studies in Education at the University of British Columbia, researching the relations between management and popular conceptions of adult literacy, and their implications for policy and practice.

Robert Fellenz, Ed.D., is Research Professor and Acting Principle Investigator at the Kellogg Center for Adult Learning Research at Montana State University. He has extensive experience in designing, conducting and evaluating educational programs for adults especially teacher training and adult literacy programs. He has served as an international consultant, and is co-editor of *Adult Literacy and Basic Education*. Robert currently serves on the board of the Commission on Adult Basic Education.

Elaine Gabor-Katz is a community educator with experience in adult literacy, school community relations and cross-cultural communication. She is a feminist research writer with an interest in policy and organizational development. She has more than ten years of volunteer experience in literacy networking organizations at the local, provincial, national and international levels, and is a strong supporter of community-based literacy. Elaine is currently completing a Master's degree in education at Ontario Institute for Studies in Education, The University of Toronto.

Carolyn Gaskin currently works for the London Board of Education. Her primary interests lie in Human Resource Development with a particular concentration on how women managers acquire their leadership skills. She is a graduate of the University of Windsor in Sociology.

Arthur Gillette was a Programme Specialist in the UNESCO Literacy Section. He holds a B.A. Magna Cum Laude from Harvard College in French Literature and a Ed.D. from the University of Massachusetts in Comparative Education. He has written numerous articles and books on Education in Cuba, Tanzania and other developing countries, and has been involved in the planning, programming and evaluation of literacy and other informal educational activities in Asia, Africa and Latin America. He is currently the editor of the UNESCO *Quarterly Museum Magazine.*

Jean-Paul Hautecoeur, Ph.D., is presently teaching at the University of Québec at Montréal after many years of graduate teaching in France. He is also Director General of Adult Education and Research at the Québec Ministry of Education. Since 1976 he has co-ordinated and developed different research projects published in ALPHA. Jean-Paul has also served as a committee member on both federal and provincial literacy research initiatives.

Jennifer Horsman, Ed.D., is a feminist literacy activist. She has recently completed a thesis on women and literacy and continues to write on these issues. She works freelance as a researcher, writer, editor and facilitator in the literacy movement.

Laurent Isabelle, Ph.D., is currently a psychologist in private practice. He has been a Professor in Educational Psychology at the University of Ottawa, President of Algonquin College of Applied Arts and Technology and Director of Education at the Correctional Service of Canada. Laurent's interests include self-directed and computer assisted learning for incarcerated adults, aptitude testing, personality inventories, career development and marital counselling.

Michèle Jean is currently Executive Director of the Employment Section, Canada Employment and Immigration Commission. She has served as Assistant Deputy Minister and General Director of Professional Development with the Ministry of Manpower and Income Security in Quebec and taught in several Canadian universities. Her major fields of interest include worker adaptation to changing technology and ways of organizing work. From 1980-1982 she presided over the Inquiry Commission on Adult Professional and Social-Cultural Development (C.E.F.A.).

Stan Jones, Associate Professor of Applied Linguistics at Carleton University, is the co-author of the *Ontario Test of Adult Functional Literacy* and of *Test ontarien d'alphabétisation fonctionnelle des adultes.*

Susan Lafleur is currently Co-ordinator of a co-operative education program at Ottawa University, assisting university students in bridging the gap between academic and work environments. She has worked as an adult educator in training and development, particularly in the high technology sector. Susan has been responsible for developing training needs analysis for management and technical training.

Diana Lohnes is a Teaching Master and Life Skills Coach in the Adult Basic Education Department of Algonquin College. Over the past two decades she has taught various college preparatory and basic orientation programs and served as Department Co-ordinator. Formally trained in Linguistics, Diana has also taught Interpersonal Communication at Carleton University. She is currently Chair of a national Program Evaluation and Literacy Assessment Project.

Dorothy MacKeracher, Ph.D., is Associate Professor for Adult Education in the Faculty of Education, University of New Brunswick. Her research has been guided by interests in aging, learning, development, women, literacy and basic education. Dorothy is an active member of the Canadian Congress on Learning Opportunities for Women and the New Brunswick, Association for Continuing Education.

D'Arcy Martin has worked as a popular educator in the Canadian labour movement since 1978. With unions and other organizations, he has been engaged in issues of tech change, gender equity and cultural democracy. During eight years with the Steelworkers, and three years with the Communications and Electrical Workers, he has designed, administered and taught union courses across Canada. As an educational activist and theorist, D'Arcy has spoken in the United States, Europe, Asia, Africa and Latin America.

Sally McBeth, a graduate of York University in Toronto, has worked for several years in community journalism and as a volunteer tutor at Parkdale Project Read. From 1983 to 1988 she co-ordinated the student writing and publishing program at East End Literacy, where she is still a member of the staff collective.

Anne Moore has been a literacy worker with Parkdale Project Read, a community-based literacy program in downtown Toronto for the last two and a half years. She is currently serving on the Board of the Metropolitan Toronto Movement for Literacy.

Claire Newman, Ed.D., is Professor Emeritus (Mathematics and Education) at Queens College of the City University of New York. She is a consultant to schools in the New York area and continues to be interested in the improvement of mathematics education for both children and adults.

Margaret O'Brien, Ph.D., is an Associate Professor at Mount Saint Vincent University in Nova Scotia where she teaches graduate level courses in diagnosis and remediation of reading problems. Her research focuses on reading difficulties of both children and adults.

Jack C. Pearpoint is president of Frontier College, Canada's oldest adult education institution. He has provided leadership in the development of literacy programs in prisons, among the disabled and with Native peoples. Jack has also been responsible for the publication of the *Student Centred Individualized Learning (SCIL)* program. He is a graduate from the University of Saskatchewan, and has worked as a Resettlement Officer in West Africa and past Director of the Projects Division of CUSO.

Lorne Rachlis, Ed.D., is Superintendent of Schools with the Ottawa Board of Education. He has worked as a teacher and principal in both evening and adult day schools and as a Superintendent of Continuing Education. He has also served as a Director of the Ontario Association for Continuing Education, and as President of Ontario's Continuing Education School Board Administrators Association.

Jeannine Roy-Poirier, Ph.D., has been involved in the field of adult and continuing education as Co-ordinator of the Cornwall Campus of the University of Ottawa, and as a Lecturer in Adult Education graduate studies. In 1982 she received the Senator Yvette Rousseau Literary Award and was President of the Canadian Association for the Study of Adult Education from 1987-1989.

Kjell Rubenson, Ph.D., is Director of the Centre for Policy Studies in Education at the University of British Columbia and holds a chair in Adult Education at Linkoping University, Sweden. His research has addressed various aspects of the relationships between adult education and the broader society including the labour market and the world of work.

Dale Shuttleworth, Ph.D., is Assistant Superintendent of Programs for the City of York Board of Education. He has pioneered policies and programs in the areas of community school development, adult and continuing education and multicultural education. He has been the recipient of several awards some of which include the Dag Hammarskjold Gold Metal for excellence in education and the Norman High Award from the Ontario Association for Continuing Education.

Judy Singh has been a special educator and researcher for a number of years. She has had a long-standing research interest in reading, both with developmentally delayed and adult learners. She has been a Tutor at the University of Canterbury, New Zealand and is currently undertaking graduate studies in special education at Northern Illinois University.

Ninbhay N. Singh, Ph.D., is Professor of Psychiatry at the Medical College of Virginia, Virginia Commonwealth University. He has edited several books and has a wide research interest that includes analysis and remediation of academic deficits in children and adults, pediatric psychopharmacology and reading.

XVI

Brian Street, Ph.D., is a Senior Lecturer in Social Anthropology at the University of Sussex, England. During the 1970's he did field research on village literacy in Iran, and has since been developing new theoretical perspectives that view literacy in cross-cultural perspective and in terms of power and ideology. He published *Literacy in Theory and Practice* (CUP) in 1985, has written numerous articles on literacy in both learned journals and more popular publications. Brian has also been a Visiting Associate Professor at the Graduate School of Education, University of Pennsylvania.

Linda Thistlethwaite, Ed.D., is currently an Associate Professor in the Department of Elementary Education and Reading at Western Illinois University. As Chair of the Graduate Reading Program, she coordinated the College Reading and Study Skills program from 1981-1987. She has served on the Training and Method Committee of the Illinois Literacy Council and is presently the Chair of the Adult Learning Division of the College Reading Association.

Alan M. Thomas, Ph.D., is currently a Professor of Adult Education, Department of Adult Education, Ontario Institute for Studies in Education, Toronto. His major interests and publications have been devoted to large scale adult education programs in labour, business and prisons; policy formation and the financing of adult education in Canada and elsewhere; and the relationship of learning and the law. Alan has worked as an international consultant in the Caribbean, East Africa, Australia, Finland and with UNESCO and OECD. He is the Former President and Executive Director of the Canadian Association for Adult Education.

Audrey Thomas, founder and life member of the Movement for Canadian Literacy, is a freelance adult educator and literacy consultant. She has taught courses in ABE for the University of Saskatchewan and the University of British Columbia. In 1988, she initiated and coordinated Project Literacy Victoria. Audrey has recently been appointed to the Provincial Literacy Advisory Committee to the Ministry of Advanced Education and Job Training.

Nancy N. Vacc, Ed.D., is an Assistant Professor of Education at the University of North Carolina at Greensboro. She recently returned from New Zealand where she was an honorary Visiting Lecturer at the University of Auckland. Her current research focuses on using microcomputers in writing instruction with young adults having a history of academic difficulties, and using microcomputers as an intervention in mathematics for developing computation skills.

Serge Wagner, Ph.D., is a Professor at the University of Quebec at Montreal. He has been involved in the field of literacy both in developing and industrialized countries for two decades. In particular he has been instrumental in the development of the popular literacy education movement in Quebec and Ontario. Serge has also conducted several action research projects with literacy learners.

Gladys Watson is a librarian concerned with issues of feminism and adult education. As a librarian she has experience in the development and management of resource centres within non-governmental organisations. Gladys is interested in exploring ways in which library science can meet literacy, community and feminist needs. Her masters degree in library science is from the University of Western Ontario.

Tracy Westell has been a literacy worker at Parkdale Project Read in Toronto for the last four years. She has worked extensively with the Ontario Literacy Coalition.

Roberta Wiener, Ed.D., is a Professor of Reading and Education at the Institute for Teaching and Education Studies, Adelphi University, Garden City, New York. Presently, she is Curriculum Co-ordinator and Program Developer and is completing post doctoral studies for social work and clinical practice. She initiated the Masters programs in Adult Learning and Development, Multicultural Education and an interdisciplinary certificate in Computers for Educators. She has also served as Associate Dean of the Institute for Teaching and Education Studies.

PART I
HISTORICAL AND PHILOSOPHICAL PERSPECTIVES

The practice of adult literacy and basic education is rooted in historical events and is guided by philosophical assumptions. This section attempts to give a background to the field of practice. Together the different chapters point out that literacy education has seldom been neutral and that both the value and the functionality of literacy is determined by political, economic and cultural factors. Another apparent theme is that learning to read and write were not always equal partners. The emphasis historically has been on teaching the skills of reading. This section also signals the importance for practitioners not only to understand the historical components of literacy education but also the backgrounds of the agencies with which they are associated.

Although most of the examples given in this section are taken from the Canadian cultural context, many of the principles which are discussed are generalizable. When examples are given beyond Canada, they are almost exclusively limited to western societies, even though the usage and evolution of literacy in other regions of the world would have been invaluable to have included in this section. The absence of such references does not in any way mean to exclude the place and richness of history and literacy in other cultures.

*Philosophies are often expressed through definitions. Such is the case with concepts like literacy and functional illiteracy. These concerns are raised in the chapter by **Audrey Thomas**. In her discussion she describes the noticeable evolution in the attempts to make literacy operational and provides a historical account of the definitional debate. Some of her major conclusions suggest that grade level completion is inadequate for definitional purposes and that adult literacy is concerned with the abilities of individuals to function within specific social contexts. With the demands of comtemporary North American society the literacy thresholds are likely to be in a continuing state of flux.*

*Having some understanding of history is important for literacy educators to comprehend and appreciate the background of present-day practices. **Draper** has presented a selected chronology of literacy events in chapter two that is Canadian and international and is expanded with an interpretive overview analysis. **Draper's** chapter six delves further into history and explores the connections between literacy and both human and national growth. Other issues explored historically include the use of literacy throughout western history, issues relating to public access for literacy, as well as the social, political and economic forces that relate to such education.*

1

*Although not always articulated as such, literacy is also embedded in social organizations. In the chapter by **Darville** two arguments are forwarded. The first proposition is that literacy is not simply one kind of skill or social relation and the second is that developing literacy is an empowerment. The author outlines the distinctions between narrative and organizational literacy and argues that in our society we need to think about literacy as empowerment in conjunction with the idea that it has more than one form. It also becomes increasingly clear that learning the skills of reading and writing have not been in isolation from the content that was used in literacy education programs.*

*One of the ways to assess the evolution of literacy education in any country is to examine the legislation and policies that have been developed relating to it. **Thomas, Taylor** and **Gaskin** review three Canadian statutes: The Technical and Vocational Training Assistance Act, The Adult Occupational Training Act and the National Training Act. Following a historical description of the different periods of federal legislative activity related to education, the authors examine specific provisions contained in the acts and the effects on adult literacy and basic education learners. These principle acts which define the approaches toward vocational training in Canada have implications for what actually occurs within literacy education classrooms. Literacy education has always been part of the political process.*

*During the 1970's in the United Kingdom, government and institutions became involved in adult literacy teaching and research. **Street** examines the definitions and activities that allowed adults to be in literacy developments. He suggests that by distinguishing between autonomous and ideological models of literacy one can better understand the underlying and often unstated assumptions about the phenomena. The author also argues for a more general theory of literacy practice and raises issues surrounding the political and academic dimensions of literacy teaching.*

CHAPTER 1:

Definitions and Evolution of the Concepts

Audrey M. Thomas

Nowadays, it seems simpler to define "Adult Basic Education" (ABE) than "literacy" in the North American context. ABE is a field which has existed for several decades. Its name has several advantages:
- it defines the target population: adult,
- it defines the program: basic education, and
- it implies the delivery of that program.

One could argue, of course, that "adult" needs further precise definition, and that what constitutes "basic education" has changed in content and scope over time. Some may also doubt that "a delivery system" is implied. By and large, however, the term "ABE" does connote a field of practice whose target population consists of those persons above the statutory school-leaving age who, for one reason or another, have, by normative standards, educational deficits which are to be redressed by a program of instruction undertaken in a setting recognized by a funding organization.

People enrolling in such programs do so for a variety of reasons, but generally, they have recognized in some way or another, their need for "more education". That education has traditionally consisted of discrete subject areas or disciplines — language arts, mathematics, science, and social studies. However, there seems to be a nagging feeling that ABE has failed, or, conversely, that society has failed ABE, because large numbers of adults are said to be "functionally illiterate" and their numbers are being swelled by youth "drop-outs" from the regular school system. Thus, we have a "literacy crisis" on our hands!

WHAT IS LITERACY?

The task of definition now becomes devilishly difficult. Given the myriad senses in which literacy is used, which one do we apply to our field? Perhaps it is easier to "do literacy", than to define it? We are faced with a concept — literacy — which is at once part of ABE, but also greater than it.

The simplest definition of literacy is "the ability to read and write", and few people would probably argue otherwise. Problems begin to surface, however, when literacy purposes are discussed. The answers to the question "Literacy for what?", determine how a literacy program is designed, implemented and evaluated. The underlying assumptions and values of the definers shape the practice. Results determine the success or failure of a program and experience may modify the initial assumptions and ultimately help change the definitions.

Coming to grips with definitions of "literacy" has become something of a preoccupation for many scholars, especially in the last decade. Technological

3

change and human resource development policies are factors contributing to the heightened visibility of "literacy" in the public consciousness and the efforts of governments at various levels to understand "the problem". One's understanding of what "literacy" or "illiteracy" is shapes policies and funding provisions. Thus, definitions become critical.

A range of definitions has emerged such that "literacy", at one end of the scale, may be defined to include only the irreducible minimum of the adult population who will likely always be illiterate, to the other end of the scale where it may be defined to encompass nearly all the adult population! Hautecoeur (1986) discusses the effects of such a range in the Quebec context.

Cervero (1985) raises the question of whose needs would be served by a common definition of adult literacy. He states:

> The effort to achieve a common definition would not be a technical process aimed at discovering the objectively best definition of literacy. Rather, it should be viewed as a clash of competing value positions, ideologies, and power structures. There can be little doubt that the winners in this struggle would be those who wish to reproduce the existing social distribution of knowledge. (p. 54)

There is no mention of reading and writing here! Literacy is a battleground — a power struggle for the control of knowledge. Valentine (1986) comments:

> . . . it must strike seasoned adult basic skills teachers somewhat curious that they are now seen as fighting the good flight and saving the nation by teaching functional literacy . . . (p. 108)

What is this "saving" power that is attributed to literacy, and how does "functional literacy" differ from "literacy"? We can agree with Bormuth (1978) that literacy has gathered around it "a certain amount of qualitative or ethical freight" (p. 124). To attempt to understand this situation, some historical perspective is necessary.

EVOLUTION OF LITERATE WESTERN SOCIETIES

Pictograms, syllabaries, alphabets and other forms of coded language have evolved for purposes of communication throughout historical time and in different locations. Reading and writing thus became necessary to understand and to produce text. In Ancient Greece, oratory was a highly prized ability and dialogue was encouraged by Socrates and Plato. However, much of what we know about Socrates has come to us through the *writings* of Plato, thus demonstrating clearly one use of literacy. Literacy gradually spread throughout the Graeco-Roman world, but its use was restricted mainly to scribes and elites. After the fall of the Roman Empire, the Church became a principal guardian of literate culture.

Language preceded literacy and separated homo sapiens from other life. Literacy had to wait for the invention of writing which took place about five thousand years ago. The Greek alphabet upon which the communication of the Western world is based, came into being about 700 B.C. The printing press was introduced in the fifteenth century, and mechanically powered printing was introduced in the nineteenth century. In the first eighty years of the twentieth century, we have seen the advent of the paperback book, the generalized use of radio, television and space satellite communications technology, while the microchip and widespread use of computers are revolutionizing nearly every aspect of our lives. Are these technological developments making literacy obsolete, or more necessary than ever? As an industrial society accommodates to the information society, there is considerable dislocation in traditional industries with structural unemployment and chronic underemployment as visible consequences. At the same time, new industries such as robotics are emerging. Will the literacy gap be narrowed or widened in our society?

It is against this kind of profound societal change that much of the discussion about adult literacy and the search for more rigorous definition has taken place.

EVOLUTION OF THE DEFINITIONS

The definition of illiteracy was relatively consistent in the Western world until the 1920s. A person who could read and write was literate; one who could not was illiterate. People had either acquired the skills of reading and writing or they had not. However, Cook (1977) in writing about the U.S.A. points out that this type of definition began to be perceived as being inadequate:

> In 1924, at a National Council for Education meeting, one educator defined an illiterate in this manner: "Clearly from a practical social point of view, it is one who has not mastered the art of reading and writing sufficiently to use it in daily life" . . . (p. 31)

Cook goes on to quote another speaker at the 1929 meeting of the National Education Association who proclaimed his violent objection "to classifying as literate . . . those who can write their names only" (p. 32). The same speaker thought that there was a chance that the 1930 census would be changed and would give enumerators instructions to inquire as to an individual's ability "to read the American newspapers — the equivalent of fourth grade English" (p. 32). Here is the germ of an idea which crystallized later into the notion of "functional illiteracy".

Definitions have been concerned with "what a thing is" or its "essential quality". The qualitative definition, however, is not sufficient for practical application. Qualitative definitions provide an ideological base or value position — a form of mission statement — but educational planners and policymakers need to know *who* has or does not have the quality. It is this applied aspect of the definition for quantitative purposes which has largely contributed to the debate about definitions today. But, in the 1940s, things were simpler. A functional illiterate was one who had completed fewer than five years of schooling. This definition may make no sense at all when applied to a particular individual (for the state of being literate depends on the balance between one's literacy abilities and situational literacy demands) but at least it supplied a crude indicator of the size of the target population. This attachment of grade level completion to definitions of illiteracy has persisted until very recently, even though the grade level threshold has gradually been raised. Adults with less than high school (grade 12) completion are the clients for ABE programs, but are such persons illiterate?

The concept of "functional literacy" gained widespread international currency in the 1950s and 1960s with the pronouncements of UNESCO. There were consolidated in 1978 into the *UNESCO Revised Recommendation Concerning the International Standardization of Educational Statistics* as follows:

Statistics of Illiteracy

1. Definitions: The following definitions should be used for statistical purposes:
a. A person is *literate* who can with understanding both read and write a short simple statement on his everyday life.
b. A person is *illiterate* who cannot with understanding both read and write a short simple statement on his everyday life.
c. A person is *functionally literate* who can engage in all those activities in which literacy is required for effective functioning of his group and community and also enabling him to continue to use reading, writing, writing and calculation for his own and the community's development.
d. A person is *functionally illiterate* who cannot engage in all those activities in which literacy is required for effective functioning of his group and community and also for enabling him to continue to use reading, writing and calculation for his own and the community's development.
2. Methods of measurement: To determine the number of literates (or functional literates) and illiterates (or functional illiterates) any of the following methods could be used:
a. Ask a question or questions pertinent to the definitions given above, in a complete census or sample survey of the population.
b. Use a standardized test of literacy (or functional literacy) in a special survey. This method could be used to verify data obtained by other means or to correct bias in other returns.
   i) special censuses or sample surveys on the extent of school enrolment;
   ii) regular school statistics in relation to demographic data;
   iii) data on educational attainment of the population.

(Thomas, 1983, p. 19)

The UNESCO definitions, being directed to an international audience, are necessarily broad. In the global context, functional literacy has been linked to community development and non-formal education projects. Mass literacy campaigns have been most successful when they have taken place within a framework of fundamental social change (ICAE, 1979). Thus, the success or failure of literacy movements and programs has been related to prevailing socio-political and socio-economic conditions. In our Western society, literacy, under the rubric of ABE, has been linked to preparation for employment — giving an individual the means to better oneself economically. Such programs tend to ignore other aspects or attributes of literacy. Scribner (1984) suggests that "*ideal* literacy is simultaneously adaptive, socially empowering, and self-enhancing" (p. 18).

Since the mid-1970s, discussion on literacy definitions have become more numerous. Definitions have been shaped according to the particular bias of the definers. Political activists, sociologists and many adult educators tend to stress the ideas of literacy as a liberating influence, a means to empowerment and self-fulfillment through active participation in the learning enterprise and in the community. Reading specialists, on the other hand, tend to look at literacy definitions from a linguistic point of view where the debate is often between "literacy as decoding" and "literacy as thinking". Somewhere in the middle of the above groups, several researchers have undertaken specific projects designed to identify specific tasks and competencies required by adults either in specific situations or in society in general.

Functional Competency

In an attempt to break away from the grade-level completion idea of literacy, the United States Office of Education (USOE) funded a research project, the Adult Performance Level (APL) Study to specify the competencies required for success in adult living. The notion of functional literacy thus gave way to "functional competence."

Functional competence was conceptualized as a set of skills and a set of five content areas in which thes kills are applied. The skills were communications (reading, writing, speaking, listening and viewing), computation, problem-solving and interpersonal relations. The content areas were occupational knowledge, consumer economics, health, community resources and government and law (APL, 1975). The study received considerable attention when its findings were published. Extrapolating its figures for the nation as a whole, the APL study infers the fifty seven million Americans do not have skills adequate to perform basic tasks. Almost twenty three million Americans lacked the competencies necessary to function in society and an additional thirty four million Americans are able to function, but not proficiently. These are alarming statistics. The study, however, has its critics.

> Cervero (1980) concluded that the APL test did not have content validity. For the APL test to have content validity, its items must adequately sample the universe of behaviours which compose functional competence . . . (p. 155). The APL test fails to meet this criterion, however, not necessarily because test development procedures were faulty, but because it is not logically possible to define this universe of behaviours without respect to a value position, a position which the test developers have chosen not to discuss. (p. 163)

In 1987, Southam News of Ottawa commissioned The Creative Research Group Limited to conduct a research study on adult illiteracy in Canada. The thrust of the study was "to provide a comprehensive assessment of the literacy performance of adult Canadians which both recognizes the complexity of information processing skills, and provides a relevant context in which to assess these skills" (p. 5). The group used a criterion measure for functional literacy and the minimum standard was determined with the aid of a jury panel. Thus, Canada received its version of the APL, although, in fact, the Group was very much influenced by the 1985 National Assessment of Educational Progress (NAEP) survey of literacy performance among American youth. They subscribed to the same definition of literacy employed by the NAEP: "Using printed and written information to function in society, to achieve one's goals, and to develop one's knowledge and potential" (p. 6).

After the results of the APL Study were made known, the term functional competency as a replacement for functional literacy became something of a vogue. This situation then appeared to open the gateway for everyone to adopt the term literacy as their own and terms such as numeracy (literacy of numbers), cartolacy (literacy of maps), visual literacy (in relation to television and film), scientific literacy, civic literacy and computer literacy were heard more and more. (Of these specific literacies only numeracy had traditionally been associated with "literacy".) The notion seemed to imply some unstated threshold of competency upon the attainment of which one would be capable of functioning reasonably well in that particular field. Until that threshold is reached, however, the individual remains functionally illiterate.

Hunter and Harman (1979) expanded the definition of functional literacy to:

> . . . the possession of skills *perceived as necessary by particular persons and groups* to fulfill their own self-determined objectives as family and community members, citizens, consumers, job-holders and members of social, religious, or other associations of their choosing. (p. 7)

Important additions to this definition are the notions of *self-perception* and *self-determined objectives* of the people themselves. The perceived need in relation to one's own objectives forms the basis upon which learning may take place. Herein lies the opportunity for genuinely individualized instruction.

Once we shift from the individual person to the larger group or society, we founded on shifting sands. Hunter and Harman go on to say:

> . . . if we take seriously the dynamic interaction between self-defined needs and the requirements of society, measurement of functional literacy becomes infinitely more elusive. Who but the person or group involved can really describe what "effective functioning in one's own cultural group" really means? Who needs to know whether skills can be used "toward personal and community development"? How is "a life of dignity and pride" measured? (p. 19)

The value-laden aspects attached to "literacy" are its definitional undoing and have come in for some harsh criticism. Levine (1982) points out the defect of "extreme elasticity of meaning" (p. 249), and says that "we have nothing more than a jumble of ad hoc and largely mistaken assumptions about literacy's economic, social and political dimensions". (p. 250). In discussing functional literacy in the Canadian context, De Castell, Luke and MacLennan (1981) commented that:

> The apparent neutrality of the concept and the vagueness of its formulation, in conjunction with its pragmatic, utilitarian appeal, attract extensive approval. Unfortunately, however, there have been few attempts to define the term rigorously. (p. 12)

Despite the criticisms, there have been attempts to operationalize "functional literacy" in specific settings. Perhaps of all the variations in literacy definitions, "functional literacy" is the variant most associated with employment or preparation for the workplace. There is a growing body of research on literacy uses and requirements in specific work environments.

Literacy Task Analysis

Researchers working on specific occupational task analysis and relationships to job performance include Sticht; Mikulecky and Winchester; and, Kirsch and Guthrie. Sticht (1975) defines functional literacy in a job-related context as "the possession of those literacy skills needed to successfully perform some reading task imposed by an external agent between the reader and a goal the reader wishes to obtain" (p. 4).

Kirsch and Guthrie (1978) stated:

> Functional literacy . . . should be kept distinct from functional competency. Literacy, whether general or functional, should not be used to represent skills or behaviours beyond those with printed materials. Agreeing that functional literacy should be limited to competency with printed materials, one is then faced with developing a theory and methodology which adequately assesses such competency in individuals and groups. (p. 491)

In 1984 the same authors confirm that reading is a complex social phenomenon conditioned by the various contexts in which it occurs. They say:

> . . . accounting for reading practices requires a contextual analysis consisting of four phases. First, the settings or contexts of interest in which reading occurs need to be identified. Second, various characteristics of the readers should be defined. Third, reading practices must be reliably assessed. Fourth, the associations among these factors need to be described. (p. 231)

> Guthrie (1983) stated: "The literacy requirement exists as a contract between people" (p. 668). The act of reading is seen as "a sort of social contract with the author" (1984, p. 353), and thus is not a solitary activity.

In their study of nurses, Mikulecky and Winchester (1983) found "superior" nurses "had a clearer sense of what they were to be doing and actually used literacy to make themselves more effective," than "adequate" nurses. "The difference between nursing groups was not so much in *what* they had available, as it was in *how* they use it" (p. 12).

Heath (1980) recorded the literacy behaviours of adults in an all-black working-class community in the Southeastern United States and classified seven types of highly contextualized literacy uses. She concluded that:

> For many families and communities, the major benefits of reading and writing may not include such traditionally assigned rewards as social mobility, job preparation, intellectual creativity, critical reasoning and public information access. In short, literacy has different meanings for members of different groups, with a variety of acquisition modes, functions, and uses; . . . (p. 132)

The researchers quoted above are trying to pin down more precisely the definitions of or provide a methodology for precise measurement of functional literacy by analyzing the uses of literacy and relationships to the target population in selected settings. It is clear that functional literacy varies in time, in space, and in relation to the needs of each individual. As Valentine (1986) says:

> When properly operationalized . . . task analysis offers a promising solution to
> the determination of common literacy demands within restricted environments.
> (p. 112)

However, there are obvious major disadvantages to this approach given the
enormous number of environments and that separate task analyses would have
to be conducted for each one. Draper (1986) stresses that:

> For literacy education to become truly functional, one would have to identify
> the skills and knowledge an individual would need to have in order to effectively
> function in one's society. To this extent, functional literacy is individualized and
> is defined and characterized by a social, economic and cultural context. It
> includes, as well, the expectations that one has of self and society. (p. 22)

Levine (1982), and De Castell et al. (1981) are also critical of operational
definitions which focus primarily on the reading aspects of literacy as being too
narrow and restrictive and therefore incapable of bringing about the transformation and empowerment of individuals which are concepts commonly tied to the
notion of literacy. In addition, De Castell et al. are concerned about the notion
of functional illiteracy within the Canadian context. Having cited various American scholars, they say:

> . . . we must be particularly wary . . . of concepts of literacy which embody a
> built-in passivity factor (e.g., functional literacy qua acquiescent consumer
> competence or restrictively defined occupational skills). The intent of literacy
> instruction in Canada must not be the creation of manipulable populace,
> characterized by passive acceptance of information and prescribed behaviour.
> (p. 16)

They call for an adequate definition of functional literacy which will consider
"not only the literacy demands of interpersonal and vocational practice, but also
literacy needs for social and political practice as determined by the demands of
Canadian citizenship" (p. 16).

We are forced to wonder with Cervero (1985): "Is a common definition of
adult literacy possible?"

CONCLUSIONS

What has been encouraging in reviewing the literature is the extent and nature
of the debate on the topic among scholars and experts and the evidence of cross-
disciplinary influences. Thus, reading specialists who formerly confined attention to the world of schooling, have entered the field of adult basic education and
have begun to look at reading within the broader social context of the adult
world. Adult activists and sociologists, for their part, have tried to become more
aware of the intricacies of reading processes. If the field has not yet reached
agreement on an *operational* definition of literacy, there appears to be more or
less general agreement on some principles:

> a. that the grade-level completion measure is inadequate for definitional pur-
>   poses;

b. that adult literacy is concerned with the abilities of individuals to function within specific social contexts;
c. that there is a literacy continuum ranging from the mechanics of learning how to decode and encode through any number of "specific literacies" to the mature utilization of literacy skills and processes for informed action and aesthetic appreciation;
d. that language precedes literacy and how one uses language should be taken into account in literacy instruction;
e. that common operational definitions in a pluralistic society are unlikely because of the underlying values and assumptions of the definers and the very varied environments which exist;
f. that literacy may indeed be empowering for some individuals and groups of people, but many seek the safer haven of "adaptation" to our contemporary society which process can, nevertheless, be self-enhancing for those individuals involved;
g. that the demands of contemporary North American society are ever changing and at a faster pace, so that literacy "thresholds" are likely to be in a continuing state of flux, and as long as some people have superior literacy skills, others who have limited skills will remain vulnerable;
h. that even people with superior literacy skills are at risk in today's labour market where more and more people are becoming unemployed and finding that their literacy levels either exceed the requirements for a large part of the economy or are not specialized enough, thus forcing a rethinking of many of the assumptions underlying literacy definitions and programs.

The Canadian Context

We have not been very adventurous with our definitions in Canada — mainly ringing the changes of current definitions from our neighbour to the South. Canadian reading specialists have tended not to be as involved in discussions and practice of adult literacy as in the U.S.A. O'Brien (1985) voices her concerns over this state of affairs and says:

> The reading community must reach out to those involved in adult literacy instruction and join with them to develop programs appropriate to the needs of the adult illiterate and which reflect the literacy demands of today's society. (p. 27)

Norman and Malicky (1986) have taken an interest in adult literacy work. In a recent study, they asked a group of adult illiterates what they thought "reading" was. They received replies such as: "sounding out words", "memorizing words", and "spelling letter-by-letter". The stress obviously was on word identification rather than comprehension. These sort of replies have been confirmed in other studies and the mismatch between lofty goals and purposes of literacy programs and the learners' conceptions of reading has been noted.

However, is this situation different from learning in other spheres? For purposes of illustration, we may make an analogy with learning to drive a car. One can become quite frustrated in the early stages of trying to drive an automobile with standard transmission. The feet do not seem to go with the various pedals at the right time. One could define driving as knowing which pedal to depress, or which gear to use in a certain situation, but once the mechanics are mastered, driving could be defined quite differently as "mobility", "freedom to travel", "pleasures of the road", and so on. Thus, with literacy, one has to master certain skills before one can enter "the magical circle of the literate" (Bhola, 1981, p. 11) or enjoy the benefits of "exchanging information through the written word" (Bormuth, 1978, p. 123), or before one sees literacy "as power" (Scribner, 1984, p. 11). But it is important in these early stages for students to realize the potential of the processes in which they are involved. Norman and Malicky (1986) make some suggestions "for a different pedagogy" for beginning adult readers.

So, where do our meanderings through the definitional maze lead us? Without doubt, it is to the individual who has perceived his inadequacy and is willing to enter into a learning situation to try to meet his needs. Meeting learners' educational needs is at the heart of the adult education enterprise. By focussing on those needs, facilitator and learner together can help close the gap until the learner can function within the jointly selected parameters.

If there are lessons to be learned from reviewing the definitions and concepts it is that the task of ABE, as ever, is to be responsive to the needs of learners and to get on with "doing literacy". It is the task of society to make that possible.

REFERENCES

Adult Performance Level Project. (1975). *Adult functional competency: A summary*. Austin: The University of Texas.

Bhola, H. S. (1981). Why literacy can't wait: Issues for the 19805, *Convergence, 14*(1), 6-23.

Bormuth, J. R. (1978). Value and volume of literacy. *Visible Language, 12*, 118-161.

Cervero, R. M. (1980). Does the Texas Adult Performance Level Test measure functional competence? *Adult Education, 30*, 152-165.

Cervero, R. M. (1985). Is a common definition of adult literacy possible? *Adult Education Quarterly, 36*, 50-54.

Cook, W. D. (1977). *Adult literacy education in the United States*. Newark: International Reading Association.

Creative Research Group Limited. (1987). *Literacy in Canada: A research report*. Prepared for Southam News, Ottawa.

De Castell, S., Luke, A., & MacLennan, D. (1981). On defining literacy. *Canadian Journal of Education, 6*(3), 7-16.

Draper, J. A. (1986). *Rethinking adult literacy.* Toronto: World Literacy of Canada.

Guthrie, J. T. (1983). Equilibrium of literacy. *Journal of Reading, 26*, 668-670.

Guthrie, J. T., & Kirsch, I. S. (1984). The emergent perspective on literacy. *Phi Delta Kappan, 65*, 351-355.

Hautecoeur, J-P. (1986). Sondage léger, conclusions lourdes. In J-P. Hautecoeur (Ed.), *Alpha 86: Recherches en alphabétisation* (pp. 243-266). Québec: Ministère de l'Education.

Heath, S. B. (1980). The functions and uses of literacy. *Journal of Communication, 30*, 123-133.

Hunter, C. S., & Harman, D. (1979). *Adult illiteracy in the United States*. New York: McGraw Hill Book Company.

International Council for Adult Education. (1979). *The world of literacy, policy, research and action*. Ottawa: International Development Research Centre.

Kirsch, I. S., & Guthrie, J. T. (1978). The concept of measurement of functional literacy. *Reading Research Quarterly, 13*, 485-507.

Kirsch, I. S., & Guthrie, J. T. (1984). Adult reading practices for work and leisure. *Adult Education Quarterly, 34*, 213-232.

Levine, K. (1982). Functional literacy: Fond illusions and false economies. *Harvard Educational Review, 52*, 249-266.

Mickulekcy, L., & Winchester, D. (1983). Job literacy and job performance among nurses at varying employment levels. *Adult Education Quarterly, 34*, 1-15.

Norman, C., & Malicky, G. (1986). Literacy as a social phenomenon: Implications for instruction. *Lifelong Learning, 9*(7), 12-15.

O'Brien, M. A. (1985). The methodology of adult literacy instruction in Canada: Some concerns. *Reading-Canada-Lecture, 3*(1), 21-28.

Oxenham, J. (1980). *Literacy: Writing, reading and social organization*. London: Routledge & Kegan Paul Ltd.

Scribner, S. (1984). Literacy in three metaphors. *American Journal of Education, 93*, 6-21.

Sticht, T. G. (1975). *Reading for working: A functional literacy anthology*. Alexandria, Va.: HumRRO.

Thomas, A. M. (1983). *Adult illiteracy in Canada: A challenge*. Occasional paper No. 42. Ottawa: Canadian Commission for UNESCO.

Valentine, T. (1986). Adult functional literacy as a goal of instruction. *Adult Education Quarterly, 36*, 108-113.

CHAPTER 2:

A Selected Chronology of Literacy Events

James A. Draper

This modern chronology of literacy events, covering about 150 years, points out a number of interconnecting factors that have influenced literacy education in Canada and elsewhere. Acquiring and retaining the skills of reading depends on the availability of reading materials. From the early 1800's in Canada, there was an increasing amount of such materials available, through newspapers, subscription libraries and eventually, free public libraries. Paralleling this was government legislation that helped to nurture a "reading society", such as the Ontario Common School Act, the Free Library Act, and various school board policies. Increasingly publicly supported institutions became involved in serving the educational needs of the adult public. Much later, a considerable amount of federal and provincial legislation was created, supporting various vocational training and other basic education programs.

From the chronology, it also becomes apparent that non-governmental, non-profit organizations (NGOs) were created to meet the social and educational needs of the population. In Canada, one can see the interweaving contributions, over many years, of such NGOs as the Y.M.C.A., the Mechanic's Institutes and later, Frontier College, the Canadian Association for Adult Education and World Literacy of Canada. For example, one can follow the influence of the 'Y' as it became involved in organizing educational programs for the Canadian militia, and then, toward the end of the First World War, in helping to establish Khaki college for Canadian military personnel in England. The 'Y' was also involved in early activities to provide educational programs to isolated construction sites, as a precursor to the Canadian Reading Camp Association.

Internationally, the influence of the Danish Folk High Schools; and the Mechanic's Institutes, the Worker's Education Association and the University Settlement Houses in England, can be seen to influence philosophical thought and innovative programming relating to adult learning, including literacy education. Many of these and other ideas and programs were appropriately adapted to the Canadian social, economic and political context.

Alternately, Canada too has its 'export' of ideas and programs: the Women's Institutes, the Antigonish Movement, the creative use of film in education such as that pioneered by the National Film Board of Canada, and the creative use of radio, such as the National Farm Radio Forum. The latter helped to stimulate the use of radio for literacy education, agricultural reform and national development in many countries of the world. Such cross-cultural, cross-national sharing has always been valued in adult education.

The first world conference on adult education was held in 1929. Since then, a considerable number of international events have taken place, especially from the 1970's, due primarily to the initiative and support of UNESCO and the International Council for Adult Education. In one sense, it was not surprising that the first UNESCO world conference on adult education was held in Denmark, nor that the second one was held in Canada, since both countries have contributed ideas internationally. Such international events have helped draw attention to the importance of literacy and education in the causes of peace, development, and self-reliance.

The 1965 conference in Iran drew attention, at the highest political level, to the implications of adult illiteracy to the development of new nations. A decade later, one of the first declarations on literacy and human rights arose from another high level conference, held in Persepolis, Iran. The establishing of the International Institute for Adult Literacy Methods in Tehran and its extensive series of publications have also made an international contribution to the documentation, literature, and research relating to adult literacy education.

World Literacy of Canada was the first non-governmental organization in Canada and one of the first anywhere that established as its primary mandate to support literacy, non-formal, and development programs in many regions of the world. Interestingly, it was this international experience that 'sensitized' members of W.L.C. to perceive the implications of adult illiteracy in Canada. Under W.L.C.'s auspices the first extensive study of adult basic education in Canada was undertaken in 1975-76. This work laid the basis for the establishment of the Movement for Canadian Literacy.

Just prior to and especially following World War I (WWI), university extension programs were being developed in Canada and elsewhere. These programs greatly helped in extending the resources of these publicly supported institutions to a larger public, thus increasing the opportunities for education by working with local people and dealing with social issues such as poverty, unemployment and illiteracy.

The first Canadian survey of adult education was undertaken in 1935, just prior to the formation of the Canadian Association for Adult Education. Other national surveys have since been conducted but none was more significant than the 1961 census, which documented the number of years of formal schooling citizens had completed. Information from this census led to a ferment of many governmental and non-governmental activities, such as the War on Poverty, the Special Senate Committee on Poverty, and various social, economic and training programs.

Indeed, the 1960's were a time of turmoil and change as groups reexamined and searched for an alternative life-style and as society dealt more seriously with the major issues of human rights and racial tensions. This decade was especially significant because society became more honest with itself as it faced the realities and inequalities within it. Canada ceased to perpetuate some of its myths, especially untruths about the quality of life and opportunities that existed in Canada. In 1953, UNESCO undertook a world survey of adult illiteracy. The Canadian government returned the uncompleted questionnaire with the comment: "Adult illiteracy is not a problem in Canada." Less than ten years later, the country could no longer mythologize its reality.

International declarations are more than rhetoric. Declarations such as The Right To Learn, The Udaipur Literacy Declaration and the Declaration of

Persepolis, for example, were attempts to mobilize thinking on the topic of literacy. The fact that national governments endorse these statements means that, to varying degrees, they can be held accountable for their implementation. All of these statements are deeply rooted in the larger declaration of human rights. The preamble and background to these public documents help to describe the breadth and depth of literacy education, the professional aspect of the work and the basic principles which guide programming and evaluation in literacy education. They are also philosophical statements that articulate goals to be achieved. These declarations have direct application to all literacy education activities, wherever they may occur. Given the generic goals for learning and for literacy education, it also becomes clear that some methods for teaching and learning are more appropriate than others.

From the chronology, it can also be seen that what was happening in literacy education in Canada was a microcosm of what was happening at the international level. In fact, the two intertwine. Changes in the functional view of literacy; mobilizing public opinion; literacy and nationalism; literacy linked to development, employment, empowerment, production and citizenship; and attempts to humanize human existence all became goals to be achieved through literacy.

Within and beyond Canada, there are regional differences. National literacy campaigns or literacy programs run by non-government and private agencies, are all part of the same social movement; guided by ideals and attempting to create and control events rather than merely responding to them. Remedial programming was no longer sufficient in meeting the demands of present-day living.

Finally, it can be seen that the chronology, incomplete as it may be, is more than a series of unrelated events. It expresses a complicated interrelationship between social forces, the creation and sharing of ideas, the needs of governments and individuals, and humanitarian goals, human sufferings and deprivation. Each person lives a history. It is as impossible to ignore the past as it is to ignore the present. Each is part of the same stream of events. Those involved in literacy education are creating history, not in isolation, but within an increasingly interdependent world.

CHRONOLOGY OF SELECTED EVENTS IN LITERACY

1792   –   Appearance of the first newspaper, *The Upper Canada Gazette*, in Newark (Niagara-on-the-Lake, Ontario).

1800   –   (June 8.) First circulating library in Upper Canada (Niagara-on-the-Lake).

1810   –   Public subscription libraries were established at York and elsewhere in Upper Canada.

1816   –   The first Common School Act was passed in Upper Canada. (Some adults took advantage of the opportunity to learn reading, writing and arithmetic.)

1825   –   *The Mechanic's Institutes were established in England.

1831   –   The first Mechanic's Institutes in Canada began in Upper Canada (Ontario) and Nova Scotia.

1844   –   *Founding of the Danish Folk High School by Bishop N.F.S. Grundtvig (a school for young adults to help farm people cope with change).
        –   *Social/University Settlements were established, Toynbee Hall, England.

1850's –   Various school boards in Upper Canada established evening classes for adults.

1853   –   First Y.M.C.A. (the "Y") opened in Toronto (later offering evening classes for adults).

1870's –   "Y" tents were established (with their libraries, writing table and lecture series) and became an integral part of summer militia camps.

1876   –   Y.M.C.A. sets up a special "Railway Department" to handle its educational and social activities in railroad construction camps.

1882   –   Free Libraries Act passed in Ontario.

1891   –   The Government of Ontario authorizes school boards to provide evening classes for anyone over the age of 14 who was unable to attend regular day school classes.

1897   –   The First Women's Institute was established at Stoney Creek, Ontario (devoted to the education of rural women and to improving the quality of rural life).

1899   –   The Canadian Reading Camp Association began working in frontier camps and communities in Ontario and elsewhere in Canada.

1900's –   Beginning of concentrated educational programs for immigrants to Canada.

1912   –   Formation of the Extension Department at the University of Alberta (later establishing its own radio station in 1925).

1917   –   The Khaki College was established for the Canadian Army in England (became a prototype for army education in many other countries).
        –   The Workers' Education Association (W.E.A.) of Canada was founded (initially established in England). (By 1924, there was W.E.A. activity in seven Ontario cities, in addition to Toronto.)

1919   –   *United Kingdom Report on Education (a political program for democracy and the concept that every adult needed continuing education).
        –   Frontier College was incorporated, to replace the Canadian Reading Camp Association.

---

*Indicates International Events.

1928 – The St. Francis Xavier University (Antigonish, Nova Scotia) establishes its Extension Department (later focusing on the development of cooperatives and becoming the Antigonish Movement).

1929 – * World Conference on Adult Education, Cambridge, England, sponsored by the World Association of Adult Education (to encourage international cooperation in adult education).

1935 – First survey of adult education in Canada.

– Founding of the Canadian Association for Adult Education (C.A.A.E.), Toronto.

1941 – National Farm Radio Forum organized (through the cooperation of the Canadian Association for Adult Education; Canadian Broadcasting Corporation; Canadian Federation of Agriculture).

1946 – Founding of UNESCO (United Nations Educational, Scientific and Cultural Organization).

1949 – *First UNESCO International Conference on Adult Education, Elsinore, Denmark (focusing on education for leisure; education for civic responsibility; international cooperation).

1953 – *UNESCO conducts a world survey of illiteracy.

1955 – World Literacy of Canada was incorporated (Toronto) to pursue work with the undereducated and illiterate in other countries and later Canada.

1958 – A graduate program in adult education began at the University of British Columbia; 1966 at The Ontario Institute for Studies in Education (O.I.S.E.), University of Toronto.

1960 – *Second UNESCO International Conference on Adult Education held in Montreal (placed literacy on the international development agenda; linked adult education and peace; was the first adult education conference where Asia, Africa, Latin America, and the Communist Block, were represented).

– *Beginning of the United Nations First Development Decade.

– A Dominion Bureau of Statistics report shows that 92% of all unemployed adults had not finished secondary school.

– The Technical and Vocational Training Assistance Act (T.V.T.A,) was passed (permitted agreements between the federal and provincial governments); followed by the Basic Training and Skill Development (B.T.S.D.) Program.

1961 – Census of Canada. Reports that over one million Canadians over the age of 15 had no schooling or less than grade 4. (Statistics also revealed that the typical functional illiterate adult was Canadian born.)

1962   –   *The Italian Association for the Eradication of Illiteracy sponsored the first international literacy conference.

1965   –   *First World Conference of Ministers of Education, to discuss adult illiteracy, Tehran, Iran.

        –   The "War on Poverty" (government programs to deal with the problems of poverty and inequality in Canada).

        –   *Beginning of the Decade Experimental World Literacy Programme (E.W.L.P.) in 11 countries, sponsored by UNESCO.

1966   –   *The First Conference on Comparative Adult Education (Exeter, New Hampshire, U.S.A.).

        –   Seminar on Adult Basic Education (Toronto). (Sponsored by the C.A.A.E. (Canadian Association for Adult Education) and Frontier College, in association with The Technical Vocational Training Branch, Department of Citizenship and Immigration.)

1967   –   Publication of *Functional Literacy and International Development*. (A Study by J. Roby Kidd, of Canadian Capability to Assist with the World Campaign to Eradicate Illiteracy.)

        –   Adult Occupational Training Act (A.O.T.). (Increases federal assistance to reduce unemployment and increase productivity of Canadian workers, with a greater focus on training; recognized the value of the B.T.S.D. Program.) (Replaces the Technical and Vocational Training Act of 1960.)

        –   *September 8 is designated by UNESCO as International Literacy Day.

        –   Creation of the federal government's NewStart Program. (Designed for the purposes of establishing action research centres in participating provinces; aimed at providing solutions to the problems of educational and socio-economical development for Canada's disadvantaged; and represented one aspect of the country's anti-poverty drive.) (By 1969, six provinces were participating in the NewStart Program, consisting of basic literacy and upgrading programs from grades 1 to 10.)

1968   –   A National Seminar on A.B.E. was held at Elliot Lake, Ontario.

        –   The first life skills course was planned by Saskatchewan NewStart. (Also, out of the Saskatchewan program, came B.L.A.D.E. — Basic Literacy for Adult Development; and L.I.N.C. — Learning Individualized for Canadians.)

1969   –   The first Adult Day School was established as a Metropolitan Toronto Department of Social Services volunteer project; later, the Toronto Board of Education assumed the financial responsibility for teacher salaries and school supplies.

1970   –   *Founding of the International Institute for Adult Literacy Methods (Iran). Publishes: *Literacy Discussion* and *Literacy Methods/ Work/Review*.

1971   –   Publication of *Adult Basic Education* (the first major book on A.B.E. in Canada). (Edited by Michael Brooke.)

1972   –   *UNESCO International Commission on the Development of Education publishes, *Learning to Be: The World of Education Today and Tomorrow*.

        –   *Third UNESCO International Conference on Adult Education, Tokyo, out of which came the International Council for Adult Education (I.C.A.E.).

1974   –   "Special Issues on Adult Literacy in Canada", published in *Literacy Discussion*. (Summer: editors: James A. Draper, J. Roby Kidd and Barbara Kerfoot; Winter: editors Michael Brooke and Gerard Clam.)

        –   Annual meeting of World Literacy of Canada, focus on adult illiteracy in Canada (Ottawa). (Out of which came the "Canada Literacy Project".)

        –   The Canada Manpower Industrial Training Program is introduced (replacing a number of previous programs).

1975   –   *Beginning of the B.B.C./T.V. (British Broadcasting Corporation) program on adult literacy. (*On The Move:* to create awareness of the problem of illiteracy; to refer persons who wished assistance with literacy skills to appropriate resources.)

        –   *World Conference of the International Women's Year (Mexico).

        –   *Second International Conference of Ministers of Education, on adult literacy (Persepolis, Iran). (Declaration of Persepolis.) (Focus on the needs of women; the needs for social development; education for liberation.)

1976   –   *N.G.O. (I.C.A.E.) Conference on Adult Education and Development (Dar-es-Salaam, Tanzania). (Nongovernmental organizations.)

        –   National Conference on Adult Literacy (Toronto), jointly sponsored by W.L.C., the C.A.A.E., and the I.C.A.E. (Release of the publication, *Adult Basic Education and Literacy Activities in Canada*, by Audrey Thomas, published by W.L.C.)

        –   The *B.T.S.D.* federal government journal on adult basic education becomes *Adult Training*.

        –   *Manpower Training at the Crossroads* conference (Ottawa). Sponsored by the C.A.A.E. and the I.C.E.A. (Institut canadien d'education des adultes).

- *Adoption of the *Recommendation* on the Development of Adult Education by the 19th Session of the U.N. General Conference, Kenya.

1977 – National Conference on Adult Literacy (Ottawa). (Convened by the W.L.C. Canadian Project for Adult Basic and Literacy Education.) Out of this Conference was formed the Movement for Canadian Literacy.

1979 – *The Mexico Declaration on the Decisive Role of Education in Development. (Sponsored by UNESCO with the cooperation of the U.N. Commission for Latin America and the Organization of American States. Spoke of the role of education as an integral part of economic, social and cultural planning.)

1980 – *Conference on professional aspects of literacy work (Arusha, Tanzania). (Sponsored by the international Institute for Educational Planning and UNESCO.) (A second conference was held in Madras in 1982.)

– Celebration by Metropolitan Toronto Library Board of 150 years of the founding of the Mechanic's Institute. (The M.I. was one of the predecessors of the Metropolitan Toronto Library, with its reading rooms, as well as courses in arts and sciences.)

1981 – *International Seminar on Adult Literacy in Industrialized Countries (England). (Promoted by the International Council for Adult Education, and supported by UNESCO, the British Council, and the U.K. Department of Education and Science.) (Organized by the National Institute of Adult Education and the Adult Literacy and Basic Skills Unit of England and Wales.)

1982 – *Udaipur (India) "Declaration: Literacy for All by the Year 2000" (initiated by the German Foundation — D.S.E.).

– *N.G.O. (I.C.A.E.) Conference on Adult Education and Authentic Development (Paris).

1983 – *International Seminar: Cooperating for Literacy (Berlin). (An overview of the World Literacy situation and major issues.) (Sponsored by the I.C.A.E. and the German Foundation for International Development.)

– *U.S.A. campaign to combat adult illiteracy.

1984 – First Collective Consultation of International Non-Governmental Organizations on Literacy (UNESCO, Paris).

1985 – *Fourth UNESCO International Conference on Adult Education (March, Paris). (Declaration: "The Right To Learn.")

– *N.G.O. (I.C.A.E.) Conference on Adult Education, Development and Peace (Buenos Aires, Argentina).

– *Conference: Reflection on the Decade of Women (Nairobi, Kenya).

-   *UNESCO: Resolutions on Literacy, General Conference of the twenty-third session (Sofia, Bulgaria). (October.)

-   Publication of *The Right To Learn*. (Report of the Work Group on Adult Literacy, the Board of Education for the City of Toronto.) (October.)

1986 –   *The first international conference on the History of Adult Education (Oxford, England).

-   *Workshop of Specialists in Europe on Prevention of Functional Illiteracy and Integration of Youth into the World of Work. (Sponsored by the UNESCO Institute of Education, Hamburg.) (Included an overview of illiteracy in industrialized countries.)

1987 –   *Founding of the Commonwealth Association for the Education and Training of Adults (CAETA) in India. Mandate to support training programs in the Commonwealth, professional development and international sharing.

-   *Second international conference on Literacy in Industrialized Countries, Toronto (sponsored by the I.C.A.E.)

1990 –   *Declared by the United Nations as International Literacy Year.

CHAPTER 3:

The Language of Experience and the Literacy of Power

Richard Darville

EMPOWERMENT AND THE FORMS OF LITERACY

This paper develops two major themes about literacy work. The first theme is that literacy is not simply one kind of skill or activity. This has become a commonplace assertion in the literature of the field. Guthrie and Kirsch (1984) remind us that literacy encompasses a diversity of purposes, materials and competencies, so that we need a "social-interaction perspective" to understand it. Cervero (1985) asserts that — although a single definition of literacy may be a convenience to managers of instruction — no single definition will suffice for guiding the practice of literacy work, or for analyzing literacy. Cook-Gumperz (1986), following Szwed (1981), writes of a "pluralistic conception of literacy." Weinstein argues:

> . . . that literacy is more than a set of mechanical skills and that the practices of reading and writing are inextricably bound within specific uses by particular actors from their different positions in the social order (Weinstein, 1984: 480).

That is, literacy is embedded in social organization. The term "social organization" points to the things people do, their social practices; and to the relations among people brought into being by those practices. Literacy's "operative meaning" derives not from individual skill but from the fact that literate skills and materials are shared among people in literate communication with one another (Havelock, 1976, 20). When people write, they produce the social organization that exists, in part, through writing. When people read, their procedures of reading are elements of social organization. Careful historical and ethnographic work has begun to display how people use different literate practices, and are tied together in different ways, when literacy is a matter of religious ritual and study, or when it is a matter of a community's own informal communication and record-keeping, or when it is used in administrative processes (Scribner and Cole, 1981; Graff, ed., 1981; Heath, 1982 & 1983; Odell and Goswami, 1982; Weinstein, 1984; Reder and Green, 1983). I want in this paper to build on the ways of thinking that this work makes available.

Empowerment is the second major theme that this paper develops. In literacy work, we have a long-standing discussion (most clearly crystallized in

25

the work of Freire, 1972; 1985) about how developing literacy is empowerment, a way that people can "name their world," give voice to the realities of their lives, gain some distance from those realities, and reflect upon them.

I want to argue that, in our kind of society at least, we need to join these two themes, to think about literacy as empowerment in conjunction with the idea that literacy has more than one form. Certain forms of literacy are part of the power of those who have power — for example, regulations, applications, contracts, invoices, signs, written speeches, identification cards, licenses, letters, memoranda, laws and judicial decisions. In asking what people learn when they become literate as an empowerment, we need to examine how the lack of this kind of literacy helps to constitute disempoweredness in our society, and how other forms of literacy are themselves alternative forms of power. These themes, the forms of literacy, and literacy as empowerment and as power, are difficult to come to terms with. We need to conceptualize clearly the various forms of literacy, so that when we say that literacy is more than one thing, we don't abandon ourselves to seeing it as an unthinkable proliferation of things.

The following pages will elaborate a distinction between two forms of literacy. In one form, prototypically narrative, people write down words that are anchored in experience as experience is lived through. In a second form, writing is anchored in organizational processes in which policies are set, work organizations determined, cases written up. We can label these forms narrative and organizational literacy. A literacy student about to visit city hall to sit in on hearings about welfare rates, when asked about how his group might write about this activity, gave two distinct answers. One was to "write about our trip;" one was to "say what was good and bad about what we heard." The difference between the story that would describe a trip to city hall, and the argument that would engage with a discussion of welfare rates, is of central importance in our understanding of what literacy is, how it develops, and how it carries power.

This set of themes also defines the audience for this paper — "literacy workers," people who define their work as the development of literacy, and whose central questions therefore revolve around what we do when we teach.[1] Their central questions do not, for example, begin with how to manage literacy work, or how to sell the issue in the political process. (Of course, literacy workers may come to be concerned with management and politics — because they set the boundaries around the space within which literacy work gets done).

THE LANGUAGE OF EXPERIENCE

It is striking that, in the face of diverse forms of literacy, literacy workers often choose, and are advised to choose, to work with a concrete and especially a narrative form of literacy. This strategy is most prominently articulated in the "language experience" approach (Kennedy and Roeder, 1975, provide a good introduction; the approach is still central in such an up-to-date compendium of literacy teaching precepts as Thistlethwaite, 1986). The language experience approach recommends the use of reading and writing which tell learners' experience. This includes both "dictated stories" — teachers' writing of stories that students tell — and students' writing of their own stories. Such stories from the outset anchor literacy in learners' actions and experiences, and in the meaning that those actions and experiences have for them. Anchoring in action and experience could be produced with other literate forms, such as lists, recipes, instructions, aphorisms and proverbs. But stories are prototypically recommended in the language experience approach. (With the terms "story" and "narrative," I mean to point to stories that relate and are anchored in personal experience, or "personal narratives.")

Learners beginning to work on writing often say: "I don't have anything to say," or, "I don't know how to explain it." Literacy workers often then listen to them, and say, "Just write that down." As they write, they write a meaning they already possess. To convey it, they use, and in time acquire facility at, an appropriate complexity of expression (cf. Gamberg, 1985).

In selecting topics and materials for learners' reading and writing even beyond the most basic levels, teachers often stick with narrative forms of literacy. It is only a reasonable extension of the wisdom of the language experience approach (whether or not we continue to use that term) to select topics and materials that anchor language in familiar action and experience. The experience involved may not be the learners' personal experience, but that of someone whom the learner can easily follow along. Thus literacy workers often choose stories of "ordinary people" — people (workers, mothers, and so forth) like or sensible to the learners — who live through the events of their lives, do one thing and then another, face a dilemma and make a choice, encounter a danger and come through it. In such stories, meaning is embedded in the action and experience of credible and familiar individuals (even if those are fictional).

It is the common experience of literacy workers that this point of departure is a powerful stimulus to literacy learning. Beginning with the familiar meaning of language experience stories, learners can focus their attention on what is, commonsensically, the first difficulty in literacy, the mechanical skill of getting the words off or onto the page. As people work on reading by reading their own stories, they know what happened next in the story, and so anticipate what words will come next on the page. Their momentum in reading leads them to forget their hesitations about reading. Students get similarly caught up in reading as they read others' stories about ordinary people. They follow the story, to see what happened. They find themselves reading words and ideas which they might not otherwise have been able to read.

Thus far, this argument has described the workings of language experience for the individual learner, as it might appear to a tutor focussing on an individual student. However, literacy is a social process — at many levels. Some aspects of this are visible within a one-to-one relationship of teacher and student. Consider this common experience of literacy work. After reading a story, a student says, "I can't read this," or, "I don't understand this," or, "I can't remember anything it said." A teacher then says what he thinks the story said. The student is startled that what the teacher says sounds familiar. He looks at the teacher quizzically as if to say, "What's wrong with you? You don't get it either?" And then he recognizes that he has read. Students learn that they *can read* by recognizing that they *have read,* that their readings make sense to others. People come to know themselves as readers by participating with others in working out meanings, in making readings. Part of the power of one-to-one tutoring is that it inexorably involves the student in this collaboration. In group literacy work, this collaboration can go on between students as well.

If we consider stories as they appear to a teacher in a classroom discussion or to a tutor in a group of students, different aspects of their workings appear. In the *social* workings of stories in literacy teaching, we see that stories lead to stories. Having read one story, students, like the rest of us, will often set off telling stories of their own that pick up on some topic within the first story. It "just happens" that people see in stories the grounds for a topical association of experiences they can tell. The concrete details of another's life lead hearers or readers to an awareness of their own lives. Narratives "stimulate by their particularity" (Creber, 1972, 130). Stories provide a "meeting-place" for all who have had the experience that the stories convey. Certain stories are "generative" in the sense that certain words are generative in the Freirian conception of literacy teaching. They work as "codifications" that objectify key elements of experience and allow reflection on them (Freire, 1971; 1985). Stories that are enchained to highly-charged stories of their readers' lives open up the expression of life-experience.[2]

A teacher or tutor can use this spontaneous topical association of stories as a self-conscious teaching device, a means to generate elaboration of the life-experiences with which learners are grappling. One can learn what story frames and character-types are highly charged for learners, by listening to learners carefully, and by using various stories and observing learners' responses.[3] The use of generative stories can work powerfully in several ways. It can even work explosively, and the teacher who would use generative stories should be forewarned. It can open up experience to expression — it can multiply stories. The telling of experience changes, and enlarges, what can be told. By opening experience to expression it can also open to reflection. It can work to coalesce the meanings of experience and explore its implications for action. The use of generative stories can produce a topical focus in literacy work, and make it, incipiently, organizing work. I will argue later that, in the long run, the generative power of stories provides a means to ground even organizational literacy in the life-experiences with which learners are grappling.

STORIES AND SOCIAL ORGANIZATION

I have referred above to "the workings" of stories. These workings, as with any literacy, are matters of social organization. The reading and writing of stories, as a distinct form of literacy, produce and express a distinct social organization. To analyze the social practices involved in the production of stories, and the relations created through those practices, is not a matter of analysis for its' own sake. An analysis of the social organization of narrative literacy provides us with a way to think about practices in teaching this literacy and its relationship to other literacies — to see both the power of language experience and its limitations. Such an analysis helps us understand how stories are grounded or anchored in experience, and so are the natural focus of language experience work, and *how* stories are generative. It helps us understand *how* the skills of narrative literacy differ from those of organizational literacy and thus what sort of teaching work can relate one literacy to the other.

To begin to delve into the social organization of stories, we can note that the teller of stories tells experience. Walter Benjamin wrote:

> The storyteller takes what he tells from experience — his own or that reported by others. And he in turn makes it the experience of those who are listening to his tale (Benjamin, 1969,87).

Stories are anchored in the experience of both teller or writer, and hearer or reader. In the telling of stories, people relate to one another through a shared orientation to experience and their understandings of experience. The story carries experience into a social relation. How does the narrative "taking" and "making" of experience that Benjamin describes actually work? Centrally, of course, narratives tell what people said, did and felt. Actions are explicitly tied to their agents, those who made what happened happen, and in that sense the narrative account of events is anchored in the lives of those who lived through them.

Furthermore, the teller of a story relates events sequentially as (or as if) they occurred in actual experience — in time, one thing after another. While the story goes on, the question is always: then what? Scholars who analyze narratives consistently emphasize that the teller intends the sequence of elements in the story to be understood as referring to a sequence of events in actual time. For example, in linguistics, Labov defines the "personal narrative" as a method of recapitulating past experience by matching a sequence of clauses to an actual sequence of events (Labov and Waletzsky, 1969; Labov, 1972). In conversation analysis, Sacks (1974) notes that in its "canonical form," narrative is constructed with correspondence to the temporal order of events reported.

Narratives' reference to experience involves not only *in what order* things happened, but *how* they happen. A reader or hearer who understands a story, who, as we say, "follows" the actions of the characters, engages in an active process of interpretation. She treats what is said as anchored in what happened, as that was lived through — as someone's experience. The teller of a story can never give an utterly complete account of what happened, so the reader must "fill in" its sense. In "making sense" of the story, she inexorably draws upon her own sense of how experience goes. She inserts what she knows about how people are and how things work, into what the text gives (Smith, 1983). She has no choice but to be reminded of her own experience.

Thus to follow a story is to orient both to the experience related, and to one's own experience that is used in interpreting what is related. Part of the attraction of stories is that while they allow one to live through things with their characters, at the same time they pull out one's own experience and sense of experience. In making sense of a story, one understands, one feels, its sense. This is perhaps especially clear when one responds to injustice in a story with anger, or to loss with sadness. The emotion is for the character, and it is one's own. The reader's experience commingles with that of the characters.

Stories not only arise within experience but also are informative about its nature. They make sense. The teller of a story selects the elements of a story so as to point to the story's significance. Likewise, in following along an unfolding story, a hearer or reader looks, as a sense-making practice, for the story's significance, for what it has to say about experience. A story that simply relates a succession of events, but without significance, will fall flat, will have no "point" (Labov and Waletzsky, 1969; Labov, 1972). A teller can be called to account for having a point. The story achieves an "amplitude" of significance because it doesn't box meaning in, but points to meaning.[4] Listeners or readers are led to their own experience partly as it is collected or grasped by the significance of the tale they are hearing or reading.

We can see still more about the social organization of stories if we look at story-telling as a conversational event. Conversational story-telling is a cooperative matter, in which the words, and the experiences, of conversationalists are linked to one another. Speaker and listeners engage with one another at the beginning of a story (e.g., "Say, have you heard . . .?" "No, tell me . . ."), and at its conclusion (e.g., "No kidding?" "Quite a character!" "That's outrageous!"). Speaker and listeners also engage with one another in relating stories and experiences. One story is often followed by another — and not by just any other story, but by one with definite ties to the one that has been told. The second story may share topic with the first. The teller of a second story may figure in it as did the teller of the first story. A second story may be tied to its predecessor through their significance — it "just goes to show you" the same thing (for analyse) in conversation analysis, see Sacks, 1974;1978).

Because stories are grounded in experience, literacy learners find them immediately accessible, and literacy teachers can rely on them as an accessible device for teaching. Learners can produce and comprehend many stories, out of meanings that are already given in their experience. Likewise the generative power of stories in a learning situation is based in the ordinary conversational practices of understanding stories as anchored in experience. Because hearers or readers of a story must use their own experience in understanding it, experiences are linked in the narrative, and stories generate other stories. Stories are linked through their topics and their significance, and so, of course, stories' generative capacity depends upon the sharing of experience among those in a circle of storytellers or learners.[5]

The discourse about language experience conveys a message of the transformative power of the act of writing. What is transformed is the writer's sense of himself as author. To achieve this transformation, we rely on a practice of encouraging students to just-write-it-down, and organize programs to allow such writing, and even the publication of such writing. This message is so important because it contradicts the ordinary relation of the illiterate or the little literate, especially if they are also poor, to a dominant literacy, that is, an organizational literacy, in which they are silenced. In this relation, their experience, even if it is written down, doesn't hold sway. And knowing that writing down one's experience doesn't count (or may be counted against one) itself generates illiteracy. Dealing fully with this situation requires that we understand the workings of the dominant literacy.

THE DOMINANT LITERACY

Any literacy is like a currency. It has a purchase on matters that it brings into a present relationship. It buys into a social organization. Its practices of reading and writing are elements of that social organization. Most of the texts that appear in our everyday lives do not directly relate us to one another or to one another's experience. Rather they relate us to one another, and to objects and events, through organizations. Organizational literacy — in, for example, job applications, Small Claims Court documents and union contracts — is concerned with effecting organizational process, not with telling individual experience. It is not about experience but about the ways that experience is managed, ordered, regulated and controlled.

Levi-Strauss pointed out that literacy was initially developed as a tool of domination. The one phenomenon always linked with the appearance of writing in human societies is "the establishment of hierarchical societies, consisting of masters and slaves, and where one part of the population is made to work for the other part." Writing

> . . . was connected first and foremost with power: it was used for inventories, catalogues, censuses, laws and instructions; in all instances, whether the aim was to keep a check on material possessions or on human beings, it is evidence of the power exercised by some men over other men and over worldly possessions (1973, 18).

In the last 600 years or so in the West, the forms of literacy now familiar to us have developed, and reading and writing abilities have spread. These developments have been part of changes in economic, religious and political organization and domination (Cipolla, 1969; Graff, ed., 1979). A dominant literacy has often been "pushed" (Johannson, 1979), by those in power, as a means of implanting ideas in a society, or of combatting ideas that contest existing power (cf. Donald, 1983; Curtis, 1985; Cook-Gumperz, 1986). In our society, the dominant literacy is that used in bureaucratic and professional organization. An interest in understanding literacy and literacy work in our society leads to an interest in understanding organizational literacy, that is, in "understanding the nature of power when power is vested in a documentary process, (Smith, 1984).

Descriptions of bureaucratic, administrative, legal, and professional language provide an important basis for understanding the social organization of organizational literacy (Heath, 1979; Campbell and Holland, 1982; Redish, 1983; White, 1983). In organizational literacy, what counts is how matters can be *written up* (to enter them into an organizational process), not how they can be *written down* (as an aid to memory or a way of relating experience). The common English idioms of verticality in writing express a fundamental difference in forms of literacy. Stories are not a tool of management. Because organizational literacy is not about personal experience, its users must not be caught up in the vortex of the immediate. They must rather be separated from the immediate and spontaneous expression of their own circumstances or of the lives of those they write about. This separation is essential to the reading practices of organizational literacy. It is part of "being literate."

Work in the dominant organizations in our society is done essentially, though not exclusively, through texts. People communicate, it is decided what really happened, and actions are taken, "on paper" (or computer screens). Even when people engage with one another face-to-face, the significance of what they say lies in what it means "for the record." Organizational literacy enables people who are dispersed in time and space to develop complementary ideas and actions. It enables them to act in concert towards the people or situations that the organization makes account of, administers, interprets, legislates for, in a probation office, a factory, or a Parliament. People using literacy to do organizational work simultaneously write, conceptualize and enact organizational processes. They make up a textually-mediated social organization (Smith, 1984).

Organizational accounts convey more than mere concepts and categories. They often describe particular events, but within an organizational framework of understanding, producing organizational narratives or "ideological narratives" (Smith, 1983). These include newspaper "stories," psychiatric "case histories" and educational "anecdotal reports." Such accounts refer to actual events, and even borrow some of the practices of the narrative, but they intend an organizational and not an experiential understanding. They refer not to experience but to the "particulars" of events, categorically relevant to their being acted on organizationally.

The dominant organizations and professions of our society share a textually-mediated character. Working in relation to one another, they organize their knowledge and take their actions in textual form. Practices for reading in various organizations are not entirely uniform. But they all pack the world into language itself, redefining events organizationally, apart from their immediacy. These literate practices are means of exercising power in our society — means not, ordinarily, available to those who become literacy learners.

I have drawn this account of organizational literacy, and of its distinctness from a language of experience, from the literature about the history of literacy, and from contemporary work in the social organization of knowledge. My intention is to make the presence of these distinct forms of literacy, and the gap between them, also visible in literacy work itself.

As teachers well know, learners often hesitate before the written word. Their hesitation involves more than a simple lack of skill. It is particularly likely to appear when they encounter an unfamiliar form of literacy, and the skills that they do have seem "out of place." Such a hesitation is commonly described as the "embarrassment" of people who don't read and write well about admitting it. But to emphasize embarrassment, without locating it in its place in the social organization, is to "blame the victims" (Ryan, 1971) for their feelings at moments when they are excluded or subordinated by the actions of others. Learners also often express anger or frustration at the language itself or at its authors. They say things like, "I always get mad trying to read that stuff," or, "They try to put you down with their big words," or, "Why don't they just say what they mean?" These commonplace expressions of hesitation, frustration and anger convey learners' sense of the gap between their literacy and the dominant literacy, their sense of what the written language is used for and whose power it serves. It is telling that the discourse about illiterates so often emphasizes their embarrassment, so seldom their frustration or anger. What it tells is that this discourse tends to be part of the dominant literacy rather than of a literacy that stands with those learning to be literate.

People in our society often feel out of place, hesitant, embarrassed, frustrated or angry, when encountering the printed word. They recognize that literacy conveys someone else's power. Indeed, in our society we all know these feelings, since they derive from a fundamental feature of our social organization. They appear in a particularly sharp form in the relations between illiterates and organizations that use literacy in their workings.

ORGANIZATIONAL LITERACY AND NARRATIVE REGRESSION

Narrative practices, as we have seen, tie actions to their agents, tie sequences of clauses to actual sequences of events, and point to the significance of events themselves. The practices used to produce and to read organizational accounts disorganize the narrative. They create a barrier for readers who depend upon narrative practices of reading, and thus make many readers "illiterate." Learners, and indeed many who do not use print by habit or daily practice, often misread organizational literacy. I will describe several instances of such misreading.

(1) Learners may not have the background knowledge that an organizational text presupposes of its readers. A simple form of this presupposing of background knowledge occurs when writers of organizational literacy delete agents of action. They leave themselves out of the texts they produce (they suppress the "I" or "we"), and they report events without naming their agents. They produce abstracted, agentless accounts through such grammatical constructions as nominalizations (*"Disturbances* followed last week's *announcement"*), participial modifiers ("of the widely *criticized"*), noun strings (*"training action plan"*), and agentless passives ("and it *was* hastily *withdrawn"*). These grammatical constructions are at the same time organizational constructions. For example, in such a standard organizational expression as, "Applications must be submitted . . .," the nominalization and the agentless passive sever activity from its agent, and thus produce an account of events that fits within the conceptual frame of an organization, not within the frame of experience (Kress and Hodges, 1979, 15-37; Ohmann, 1976).

If the agents of actions are deleted from texts, then readers must "fill them in" as one of their practices for reading the texts. In order to fill them in, readers must use a background knowledge of how actions are done and who would do them. Organizational literacy poses a barrier to people who do not have such background knowledge, and renders them illiterate.

(2) As we have seen above, a narrative practice, "just writing it down," is in a sense "natural." So is the counterpart practice of reading as if what is on the page were an individuals experience or thought. Because of the naturalness of this practice, people are apt to use it even when the texts they are reading intend other practices. Using a narrative practice when organizational practices are intended constitutes a "narrative regression." One aspect of the narrative regression involves temporal sequences. Those who use the reading practices of narrative literacy will misread conventional newspaper "stories" (or even fictional stories that use a flashback technique). Asked to tell events in the order that they happened, or to say which event happened before another, students often mistakenly recount them in the order that they appear in the text. They don't realize that the order of their actual occurrence has been undone in their reporting. (For a detailed account and other examples, see Darville, 1985).

(3) Again, organizational literacy presumes an organizational framework for understanding. Even filling out a job application skillfully requires reference to the organizational process in which the application is embedded. Thus we can understand new readers with application forms who say, "Date of application?" Whats that mean? What do I put there?" Readers can not assign a meaning to this category if they do not understand how the form may be used within an organizational process, perhaps by being filed by date. We can see the same process at work in people's oral accounts of their decisions in filling out job applications (as analyzed by Holland and Redish, 1982). Some "expert" users of applications describe what they do with reference to the intentions behind the application and the way it will be used in an organizational process. They selectively describe their lives and experiences, not with regard to what the questions on an application literally ask, but paying heed to "what they're looking for" or "what will get you points." "Novice" users, however, are "more constrained by the individual items," and, for example, leave out favourable information about themselves because the form doesn't ask for it.

(4) We can also see the narrative regression in many more general classroom events. When learners deal with texts such as newspaper articles, bureaucratic forms, or political pamphlets, their understanding may fall apart. They may say nothing. They may say, "I can't read that," (although they produce a fluent oral performance of it), or, "I can't remember anything I've read." They may "just have a hard time following instructions." Learners (as well as their tutors or teachers) may suffer bewilderment at a reading in which meaning remains opaque, and words seem, incalculably, to mean more than they say.

Likewise, student discussion of legal or political issues may not be pitched at "the right level of abstraction." Students sometimes report how they came to know about news events, rather than "what happened." They focus on individual moral considerations about some issue, rather than, say, the social effects or intentions of law. They read only personalized accounts in newspapers, or they make personalized readings of newspaper stories or bureaucratic documents if, for example, they interpret people as agents of their own actions, with distinct feelings and desires, rather than as agents of an organization.

(5) Learners will often use narrative or experience-anchored procedures in ways that traditional teachers, at least, find "inappropriate." An organizationally set instructional routine diverges from experience, necessarily. Thus a student doing drills on verb inflections encounters the exercise sentence, "This soup (need/needs) salt," and says, "That sentence is wrong. Salt is bad for you." If teachers want the content and sequence of classroom activities to follow a predetermined lesson plan, they may be frustrated by learners who make the content and sequence depend upon experience. Students commonly respond to reading passages not by focussing on "the point" stated in the curriculum guide, but by telling stories that the reading reminds them of. They make connections between situations through "configuration links," relating one whole scene to another whole scene, rather than by using labels for features of situations (Heath, 1982).

The significance of narrative regression is *not* that working class people who have difficulties with schooling possess a language that is "restricted" in the range of listeners or readers to whom it is addressed and sensible (Bernstein, 1971), or a language that has not developed "abstraction." (Edwards, 1976, provides a useful overview of theory and research on these themes). Narrative regression does not indicate any incapacity to abstract, or to speak or think apart from an immediate context. Abstraction is not a thing in itself, apart from the social organization in which it appears. Many who are little practiced at academic or bureaucratic abstraction create powerful abstraction by metaphor, or discuss abstract problems of love, learning, and so on. In organizations such as unions or churches that serve their own purposes, they are powerfully articulate (cf. Rosen, 1972). But when abstraction arises within an unfamiliar organizational frame, or within unfamiliar scientific conventions, and when it views immediately experienced events from outside, for purposes of knowing or controlling them, it can create what looks like "restrictedness" in these same people. Certain forms of literate abstraction generate "illiteracy."

TELLING STORIES AND TELLING MORE

The splitting off of the language of experience from the literacy of power is present at the very heart of literacy teaching and learning, in more ways than this brief paper can elucidate. We who do literacy work need to learn to observe, conceptualize, and even research these forms of literacy and the gap between them, in our ordinary work. To do so, we need to take seriously Weinstein's observation that practices of literacy are tied up with specific uses and users of literacy, and their locations in society. Being in a "location" in society is in part a matter of what you know, and how you know and communicate — including how literacy is for you a tool of knowing and communicating.

All of us, literacy learners included, are in a location to use narrative literacy to record our experience and share or exchange it with others. Just writing it down gives us the power of authorship, the power of reflection on what we have lived through, and the power to communicate to people at other moments in time and space. Language experience is then a progressive (empowering) teaching process, in at least these senses. The language experience approach is in part a reaction to the exclusion of learners (and others) from the distinct literacy of power. When students use material that conveys *their* lives, this undercuts any sense that literacy only belongs to other people. This reaction is valuable, indeed essential.[6] But it is also curtailed. In it we are still reacting — to a situation in which literacy dominates, by treating people's response to their domination as the problem to be dealt with. We work with a form of literacy which doesn't appear to be touched by organizational power, in an enclave of "experience."

Language experience does not extend to the uses of literacy as a means of power in the organizations that dominate our society. And the empowerment of language experience becomes condescension and disempowerment when we treat students merely as repositories of personal experience; or when we act as if, once they write their stories, they are empowered, and we have done what we can do. The story is the strength of the illiterate and the poor. They know the story. We mostly middle class literacy workers may not have much to teach them about that. Indeed we may have a lot to learn. But insofar as we are administratively competent, we do know certain organizational practices of reading and writing. They are something that we do have to teach — and that in teaching we can come to know better.

Progressive literacy workers have been, I think, reluctant to engage in systematic discussion of extending literacy beyond the rudimentary skills and personal expression, because we do not have terms for such a discussion. We do have a critique of the dominant conception of organizational literacy as "functional" or "competency-based," in work such as that of Griffith and Cervero (1977), Collins (1983), and Kazemak (1985). This critique is twofold. First, an external description of skill, devised for purposes of "managing instruction," silences learners; it does not arise from their experience, their life problems, or their questions. (Functional literacy, as usually conceived, rules out learners' stories). Second, a description of skill devised in the context of a management of instruction can't really grasp the practical competences that will be exercised in the contexts of actual performance in life and work.

I would add that the conception of "functional literacy" fails to provide a grasp of the character of organizational, power-carrying literacy, as a distinct form. It doesn't let us see the distinctness of organizational literacy, so that we could see what teaching might move across the gap that separates it from narrative literacy.

Literacy work needs means of dealing with organizational literacy — without abandoning the gains of language experience and the anchoring of literacy in everyday life. I want here to discuss, programmatically, a way of thinking about building on language experience. My aim is to suggest that we can do better than to lead people to "acquire" a functional literacy that starts outside their experience and purposes; we can assist people to "develop," beyond a personally expressive literacy (cf. Kazemak, 1984; 1985), an organizational literacy that starts within their experience and purposes. Learning the practices of organizational literacy can be grounded in learners' immediate experience, related in narratives.

The question to ask is: from what location would literacy learners use organizational literacy? They are not, as a rule, about to become bureaucrats, teachers or lawyers. They do not need the same literacy or the same knowledge as those who operate the dominant organizations. They will, however, continue to deal with bureaucrats, teachers and lawyers. Functional literacy, being administratively competent in the sense of being competent to be administered, *is* important. Practices of reading and writing, as the means whereby we articulate ourselves to organizations (cf. Smith, 1984), are essential to "participation" in one sense. They make up a knowledge constructed from the location of those who want to fit into organizational frameworks of activity and literacy.

But a "functional" knowledge of the practices of organizational literacy can be explicitly constructed from the location of those on whom these practices are used. Literacy learners have commonly for years or lifetimes confronted organizations and their literate practices as standing over and against them — on the job, in dealings with government agencies, and in contact with educational or social work and psychiatric interventions. This experience is the basis of a distinct educational task, one central to adult literacy education.

A first step beyond simply telling stories must be, paradoxically, to defend their autonomy. We need to tell and to respect accounts of experience, not only in isolation, but also facing up to the dominant organizations. Juxtaposing people's own stories with the organizational forms that would redefine them breaks the silencing of experience by those organizational forms. Insisting on how we write it down is a defence against being disappeared in how they write it up. So the student's story should be contrasted with the school records, the worker's account with the foreman's, the patient's testimony with the psychiatrist's case history, or, as Brecht (1977) shows us, people's history with the history of kings and generals ("Who built Thebes, with its seven gates?/ In books we find the names of Kings./ Did the kings drag along the lumps of rock?").

As noted above, stories' generative power can collect and concatenate experience. In stories, the social character of experience arises collectively, rather than being defined by organizational categories. In the narrative literacy process, a theme or frame can be leached out of a series of linked stories, and articulated to state what that collection amounts to. The process can, in short, coalesce the meanings of experience and explore its implications for action. A narrative frame can then point forwards toward other uses of literacy.

Thus the narrative process can provide an approach to organizational literacy as learners need to deal with it. Experience itself leads up to organization, at those moments when organization penetrates into experience. Organizational language, by leaving implicit its own frame and by describing actions without naming their agents, often makes it hard for people to see how they are regulated, and thus how they might deal with regulation. Starting from a collection of stories of and by those who are regulated can make visible how regulation works, and how it can be resisted. Embedding an approach to organizational knowledge in people's experiences and stories can display how ordinary people can come to want and to develop that knowledge for themselves.

All this suggests a way of working with learners' stories and building on them — in dialogue that takes place in classroom or tutoring situations. It also suggests a way of developing materials for learners — by composing stories which lead up to organization, when their characters find themselves in situations where they need organizational knowledge and need to read or write organizational texts. (For an example of such material, dealing with buying and working, and so with the law of consumer and labour contracts, see Darville, 1981). Finally these thoughts suggest a way of developing materials for learners — by composing stories which show the tension and opposition between experience and its organizational rendering, and support people in defining their own lives and qualities, apart from how those have been defined by organizations. (A work for adult literacy students describing how school organization penetrates into the lives and stories of those who become school failures, and, later, adult literacy students, is Darville, 1982).

Collecting and concatenating stories, displaying the commonalities of experience, can also begin a process that goes beyond adapting to organizational frames. That is, people can begin to ask how society works so that they have common experience — what, politicians, judges, business people, teachers, etc., do, that create the circumstances of their lives. Naming common experience, and the organizational processes that have constructed it, can lead to new understanding of individual experience. Confronting organizational literacy with actual life experience may ultimately support demands that organizations serve life rather than merely managing it, and thus to action in community groups, trade unions, churches, Indian bands. Of course, this action must take place in a society saturated with organizations and their literacy. So acting must mean, among other things, literate action — producing letters, pamphlets, petitions, newsletters, books, manifestos, that enable people, beginning from their experience, to participate together in creating the conditions of their lives. Literacy work in the long run means producing a new literacy that is capable of such action, capable of bringing together the language of experience and the literacy of power in new forms of organization that begin in people's experience and not in a bifurcated management over it. Such a project is of course beyond the grasp of literacy work itself, but literacy work has essential insight, skill and knowledge to contribute.

NOTES

1. This paper is, in part, an effort to come to terms with a number of years of experience of teaching literacy and of writing for literacy students. It also reflects many hours of conversation and debate with other literacy workers, and with others (sociologists, public legal educators, feminist organizers) interested in the fractures of language in our society. Although they are not the only ones, I want to mention Harold Alden, Evelyn Battell, Sandy (Clive) Cameron, Linda Forsythe, Nancy Jackson, Christopher Knight, Mary Norton, Carol Pfeifer, Michael Szasz and Frances Wasserlein.
2. The parallel to generative words is not exact. With generative words, syllables, the elements of words, are separated and recombined. With stories, event and significance, the elements of narrative, are separated and recombined.
3. I was first forcefully enough struck by the generative power of stories to conceptualize it, in reading, with students, stories of bullies and their victim (Dahl, 1979) and of a child treated cruelly by parents (Hart, 1977).
4. Provocative accounts of the "amplitude" that narrative achieves, as Walter Benjamin puts it, are offered by Benjamin (1969, esp. 89) for the classic art of storytelling; by Ricoeur (1978) for the parables of Jesus; and by Shah (1971) for the Sufi tales of the Mullah Nasrudin. Didion (1978) makes a chilling portrait of everyday contemporary events that can not be redeemed by any narrative significance.
5. There are many kinds of stories, and many questions about which of them are actually told and heard in literacy classes: which of them teachers are prepared to hear (cf. Sola and Bennett, 1985; Michaels, 1986); which of them students don't tell because they're in a school context, or because there are also men, or white people, or older or younger people, in the room; which of them are already penetrated by organizational processes and categories. I don't take up these questions here, focussing instead on the differences between stories generically, and the forms of literacy that stories don't get us to.
6. An exciting movement of working class and community publishing sees the publication of student (or other working class) writing as a demystification of the production of print and a disestablishment of the category of "literature" (see Morley and Worpole, eds., 1982).

REFERENCES

Barthes, Roland (1982), "Introduction to the Structural Analysis of Narratives," in Susan Sontag (ed.), *A Barthes Reader.* New York: Hill and Wang.
Benjamin, Walter (1969), "The Storyteller: Reflections on the Work of Nikolai Leskov," in *Illuminations.* New York: Schocken, 83-110.
Bernstein, Basil (1971), *Class, Codes and Control, Vol. I. Theoretical Studies Towards a Sociology of Languge.* St. Albans: Paladin.

Brecht, Bertolt (1977), "A Worker Questions History," in Martin Hoyles (ed.), *The Politics of Literacy.* London: Writers and Readers Publishing Cooperative, 62.
Campbell, L.J. and V. Melissa Holland (1982), "Understanding the Language of Public Documents, Because Formulas Don't," in Robert J. DiPietro (ed.), *Linguistics and the Professions.* Norwood, N.J.: Ablex.
Cervero, Ronald (1985), "Is a Common Definition of Literacy Possible?," *Adult Education Quarterly* 36:1, 50-54.
Cook-Gumperz, Jenny (1986), "Literacy and Schooling: An Unchanging Equation?" in Jenny Cook-Gumperz (ed.), *The Social Construction of Literacy.* Cambridge: Cambridge University Press, 16-44.
Cipolla, Carlo (1969), *Literacy and Development in the West.* Harmondsworth: Penguin.
Creber, Patrick (1972), *Lost for Words: Language and Educational Failure.* Harmondsworth: Penguin.
Curtis, Bruce (1985), "The Speller Expelled: Disciplining the Common Reader in Canada West." *Canadian Review of Sociology and Anthropology* 22:3, 346-68.
Dahl, Roald (1979), "The Swan," in *The Wonderful World of Henry Sugar and Other Stories.* New York: Bantam, 71-95.
Darville, Richard (1981), *Can We Make a Deal?* Vancouver: Legal Services Society of British Columbia.
_____ (1982), *It Takes Two to Fail.* Victoria: British Columbia Ministry of Education.
_____ (1985), "Telling Stories and Telling More: Literacy as a Social Relation," Paper Presented at the Meetings of the Canadian Sociology and Anthropology Association, Montreal.
Didion, Joan (1978), *The White Album.* New York: Bantam.
Donald James (1983), "How Illiteracy Became a Problem (And Literacy Stopped Being One)," *Journal of Education* (Boston) 165:1, 35-52.
Edwards, A.D. (1976), *Language in Culture and Class.* London: Heinemann.
Freire, Paulo (1972), *Pedagogy of the Oppressed.* New York: Herder and Herder.
_____ (1985), "The Adult Literacy Process as Cultural Action for Freedom," in *The Politics Of Education.* South Hadley, Mass.: Bergin and Garvey.
Gamberg, Ruth (1983), "Has Writing Been Underestimated?" *Literacy/ Alphabétisation* 8:3, 4-7.
Graff, Harvey (ed.) (1981), *Literacy and Social Development in the West.* Cambridge: Cambridge University Press.
Griffith, William S. and Cervero, R.M. (1977), "The Adult Performance Level Program: A Serious and Deliberate Examination," *Adult Education* 27, 209-224.
Guthrie, John T. and Irwin S. Kirsch (1984), "The Emergent Perspective on Literacy," *Phi Delta Kappan* 66:5, 351-55.
Hart, Tom (1977), "Amanda," in *Safe on a Seesaw: A Book of Children.* London: Quartet.
Havelock, Eric (1976), *The Origins of Western Literacy.* Toronto: Ontario Institute for Studies in Education.
Heath, Shirley Brice (1979), "The Context of Professional Languages: An Historical Overview," in James E. Alatis and G. Richard Tucker (eds.), *Language in Public Life.* Washington, D.C.: Georgetown University Press, 102-18.
_____ (1982), "Protean Shapes in Literacy Events: Ever-Shifting Oral and Literate Traditions," in Deborah Tannen (ed.), *Spoken and Written Language: Exploring Orality and Literacy.* Norwood, New Jersey: Ablex, 91-117.
_____ (1983), *Ways With Words: Language, Life and Work in Communities and Classrooms.* Cambridge: Cambridge University Press.
Holland and Redish (1982), "Strategies for Understanding Forms — and Other Public Documents," in Deborah Tannen (ed.), *Text and Talk.* Washington, D.C.: Georgetown University Press, 1982, 205-218.
Johansson, Egil, "The History of Literacy in Sweden," in Harvey Graff (ed.), *Literacy and Social Development in the West.* Cambridge: Cambridge University Press, 151-182.
Kazemak, Francis (1984), "Adult Literacy Education: An Ethical Endeavour,"*Adult Literacy and Basic Education* 8:2.
_____ (1985), "Functional Literacy Is Not Enough: Adult Literacy as a Developmental Process," *Journal of Reading* 28:4, 332-35.
Kennedy, Katherine and Stephanie Roeder (1975), *Using Language Experience with Adults: A Guide for Teachers.* Syracuse, New York: New Readers Press.

Kress, Gunther and Robert Hodges (1979), *Language as Ideology.* London: Routledge and Kegan Paul.

Labov, William (1972), "The Transformation of Experience in Narrative Syntax," in *Language in the Inner City,* Philadelphia, University of Pennsylvania Press, 354-396.

_____ (1982), "Speech Actions and Reactions in Personal Narrative," in Deborah Tannen (ed.), *Analyzing Discourse: Text and Talk.* Washington, D.C.: Georgetown University Press, 219-47.

Labov, William and J. Weletzsky (1969), "Narrative Analysis: Oral Versions of Personal Experience," in J. Helm (ed.), *Essays on the Verbal and Visual Arts.* Seattle: American Ethnological Society.

Levi-Strauss, Claude (1973), "'Primitive' and 'Civilized' Peoples: A Conversation with Claude Levi-Strauss," in Robert Disch (ed.), *The Future of Literacy.* 15-19.

Michaels, Sarah, "Narrative Presentations: An Oral Preparation for Literacy with First Graders," in Jenny Cook-Gumperz (ed.), *The Social Construction of Literacy.* Cambridge: Cambridge University Press, 1986, 94-116.

Morley, Dave, and Ken Worpole (eds.), *The Republic of Letters: Working Class Writing and Local Publishing.* London: Comedia Publishing Group, 1982.

Odell, Lee and Dixie Goswami, "Writing in a Non-Academic Setting," *Research in the Teaching of English* 16, 201-14.

Ohmann, Richard (1976), "Writing, Out in the World," in *English in America.* New York: Oxford University Press, 172-206.

Ong, Walter J. (1981), "Literacy and Orality in Our Time," in Gary Tate and Edward P.J. Corbett (eds.), *The Writing Teacher's Sourcebook.* New York: Oxford University Press, 36- 48.

Redish, Janice C. (1983), "The Language of the Bureaucracy," in Richard W. Bailey and Robin Melanie Fosheim (eds.), *Literacy for Life.* New York: The Modem Languages Association, 151-174.

Reder, Stephen and Karen Reed Green (1983), "Contrasting Patterns of Literacy in an Alaskan Fishing Village," *International Journal of the Sociology of Language* 42, 9-39.

Rosen, Harold (1972), *Language and Class: A Critical Look at the Theories of Basil Bernstein.* Bristol: Falling Wall Press.

Ricoeur, Paul (1978), "Listening to the Parables of Jesus," in Charles E. Reagan and David Stewart (eds.), *The Philosophy of Paul Ricoeur.* Boston: Beacon, 239-45.

Ryan, William (1971), *Blaming the Victim.* New York: Pantheon.

Sacks, Harvey (1974), "An Analysis of the Course of a Joke's Telling in Conversation," in Richard Bauman and Joel Scherzer (eds.), *Explorations in the Ethnography of Speaking.* Cambridge: Cambridge University Press.

_____ (1978), "Some Technical Considerations of a Dirty Joke," in Jim Schenkein (ed.), *Studies in the Organization of Conversational Interaction.* New York: Academic Press.

Scribner, Sylvia and Michael Cole (1981), "Unpackaging Literacy," in Marcia Farr Whiteman (ed.), *Writing.* Hillsdale, N.J.: Lawrence Erlbaum, 71-87.

Shah, Idries (1971), "The Subtleties of Mullah Nasrudin," in *The Sufis.* Garden City, N.Y.: Anchor, 63-110.

Smith, Dorothy E. (1974), "The Social Construction of Documentary Reality." *Sociological Inquiry* 44,257-268.

_____ (1983), "No One Commits Suicide: Textual Analysis of Ideological Practices." *Human Studies* 6, 309-59.

_____ (1984), "Textually-Mediated Social Organization." *International Social Science Journal* 36,59-75.

Sola, Michele and Adrian T. Bennett, "The Struggle for Voice: Narrative, Literacy and Consciousness in an East Harlem School," *Journal of Education 167:1 (1985), 88-110.*

Szwed, J. (1981), "The Ethnography of Literacy," in Marcia Farr Whiteman (ed.), *Writing.* Hillsdale, N.J.: Lawrence Erlbaum.

Thistlethwaite, Linda (1986), "The Adult Beginning Reader: Assessment, Discussion, Instruction," *Lifelong Learning* 10:2, 4-7.

Weinstein, Gail (1984), "Literacy and Second Language Acquisition: Issues and Perspectives," *TESOL Quarterly* 18:3, 471-484.

White, James Boyd (1983), "The Invisible Discourse of the Law: Reflections on Legal Literacy and General Education," in Richard W. Bailey and Robin Melanie Fosheim (eds.), *Literacy for Life.* New York: Modern Languages Association.

CHAPTER 4:

Federal Legislation and Adult Basic Education in Canada

Alan M. Thomas
Maurice Taylor
Carolyn Gaskin

PART I

Popular versions of the control and administration of education in Canada allow little room for considerations of federal participation in "basic" education of any kind, with the possible exception of provisions for Native Canadians. "Basic" education, which must deal with the mastering of literacy, numeracy, and elementary social skills, is surely the domain of the provinces, as clearly established by the British North America Act (1867) and subsequent judicial decisions. To be sure, the federal government has played, and continues to play, a major role in the wider reaches of "basic" education, adult and otherwise. These activities, represented by such agencies as the Canadian Broadcasting Corporation, and indeed the regulation of all broadcasting, the National Film Board, the museums, galleries, and supportive activities of the Canada Council, play an immense and powerful role in the continuing socialization demanded of all modern societies. But when it comes to specific instruction characteristic of training and education, that surely has been and is dominated exclusively by the provinces.

Any reply to that assertion has to be guarded and qualified. While the provinces have, by means of their monopolization of familiar and conventional educational delivery systems, maintained the higher profile, the fact is that the provision of basic education for adults has been defined, and relentlessly driven — at least until recently — by the efforts of the federal government.

So much is this the case that Canada is rapidly approaching a time when the basic responsibilities for the maintenance of systems of genuine "continuing education", available to all ages, for multiple purposes, defined both individually and collectively, will have to be re-examined and reassigned. Nothing prompts that argument more cogently than an examination of the provisions for adult basic education in Canada, and the "stealthy" incursions of the federal government.

Adult Basic Education has been defined elsewhere in this volume. From one point of view, it is simply the adult equivalent of elementary education, traditionally considered, in western societies, as that education necessary for the entrance of the young to the society as a whole. The character of those societies has determined that this initial education be concerned primarily with literacy with respect to printed information; numeracy, and basic "lifeskills".

It is assumed, or more accurately, hoped, that the other dimensions of the child's life, family, neighbourhood, economic circumstances, each one a source of learning if not teaching, will be reasonably supportive of the objectives pursued by the school.

Such is not the case with respect to basic education for adults. What has formed this enterprise primarily has been the need for entry to the work force, rather than the society as a whole, and a realization that the other dimensions of the adult's life are likely to be unsupportive if not downright hostile to the efforts of the educational enterprise. Since the turn of this century the developments in the economy have, with increasing relentlessness, altered the demands for skills necessary not only to enter but also to remain in the work force, the character of adult basic education has changed more frequently than has the character of elementary education for the young, despite the much greater public attention directed to the latter. For understandable reasons, perhaps, the provinces, until quite recently, seem to have clung to the promised potential of compulsory education of the young, hoping that the demands for education by adults would eventually decline. The need for "elementary education" would have been taken care of for all citizens as children and young people (Thomas et al, 1979:89).

Nevertheless, with its repeatedly acknowledged responsibility for the state of the national economy, and for employment, the federal government has been obliged to respond to the circumstances of certain groups of individuals with respect to their ability to participate in both. As the century has progressed, the federal response has had to be increasingly in educational terms, or, at least in terms of the needs of larger and larger groups of individuals, primarily adult individuals, for access to opportunities to learn knowledge and skills they do not possess.

While our attention can be focussed on the three inclusive pieces of legislation of the past three decades: The Technical and Vocational Training Assistance ACT (TVTA) 1960; The Adult Occupational Training Act (AOTA) 1967; and the National Training Act (NTA) 1982, those developments do have a history. A glimpse of that history helps to explain their character, and may assist us in planning for the next stages.

PART II

Federal legislative activity can be divided into roughly three periods with respect to educational adventures.

The first period extends from the passage of the Agricultural Instruction Act (AIA) 1913, to the Youth Training Act (YTA) 1939. This period includes, amongst others, The Technical Education Act (TEA) 1919, and the Vocational Education ACT (VEA) 1931. The unabashed use of the word "education" is to be noted. Provincial sensibilities had not yet sharpened.

The second period extends from the introduction of the Youth Training Act (1939), to the passage of the Adult Occupational Training Act (1967). These twenty-eight years were years of growing and varied educational activity by the federal government. In fact, the government was accumulating a variety of experience in dealing with the stimulation, financing, and delivery of educational services, in conjunction with increasingly independent-minded provinces. It was, simultaneously, learning to cope with a larger working population with greater diversity of every imaginable kind, especially diversity in educational and training experience.

Principal acts in this period included: The Unemployment Insurance Act (UIA) 1930; The Vocational Training Coordination Act (VTCA) 1942; The Veterans' Rehabilitation Act (VRA) 1945; The Children of War Dead (Education Assistance) Act (CWDA) 1953; The Technical and Vocational Training Assistance Act (TVTA) 1960; The Vocational Rehabilitation of Disabled Persons Act (VRDP) 1961; The Youth Allowances Act (YAA) 1964; and the Canada Student Loans Act (CSLA) 1964. Not all, obviously, are devoted to adult basic education, but each one represents further assertion of federal interest in some areas of education, though by then the word "education" was rarely used. Each contributed to the experience reflected in the final and most ambitious phase of federal participation in education, and particularly in the basic education of adults.

The third and final period has been dominated by the two landmark acts of the past twenty years: The Adult Occupational Training Act (1967), amended in 1972 and repealed in 1982; and the National Training Act introduced in 1982, and still the determining piece of legislation. At the same time approximately as the AOTA was introduced, the federal government entered into an agreement with the provinces to pay half of the cost of post-secondary education. This accord, for the next twenty years, separated the federal government's concern for assistance to the provinces for purposes of the provision of conventional educational resources, from its interest in training/education devoted to older groups in the population, and more narrowly directed to immediate employment. It would appear that the federal government believed that having relieved provincial concern for the former, it was freer to move ever more independently of provincial governments with respect to the latter.

In the first period educational legislation was devoted primarily to matters of substance, such as agriculture and/or industry, the promotion of which required support of an educational character. Both are areas of joint federal and provincial responsibility.

The preamble to the AIA states: "Whereas it is desirable that encouragement be given to agriculture in all the provinces of Canada, and whereas great and permanent benefit will result through education, instruction, and demonstration carried on along lines well-devised and of a continuous nature; Therefore . . ." (Queen's Printer, 1913:135). The TEA states: "technical education, means and includes any form of vocational, technical or industrial education or instruction, approved by agreement . . ., as being necessary or desirable to aid in promoting industry and the mechanical trades and to increase the earning capacity, efficiency, and productive power of those employed therein." (Queen's Printer, 1919:3933) The third act, the VEA, shows signs of considerable haste in its drafting — it was 1931 — and leaves almost all matters of substance to the regulations. However, the definition in the TEA, with its reference to both the benefit to the enterprises, and to the workers that made them possible, reflects the emergence of a dual concern that has been troublesome and difficult to reconcile ever since.

In addition, the lumping of the term "vocational", which suggests education/training for any form of employment, with the two other terms "industrial" and "technical", conveying the idea of objectives associated with specific domains of enterprise, suggests the growing inclusiveness of federal concern for all forms of employment.

The foundations for federal enterprise in education, and for future federal/provincial relationships, are to be found in these three acts. The first is the dependence upon provincial delivery systems, and the corresponding necessity of seeking agreements with individual provinces. Fixed sums of money were to be made available to cooperating provinces over fixed periods of years. In the TEA, the first mention of the tying of federal grants to actual provincial expenditures appears. It does not appear in the VEA, perhaps an early victim of the depression and provincial financial hardship, though it was to reappear as a fixture in later legislation.

Federal control through specific terms of agreement and reporting intensifies in each subsequent act. While no specific reference is made to participants, whether adult or youth, it can be inferred that the population sought after is other than that reached by formal schooling, with the exception of the students of veterinary colleges singled out for assistant in the AIA. In each subsequent act there are more frequent references to the procedures for expending funds carried over from a previous year. What this suggests is that, despite the opportunity of one hundred percent federal funding, not all the provinces were exhibiting the initiative in undertaking the programs for which the federal government had hoped. This frustration grew, and became a dominant factor in the late nineteen-sixties.

The second period of legislative activity related to education, between the years 1939 and 1967, displayed developments of two distinct kinds. Few of the acts in either category were exclusively concerned with adult basic education, some not at all. However, each reflected a steady growth in federal initiative, and each contributed opportunity for increased federal experience in the management of education in Canada. The foundations for the following stage are clearly apparent.

The first of the two categories includes a group of acts that identify specific groups of individuals as recipients of special services or benefits. The second category includes three major acts dealing, potentially at least, with all adult Canadians in terms of their relationship to employment and the labour force. What each of these latter acts reveals is the steadily increasing degree to which that relationship involves access to learning and education, or the lack of it.

In the first category, groups of individuals are defined in terms of specific age; youth; specific circumstances; veterans; specific condition; the disabled; and a combination of age and circumstance, as in the case of Children of the War Dead. The matter of age makes its first appearance in the YTA, where youth is defined as 16-30 years, a generous definition by any measure, and without doubt reflecting the experience of the depression years, as well as the apprehension about the war to come. The YAA, a quarter century later, defines youth as 16-18, though it does not restrict the benefits to that limited period of years. All future legislation form the federal government dealing with education/training touches on this problem, which is a thorny problem indeed. Lurking always in the background is the reluctance to be perceived to be invading the provincial domain of exclusive authority over "in-school" youth.

A second emerging practice pervading most of this legislation is the tying of all benefits to successful attendance at school. Where individuals, or groups of them, are the principal concern, their decisions about the type and duration of the education to be pursued are determining. This is the case provided the program selected falls into provincially determined educational categories, such as programs directed to secondary school leaving certificates, or university programs leading to a bachelors degree. This is in contrast to later versions of the other category of legislation in this period, where most adult basic education is to be found, where the duration of the educational program is fixed by the legislation itself.

Dependence upon provincial delivery systems, predominantly educational systems, was steadily enlarged as successive acts emerged in this period. The one exception was the YTA, where municipalities were involved in providing work/learning programs, a practice that reappears in later legislation. However, the methods of financing displayed dramatic alterations. Instead of providing formula-based sums of money to provinces over fixed periods of time, with the exception of the VRDPA, money was provided directly to individuals in the various groups, at their request. Funds were provided directly by the federal government to individuals for tuition (CSLA), for a living allowance while attending school (YAA), or both (DVA, CWDEAA). In this manner, the federal government was adding the stimulation of consumer demand to its efforts to win provincial support for its educational goals. In the case of DVA further federal assistance was made available to educational providing agencies that had been selected by veterans. Therefore, despite the continued dependence upon provincial delivery systems, the federal government was accumulating experience in dealing directly with individual citizens in the pursuit of its learning and educational objectives. This experience was to become a major factor in the introduction of the AOTA in 1967.

An additional direct result of these varied financial experiments was the evolution of a new variety of relationships with the provincial governments. They ranged from the already familiar agreements of the previous period, for example in the VRDPA, to the absence of any formal agreement, for example in the DVA and the CWDEAA, despite the nearly exclusive use of provincial educational delivery systems. However, the federal insistence on increased specificity, greater control, and better evaluation was characteristic of even the familiar types of agreements. For the first time in educational legislation, the practice of "matching" grants made its appearance, in legislation in both of the categories of this period. What appears to be the case is that the federal government had decided that its interests in learning and education were or should be the interests of the provincial governments as well. What was needed, therefore, was incentive and encouragement, rather than the permissiveness implied by one hundred percent financing.

The second category of development in this period contains three landmark acts: the UIA (1940); the VTCA (1942); and the TVTA (1961). Unlike the other group, these acts deal with the circumstances and conditions of employment or the lack of it, and therefore are addressed to the entire population of Canada insofar as it is involved in conventional employment. The reference to domains in the UIA, and implicitly in the other two acts at the outset, does have the effect of excluding some workers, notably housewives.

The UIA established three main factors of interest to us. It introduced the principal of federal dealing with individual citizens in a context that was to become increasingly related to learning and education on a much larger scale than the acts of the first category. It established an independent federal structure of employment and information offices throughout Canada, which in various guises in the future allow the continuance of direct contact with individual citizens for purposes of training/education, and counselling. Finally, by implication at the very least, it established the direct connection between some form of training/education, and employment, and the legitimacy of a direct federal interest in that connection.

> 28. The receipt of insurance benefit by an insured person shall be subject to the following statutory conditions, namely —
> (iv) that he proves that he duly attended, or that he had good cause for not attending, any course of instruction or training approved by the Commission which he may have been directed to attend by the Commission for the purpose of becoming or keeping fit for the entry into or return to employment.
>
> (Queen's Printer, 1940:189-223)

The VTCA (1942) displayed most of the characteristics of legislation passed during wartime. Inclusions were as global as possible and much was left to the Minister's discretion. It enlarged the role of the federal government in three main ways. The first was by means of the definition of vocational training:

> "Vocational training" means any form of instruction the purpose of which is to fit any person for gainful employment or to increase his skill or efficiency therein, and, without restricting the generality of the foregoing, includes instruction to fit a person for employment in agriculture, forestry, mining, fishing, construction, manufacturing, commerce, or in any other primary or secondary industry in Canada.
>
> (Queen's Printer, 1942:5357)

The needs of individuals were at least equal to the needs of particular domains of enterprise. In this case the act specified that adults, and no longer just youths, were included.

Second, for the first time, an "educational" identification of the "training" involved was specified by reference to: "training on a level equivalent to the secondary school level" [Sec. 4(1)(e)]. With these two measures the door was open to the development of adult basic education under federal auspices.

Finally, there was the nature of the agreement with the provinces. No time limit, or financial limit was stated, but cost-sharing of varying dimensions was made explicit. In addition, there was the creation of a Vocational Training Advisory Council, a phenomenon to be found with increasing regularity in subsequent training legislation. The Council represented both the opportunity to seek consultation beyond the provinces, from representatives of employers and employees, and to include some of the provinces at least, in ongoing implementation and adjustment of the act.

The final step in this stage of development was represented by the TVTA (1960). This act brought the persistent attempts of the federal government to further its training/educational aims by the exclusive use of provincial educational delivery systems, to its concluding phase. Technical and vocational dimensions, heretofore considered distinct, were joined, and training was considered to include the same activities and domains as in the previous act.

However a new distinction was added by stating that any form of instruction leading to employment excluded training leading to university credit. Otherwise anyone pursuing technical/vocational training/education from secondary school level and upwards, and in any approved setting, was eligible for federal assistance. The scope was even more widely defined by clauses authorizing support for the training of instructors, including for the first time in this category of legislation, provisions for living allowances, and for substantial federal sharing of capital expenditures undertaken by the provinces. Adults were specifically included by reference to persons over regular school leaving age, which age was left to provincial determination.

It is clear that the federal government either believed or hoped that by maximizing the educational systems of the provinces, both in form and content, and by extending them to additional individuals in those provinces, namely adults, that the demands on it for an expanding economy and full employment could be met. Within the stated term for this act, six years, it became apparent that the goal could not be achieved. It was partly due to problems associated with basic education for adults, or the lack of it, that the failures began to manifest themselves (Thomas A. 1983)

Involved in the identification of millions of Canadians with minimal levels of literacy, and of other skills necessary for the successful entry to skill training programs, were the demands of the economy of the late sixties. It was becoming apparent that the full employment, characteristic of the "industrial" era at its best, was no longer achievable. The gap between emergence from existing educational programs, even those maximizing the "training" supported by the federal government, and successful entry into the labour force, was growing relentlessly.

In addition to technical development occurring within generations of working lives, which necessitated, for some, multiple retraining, traditional skills were being eliminated entirely. New jobs demanding the use of multiple skills and improved basic education were multiplying. It was no longer possible to depend upon early schooling to provide even sufficient basic education for a lifetime. Such world authorities as UNESCO and the Organization for Economic Cooperation and Development were promulgating the need for "lifelong learning" and "recurrent education" with the elaboration of appropriate public policies. During the last years of the TVTA, most provinces had been exploring the introduction of a whole new educational level of colleges with the purpose of extending initial schooling for those individuals who, for whatever reason, did not continue on to university. Most of the provincial governments expected that these colleges, whatever their specific form, would be financed basically by means of the formula funds flowing from the implementation of TVTA.

This expectation did not reflect the intentions of the federal government. All of these developments, plus the uneven impact of TVTA in the different regions of Canada, had inclined the federal government to become increasingly impatient with its nearly exclusive dependence upon provincial educational delivery systems.

The final period of legislative activity, dating from 1967 to the present, has been dominated by two pieces of legislation: the AOTA (1967) and the NTA (1982). Each of these acts extended the independence of the federal authority, with respect to training/education, and each has had impressive consequences for adult basic education.

The AOTA introduced into the area of general training/education, practices that had been developed in the "individual-centered" legislation of the previous period. The federal government would directly with individual citizens, through its already established offices across Canada, designed originally to engage in employment placement and counselling. At the request of a citizen seeking retraining for employment, the now named "Manpower Officer" would purchase, on behalf of that individual, training of up to 52 weeks or 1820 hours of part-time instruction. Purchases were to be made primarily, if not exclusively, from provincial or municipal authorities. Provincial governments were to be "reimbursed" for actual purchases or to be paid at an agreed upon rate. Citizens eligible for such training had to be one year over the school leaving age, and not have attended full-time school in the previous twelve months. Original eligibility for the associated training allowance was restricted to adults who had been in the labour force without substantial interruption for three years, and who had dependents. Both of those conditions were amended in 1972 to allow for housewives wishing to enter the workforce, and for single persons without dependents, to participate.

An additional mechanism was the right of the federal authorities to engage in agreements with employers, not only to support, financially, the training of employees in "generic" skills on site, but also to pay for training arranged by employers for their employees off the premises. However, the federal authorities were obliged to seek assurance that any courses proposed by an employer, or later any groups of employers, had been subject to "consultation" with the appropriate provincial government. A similar authority was left to the provincial governments with respect to the federal use of any other private sources of training: the agency had to be registered by the province, and approval obtained.

A final thrust of federal independence was to be found in section 12:

  (1) The Governor-General in Council may make regulations,
     (a) defining the expressions "instruction designed for university credit", "full-time instruction", "part-time instruction", "labour force", "training on the job", and "regular school leaving age" for the purposes of this Act.
     (b) specifying for the purposes of this Act, the circumstances under which an adult shall be deemed not to have attended school on a regular basis for any period.
     (c) prescribing, for the purposes of subsection (1) of Section 5, the method of determining the costs incurred by a province or a provincial or municipal authority in providing training in an occupational training course to adults . . .
                      (Queen's Printer, 1967:1210-1211)

Previously these definitions were mostly left to the provinces and the practices of their delivery systems. For purposes of capital construction low cost, long-term loans could be arranged, but grants and cost-sharing had been eliminated.

The most immediate effect of this act was to offer a new definition of who was an adult in Canada, and to introduce a new "school year" of 52 weeks as compared to the approximately 38 week provincial school year. What was significant about this determination was, not so much the contrast in the length of the two school years, as the fact that the legislation required the tying of educational achievement to specified time periods, which bore no obvious relationship to the time that might be required by different individuals tackling different learning goals. Subsequent evidence seems to suggest that it has been precisely the least well-educated individuals, those in need of adult basic education, that have suffered the most from this specification.

The NTA (1982) largely extends the freedom of action of the federal government. A major influence on the determination to become more independent of provincial delivery systems had presented itself in 1968 with the OECD review of the Canadian Manpower Training System (OECD, 1969). The Review had been positive with the exception of one characteristic of the program. The reviewers expressed amazement at the proportion of manpower training (80%) carried on in formal educational settings, as compared with the proportion (20%) carried out on the shop floor. The federal government had been making strenuous efforts, even within the terms of the AOTA to reduce the proportion of institutional training, and the NTA allowed them very much greater freedom to do so.

Many of the same provisions and definitions are repeated, though in the case of the federal government contracting for training with employers or with a "non-profit" organization, or in fact utilizing any alternative to provincial delivery systems, the province must be notified and register an objection within a specified period. The initiative seems more firmly in federal hands, since presumably a province is not going to say no forever. The Act also contains a provision for the federal government, "after consultation . . . with the governments of such provinces as it considers will be most effected, thereby [to] declare, by order, any occupation to be an occupation of national importance, if it is satisfied that there is or will be a national or regional shortage of workers in that occupation sufficiently serious to justify the special action" (Queen's Printer, 1982:3194). Presumably this represents a further attempt to overcome the regional variations that have plagued, in the federal view, the earlier dependence on provincial initiatives and delivery systems. With this Act still in force it is impossible to achieve the same evaluation as with respect to the earlier ones. However, it is possible to assess some aspects of the development of adult basic education during this third legislative period.

Initially that part of the program met with some success. It was acknowledged that many of the eligible trainees were not sufficiently educated to enter the skill training programs. More elementary programs were introduced, including Basic Training for Skill Development (BTSD), Job Readiness Training (JRT) and Work Adjustment Training (WAT) designed for individuals at the bottom of the scale. The availability of living allowances provided by both Acts, made it possible for many more from the poorest circumstance than previously, to commit themselves to full-time training. Nevertheless, from a high of 55,671 for all of Canada in 1972-73, the total declined to 29,170 in 1984-85 (Table 1). Even at its height, the program included only a tiny portion of the functionally illiterate in Canada. While the numbers of older workers have increased in the same period, indicating that a larger proportion of older adults are being included, the proportion of those with the least schooling, grades 1-7, declined from 19.4% in 1972-73 to 7.2% in 1984-85. And, despite the increase in the number of women entering the labour force, the percentage of women trainees has remained approximately the same over the twelve years represented (Table 2). It is difficult to believe, given the economic circumstances of the period involved, that the total number of functionally illiterate adults in Canada has dramatically declined, or that substantial numbers of them have found employment and therefore have not presented themselves for training.

Table 1
Institutional Training Summary:
Number of Trainees in Basic Training for
Skill Development Programme
1972–1985

Year	Type of Training (B T S D)*
1972-73	55,671
1973-74	52,684
1974-75	47,791
1975-76	45,889
1976-77	44,010
1977-78	43,960
1978-79	39,995
1979-80	37,459
1980-81	32,589
1981-82	28,972
1982-83	28,155
1983-84	28,686
1984-85	29,170

*Includes BJRT and WAT (Canada Manpower, 1986)

Source: Canada Manpower Training Program, National Training Program, *Annual Statistical Bulletin, 1976-77 – 1984-85.*

Table 2
Institutional Training Full Time Trainees
Characteristics Summary in Canada
1972-85
(Percentage)

CHARACTERISTIC		Fiscal Year					
		1972-73	1973-74	1974-75	1975-76	1976-77	1977-78
SEX	MALE	70.3	64.1	65.0	66.1	67.1	68.1
	FEMALE	29.7	35.9	35.0	33.9	32.9	31.9
AGE	19 AND UNDER	11.1	12.3	13.2	14.1	12.5	11.9
	20-24	33.1	34.4	37.2	37.6	40.0	40.0
	25-44	44.1	42.6	41.0	41.0	41.0	41.5
	45+	11.7	10.7	8.6	7.3	6.5	6.6
EDUCATIONAL LEVEL [1] (Years of Schooling)	1-7	19.4	17.0	13.0	14.1	12.1	11.6
	8	15.1	13.0	11.5	13.4	12.8	12.8
	9	16.1	16.3	17.1	16.2	16.2	16.5
	10	17.3	17.3	18.1	19.3	20.3	20.3
	11	14.1	12.1	8.9	12.5	13.2	13.5
	12	14.7	16.0	13.0	14.7	15.5	16.4
	13	0.8	2.8	7.8	3.7	4.1	3.6
	14+	2.5	5.5	10.6	6.1	5.8	5.3
LABOUR FORCE STATUS [1] (Prior to Training)	EMPLOYED	37.2	36.7	35.7	20.2	19.2	18.7
	UNEMPLOYED	55.5	54.2	52.9	66.0	66.8	66.5
	NOT IN THE LABOUR FORCE	7.3	9.8	11.4	13.8	14.0	14.8

		1978-79	1979-80	1980-81	1981-82	1982-83	1983-84	1984-85
SEX	MALE	66.6	67.5	69.2	70.9	74.3	73.4	169.4
	FEMALE	33.4	32.5	30.8	29.1	25.7	26.6	30.6
AGE	19 AND UNDER	11.7	10.7	9.8	8.1	7.0	6.0	4.7
	20-24	42.4	42.1	42.3	42.3	40.9	38.6	35.8
	25-44	40.9	42.3	43.1	45.1	47.7	50.2	53.5
	45+	5.0	4.9	4.8	4.5	4.4	5.2	6.0
EDUCATIONAL LEVEL[1] (Years of Schooling)	1-7.	8.5	8.6	9.6	7.5	6.8	6.5	7.2
	8	11.2	10.2	9.8	8.9	8.7	8.2	8.0
	9	15.4	14.4	13.4	13.0	12.0	11.8	11.3
	10	21.4	20.5	20.1	19.0	18.4	17.6	17.5
	11	14.7	14.5	14.1	15.6	15.2	14.6	13.7
	12	18.9	20.9	21.7	24.1	28.5	30.2	30.4
	13	4.1	4.5	4.5	5.5	5.3	5.4	5.6
	14+	5.8	6.4	6.8	6.4	5.1	5.7	6.3
LABOUR FORCE STATUS[1] (Prior to Training)	EMPLOYED	14.7	13.7	11.8	15.6	11.2	11.1	11.5
	UNEMPLOYED	71.5	72.3	72.7	69.5	76.4	78.1	76.9
	NOT IN THE LABOUR FORCE	13.8	14.0	15.5	14.9	12.4	10.8	11.6

(1) Not documented for Apprentice trainees since January 1, 1975.

Source: Canada Manpower Training Program, National Training Program *Annual Statistical Bulletin* 1976-77 to 1984-85

PART III

Two explanations are possible. The first is that the federal government has become convinced that adult basic education is truly elementary education of a formal nature, for adults rather than children. For that reason it falls within the domain of the exclusive responsibility for education claimed by the provinces. In short, after prolonged disputes with the provinces over educational jurisdiction, the federal authorities seem to have concluded that adult basic education must be accepted as fully within the responsibility of the provinces, and, in addition, it is their clear responsibility to pay for it. Some credence can be attached to this conclusion by evidence of the fact that the number of adults has increased substantially in programs offered by school boards in some provinces. In Ontario, for example, there are more than 16,000 full-time, daytime, students, of 22 years or more, in secondary schools. The increase has been on the order of 800% in approximately the same period as that covered by Tables 1 and 2 (Ministry of Education, Ontario, 1986).

Many of these adult secondary school students are being supported by Unemployment Insurance benefits. We might conclude that in these cases the original UIA had reached its full potential, if the provision of such benefits to such students seemed uniform across Canada or even within specific regions. There seems no evident interpretation of the UIA that would prevent such support, and indeed it seems a logical extension of its intentions, but clarification and consistency is badly needed. The fact that two thirds or more of these students, at least in Ontario, are women, may explain, without necessarily justifying, the lack of growth in numbers of women in the federal programs. It certainly seems to suggest the need for a variety of available responses to these learning needs.

The same province has been engaged in transferring some funding for the support of those students from the Colleges of Applied Art and Technology (CAAT) to the school boards during the same period. Functionally speaking, there is strong evidence from adult education research in Canada, and elsewhere, to support those developments, in terms of the likelihood of local agencies, public and private, serving this population of learners more effectively than others.

A second possible explanation relates to the consequences of transferring the pursuit of particular learning objectives from formal "academic" providing agencies, to the milieu of the users or employers of individuals who are achieving or have achieved the particular learning objectives. There is a good deal to be said on behalf of such a transfer: the users understand the character of the desired skills and their applications; they can more easily find or develop instructional resources; and they have a high interest in making use of the successful learners. However, there are also disadvantages. The principal one is that the demands of immediate production will gradually take precedence, growth will dominate the need for equity or even stability, and increasingly the easiest and least expensive to train will receive the training. The others, making up most of the population requiring some form of basic education, will be left to someone else.

What is likely is that both conclusions apply, and that both sets of circumstances have contributed to the steady reduction of the role of the federal government in the basic education of adults. Whether that is the correct response to the long and short term objectives, which both levels of government say that they espouse, is a matter of debate and conjecture. It does appear, however, that substantial numbers of adults are being left out of available educational opportunities.

What can be witnessed from this brief elaboration of federal legislation is the steady enlarging of federal initiative and direction with respect to education in Canada. Initially the attempts and legislation that appear are hardly more than encouraging and enabling. However, as the century progressed, and the economy and employment, for which the federal government is clearly held responsible by the Canadian voter, became more and more dependent upon the opportunities for Canadian workers, at all levels, to learn and relearn skills, it was perceived to be necessary by the federal government to assert and achieve increasing measures of control. In the most recent stages of this development, the federal government has abandoned provincial educational delivery systems as the sole mechanism for managing the learning objectives it seeks, and turned increasingly to the utilization of other means of management and delivery. To a certain extent, reluctantly, provincial governments have followed suit. The next stage in our understanding of the response to the needs for basic education for adults will probably be better pursued by examining legislation at the provincial level.

The need for basic education for adults presents some particularly engrossing problems. The bulk of the population in need of such education is native born. The problem cannot be attributed to immigration and the school systems of other countries. Can it then be attributed to the failure of the Canadian educational system as a whole, at least for the Canadians with poorer backgrounds? There is a certain amount of evidence to support that view, and it might appear that the most recent decisions of the federal government are based on such a conclusion. However, another conclusion seems more likely.

A general view of the achievement of literacy and numeracy is that once accomplished it is permanent. Little attention, until recently, has been paid to the existence of powerful out-of-school supporting systems that maintained and increased those skills. However, the rapid spread of non-print means of communication throughout the society has made the function of those supporting systems evident. While many have been retained in the upper levels of employment, it is the lower levels that have experienced the decline most severely. What is likely is that many of the individuals now in need of basic education, have been, at one time, functionally literate. But, their experience since leaving school has been such as to allow those skills to decay, without their really noticing. The uneven decline in types of employment has thrown large numbers of such individuals out of work, unable to fill new jobs which require higher levels of literacy.

Canada, in the company of other industrial societies, has recently acknowledged the extent of illiteracy amongst its adult population. The reaction of the first half of this century, which was to write off the undereducated adults and concentrate on the children, is no longer tenable, if it ever was. Existing generations of adults can maim or destroy societies, to say nothing of destroying the world. What will not work either, are large scale blitz-programs aimed at eliminating illiteracy permanently in one massive effort. The existence of fluctuating degrees of illiteracy of various kinds is a permanent aspect of the

Canadian population, at least as far as can be foreseen. Past experience tells us that it is, and will be necessary to maintain a variety of continuing responses to the problem at all levels of the educational system and beyond it in the private commercial and voluntary sector. This will require the active response of all levels of government in the direct and indirect provisions of support of opportunities to acquire various forms of literacy.

It would be better if this response were better organized and coordinated than it is now, though some interesting and useful steps have been taken. The rationalization in the formal school system to provide for certain levels of educational achievement for all, regardless of age or condition, is one such promising development. The shift from total dependence upon the formal system for the provision for all learning needs, to a much more varied universe of provision, is another. What is now needed is some more effective and clearer articulation of the various levels of government in these developments. The federal government can no longer disguise its educational activities under the rubric of training; the provincial governments can no longer blame the federal government for educational inadequacies that are its responsibility.

It is interesting that the provision of basic education for adults should have played and will continue to play such a critical role in these developments. However, it is undeniable that adult basic education is essentially political in its means and ends, and it is a wise society that acknowledges that fact and attends to it with energy and commitment.

REFERENCES

Government of Canada. (1967). *The Adult Occupational Training Act*. Chapter 94. Ottawa: Queen's Printer.

Government of Canada. (1913). *The Agricultural Instruction Act 3-4 George V.* Ottawa: Queen's Printer.

Government of Canada. (1982). *The National Training Act*. Section 2(3), Chapter 109. Ottawa: Queen's Printer.

Government of Canada. (1919). *The Technical Education Act*. Section 2(c), Chapter 193. Ottawa: Queen's Printer.

Government of Canada. (1940). *The Unemployment Insurance Act 4 George VI*, Chapter 44. Ottawa: Queen's Printer.

Government of Canada. (1942). *The Vocational Training Coordination Act*. Section 2(c), Chapter 286. Ottawa: Queen's Printer.

Government of Ontario, Ministry of Education. (1986). *Secondary School Enrolment by Age and Sex, Preliminary Figures*. Toronto: Ministry fo Education, Ontario.

Organization for Economic Cooperation and Development (OECD). (1969). *Canada: Country Review, Manpower Training*. Paris: OECD.

Thomas, A. M. (1983). *Adult Literacy in Canada: A Challenge*. (Occasional Paper 42). Ottawa: Canadian Commission for UNESCO.

Thomas, A. M., Holland, J., Keating, D., McLeod, B. (1979) *Boards of Education and Adult Education: A Functional Definition for Boards of Education in Ontario*. Toronto, Ontario: Ontario Institute for Studies in Education, Department of Adult Education.

CHAPTER 5:

Literacy – 'Autonomous' v. 'Ideological' Model

Brian Street

The sudden perception of "illiteracy" as a "problem" in the 1970s in England led to government money and institutions being directed towards adult literacy teaching and research. Literacy had previously been subsumed under "schooling" both in terms of the concepts applied and the finance available and it required a shift at both levels for it to include adults. I would like to examine both the definitions and activities that this shift involved in the light of recent developments in general theory about literacy.

THE POLITICAL DEBATE

Levine, in an SSRC study of adult illiteracy in Nottingham, describes how the approaches to the "problem" changed over time. At first, he says, researchers followed a "policy" orientation, concerning themselves with questions of "aggregate provision" and "aggregate need" (Levine, 1980, page 3), as part of a strategy to mobilize support and funds. This stage was followed by "action research". Those adults who had come forward for some literacy training had often done so hesitantly and wanting privacy and as a result teaching had become organized on a personal "one-to-one" basis. "Action" researchers, then, had been asked to provide those responsible for the overall organisation of the new provision with evidence of what was actually going on in these private sessions. More recently a debate has arisen regarding the "political" dimension of adult literacy teaching. Mace, for instance, whose book *Working with Words* has been seminal in putting literacy on the political agenda, at least of the left, emphasized the "loss of self esteem" which, she claimed, adult illiterates had suffered as a result of bad schooling experience and she proposed that literacy programs should be directed to the explicit political aim of "comprehensive resocialization". *Tribune* reviewed her book under the headline "Literacy as a Political Issue" and lent support to her attempts as "helping the student to regain his (sic) self confidence in a learning relationship established on the basis of trust and mutual respect" (22 June, 1979). This involved doing more than simply inculcating skills in "consuming print" but was a whole education so that the student would "no longer see his illiteracy in terms of a personal failure, marking him as an incompetent devoid

---

*This article was first published in "Literacy Teaching Politics" No. 2, and we are grateful to the editorial collective for permission to reprint it here.

of moral virtue, but in terms of an educational system which had failed him in the past."

Levine has questioned Mace's approach and asked whether the people who came to literacy programs actually saw themselves in the terms she posed. He wonders whether many of them in fact under-estimated their "problem" or simply did not experience any difficulty, until some crisis occured for them. The kind of situation he has in mind is exemplified by the experience of an individual I encountered at a Brighton literacy centre. He was a mechanic who had been used to handing out MoT forms to customers on the basis of his ability to "read" the layout of forms and the few conventional terms which they employed. One day a customer returned, telling him that his MoT form had been wrongly filled in and he discovered that the Ministry had changed the format. At that point he decided that he needed more general literacy skills, to enable him to adapt to such changes; those he had successfully exercised for many years seemed no longer adequate. Levine would argue, rightly I believe, that individuals such as this had not perceived themselves as "deprived" and did not lack "self-esteem", so that Mace's approach would not, adequately cater for their particular experience and demands. However, he uses this, unjustifiably I believe, to reject the larger political framework offered by Mace. He writes

> ". . . if prisons, schools and other similar formal organizations commanding considerable resources find comprehensive resocialization a problematic and often impossible task, is it not overambitious to attempt it via very limited contact with students, limited finance and predominantly part-time and volunteer personnel?"

This, I feel, misses the point. It was precisely because of the kind of socialization offered in formal establishments that the problems to which Mace alludes occurred. She does not expect those establishments to offer any help since they are the cause of the problem. The institutional framework and its establishment ideology, in her view, failed to give working people the confidence and learning experience that would raise their political consciousness as she would like. The adult literacy programs were therefore a way of compensating not for the "cultural deprivation" of class and family background, as educationalists following Bernstein would seem to suggest was needed, but for the failings of establishment education. It might be over ambitious for political activists to use the adult literacy programs in this way, but not for the reasons proposed by Levine.

A THEORY OF LITERACY PRACTICE

However, Levine does highlight a crucial problem in Mace's approach. A project for altering individuals' consciousness, which is all that Mace, in the end, offers us as a form of political action with regard to literacy, will remain marginal if it fails to challenge the central establishments themselves. We have to ask, in this as in other areas, is it right to opt out of the establishment institutions and to work instead at "comprehensive resocialization" in alternative sites of struggle? Or does this deflect our energies from the major task of changing those institutions themselves? In order to act on this larger front, I would argue, we need a more general theory of literacy practice, a theory which combines understanding of just how establishment institutions are really "depriving" working people (without falling into the "cultural deprivation" trap) with understanding of why the participants themselves do not necessarily perceive it in that way.

From this perspective Levine's work does pose a challenge to Mace and to the main direction of radical thinking with regard to literacy. We would do well to listen when he tells us that many people's experience of establishment institutions and practices does not necessarily entail loss of "self-esteem" or feelings of inadequacy. Middle class radical intellectuals might sense that they would feel such a loss if they were in those circumstances but that, as the anthropologists would say, is "if I were a horse" kind of thinking. Such a framework blithely ignores "folk models" or relegates them to the level of "false consciousness" and thus prevents us from coming to grips with just why that experience leads the participants to that particular conception of it. Levine's findings remind us that solutions to political problems cannot be extracted from such "if I were a horse" kinds of approach.

A theory of literacy practice that adequately explains the situation which large numbers of adults currently find themselves in cannot be satisfactory if it rests on the simple belief that "they" have been directly deceived and that there is nothing in their situation that might reasonably lead them to the conceptions they evidently hold about it. Rather I would propose that we should examine that situation as an anthropologist would a culture or sub- culture, making explicit judgements we would make from our own cultural and structural situations in order to discover how and why the structures to be identified there generate particular conceptions and perceptions amongst the actors themselves. From a radical perspective that project, then, requires a theory of literacy practice that is not embedded in the dominant establishment uses of, and assumptions about literacy in this culture.

'AUTONOMOUS' AND 'IDEOLOGICAL' MODELS OF LITERACY

In order to disembed ourselves from that dominant ideology we firstly have to make it explicit. I will suggest in this article a way of examining the underlying and often unstated assumptions about literacy held in our culture by offering a distinction between what I term "autonomous" and "ideological" models of literacy. The "autonomous" model assumes a "neutral". "autonomous", "technical" character for literacy which, I argue, is misconceived and which leads to misrepresentations of the actual practice of literacy, whatever the political persuasion of those employing it. A radical project for literacy acquisition and use must, then, reject the "autonomous" model. Those who subscribe to this model are, despite their claimed "neutrality", doing no more than revealing their faith in the powers and qualities of literacy peculiar to their own kind of capitalist society and to the academic sub-culture within it, to which most of them belong. Some examples from recent academic work on literacy will make the point.

Olson and Hildyard, for instance, have argued that written forms enable the user to differentiate the logical form the interpersonal functions of language in a way less possible in oral discourse. To support this argument they make use of Patricia Greenfield's research amongst the Wolof of Senegal. She applied aspects of Bernstein's concepts of elaborated and restricted codes to schooled and unschooled children and concluded that unschooled children lacked the concept of a personal point of view and the cognitive flexibility to shift perspective in relation to concept-formation problems.

The claim that unschooled Wolof children have not developed the "logical functions" of language is, in fact, no more than a statement that the conventions in which their thinking is expressed are different from those of the researcher herself. But Greenfield tries to claim more than this, as do Olson and Hildyard. They attempt to maintain that their own conventions are superior. However, they do not do so directly, as earlier writer's in the "great divide" tradition did. Instead they do so indirectly by appealing to the supposed intrinsic and culture-free nature of literacy. If they can establish that literacy in itself constructs superior logical functions, then it will follow that those without it have inferior logical functions. The assertion is supposedly absolved of its racist and ethnocentric connotations by the neutrality of literacy. "Scientific" tests for cognition can be conducted not on social groups and individuals as such, with all the political implications that involves, but on a newly constructed, a-social category of "literates" and "non-literates", as though the culture they belonged to were incidental. The implications of the findings can then be claimed to follow directly from scienfific experiments conducted in an open-minded way with no prior assumptions. The fact that the Wolof turn out to be less "logical" when in their own environment than when in contact with Europeans just happens to follow from the tests, whatever we might want to believe. The great divide has been re-established by the appeal to literacy, apparently without the offensive appeals to inherent cultural and intellectual superiority that discredited its early phases.

Goody, in fact, explicitly claims that the distinction literate/non-literate can be used as a modern substitute for the "great divide!" of earlier periods. It is, he believes, similar to but more useful than that traditionally made between "logical" and "pre-logical". This, he claims, is because of the inherent qualities of the written word — writing makes the relationship between a word and its referent more general and abstract, it is less closely connected with the peculiarities of time and place than is the language of oral communication. Writing is also "closely connected to", "fosters" or even "enforces" the development of "logic", the distinction of myth from history, the elaboration of bureaucracy, the shift from "little communities" to complex cultures, the emergence of scientific thought and institutions and even the growth of democratic political processes.

All of these writers are, in fact, privileging their own particular ways of thinking, acting and writing at the same time as claiming neutrality for such claims. They fail to see that even if it were possible to isolate "autonomous" features of literacy (and this has yet to be demonstrated, since any feature so isolated only has meaning in terms of its social context), there still remains the problem of the relationship between these features and the ideological and political nature of literacy in practice.

Writers whom I identify as developing an "ideological" model of literacy avoid these dangers by recognising the social nature of literacy practice and by concentrating on the social structure and the ideology in the context where literacy is being acquired and purveyed.

HISTORICAL PERSPECTIVE

Michael Clanchy, for instance, who is an historian, describes the shift from memory to written record in Medieval England in such a way as to highlight the social and ideological nature of literacy practice. He argues that the shift was facilitated by the continuing "mix" of oral and literate modes and that written forms were adapted to oral practice rather than radically changing it. He shows how the Norman Conquerors deliberately fostered a "literate mentality" through the development of central bureaucracies and written records, for their own political purposes. As newcomers they could not establish claim to land through local custom and practice, folk memory or indigenous symbols, as the natives did, so they made land rights dependent on written documentation, which they could control. Such examples remind us to be sceptical of claims for the "neutrality" and "objectivity" of written forms and procedures and to look more closely at who controls them. Clanchy's careful documented account emphasises the necessity of examining the real social practice involved rather than attempting to infer the nature of literacy itself from introspection or experimentation.

Harvey J. Graff, a social historian, likewise provides a basis for an alternative, more socially based view of literacy. He challenges what he calls the "literacy myth" whereby it is contended that literacy of itself will lead to social improvement, civilization and social mobility. With reference to 19th century Canada he analyses the statistics for occupational and ethnic groupings in relation to evidence of their respective literacy achievements. He discovers that literacy itself made very little difference to occupation and wealth as compared with the significance of ethnic and class origin. He argues that the presentation of literacy as "autonomous" and "neutral" was itself part of the attempt by ruling groups to assert social control over the potentially disruptive lower orders. This encouraged these people to send their children to state schools even though in reality what they learnt there was anything but "neutral" and, as Graff can now demonstrate, there was really nothing in it for them. In practice literacy was taught, for instance, by making students read aloud from textbooks while the teacher "corrected" their pronunciation. This was a means of homogenizing the different dialects and making them conform to the standards of the ruling class, as well as of maintaining discipline in the classroom, but it did little for their "development" or even for their command of literacy. Schooling and the techniques for teaching literacy were, then, forms of hegemony and in such a context it would be misleading to represent the process of literacy acquisition as leading to greater "criticalness" and logical functioning.

In recent work in sociolinguistics a similar scepticism about establishment claims for literacy can be discerned. Early linguists like Bloomfield argued that written forms were merely extensions of spoken forms. More recently sociolinguists have challenged this view and argued that linguistic models have been too heavily based, implicitly, on specific written forms that do not in fact provide useful general models for language and speech. Crystal notes that written language forms represent special cases of language use, with their own conventions and rules. But he sees this "independence" from oral forms of language as socially based and understandable in terms of the conventions and rules, not as "autonomous" in the sense described above. Particular forms of writing, such as the literacy conventions of English academic written language, have been taken as the basis for general descriptions of language. It was from these forms that the "grammatical rules of school textbooks" were elicted, at least until the work of theoretical linguistics in this century. That work provided the basis for descriptions of the conventions used in different language contexts and thus for distinguishing language used in everyday informal conversational ways from formal utterances, of which academic English was a special case. This provides a basis also for recognizing the conventional nature of different literate practices; academic written English is no more useful as a general model for written forms than it is for spoken.

The writers I am referring to as exponents of an "ideological model" of literacy do not always make explicit their rejection of the "autonomous" model and they do not necessarily couch their arguments in the terms I am adopting. Nevertheless, I would maintain that the use of the term "model" to describe their perspective and what they oppose is helpful since it draws attention to the underlying coherence and relationship of ideas which, on the surface, might appear unconnected and haphazard. The models serve in a sense as "ideal types" to help clarify the significant lines of cleavage in the field of literacy studies and to provide a stimulus from which a more explicit theoretical foundation for descriptions of literacy practice and for cross-cultural comparison can be constructed.

LITERACY CAMPAIGNS IN THE UK

How, then, does this academic work on literacy relate to the actual practice of different literacies in the UK and specifically to the ways in which the Adult Literacy Campaigns have been conducted here in recent years? There has, in fact, been little explicit connection between them. On the one hand, those involved in the day-to-day practice of teaching adult literacy have had little time, or often inclination, to devote to an apparently jargon-ridden, ivory-tower set of theories of the kind I have been discussing. As one literacy worker put it to me. "I just use my intuitions." On the other hand, those producing the theories and ideas cited above, have indeed operated at a remove, institutionally, conceptually and in terms of their empirical interests even, from the workers "in the field". The substantive data on literacy practice to which they do refer ranges from Medieval England to contemporary Africa and Asia, but it pays little attention to what is happening right now in the UK. Questions regarding the political and ideological nature of literacy practices, which they have posed in relation to other times and places, have scarcely been confronted by them or others with regard to the UK. Research here, as Levine points out has been either "policy oriented" or conceived in terms of the "social problem" approach. Subserving these aims has been a considerable academic literature, particularly within experimental and developmental psychology, on reading skills, spelling, dyslexia, etc. As Stubbs points out ". . . most theories of literacy have been related to instructional techniques." The ideological model of literacy, then, has, for a number of reasons, scarcely penetrated studies of literacy practice in the UK. What we find here in terms of political and ideological debate are such arguments as that between Mace and Levine regarding the extent to which "illiterates" see themselves as deprived, whether individuals or institutions are "to blame" and, most recently, the relationship of literacy to job prospects. These are all important questions, but it is difficult to see how any of them can be resolved without recourse to a larger theoretical framework that would put them into perspective.

SPECIFIC SKILLS AND KNOWLEDGE FOR SPECIFIC PURPOSES

One area, however, where some attempt has been made to apply aspects of the ideological model of literacy, albeit implicitly, to the practice of literacy teaching in the UK has been within the Adult Literacy and Basic Skills Unit (ALBSU). In doing so this work provides some answers to the challenge posed by Levine: instead of approaching adult "illiterates" as "lacking in self esteem" and "in need of comprehensive resocialization", as Mace would have it, the unit would offer adults specific skills for specific purposes, respecting their own perceptions of what they need and putting a lot of its theoretical effort into providing a political and ideological framework in which that choice is possible and meaningful. Resource Centres and even temporary caravans in city centres, for instance, provide a resource to which passers-by can come to discover what is available and to relate it to their own perceived needs; some "clients" may attend only once and never return, others may discover something they are looking for and then sign up for more substantial courses. The courses, however, remain more of a resource and more student- oriented than anything they are likely to have encountered at school.

This framework is reflected in the pedagogical theory purveyed in the Unit's teaching books. A primer for teachers entitled *Working Together — An Approach to Functional Literacy* gets beyond the limitations of its title, notably those of "functional" theories of literacy, and succeeds in conveying some of the ideas that I have described in terms of the "ideological" model. The pamphlet begins by stressing that literacy is *doing*, it is only meaningful in practice. The authors have found it necessary to stress this fact as a result of realising the differences between the needs of adults regarding literacy and the kind of literacy normally imparted to children in schools. They write:

"Most tutors, teachers and organizers (in adult literacy) are dissatisfied with the use of school children's books because:

> 1. In the adult world we DO things with reading and writing. You cannot DO much with children's books except sit and read them.
> 2. Ploughing through children's reading books tends actually to be slower because it takes longer to get to the words and phrases an adult might urgently need to learn to read and write". (ALBSU, 1981, page 5).

Many teachers at school would, of course, express similar criticisms of the value of the material for children themselves. The ALBSU pamphlet proposes, then, that teachers begin by "helping their students to define their needs and interests". This is not to suggest abandoning "previous teaching strategies, concerned with teaching the relationship between sounds and letters or spelling skills," but "the object is to put these skills into a more relevant setting" *(ibid.)*. A lot of time has, then, to be devoted to establishing what particular literacy practice individuals are interested in or "need" and this inevitably involves some analysis of their social position and of the social context within which their practice has relevance. In this sense, then, adult literacy tutors are employing something more akin to the "ideological" model of literacy than to the "autonomous" model which, they suggest, is still being employed in schools.

The value of the list is that it directs us towards aspects of literacy practice that tend to be ignored both in traditional teaching situations and in much of the research in the field. The question of what literacy actually is in specific contexts is made problematic for both the teacher and the researcher and both are forced to move away from a rigid conception of a fixed set of technical skills to be imparted across the board. For the researcher, for instance, the nature of the format and layout of written material, to which the list draws attention, raises questions which provide a concrete basis for cross-cultural comparison that might be more interesting than those raised by comparison of more traditionally-isolated literacy skills, such as "spelling", etc. With regard to my own anthropological fieldwork in Iran, for instance, it suggests a way of comparing the traditional "Qoranic literacy" taught in the mountain village I studied, with the recent development there of commercial uses of literacy. In the "maktab" or "Qoranic school" students had learnt in their reading of sacred texts about various conventions regarding layout and format that I argue elsewhere (Street, 1983), served them in good stead when the need arose to expand commercial literacy practices. Some religious texts, for instance, would display sections of print at an angle across the page, indicating a specific relationship between that section and the main body of the text displayed in the more familiar way. Words would also be placed in specific columns alongside the main text, indicating commentary or section headings, etc. These conventions were as significant for "reading" the meaning of the text as a whole as were the literal "words on the page". In learning to interpret and use these conventions, students acquired "hidden" literacy skills and knowledge, of the kind highlighted by the ALBSU list. Some of them were able to transfer these skills and knowledge to the different literacy practices associated with the commercial expansion of the village and thus to establish positions of influence and power in the new circumstances following the oil boom of the 1970s. In "commercial" literacy, for instance, local entrepreneurs had to keep records of deals struck with other villagers and with town middlemen, and this required knowledge of how to lay out a page of a notebook, etc. using columns, lists, tables, underlining, headings, sections and sub-sections as means of conveying meaning. It was a knowledge that those literate in other contexts have not necessarily developed to such an extent and which varies according to culture, circumstances and the individual's role. ALBSU tutors suggest that it is a knowledge that is not explicitly taught in English schools, where the emphasis tends to be at the level of relating sounds to letters, and of learning the "literal" meaning of the "words on the page".

In the list of literacy "skills" described by ALBSU, then, the concept of "skill" appears to have a broader connotation that in the "autonomous" model. The authors point out, for instance, that "the skills are only relevant when a context has been created for them" (p. 23) and that any such list must always be "incomplete" *(ibid.)* "New" and different skills will continually be developed in new and different contexts and the tutor is advised to continually add these to the list. They also point out how many of these skills are "hidden" social skills rather than explicit technical or "cognitive" processes. Parents and teachers alike may often not recognize this and instead expect to see literacy skills openly displayed, as for example with the superficial memory exercise of repeating the letters of the alphabet. The authors argue that it is "nonsense" to believe that such exhibitions mean that the reader is "well on the way". Whereas a lot of parents with very young children *think* that they taught their children to read by this method before they went to school", in fact "what actually happens is that parents have done lots of other things which convey the 'message', and have got their children so interested in reading that the process got started without any conscious effort." The children have, in fact, been socialized rather than trained in knowledge of literacy. They have, for instance, "learned the purpose of print" (*ibid.*, p.22) and it is such knowledge that is the basis of their "skills". That knowledge is, clearly, social knowledge, and the skills are social skills, their significance and content vary across cultures and over time and space.

Adults who come to literacy programs in the UK tend often to be asking for help in these kinds of skill and knowledge. In their daily lives they are often called upon to "skim" a text, whether it be a leaflet, a newspaper or the instructions included with some technical object, to fill in a form which involves such "hidden" skills as "understanding the concept of the box" rather than simply the explicit ability to relate sounds to letters; and to "read" format and layout in order to interpret factory warnings and instructions, city signs and symbols (c.f. Graft), or labels on bottles.

One outcome of this broadening of what is included under "literacy skills" is that Adult Literacy Programs can concentrate on specific skills for specific purposes. They need not be drawn into imparting as integral to literacy, conventions that are in fact only those of a particular culture or sub-culture. The classic case is that of "academic" literacy practices which are often treated in schools as if they are "universal" and vital. Olson and others would, as we have seen, associate these conventions with "logic", "rationality", "objectivity" and "intelligence". If this were really the case then clearly we would want everyone to have equal access to that particular kind of literacy. If, however, as Labov, Street and others have argued, these grandiose claims for "academic" literacy am merely those of a small elite attempting to maintain positions of power and influence by attributing universality and neutrality to their own cultural conventions, then we could do without them and suffer no great loss. This is, in fact, the case; "logic", "objectivity", etc. are equally possible in other literacy conventions, other forms of discourse and other media of communication than those practised by the specific academic sub-culture that much schools literacy is modelled on. ALBSU can, then, legitimately concentrate on teaching specific skills and knowledge for specific purposes without depriving their students of skills that are crucial to their full development self-expression and participation in society.

CULTURAL DEPRIVATION

This point was of central importance in the "cultural deprivation" arguments of the 1970s, although it was not often made with specific reference to literacy. The dilemma for progressive workers at that time was how to reject the claim that certain cultures or sub-cultures, such as working class families, were "deprived" at the level of "logic", "abstraction" and basic intellectual skills, while recognizing and struggling to change the fact that they were "deprived" in terms of access to power and wealth, which in this culture are linked to certain linguistic and literacy performances. Bernstein, for instance, saw this latter kind of "deprivation" as linked with differences in language "codes" amongst different classes and social groups but then appeared to give credibility to the idea that this was also linked to the former less relative kind of "deprivation".

What makes these claims significant for our present interest is the similarity between Bernstein's claims for certain "codes" and those put forward in the "autonomous" model of literacy for the consequences of reading and writing. Thus his description of "elaborated" code, which working class children were supposed to lack, is not just of relative, culture-specific skills and styles but includes the "deeper" abilities such as "abstraction" and "logic" which some researchers have attempted to link with literacy. However much he claims that he is not making value judgements, then, his actual description of the consequences of employing different codes, does include qualities, the lack of which is bound to lead to judgements of inferiority and would, indeed, call a person's very humanity into question. All who use language do in fact engage in abstraction and, as anthropologists have demonstrated, "logic" is to be found in all cultures, accounts of its absence in specific groups being due often to misunderstanding on the part of travellers and observers from alien cultures. Similarly, Labov has shown, in relation to black, working class sub-cultures in New York, that the lack of "logic" attributed by middle class teachers and testing processes to many black youths there is often no more than mistaken interpretation of the rules and conventions of an alien language use and dialect — youths labelled "sub-normal" and "illogical" turned out to be perfectly logical and intelligent once the tester had learnt to understand these cultural rules and conventions.

One might expect that any researcher who still poses the problem of cognitive difference across cultural groups must at least confront this literature and take account of these arguments. However, those writers I have cited as offering an "autonomous" model of literacy and who appeal to literacy as the basis for cognitive difference do not do so. They do not do so, I would argue, because they believe that the model of literacy they are employing insulates them from such arguments. The supposedly technical and neutral nature of the "autonomous" model of literacy which they employ appears to absolve them from the charge that they are making ideological claims about cultural difference. They can argue, whether implicitly or explicitly, that this new version of the "great divide", the division between literate and non-literate, does not discriminate between cultures but simply between technologies. Since technologies are "neutral", then no aspersions are being cast on individual members of cultures which happen to lack a particular technology and are thus taken to lack certain intellectual advantages. Where Levy-Bruhl's version of the "great divide" theory claimed differences in cognitive *capacity* between members of different cultures, those appealing to literacy simply claim differences in cognitive *development*. The suggestion is no longer that a culture has acquired such technological skills as literacy because it is intellectually superior, as earlier racist theories had argued. Rather, it is claimed that a culture is intellectually superior because it has acquired that technology.

Appealing as this sounds, it is not, I contend, tenable. The argument must still confront the anthropological and linguistic evidence for intellectual development as well as capacity in different cultures. It cannot side-step that challenge by claiming to be neutral and value-free because of its appeal to the technology of literacy. That technology is, in fact, ideologically charged; any version of literacy practice has been constructed out of specific social conditions and in relation to specific political and economic structures. A statement about cognitive difference based on assessment of the nature of literacy is as socially-embedded and open to challenge as are statements about cognitive differences based on race, ethnicity and class.

The fact, then, that many people in this culture do not read or write much, or do so in different ways than academics, does not mean that they lack "logic" or the ability to abstract any more than does the fact that they speak "nonstandard" English. There is no need to associate the evident material deprivations suffered by many working class and ethnic groups with the "cognitive" deprivation associated by Bernstein, Goody and others with lack of "logic" and the "great divide". We should not, then, be concerned if "academic" literacy is not part of the core curriculum — lack of it will not do any harm to students intellects.

PROVIDE WHAT THE PEOPLE WANT APPROACH
However, this still leaves us with the political problem (and it is a political rather and an "academic" one) that "academic" literacy happens to be a source of wealth and power in the particular culture we inhabit If we ignore it — leave it to the middle classes as it were — then we can hardly complain if they continue to exercise hegemony through it. There are, I believe, two major answers to this dilemma. Firstly, we need to build institutions which enable people to acquire what they say they want and not what teachers, radical or otherwise, think they want. Levine, as we have seen, can provide useful information on what people say they want and more research of this kind is clearly essential to this project. The development of the kinds of "hidden" literacy skills listed by ALBSU and which people say they come to adult literacy classes for, will itself make a contribution to their ability to exercise power in the system as constituted at present. The person who can fill in forms, for instance, has the power to extract funds from institutions, run garages and make use of bureaucratic processes for their own particular purposes and organizations. This response is currently being advocated with positive results by many progressive elements within adult literacy courses, whether set up under MSC programs, LEA or WEA funded or directly under ALBSU.

It has, of course, dangers of the kind previously identified in radical critiques of "consumer" education in general. It could be argued, for instance, that people may have been indoctrinated into asking for the "wrong" things. As I have suggested, I am suspicious of this argument and believe that people are generally more aware of their interests than middle class researchers and "providers" give them credit for. However, there is some point in the argument that crude response to "consumer" demand simply reproduces the social framework and is not what radical activists are about. Radical critiques of Bernstein's approach did point out that the political program which followed from it simply offered a prospect of access to power structures as they currently existed rather than any way of changing them; the notion of "giving" working class adults or school children (and the problems there presumably require further elaboration) whatever literacy skills they wanted, might similarly be seen as creating the illusion that this would change their fundamental disadvantage as a group when all it does is give individuals greater facility within the system. I would hope, however, that we do not have to relive all of the earlier struggles and debates about education in general when considering literacy strategies; one of the functions of this article is to attempt to clear away some of the "dead wood" and to at least bring debate about literacy up to date, if not attempt to move it further ahead. As regards literacy, there are in fact positive aspects of the "provide what people want" approach which are embodied to some extent in the ALBSU approach and they should not be so readily discarded by those on the left. The "ideological" approach to literacy is, I would argue, more complex than some of the earlier "compensatory" or "consumerist" theories of education. It involves, for instance, constructing a framework within which demand takes on a different meaning than it does in establishment institutions. The "choice" of literacy skills and knowledge being proposed by the ALBSU list or being offered through such institutions as one-to-one teaching, caravans in city centre sites or "Write First Time" sessions in which students produce their own texts rather than consume those provided by the teacher is clearly of a different kind and range than that available in schools. One immediate and practical answer to the dilemma posed above is therefore to challenge hegemonic use of elite literacy practices at base — within schools and other establishment institutions themselves — by introducing the ALBSU approach there.

Nevertheless, it is clear that however effective in itself, the ALBSU approach would remain marginal if it were not accompanied by more radical proposals. The second answer to the dilemma posed above, then, is both more difficult and more crucial in the long term, since it involves changes at the level of ideology within the institutions themselves. A step in this direction would be achieved by the dissemination of the "ideological" model of literacy more widely amongst those responsible for the organization of these establishments as well as amongst those engaged in day-to-day literacy teaching in them.

REFERENCES

ALBSU (1981) *Working Together — An Approach to Functional Literacy*.
Bernstein B. (1971). *Classes, Codes and Control*, RKP.
Clanchy M. (1979). *From Memory to Written Record*, E. Arnold.
Evans-Pritchard E.E. (1937). *Witchcraft, Oracles and Magic Amongst the Azande*.
Goody J. (1966). *Literacy in Traditional Societies*, OUP.
Graff H. (1979). *The Literacy Myth*, Academic Press.
Greenfield P.M. (1972) "Oral or Written Language; the Consequences for Cognitive Development in Africa, US and England". *Language and Speech*, 15.
Horton R. (1967), "African Traditional Thought and Western Science". *Africa*, Nos. 1 and 2.
Keddie N. ed. (1973), *Tinker Tailor. . . The Myth of Cultural Deprivation*, Penguin.
Levine K. (1980). *Becoming Literate*, SSRC.
Levi-Strauss C. (1966). *The Savage Mind*, W and N.
Labov W. (1973), "The Logic of Non-Standard English" in N. Keddie ed.
Linell P. (1982), *The Written Language Bias in Linguistic Theory*, Linkoping.
Mace J. (1979), *Working with Words*, Writers and Readers/Chameleon.
Olson D. and Hildyard A. (1978) "Literacy and the Specialization of Language. Some Aspects of the Comprehension, and Thought Processes of Literate and Non-Literate Children and Adults". Ms. The Ontario Institute for Studies in Education, Toronto.
Polanyi M. (1962), *Personal Knowledge*.
Street B. (1979). "Literacy, Commerce and the 'Qoranic School' in an Iranian Village". Ms.
Street B. (1975), The Mullah, The Shahnameh and the Madrasseh: Some Aspects of Literacy in Iran", *Asian Affairs* 62.
Street B. (1982), "Literacy and Ideology", *Red Letters* Vol. 12.
Street B. (1984), *Literacy in Theory and Practice*, CUP.
Stubbs M. (1980), *Language and Literacy; The Socialinguistics of Reading and Writing*, RKP.
Wilson B. ed (1970), *Rationality*, B. Blackwell.

CHAPTER 6:

A Historical View of Literacy

James A. Draper

Tracing the historical and philosophical roots of literacy enables educators to understand the development of current practice. As literacy is part of a cultural, political, and economic context, so literacy education is part of the larger, global movement towards human rights and human equality. Throughout history, literacy has never been neutral — it has been an expression of national and political values. There is an integral connection between the development of national literacy and the value the state places on individual growth. To illustrate these connections, this chapter describes aspects of the development of Western English language literacy.

UNDERSTANDING HISTORY

It is our present day questions that guide us in looking at the past. Because learning is integral to our humanity, our history can be traced through the development of human learning and communication. All societies have communicated with each other, although a written alphabet is a relatively new invention. Literacy is part of the broader framework of human communication, just as adult literacy is part of the framework of adult education.

The history of adult education is a long and rich one. Welton (1985) points out that, compared with political history, "social, cultural, and intellectual history are relatively late arrivals on the scene". Grattan (1955) writes about the learning of preliterate society, then traces adult education and literacy through 2500 years, covering the major periods of Western history. Clark and Brundage (1982) describe adult education opportunities in Canada, including the programs available for under-educated adults. While there is considerable literature on the evolution of adult learning and education, it is not the purpose of this section to review this general, although relevant material.

Legge, (1986: 74-76) reporting on the first conference on the history of adult education, emphasizes the importance of historical insights for "the development of wisdom, attitudes, and perspective". The history of literacy provides a background for current values, programs, and beliefs. Through history, we can distinguish the commonplace from the unique and understand individual or institutional roots. An historical perspective is a way of stretching our identity, enabling us to grasp what Kidd(1979) refers to as our heritage, assess change, and prepare for the future.

The UNESCO document, *Development of Adult Education* connects the goals of adult education with the local and international goals of literacy:

Developing a critical understanding of major contemporary problems and
social changes and the ability to play an active part in the progress of society
with a view to achieving social justice; and increased awareness of, and giving
effect to, various forms of communication and solidarity at the family, local,
national, regional, and international levels. (UNESCO: 1976)

Many other such statements from modern history link literacy to the implementation of the Universal Declaration of Human Rights. The UNESCO
document goes on to say that adult education should be designed for men and
women "to acquire basic knowledge (reading, writing, arithmetic, basic understanding of natural and social phenomena), but also make it easier for them
to engage in productive work, to promote their self-awareness".

Selman (1986), a Canadian adult education historian, observes that:

Students of the craft of history tend to fall into two categories: those who
stress the primacy of telling the story of the past, 'how it was', a descriptive or
narrative approach; and those who emphasize the interpretive function of the
historian.

In fact, the history of adult literacy education needs both narration and
interpretation. Carr (1961: 105) emphasizes that "history is a process of
selection"; the aspects are chosen from a particular point of view. He points
out that historically "society and the individual are inseparable; they are
necessary and complementary to each other, not opposites." This relation is
well illustrated through literacy education. Individuals are molded by society,
and they exert a reciprocal influence on the larger social context, including
their conditions of illiteracy and poverty.

Some examples from the historical literature on literacy are given to illustrate
how literacy in society evolved, the political and other forces that helped to give
it meaning, and how literacy expressed social and individual values.

HISTORICAL APPROACHES TO ADULT LITERACY
Different approaches to literacy have developed throughout recent history.

Development Approach:
Since the United Nations First Development Decade in the 1960s, different
views have emerged about the meaning of national development and its relationship to literacy. Following World War II, the prescription for the development of new nations was a Western model focussing on production, large-scale
economic projects, and the exploitation of natural resources. The development of people seemed to be secondary, except the extent to which they
contributed to production. Learning and education programs for adults were
limited because the western model emphasized expansion of the formal education system for children.

E. F. Schumacher, in *Small is Beautiful* (1974), describes the movement
towards a more humanitarian view making people as learners central to development. This change in the meaning of "development" had a major impact on
literacy education. Instead of imposing inappropriate, large-scale technology,

there was a trend towards adapting appropriate, small-scale, and labor-intensive technology. This shift influenced the acquisition and application of knowledge and literacy.

Traditional Approach:

This approach to literacy took the view that learning to read and write had an innate goodness in itself (Draper, 1974: 659-673). The content of what was read was irrelevant and unrelated to the practicalities of daily life, except, perhaps, philosophically or morally. Classical literature was read extensively, and rote learning was the methodology.

Religious Approach:

The purpose for literacy was to read the holy scriptures in order to propagate "the faith". The content was limited to religious materials, and the focus was usually on reading rather than writing skills.

Work-Oriented Approach:

UNESCO coined the term "work orientation", which was related to increasing production. The incentive to learn was economic. Content was important and narrowly confined to employment and production.

Social-Change Approach:

Paulo Friere has been a most vocal proponent of the social-change approach to literacy. The learner is enabled to participate in a class struggle to overcome oppression. The learners become aware of relevant issues, examine them in light of their "personal worlds", and then see them in political dichotomies: between the oppressed and the oppressor, between those who have and do not have power and formal education.

Life-Oriented Approach:

The focus of this approach is on the development of the learners' ability to learn, think, solve problems, and develop coping skills. This approach goes beyond the acquisition of knowledge, stressing the application of this knowledge to daily living. The context goes beyond the world of work to embrace the whole life experience.

These approaches illustrate how literacy was perceived — i.e., to read the word for its own sake; to read the word of God; to read about work; to read about the world and to change it; to read in order to improve the quality of daily living. Each approach differs according to the learner's motivation, the content of the learning materials, and the relevance of the learning to daily living. The role of the teacher or facilitator also varies, as do the methods used for teaching and learning, ranging from learning as an exclusively individual enterprise to learning that includes group interaction. Each approach to literacy education requires a "political decision". The trend in many regions of the world today is towards a more learner-centered approach such that all learners are involved in deciding what, where, and how learning will take place.

The debate about the "functionality" of literacy is perhaps one of the most significant historical issues. "Functional" from whose point of view? And what end? Levine points out:

In the earliest UNESCO documentation (1947), the term 'literacy' was not qualified; rather, it signified one of the requirements for the establishment and maintenance of human and civilized values. Thus, the skills of reading, writing, and counting, are not an end in themselves. Rather they are the essential means to the achievement of a fuller and more creative life. (Levine, 1982: 249-265)

The history of literacy reveals different responses to the question, "To what end?", including the promotion of materialism, dependency, independence, religion, morality, family, migration, immigration, survival, preservation, change, urbanization, a welfare state, cultural pluralism, indoctrination, leisure, liberation, and depersonalization. The list goes on. The words express values and goals which, in turn, determine action.

The historical vocabulary of literacy (i.e., the words coined and used at a particular time) reveals the prevalent perceptions. These perceptions then need to be placed in the social, cultural, economic, and political context of the past. To participate in literacy education is to shape the future. Literacy has a social as well as a personal value.

THE PLACE OF LITERACY IN HISTORY

Describing the "Literacy Revolution in the West", Cipolla (1969) emphasizes that writing was not a sudden invention. The Sumerians, for instance, as early as the third millennium B.C.E. (Before the Common Era), had developed a "script". Perhaps one of the most creative thoughts in history was that "a written sign must represent a sound". The development of literacy was greatly determined by the requirements of trade, diplomacy, accounts, and revenues. The development of an alphabet had a practical, recording function. However, the practice of writing failed to filter down through the social strata to the majority of the peasantry who were striving to meet their basic survival needs:

The craft of reading and writing remained the sacred monopoly of small elites. By 1750, at the dawn of the Industrial Revolution, almost 5000 years had elapsed since the first rudimentary appearance of the art of writing. Yet more than 90 percent of the world's population had no access to the art. (Cipolla, 1969:8)

Literacy developed its own traditions and was used in particular ways for particular purposes. However, the meaning and importance of literacy were adapted to changes in technology, such as open-sea navigation devices and the invention of new weapons for war, which required more widespread literacy. Increasingly, literacy was related to the balance and the use of power which in turn, influenced trade and commerce. One outcome of these technological and social changes was a decrease in the control exercised by the church, which had previously "a virtual monopoly on literacy and education, especially from the 6th to the 11th centuries". (Cipolla, 1969:43)

Literacy was at first primarily an urban phenomena since cities were the centers of trade, commerce, and manufacturing. As early as the 13th century, literacy became a precondition for employment, leading to legislation governing these matters.

It was in the 13th century too that the techniques of making paper and grinding spectacles were first developed. In addition to the more obvious consumption values as a consumer product, the more subtle value of literacy as an instrument of investment came to be recognized. The buying and selling of books and of literacy skills increased. One could now link material benefits to being literate, or "one may desire education for one's own spiritual enjoyment and/or emulation" (Cipolla, 1969: 42)

The traditional desire (for) "education for one's own spiritual enjoyment and/or emulation" persisted, at the same time as the work approach was emerging, linking material benefits to literacy (Cipolla, 1969: 42). The development and diffusion of technological innovations increased the investment demand for literacy. "The growth of an urban society and the growth of schools and literacy were related phenomena". (Cipolla, 1969: 49)

As early as the 13th century, Cipolla observes that: "The areas that experienced higher rates of economic expansion and more revolutionary social change were also areas in which schools and teachers were relatively more numerous" (Cipolla, 1969: 42-45).

The school curriculum in the 16th century taught reading before writing (Graff, 1981: 203-260). A larger proportion of society could, therefore read the thoughts of others without sharing their own thoughts through print. However, opportunities for literacy education expanded during the 16th century in England:

> There was an increase in literacy among yeomen, craftsmen, and women in the middle class; and even lower classes began to take advantage of opportunities to become literate for religious or vocational purposes. (Rafe-uz-Zaman, 1978: 38)

Certain geographical areas were, and continue to be, more favored with privilege, growth, and power. In earlier days, the pressure for literacy was also linked to expressions of loyalty to the ruler, relating literacy to propaganda and security as well (Cressy, 1980: 64-142). Increasingly, the illiterate experienced problems over oaths of loyalty.

As a commodity or skill to be acquired, the increasing demand for literacy and the increase in the provisions for becoming literate had far-reaching effects. The response to the intensified demand for literacy was expanded provisions for becoming literate. The changed proportion of literate members altered the social fabric. Cipolla (1969: 36) points out that the spread of literacy was accompanied by more social programs concerned with public health, but also added to health problems, for example, crowding children into filthy, poorly ventilated rooms had led to the spread of disease and improvements in diagnosis.

As the division of labour grew between those with and those without literacy skills, negative attitudes developed about those who could not read and write. Society was perceived to be divided into the vulgar, illiterate masses,and the literate elite. Those who were unlettered were also considered unfit for a variety of economic and social functions. Society developed a moral obligation to equip its members, especially the young, with basic literacy. Literacy gradually acquired moral overtones — something 'right' to possess and 'wrong' to lack.

The eventual establishment of schools for adult literacy, as with the establishment of schools for children, paralleled the rise of evangelism and well-intentioned philanthropy among the growing ranks of the middle class (Grattan: 1955). There arose a superior, "do-gooder" attitude among the literate, moralizing elite toward the poor and illiterate. Literacy became associated with being civilized and was seen as a means of cultural diffusion. Later, such attitudes spread with colonialism to Africa and to other parts of the world.

Historically, being poor was also linked to being 'sinful'. Since the poor were also illiterate, one way to combat sin was to teach them to read and write. In 1830, the newly-formed Mechanic's Institutes were designed to help each member:

> To acquire a more perfect knowledge of arts and sciences as a means of securing him against the temptations to which the youth of our city are exposed, by opening to him the way to rational enjoyment, which cannot fail to strengthen his virtue while it mingles instruction with amusement.

This statement is comparable to one made by the Kingston (Ontario) Superintendent of Schools in 1852:

> Public education will not only show the deformity of vice, but elevate the social state of the poor —assimilating them in habits, thoughts, and feelings to the rich and educated. (Globe & Mail, Dec. 19, 1988:7)

Havelock (1976) points out that the advancement of literacy had more than technological obstacles to overcome: "The alphabet had to be confronted in the arena of politics as well." Grattan (1955:65) describes the debates going on in England during the early 1800s over the question, Shall the laboring poor be literate? One argument was that the ignorance of the lower classes was divinely sanctioned and should not be tampered with (Webb, 1978: 39). The opposing argument held that:

> Literacy made the poor more efficient as producers without being less interested in productive labor; that it reduced crime; that it gave those who possessed it a beneficial sense of personal worth and strengthened their morals; and, of course, it reinforced religious principles (Grattan, 1955: 75).

By way of a compromise, the teaching of reading and sometimes writing were duly accompanied by the instillation of "cleanliness, temperance, honesty, and the habit of regularly attending church" (Grattan, 1955: 76). Still, "as late as 1850, about half of the adult population in Europe could neither read nor write" (Cipolla, 1969: 55).

The history of literacy has not been a linear progression upwards from a society with few to a society with many literate members. Cressy (1980) states:

> There appears to have been no steady cumulative progress in the reduction of illiteracy among men in the early modern period. Nor did the different social groups maintain the same level of illiteracy in relation to each other at all times from the 16th to the 18th century.

In Europe during this period there was an overwhelming number of illiterates; by contrast, in the fourth and fifth Century B.C.E., "most Athenian citizens were literate" (Cipolla, 1969: 38). Discussing the rise and fall of literacy over the centuries, Rafe-uz-Zaman adds another dimension:

> Literacy and reading expanded when revolutionary literature appeared in revolutionary times (referring to 17th century England). Apathy gave way to involvement and involvement necessitated literacy... Many who had awakened to literacy in the revolutionary period found nothing in the Restoration to sustain their interest. Literacy had stimulated the masses and knowledge of this instilled fear in the upper classes. To counteract the possibility that the lower classes would again fall under the sway of revolutionary thought, attempts were begun to indoctrinate the lower classes with 'true morality', and basic education began to be used as a tool for subordinating the masses through the charity schools of the 18th century, which had the limited goal of equipping students to read the Bible and to interpret it in the way the upper classes did. (Rafe-uz-Zaman, 1978: 39)

Graff (1978) points to a chain of cause-and-effect operative in the late 18th through the 19th centuries, that is, the development of social theories led to the promotion of schooling for the masses, leading, in turn, to the creation of public systems for mass education. Until recent times, the history of literacy was more a history of adult education than that of children and youth.

In the 1980s, a UNESCO (1984) report commented on the early years of literacy education:

> For a long time, literacy activities were chiefly carried out by small organizations, even individuals, with particular target groups: nomads, gypsies, barge people's children. The arrival of immigrant populations strengthened the idea that residual illiteracy affected only foreign groups, and a few national groups of limited size and special characteristics.

The focus for most literacy education activities was on minority, (often visible minority groups) overlooking the literacy needs of the members of society at large. Since many, if not all, the industrialized countries had had compulsory schooling legislation for many years, adult nationals were presumed to be literate. Illiteracy in less-developed countries, many of them new nations, was apparent. The failure to recognize the need for remedial adult literacy in industrialized countries has compounded the problems of tackling this social issue today. (I.C.A.E., 1988).

HISTORICAL IMPLICATIONS
History is the story of individual men and women, of agencies and institutions, of values, of causes and movements, of beliefs and philosophies, and of relationships between individuals and between nations. The history of literacy is one of individual empowerment. According to Furet and Ozouf (1981: 214-232), the specific development of literacy from the 16th century is a history of "three centuries of cross-fertilization".

Literacy has an ideology influenced by material or spiritual fulfillment, functioning to refine society and to make it more just. Literacy education has historically reached out — to cultural or linguistic minorities, migrants, the handicapped, the elderly, the unemployed, the incarcerated, and the socially or economically disadvantaged. The extension of literacy is not only an extension of the larger society but also a reflection of it.

Throughout history to the present, illiteracy has been determined by and interpreted as part of a nation's cultural dynamics — associated with poverty and unemployment. Comparative studies correlating literacy with employment, reveal differences between developed and developing nations. Whereas in industrialized countries, literacy education is intended to promote employment, in almost all the developing nations, the majority of the poor and illiterate are "employed" in attempting to survive on a piece of land — likely not their own. In a traditional agricultural society, employment does not require literacy and poverty is not the result of unemployment. Nor is illiteracy just a rural problem; it is a social expression of larger political and economic policies. The cause and effect of literacy needs to be further examined.

The present body of literature and research are only a beginning. More needs to be understood about the barriers to learning, about the ways in which newly acquired literacy skills are used, about the values learned through literacy education, and about the experiences of other regions and countries. A career in literacy education requires more theorizing and research. For example, Bhola (1981: 6-23) has developed a taxonomy of "literacy effects" which can be used by policy-makers and planners in promoting literacy education in the service of national development.

Beyond the economic argument, the history of literacy education is the story of individuals striving to improve the quality of their lives through the acquisition of knowledge, skills, and values. Literacy, or illiteracy, has been influenced by the social and economic context, which determines the values and functionality of learning. Literacy has been used to define civilization and the attributes of the 'cultured' society; and at times this has also meant literacy in a second language such as French or Latin.

The early development of adult literacy education was "a period of scattered, informal beginnings, under private and voluntary auspices"(Selman, 1984: 7-16) In the past, as in the present, the non-government, nonprofit, and community-based organizations have played a key role in literacy education. Even as recently as 1984, UNESCO argued that "NGOs should be the advocates for illiterates". Such agencies require a constellation of characteristics to sustain their growth, vision, and value in this vital role.

Literacy has never been neutral, but has always had some practical or spiritual application — even a religious or commercial function of indoctrination. Literacy education has played an important part in sweeping social change:

> The Industrial Revolution, occurring first in England, then throughout Western Europe and North America, was an upheaval that produced the need for writing and computational skills, particularly for armies of clerks, secretaries, and salespersons, and provided the opportunity for people to be educated considerably beyond their previous expectations. (International Encyclopedia of Education: 1985)

CONCLUSIONS

Traditionally, much of the spread of literacy was undertaken by unpaid volunteers and has been associated with class struggles. The teaching of values has been accompanied by the teaching of content; and decisions about content were crucial, political ones. Increasingly, literacy became associated with liberal education, as well as progressive education and humanistic philosophy (See Elias & Merriam, 1980). Literacy education has been both reactive and proactive, both remedial and preventive.

The ups and downs of literacy were often the social indicator of the ups and downs of a nation, revealing changes in social and economic conditions. The Great Depression of the early 1930s provides a recent example. Literacy too, was seen to be a way of seeking truth. History informs decisions about how present-day literacy programs might be influenced, perhaps reconceptualized, and even further understood.

REFERENCES

Bhola, Harlans S. (1981) "Why Literacy Can't Wait": Issues for the 1980s, in *Convergence*, Vol. XiV, No 1.

Carr, E. H., (1961) *What is History?*, New York: Penguin.

Cipolla, Carlo M., (1969) *Literacy and Development in the West*, Books, England: Penguin Books Ltd.

Clark, Ralph J. and Donald H. Brundage, (1982) "Adult Education Opportunities in Canada", in *Adult Education Training in Industrialized Countries*, by Richard E. Peterson, et al., New York: Praeger.

Cressy, David, (1980) *Literacy and the Social Order (Reading and Writing in Tudor and Stuart England)*, Cambridge: University Press.

Draper, James A., (1974) "A Commitment to Development and International Education: Some Examples from Canada", in *Literacy Discussion*, Winter.

Elias, John L. and Sharan Merriam, (1980) *Philosophical Foundations of Adult Education*, Malabar, Florida: Robert E. Kreiger Company.

Graff, Harvey J., (1978) *Literacy in History*, Literacy Bibliographies 11, Tehran, Iran: The International Institute for Adult Literacy Methods, February.

Graff, Harvey J., (1981) "Literacy, Jobs, and Industrialization: The Nineteenth Century", in *Literacy and Social Development in the West (A Reader)*, Cambridge: University Press.

Grattan, C. Hartley, (1955) *In Quest of Knowledge: A Historical Perspective on Adult Education*, New York: Association Press.

Havelock, Eric A., (1976) *Origins of Western Literacy*, Toronto: The Ontario Institute for Studies in Education.

International Council for Adult Education, (1988) *Literacy in Industrialized Countries*, Toronto: ICAE.

International Encyclopedia of Education, (1985) "Adult Education: An Overview", in *Research and Studies* Vol. 1.

Kidd, J. Roby, (1979) *Some Preliminary Notes Concerning a Enquiry into the Heritage of Canadian Adult Education*, Occasional papers in Continuing Education, Vancouver: Centre for Continuing Education, The University of British Columbia.

Legge, Derek, (1986) " First Conference on History of Adult Education", in *Convergence*, Vol. XIX, No. 2.

Levine, Kenneth, (1982) "Functional Literacy: Fond Illusions and False Economies, in *Harvard Educational Review*, Vol. 52, No. 3.

Rafe-uz-Zaman, (1978) "Why Literacy?" Special Issue of *Literacy Discussion*, Spring.

Schumacher, E. F., (1974) *Small is Beautiful*, London: Abacus.

Selman, Gordon, (1984) "Stages in the Development of Canadian Adult Education", in *Canadian Journal of University Continuing Education*, Vol, X, No. 1.

Selman, Gordon, (1986) "Origins of Adult Education in British Columbia: Insights for the Present Period", in *Proceedings*, Antigonish, Nova Scotia: Canadian Association for the Study of Adult Education.

UNESCO, (1976) Recommendation on the *Development of Adult Education*, Ottawa: Canadian Commission for UNESCO.

UNESCO, (1984) *Final Report and Recommendations: First Collective Consultation of International Non-Governmental organizations on Literacy*, Paris: UNESCO House.

Webb, R. K., (Spring, 1978) *The British Working Class 1790-1848: Literacy and Social Tension*, London: George Allen and Unwin Ltd., 1955 (also quoted in *Literacy Discussion*).
Welton, Michael R., (May, 1985) "In Search of a Usable Past for Canadian Adult Education". in *History Bulletin*, Halifax: Dalhousie University.

PART II
THE ADULT ILLITERACY DIMENSIONS

The dimensions of adult illiteracy are multi-faceted. This section provides confirmation of a point that has important implications for all practitioners: there are various categories of adult illiterates who need to be understood before they can be helped.

*For example, **Roy-Poirier** addresses the special needs of the Franco-Ontarians as a cultural linguistic group whose concerns are compounded to some extent by functional illiteracy. She also mentions some of the barriers for Franco-Ontarians' past and present participation in literacy education programs. Through an interesting historical account she outlines some of the reasons why a minority group such as this one has limited access to formal education, concluding with a number of possible scenario's to help alleviate illiteracy and generally improve Franco-Ontarian life.*

*With the growing awareness of adult literacy and basic education in Canada, there are now a variety of programs and activities offered across the country. **Anderson** describes the numerous provincial programs now in place to help the different types of basic learners. She suggests that the focus of each provincial program reflects the adult education philosophy of the sponsoring agency. In addition, she also stresses that many under-educated adults will have less difficulty in becoming active learners if basic education programs become an accepted and integral part of the lifelong learning continuum.*

*Another important community is that of the labour movement. **Martin** outlines the social background which influences the value of books and the place these have in one's life. He presents the idealism of the educator applied to working with union members, although these expressions of principle are applicable to a wide field within adult education. He also comments on the relevancy of content and spirit to adult literacy and basic education, integrating various goals and outcomes of learning. He makes the point that there is a need for critical popular education and concludes that we all operate within institutional and historical limits.*

*Previous mention has been made in this book of the various political, social and cultural factors which influence adult learning. Scientific and technological changes affect the working and private lives of each person and therefore become not only the context for learning, but may also form the content. One learns the content in order to cope with and understand change. These changes offer both a potential as well as a challenge to society. **Jean** discusses the implications of these changes to adult education and raises issues on the need to equip adults both to handle technology and to participate in decision-making about it.*

*Increasingly, community-based programs are becoming the centres for literacy education. **Gaber-Katz & Watson** make some comparisons between these programs and the more traditional ones. A community-based setting has a number of advantages, including the geographical proximity to the adult learner. They outline in some detail the structure and philosophy of these programs as a way of guiding others in setting up similar programs. Such guidelines include the selection and role of tutors, resource centers, material production and the focus on the adult learner. One might predict a trend toward more literacy education occurring within the communities in which people live.*

*In Québec, as in other parts of Canada various literacy offensives are being waged by educators, volunteers, and social activists. **Hautecoeur** describes the current literacy paradox in Québec — the gap between supply and demand. He questions whether the resources made available for literacy education have been utilized effectively. He also calls for more stringent program evaluations, and discusses five explanations for the very low participation rate in basic education programs, suggesting some helpful strategies.*

CHAPTER 1

The Case of The Franco-Ontarian Illiterate: A Historical Perspective

Jeannine Roy-Poirier

Literacy is a right, but millions of people are still unaware of that right. (UNESCO declaration)

The 1987 Southam Literacy Survey Inc. which tested 2,398 adults in their homes with a battery of more than 40 literacy-related questions estimates that over 4.5 million Canadians have a level of schooling of less than Grade nine and that half of these identified are fifty-five or older.[1] Furthermore, this survey estimates that 1,600,000 illiterates reside in what is considered to be the prosperous province of Ontario. These statistics indicate that about twenty-four percent of Ontario's adults have less than Grade nine education, and as such, are considered to be functionally illiterate. This rate is increased when it relates to the Franco-Ontarian population, varying between 25.2 percent in the eastern region which takes in the national capital region, to 45.7 percent in the north-west region of the province (Churchill et al.,1985). As such, this exposé will deal specifically with illiteracy among Franco-Ontarians.

In preparing for this exposé, several sources were searched: historical theses and books, Ministry of Education documents, publications from national and provincial Francophone organizations, popular or community literacy groups, discussions with teachers and colleagues in the field of Adult Education. Based upon the reading of the documents and the verbal information obtained, I attempted to 1) analyze or conceptualize the phenomenon of illiteracy among Franco-Ontarians, 2) present the findings in a logical and interesting fashion, reflecting the realities of a people who have known and survived numerous hardships.

The exposé will cover the following areas. First and foremost, we will touch upon the problem of definitions and statistics. Also included will be a brief profile of the Franco-Ontarian illiterate. Since as a historian, I believe that the present is intimately related to past events, four dimensions of Franco-Ontarian history will be presented: political, economic, socio-cultural and educational. This will be followed by a brief description of the illiteracy problem and the remedial measures now in place, as well as the difficulties still encountered. Last but not least, I will end this exposé with three scenarios depicting possibilities for the future.

PROBLEM OF DEFINITIONS

Defining terms such as illiteracy and Franco-Ontarian can present some difficulty. As such, I will attempt to illustrate this point by referring to a limited number of definitions which in turn will lead to a definition of the Franco-Ontarian illiterate. This exercise will hopefully eliminate as much ambiguity as possible.

Undoubtedly, the most comprehensive and widely used work on adult illiteracy in Canada has been that of Audrey Thomas. She clearly specifies that "literacy is a concept which is relative to the social, economic and political contexts in which human beings find themselves". This statement is particularly relevant in this exposé, since in writing about an identified linguistic minority group, certain social, economic and political dimensions will surface, as well as historical and educational facets of Franco-Ontarian culture.

Thomas draws a distinction between the basic illiterate and the functional illiterate. She defines as basic illiterate, a person "who cannot with understanding both read and write a short simple statement on his every day life". On the other hand, a person who is functionally illiterate "cannot engage in all those activities in which literacy is required for effective functioning of his group and community..." Because of her reference to the group and the community, Thomas' definitions appear to be sufficiently broad for direct application to the Franco-Ontarian minority. In fact, La Fédération des Francophones Hors-Québec Inc. uses identical definitions (Letourneau, 1983). Le Conseil de l'Education Franco-Ontarienne defines the functional illiterate as a person who has not pursued studies beyond the elementary school level (Churchill, 1985). This latter definition facilitates the identification of illiterates since it is based on a more precise and quantifiable standard.

The second term, Franco-Ontarian, also requires careful definition, in view of the mobility of Canadians across the country. Since the experiences of native Franco-Ontarians, that is, of Francophones born and educated in Ontario differ from those who were born and educated elsewhere, it is essential to make the proper distinctions. A report published by the University of Ottawa attempts to define the term Franco-Ontarian. Since this particular study applies to university students only, it identifies as Franco-Ontarian, the Francophones who have completed their secondary education in Ontario. However, in this exposé, the term Franco-Ontarian relates to all Francophones who were born and raised in Ontario.

THE PROBLEM OF STATISTICS

The problem of statistics stems most frequently from that of definitions, since numbers will vary considerably, depending on who can be identified as falling within a specific category. When writing about Franco-Ontarian illiterates, the problem is further compounded by regional differences on the one hand, and by the unequal distribution of Francophones throughout the province. Franco-Ontarians constitute a very distinct minority, in fact they are the largest francophone group outside of Quebec (Churchill, 1985). The following table illustrates the distribution of Francophones in Ontario.

Table I
Percentage of Designated Area Population which is French Mother Tongue
by Region, Ontario – 1981

Region	%	Total FMT	Total D.A. Population
North-West	21.4	3 750	17 557
North-East	28.0	150 900	538 493
East	23.2	173 645	749 493
Centre	2.0	56 560	2 844 008
South-West	8.3	20 305	245 698
Total	**9.2**	**405 160**	**4 395 249**

Source: Office of Francophone Affairs, Ontario Statistics 1986, revised version 1987, Government of Ontario, Ministry of Treasury & Economics. Special Tabulations from Statistics Canada, 1981.

The highest proportion of Franco-Ontarians who regularly use the French language is located in the eastern part of the province, although numbers in the northern and the Ottawa-Carleton regions are higher because of their greater population base.

A comparison of Ontarians having less than Grade nine education, that is considered to be functionally illiterate is contained in the next table.

Table II
A comparison of Francophones and Non-Francophones between the ages of
25 and 64 living in Ontario who have less than a Grade 9 education.

	Francophones		Non-francophones	
	Total	Percent	Total	Percent
Ontario	50,355	(31.2)	685,966	(16.8)
East	18,436	(25.2)	66,744	(13.1)
North-East	21,665	(39.5)	44,300	(20.5)
Central	6,305	(26.9)	448,635	(16.8)
South-West	2,395	(33.8)	103,680	(17.5)
North-West	1,290	(45.7)	22,200	(20.8)

Source: 1981 Census as reported in the Stacey Churchill report, p. 184; also in *Les Francophones tels qu'ils sont,* ACFO, 1986, P. 30.

This table clearly indicates that the percentage of Francophone illiterates in Ontario is almost double that of non-Francophones.

PROFILE OF THE FRANCO-ONTARIAN ILLITERATE

The specificity of the Francophone illiterate was brought out at a seminar held at Val Morin, Quebec in March 1983 (Letourneau, 1983). A holistic picture of the problem appears in the report: the illiterate is perceived not only as a person who has reading and writing deficiencies, but also as one whose general personal, social and economic level is at a low ebb. Previous educational experiences for many were painful, since the traditional school system did not meet their needs. This is particularly true of Franco-Ontarians, since a complete education in their own language was virtually impossible after 1912 following the imposition of Regulation 17.

The most common causes of illiteracy cited by UNESCO are poverty, hunger, isolation, lack of funds for education and externally imposed education systems. After 1912, Franco-Ontarians definitely became the victims of the latter three conditions, isolation, lack of funds for education and an externally imposed education system. Although some succeeded in functioning at a respectable level, the opportunities for economic and social mobility have been greatly limited.

Tracing the links between a social problem such as adult illiteracy and past events presents a challenge in historical analysis. What is far more difficult however, is to assess the extent to which such historical events came to exert an influence on such a problem. The critical point arrives when people, as a minority group, become aware of the historicity of their collective existence and of their past and present social environment. As such, in this part of my exposé, I will attempt to look at four dimensions of the Franco-Ontarian historical reality: the political, the economic, the socio-cultural and the educational.

The Political

The minority status of Franco-Ontarians can to some degree be historically traced back to 1759 when James Wolfe, as commander of the British expedition was sent to Canada to wrest the power from the French. During September of that year, Wolfe engaged the French in the battle which gave the British supremacy in Canada. At the time of this historical battle, a few hundred families of French origin were already living in the region now known as Ontario: along the river front regions of the Detroit River (which in 1796 became American territory), and around Fort Frontenac, commonly known as Kingston. Canadian historian and educator Arthur Godbout reported that the French population in Ontario at the beginning of the English regime was in the proximity of "a few thousand souls" (Godbout, 1977). Some twenty years or so later, another major historical event had a direct impact on the numerical and particularly on the economic status of the French-speaking population of the province. In 1783, following the signing of the Treaty of Versailles in September of that year, citizens living south of the border who wished to remain loyal to the British Crown, emigrated in large numbers towards northern soil. Known as United Empire Loyalists, their loyalty to the British Crown was richly compensated, as vast expanses of land were granted to them, according to their military rank (Harkness, 1946).

Godbout estimated that by 1790, more than ten thousand Loyalists had been established as such between Montreal and Detroit. In 1791, this territory was divided into Upper (primarily the Ontario region) and Lower Canada (primarily the Quebec region), with an English majority in the former, and a French majority in the latter. Thus came into play the first assimilating forces of the francophone population in Upper Canada, particularly in the Fort Frontenac area. The large numbers of Francophones in the Detroit-Windsor area made assimilation more difficult.

However, the new administration was far from being inimical to the French. In fact, near the end of the century, the British government, at the recommendation of Governor Simcoe, is said to have offered extensive areas of land in Upper Canada to French noblemen who sought to escape the consequences of the French revolution. Several returned to France, and others moved on, towards Lower Canada, later known as Québec (Godbout, 1977).

The Economic

The British were quite intent on having some of the land placed in French hands. Accordingly in 1803, a government agent by the name of Smith had a proclamation translated in the French language to inform Francophones of their rights to acquire Crown land.

Meanwhile, social and economic conditions in Lower Canada (Québec) were not too favourable to the majority of its inhabitants. As a result, it is estimated that more than one million immigrated to the United States between 1850 and 1900 (Chevrier,1980). During the same period, sixty-two thousand Québecois established their homes in Upper Canada, particularly within the boundaries of Glengarry, Stormont, Prescott and Russell, the South-East region of Ontario. Seeking better living conditions, these new immigrants encountered numerous difficulties. Most of the land already belonged either to the United Empire Loyalists or to the large numbers of Scottish immigrants who came to Canada in 1804, accompanied by their spiritual leader, the Reverend Alexander Macdonell (Harkness, 1946). A close look at a historical atlas of Stormont, Dundas and Glengarry reveals that most of the farms were indeed the property of British, Scottish and German descendants. Very few farms were registered under French names. Although some of the new immigrants eventually succeeded in buying land, most were forced to locate in urban areas, working as labourers in the mills of Eastern Ontario, and the mines of Northern Ontario.

The Socio-Cultural

The great influx of Francophones to Upper Canada led to a number of changes, demographic and otherwise. Within the eastern counties such as Stormont, Dundas and Glengarry, Canadians of British, Scottish, French, Irish, German and Dutch ethnic origins inevitably lived side by side. Their hopes, aspirations, their conflicts and problems of cohabitation have inspired the pens of novelists.

Although the early pioneers of varied backgrounds shared a common goal of basic survival, their cultural differences were many, – unfortunately serving to divide their energies, and weaken the wheels of progress and development.

First of all, there were linguistic differences – and since culture and language are so intimately intertwined, the British, the French, the Scottish, the German United Empire Loyalists, all sought to maintain their cultural roots.

Then, there were basic philosophical differences. The spirituality of Roman Catholic philosophy differed from the perhaps more materialistic and pragmatic views of the Protestant ethic (Weber, 1976). But undoubtedly, one of the most divisive and harmful differences lay in the Irish-French Roman Catholic struggles, particularly within the ecclesiastical hierarchy. Historian Robert Choquette (1977) gives vivid and detailed accounts of such conflicts which, unfortunately entered the political arena. Irish Catholic bishops supported the concept of an all-English Ontario, while, in opposition, the Francophone church leaders fought ferociously to preserve the French culture in Ontario.

In spite of valiant attempts by Egerton Ryerson and other political leaders to assure equal linguistic rights to Anglophones and Francophones, passions became increasingly heated, and eventually erupted in 1912 with the imposition of Regulation 17, which spelled the death knell to French schools and education for several decades.

In 1901, illiteracy rates were already higher among the Francophone population in Ontario. A comparison of illiteracy in the counties of Stormont, Dundas and Glengarry reveals that 23.4 percent of Glengarrians (55.9 percent French), and 17.7 percent of Stormont inhabitants (26 percent French) could neither read nor write. Meanwhile in neighbouring Dundas where the French population was a mere 6.2 percent, 8.9 percent of its citizens could neither read nor write (Roy-Poirier, 1983).

Large families among Roman Catholic Francophones, seen as a blessing from an economic point of view, may have contributed to their generally lower level of education. Moreover, schooling was perceived as a deterrent from religious practice. I have personally listened to several accounts of elderly francophones who were withdrawn from school at a very early age to work on the family farm, or as labourers. Financial conditions allowed very few to attend school on a regular basis. The scarce monetary resources of Francophones were being used to primarily purchase farms which had originally been given to anglophone United Empire Loyalists by the British Crown. With very few exceptions, the only Franco-Ontarians who became educated did so through religious vocations, as nuns or priests.

The Educational

Prior to 1900, French and English education had basically equal status and endured similar difficulties. In fact, when the government of Upper Canada made the decision in 1816 to fund common schools, French schools were established on the same basis as English schools; funds were distributed fairly to both linguistic groups (Godbout, 1977). Throughout Ryerson's mandate as Superintendent of Education in Upper Canada, French education received fair and equal treatment. In 1883, twenty-seven schools in Upper Canada were exclusively French (Choquette, 1977).

However, during the latter part of the century, the linguistic war was about to erupt. Prior to 1850, the majority of Roman Catholics in Upper Canada were of Irish or Scottish origins. As mentioned earlier, the massive immigration of French Catholics to Upper Canada between 1850 and 1900 brought about demographic changes, particularly in the eastern counties of Prescott, Russell, Stormont and Glengarry. Religious wars were taking place on different fronts. Protestant United Empire Loyalists feared the growth of Roman Catholic power. Meanwhile, the Irish Catholic and French Catholic bishops extended their language battle to the political front. Linguistically, the Irish bishops joined forces with their English-speaking Protestant counterparts to fight the French-speaking bishops and educators. Pressures were being placed on the government from both sides. Gradually, laws were introduced to erode French education.

In 1912, the declaration of Regulation 17 drastically limited the use of the French language in all schools of Ontario.Until then, Franco-Ontarians had had no reason to regret their separation from French Lower Canada in 1791 (Godbout, 1977). In fact, many preferred the fair play of the British at the time, than the iron-fisted tyranny of their own leaders in Lower Canada. Regulation 17 was further entrenched in 1915, when the Chief Justice of the Supreme Court of Ontario declared it valid, removing all natural and constitutional rights of the French language in Ontario. Anyone who defied the law was either jailed or payed a stiff fine (Choquette, 1977). .

Even more hostile to Francophone rights, the Irish and Scottish Catholic bishops continued to oppose the French-speaking ecclesiastics. In 1917, the situation was presented to the Vatican. Basically, in-fighting among Catholics was to be the most destructive force against Franco-Ontarian culture.

This marked the beginning of an era which disallowed Francophones an education in their language, and which promoted prejudice against them in all schools of Ontario, except in separate or private schools. There are reported incidents in the 1940's of elementary school children receiving harsh corporal punishment for speaking French even in the school yards during their recess periods. Times were hard; many verbal and legal battles were fought.

It was not until July 1968 that the law was changed by the Robarts government, officially permitting the teaching of French in all educational institutions of Ontario. In the interim, thousands of Ontario citizens had become the "lost generations" of uneducated, undereducated, or simply assimilated (Churchill et al., 1985)

The Illiteracy Problem

In 1977, La Fédération des Francophones Hors-Québec published a report on the educational level of citizens of Ontario, indicating that 38.1 percent of Francophones had a maximum of eight years schooling in comparison to 27.2 percent of the entire population.

More recent figures indicate that about twenty-four percent of Ontario's adults have less than a Grade nine education. Slightly more than fifty percent of Ontario's illiterates are older than fifty-five years of age.

About twenty-five are under the age of forty-five. Francophone groups are over-represented at thirty-five percent (Wright, 1986).

It has been noted time and again that "poverty and education play major roles in deciding whether illiteracy is transmitted from one generation to the next."[6] This phenomenon perhaps explains in part the high level of illiteracy within this particular group.

REMEDIAL MEASURES AND THE DIFFICULTIES ENCOUNTERED

Although illiteracy has always existed, only within the past decade or so has society in general become conscious of its reality. In fact, recent social awareness, made possible through the media, conferences, adult education courses, has given Adult Basic Education an unprecedented degree of importance. Ontario community colleges, adult day schools and community literacy groups such as Alfa-Action in Hawkesbury, La Magie des Lettres in Ottawa and others are attempting in modest ways to provide services for Francophone illiterates. There exist at present more than 175 community literacy groups in Ontario, twenty or so of which are Francophone? The demand for more services far exceeds the funds available. Of the $4.2 million allotted to the Ontario Community Literacy Programme in recent years, $850,000 went to the Francophone sector. To meet the requests of the various communities, $3 million is required within the francophone sector alone.

Problems also centre around the dependency on volunteers, inadequate methodologies and teaching material, as well as the recruitment of illiterates. A study by Déry and Jones, (1985) whose purpose was to design a method of needs analysis directed at Franco-Ontarian illiterates, brings to the fore the "pedagogical desert" which French literacy educators face in Ontario. Déry and Jones particularly emphasize the paucity of "adult" material and the reliance on methods adapted for children, a reality which in many ways, acts as a barrier. An attempt by Dallaire, Compain and Quéry[8] to design a "unique and different" learning tool may help to fill the gap of inadequate teaching material aimed at the Francophone illiterate. Their product was made available in March of 1987. A French language literacy programme has also been designed at Northern College. Further material is in the planning stage, in conjunction with the French network of TV Ontario and local community literacy groups.

Other difficulties have also been identified, for example the absence of a community development tradition such as exists in Anglophone sectors, especially in libraries which have been more involved in literacy work (Wagner, 1987). A resource centre of material intended for the anglophone sector is located at the Ontario Institute for Studies in Education in Toronto. There is no such centre for Francophones. Also, throughout the twentieth century, Franco-Ontarian energies have been directed towards the acquisition of French language instruction for the young; as such adult education in the Francophone sector is vastly underdeveloped. At the post-secondary level, the lack of a Francophone community college has also been a hindrance. Corrective measures are in the horizon with the foreseen creation of a French language community college.

The 1960's have brought progress in terms of educational opportunities for Francophones. However, this progress has been described at times as being only "a hodge-podge collection of measures designed more as palliatives than as cures to a linguistic malaise "(Savas, 1988). The emergence of the French Language Services Act (Bill 8) in 1986 designed to provide to Franco-Ontarians full access to government services in their own language is a means aimed at correcting some of the anomalies.

In September of 1987, the Ontario Ministry of Skills Development acquired the responsibility of basic literacy programmes for adults. Within the Literacy Branch of this ministry, coordinator Richard Hudon oversees the operation of the Ontario Community Literacy Programme for Francophones. For the first time in the history of Ontario, francophone adult illiterates have legal and official access to the acquisition of reading and writing skills.

Five other ministries share in the responsibilty of literacy training: Ministry of Education, Ministry of Citizenship and Culture, Ministry of Correctional Services, Ministry of Colleges and Universities, and the Ministry of Social & Community Services.

SCENARIOS FOR THE FUTURE

In what directions will Franco-Ontarians move in the future to alleviate illiteracy and to improve their lot in life generally? I will describe three brief scenarios which in some respects depict the present situation and the possibilities which could ensue. To add a bit of humour, I have entitled the scenarios as follows: The Squeeze, The Displacement and the Proaction for Change.

The Squeeze

The squeeze presents itself on two fronts, the financial and the socio-cultural. First of all, the squeeze for funds at all levels of education has been upon us for almost a decade. In September 1986, the Honourable Lily Munro, Ontario Minister for Citizenship and Culture announced a major project aimed at eliminating illiteracy in Ontario. How much of the funds will go to Francophones will greatly depend on the ability of groups and institutions to mobilize and to claim their fair share in the years ahead.

The squeeze presents itself also at the socio-cultural level. Since few Franco-Ontarians have attained a higher level of education, positions of power, money and prestige in Ontario have been and will continue to be held primarily by Anglophones (men and women), and by better educated male Québecois who have experienced great economic opportunities by immigrating to Ontario during the past few decades or so. Native-born Franco-Ontarians tend to be found in the lower-paying clerical and custodial jobs. The situation will be particularly grave for Franco- Ontarian women, illiterate as well as literate. A recent report reveals that "in terms of who earns and who earns the least, there is a sex-related income pattern which does not favour women in Ontario, and most especially not Francophone women" (Savas, 1988). The report specifies that the pattern from the highest to the lowest income levels shows Ontario males at the top of the pyramid followed by Francophone males, Ontario females and then Francophone females. In contrast with their male counterparts, Quebec women have suffered Napoleonic-style oppression of their own; in fact, they were granted the vote in 1940 only (Gagnon, 1983). As such, as new arrivals in Ontario, they tend to have a clearer understanding of the difficulties expressed by Franco-Ontarians.

The Displacement

Will the French language survive in Ontario? Yes, of course. Perhaps not through the Franco-Ontarians themselves, but rather through the present enthusiasm of Anglophones who recognize the advantages of a bilingual education for their children. Franco-Ontarians, who have been sensitized to their economic deprivation and the "squeeze" situation, often become easy victims of the assimilation process. This could be most prevalent among the illiterate Francophone population, who through lack of motivation generally, and the absence of effective programmes will join classes which will teach them the language of the majority. This fact was brought out in a recent article which indicates that "One third of Ontario's Francophone population can't read and write French. Although this segment of the population may well be literate in English, statistics show that they are having problems with their mother tongue."

The Proaction for Change

The third scenario is built on the Proaction for a Change paradigm of Boshier (1986). Because of their past history, Franco-Ontarians have either been apathetic or highly reactive. In the present context, will it be viable for Franco-Ontarians to maintain the reactive stance which became necessary for cultural survival after 1912?

A proactive scenario coupled with a collective effort could in the words of Moses Coady, make them "masters of their own destiny" (Coady, 1939). It could uproot illiteracy within their own culture and give men and women a sense of self-esteem and dignity. The present Francophone community literacy programme emphasizes a collective or group approach aimed at reinforcing the social and political dimensions of the learning situation. Also, the oral communication tradition of Francophone illiterates must be taken into account and valued as a strength.

A proactive stance is also essential from the Anglophone point of view. A holistic, rational and objective comprehension of the serious problems which Franco-Ontarians (in spite of being a part of one of Canada's founding nations) have endured through many decades is vital along with the continued political will to put into place the necessary corrective measures.

Through the principles of adult education which favour a more humanistic, (Brundage & MacKeracher, 1980) democratic, (Knowles,1985) and pleasurable" (Dufresne-Tassé, 1979) approach to education and life in general, Franco-Ontarians may be able to pick up the pieces of their past, and work towards a more optimistic future. Effective affirmative action programmes, specifically directed at Franco-Ontarian women will give them the opportunity to overcome their particularly difficult situation of "being" as a double minority. Linguistic roots can be denied for economic reasons but gender cannot!

CONCLUSION

In presenting the case of the Franco-Ontarian illiterate, several aspects were taken into consideration. First of all, the problem of definitions and of statistics led to a profile of the Franco-Ontarian illiterate. Then followed a review of four dimensions from the historical past: political, economic, socio-cultural and educational. From the past to the present and through causes and effects, we looked somewhat at the problem as it exists in 1988, as well as the remedial measures now in place. The exposé ended with three brief scenarios for the future.

Because of the inherent difficulties linked to a minority status, such as small numbers, the dispersiveness of the population and in many cases, socio-economic difficulties, easy solutions to illiteracy among Franco-Ontarians may not be easily found. However, as society moves towards a greater awareness of the ill-effects of illiteracy in general, it may be possible to alleviate the problem somewhat - and hopefully in the future, eradicate it completely.

NOTES

1. Southam Literacy Survey, as reported in the *Ottawa Citizen,* September,1987.

2. Groupe de travail sur les services universitaires en français, the results of which were published in *L'Université d'Ottawa et la Francophonie Ontarienne,* Ottawa, 1985.

3. As reported in The *UNESCO Courier,* June, 1980.

4. In a *Historical Atlas of the Counties of Stormont, Dundas and Glengarry, Ontario,* compiled, drawn and published from personal examinations and surveys by H. Belden, & Co., Toronto, 1879.

5. One such novelist was Dorothy Dumbrille author of several books, including *All This Difference,* Progress Books, 1945.

6. As reported in the *Ottawa Citizen,* September, 1987.

7. Information was obtained in a government document, *Alphabétisation, base de la croissance.* Ministère de la formation professionnelle, Ontario.

8. Report published at the University of Ottawa, Ottawa, Ontario, in the *Gazette,* Vol. XXI, 16, 1987.

9. According to a newspaper article, "Francophones learn their own language", in *The Evening Tribune,* Welland, Ontario, September 7, 1988.

10. Dufresne-Tassé stresses in most of her writings the role of pleasure in adult learning, which frees the energy required for action.

94 JEANNINE ROY-POIRIER

SELECTED REFERENCES

Association canadienne française de l'Ontario (1986). *Les francophones tels qu'ils sont: regard sur le* *monde du travail franco-ontarien.*
Boshier, Roger (1986). "Proaction for a Change: Some Guidelines for the Future". *International Journal* *for Lifelong Education.* 4:11.
Brundage, Donald H. and Dorothy MacKeracher (1980). *Adult Learning Principles and their Application* *to Program Planning.* Toronto: Ministry of Education.
Chevrier, Bernard (1980). "Early French Canadians in Ontario". Cornwall, Ontario: *Standard-Freeholder,* August 7.
Choquette, Robert (1977) *Langue et religion: histoire des conflits anglo-français en Ontario.* Ottawa: Editions de l'Université d'Ottawa.
Churchill, Stacey et al. (1985). *Education et besoins des Franco-Ontariens: le diagnostic d'un système* *d'éducation, Volume 1.* Toronto: Le conseil de l'éducation franco-ontarienne.
Coady, M. M. (1939). *Masters of Their Own Destiny.* New York & London: Harper & Brothers Publishers.
Déry, Lucie and Stan Jones (1985). *Etude de besoins Pour le développement d'un test ontarien* *d'alphabétisation fonctionnelle des adultes en langue française.* Ottawa, Algonquin College.
Dufresne-Tassé, Colette (1979). *La jatte d'abricots: notes sur la relation motivation, apprentissage chez* *l'adulte.* Montreal: Université de Montréal.
Gagnon, Lysiane (1983). *Vivre avec les hommes: un nouveau partage.* Montreal: Québec/Amérique.
Godbout, Arthur (1977). *L'origine des écoles françaises dans l'Ontario.* Ottawa: Les Editions de l'Université d'Ottawa.
Harkness, John Graham (1946). *Stormont, Dundas and Glengarry: A History.* 1784-1945. Ottawa: Mutual Press Limited.
Knowles, Malcolm S. & Associates (1985). *Andragogy in Action: Applying Modern Principles of Adult* *Learning.* Jossey-Bass Publishers.
Letourneau, Léo (1983). *Analphabétisme chez les francophones hors Québec.* Ottawa: La Fédération des francophones hors Québec.
Roy-Poirier, Jeannine (1983). *Le rôle et les fonctions d'agents agricoles dans Stormont, Dundas et* *Glengarry de 1907 à 1917.* Montreal: Université de Montréal. Ph.D. thesis.
Savas, Daniel (1988). *Socio-Demographic Characteristics of the Franco-Ontarian Community.* Report 1, Spring.
Thomas, Audrey (1983). *Adult Literacy in Canada – A Challenge.* Occasional Paper 42, Ottawa: Canadian Commission for UNESCO.
Wagner, Serge (1987). *Documents d'appui pour l'alphabétisation communautaire chez les* *Franco-Ontariens,* étude produite pour la direction du programme Alphabétisation communautaire Ontario.
Weber, Max (1976). *The Protestant Ethic and the Spirit of Capitalism.* New York: Scribner.
Wright, G. H. (1986). *Project Report: For Adults Only.* Toronto: Ministry of Colleges and Universities.

CHAPTER 2:

Adult Basic Education Programs in Canada

Ethel E. Anderson

Adult upgrading programs in Canada are not new. As early as 1855 the Toronto Board of Education was offering basic literacy and numeracy courses for adults (Toronto Board, 1978) and in 1903 Frontier College was providing literacy and continuing education to workers in remote areas of Canada (Morrison, 1974). What is new however, is the growing recognition on the part of the public, governments, and private corporations that Canada has a significant undereducated adult population and adult basic education programs are necessary. This growing awareness has resulted in a variety of programs being offered across the country.

The majority of adult basic education (ABE) programs in Canada are government sponsored. Many receive direct funding from either the federal or provincial governments while others receive indirect support through government sponsorship of students. A few programs, primarily volunteer ones, rely on financial support from individuals and/or community groups. The focus of the different programs often reflects the adult education philosophy of the sponsoring agencies.

ROLE OF THE FEDERAL GOVERNMENT

Thirty years ago ABE programs were rare in Canada. There were employment opportunities for most people regardless of their level of education and a grade eight was often deemed a sufficient level of education. This situation started to change towards the end of the 1950s when Canada's unemployment rate started to rise and level of education became a criterion for employment. Adults with limited formal schooling were at a disadvantage in the increasingly technological work environment.

The federal government responded to the higher unemployment rates and the need for a better-trained work force by implementing the Technical and Vocational Training Act in 1960. This act provided funding for programs that would prepare adults for employment. Although academic upgrading was not funded, it soon became clear that many of the unemployed could not qualify for the technical and vocational courses unless they had an opportunity to upgrade their academic skills. The Technical and Vocational Training Act of 1960 was replaced by the Adult Occupational Training Act of 1967. This act covered the Canada Manpower Training Programs which enabled undereducated adults to upgrade their education to a grade eight or higher level through the Basic Training for Skill Development (BTSD) program before entering the technical courses. Many of the BTSD programs were offered through vocational centres or community colleges and theoretically were open to all adults. However, the fees for these programs made attendance impossible for most undereducated adults unless they were sponsored under the Canada Man-power Training Program. The adults who were sponsored were those who were most likely to complete their upgrading in 52 weeks or less and were deemed to be employable, but for many adults, particularly those with limited literacy skills, the 52 week time frame was not realistic.

In 1982 when the federal government passed the National Training Act which emphasized training, primarily at the post-secondary levels, for the high technology sector, funds going to adult upgrading programs were re-allocated. In many provinces the deliverers of ABE programs had relied heavily on federal funding and the withdrawal of this support meant that many ABE programs were terminated. Although the Canadian Jobs Strategies, implemented in 1985, was designed to provide a combination of skill development and job experience for people who already had a basic education, some undereducated adults seeking employment have been sponsored for basic upgrading as a first step in their training. This change is a result of a 1988 recommendation that more funds be allocated to basic upgrading programs under the Job Develop-ment and Entry/Re-entry Programs.

Since education is a provincial responsibility, the federal government's in-volvement in ABE programming has been in response to specific problems in areas where it has jurisdiction, such as unemployment or prison recidivism.

In 1988 the federal government expanded its ABE role when it designated $110 million, over a five-year period, to support literacy initiatives. In keeping with the federal government's hands-off approach to education, direct pro-gram delivery is not funded. Instead, these funds are being used to support the development of new literacy projects by the voluntary and non-governmental sectors, joint initiatives with the provinces, and the organization and mainte-nance of the National Literacy Secretariat. This new funding has resulted in an expansion of literacy activities across the country.

ROLE OF THE PROVINCIAL AND TERRITORIAL GOVERNMENTS

The provincial governments have responsibility for education but the amount and degree of support for ABE varies from province to province.

British Columbia

The main deliverers of ABE in British Columbia are school boards and colleges. The funding for these programs is provided by the provincial Ministry of Education.

Under Continuing Education, the Ministry of Education provides a variety of programs identified as ABE. Included under this heading are GED prepara-tion, Adult Special Education, Basic Literacy, B.T.S.D., and other programs that offer the basic skills of reading, writing, spelling, and comprehension (B.C. Ministry of Education, 1983). As a result of the 1984 initiation of a certification and articulation project (Fraser, 1984), all levels of ABE have been clearly identified and delineated and certificates for the different levels have been developed.

The term ABE Fundamental is now used to identify programs designed specifically for adults who have less than a grade eight equivalency. These programs are offered by community colleges and school boards using class-room settings where students have an opportunity to interact while working on individualized programs. To assist teachers in developing these programs the *Native Literacy and Life Skills Curriculum Guidelines* (British Columbia Ministry of Education, 1984) and the *Adult Basic Education Literacy Curriculum Guide* (British Columbia Ministry of Advanced Education, 1987) have been developed.

Alberta
The province of Alberta provides financial support to a variety of ABE programs through Alberta Advanced Education. This ministry of the provincial government funds upgrading programs offered by the Alberta Vocational Centres, local school boards, community colleges, community vocational centres, and Further Education Councils.

The majority of programs offered by the Alberta Vocational Centres, school boards, community colleges, and community vocational guidance centres provide individualized instruction in a class setting. The programs offered may be full- and/or part-time. In order to assist adults to participate in the full-time upgrading programs, the provincial government's Department of Manpower provides a training allowance. This allowance is available to adults enrolled in any full-time ABE program.

The Further Education Councils also play an important role in ABE in Alberta. These councils receive administrative grants from the Further Education Service branch in order to

> coordinate further education programs at the local level and to encourage the delivery of part-time Adult Basic Literacy and English as a Second Language programming throughout the province (Alberta Advanced Education, 1984).

In most communities one-to-one volunteer tutoring programs are established. Often a school, library, or college acts as the hosting agency and the grant money is used for course materials and the coordinator's salary.

To assist community groups in their development of one-to-one volunteer tutoring programs, the Further Education Services Branch developed an instructor's training manual and the Alberta Educational Communications Corporation (ACCESS) has developed a tutor-training series. Funding from the Secretary of State, matched by the province, has also been used to develop additional training programs for tutors.

Saskatchewan
ABE programs in Saskatchewan are offered through the regional colleges, the Saskatchewan Institute of Applied Science and Technology, some school boards, the Regina Public Library, and various volunteer groups. These programs are funded with grants from the Department of Education (Saskatchewan Department of Education, 1987).

In Saskatchewan, as in British Columbia, the term ABE covers adult upgrading programs from a basic literacy level to a grade twelve equivalency. Life skill and job skill programs are also included. In 1983, an ABE curriculum guide for communications, mathematics, science, and social studies was developed. Adults who complete the grade ten to twelve part of this program receive special certificates.

The regional colleges are the major providers of ABE programs, but few offer basic literacy. The basic literacy programs that are offered by the colleges are outreach programs that rely on volunteer tutors. The programs offered at the colleges, whether full- or part-time, are aimed at adults who are functioning above a grade five level. Adults who qualify for the Saskatchewan Skill Development Program, a cooperative venture between the colleges and the Department of Social Services to provide academic upgrading to adults who are on social assistance, receive financial support from the Department of Social Services.

In 1986 the Department of Education established the Saskatchewan Literacy Council to coordinate literacy efforts throughout the province. A major emphasis has been on one-to-one volunteer tutoring efforts. This initiative was one of the first programs funded under the new federal government's National Literacy Secretariat.

Manitoba

The Adult and Continuing Education Branch of the Manitoba Department of Education is responsible for ABE within the province.

Prior to 1982 and the withdrawal of CEIC funding, colleges were the main providers of ABE programs in Manitoba. Although some colleges continue to offer ABE, the programs are at a grade seven level and above.

In 1984 the Adult and Continuing Education Branch implemented the New Initiative Program which provides small grants to communities interested i developing literacy programs. The programs are developed in cooperation with school boards or other community groups. Most of these programs provide an individualized program on a part-time basis (six hours or less per week) using paid literacy workers (Manitoba Department of Education, 1988). In 1986 approximately 200 adults participated in these literacy programs (Manitoba Department of Education, 1987).

Ontario

In Ontario the Ministry of Education and the Ministry of Skills Development are the two primary sponsors of ABE programming with the Ministry of Skills Development also having responsibility for coordinating literacy efforts within the province.

The Ministry of Education provides continuing education grants to school boards offering ABE programs. To encourage school bord involvement in ABE, the Ministry of Education provides additional funding so school boards can accommodate low enrolments in the ABE classes. Over a third of the school boards in Ontario use these grants to provide adult basic literacy and ABE programs. These include day and evening classes where students work on individualized programs as well as one-to-one tutoring and/or small group sessions.

The Ontario Ministry of Education also provides ABE courses through distance education for adults who are unable to participate in other programs. Using print, audio tapes, and the telephone, adults are able to take basic literacy as well as English courses starting at a grade four reading level.

The Ontario colleges of applied arts and technology provide ABE programs as part of the Ontario Basic Skills Program (OBS). This program, which was designed specifically for "adults who face barriers to skills training by virtue of being educationally disadvantaged" was initiated by the Ontario Ministry of Skills Development in 1986 (Ontario Ministry of Skills Development, 1986). Although academic instruction from a basic literacy to a grade 12 level is offered as part of this program, the focus is on preparation for the work force. Financial assistance for child care, transportation, and accommodation is available to participants in the program (Ontario Ministry of Skills Development, 1986). The Ministry of Skills Development also supports ABE programs sponsored by business and labour through the Ontario Basic Skills in the Workplace program.

In addition to the OBS and OBSW programs, the Ministry of Skills Development supports community based literacy programs. The Ministry provides training and consultative services as well as funding through the Ontario Community Literacy grants. These grants are intended to help community groups cover the cost of the development and delivery of basic literacy programs.

Quebec

The Quebec Ministry of Education is responsible for ABE in the province. The *Continuing Education Program Policy Statement and Plan of Action*, released in 1984, presents the Ministry's position on adult literacy programming and ABE, as well as adult education in general.

A majority of the ABE programs in Quebec are offered by the regional school boards. These programs, which are funded with Ministry of Education grants, provide instruction from a basic literacy to a grade six equivalency in a small class setting. The classes, which may be full- or part-time, are provided free of charge.

In addition to the school board programs, some volunteer community education organizations that provide basic literacy instruction are also funded by Ministry of Education grants. In order to qualify for funding from the Ministry of Education, however, these organizations must follow the French and English adult literacy curriculum guidelines that are presently being developed by the Ministry.

Atlantic Provinces

For the past twenty years the main providers of literacy and basic upgrading in the Atlantic provinces have been the volunteer literacy councils. In some instances, the volunteer literacy councils in cooperation with local school boards or colleges co-sponsor ABE programs.

Although the provincial government of New Brunswick through the Department of Advanced Education provides funding to the colleges for ABE, a majority of the college programs are for adults functioning above the grade eight level. The literacy and basic upgrading programs that are offered by the colleges are one-to-one volunteer tutoring programs with the colleges providing funding for coordinators and materials. The Laubach literacy materials are used in most of these programs as well as in the literacy programs offered by the volunteer literacy councils.

A similar situation exists in Nova Scotia where ABE programs are provided by the school boards and the volunteer literacy councils. The provincial government's Department of Education funds the school board programs. In larger centres, such as Halifax, the school board ABE programs include day and evening classes. These classes may meet in libraries or other satellite locations depending upon the needs of the group being served. In smaller centres where classes may not be feasible, boards offer literacy instruction and basic upgrading with the help of volunteer tutors and the Laubach literacy materials. To provide coordination of the literacy activities in the province, the Nova Scotia Department of Advanced Education and Training is developing a literacy delivery system.

In Prince Edward Island most of the ABE programs are provided by literacy councils, although one college and a few school boards do offer adult upgrading classes.

Newfoundland

Adult Basic Education in Newfoundland is the responsibility of the provincial government's Department of Career Development and Advanced Studies. Until recently most of the province's ABE programs were offered at vocational centres and high schools throughout the province. However, with the new reorganization, colleges will assume greater responsibility for ABE delivery.

Yukon and North West Territories

In the Yukon, the Department of Advanced Education is responsible for ABE. It, in cooperation with the Secretary of State, supports the Yukon Literacy Council and the Yukon College program.

In the North West Territories where the Department of Education is responsible for ABE, upgrading programs including basic literacy are offered through continuing education.

THE ROLE OF OTHER AGENCIES

Although the primary providers of ABE programs in many of the provinces appear to be the colleges, school boards, and vocational centres, other important players are the non-profit volunteer tutoring organizations. Without organizations such as Frontier College and Laubach Literacy of Canada, adults in some areas of Canada would have no access to literacy instruction.

Frontier College

Since 1903 when it placed its first labourer-teachers, Frontier College has been providing educational opportunities to Canadian adults who are out of the "main stream" (Morrison, 1974).

For a number of years, Frontier College's main work was with labourers in isolated situations such as lumber camps. Although the college continues to provide labourer-teachers, in 1976-77 Frontier College began offering literacy programs in what it terms the "new frontier". The first of these was a one-to-one literacy tutoring program in a Manitoba prison. This program has served as a model for others across Canada.

Another "new frontier" was Independent Studies, a literacy tutoring program developed for physically disabled adults. This program is now offered in cities across Canada.

In addition to these "new frontier" efforts, Frontier College continues to offer literacy tutoring programs to adults and young people in communities where literacy programs are needed.

Laubach Literacy of Canada
In the three Atlantic provinces, the Laubach Literacy Councils made up of volunteers are the main providers of literacy programs. The first Laubach Literacy Council started in Nova Scotia in 1970 and others were soon established. There are now Laubach Literacy Councils in every province in Canada.

Laubach Literacy of Canada, which is affiliated with Laubach International based in Syracuse, New York, provides training and materials to volunteers who want to serve as literacy tutors. The administration of the councils as well as the tutor-training and the tutoring are all done on a volunteer basis.

SUMMARY
The last decade has seen a growing awareness of the need for ABE programs, not only as a means of alleviating economic problems but also as part of a continuum of life-long learning. The federal, as well as the provincial governments are becoming more involved and the number and variety of ABE programs available across Canada has increased significantly from the 250 identified in 1978 (Anderson et al., 1978).

There are, however, areas of Canada where there are no ABE programs. In order to ensure that all undereducated adults have an opportunity to continue their education, there will have to be continued commitment to ABE and continued cooperation among governments agencies, voluntary groups, community organizations, business, and labour. It is through these combined efforts that innovative ways of providing educational opportunities to Canadians will be identified.

REFERENCES

Alberta Advanced Education, (1984). *Annual Report 1983-84*. Edmonton, Alberta: Government of Alberta, pp. 44–50.

Anderson, Ethel E., Audrey M. Thomas and Carolyn Youseff, (1978). *Directory of Adult Basic Education Programs in Canada*. Toronto: Movement for Canadian Literacy.

B.C. Ministry of Advanced Education, (1987). *Adult Basic Education Literacy Curriculum Guide*. Victoria, B.C.: Government of British Columbia.

B.C. Ministry of Education, (1983). *School District, College and Institute Continuing Education Data*. Victoria, B.C.: Government of British Columbia.

B.C. Ministry of Education, (1984). *Native Literacy and Life Skills Curriculum Guidelines*. Victoria, B.C.: Government of British Columbia.

Fraser, Bruce, (1984). *Adult Basic Education Articulation*. Victoria, B.C.: Government of British Columbia, pp. 14–17.

Government of Quebec, (1982). *Learning: A Voluntary and Responsible Action Summary Report*. Quebec City: Commission d'etude sur la formation des adultes p. 48.

Government of Quebec, (1984). *Continuing Education Program Policy Statement and Plan of Action*.

Manitoba Department of Education, (1987). *Annual Report 1986-87*.

Manitoba Department of Education, (1988). *Manitoba: Progress in Literacy*.

Morrison, Ian, (1974). "Meeting Poverty through Education: A Canadian Experience", *Literacy Discussion*, Summer, 1974, pp. 201–210.

Ontario Ministry of Skills Development, (1986). *Ontario Basic Skills Program Guidelines*. Toronto: Government of Ontario, p. 2.

Saskatchewan Department of Education, (1987). *A New Beginning: A Background Paper on Adult Illiteracy and Undereducation in Saskatchewan*.

Toronto Board of Education, (1978). *Toronto Board of Education Continuing Education Department Report*.

CHAPTER 3:

Conscious Romantics: A Trade Unionist's Reflections on the Politics of Learning

D'Arcy Martin

Remember. You must share this poem. It brings good luck. Send no money. Don't ignore it.[1]

Consciousness, being truly awake and alert, can only be developed by the careful application of cultural logic. It can't be pushed along like a donkey, it can't be prodded by shocks, electrical or emotional, and it can't be humiliated into action.

The job of the poet is to ring the bell. The job of the adult educator is to open the curtains and let the light, which has always been there, flow into the dark.[2]

THINK TWICE

It's in the playground that we learned the difference. Certainly by the age of nine. The street smart and the book smart have different costumes and different languages.

In adult education courses, participants and teachers stare at one another across the same experiential gulfs we discovered as children. And whichever group we belonged to back then, it's clear that all adult basic educators start from the book-smart pole at the beginning of a course. Whether our "expertise" derives from experience or from formal study, it has been recognized by naming us as educators. We should think twice about what this means.

Authentic adult basic education is a job for conscious romantics,[3] people who have a vision of social justice, and practical experience of the difficulties in bringing it about. We work with those adults who have been expelled earliest from formal education, who associate teaching with negation and humiliation. And we ourselves are often over-extended by the multiple strains of our work — how many high school teachers have to hustle grants just to keep their classrooms open?

Yet when trade union and other adult basic educators gather, the raw, impolite facts of our work are often screened out of the conversation. Our communication patterns recall the properties of water, so carefully memorized as adolescents — colourless, odourless and tasteless.[4]

I suspect it's because we don't take seriously enough the tensions built into our own learning process. The source of the tension is our status as go-betweens. Our challenge is to direct the flow of ideological traffic between the powerful and the powerless, without ourselves being run over.

Keeping track of these contradictions in our role means we have to think carefully. Think twice.

After all, my work has different imperatives than that of the union stewards in my courses.[5] The "engineered anxiety" of workers in the telephone system, members of my union, is different from my stress as a worker educator. For them, the issues are productivity pressure, electronic surveillance, income insecurity. For me, the porous wall between employment and voluntary social action, the disorientation of constant travel, the pressure on family life are anchored in a different work process. While we share a commitment to social unionism and a stake in the union's organizational life, no one is helped by the pretence that our work lives are identical.

As educators, our raw material is ideas, and our product is words and images. This product, I would argue, is intrinsically equally valuable to that of other workers. And since we have chosen this craft, even for a time, we shouldn't talk only to the walls, or only with the participants in our courses. We should take over our own stress factory.

This means developing some common language among literacy workers, teachers of English as a second language, vocational instructors and trade union educators. For us all, a critical popular education movement can evolve only speaking and listening carefully with on another. In that spirit, I will draw on my trade union experience in sketching some principles of popular education.

OTHER WORKERS

Out of burlap sacks, out of bearing butter
Out of black bean and wet slate bread,
Out of the acids of rage, the candor of tar,
Out of creosote, gasoline, drive shafts, wooden dollies,
They Lion grow.[6]

The living room walls were covered with certificates. High school graduation, welding courses, Augusta's university degree, lovingly packed when they immigrated from Nigeria.

But one small label stood out. It was a piece of masking tape starting to peel off the base of the table lamp, with a price of $20 marked on it in ballpoint pen.

Zeke and Augusta were selling the contents of their house, part of the stake they had built in five years of hard work. This small mining town in the interior of B.C. was just the first stop in the road to their dreams.

Now they were ready to move to an urban centre. The down payment on their new house had been mailed to London, Ontario, and Augusta's transcripts had been accepted at the university. Zeke was ready to take a pay cut, working as a welder at 30% less than his current rate at the coal mine. Selling their house and furnishings would give the nest egg needed to carry them through this next phase.

But then the strike started. It had been on for six weeks. Housing prices had dropped, because it was anyone's guess how long the strike would last. And they were in limbo.

They were solid union supporters. Zeke was sick of being treated like a dummy by the company, and Augusta knew that the safety hazards in the mind had to be challenged. They hadn't flinched since the strike vote. But underneath was the sense that their plans and hopes were being ground up in a conflict not of their making.

They were workers. As a worker educator, I could have dished out some abstract rhetoric of solidarity and struggle as my contribution. It would have made no sense to them at all. Their personal solidarity as a couple[7], and their status as immigrants of colour were basis on which any real identification with the other workers in the strike would have to build.

Strike education for us meant bringing these realities to the surface. It meant articulating the individual needs and situations of each striker.

In automobile lore, this is called customizing. It's a luxury, for a small market. For a popular educator, this is a necessity. Not just as tactics but as ethics.

The time and place of this story was a strike in a small mining town. But the time for this couple was the eve of a move, and the place was their living room, with a price tag on all that they owned.

The educational job here was to synchronize Zeke and Augusta's watches with those of the other strikers. It was to unite, join, merge — to build collectivity by establishing shared meanings. If we are to anchor general ideas about popular movements in people's lived experience, this is first and central. It's a precondition to democratic educational leadership.[8]

Then we can begin to draw together the needs of young and old, of men and women, of native-born and immigrant, of employed and unemployed. We can legitimately talk about the educational moment in the process of building popular movements.

CONSCIOUSNESS RAISING ON A CROWDED STAGE

> At a certain point you have to recognize the work of your own hand in your confinement.
> Learn to untie the ropes by re-tracing the moves.
> Look for clues you've left yourself on the way in.
> Be aware of knots you've tied particularly tight — they're the hardest to undo because you meant it that way when you were doing it.
>
> Only read books when you have to.[9]

To make sense of the adult basic education drama, we need to know who is on stage. There are three starring roles, those of participant, educator and sponsor.

For liberal or "facilitating" adult education, the centre of attention is the participant. Usually, however, the learner is treated as an individual rather than situated in the dynamics of social power.[10]

In trade union education, the participants are members, already active in the "union culture"[11]. I have introduced Zeke and Augusta to remind us that union members in Canada are a very diverse group.

The conventional image of "unionist" is of a white man, middle aged, employed full-time in a stable, industrial job. But this image is already a generation behind the facts. Today, more and more, unionists are on the move, across regions and economic sectors.

Increasingly, women are working outside the home, in unionized information/service jobs. Their involvement is part of the reason why unionization in Canada has risen from 30 per cent of the workforce to 40 per cent in the last generation. And their energy has propelled a woman to the national presidency of Canada's labour movement.

An adult educator with an outdated image of "unionist" could not be effective in Canada today. Workers may lack book-smarts, but they know which way the wind is blowing.

Reflecting on the education drama also means casting the educator. Most good mystery novels centre on the question of agency — whodunit? In adult basic education, it's usually a woman. After all, work in this field is relatively low in pay and prestige, precisely the areas of the economy where women tend to be ghettoized.

Recognition by the labour movement of the working conditions among adult basic educators has been rather belated and cautious. Yet the recent policy statement by the Ontario Federation of Labour indicates the possible coalition around literacy:

All over Ontario, groups of people are working to provide literacy training. These people work hard under grossly underfinanced conditions because they are strongly committed to improving the lives of people. All of us in the trade union movement know people in our own organizations who have struggled with the enormous disadvantage of being unable to fully use printed materials. . . We should seek to launch a literacy drive which operates in the workplace, during working hours. This drive should take on the charter of a major campaign and must follow the fundamental principles of adult education — democratic control by the participants over methods, approaches and the materials to be used.[12]

As we engage in dialogue around an area of common interest, such as literacy, the differences in institutional stake will also emerge. Some of us are better paid than others. Some of us are identified directly with the participants in a social movement — union, women's group, community organization, etc. Our sympathies, friendships and incomes are intimately tied to the fate of that movement. Often, as in the labour movement, the educator has come into an educational staff position by rising through the ranks.

Others are professional educators, for whom popular organizations are allies rather than employers. Seeing participants as a constituency or clientele rather than a universe confers on these people a very different stake in discussions. At times their critical distance raises the level of debate. At others, the division of labour becomes a dialogue of the deaf.

Another factor to consider in the position of the educator in the institutional hierarchy. One of the paradoxes of organizational life is that the best popular educators are all too often "promoted" into categories such as researchers, policy-maker or administrators.[13] While they may thereby become invaluable strategic allies for the adult basic educator, they also lose direct contact with the central educational encounter. Gradually, their educational views tend to drift into nostalgia and paternalism, until institutional debate brings into sharp relief their loyalties, and it is clarified once again "which side are you on?"

For critical adult education, then, it is necessary to think in stereo — to locate both participants and educators in social context. Only then can authentic dialogue take place. And only then does a shared praxis become possible.

Once we have clarity on the social identity of the learners and the educators, the third actor appears — the sponsor. For those who think in terms of academic freedom, this may be a distasteful matter to raise, but such people would be ineffective as adult basic educators in any case.

In practice, it takes a sponsor to bring educators and learners together. This is not to negate the value of self-directed and individual learning. But programs of adult basic education invariably are conditioned by the educational, political and economic contradictions of a sponsor.

This may mean navigating through the internal political rivalries of a union, or challenging the constraints imposed on a vocational training agency by its dependence on government funding, or debating with community college staff about their condescending stance towards workers. Whatever the disciplines involved, failure to reflect critically on the sponsor of adult basic education is naive. It can also lead to heartbreaking surprises . . . a Waterloo of illusions.[14]

In practice, then, adult basic education requires a cast of three characters — the participants, the educator and the sponsor. In theatre terms, it is a "three hander". Inevitably, there will be some tensions among these three actors.

Consensus models of education, which associate tension with negativity, will tend to supress this fact. Dialectical models, which associate tension with energy, will yield more insight and inspiration for practitioners of adult basic education.

Indeed, the momentum and dynamism of any adult learning program is generated by the interplay among these three roles. A responsible actor in popular education is constantly dealing with the kaleidoscopic shifts in personal and social relations which result. By ruling out any of the three "who's" in the cast, the richness and transformative potential of the educational drama would be lost.

KNOWING, FEELING AND DOING

I wanted to swim in the most ample lives,
The widest estuaries,
And when, little by little, man came denying me
Closing his paths and doors so that I could not touch his wounded existence
with my divining fingers

I came by other ways.[15]

In adult education, we need to conduct ourselves by knowing, feeling and doing. This means breaking the tyranny of the cognitive, situating information as only one level of the educational encounter. The levels of emotion and skill must be dealt into critical popular education with equal force.

In the silicone age, the most discounted of the three is feeling.[16] Yet it is the key to generating any popular resistance to dominant ideas.

When an educator says "free trade" or "abortion" or "pollution", each of us hits a different level in our emotional thermometer. It would take some discussion to reach a consensus on ranking their priority as content for adult basic education.

The challenge is for us to do in our reality what Paulo Freire and other popular educators have been doing in the intricacy of Latin American society — act upon generative themes[17]. This means first identifying a part of collective experience which participants acknowledge as important, be it bingo or grievances or alcoholism. Educational leadership means moving perceptions of the theme from naive to critical understanding, and then to transformative action, by a process of conscious dialogue.

In addressing each theme, the process of naming will be central. As with the "naming of cats" in T.S. Eliot, there will be different layers involved.

Further, we need to develop the courage to propose, to assert possible ways that they could reflect on the issue and incorporate their conclusions into shaping their own lives. While currently fashionable, it is misleading and irresponsible to suggest that a dream of change, and the commitment to act upon it, is without value.[18]

Many of the "communications difficulties" experienced by adult basic educators, in unions as well as formal educational institutions, can be traced to the separation of knowing from feeling from doing. Let us consider how each is distorted when cut off from the others.

The first approach, heavy on knowing, we might term "research-driven". Its central commitment is to the content of a social issue, whether racism, sexism or class bias. Its energy and skill go to studying the matter and confronting people with findings.

The reaction of participants and sponsors to this stance is usually to plead overload and hence justify paralysis. In one workshop on technology where I myself erred on this side, a participant commented, "I came looking for a glass of water, and found I was dealing with a fire hydrant." The resulting confusion contradicts the stated goal of the educator, to achieve collective clarity on the issue.

The second approach, heavy on the affective level, we might term "feeling-driven". Its central commitment is to group process and psychic empowerment. Here, the educator's energy and skill goes into listening, and into shepherding the group towards an intuitive consensus based on information already present among the participants. If one seeks a glass of water here, a hug may be the only result.

The reaction of unionists and participants in other popular movements to this approach is to wonder "where's the beef?" Often participants will retreat to the safe ground, to the cognitive level, by pressing for accurate data, for statistics and specifics. And they regard with suspicion the claims of the leader that there are no externally-set, hidden agendas. Their withdrawal contradicts the stated goal of the educator, to build a common set of feelings.

The third approach, heavy on the skills and action developed by participants, may be termed "output-driven". In its dichotomized form, it seeks a public outcome, whatever the price is cognitive accuracy or affective cohesion. Behavioural standards are set, and quantifiable results are then fed to the educational and political sponsors of the educational encounter. This is an instrumental approach to popular education, analogous to those who assess the value of a theatre production by computing the number of "bums on seats".

Educationally, it is clear that each of these approaches withers in isolation. Politically, the separation serves to push away the real fear . . . informed and effective social action by learner in popular social movements.

Most administrators in the adult basic education system claim social neutrality. Among many adult educators, there is a strong, if misguided, sense that "professionalism" means withdrawal from the learning process at the point where people begin to test their knowledge and feelings in action. Rather than an integrated educational praxis, this results in sterile discourse, sensed and treated as such by participants.

Certainly, workers like Zeke and Augusta were not seeking "neutral" education when they came to a course in the middle of a strike. They wanted support and shared risk, and had a right to find it. But the willingness to stake a social and ethical ground, to take a stand, can emerge in much less dramatic and polarized situations. And the educator who dodges at this point based on a professional self-image triggers the same silent sneer that the street smart, the powerless, have always reserved for the spineless among their social "superiors".

A socially engaged and responsible educational strategy means working in three dimensions at once — developing a solid grounding in the content of issues; charting the emotional snakes and ladders along the route; and setting an internal compass of skill which can culminate in effective individual and collective action.

This synthesis is in fact a synergy. One alone yields addition; with two in combination, we can achieve multiplication; only with all three operating simultaneously can we generate the educational algebra of authentic social transformation.

EXIT, STAGE LEFT

. . .you can't escape, there's nowhere to go.
They have made this star unsafe, and this age Primitive; though your mind is somewhere else,

Your ass ain't.[19]

Among adult basic educators in Canada, it is time to compare dreams. We should stop settling for less. When we start, then, we need to make peace rather than war among ourselves.

We also need to get specific. In trade union life, people are constantly forced to say what they want. Proposals (or "demands", as the media usually say) are the starting point of all collective bargaining. And in grievance handling, stewards know that no arbitrator is empowered to award a remedy which has not been requested. In these very immediate ways, setting specific objectives is an integral part of the union culture.

The most concise and progressive statement so far of labour's educational agenda is the policy paper of the Ontario Federation of Labour, "Life-Long Learning". It proposes a six-point program of action, based on this premise:

As the representatives of working people and their families, the labour movement must take a highly activist approach to the process of life-long learning and its institutions. We must argue that all of our society, all working people, have a fundamental right to participate in and shape the programs and institutions which make life-long learning possible.[20]

In the process of shaping together the programs of adult basic education, a sense of proportion is also needed. We all operate within institutional and historical limits. We know that the primary educator for adults is experience, perhaps followed by the mass media. Only in the third instance do structured sessions enter the politics of perception. That's why a popular educator who doesn't intervene in these first two levels is conceding the centre of the room to the establishment, and conducting the battle for hearts and minds in the corners only.

Critical popular education does not only look at the surfaces of a room. It goes beneath the furnishings and colouring. It encourages learners to understand the principles of construction. Only in that way are people empowered, equipped both individually and collectively, to renovate, to demolish, to construct according to their own objectives.[21]

In the education program of the Communications and Electrical Workers of Canada, four objectives have been established to guide our practice — dignity on the job, democracy in the union, responsibility in the society and building on the grassroots.[22] In coming years, our educational practice will refine and develop this statement. But in its current form, it still provides some charts by which we can plan the educational journey. And it ensures that each participant in a union course has the power, the mandate, the obligation to speak their knowledge, to express their social passion, to apply their skills to the task of building a better world.

As conscious romantics in adult basic education, we address the learning needs of the most oppressed sectors in society. Of course, there are substantial forces lined up to ensure that romantics of any sort do not challenge the status quo. Our work, then, will have to take particular shape in each educational site. Our energy will have to be applied in a focused, customized way.

That our vision is not precise and detailed at this point need not stop us from proceeding.[23] But critical popular educators need to mobilize energies around a shared vision, not merely divide up tasks. In other words, objectives should be driving tactics, rather than the other way around.

As a concluding statement of objective, from a conscious romantic who has pioneered in her own generation of adult educators, we might listen to Doris Marshall:

> I want to see ordinary people feeling their own worth as human beings and recognizing the same worth in other ordinary people, so that the resources of the world can be used together. This cannot be brought about from the top down, but only by ordinary people imbued with their own power.[24]

NOTES & REFERENCES

(1) Daniel David Moses, "The Chain", unpublished poem based on the format of a chain letter, 1986.

(2) Catherine Macleod, "Cultural Logic", in *A Working Class Girl's Album of Adventure* (Charlottetown, PEI: Ragweed Press, forthcoming).

(3) This phrase was introduced to me by Richard Swift of the *New Internationalist* magazine.

(4) This reference was made by Rosa Paredes of Venezuela, at a meeting of the Executive Committee of the International Council for Adult Education, in Sri Lanka, October, 1986.

(5) The most comprehensive steward course now available is the week-long program designed by Barbara Thomas, Dan Mallette and myself for the Canadian Labour Congress (Ottawa: C.L.C., 1986).

(6) Philip Levine, "They Feed They Lion", *Selected Poems* (New York: Atheneum, 19840, p. 81.

(7) For a challenging sociology, and an often lyrical defence of the couple, ("the smallest social unit capable of resistance"), see Francesco Alberoni, *Falling in Love* (New York: Random House, 1983).

(8) "The coordinator is not just a participant and the process of the program is not spontaneous. The coordinator's role is to ensure that the process — what happens and how it happens — encourages learning and the development of leadership in the group." Rick Arnold and Bev Burke, *A Popular Education Handbook* (Toronto: CUSO and OISE, 1983).

(9) Catherine Macleod, "Freedom Exercise", in *op. cit.*

(10) See Alan Thomas's article and my critique, both published in *Learning in Society* (Ottawa: Canadian Commission for UNESCO, 1984).

(11) The concept of "union culture" is developed in my article "Public Policy Debate: A view from the 'union culture'", in the magazine *Optimum* (Ottawa: Supply and Services Canada, 1985).

(12) Jo Surich, Glenn Pattinson et al., "Life-Long Learning", policy document 3 at the 30th annual convention of the Ontario Federation of Labour. (Toronto: O.F.L., November 24-27, 1986), p. 4.

(13) In union life, we have the parallel experience of fine activists being "promoted" into management. This pattern is consistent with the pathologies described in Michael D. Cohen and James G. March, "Leadership in an Organized Anarchy", *Leadership in Ambiguity* (New York: McGraw-Hill, 1974).

(14) This phrase, from the Brazilian sociologist Fernando Henrique Cardoso, is cited by Isabel Hernandez in her evaluation of the World Assembly of Adult Education, held in Argentina in November, 1985.

(15) Pablo Neruda, "Heights of Macchu Picchu", part IV (London: Jonathan Cape, 1972, p. 22).

(16) The fear of passion exhibited by modern institutions is well captured by Alberoni: "Confronted by the nascent state, even in its most minute form, the institution is shaken in its certainties. Reproducing the event in which the institution is born, revealing the forces that nourish it in their fundamental purity, the nascent state creates a situation of mortal risk. All social mechanisms, all the wisdom of tradition, now have only one aim: to try to suppress it, to render it impossible." *op. cit.*, p. 82.

(17) "The program content of the problem-posing method — dialogical par excellence — is constituted and organized by the students' view of the world, where their own generative themes are found. The content thus constantly expands and renews itself." Paulo Freire, *Pedagogy of the Oppressed* (New York: Herder and Herder, 1971), p. 101.

(18) "Everyone knows that this element of goodness exists, that it can grow, or that it can die, and there's something particularly disingenuous and cheap about extricating oneself from the human struggle with the whispered excuse that it's already over". Wallace Shawn, "Reflections after writing a play in the age of Reagan", *American Theatre,* September, 1986, p. 49.

(19) Imamu Amiri Baraka, cited in Elissa Melamed, "Reclaiming the Power to Act", *Therapy Now,* Summer 1984, p. 8.

(20) Jo Surich, Glenn Pattinson et al., *op. cit.,* p. 1.

(21) This image is paraphrased from the Nicaraguan adult basic educator Eduardo Baez, in a presentation to the ICAE conference in Sri Lanka (see above, note #4)

(22) The full text of the statement is as follows:

"Dignity on the job — As union activists, we need to feel confidence in ourselves and our backup team. We need skills to educate, organize and represent fellow workers effectively. And we have the right to accurate information about the economic, technological and political forces which affect the security and quality of our jobs.

"Democracy in the union — We equip workers to raise their voices on the job, and we do not silence them in the union. Our education program is participatory. It builds on the creativity and experience of the members. To be a healthy and effective organization, new ideas from the rank and file must be supported and refined. That's part of our educational process.

"Responsibility in the society — Ours is more than a business union. It is part of the broad movement for social progress in Canada. When we study contract language and grievance procedure, it is within this context. The issues of the day, such as free trade and pay equity, are an integral part of our education agenda. And the skills to debate them in public, in the media, are central to modern unionism."

"The grassroots, something to build on — Information is power. Our program aims to empower rank and file union members. By developing confidence and skills they can defend and extend the rights of all workers."

"Thinking Union Bulletin #1", (Toronto: Communications and Electrical Workers of Canada, September, 1986.)

[23] "In the varied topography of professional practice, there is a high, hard ground which overlooks a swamp. On the high ground, manageable problems lend themselves to solution through the use of research-based theory and technique. In the swampy lowlands, problems are messy and confusing and incapable of technical solution. The irony of this situation is that the problems of the high ground tend to be relatively unimportant to individuals or to society at large, however great their technical interest may be while in the swamp lie the problems of greatest human concern." Donald A. Schon, "Toward a New Epistemology of Practice: A Response to the Crisis of Professional Knowledge", paper presented to the Global Learning Symposium, Toronto, April 28–May 1, 1985. It has since been published in Alan Thomas and Edward Ploman eds., *Learning and Development: A Global Perspective* (Toronto: OISE, 1986).

[24] Doris Marshall, speaking to the core team of the Doris Marshall Institute for Education and Action, Toronto, November 17, 1986.

CHAPTER 4:

Implications of Technological Change for Adult Education*

Michèle Jean

Since prehistoric times, we have been developing science and technology to make our work and daily life easier. Until the last few years the main contribution of machinery has been motor power, which lessened the need for physical labour. But we are now passing from the era of simple machines to the era of elaborate machines which deal with information. This evolution, sometimes called the technological revolution, already affects every area of our life: in the factory, in the office, at home and in cultural pursuits. Slowly, work, education and recreation are being transformed. Every type of worker is affected in some way: executives, labourers and service personnel. Thus our reactions to scientific and technological progress - the ability of the human being to adapt and to make the best use of it - become particularly significant. For we are witnessing the dawn of a new era, greeted by some as one of great promise, while others warn of great danger.

THE IMPACT OF TECHNOLOGICAL CHANGE

The impact of technological progress on human society has probably been the greatest focus for the energies of sociologists and anthropologists (among others) over the last decade. Perhaps the headiest promises and the direst predictions have been reserved for information and communication technologies, especially television and microtechnology. But all areas of scientific research and progress have been similarly scrutinized, by the prophets both of doom and of salvation. Each have given their point of view on the progress foreseen in physics (especially nuclear physics), biotechnology, and even medicine.

Modern technology has taken a giant step over the last few years. We have reached a point where micro-computers can endow common machines with artificial intelligence. This intelligence, while limited, nevertheless makes these machines self-sufficient to the point that they can substitute for human beings, or at least significantly help with a host of particularly fastidious or repetitive tasks.

Only in the last few years have we begun to see practical applications of the new technology in our factories, offices, and homes. We now have at our disposal personal computers, specialised networks providing access to data banks, video games, transactional and interactive services - not to speak of even more ambitious administrative technologies, robotics, and computer-assisted manufacture. It has become possible in the last few years to get a

*Published in *Adult Education: International Perspectives from China*. London: Croom Helm, 1987. Reprinted with permission.

personal computer or an 'intelligent terminal' at a fraction of the cost one would have had to spend to buy a computer. We can see that prices will continue to fall over the next few years, assuring that microtechnology, telecommunications and associated technologies will expand at an unprecedented rate over the coming decades.

These machines are also becoming more and more flexible. Their memory banks can hold all the information we need to manage our personal affairs. They can offer access to data banks thousands of kilometres away, giving information on the widest range of subjects. Consider the potential of experimental projects in several countries that in a few years will allow people to deposit or withdraw money from a bank through their home terminals, go 'teleshopping', or make use of professional medical, commercial or scientific services. Although many uses are not yet commercially viable, the list of possible applications is virtually inexhaustible. Consider all the tasks technology could handle that have traditionally required hours of finicky work.

The predictive sciences have been active in drawing optimistic or pessimistic scenarios of our future: for everyone wants to know what his or her universe will be like a few years down the road. In Canada, as everywhere, reports proliferate on the expansion of technology, the speed with which it is brought into the workplace and the educational system, and the policies and legislation around it. We really are seeing a change in society. With recent scientific and technological progress, especially in the field of microtechnology and telecommunication, it is clear that human society will evolve within a framework dominated by technology. So we must examine the implications of such change, and what consequences may flow from it.

POTENTIAL AND CHALLENGES FOR SOCIETY

We sometimes seem to forget that all this change is brought about by and for human beings, not only to increase productivity but also to improve the quality of life. Nevertheless, with our brief experience in the field, we are beginning to get a clearer picture of the impact of these new technologies.

The stakes seem immense: will knowledge, and thus power, be concentrated, or spread? Will thought and culture become robot-like, or information be shared for a convivial society? Will private life and human relations be diminished, or will community life grow? A look at the past suggests the real risk that the most pessimistic scenarios will carry the day. Through the ages, technological progress has for the most part served to concentrate power and knowledge in the hands of the few. Certainly, one cannot deny that there has been progress in access to education, access to consumer goods, the spread of culture, and the improvement of general health. But the realities of human beings becoming alienated, dislocated from their environment and powerless in the face of change; of the real intellectual and material poverty of millions of people: these leave us skeptical over the potential for improvement offered by the new technology.

These changes also threaten to widen the gulf between North and South. The same thing happens when countries as within them: the vendors of technology impose their language and their culture, thus making it even harder for many human communities to maintain their autonomy and catch up to the rest of the world. We do not yet measure the social consequences of these changes very well: carried away with enthusasim for the potential of technology, we tend to minimize negative effects. When one looks at the question from the point of view not only of States and the economy, but also of the individuals who will have to undergo the changes, the contradictory effects of computerizing society become more disturbing. The computerization of the office and the factory will wipe out a large number of jobs, and change the organization and the very nature of work. Thousands of workers will face the de-skilling process, and a few will face over-qualification. Work at home will become more common. Teaching will be transformed.

The capacity of people in the future to appropriate this new environment will depend largely on the tools they have been given, especially in their early and continued education. It is not enough simply to ask what the consequences of technology will be. We must above all ask ourselves, given these consequences, if current formal and non-formal education of children and adults is adequate, and what educational planning strategy we should use. Once past the first wild spate of invention and spread of new machines, business and political leaders are beginning to realize more and more that human potential is the touchstone of a successful technological revolution. In a number of industrial sectors, and in many offices which began with indiscriminate computer or robot installations, people are now starting to use more humane and appropriate strategies and training. Here adult education, within a perspective of lifelong education, comes into play.

IMPLICATIONS FOR ADULT EDUCATION

When adult education began in Canada at the end of the 19th century, it was a tool for thousands of workers to gain knowledge, especially in agriculture. Nonformal education, in particular, allowed them to keep up with developments in their field and learn new techniques. Later, with industrialization, professional training in schools and in the workplace was developed for youths and adults. Adult education, over the years, has been a way for concerned client groups to cope with change. It has allowed several groups to prepare themselves not only for their work, but also for fuller participation in making social decisions.

The technological revolution does present us with change but also, in some ways, with continuity. As the American author Richard Bolles pointed out, when speaking of the future we should not paralyse people by speaking only of changes and not of those things which are, and will remain, necessary: the need to know how to read and write, to be innovative and creative, to have a critical awareness.

Education must be able to respond to the needs of thousands of adults for basic and professional training. Nations must take a chance on the development of human potential, which will involve adults in decisions on their own education. Thus, to avoid the trap of overly narrow and rapidly outdated professional training programs, or of short-term reform we must press governments for careful development and educational planning. Planning should tie into global policies, taking into account all facets of the life of adults which relate to education. Such policies must examine and coordinate all the educational initiatives necessary, not only for an improved work life but for recreation, culture and society.

Since the contemporary reorganization of work life will entail shorter work-ing times, we cannot reflect about work without considering leisure time as well. Such policies will allow projects to be oriented to society, and the adult population to take a hand in defining their future, as long as planners take the trouble to build consultation mechanism into the process.

The 'educative society' we have been talking about for decades really must be put in place now. One result of the development of technology is increasing consciousness of the need for a real system of lifelong education. In Canada, in the space of two years, I have noticed enormous changes in attitude. Business leaders, executives and political men, having themselves had to face in their day-to-day work the inadequacy of their own training to use micro-technology, have to some degree experienced the fears and anguish they have put their employees through all along: the fear of losing one's job, of being underquali-fied; the lack of effective educational responses.

We must make education one pivot of the technological revolution. Starting from that point of view we can build programs to teach the new disciplines, and to adapt older disciplines to deal with change. Education has five main roles to play in this process:

> training qualified man-power and re-training people in line with technological change;
> organizing instruction in the new computer disciplines;
> introducing young people and adults to the computer as a tool for action and learning;
> adapting cultural models (ways of thinking and acting) to technologi-cal change;
> training teachers to be able to introduce programs and information into computer systems which are appropriate to a given culture.

In relation to this:

> In the sectors in which the new technology is being widely and rapidly applied, the determination of both early and continued education which the educa-tional system should guarantee should not be based simply on observation of current processes of production and employment structures. Quite a bit of foresight is also necessary. Timetables for implementing adapted early educa-tion programs may be inadequate for pressing needs. Continuing education offers the fastest way to introduce new training programs but these are generally too short, too expensive and too superficial to make up entirely for the lack of initial training... (Malan, 1983:3)

So we must take a different approach to the connection between work and education; we must see it as a process in which many elements besides training play a role: age, sex, social class, seniority, management styles, etc. This leads us to consider diversifying educational activities, and to pay more attention to the methods through which technology is transferred. Technological training alone is not enough: we must also ensure that the technological culture is appropriated, through the development of critical judgement and logical thought as well as the ability to communicate. We must therefore link social apprenticeship to technical apprenticeship, especially, in countries which have to absorb foreign technologies:

> Apprenticeship should not be considered as a passive process depending solely on the level of the workers' initial training and the time spent in accumulating experience. In the progressive management of a system of production, the body of workers come to new know-how, to weave new information networks among their members, to create new reflexes and behaviours. Apprenticeship is an active and productive process. (Perrin, 1983)

Thus, in transfers of technology, one must take into account the specific technical skills of the workers, and apply them to familiarity with the technical structures of the recipient countries. Nowadays, as several studies have pointed out, technical know-how is no longer merely the result of individual action, but has become an ongoing collective creative process.

In any case, it is important to leave behind a compartmentalized approach to work/training/leisure, and to develop overall adult education policies which aim to link the economic, social and cultural life of the individual. Research should be undertaken to "spell out the connections between society and technology within the education system, considered in all its aspects, especially its cognitive, cultural and social functions" (Reiffers, 1983:1). For although the educational system must respond to needs for manpower, it must not orient itself solely to economic efficiency at the risk of satisfying only a very narrow spectrum of social needs.

We are thus brought back to the issue of social change. For adult education, this means that "if adults are not involved in developing societies of their choice, computerization, instead of being an enriching and liberating factor, will merely engender a growing dependence of individuals on machines, and will throw a large part of the population into a sort of 'social vacuum' ". The role of adult education thus consists of equipping adults both to handle technology and to participate in decision-making about it. We must also look for ways to prepare adults for more free time, for methods of work-sharing. Study-leave policies must be developed which will serve both for professional re-training and to enlarge our cultural world. We must introduce trainers and adult educators to the new technologies and to research on adult learning.

The response to these possibilities depends largely on whether governments want to move towards a more equitable sharing of knowledge and power, or to a growing concentration. Our response to these questions will influence, for better or for worse, the future of the women and men who live on this planet.

REFERENCES

Institut Canadien de l'education des Adultes, and Centrale de l'enseignement du Quebec, (1983), "Negocier le virage technologique", proceedings of a seminar on tele-communications held in Montreal in February 1983, Montreal, pp. 267.

Malan, Thierry, (1983), *Politiques de developpement economique et sociale et planification de l'education en France*, Paris. photocopy, unpublished, 24pp.

Quebec, (1982), *Apprendre: Une Action Volontaire et Responsable*, final report of the Commission d'etude sur la formation professionnelle et socio-culturelle des adultes, Editeur officiel du Quebec.

Quebec, (1984), *Un projet d'education permanente, Enonce d'orientation et plan d'action en education des adultes*, Editeur officiel du Quebec.

Quebec, Ministry of Education (1983), *Rebatir L'avenir*, report of the working group on telecommunications in education (working paper), photocopy.

Perrin, J., (1983) "L'apprentissage des savoir-faire industriels peut-il etre integre dans une planification de l'education," Grenoble, photocopy, unpublished.

Reiffers, J. L., (1983), rapporteur, report of working group 1: "Les implications pour la planification de l'education des politiques de developpement technologique," seminar of the International Institute for Educational Planning, Paris.

Seaborg, Eric, (1983), "They have seen the future", *The Futurist*.

Trudel, Lina, (1982), *L'informatisation: pour le meilleur ou pour le pire*, paper presented to the conference "Towards an Authentic Development: The role of Adult Education", Paris.

CHAPTER 5:

Community-Based Literacy Programming – The Toronto Experience

Elaine Gaber-Katz
Gladys M. Watson

A community-based literacy project is one in which members of a community share locally the responsibility for providing adult literacy education.[1]

Throughout Canada, literacy education has generally been provided by educational institutions such as school boards, community colleges, and libraries, or it has been provided by local affiliates of national and international volunteer literacy organizations such as Frontier College, Laubach Literacy of Canada, and Literacy Volunteers of America (LVA).[2] In Toronto, this has also been the case but, in recent years, community-based literacy programs have developed as an alternative.

Community-based literacy programs are now providing learning opportunities for adults in several areas of the city of Toronto. These programs view the acquisition of reading and writing skills in the context of a larger goal: to encourage all members of the community to participate fully in society. All the elements of the program — organizational structure, setting, program design, methodology, and materials — are shaped by this goal. Philosophically, the concepts of "community development", "organic growth", "empowerment", and "holistic education" are seen to be central to community-based literacy. Pedagogically, these programs aspire to a vision of learning in which students acquire basic reading and writing skills in ways that will best meet their individual needs and increase their potential to participate in the life of the community.

Learners are the focal point of community-based programs. Their needs and aspirations shape the content and direction of the programs. Given this learner-centred approach, staff and volunteers in community-based literacy programs know that it is vital that they understand the students who participate in the program in order to prepare an appropriate educational program for them.

Staff and volunteers begin to learn more about the experience of illiterate adults, when they listen to the reasons adult learners give for never having learned to read:

- "I missed school because I had to work."
- "I had to take care of the younger children in my family."
- "I never attended school regularly in my home country and never had time to attend classes before now."

- "The schools/teachers said I couldn't learn."
- "I never liked/understood/learned in/related to school."
- "I was too ill/handicapped to attend."
- "My parents didn't care. They couldn't/didn't read."
- "I was too depressed/too active/too quick tempered so they gave me medication/sent me away, and I missed a lot of school."
- "I was too slow/too stupid/too unkempt/too wild/too scared and they sent me away to a training school/a school for the mentally retarded/a home teacher/an opportunity class."[4]

The majority of adults who have had these experiences have less than grade eight education. In Toronto, they comprise 135,000 adults or 22 per cent of the adult population. A small, but still significant, number of adults with reading and writing difficulties may have attended vocational high school. Although they are not reading at a grade eight level, they have formally completed grade eight or higher, and therefore are not counted as part of the city's statistics on illiteracy.[5]

It is important to recognize that the majority of adult literacy students are found in the lowest socio-economic sector. Members of community-based literacy programs know this and understand that one cannot separate the issue of illiteracy from the issue of poverty. Students who come to literacy programs may have many pressing needs that distract them from their desire to learn. They may have problems with housing, health, (un)employment, and even hunger. Community-based literacy programs assert that the problem of illiteracy cannot be confronted without also addressing poverty.

Community-based literacy programs recognize and address two manifestations of the problem of illiteracy. First, literacy learners state that they have difficulties functioning in our print-oriented society. They do not have full access to information and are not "heard" by those who are literate. Second, illiteracy indicates that a significant percentage of the population is unable to participate in our democratic society. In a community-based literacy program, learning to read and write is viewed as more than a technical problem; it is seen as a problem with a relationship to the social context in which it exists. Given this shared perspective on the social dimension, community-based literacy programs tend to have elements in common. Here, we describe some of these elements as they appeared in community-based literacy programs in Toronto as of 1986.

ORGANIZATIONAL STRUCTURE

Community-based literacy programs intentionally remain small in size, to ensure that staff members know everyone in the program personally and are familiar with individual learning needs. The largest of the programs in Toronto serves approximately seventy-five learners and the smallest no more than twenty. Direction for each of the programs comes from its volunteer board of directors, with board members drawn from experienced tutors in the program and from the local community. The provision of tutoring is primarily through volunteers who are trained by experienced practitioners to tutor in both one-to-one and small group situations. Community-based programs are financed through a combination of public and private funds, with budgets that range from $30,000 to over $150,000.

FRIENDLY COMMUNITY SETTINGS

"I just come in here and do things — straighten up the books, clean up. At first, I didn't. Then somebody said, 'You can come in here any time.' That's why I like it here — it's friendly." (a literacy student, *Let's Get Together*, p. 7)

Community-based literacy programs in Toronto are situated in densely populated sections of the downtown city core, in areas where there are a large number of adults who are illiterate. On contrast to the large institutional programs, community-based literacy programs are usually located in small premises in community settings, such as rooms in settlement houses, libraries, churches and community centres. Most of the programs have space which is provided free of charge by the host organization. Most of the programs are easily reached by public transit, and most are close to other community services. Only a few of the community-based programs are accessible to disabled students, although some have accessible meeting space available elsewhere in the building.

In most cases, although the space is small, the programs have considered their needs and planned out floor space and furnishings accordingly. The space is generally flexible enough to accommodate a variety of needs and activities, such as one-to-one tutoring, small groups and classes, individual studying and reading, staff interviews with students and tutors, tutor training, production of materials and publications, a resource collection, a children's area, an office, social events, and meetings. Most programs have comfortable chairs and couches, fold away tables, and a coffee pot which is always hot. With donations, often in-kind, some programs have equipped their literacy centres with office and training equipment such as video cassette recorders, cameras, light tables for materials production, tape recorders, typewriters, and computers. Because the philosophy of community-based literacy links learning to read with participation, these programs have developed, over a period of years, literacy centres which encourage participation and are well used.

Community-based literacy centres are usually open five or six days a week, throughout the day and most evenings. Some students and tutors meet regularly in the centres, although much of the tutoring takes place in the home or elsewhere in the community. What is important about the literacy centres, is that students, tutors, and visitors can drop in any time, without calling first for an appointment, to talk to staff about their ideas or concerns. At any one time in a community-based literacy centre, there is likely to be a variety of students, tutors, volunteers, and staff involved in reading lessons, office work, newsletter production, curriculum development, and interesting discussions. Unlike students in classroom programs or most one-to-one volunteer tutoring programs where staff are only available during classroom hours or at prearranged times, participants in community-based literacy programs have the opportunity to visit the centre at any time and become involved in the day-to-day aspects of the program.

PROGRAM DESIGN

In order to fully grasp the significance and contribution of community-based literacy programming, it is first necessary to have an understanding of the kind of programming elsewhere. Whereas the community-based programs are located in non-institutional settings and involve locally trained volunteer tutors, larger institutional programs usually consist of classroom instruction, given by qualified teachers using highly structured curricula. In these institutional programs, many aspects of the program, including the setting, the teaching methodology, and the classroom materials, are similar to what has been offered to illiterate adults in their schooling as children. And in the case of other volunteer tutoring programs such as Laubach Literacy Canada and Literacy Volunteers of America, a trained volunteer tutor is matched with each adult learner. The teaching methodology, although it varies from program to program and among individual tutors, is usually highly structured, using commercially prepared materials, controlled vocabularies, and a phonics-based approach.

Community-based literacy programs take a very different approach. Their programming is flexible since **the ultimate goal is to provide the kind of learning environment which best meets the needs expressed by the students**. At the heart of all community-based literacy programs is the one-to-one tutoring component. One-to-one tutoring is most often preferred by students who lack confidence in their ability to learn. They find individualized instruction does not threaten them with the potential humiliations of the classroom. Students also appreciate the opportunity to progress at their own pace, learn in their own way, and use reading materials that meet their personal reading needs. But not all students prefer one-to-one learning situations, and community-based literacy programs have come to recognize the disadvantages of offering this mode of instruction exclusively. There are, for example, some misgivings about the isolation that one-to-one tutoring sometimes promotes, about the dependency that may develop between a student and a tutor, and about how to monitor the consistency and quality of one-to-one instruction. In response to these concerns and students' requests, programs are offering different kinds of small group learning opportunities, ranging from Saturday drop-ins to student writing groups.

The underlying desire to put the interests and needs of students first creates an atmosphere in community-based programs that is hard to describe. In part, it is the strong feeling of respect for the learners which staff and tutors project. They believe that their role is to create an environment which allows students to articulate for themselves what they need. Learners' educational interests and needs form the basis of the program: staff and tutors make sure that learners aer heard and taken seriously. This is often not an easy task. Adults who are illiterate are so accustomed to being left out that initially they are often not confident in their ability to understand and make decisions about their curriculum. Furthermore, many tutors initially find this approach quite unconventional. They are so used to the concept of "teaching" as directing and controlling someone's learning that it can be difficult for them to know exactly what their role as tutors in a community setting will be.

But the atmosphere of the community-based literacy program helps to relieve many of these apprehensions. New learners and tutors are likely to meet experienced students and tutors who can allay their fears and inspire by example. The mood of the literacy centres is particularly exciting and stimulating when students volunteer. Through volunteering, students often learn new skills which are shared and used in a variety of ways within the centre.

Another quality which infuses the atmosphere of the community-based literacy program is trust — the ability of the organization as a whole to inspire confidence, take risks, and at the same time accept responsibility. All of the procedures used in the day-to-day work of the organization reflect this approach.

Referrals

While most students hear about community programs by word-of-mouth or from social service agencies, initial interviews are set up for students only after they have personally contacted the program. Staff may handle referrals from adult protective services workers, welfare workers, probation officers, or children's aid workers, but only by asking that the student themselves call or visit the programs independently and voluntarily.

Student interviews

Most programs follow up the initial inquiries by arranging an interview with the students to discuss their backgrounds, experiences, literacy skills, and educational goals. This interview also includes discussion and informal questions about educational background, current reading and writing skills, and preferences for one-to-one or small group tutoring. It also serves as an orientation to the program, giving students an opportunity to learn more about the centre which can help them decide whether this is the most appropriate program.

Throughout the interview, staff may take notes on a prepared interview form. In some programs these notes are kept to a minimum and are sometimes read back to students so that they will know what is being written down. Questions are also kept to a minimum. The atmosphere is professional, yet informal. Students are informed that they have complete access to their files and staff offer to help them at any time to read the contents. In many instances, they are also informed that no social service agencies or other persons will be given information about their involvement in the program. Students, rather than staff, are responsible for updating other people and agencies about their participation and progress in the program.

Tutor Training

The tutor training sessions of community-based literacy programs vary greatly in terms of format and resources. Tutor training sessions can change frequently over the span of one year, even within the same program; nevertheless, there are two objectives that are common to most community-based tutor training programs. The most important objective is to introduce the learner-centred approach to the tutors. The training stresses the importance of tutors finding out about their students personally: in what they are interested, what they can read, what they enjoy reading, what makes them comfortable or uncomfortable in a learning situation, what they want to learn, and how they learn best. The students are the best source of information about their strengths and abilities, and tutors are encouraged to see their students as knowledgeable about how and what they need to learn. After the tutors find out this information, it is equally important that they follow through by acting on the information throughout the course of the tutoring.

The second objective of the tutor training is to convey to the tutors that respect for learners is the key to successful tutoring. Tutors are encouraged to understand that they have certain literacy skills to share with their students, but they have no right to impose their values or lifestyles on the students. Students, especially those who frequently come into contact with social service agencies, have been counselled endlessly about nutrition, appropriate social/ sexual behaviour, body language, lifestyle, coping mechanisms, family arrangements, and so on. Community-based programs seek to promote tolerance for how people live and a respect for students' right to privacy. Tutors are encouraged to accept their students as they are and to concentrate on helping the learners articulate for themselves what they think needs changing in their lives.

Contact with students and tutors

From the very beginning, students are involved in saying what learning situation suits them best. After they are matched with tutors, the staff feel it is important to maintain their connection to the students rather than to simply monitor the tutoring relationship through contact with the tutor. Often, in alternate months, both students and tutors are contacted to discuss materials, frequency of tutoring sessions, student progress, and any problems or concerns. After tutor-student pairs work together on a weekly basis for six months, staff hold individual review meetings with students to help students evaluate their progress, their tutors, and the support they received from the program. This method provides students with a way to be involved in their own evaluation process. Most programs use this method and find it to be very successful.

MATERIALS AND RESOURCES

As a result of their learner-centred approach, community-based literacy programs have proved to be highly eclectic in their selection and use of learning materials. Community-based programs have actively involved learners, not only in the selection of materials, but also in the writing and publishing of materials. Most of the programs have organized their materials into resource collections. Although these collections are relatively new and not yet fully developed, they are valuable resources used by students, volunteers, staff, interested individuals, and the community. The collections tend to consist of four types of materials.

(1) Functional materials

Almost every program has a collection of functional materials which includes "found" materials such as bank deposit slips, job application forms, legal agreements, food labels, government documents and so on. In one program, the collection of functional materials is displayed in brightly coloured bins occupying an entire wall from ceiling to floor. Along with "found" materials, non-traditional materials such as board games, flash cards, student-generated stories with word games, and learning kits are also available. Functional materials need periodic updating and reorganizing, and in most of the programs, students and tutors are encouraged to assist with this work as well as contribute new materials.

(2) Student materials

The student materials are a highly valued part of the collection. There is general agreement that there is a dearth of quality reading materials for adults who are learning to read. In response to this, most community-based literacy programs have made a special effort to seek out stories written by students themselves, not only from literacy programs in Canada but also from other countries, particularly England and Australia. These materials are at a beginning reader's level and yet reflect adult concerns in content and tone. Some books designed for the beginning reader consist of one or two lines per page, accompanied by a carefully selected photograph or illustration which provides clues to the text. In addition, easy-to-read pocket books, and magazines and periodicals which range in level of difficulty are also available. A wide range of titles assists in meeting a variety of reading interests, aids in choosing books for tutoring sessions, and provides opportunities for independent reading. Some programs colour code student materials according to level of reading difficulty, making the collection easy for students to use. In fact, students and tutors are often involved in organizing and shelving the books.

(3) Teaching materials

In each collection, there are copies of commercially prepared reading courses and structured workbooks on spelling, grammar, and numeracy which are used as needed by students and tutors. Usually, there are several complete sets of the well known reading programs from national and international literacy organizations such as Laubach Literacy Canada and Literacy Volunteers of America. Most programs assist their tutors to use these workbooks in creative ways. For example, tutors learn to apply the reading strategies from the workbooks to materials generated by the students themselves. In some cases, teaching materials are being purchased by the Toronto Public Library and housed in the literacy centres as "non-traditional deposit" collections. This means that the materials are on permanent loan to the literacy programs. In this way, the library system is becoming a helpful resource for literacy work. The community-based programs assist in the selection of the materials through participation in the Toronto Public Library Literacy Advisory Committee.

(4) Tutor resource materials

The tutor resource collections include works on education and literacy theory for the professional development of tutors and staff. They may be books, articles, newsletters, journals, audio tapes, photographs, slides, films, or video tapes. These tutor resource materials address questions related to the philosophy of teaching, the politics of literacy, and the practical concerns of tutoring. Some programs have collections of resources that complement their tutor training programs and are used for particular workshops: selected articles from journals and magazines, government policy documents relating to adult basic education and literacy, and a range of tutor training manuals. Most community-based programs maintain press files on literacy issues, as well as files of media coverage on their respective programs.

STUDENT INVOLVEMENT IN THE PROGRAM

Community-based programs thrive on student participation and give it a high priority. Many of the components of the program such as tutor trainings, meetings, and workshops are frequently re-assessed and revised according to whether they hinder or assist in the attainment of this goal.

Learners become involved in producing curriculum for the programs by writing their own stories, often working in small groups to prepare them for use by others. To supplement the stories, students create learning activities such as crossword puzzles, cloze exercises, word games, and comprehension questions, collaborating with others to produce them in easy-to-use formats.

Student-writing programs are successful vehicles for bringing students into the centres. Once there, they find many other avenues to participation. In one program, a student-leadership group has formed and calls itself the "Students for Action" group. They meet regularly with staff to plan their involvement in the program. Some of the responsibilities they have assumed are to plan special events, such as apple picking trips and drama nights; to support students who are active members of committees and the Board of Directors; to organize participation in International Literacy Day events, such as making buttons and placards and speaking at press conferences; and to network with other students through phone-trees and easy-to-read newsletters. Students in all of the programs act as resource people in a multitude of ways. In tutor training sessions, they talk about the issue of illiteracy. In community education meetings, they describe the process of student-writing. At conferences and workshops, they speak about many aspects of community-based literacy. Often they are a part of the centre's involvement in "plain writing" activities, consulting with agencies and public institutions in order to make their publications easier to read. In some programs, students are trained to attend interviews with new learners to help them feel comfortable and provide them with first-hand information. Many students enjoy tutoring others who are less advanced, and some programs encourage students to assist beginning readers in group sessions. This has led to remarkable improvements in the oral reading skills of the students who are tutoring. In one program, after several years, a few advanced learners became committed volunteers.

Students who volunteer to help out in the offices of community-based literacy programs learn to use equipment they have not encountered before. This has proven to be highly motivating and students who read technical instructions aloud often quite unconsciously reveal that they learned new words and concepts in a relatively short length of time. Participation in student-writing programs also helps them become experienced with photography, typing, lay-out, and materials production as they help produce booklets, flyers, and magazines.

Some students gain the confidence needed to make oral presentations to the media or to large groups of people. Students also give readings of their writing at special events. They may practice for weeks in order to gain the confidence to read aloud at a special event which might draw more than one hundred people. There is a feeling of exhilaration at events such as these, when the audience, tightly packed into a large room, patiently and silently waits for the nervous adult new reader to commence reading. The room can vibrate with a tension and apprehension akin to fear, until it eventually explodes into applause at the conclusion of the reading.

As a result of the successful experiences that community-based literacy programs have had with student participation, this dimension continues to grow as the programs challenge themselves to learn new ways to involve non-readers in all areas of community-based literacy work.

CONCLUSION

These are some of the elements which comprise community-based literacy programming as it has been practised in a number of community-based literacy programs developed during the lat decade in Toronto. As these programs continue to grow and change, and as new programs are initiated, it will be important to document[6] and publicize this work, since in future these programs are likely to be seen as exemplary modes of adult community education.

NOTES:

1. Toronto Curriculum Working Group. *Community-Based Literacy in an Urban Setting: A Model*. Toronto: unpublished paper, 1984.
2. Thomas, Audrey M. *Adult Illiteracy in Canada: A Challenge. Canadian Commission for UNESCO Occasional Paper no. 42*. Ottawa: Canadian Commission for UNESCO, 1983.
3. This article was written in 1986 with reference to five community-based literacy programs operating in the city of Toronto at that time:
   - Alexandra Park Learning Centre
   - Adult Literacy for Action (ALFA)
   - East End Literacy
   - Parkdale Project Read
   - St. Christopher House Literacy Programme
4. Based on hundreds of intake interviews which Elaine Gaber-Katz conducted over a period of several years while working in a community-based setting.
5. East End Literacy Evaluation Committee. *East End Literacy: A Model for Delivery*. Toronto: unpublished paper, 1984.
6. The authors of this article conducted a study of community-based literacy programs in the Toronto area in 1987-88. The results of this study will be forthcoming in a book on community-based literacy.

CHAPTER 6

Generous Supply, Barred Demand: The Current Paradox of Literacy

Jean-Paul Hautecoeur

"The measure of success (of literacy education) should be the number of adults who enroll in learning programs, as well as the number of readers who have achieved competence, thereby acquiring the means to change their living conditions".   Jonathan Kozol

THE GAP BETWEEN SUPPLY AND DEMAND

In those territories conquered in the cause of literacy education, we are apt to recall the numerical scale of the illiterate population, as well as the distressing psychological and social condition of those who are "victims" of illiteracy. Or else we deplore the huge cost to industry and society in general of the massive illiteracy rate in the Canadian population. In both instances, a public alarm is sounded, the pathology is diagnosed, and the failure of public or private authorities to take the issue seriously enough is regretted. There are calls for recognition of the scale of the "drama", "crisis" or "peril"; there are demands for consequent investments, and appeals for a national plan of action in the struggle against illiteracy, for mobilization of the business sector, etc.

Such is an outline of the offensive being waged in Canada, often in unison, by professional educators, literacy volunteers, social activists, the business sector (especially paper, books, any printed material which is produced and sold), and a few political figures. A comparable situation prevails in Quebec, where professional educators are more heavily represented, whilst the involvement of the private sector and volunteer organizations is weaker. There, virtually the entire field of literacy education has, in one way or another, become associated with the "Ministère de l'Éducation", Québec.

It is now estimated that one Canadian adult in four, is "functionally" illiterate - almost one in three in Quebec and in the francophone population of Canada [1]. These figures compare with recent American estimates.[2] They are still lower than the French estimates, which amount to 50 to 70% of the population.[3] The validity aspect of this information is of little consequence for the time being.

What is important to note here, is that these statistics are circulated, in large part by the media and that they are, for all intents and purposes, made official by government: aided and abetted by hyperbole they become undeniable. At the same time, and as a corollary to these statistics, this deprived population is seen as being in urgent "need" of literacy education and a no less urgent need for "preventive measures" is being forced upon the young people of school-age. Inflation of need follows that of figures: the urgency of intervention becomes more pressing as the diagnoses become more alarmist (Ministére de l'Education, Québec, 1987)

The logical consequence of the demands from various increasingly influential pressure groups is a more consistent commitment from the governments, the growth of resources, and the development of services. This is where we stand at present, both in the province of Quebec and other provinces. Governments have been made aware of the problem; they are putting means of intervention into place, and are increasing the resources for information, organization and education. Very unevenly, to be sure, but the growth is progressive, which is not the case in most social and educational sectors.

In Quebec, the Ministère de l'Éducation has implemented a literacy program which, in theory, provides school boards with the means to increase their educational activities in accordance with demand. The model is rigid: it imposes unitary administrative standards, gives school boards a virtually monopolistic regional power in the literacy field, etc. Even though it by no means comprises all those virtues readily ascribed to it by outside observers, this program assures adults, in principle, the same accessibility to education as those of school age. This is already a great deal in the formal terms of the right to education.

However, there appears to be a major problem — not within the system, but alongside it — in the way in which it is being used. In actual fact, it is observed that demand does not accompany supply of services. The population on which an imperative and urgent "need" had been projected is not coming forward. If costs are increasing considerably, this is due less to an actual increase in literacy education enrolment than to a growth effect endogenous to the system.

"The problem is that we are looking for "clientele": that is the subject of this reflection.

Firstly, it will be a case of establishing the problem and defining the terms in which it is being presented. A 1986 survey of most organizations involved in literacy education in Quebec provides an opportunity to do this. It will then be a question of attempting to understand the causes, and approaching the probable and plausible significances. We will have to ask ourselves what can be done in order to ensure that the resources made available for literacy education be utilized more effectively for that purpose. Some elements of response will be given throughout the text, but not a new global plan for Quebec. The latter is to be drawn up collectively following more stringent evaluations of the present programs. We have not yet reached that stage.

THE ESSENCE OF THE PROBLEM
In an inquiry designed to record all the literacy education activities in Quebec[5], respondents were asked to draw up a self-evaluation of their interventions, namely, to list those which they considered to be their successes and failures. The following information was drawn from the analysis of these responses to some 180 questionnaires. (Blais, Hautecoeur, Lépine, 1988)

According to Lucie Lépine, "it is at the recruitment level that one feels most strongly the obstruction in the extension of the offer of services" (also called "opening of the network" in educational jargon). When many organizations are listing recognition of the literacy phenomenon by the state and the general public as being among their evident successes, the sensitivity of educational institutions to the "urgency of needs", and, in some cases, the priority given to literacy in adult education, many organizations acknowledge that detection and recruitment are a "heavy challenge to take up". The difficulty of linking up those who represent the hidden part of the iceberg presents a large problem. This implies that the submerged and infinitely more voluminous portion of the iceberg remains untouched.

With regard to the presumed pool of "needy" people in a region, it is acknowledged that enrolment rates are low. "The majority of organizations have not attracted the desired number of individuals concerned given the proportion of illiterates in their area". In some cases, the failure is patent: local anglophone literacy councils easily recruit volunteer tutors, but few volunteers for literacy education, with the result that they are sometimes led to abandon literacy education or even to reorientate themselves within a school environment in order to implement preventive measures.

In rural areas, a decline in enrolment is observed if a vigorous campaign is not maintained. It is recognized that, "the number of enrolments is not proportional to all the energy expended in campaigning". "The extreme difficulty of recruiting "pure" illiterate adults who are isolated psychologically, socially and geographically is an invariable feature of the evaluations". In some cases, "the educational centres have had to be closed, since a sufficient number of candidates were not recruited, and neither was there the possibility of joining the group to those of other municipalities".

As has long been observed in the schools, a phenomenon of "creaming", or "exclusion of the most deprived", has also been observed in literacy education. Many people declare that "joining the clientele of the most deprived is not their priority". "Over-educated concepts have engendered a certain selection from the public and . . . a residue of illiterates".

Again, however, the easier recruitment of young people in special education courses (with a financial incentive), and restricted minorities, such as the perceptually, handicapped or allophone immigrants, has served to compensate for the decline in enrolment by "ordinary illiterates". It is a fact that many school boards have specialized in the functional education of the handicapped. Literacy education was a promising territory for this population, as well as for those allophones who are seeking to learn written French. Without these compensations — and many others which I won't mention here, it is to be feared that enrolment rates would often have declined, leaving the school boards with a slack period, a drop in employability, etc.

It is a clearly established fact: the offer of services is far from creating the expected demand. In Quebec, the cost of the literacy education program was estimated at $23.5 million in 1988-89, and the number of persons who had enrolled again during that same year is estimated at 15,000. It is also known that the number of enrolments is overestimated in relation to the number of persons who actually attend the writing workshops.

If one considers that the pool of the adult population identified as illiterate and semi-literate (Hautecoeur, 1988) is about 1.5 million individuals (29% of the adult population), the literacy education program is reaching no more than

1% per year. This rate is not atypical: it is comparable with the rates noted in the United States and in Europe. Though we may find this deplorable, we must try to understand it.

WHY AREN'T THE PEOPLE COMING FORWARD?

There are several courses to be charted, each of which would merit an in-depth survey. I shall outline them first before commenting on each of the arguments.

- Firstly , one might say — and there are those who do not hesitate to do so — that if, after all this barrage of information, and this generalized offer of free services, few — if any — people show up, this means that the problem did not exist. Illiteracy has been blown up out of all proportion: it is time to revert to a realistic picture, and invest in education wherever it is profitable to do so . . . .
- Literacy education professionals develop the argument of insufficient re-sources, particularly for the essential work of pre-literacy: information, campaigning in the field, community action . . . The Ministry of Education program has favoured training at the expense of socio-cultural intervention, hence the recruitment difficulties . . .
- From a more critical point of view — or even that of common sense — one might ask whether the services offered are truly adequate. If they are not stimulating any demand, it is because they are not attractive! The institu-tional literacy education program is in question here. This question is un-folding on a basis while technical, is also political.
- One currently encountered argument imputes recruitment difficulties — the "broken date" — to the very nature of illiteracy: it is an invisible reality because it is hidden, shameful, repressed and kept private. Strategies, serv-ices and personal must be adapted to the distressing nature of the phenome-non. This requires resources and facilitating conditions and, above all, adequate facilitators and tailored solutions . . .
- Lastly, the defeat of the traditional approach to literacy education is due to its archaism, as well as to the inactivity of the industrial-commercial sector and the public authorities. The pressing need is for basic education adapted to the needs of the modern community and new job conditions. The problem of recruitment must be replaced by that of adapting to the offer of service. This is the point of view of the business sector.

I am going to comment briefly on each of these attempted explanations which refer to different ideologies of literacy education, and these latter to particular social groups. One might easily apply in Quebec what J. F. Lae and P. Noisette were saying about the French situation: "Whatever is said and done in terms of the struggle against illiteracy teaches us far more about those who are talking or doing than about a subject which none of them has managed to grasp". (Lais & Noisette, 1985)

THE ILLITERACY PROBLEM HAS BEEN OVER-INFLATED

This is often a conservative, not to mention reactionary, argument. It consists of affirming that everyone, or nearly everyone, has had the chance to go to school and that, consequently, illiterates are reduced today to a few unlucky, sick, handicapped, feeble, maladjusted and under-educated older people, and certain Third World immigrants.

It is also a prejudice supported by the strict sense of the French word and its older meaning. The stereotype of the illiterate is that of a peculiar individual, lost in town, who scarcely knows how to sign his name: a hybrid of idiot, peasant, handicapped person, poverty-stricken wretch and simple-minded outsider.

In Quebec, only one generic term — illiteracy — is used to designate the multiple incidences of deficit or incompetence in written communication and in the activities in which the latter is required. While the French have introduced a new concept of illiteracy, the better to cover this variety of situations and usages, anglophones qualify the equivalent term of illiteracy differently (basic — functional — cultural — technical . . .), the polymorphous usage of the single concept of illiteracy can lead to a great deal of misunderstanding.

It is true that we could go on discussing the limits of illiteracy indefinitely. In the radical or full sense — that of degree-zero of written communication (for a population or individual), ambiguity vanishes and the number of persons to whom one might apply the term is minute in this country. Then, we speak of "functional" illiteracy or, as I was able to suggest following the survey on literacy in Canada, of "semi-illiteracy[5]. Scientifically speaking, there is no limit to functional illiteracy, to semi-literacy, to illiteracy: their definitions, their perceptions and their current representations are, above all, social, as are those categories of the population which they designate, and the numerical scales which they imply.

These perceptions and these social categories are changing. Only 10 years ago, it would have been inconceivable to apply the attribute of illiteracy to $1/4$ or $1/3$ of the adult population. Things have certainly changed, as have the words and numbers. The concept has been rapidly vulgarized: the item which it designates has been extended, and its "pathological" or exceptional character has attained normality, even familiarity. The adventure of this phenomenon is far from over.

From a semantic or terminological point of view, one may contest the extensive uses of the concept. From the viewpoint of effectiveness in communication, or even from an elitist position, one may also wish to raise the "acceptable" threshold of linguistic performances to a significant degree. However, one must establish what has been clarified by opinion, namely, in the sense that the strong institutions retain it. For some time this becomes the common sense. For from this angle, neither the problem nor the rate of illiteracy has been over-inflated: they exist in the manner in which they are defined at the present time.

Illiteracy, like madness, is defined as such by a society at a given time. In North America, and increasingly in Europe, it fluctuates between one adult in five and one adult in three. It is a fact. So, we are left with the problem: why is the "clientele" absent?

RESOURCES ARE INSUFFICIENT:
"PRE-LITERACY" HAS BEEN SACRIFICED

This is what literacy tutors are saying in their evaluations. Recruitment problems are partially imputed to the new literacy program. In reality, they are older. They date from the first budget cuts in worker education, in the very place where literacy got its start. However, the new program exacerbated the difficulties, particularly in rural and semi-rural areas.

The administrators were delighted at the introduction of the new model of operation: "opening of the network", "the open coffer", the integration of literacy into the general training program of the Ministry of Education. Management was simplified, resources promised to be more generous, we were passing from short term to medium-long term, and the principle of accessibility for all was guaranteed. Furthermore, literacy was put back onto the school course which leads straight to the secondary school diploma.

However, this model can only be implemented after the adults have shown up. It excludes virtually all community action work. It divides literacy intervention into two: training and campaigning; the first being standardized and subsidized, the second left to the volunteer. It discourages field work in favour of a quantitative management of the stock and internal resources within the system. It favours urban centres, where population density renders community involvement less essential for recruitment purposes.

The paradox of this program is as follows: while the supply is wide open, the demand is barred. Nevertheless, there are means of ensuring the maintenance, or even growth of labour by annexing the "clientele" from worker groups in exchange for salaried education; by streamlining education in accordance with the profile of the new, "special clienteles" (young people in special courses, handicapped persons, allophones), or, on the other hand, by opening it completely to personal and social skills courses (what they were called before the community-based education — "l'éducation populaire").

Thus, though it is true that resources are insufficient on the campaign front, the solution to the recruitment problem would not be guaranteed merely by increasing these resources. Literacy education has undergone a transformation: from community action and community-based education to an integrated special education and specialized training program. It is this systematic tendency as much as the deficit in resources which explains the stagnation in the demand for services.

THE SERVICES OFFERED ARE INADEQUATE

Here, I will borrow an argument from Jonathan Kozol, since the alternative discussion on literacy education has become less loquacious in Quebec in recent years. This is partly due to the situation referred to briefly above: the new program has given increased power to the school boards, which have annexed (or created) a large number of autonomous organizations. At the same time — namely, during its crucial and alternative function — the "community" discussion of literacy education was integrated with the institutional discussion.

According to Kozol (1986), implantation of literacy education facilities at worker level, and hence the participation of interested parties, could depend on the replies given to the following three questions:
• who decides on the objectives and strategies for recruitment and training?
• who is in charge of recruiting, and what direction is being followed?
• where, in which environment, are the activities taking place?

Community action strategies which mobilize local resources and people in the field should be remunerated, and not based on volunteerism. This is the only way to motivate and involve worker facilitators who come from the same walk of life as the illiterate individuals. According to Kozol, (1986) "among those who are living on welfare, many would be perfect candidates to work in training, organizational and campaigning work". This had already been mentioned in the *Declaration of Persepolis in 1975:*

> (The literacy tutors) should not be incorporated into a specialized, permanent professional body, but recruited as closely as possible to the population which is to receive literary education, and should come from the same socio-professional class, or from a similar walk of life, in order to promote the dialogue.
>
> This mobilization will be all the more effective when it makes more room for initiatives from the target population, and for an understanding with them, instead of abiding by bureaucratic decisions imposed from elsewhere, and from above.
>
> Interested parties will be all the more motivated when each community is given the opportunities to implement the literacy project itself. . .

It is clear from experience that the most effective recruitment is that directed by the participants in literacy education whenever the conditions of the latter are favourable and attractive: word of mouth, friendly door-to-door visits, and not the "Electrolux Method", or television advertising. We know that it is necessary to go out and look for people in the places where they are at ease, without external constraints (a long-time literacy tutor told me that he was recruiting a lot of young people in the parks on the East side of town). Again, it is a known fact that a neighbourhood house, community centre, or shelter, are social centres suited to the establishment of literacy activities.

In Quebec, it was decided to support the development of literacy education within the school system rather than in society; (perhaps "choice" did not play a decisive role: traditions, structure and organizational logic were equally involved). Such orientation obviously had some advantages from an organization point of view, from a corporate and even union viewpoint as far as teachers were concerned, or from the aspect of access to the infrastructures and services of the school system. However, it has marginalized the autonomous movement of worker education. For several years, it has been noted that this has led to a form of annexation of the worker organizations by local school boards.

It should come as no surprise that services offered by school boards are receiving no more than average public acceptance. The institutional model does not promote large-scale recruitment from those working sectors of society which are culturally distant from such an organization of services.

We must ask ourselves in what measure literacy education may otherwise attain its objective of 'special education' — access to secondary education, at least for younger, under-educated people. We have no information on this theoretical objective borrowed from the literacy education program at the time (1984) when it was decided to integrate it with general education rather than with community-based education. These evaluations become indispensable when one observes that the growth of investments does not correspond with an increase in demand, nor with the realization of the objectives which we had set for ourselves.

THE NATURE OF THE PROBLEM EXPLAINS THE ABSENCE AND THE SILENCE

One of the arguments most frequently used to justify the special treatment represented by literacy education is that of an invisible, stigmatized "clientele". This clientele is unseen because it is hiding itself; it is hiding because it is afraid of being revealed, and is ashamed of its inferior image. It does not come out from its retreats unless it is discovered, or the pressure becomes too great. In such an instance, it is essential that the services offered be adapted, and tailored to the image of individual or small-group therapy.[6]

Hence, for example, the 'pairing' approach favoured by the anglophones, and also the various forms of individualized assistance which plays an important part in the discussions of literacy tutors, as well as in "pre-literacy". Here, "pre-literacy" is not interpreted as the "all-terrain" (Le Soleil, 1988) of community action or community-based education, but as an office consultation between a patient and healer. Curative and preventive therapies which call in re-education professionals (Blais et al, 1988) respond to the diagnoses of pathology. Along with these, a greater number of available, unpaid personnel are needed on a voluntary basis, just as in the health system. Everything takes place in an institution — a place far removed from the everyday ordinariness of communication.

It is not surprising that, in the light of this logic, the trend has become one of identifying literacy with special education, curative, identifying its public to a physically and/or mentally handicapped population, and the school to be a rehabilitation institution which requires appropriate staff, adapted operational standards, and additional funding. Since there is a tendency to reduce the illiterate population to its most disadvantaged fringe, one may justify the limited recruitment in terms of the special quality of care required. If there is a problem of demand, it is certainly not due to the poor quality of the services offered, but rather to the symptom of illiteracy being perceived as an individual psychosis.

THE PRESENTATIONS OF THE PROBLEM AND THE INTERVENTIONS ARE ARCHAIC

An editorial by an influential group in Canada states:

> Make no mistake about it. As long as literacy remains bogged down in the volunteer committees of the nation, it will not find its way into either the workshops or the secretariats. At the moment, literacy is nothing more than just another voice raised in the fundraising chorus, along with orchestras, community centres and diseases.
>
> Though all these activities are for good causes, literacy education itself is different. Literacy in the workplace is a goal which should be of serious interest to every business. It is a fundamental matter for each company, as our study on the costs of illiteracy will shortly prove. . .
>
> If we love our country, and if we want it to prosper, literacy in the workplace must become an essential priority. . .

In another editorial, the president of this group of business people suggested that 'literacy' be given another name, since this latter had an archaic connotation which in no way induced workers to acknowledge their incompetence, employers to invest in staff training, nor governments to make it a national priority. The concept and the activities which it designates should be reassessed and updated in order to bring literacy out of the social and health-services rut, which hinders adaptation of the offer of services to the demands of the labour market as well as the development of that demand.

According to this technological concept of the qualifying needs of the labour force, literacy is a group of information-processing skills which may be applied to different purposes within multiple contexts".[*] This is far removed from the A B C of school literacy, from the objective of self-direction as inspired by clinical rehabilitation, and also far from the ideas of social justice of transformation of social relations embodied in militant literacy education. Therefore, it will be the historic and synchronic laws of the job market which will dictate the courses to be followed, as is now being widely proclaimed all over Canada.

> It is clear that the degree of technological innovations attained, and the competitive level of the advantages offered to Canada's trading partners, will depend on availability of sufficiently-trained, competent and adaptable manpower. . . As the OECD noted, "even where certain tasks do not require major qualifications, a reserve of contingent competences is necessary in order to provide the worker with the required flexibility and adaptability which will enable him to hold a variety of jobs over a longer term . . .(Ottawa, 1988)

If this training imperative must still be called "literacy education", it effectively addresses a very large pool of workers which is directly recruitable in business and employment centres. It is sufficient to point out the criteria on employability, to put pressure on the labour force to participate in a training or refresher course, or to offer adequate services within the framework of the company in order to obtain co-operation from the government, from companies which specialize in training and retraining services, and from the unions — which may eventually assume this function of adaptation of the workforce to the mobile job market.

Such a program will not be introduced without problems. From this viewpoint of a company a country's workforce however, the recruiting problem is no larger just because one is dealing with a population which is captive, dependent and under pressure. The new test will rather be one of offering training services which are adequate and effective for the new demand.

The prime objective of this growing discussion is the active population, integrated in the work force and minimally qualified. It renders the notion of literacy more complex and technical, in order to better highlight the minimal prerequisites for professional qualification. It considerably increases the illiterate population from above, and its training methods are only designed for workers participating in the job market, illiterate by technological downgrading rather than by sociological marginalizations. This latter, the chronically illiterate population, usually on the fringe of socio-economic exchanges, will find its exclusion confirmed. It is evident that the problem of the demand for training services is far from being settled. On the contrary, selective supply, risks accentuating the social division.

THE RISKY BET OF THE PRESSURE OF SUPPLY AND DEMAND

Most of the above attempts at explanation were also presented as special solutions to the problem of a deficit in the demand. I will conclude with a displacement of the problem: in attempting to put myself no longer on the side of the professionals or the purveyors of services, but on that of the sought-after "clientele" — the side of the victim.

We must ask ourselves how illiteracy is experienced by those designated as victims. What is it like in everyday life? For it may well be that the massive phenomenon which we deplore today, and which we loudly claim to have 'discovered', was created prior to having been scrupulously recorded. It is quite possible that we were betting on the pressure of the supply in order to create the demand. Would the problem merely be one of marketing: making the pressure more effective?

It is often said that there is a 'hard core' of illiteracy, represented by that population which is stigmatized by its exclusion from written communication, a more or less generalized exclusion from all communications with the outside world. We would tend to identify this population with the dramatic picture given it by clinical discussion. We may expect to encounter it in the literacy education organizations (where the journalists are also looking for it). In principle and by priority, literacy services are directed at the group most directly involved. Although it is difficult to quantify precisely, we can, by cross-checking the surveys, estimate it at some 10% of the adult population, about 500,000 persons.[9]

Theoretically, this would be the pool of people in which the "need" for literacy education is most evident, because it is most profoundly felt and suffered. In reality, this is not necessarily the case. The need for literacy or normal communication is normative: it is socially imposed — the school makes it a categorical imperative, the purveyors of services project it upon the targeted public. However, the public is fickle. It contrasts its differences with prescribed need and Epinal illustrations.

We could have mastered the exclusion to the point of feeling right at home in it: the role of the illiterate — interiorized, assumed, adapted — is played as such both in public and in private. "Illiteracy and failure end up by becoming constitutives of a person's social status and character", writes J. P. Vélis. Quoting his psychological interlocutor, he continues: "There are those who willingly put themselves in the position of welfare recipient. It is not unusual to find young people and adults who say, right from the start: "I am illiterate", and who use every means to demonstrate it! It is a badge of recognition; besides, the change of status may be perceived as a threat: beginning any kind of education is out of the question."[10]

Delinquency may also have been adopted as a way of life in which illiteracy is not only normal, but a distinguishing mark. This trademark of opposition is learned from peers at school until they leave to live in the underground. It may be cultivated by the affirmation of other means of communication: slang, and music. I gave a fascinating image of this in the personage of Ti Pit (Hautecoeur, 1984) who, like so many others, ends up as a recluse. W. Labov (1978) has described in great detail the language, values and phenomenon of these sub-cultures by demonstrating that exclusion is overcome here through refusal to participate or assimilate at all, in the ostentatious manner of the aggressive affirmation of its difference.

There are many other sets of personalities in this portrait gallery. However, the most numerous ones are less marked. The further away one moves from the "hard core" of illiteracy, or from radical exclusion, the more the perception of anomaly is blurred. If the social differences are indeed well perceived as inequalities, they are not attributed to "illiteracy". It is necessary to have been educated or to have climbed the socio-professional ladder in order to valorize written objects and graphic communication. This method of social promotion must be valorized in order to recognize oneself as illiterate, or to desire to escape from it. It is necessary to know or believe that, through writing, one can change one's life in order to get involved in a learning experience.

This is not the case for the majority of people who the surveys have been able to identify as illiterates.

According to the survey on literacy in Canada, half the respondents in Quebec did not feel that it was very important to know how to read well, write well or even speak well, nor to have attended a secondary school; 60% did not feel that it was important to read to children; 44% stated that they had not read a book during the previous six months; 62% had never written a letter more than one page in length; 77% had never been in a library. 38% did not deem it important to know how to read or write in order to work; 89% declared that they had never been penalized because of reading and writing.

A significant division between men and women should be mentioned. In practice, as in the representations, illiteracy is clearly more a masculine than a feminine fact. (Blais et al, 1988)

Thus, we are far from being an "all-written" society, and far from a cultural consensus on the importance of literate competence. For large numbers of people, literacy or semi-literacy does not seem to be perceived as a handicap. Whereas 37% of the respondents to the aforementioned survey acknowledge that they need help in order to read or write (M: 41%, W: 33%), only 11% acknowledged that they had been penalized because of their illiteracy. Help and recourse to the service of another party in order to read and/or write is not always perceived as an admission of inferiority or dependance.

According to these few facts, it is clear why the "need" for literacy (on the basis of which many literacy tutors are justifying the adequacy of their facilitation) is more of an external pressure than a manifest fact of daily life for one third of the adult population. Illiteracy is a definition given by the educated or moderately schooled classes. 'The division of society according to this socio-linguistic division is indeed real and perceived by the poorer classes', (Labrie, 1987: 41-44), but may not be seen as such by others.

It should not be assumed that an offer of training or re-education will be perceived as a desirable service, or as an aid to individual promotion. In fact, the more one participates in the exchanges and values of the "active" society (producer, communicator, writer), the more one also participates in the training activities which it implements. "Le Conseil Supérieur de l'Éducation" of Québec recalls this paradox:

"Among those persons with an elementary school education, one adult in 20 is involved in educational activities; among those with a university-level education, we find 4 adults out of 10. . . .
    Participation in adult education is closely linked with the situation concerning the job market: the more active one is therein, the more one participates in educational activities. . . .

A certain basic education is virtually part and parcel of the emergence of a taste for getting involved in an educational process, not to mention the capacity to perceive the importance of it. . . .

The essential point is that the imposing apparatus of adult education is nowhere near connecting those population groups whose need of education is most urgent. . . . (Québec, Feb 1987)

We are back at square one, but we have explored the deficit in demand. It has been recorded. It has been partially explained. What is to be done if the proclaimed objective is the "struggle against illiteracy", or even the participation of the greatest number of individuals in cultural, economic and social life?

Schematically, there are only two ways: increasing the pressure on the offer is the marketing strategy, or, assessing the field in order to find the conditions which are most acceptable and most desirable for the joint management of supply and demand. I fear that at present we are on the first track rather than the second. We are "struggling against illiteracy" instead of seeking better conditions for a less unequal development of resources and competences.

NOTES

1. Cf. The Creative Research Group, *Literacy in Canada — A research Report*, prepared for Southam News, Ottawa, 1987; *Literacy in Quebec — A Research Report*, prepared for the Gouvernement du Québec, Ministère de l'Éducation, Québec, 1987.
2. According to Jonathan Kozol, "25 million American adults are unable to read the anti-poison warning on a box of pesticide, a note from their child's teacher, or the front page of a daily newspaper. The reading ability of 35 million others is not even at the level required for survival in our society. Together, these 60 million individuals represent more than one third of the adult population", *Illiterate America*, Anchor Press/Doubleday, NY., 1985.
3. The Association française pour la lecture (AFL) estimates that from "50 to 70% of the population finds itself excluded from all forms of written communication", as quoted by Jean-Pierre Vélis, *La France illétrée*, Éditions du Seuil, Paris, 1988.
4. Here, for example, is what the National Advisory Board on Science and Technology had to say: ". . . it is essential that the Government of Canada maintain its leadership in order to ensure that this problem is resolved with *extreme urgency*. There is no excuse for a country like Canada, with its resources and talents, to be tolerating the level of illiteracy which exists at present", *Technolgical Advance and Social Change: A Report by the Industry Committee of the National Advisory Board on Science and Technology*, Ottawa, 1988.
5. "Poids et mesures..." op. cit; see also François Furet, Jacques Ozouf, *Lire et écrire*, Editions de Minuit, Paris, 1977.
6. For an official copy of this discussion, see the *Guide d'intervention sur mesure en formation de base*, Document I, Direction générale de l'éducation des adultes, Ministére de l'Éducation, Québec, 1987 (pp. 33-34).
7. Extract from the editorial *Newsletter, Business Task Force on Literacy*, Vol. 1, No. 2, January 1988.
8. In the United States, a Council of Employers for the development of literacy (connected with the McGraw-Hill Group) defines literacy as, "the ability to process information, understand it, and apply it to defined tasks ... 14 million workers have a reading level equivalent to Grade 4, and 23 million (20%) only have a Grade 8 level. However, studies indicate that 70% of the reading material required for a sample of jobs across the nation require a level of comprehension corresponding to at least Grade 9 . . ." "Illiteracy Seen as a Threat to U.S. Economic Edge", *The New York Times*, 7-8-1988.
9. For example, those unable to read newspapers were estimated at 8%; the adult population declaring less than 5 years of schooling at 6%; the failure rate for the most elementary test of linguistic competence at 8%; the rate of adults who acknowledge that the inability to read and write has penalized them at work or in life, at 11%; the average failure rate in a series of 7 simple tests of linguistic competence, at 12% . . .
10. La France illettrée, op. cit., pp. 146-147.

REFERENCES

Blais, Hélène, Hautecoeur, Jean-Paul, Lépine, Lucie, (1988), *Recherche-action sur le développement de l'alphabétisation au Québec: Évaluations*, Direction générale de l'éducation des acults, Ministère de l'Éducation, Québec.

Des priorités en éducation des adultes, Conseil supérieur de l'Éducation, Québec, Feb. 1987.

Hautecoeur, Jean-Paul, (1984), *Anonymus Autoportraits*, Éditions Saint-Martin, Montréal.

Hautecoeur, J. P., (1988), "Poids et mesures de l'analphabétisme au Québec", ALPHA 88, under the direction of J. P. Hautecoeur, Ministry of Education, Québec.

Kozol, Jonathan, (1986), *Where stands the Republic? Illiteracy: A Warning and a Challenge to the Nation's Press*, Cox Newspapers, Atlanta.

Labrie, Vivian, (1987), *Alphabétisées! Quatre essais sur le savoir lire*, Institut québécois de recherche sur la culture, Québec.

Labov, William, (1978), *Le parler ordinaire*, Éditions de Minuit, Paris.

Lae, Jean-François, Noisette, Patrice, (1985), *Je, tu il, elle apprend*, La Documentation française, Paris.

Le Soleil "CECQ donne gratuitement au public des cours d'alphabétisation", September 9th, 1988.

A National Literacy Skill Assessment: Planning Report, Special Projects Group, Statistics Canada, Ottawa, 1988 (p.V).

Recherche-action sur le développement de l'alphabétisation au Québec, Direction générale de l'éducation des adultes, Ministère de l'Education, Québec, 1987.

Part III
ELEMENTS IN
THE PROGRAM PLANNING PROCESS

Adult educators are now finding themselves in a period when reform, innovation and modernization are collectively challenging traditional approaches to planning educational programs for adults. Since the publication in 1950 of Tyler's Basic Principles of Curriculum and Instruction in which he outlined a decision-making framework, there now appears to be a substantial body of literature on both traditional and innovative practices in program planning for adults.

Whether implementing the institutional model of program planning or the developmental process model, there are certain major decision points that a planner must take into consideration especially in an adult literacy and basic education environment. Some of these decision points are concerned with establishing general directions and procedures, program objectives and experiences, learning needs and evaluation practices. The purpose of this section is to examine these steps and their implications for both the adult educator and student learner.

One of the tasks in the planning process is deciding on appropriate instructional resources. McBeth outlines a successful approach to the development of learning materials in a community-based reading centre. Encouraging a learner-teacher partnership in the creation of a curriculum and viewing the learner as a curriculum planner and writer are strategies for assuring program participation. Throughout the chapter, she draws on the experience of students, volunteers and staff and demonstrates how the production of learning materials can be integrated into every aspect of the teaching-learning exchange.

Askov also addresses a step in the program planning process — the identification of instructional techniques. Various approaches to reading instruction categorized by their emphasis are described as they apply to teaching adult beginning readers. For example, language experience and individualized reading are discussed under the category of meaning-getting, and phonics and linguistics are discussed under the decoding emphasis. In addition, considerations in selecting computer software for beginning readers are provided along with a list of educational computer journals.

An awareness of the technological developments of the field can be instructive in planning adult literacy and basic education programs. Wiener examines the role of computers in education with respect to the recent research findings on cognitive measures and their andragogical implications. Concerns with regard to gender issues and the need for demystification of educational computer involvement are also-raised.

She defines the different types of computer-assisted instruction (CAI) programs and provides a practical checklist for basic education instructors to use in evaluating CAI materials.

Another procedure in program planning is the analysis of the client system to be served and the methodologies to be implemented. Conger and Cameron discuss the development and application of a life skills training program for various basic education populations. This approach provides the learner with problem solving behaviours that help in the management of changes occuring in the workplace, home and community. Philosophical foundations and different learning theories incorporated in the life skills instruction are also depicted. In addition, various life skills programs for youth, natives, women and special needs groups are described.

Often linguistically different people become the focus of new programs and different methods emerge to meet their needs. Burnaby and Bell discuss the characteristics and needs of the majority of well educated English Second Language (ESL) learners and the methods commonly used to teach them. As well they describe the characteristics and needs of those ESL learners who have special problems with respect to literacy in English and various forms of teaching. The authors also raise the issue of increased co-operation between people in the fields of ESL and ABE.

One of the most important steps in program planning is sequencing learning activities and events in a curriculum so that students can meet their own goals. Brown proposes a core literacy provision of three elements which consist of functional literacy, mastery of English and writing. Together these strands can create a dynamic process within which students can work towards chosen goals. She also argues that if practitioners were in touch with literacy theory then they would be able to offer a better student-centred service.

Formulation of an administrative plan is often cited as an important step in the program planning process. Lafleur explains an organizational approach to structuring a company wide training program using the Rubic cube as the model. The major components consist of networking job descriptions, skill requirements, courseware and evaluation at the appropriate level of competency for all employees. Not only can the model be used to identify job skills and update job descriptions but it can act as a planning aid between a department manager and employees to explore career path opportunities.

CHAPTER 1

Creating Curriculum: A Learner-Centred Approach

Sally McBeth

Everyone who works in the field of adult basic literacy is concerned about the lack of learning materials — especially those who work with adults who are approaching reading for the first time, or adults who learn very slowly. Sometimes an adult comes to a literacy program with the stated intention of keeping one step ahead of his or her school-age child. This is an important example of how a child's curriculum can form a part of the adult's. Usually, however, adults are baffled and demeaned by the playful irrelevance of children's learning materials. They have come to literacy instruction because they are grown up people trying to cope with a complex world. Moreover, their experience in the primary grades has often been traumatic. No amount of brightly-coloured, fantasy-filled primers and workbooks will convince them that reading and writing are "fun." They need learning materials that will help them function more independently and encourage them to persist with learning. They are invariably willing to persist, provided they see a link between the materials they are using and the needs and goals that compelled them to come to a literacy program in the first place.

Seen in this way, there is no real "lack" of learning materials for adults. They are all around us: street signs, banking forms, letters from a relative, the telephone bill, a recipe, the instructions on a bottle of medicine. More properly stated, the problem with learning materials in adult basic literacy is that each learner requires a substantial component of the curriculum to be tailor-made to his or her needs.[1]

Many would-be literacy teachers are daunted by the prospect of designing and producing original materials. Yet materials production can be the most exciting and rewarding of literacy activities, provided the instructor is prepared to relinquish much of the authorship of the curriculum to the learner. To put it another way, curriculum design and materials production are not "extra" activities that go on in preparation for instruction. Rather, they are a crucial part of the learning process itself, which the learner and the teacher enter into as a partnership.

WHAT DOES THIS MEAN IN PRACTICE?

East End Literacy is a community-based reading centre in Toronto, Canada. This organization has been training volunteer tutors to provide one-to-one and small group instruction to adult learners since 1978. In 1982 East End Literacy also began to publish learning materials for adults. In this article, we will draw on the experience of our students, volunteers and staff to show how the production of learning materials can be integrated into every aspect of learning and teaching. Although our work in materials production has taken place in a community setting, we think classroom teachers will find many new and interesting ways to apply these ideas to their own situations.

THE LEARNER AS CURRICULUM PLANNER: EVERYDAY MATERIALS

When Mary Evans came to East End Literacy, she was extremely skeptical about learning to read and write at the age of 25. Over coffee with Vivian, a staff member, Mary described her experience with schooling.

"I got kicked out of school when I was 10 years old. I took asthma attacks and they didn't listen to me . . . I tried (other schools) but my reading wasn't good enough."

Mary's reading *was* good enough to read *Green Eggs and Ham* or *Go, Dog, Go* to her two small children. But she wanted to read harder books, for her kids and for the daycare job she someday hoped to get. Mary would also need to read textbooks for an Early Childhood Education course, but she felt she wasn't ready for that yet.

In the meantime, there were a number of skills related to parenting and home management that Mary wanted to work on:

I'd like to put a shopping list on the wall, and know what it says when I go shopping. I need help with spelling brand names, and with reading labels in No Frills stores. It's cheaper there, but it's hard to know what's in the boxes when there's no pictures.

"I'd like to knit and cook better, but the instructions are hard to read sometimes.

"I cash my whole (mother's allowance) cheque at the beginning of the month. It would be nice to have a bank account and be able to write cheques."

By the end of the interview, Mary and Vivian had discussed a lot of everyday materials she could use with her tutor. When it came time for Vivian, Mary and her new tutor, Susan, to sit down and write a learning play for the first six months, Mary came up with the following goals:

• To help her children with schoolwork. Materials would include her kids' homework, report cards and information sent home from teachers.

• To write notes to friends, family and her children's teachers.

• To read and understand knitting and crocheting instructions and recipes. Mary would find the patterns and recipes she wanted in illustrated magazines.

• To write and understand shopping lists. Susan and Mary decided to draw their own flashcards for practice and then spend time shopping together.

• To learn the mathematics needed for shopping, banking and bowling. For this they would use price lists, bowling score cards, bank forms and adult-oriented math books available from East End's student library.

After several tutoring sessions, Mary also decided she would like to write some of her own stories in the form of a journal. As their work together progressed, it became clear that Mary's journal would help her with more than just writing skills. She had many problems with her ex-husband and her kids, so sometimes the tutoring sessions were devoted to discussing and writing about these problems. Susan helped Mary to understand legal documents that affected her, such as those relating to her ex-husband's visitation rights.

After six months together, Mary and Susan again met with Vivian to review her progress. Mary said she felt more confident reading to her kids and dealing with their teachers. She noticed a marked improvement in her technical skills: "I understand about vowels and pronunciation, and how to read around difficult words, then work them out. And I keep score better at bowling — even my girlfriend noticed!" Mary and Susan went on to develop a new set of goals for the next six months.

There are a number of ways in which everyday materials contributed to Mary's success. First, they related to her life, so that work done in a tutoring session was reinforced in her daily activities, and she could see immediate benefits from her new knowledge. For her part, Susan, the tutor, was relieved to learn that the burden of instruction was not on her shoulders alone, but rather that Mary could guide her to the places where instruction was truly needed. Most important, setting her own goals and choosing her own materials gave Mary a sense of control over her learning, and helped her to banish the feelings of inadequacy that she had carried with her since childhood.

THE LEARNER AS CURRICULUM WRITER:
EXPERIENCE STORIES AND THEIR APPLICATIONS
Experience Stories

From the moment Rob and his tutor, Anne Marie, began to work together, she sensed he had a strong desire to express himself in spoken and written form. A likeable man in his early twenties, Rob had a rich vocabulary and many issues he was anxious to discuss: his past, his family, schooling, work.

Although he was verbally gifted, Rob could read only a few words by sight. At first, Anne Marie thought their initial meetings would be "getting to know each other" sessions that would eventually lead to formal reading aloud from simple books. But they could find no basic readers with interesting subject matter. She began to realize that the reading material of most interest to Rob was inside his head. He could not write, but he could supply her with a text if she would agree to be his scribe. Here is a part of Bob's story:

> When I was 18 years old,
> my teachers told me I learned too slowly.
> I could not read and write very well.
> They said it was time for me to learn a job.
> They sent me to a sheltered workshop.
> My first job at the workshop was packing,
> I put together a package of soap, shampoo and bath oil.
> At a workshop you are always watched.
> The staff check the work and stop fights.
> At first I got into a lot of fights.
> I didn't want to talk to anyone.
> Everyone ordered me around.
> But after a while,
> I began to get along.[2]

Over many weeks Rob and Anne Marie wrote several versions of this story. Each segment was printed on a large sheet of lined paper and used for reading practice. Here is how the process works:[3]

1. The learner chooses the topic and begins to speak about it. The tutor repeats what the learner has said and gets agreement from him that those are the words he wishes to see written down.

2. The learner follows along as the tutor prints his words clearly on lined paper. The tutor makes no attempt to alter the learner's style of speaking or to correct grammar. She may, however, "break" the lines between sentences or clauses to keep the lines short and facilitate reading.

3. The tutor reads the segment aloud, gliding her finger beneath the words as she reads.

4. The learner and the tutor read together, the learner using his finger to follow beneath the words if he wishes. There may be much repetition and backtracking at first. Once a difficult word has been decoded, it is good to go back to the beginning of the sentence and read the word again within its context.

5. The learner reads alone.

The benefits of writing experience stories with children are well know.[4] Adapting this method of materials production to literacy work with adults has uncovered many additional benefits. Rob, whose experiences in school left him feeling that his potential was underrated, now felt he was making a valuable contribution to his own learning. And when Rob was the author or his own text, there was no danger he would find it boring, childish or irrelevant. On the contrary, he was excited to see his own ideas on the printed page and repeatedly passed his manuscript around to staff and students at the reading centre. Since many of East End Literacy's adult learners had worked in sheltered workshops, the manuscript generated much discussion and was eventually published in book form as part of our *New Start Reading Series*.

Rob's transformation from a person with shaky faith in his learning ability, into an author aggressively promoting his own manuscript is of particular interest to those of us at East End Literacy who worked in our publishing program. Illiteracy is often described as a "culture of silence." Learning that thought can be made visible through writing, and that writing is valued by others, creates a revolution in the mind of the newly literate adult. As Rob participated in the preparation of his manuscript for publication, it was apparent that he was changing the way he saw himself in the world.

COLLECTING MATERIALS

Not all adult learners want to publish a book as much as Rob did, but many learners like the idea of making available to others the materials they have designed or written themselves. This might simply mean printing a story on large sheets of paper and taping it to the wall for others to read. It may mean lending another student a picture dictionary made by hand and no longer needed. Or, it could mean turning a list of words into a crossword puzzle, running it off on a copy machine, and passing it around.

It is always helpful to make these materials available to other learners and tutors. At East End Literacy, student- and tutor-made materials are stored in plastic bins along one wall of the "reading centre" room. Organized into categories such as Housing, Banking and Spelling, the bins contain extra copies of everyday materials and exercises that learners and tutors have found useful.

PLAIN ENGLISH

Sometimes the materials adults need to master are written in language that would confuse even a college graduate. The legal documents Mary and Susan worked with are a good example. East End Literacy staff organize "workfests" where volunteer tutors help to rewrite pamphlets and documents in plain English. Literacy learners play an important role in plain English translations because they can identify the areas of difficulty and offer ways of saying the same thing in ordinary language.

EXERCISES

Literacy instructors often mistakenly believe they have to stay up late at night preparing spelling games, "cloze" exercises, flash cards and the like, in order to enrich the curriculum of adult learners. In fact, adults learn more, and have more fun, when the instructor simply supplies them with the concepts and the construction tools needed to do this themselves. We have found this is especially enjoyable as a group activity. On Wednesday nights a group of adults, tutors and staff meet to develop experience stories around a theme for our student magazine, *The Writer's Voice*. Once the writing and editing are done, we pass out graph paper, white-out, rulers, scissors, and glue, and the learners set about developing "word games" from the vocabulary contained in their stories. These are eventually published alongside the stories in *The Writer's Voice*.

It is particularly important to listen to adult learners when making up comprehension exercises. If we accept the definition of reading as "getting meaning from print," then it is not enough to pose questions to the adult learner that only require using the faculty of recall.[5] We came upon a vivid illustration of this point when East End Literacy Press was field testing the following story by Hank Guindon for the *New Start Reading Series*:

> In 1960, I lived in Hamilton, Ontario. I was 24 years old. I went to a New Year's party. As I was walking home, I heard a women scream, so I ran to help her. Two men were slapping her face and kicking her. I grabbed one guy and three him against a brick wall. The other guy ran away. I chased him. I grabbed him by the hair and pushed his face into a brick wall. After that, I knew he wasn't going anywhere. I called for help. Police Officer Hudson was walking his beat. He called a police car. The police car took the two guys to jail. The woman was taken to the hospital. A week later the two guys went to court. They got two years each. They swore they would get me when they got out. I gave them my address. One guy was 42, one was 43. But any guy who does that to a women it not much of a man. After a few days, a newsman came to the cotton mill where I worked. He took a picture of me. Two or three days later, I got a call to come to City Hall. I stood in front of judges and police. A judge made a speech. He said I was a good citizen. He shook my hand and gave me a citation.[6]

We tested this story in a variety of literacy and English as a Second Language programs. We found that women who had been the victims of male violence found it very satisfying reading. On the other hand, a literacy instructor who worked with ex-prisoners reported that they were offended by the story. They felt the jail sentence was too long for the crime committed, and they objected to the vigilante violence meted out by the hero. "Criminals should not be punished twice," they said.

Our point here has nothing to do with what should have happened that fateful New Year's of 1960. As publishers, we were excited by the level of discussion the story promoted. Literacy instructors did not have to belabour their classes with questions like "How many years did the two guys get?" Because the story was interesting, clearly laid out and illustrated, and relevant to the lives of the learners, they spent a minimum of time grasping its content and moved quickly to examine its underlying message. We believe that, given good materials and an instructor who is willing to stand back and listen, literacy learners will invariably choose to develop their skills in critical thinking.

THE LEARNER AND THE AUDIENCE
Editing

An adult who writes an experience story is concerned primarily with self expression. The story may contain idiosyncracies of grammar, unnecessary detail, obscure local references and so on.[7] Since the reading audience is composed solely of the learner and the tutor, these idiosyncracies do not matter — in fact, they aid the learner in reading because they contain familiar patterns of speech.

When the learner decides to make a story available to others through publication, an opportunity arises to think about written language as a means of communication. A learner who is encouraged to join in the editing not only gains from the process, but also contributes a great deal to the final product.

When East End Literacy Press decided to produce a series of basic readers, we asked Hank Guindon if we could use his experience story, *New Year's 1960*, as the first book in the series. Hank became a member of the production group responsible for the editing and design of the book. Hank's involvement as an editor helped us to make the story accessible to beginning readers without reducing the manuscript to nonsense.

We did not attempt to create a perfectly "controlled" vocabulary because we did not want to destroy the author's natural style, or to make the story monotonous. The danger of overly controlling vocabulary is easily seen in the following passage, taken from a commercially produced workbook for adults.:

> This is Al Smith. He's not tall, and he's not short. He's not thin, and he's not fat. He can talk as much as the next man, or he can just sit and let his pals do the talking. And Al has lots of pals.
>
> Dan Walker and Ned Black are pals of Al's. Dan is a talker. He can't stop talking. But Ned is shy. He never talks if he can help it.
>
> Al and his talking pal, Dan Walker, are having a drink at the drugstore. Al sips his drink as Dan talks. This is what Dan tells Al. "Al, I've got this girl, Nell. What a talker! She can't stop talking. Talk, talk, talk! When I'm with Nell I just sit. She talks more than I do. I've had all I can stand. What can I do?"[8]

The language in this passage is supposed to be easy to read, but it is nothing more than a vehicle for a list of words. The repetition and oversimplification distract the reader from the story line, such as it is. Books like these offend and humiliate adult learners.

Although we tried to make Hank's book as easy to read as possible, Hank's contribution was to ensure that the vocabulary remained authentic. For instance, Hank's original manuscript contained the sentence: "In front of the commissioner of police, I got a citation." Clearly, "commissioner" and "citation" are difficult words to include in a basic reader. To help us simplify the text, we discussed with Hank what had happened at the award presentation. He described the experience of standing in front of a group of dignitaries and related what the commissioner had said. In the course of this discussion we realized that the commissioner had the status of a judge. Using Hank's words, we changed the sentence to: "I stood in front of judges and police. A judge made a speech. He said I was a good citizen. He shook my hand and gave me a citation." We chose not to change the word "citation," however, because no simpler word could convey its formality and importance.

Hank's role as a member of the production group helped him to learn new writing skills. Prior to coming to Easy End Literacy, Hank had almost no notion of the role of punctuation. During the editing process we repeatedly asked Hank to read various edited versions of the manuscript out loud. This helped us to punctuate according to the natural pauses in his reading; it also gave Hank a better appreciation of the roles of punctuation and the reasons for them.

Hank learned about the process of polishing and refining his writing. He discovered that his own words, once written down, were not immutable, but that they should be clarified out of consideration for the reader. A beginning reader himself, Hank knew there was a shortage of basic reading material for adults. Like Rob, he was proud of the fact that his story was going to be read by others. Hank's experience as an editor made him see how, by communicating his story well, we could help someone else get a new start at reading.

DESIGN

When we leaf through the pages of a magazine, most of us don't realize that an army of professional designers and illustrators have been at work to influence our reading decisions. Whether we merely glance at a picture and scan the headline, or start reading an article and continue through to the end, our decisions are very much influenced by the way the article is presented on the page.

Adult learners at East End Literacy have taught us a great deal about how the design of some learning materials motivates them to continue reading while others seem to discourage them. We have learned, for example, that even relatively advanced students dislike crowded pages, small print, and busy layouts. When confronted with materials like this, they often say they can't read them, before they even try. This problem is easy to avoid when learners and instructors create the materials together. When producing our student magazine, *The Writer's Voice*, we often print the stories out by hand and ask adult learners to cut them up and arrange them on a "mock-up" page in a way that they think will make them easy to read. We find it very helpful to break the lines of the story at places where there are natural pauses in the reading, to leave lots of space between lines, and never to allow the lines of print to become too long.[9] This helps to prevent the learners from getting lost in a line of print and makes it easier to find the beginning of the sentence if it is necessary to start over.

Illustrations and photographs are an excellent way of providing clues to the text. Since experience stories often concern family and friends, many learners can supply photographs to illustrate their stories. Adults who like to draw can be especially effective in helping to provide clues to the text.

When we designed the *New Start Reading Series*, we decided to turn Hank Guindon's *New Year's 1960* into a photostory.[10] We wanted to have a picture on each page of the book that would help the new reader understand the words it accompanied. We asked a group of adult learners to help us design the book. First we made sure that everyone was familiar with the story. Then we made "storyboard" sheets with each line of the story printed beneath a blank square.

We asked the learners to sketch into the squares their own visualization of the action. We then "cast" several members of the group as characters in the story and practiced acting out the scenes they had sketched in the storyboards. We found locations in our neighbourhood that fit the story, and photographed our actors as they played through each scene. After the photos were developed the group met to choose the ones they through illustrated Hank's story best.

THE GREATEST BENEFIT. . .

This project was a lot of fun and we were all proud of the result. However, before we prepared *New Year's 1960* for publication, we wanted to know what learners in other programs would think of it. We sent "mock-up" versions of the book to a number of literacy and English as a second language programs throughout Ontario, along with a questionnaire. The response was what we had hoped for. "Entry level" or "basic" students found the book interesting and easy to read; we knew that Hank's book could provide many adults with the experience of mastering their first book.

The learners at East End Literacy who took part in this project learned a lot about how a publication is made. They were proud of this new knowledge, and began to look at other books with a more critical eye. Making a publication themselves had demystified books for them and made them feel less intimidated by print material in general.

We have come to believe that the greatest benefit of making adult learners the creators of their own learning materials is the change it brings about in the way they see themselves. They become participants in a culture in which their ideas and experiences can be shared with others through the medium of print. Helping them to become a part of this culture is, to us, one of the great goals of literacy work.

NOTES & REFERENCES

The author acknowledges the valuable contributions to this chapter of these members of East End Literacy:: Betsy Alkenbrack, Karen Diver, Anne Marie Greenaway, Ruth Wehlau.

[1] The need for individualized curriculum in adult basic education is not a new idea. In 1880, James Hughes, School Inspector for the Toronto Board of Education, wrote in a report: "The mode of instruction in the evening school was necessarily individual; for owing to the imperfect education of most of the pupils, it was found hardly possible to establish any mode of classification that would work as regards to the greater number of them." Quoted in *The Right to Learn: The Report of the Work Group on Adult Literacy*, Toronto, Board of Education for the City of Toronto, 1985, p. 4.

[2] Collie, Robert, (1985), *Getting Along*, Toronto, East End Literacy Press, pp. 3-11.

[3] For a film demonstrating the uses of experience stories in tutoring adults, see *Teaching Adults to Read*, Adult Literacy and Basic Skills Unit, London, England, 1977. This film is available in many parts of Canada through the public library system.

[4] See Donald H. Graves, (1983), *Writing: Teachers and Children at Work*, New Hampshire, Heinemann Educational Books.

[5] See Roger T. Cunningham, (1977), "Developing Question-asking Skills," in *Developing Teacher Competencies*, ed. James E. Weigand, Englewood Cliffs, New Jersey, Prentice-Hall, pp. 81-130.

[6] Guindon, Hank, (1985), *New Year's 1960*, Toronto, East End Literacy Press.

[7] Literacy instructors are sometimes unsure whether experience stories told in dialects such as those of learners from West Indies should be made to conform to standard written English. We feel that the most important thing to consider is the learner's intended audience. There is such a shortage of basic reading material for dialect speakers that their own stories are very valuable left as they are. If, however, a learner of English as a second dialect wishes the story to be read easily by an audience of non-dialect speakers, the instructor and the learner have gained an opportunity to study the differences between the grammatical rules of the dialect and those of standard written English.

[8] Buchanan, Cynthia Dee, (1966), *Programmed Reading for Adults, Book 6*, Sullivan Press, pp. 32-33.

[9] We are indebted to Sue Shrapnel and her colleagues at the Hackney Reading Centre in London, England for much useful information on effective ways to produce and publish student writing.

[10] For more information on the use of photostories in adult education see Deborah Barndt, Ferne Cristall and dian marino, *Getting There: Producing Photostories with Immigrant Women*, Toronto, Between the Lines, 1984.

CHAPTER 2:

Approaches to Reading Instruction for Adult Beginning Readers

Eunice N. Askov

Low-literate adults who are functioning at the beginning reading levels are likely to have met with failure and frustration in school in trying to learn to read. In selecting an approach to reading instruction, the teacher or tutor must always keep in mind that the adult learning to read is a "fragile learner." Successes must be built in from the beginning. Small incremental steps — with success at each step — are necessary.

The usual approach in selecting a method by which to teach reading is to pick one that is familiar to the teacher and convenient to the setting. However, in this case the adult learner should be the first consideration. Information about past experiences in school can be helpful — for example, asking how reading was taught in school and how the adult thinks s/he can learn best. Often adults have insights into their own learning skills that children lack; reading instruction can be geared to the person's strengths rather than weaknesses.

For example, if an adult student says that s/he cannot remember letter sounds — or has difficulty hearing the differences in sounds — a phonics approach would not be appropriate. That individual might do better with a visual or whole word approach to instruction. Conversely, if the individual has trouble remembering whole words, a phonics approach may help the adult student to learn to decode or sound out words.

DESCRIPTION OF THE APPROACHES

A teacher can use diagnostic information gleaned from a variety of sources to plan instruction focused on students' needs but utilizing their strengths. This instruction may be carried out within a group reading instructional program or on an individual basis such as in a tutoring situation.

The various approaches to reading instruction may be categorized by their emphasis — whether on getting meaning or on decoding or sounding out the words. Rarely are approaches kept pure in practice; this categorization is for discussion purposes as shown in Figure I.

Meaning-getting Emphasis		Decoding Emphasis
Language Experience (LEA)	Reading Textbooks	Phonics
Individualized Reading		Linguistics

Figure I. Continuum of Approaches to Reading Instruction

We consider these approaches especially as they apply to teaching adult beginning readers. More information on the approaches, but as they are used with children, may be found in various textbooks related to reading (for example, Miller, 1984).

Reading Textbooks

Reading textbooks vary in their emphasis. Some emphasize decoding skills while others stress meaningful context as an aid to word recognition. Usually the teacher's overview indicates the emphasis in a particular reading series. We have placed them in the middle of the continuum because most reading textbooks are eclectic, incorporating a variety of approaches to reading instruction.

The problem with reading textbooks is also an advantage — namely, that they are intended for any adult of a given reading level. This feature makes them easy to use with average learners in a typical setting. They become less satisfactory, however, when used in atypical situations, such as on an Indian reservation, or with atypical learners, such as learning disabled adults.

Most reading textbooks offer instruction within a functional context. The narratives often focus on success stories of newly literate adults facing the literacy demands in their daily lives. Attempts are made to teach coping skills along with reading skills, such as reading newspaper advertisements. Many of the stories tend to have moralistic outcomes, such as inculcating appropriate behaviours in order to get and keep a job.

While the use of minority role models in the stories is undoubtedly a positive factor, most reading textbooks appear to be oriented toward middle-class values. The situations which are portrayed in the stories sometimes lack the flavor of reality. Some textbooks focus almost exclusively on narrative materials rather than finding a balance between fiction and non-fiction.

Reading textbooks are undoubtedly the easiest approach for a teacher or tutor to use. All the materials, including vocabulary, comprehension, and study skills instruction and exercises, are provided. Therefore, reading textbooks are well suited even for the volunteer tutor. They are also appropriate for the average adult learner who does not have unique learning difficulties.

Reading textbooks usually employ an analytic approach to teaching phonics. Students first learn whole words by sight. After they have learned several words containing the same sound, they are led to generalize about the sound made by a particular letter or letter combination. Some students, especially those who may have been in special education classes, are unable to learn phonics by the analytic approach. These students may benefit from synthetic phonics programs in which they learn sound separately and then learn to blend the sounds together. Phonics is described in the next section.

Phonics

Phonics emphasizes the decoding process (see Figure I). The difference between the analytic and synthetic approaches to teaching phonics may be illustrated by the following example. In the synthetic approach students would not learn the word *cat* until they had learned each letter sound separately. They would then be taught to blend "kuh-a-tuh" by saying the sounds quickly together. By contrast, in the analytic approach students might learn the word *cat* as a whole in association with a picture. After they had also learned such words as *can* and *cow*, their teacher would ask them to conclude what sound is the same in all three words. These words would then become the basis for teaching the *c* sound.

The synthetic approach is deductive — the teacher tells the students the phonics generalization and lets them apply it to new words. The analytic approach is usually inductive — the students draw the generalization after being presented with specific examples. Some students seem to need the structure of the synthetic approach, finding it difficult to draw generalizations on their own. They may also benefit from the more intensive drill and practice of the synthetic approach.

Phonics in either the analytic or synthetic form is part of almost every reading program today. Research in the 1960s, while producing mixed results in terms of the best approach to reading instruction, indicated that early, intensive phonics programs for children produced higher reading achievement (Chall, 1967). As a result of these research findings most reading instructional systems for children incorporate more phonics instruction earlier in their reading systems. Many young adults today have had a heavy dose of phonics in the elementary grades.

The widely used reading series published by the Laubach Literacy Action (New Readers Press) is based on synthetic phonics. Each letter sound is presented separately and then in combination with other sounds to create words. The series has been used widely in this country and in developing countries by volunteers who lack expertise in reading pedagogy. Following a training period of approximately ten hours, the volunteer is equipped to use the textbook series which brings the student up to about a third grade reading level upon completion. The advantage of this series is that it can be used by those lacking specialized training in reading instruction.

We are convinced, however, that some people, because of auditory processing problems or some other factor, are simply unable to learn to read by applying phonics generalizations. The author recalls one student who, after one year of synthetic phonics instruction, still said *ah* for the short *a* sound. When his teacher switched to a whole word approach reinforced by tracing, he not only learned the words in his own stories, but he also recognized the words in new contexts and retained them the following year. As a rule of thumb, if students have had phonics instruction in school and they are still unable to apply phonics generalizations in attacking new words, we recommend another approach, accompanied by tactile/kinesthetic reinforcement. In other words, students can learn new words by tracing over the letters (written in crayon or some type of rough surface) and by copying and writing them numerous times.

Linguistics

Linguistic approaches to reading have been handicapped by confusion of terminology. Almost every reading series claims to be "linguistic," or to follow linguistic principles. What is meant is that the materials reflect a knowledge of the structure of our language.

When we speak of the linguistic approach to reading instruction, however, we think primarily of the materials that have been developed on the basis of the work of C. C. Fries. Popular in the late 1960s, the materials emphasize decoding rather than meaning-getting in the initial stages, like phonics. However, unlike phonics, instruction in word recognition occurs through the visual modality. Students learn the word *cat*, for example, as a spelling pattern or whole word. They also learn *fat, mat,* and *Nat* in the same lesson. Through instruction in the *at* spelling pattern, students learn new words by "minimal contrasts" — that is, by learning new words that differ only in one letter. The sounds are thus not isolated or taught synthetically.

After students have mastered the basic decoding skills, the linguistic materials place greater emphasis on meaning; they appear similar to reading textbooks. They still introduce new word elements by spelling patterns, but they also stress comprehension.

The linguistic approach has been effective primarily with those who have had difficulty with phonics. It is particularly successful with non-native speakers, who are often confused by phonics because the sounds in English are different from those in their native language. Because students easily learn spelling patterns, and hence words following those patterns, they experience some immediate success. The linguistic approach is more structured and controlled than meaning-getting approaches but less meaningful to the individual reader.

Language Experience Approach (LEA)

Of the meaning-getting approaches, in which the content of the material becomes the cue to word recognition, the language experience approach (LEA) is the most highly meaningful and personal to the student. The student's own writing — or that of a group of students — becomes the reading material through which reading instruction is offered.

In using LEA, some sort of stimulus — perhaps a picture, a common concern, or event, a field trip, or a movie — first introduces the topic. Sometimes reading material written by a professional author or another student becomes the stimulus. Discussion following the stimulus is important in bringing out the vocabulary and concepts to be used. The student or a group of students dictates a story that recaps the main ideas from the discussion. The teacher or tutor records the story on a chart or chalkboard. Because the story is written by the student, he or she has little difficulty with word recognition. Upon encountering an unknown word, the student rereads from the beginning to recapture the flow of the story, usually recognizing the words from the ample clues in the context.

After the student has reread the story several times for several days, the instructor selects high-utility words from the story to present in isolation and in new contexts. Word recognition skills can also be taught using words from the student's story.

We consider LEA to be a very appropriate instructional strategy with beginning adult readers. Students are usually motivated by their own writing, particularly when their stories are bound together in a "book" to be shared with others students in a classroom library. The teacher can present the word recognition skills needed by the students, not necessarily those presented with a given story in a reading textbook.

Students should be encouraged to do their own writing to record their ideas. They should spell words as well as possible using their word recognition skills.

Independence in these attempts is important in helping students apply their skills. Later writing can be "edited" to correct spelling and grammatical errors. Reading and writing complement each other; development of one benefits the other. Daily writing programs, used frequently in some parts of the United Kingdom, Canada, and Australia, seem to improve the development of word analysis skills in reading.

LEA must be supplemented with other readings — written not only by other adult students but also by established authors. Reading books to the students can stimulate discussion and creation of LEA stories. Reading appropriate books on their own encourages students to apply their growing skills independently. Individualized reading forms a natural follow-up to LEA as students mature in their reading skills.

This approach is used effectively at the Lutheran Settlement House Women's Program which is located in a transitional neighborhood in Philadelphia. Students dictate or write their own stories in response to themes presented in pictures, other students' writings, or community information bulletins. Key words are placed on the chalkboard as an aid to writing. The topics are relevant to their lives. Since over half of the women in the program have suffered abuse, the topic may, for example, deal with domestic violence. Instructors make an effort not to be judgmental or offer solutions; the students' feelings are accepted.

Once the student has constructed a skeleton for a story, it is shared with the rest of the group. The other students question the writer to help her develop the content of the story. The student then rewrites the story, expanding it in line with the advice of the group.

Only after the content has been developed is editing for mechanics allowed. At this point other students may offer corrections to spelling and grammatical errors, or suggest more effective ways of presenting the content. In other words, the focus on the mechanics comes last, not first.

The instructor then uses the student's stories as the basis for word recognition and comprehension exercises. Stories and exercises have been published in books available for purchase from the Lutheran Settlement House Women's Program, 1340 Frankford Avenue, Philadelphia, Pennsylvania 19125.

Individualized Reading

Individualized reading, like LEA, emphasizes meaning as a cue to word recognition. Students select their reading material, read at their own pace, and discuss the material in individual conferences with the teacher or tutor. This approach works best after readers have reached some proficiency in reading, about a second-grade reading level.

Individualized reading includes students' silent reading, followed by an individual conference at the completion of the book. In the conference, the teacher or tutor checks the student's comprehension through questions and discussion. The student might be asked to read a portion aloud to check application or word recognition skills. The final step in the conference is selection of additional reading material with guiding questions and prereading motivators (Hunt, 1971).

A variation of this approach is SSR, Sustained Silent Reading (McCracken, 1971). As a supplement to another approach SSR offers students frequent opportunities for uninterrupted reading. Students simply read at a given time during the instructional period. The teacher or tutor also reads as a role model. The instructor might keep a record of the number of books read or time spent reading outside class to encourage further reading. SSR has proven useful in building fluency in application of reading skills. It is based on the premise that students learn to read by reading.

We heartily endorse meaning-getting approaches for adult beginning readers. Because reading has not been pleasurable or easy, adult readers often avoid it. We have found that making reading personally meaningful to students has made them want to read. Increased reading time results in improved reading skills.

Let us sum up this discussion of instructional strategies by saying that most adult beginning readers benefit from some combinations of decoding and meaning-getting activities. Reading textbooks, which have both elements, are popular for teaching average learners but have limited usefulness for teaching learners with severe reading problems.

Therefore, we endorse an eclectic philosophy, using anything that works. No single instructional approach works with every student, nor is every teacher or tutor equally adept with every approach. Our advice is that you have a variety of approaches to instruction in your "bag of tricks." You must be sensitive to the needs of individuals to decide upon the most effective strategy for each learner.

COMPUTER TECHNOLOGY

The computer is a tool for instruction, not really an instructional approach. Just as the slate was for pioneers learning to read and the chalkboard is today, the computer can be used in both decoding and meaning-getting approaches. Because it is just a tool, the computer is only as effective as the instructional programs written for it. The lesson we learned from teaching machines in the 1960s is that students learn best from machines in small doses. The instructor controls the use of the tool. If the instructor uses a computer effectively, it can become a very significant technological aid in the classroom.

Software companies continue to spring up in basements and garages. These new companies are peddling software that is quick and relatively easy to create because elaborate, long-term curriculum development requires extensive funding and expertise. As when buying a car, the teacher or tutor who wants to purchase software should shop around to find the best bargains. Although car dealers allow you to test drive a car before buying it, many computer companies do not send software to potential customers on approval.

The best alternative for the teacher seeking good educational software is to join a consortium that purchases and/or reviews commercial software. In some states the department of education has organized this service, which lets the teacher know what is "under the hood" of the software package. (Shiny chrome on the outside may convey a false promise of effectiveness and usefulness!) Finding out what others have used effectively is one solution to the problem. Reading educational computer journals is another. (See the list of journals at the end of the chapter.) Seeing the software demonstrated at professional meetings and workshops is probably the best way to know what a particular software package will do.

But what should you look for in software to teach reading to adult beginning readers? Whether you are looking for educational games and practice materials or computer courseware (more or less a complete curriculum), you need to keep some special considerations in mind.

Software for Adult Beginning Readers

The process of learning to read has somehow gone wrong for the adult who has not learned how to read; the computer offers a new route to learning that is not yet fraught with failure. It is important, therefore, that the software be effective. If the student fails again, this time using the computer as an instructional tool, feelings of failure will be reinforced and reading will be rejected.

Software for adults must be adult in nature. Most available software has been developed for school-age students. If not clearly inappropriate in format and presentation, it may be useful for adult beginning reading instruction. Sometimes minor adaptations make it acceptable to the adult learner.

More important than the obvious features of adult format and content is the incorporation of principles of adult learning. Adult learners need to have a sense of controlling their own choices; software that offers no options is not appropriate for adults. The adult should feel that s/he is determining what the machine should do, not vice versa. Through this ability to control and make choices, the illiterate adult may feel empowered — in control of his/her own decisions possibly for the first time. It is important for software to enhance the adult's feelings of self-worth by encouraging choices in learning. (See Knowles' concept of andragogy.)

Some software programs do not permit a student to enter a wrong answer; the computer simply does not respond until the correct answer is entered. While this may be appropriate with very young children or with severely retarded individuals, it seems to encourage random guessing. On the other hand, programs ought not say to the student, "You're wrong!" We prefer those programs that provide branching to reteach concepts, yet give the user the sense of having control rather than being controlled. The student should be able to choose activities within a given lesson or decide which activities to do first.

Directions to the student should be simple and easy to follow. In programs for non-readers, however, printed directions can be a real problem. Even if a program offers good examples of what the students are to do, non-readers may not know how to respond. Some software packages have used speech synthesizers to get around this problem. Speech synthesizers can also be very useful in teaching reading to non-native speakers, who especially need auditory as well as visual input in learning to read English.

Good software should be designed to guarantee success. If a student answers incorrectly, the program should contain branches to route the student through instruction on prerequisite skills. New material should be introduced at a pace governed by the student's rate of mastering prior material.

For the student to achieve success, good diagnostic tests, administered on the computer or by the teacher, must be part of the software curriculum. Unless the student is placed appropriately according to reading level and skill needs, learning on the computer will not be effective. Likewise, mastery tests must be built in so that both the teacher and the student can see that progress is being made.

Another concern in selecting software is whether the programs are to be used by individuals or groups. Software intended for group use offers both wider usage of the computer and socialization. For non-native speakers the language interaction of group members can have important benefits in helping them learn English. Discussing tasks on the computer can also help withdrawn or unsure students. In a group of mixed abilities, however, the better readers may set the pace in the learning process, leaving slower learners behind. If that happens, the slow learners cannot feel any better about themselves by using a computer. The decision about group versus individual use has to be made locally, considering the students for whom the software is intended.

Most software designed for adults is intended for use by individuals. Therefore, it should individualize instruction, responding to the strengths and weaknesses demonstrated in the individual's responses. This interactive capability of the computer should permit instruction to be tailored to the individual student as no other instructional tool can be. Good software capitalizes upon this capability.

Good software should allow the teacher or tutor to modify it to "fit" a particular student or a local situation. For example, some software programs allow the instructor to enter vocabulary words that are particularly relevant to the student or curriculum. Those words become the focus of instruction. It is also possible to personalize the software by using the student's name and incorporating words that pertain to a subject of the student's personal interest.

Another consideration in selecting computer software is whether the instructor wants computer management of instruction (CMI) in addition to computer assisted instruction (CAI). CMI offers the benefits of record-keeping so that students can begin a lesson where they left off in the previous session. CMI also keeps track of the results of diagnostic and mastery tests for each student and provides class records if appropriate. Many CAI software packages include a CMI component. As microcomputers become more powerful, they will be able to utilize more sophisticated record-keeping systems and manage more data. The teacher or tutor needs to be aware of the capabilities of the particular available computer when selecting software, to know whether it will handle a particular CMI software package.

The role of the teacher is an important and final consideration. Since adult beginning readers are "fragile learners," most of whom have already experienced failure in learning to read, a close relationship with a teacher or tutor is essential. Instruction on the computer should not be considered sufficient for learning. (At higher levels students can learn on a computer with little or no intervention by an instructor. The illiterate adult, however, usually lacks the confidence necessary to use the computer independently, especially in the initial stages. Once s/he learns how to operate the machine, then s/he can become increasingly self-sufficient in learning.) Suggestions for the instructor are an important consideration in selecting the software. Not only should a teacher's manual contain information on the mechanical aspects of using the software but also teaching suggestions on activities that will help the student transfer learning on the computer to his/her daily life.

A sample software evaluation form, developed by the Merrimack Education Center, is provided as an example. Teachers or tutors selecting software are advised to use a checklist of criteria so that decisions can be made objectively and systematically.

ADULT LITERACY AND TECHNOLOGY PROJECT

Funded by the Gannett Foundation, beginning in the Fall of 1986, the Adult Literacy and Technology Project offers assistance to teachers and tutors who want to use technology for instruction and/or management. Coordinated by the Institute for the Study of Adult Literacy at The Pennsylvania State University, on behalf of the national Steering committee on Adult Literacy and Technology, the project has two missions: training and communication. A network of technology consultants provides technical assistance to adult literacy and adult basic education programs; an audio-visual training package orients the new user to possible applications of technology. Communication is facilitated through quarterly newsletters, Litline (an electronic bulletin board through the U.S. Office of Education), and national conferences. Evolving technology is tracked to explore possible new applications of technology to adult literacy instruction. Evaluations of software are regularly conducted to inform teachers and tutors about the strengths and weaknesses of existing software for adult learners. Current information may be obtained from the Institute for the Study of Adult Literacy.

You, as a concerned teacher or tutor, need to stay informed about developments in computer technology. Progress is being made every day in increasing capabilities while bringing down costs. It is exciting to know that you will have opportunities for using technology in ways that we have not even contemplated.

REFERENCES

J. S. Chall, (1967), *Learning to Read: The Great Debate*, New York, McGraw-Hill.
C. C. Fries, (1963), *Linguistics and Reading*, New York: Holt, Rinehart & Winston.
L. C. Hunt, (1971), "Six Steps to the Individualized Program (IRP)," *Elementary English* 48, no. 1, 27-32.
M. S. Knowles, (1980), *The Modern Practice of Adult Education: From Pedagogy to Andragogy, Revised and Updated*, Chicago: Follett Publishing Company.
R. A. McCracken, (1971), "Initiating Sustained Silent Reading," *Journal of Reading* 14 no. 8, 521-524, 582-583.
Merrimack Education Center, *Computers in Adult Education: A Planning Guidebook*, Chelmsford, MA: Adult Education Computer Applications Project (101 Mill Road), n.d.
W. H. Miller, (1984), *Teaching Elementary Reading Today*, New York, Holt, Rinehard & Winston.

SELECTED LIST OF EDUCATIONAL COMPUTER JOURNALS (U.S.A.)

C.A.L.L. Digest
KAIRINSHA International
2024 Center Avenue
Fort Lee, NJ 07024

Computer Learning Classroom
Subscription Department
5615 West Cermak Road
Cicero IL 60650

Computers, Reading, and Language Arts
Department M2
PO Box 13247
Oakland, CA 94661-0247

The Computer Teacher
International Council for Computers in Education
Department of Computer and Information Science
University of Oregon
Eugene, OR 97403

*Creative Computing: Magazine of Personal
Applications and Software*
PO Box 5214
Boulder, CO 80321

Educational Computer
3199 De La Cruz Boulevard
Santa Clara, CA 95050

Educational Computer Magazine
PO Box 535
Cupertino, CA 95015

Electronics Learning
Scholastic, Inc.
50 West 44th Street
New York, NY 10036

MECC Uses Newsletter
MECC Publications
2520 Broadway Drive
St. Paul, MN 5113

Personal Software
PO Box 2919
Boulder, CO 80321

Computer Assisted Instruction (CAT): Current Issues, Gender Implications and Future Directions

Roberta B. Wiener

Computers as educational tools are here to stay. It is unlikely they will ever be relegated to the dustbins of forgotten technology such as talking typewriters or TV in the classroom. Computers and education will not have such an ignominious future. "Minis," "micros," "monitors," "mainframes," "word processors," are not merely part of a new and passing lingo — they as much a part of the necessary paraphernalia of the classroom, especially for the adult populations, as desks, film and audio cassettes, pocket calculators, and even textbooks.

That we are in the midst of a high tech revolution, that has become an educational phenomenon and not a passing fad, must now be obvious to all educational institutions. This poses very real problems for educators who are pressured to do "something" with computers but who have no guidelines, little or no computer knowledge (literacy), few ground rules and a paucity of relevant research data. At first this was understandable, there were few studies and many of those left more questions unanswered than answered.

The research is beginning to mount and the popular press, and professional journals are bringing the data and information to the public and the professional educational community. Bracey (1982) has summarized the effectiveness of Computer Assisted Instruction (CAI) in 51 different research studies. It appears that most researchers he cited were interested in measurable, cognitive outcomes. Did students using a computer learn more than other students using more traditional instructional materials? Research into the social, motivational, and affective areas should receive more attention, especially as it relates to the basic skills learner who in many cases has experienced much failure in the past. Preliminary investigations seem to point to very high involvement with computers and extremely positive motivation and interaction with adult populations (Buckley, 1983). Increases in motivation and interest in computers with some high school students may translate, be channeled, to decrease the dangerously high and increasing drop out rates (Pressman and Rosenbloom, 1984).

Bracey (1982) cites some encouraging research results: 1) students either learned more, retained more, or learned the same, but faster, using the computer; 2) CAI improved retention when students were tested after the computer program ended; 3) in math, students who had access to the computer for only ten minutes a day scored significantly higher than those who did not and twenty minutes a day doubled the gains.

A number of studies looked at CAI use in reading and comprehension (Carver and Hoffman, 1981), writing (Schwartz, 1980 and Pappert, 1980), and adult literacy (Buckley, 1983, Caldwell, 1980). The results allow us to proceed with some confidence. There does seem to be improvement in teaching of literacy with computer based programs. Older students using computers achieved mastery levels in less time. Those using word-processing software programs find them extremely helpful — turning writing, and editing — what some students believe a messy chore of changing, crossing out, rewriting — into a neatly organized and simplified task (Solomon, 1985).

If we look at benefits other than cognitive ones, we encounter expectation, assumptions, and interesting, but not always positive, outcomes. Will technology be available, for example, to all socio-economic groups? Some studies indicate that richer communities, predictably, invest considerably more money in computers both at home and in the schools. (Johns Hopkins, 1983; Becker, 1985). McGinty (1985) has pointed out rather dramatically, that computers have gone beyond classrooms and have "invaded the home." Their purpose, he goes on to say, has changed from the simply recreational to the educational. This requires additional knowledge — moving from simply acquiring computer literacy, to acquiring the ability to evaluate software when making purchases. There are some communities McGinty tells us, with software lending libraries that have developed parent/child literacy programs and even provide prepared forms for parents to use as guides to evaluate software.

Several educators have serious concerns with regard to gender and computers. Computer classes have more male than female students, and this seems to hold true for computer camps, as well as interest in computers in the home. Recent studies have looked at male/female enrollment in computer classes and have provided some interesting data. Female enrollment was only 25% in computer classes in one study (Linn, 1984) and was highest in introductory courses (34%), decreasing in intermediate courses such as those teaching BASIC (19%). Another study concludes that skill with computers is more socially approved and offers more social incentives in the culture of adolescent males than females (Chen, 1986). Thus, stronger male bonds develop and reinforce males' greater self confidence with technology. Chen suggests using computers (CAI) in subject matter content, i.e., English, Science, Math, History, subjects other than programming, so as to engage and encourage female interest. Eccles (1986) points out that there are psychological barriers, as well, that contribute to women's underrepresentation in certain high-level and scientific careers. This reflects institutional influences and "the impact of rigid gender-role socialization on the determinants of these choices." She further shows, against popular mythology, through a most interesting research model, that women seeking relatively low level math related careers *did not* lack confidence in their math abilities nor did they consider math any harder than women seeking math as a career! Eccles suggests effective intervention programs and comprehensive career and life-role counseling programs to help women assess and reevaluate decisions and understand the stereotypes of various occupations.

We know that software has now become so simplified that people with little or no training are successfully using software kits and discs. Perhaps this success is also due to the fact that users find computers "more humane, more patient, and less critical than humans." (Bracey, 1982)

If there is more provision for computer use in the home and in the school, how can the computer phobic educator, or the non computer literate teacher gain the modicum of knowledge needed for students to comfortably engage in CAI materials? We can no longer afford the unfortunate (and too true) stories of computers in closets because a teacher does not feel competent or "computer literate" and therefore does not use the micros nor does he or she allow the students to do so.

Computer awareness is not like pregnancy; you CAN be a little computer literate! If you become familiar with some of the terms and can boot (turn on or engage the computer), reduce your anxiety around the machines and recognize some of the terminology, understand how computers affect our society and what problems can and can't be solved by computers, then you are well on your way to being initiated.

First, and foremost, educators must not allow themselves to be intimidated by an inability to "program." Using CAI materials and the ability to program are very different tasks and shouldn't be confused with one another. Aren't there many people who take terrific pictures without the least knowledge of or interest in developing negatives? Don't most of us enjoy movies without the ability to write or direct a script or process the fill? To extend the analogy further: everyone is literate on some levels and in some areas but fairly illiterate in others. A sentence in *Scientific American* reads "To understand the structure of any given schechtmanite alloy in terms of three dimensional Penrose tilings, one must devise a way of decorating or filling, the two rhombohedrons with atoms in such a way that an agglomeration of rhombohedrons would contain the correct proportion of atoms to crystals" (Nelson, 1986). To the physicist this may not seem obscure, to most of us it is barely intelligible. We have few of the literacy skills needed, i.e., either prior experience with the topic, or the specialized vocabulary and concepts necessary for comprehending the technical material. If we pick up a pharmacological journal, we will probably experience similar difficulty for the same reasons. So it is with computer literacy. Programmers are highly literate in computer and assembly languages; photographers are highly skilled at cropping and developing film and educators are comfortable and expert with the language of pedagogy or andragogy.

The teacher who can use the computer in the classroom to help students learn more effectively with appropriate software and courseware, who knows how to select these materials, is literate to some degree — enough not to be defensive about lacking programming ability. There is no need for that teacher to know how to program, anymore than she needs to know how the typesetter puts together the print to make a textbook (Wiener, 1984).

SOFTWARE

How can we know what's good and effective software? How can we evaluate these programs appropriately? What are some of the guidelines? Software has moved from an incidental business to a booming one ... totalling $13.14 billion dollars in 1981 and probably doubled by now (Pollock, 1981). There is so much available the educator needs assistance in selecting the good from the bad, the useful from the dreadful. Computer journals do an excellent job of evaluating new software each month, in each issue. The articles are written for the non computer expert, for the uninitiated or barely computer literate.

Can teachers evaluate CAI material for themselves? Why not? Most educators would not be uncomfortable if asked to select a new text. They would make a judgment based on readability, clarity, diagrams, pictures or graphs, and the suitability of content to student needs. They might also ascertain if the text had a table of contents, glossary, italics and/or bold print.

Should teachers look for the same things in software? Yes, but the mode of delivery and the terminology differs. (I'm convinced computers engineers and programmers created the language they did to mystify all outsiders.) First, one must define and clarify the five different types of CAI programs that are available. They are 1) tutorials, 2) drill and practice, 3) demonstrations, 4) simulations, and 5) instructional games.

Tutorials

These programs are similar to one-to-one instruction. The computer presents the information and asks a series of questions Socratic style. The student's response determines if additional information will be provided. If the program is well written it will BRANCH when an error is made. The branching provides additional information, teaching, or explanations and allows students a chance to try again after relearning.

Drill and Practice

Generally used to reinforce basic, discrete, and specific skills in math, spelling, and grammar. Although often denigrated, drill and practice software often takes the boredom out of certain routine tasks such as multiplication table reviews or splintered skills practice in reading.

Demonstrations

These are especially useful in math and science where hands on demonstrations are traditional. Students can manipulate one variable and watch the effect on other variables on the monitor. It is particularly helpful when danger is involved (corrosive, explosive or toxic substances, radiation or heat). It is also practical for genetic studies, population and demographic displays, economic and social predictions. Especially appropriate for the computer screen are the visual depictions and movements of planets, circulatory and nervous systems, ocean currents, atomic structures, chemical equations, and the food chain.

Simulations

Realistic situations are created for concepts that are frustratingly abstract to some students. This is not at all rote learning; on the contrary the students become involved in the learning process through alternative and decision-making strategies. In stimulation courseware a particular environment is designed, e.g., World War I, a food stand or an ecological environment. Students then vary inputs to see what can happen. They hypothesize and manipulate the variables to see how this can affect the situation and then immediately observe the outcome. (If they charge a higher price for the food, will they be competitive enough to get back their original investment? Will they make a profit?) Concept development and insights into cause and effect relationships are gained with this type of courseware. Water pollution studies, physical science problems, historical and social situations lend themselves to simulations.

Constructional Games
Games are not merely fun but they provide a clear set of rules which when followed result in the determination of the winner. This is an excellent motivational strategy especially for reluctant learners. Some educators, however, are uncomfortable with the use of games in teaching. Others believe it is an essential ingredient for all age groups and support Zamora (1982) who warns, "In the future . . . those of us who make a distinction between learning and recreation will not know much about either."

Courseware must be previewed to determine the CAI type and if that format will meet a particular classroom need. Some students need drill and practice with specific linguistic patterns; some do very well with tutorials which focus on literal comprehension.

Once it is determined that the program has potential for a particular educational environment then the next step is evaluation. The following checklist may prove helpful in covering at least four significant areas: program operation, program content, student outcomes, and educational/pedagogical concerns.

CHECKLIST

Program Operation
1. Is there good DOCUMENTATION? The documentation for CAI is equivalent to the teacher's manual. It should discuss the scope of the program and in a useful and readable form provide instructional information, descriptions of the objectives and the content and follow-up suggestions and activities. The type of management system should be described and there should be clear examples taken directly from the frames.

2. How are the users' (students) mistakes handled? Is branching built in for reteaching or explaining errors to the students? Can the students go back to one specific part of the program that is particularly troublesome or difficult or must they go through the entire program when there is an error?

3. Are the operating procedures available and clear?

4. Are there graphics? How well are color, sound and graphics used? Can sound be optional? Can it be turned off when a quiet environment is needed?

5. Is the frame display effective?

6. Is there good resolution? (Are the letters fuzzy or clear and distinct?)

Program Content
1. Is content suitable for your students?
2. Is it accurate?
3. Is it educationally significant?
4. Is the presentation clear and logical?
5. What VALUES are conveyed? Is aggressive behaviour encouraged? This area should be carefully examined, especially in instructional games. If graphics depict guns shooting down people or errors, punching out a wrong answer, etc. would you accept this in a print medium? If it is offensive in print and one doesn't wish to promulgate these values on a page in a book, then why accept it in a computer program? Additional areas to be alerted to include racism, sexism, and ethnocentrism, and ageism.

Student Outcomes
1. Can students operate the program easily and independently?
2. Will this program be interesting to your students? Will they enjoy using it? Is it self-motivating and rewarding? Will it enhance self-esteem as well as learning?
3. How well will students learn what the program intends to teach?
4. Are there any unintended and undesired learning outcomes?
5. How effective is the program compared with noncomputer material?
6. Can the student control rate, sequence, and directions?

Educational and Pedagogical Concerns
1. What types of reinforcement or feedback does the program provide?
2. Is the program passive, active or interactive?
3. Are graphics rewarding errors or correct responses? If graphics, after an incorrect response, are too interesting or funny then students are not too subtly rewarded and encouraged to make wrong responses. (It is better to respond with a print "No" or "wrong answer" than a graphic display for an error. Graphics should be saved for correct or learned responses.)
4. Is the courseware self-contained or is teacher assistance required?
5. Can the program be used individually or with small groups or the entire class?
6. Does the program tap different learning styles?
7. Is a management system built into the program? Are there separate paper and pencil record systems?
8. Are there tasks that follow up the program that can be done at one's desk away from the computer to integrate and extend learning?
9. Is the program designed primarily for remediation, enrichment, or diagnosis?
10. Is the program appropriate for special populations, i.e., bilingual, visually impaired, learning disabled, adults?

To complete initiation into the world of educational computing one must be knowledgeable of where to go for additional information. What is available? Where can one get data? Reviews? Assistance? There are now many avenues open to the interested educator or consumer of CAI materials. Educational agencies, governmental and private, abound, which provide tapes, films, summer training seminars, technology fairs and linkages with other state organizations. There are Users Groups that focus on their special interests groups (i.e., teachers, accountants, language buffs) which share discs, pitfalls of programs, activities, and special concerns. Computer stores and computer journals can provide the names and contact persons for these groups. Many of the computer journals are on the market that are not written for the technocrat or computer scientist but are designed for and speak to the educator and classroom teacher. These include: Electronic Learning; T.H.E. (Technical Horizons in Education); Teaching and Computing; Computers, Reading and Language Arts; and Classroom Computer News. Software clearinghouses seem to be very helpful and the addresses and contact persons are listed in the computer journals. The publishing house of McGraw Hill has an excellent film for rent or sale called *Don't Bother Me I'm Learning* which shows computer use in various school and community settings, with a delightful section devoted to senior citizens and their initial fear and later joy using computers. Some unusual, witty, and very helpful books have recently been published that can entice the uninitiated on an intellectual, humorous, or self-help level. A list and precis of some exceptional books can be found at the end of this chapter.

To summarize, four areas should guide evaluation: the program itself, one's own teaching goals, the students' needs and sound educational principles. One should not feel too badly if a compromise has to be made, however. There have been times when a textbook or tradebook is selected because it was better than the alternatives, but wasn't perfect. Obviously, good judgment is important. If in previewing a CAI program on W.W.II one finds it omits the mention of Nazis it will be found lacking in content and won't be purchased. On the other hand, if the chart on DNA is not in color, it might be selected because it meets other criteria and the lack of color does not seem to significantly compromise learning or the program.

The computer, for many of us, will be most useful as a tool. Without the use of a word processor it would take this author and other writers hours, if not weeks, longer to compose and edit our work. For many students the friendly, ever so patient and non-threatening computer allows for the learning of tedious and difficult concepts. For some the computer is motivating. It does not reek of past failures and it seems adult and advanced to sit at a monitor and work at a task — no matter how simple or complex. If self enhancement and self actualization are truly the goals of education, the computer can be useful. When used as a tool, a sophisticated typewriter or an interactive and dynamic textbook, as in Computer Assisted Instruction, computers provide a motivating alternative means of learning.

There are few who will use computers or interact with them in ways that will allow them to "think about thinking" as Papert (1980) envisioned. But if teachers take computers out of the closet and allow students to use them to problem solve, learn decision-making strategies, move from basic to critical thinking skills, and turn on to learning and literacy then I think they are worth learning about. Of course, computers are not a panacea, but it does seem that teachers and educators who know something about computers, not necessarily how to program, but how to use them effectively, how to evaluate available commercial programs, how to distinguish a good program from a poor one, how to use CAI creatively and appropriately will be able to help learners more than those who are uninitiated and computer illiterate.

REFERENCES

Becker, H. (1985). "How Schools Use Microcomputers: Results from a National Survey", *Children and Microcomputers*. Chen & Paisley (eds.). Sage Publications, Beverly Hills, pp. 87–108.

Bracey, G. (1982). "Computers in Education: What Research Shows", *Electronic Learning*, Vol. 2 (3), pp. 51–55.

Buckley, E. (1983). "CAI for ABE Students", Unpublished manuscript.

Caldwell, R (1980). "A Comparison of Using Computer-based Education to Teach Literacy and Numeracy Skills from Programs of Adult Basic Education", (Report No. CE-026-862). Boston, Mass: American Educational Research Association (ERIC Document Reproduction Service No. ED 194 721).

Carver, R. and Hoffman, J. (1981). "The Effects of Using a Computer Based Instructional System", *Reading Research Quarterly*, Vol 16 (3), pp. 374–390.

Center for Social Organizations of Schools, School Uses for Microcomputers, Report from *National Survey*, Issue No. 3, Johns Hopkins University, Baltimore, April 1983.

Chen, Mi Hon (1986). "Gender and Computers: The Beneficial Effects of Experience on Attitudes", *Journal of Educational Computer Research*, Vol. 2 (3), pp. 265–283.

Eccles, Jacquelynne S. (1986). "Gender Roles of Women's Achievement", *Educational Researcher*, Vol. 15 (6), pp. 15–19.

Linn, M. C. (1984). *Fostering Equitable Consequences from Computer Learning Environments*. University of California, Berkeley.

McGinty, Tony (1985). "Making the Home School Connection", *Electronic Learning*, Vol. 5(3), p. 31.

Nelson, David R. (1986). "Quasicrystals", *Scientific American*, Vol. 225 (2), pp. 42–52.

Papert, S. (1980). *Mindstorms, Children, Computers and Powerful Ideas*. New York: Basic Books.

Pollack, A. (1981). "Computers: The Actions in Software", *New York Times*, Sec. 3, p. 1.

Schwartz, H. (1980). *Teaching Stylistic Simplicity with a Computerized Reading Formula*. Michigan: Oakland University.

Solomon, Gwen (1985). "Writing with Computers", *Electronic Learning*, Vol. 5(3), p. 39.

Vockell, E. (1985). "Computer Literacy for Educators: An Applied Programming Approach", *The Seminar*, (newsletter) Macmillan Publishing, Vol. 1, p. 6.

Wiener, Roberta B. (1985). "Evaluating Software: A Guide for the Uninitiated", *Lifelong Learning*. Vol. 7 (7), p. 16.

CHAPTER 4:

Life Skills

D. Stuart Conger
Sharon E. Cameron

Life Skills training has become an integral and prominent component of adult basic education in Canada. The first course in Life Skills was developed in Saskatchewan about 1970. Since that time life skills courses have been taught in all regions of this country (as well as in several others), and in a great variety of personal and social developmental programs. Life skills training is dedicated to the development within the individual of appropriate self-management skills and, in this way is very much in keeping with the philosophical basis of adult education in a free society.

Life skills are the appropriate and responsible utilization of problem solving behaviours in the management of one's life. The assumptions and values underlying this definition are that many people who engage in self-defeating behaviours in their personal, social, vocational, educational and community lives flounder because they lack the skills that characterize competence in these domains. They are not viewed as sick or under-developed but simply as currently lacking the competence and, uncertain about how to acquire it, or apprehensive about managing their own lives. The life skills problem-solving behaviours include a relatively small number of skills usable in many life situations. Appropriate use requires an individual to adapt the behaviours to time and place. Responsible use requires maturity or accountability. As behaviours used in the management of personal affairs, the life skills apply to five areas of life responsibility: self, family, community, use of leisure time, and work.

THE LIFE SKILLS COURSE

The development of the original Life Skills Coaching Manual (Himsl, 1973) commenced in 1969 and was completed in 1973, following three generational changes. The design has been generally followed in subsequent specialized courses of Life Skills addressed to women, to youth, to refugees and other disadvantaged immigrants, to inmates of penal institutions, and to other special needs populations.

The Life Skills course recognizes that true learning (behavioural change) occurs when the learner has: (1) a clear understanding of his/her goals, (2) a clear description of the new behaviours, and (3) an understanding of those conditions which make the behaviours acceptable. The concept of these new sought-for behaviours as skills makes a happy fit with the recognition of "learning as changed behaviours".

Philosophical Foundations

In the initial planning of the Life Skills course the developers found it necessary to determine what they considered to be the appropriate philosophical model for the program. The Saskatchewan Life Skills program represented a mix of 'process' models rather than 'product' models which were articulated by Melling(1980):

1. Process Models:

The Experimental Model calls for open-ended learner activities incorporating a range of skill and knowledge demands.

The Reflective Model develops the student's ability to perceive data and relationships in alternative ways, make and check generalizations, and develop conceptual frameworks.

The Counselling Model recognizes the importance of the affective domain which helps students reflect on experiences, to increase understanding and control of his/her own behaviours and feelings; as well as others; to distinguish between emotional and cognitive elements in such matters as decision-making.

2. Product Models
Historical start-up

Winthrop Adkins and Syndey Rosenberg originally described the outline for Life Skills lesson plans in a proposed training program for disadvantaged youth in New York city. Project TRY - (Training Resources for Youth) was not continued so the authors did not prepare an actual course on Life Skills.

The Saskatchewan NewStart course, field-tested in the winter of 1969, concentrated on human relations skills. The adult learners did establish better relations and communications with personnel in the training centre and in their own homes. However, the learners' other problems still remained as they had before enrollment. For this reason it was decided that the course must be rewritten to include other skills required for life.

Adkins and Rosenberg (1969) helped the 'NewStart' developers to understand more completely the theory they had articulated, and to critique the draft lesson plans. A final element was added to develop a five stage lesson plan, as follows; stimulus, evocation, objective inquiry/skill practice, application, and evaluation. The skill practice activity ensured the students had ample opportunity to practice their new skills in the classroom.

By 1972 Saskatchewan NewStart was largely satisfied with the training curriculum that it had prepared and undertook an extensive dissemination program throughout Canada and to some extent in the United States.

Learning Theory

Moore and Anderson (1969) outlined four characteristics necessary to enhance adult learning environments. These were as follows: Perspectives Flexibility; Autotelic Flexibility; Productive Flexibility; Personalization Potential.

Perspective flexibility takes place in an environment which . . . "both permits and facilitates the taking of more perspectives toward whatever is to be learned,". . . with all four characteristics actively present.

Autotelic flexibility is necessary to protect learners against the serious consequences of taking psychological and social risks while working in the group, through developing a safe learning environment where they can try things out, without fear.

Productive flexibility uses material which "frees the learner to reason things out for himself and . . . from depending on authority". (Moore and Anderson, 1969).

Personalization potential refers to learning environments which are: a) . . . "more responsive to the learners activities; b) permits and facilitates the learner's taking a more reflexive view of himself as a learner." (Moore and Anderson, 1969).

Counselling Theory

Life Skills training may be viewed as a form of structured group counselling or as an educative approach to counselling. Furthermore the students needed to learn the same skills that counselors use, such as: attending behaviours (Ivey, 1971), non-verbal cues, body posture, paraphrasing, and reflection of feeling; also the counselor's relationship skills (Carkhuff 1969) of empathy, confrontation, genuineness, and respect among others.

It also reflected the use of interventionist models such as Reality Therapy and Transactional Analysis. During the Life Skills developmental period the War on Poverty focused its attention on the "culture of poverty" and the inappropriateness of non-directive counselling for the poor. The Life Skills model incorporated innovative counselling methods designed to help people learn personal and social competencies so that they could enter the middle class.

The Process Dimensions

Life Skills training integrates three process dimensions: (1) student response to content, (2) student use of group, and (3) problem solving.

1. The Student Response to Content Dimension

In responding to this dimension, the student may react first in any one of its three domains: (1) the cognitive, (2) the affective, or (3) the psychomotor. When he or she reacts in the cognitive or knowing domain, this might include rephrasing a sentence in one's own words, summarizing the happenings of the lesson, or combining the rather simple act of recalling with the more complex act of synthesizings. Or s/he might relate the discussion in a lesson to an experience in home life, thereby contrasting and comparing; or linking the items in one lesson to those of another, thereby showing relationships. Any manipulation of course content, such as representation or recall, explanation, analysis, application, synthesis or evaluation represents a cognitive or knowing response.

Students also respond on this dimension with affect or feeling. The affective response may occur before, at the same time, or after the cognitive or knowing response. Life Skills training recognizes the affective reaction and encourages its expression and control. At the worst, unexpressed or suppressed feelings inhibit the development of behavioural change and prevent the student from facing him/herself and others.

At the best, expressed feelings can open the student to new understandings of those around and help the learner recognize that others have the same fears and uncertainties. Yet they manage to function. Furthermore, the student soon comes to the realization that the mere expression of feelings often assists in controlling them. At one extreme, s/he may blurt out that some things look stupid, reject lessons, or participate passively. At the other extreme, s/he may speak loyally of the group and the activities of the lessons, may defend the activities of the course and the group against outside criticism and enthusiastically tell others what s/he has learned. Though such expressions of feelings and attitude demand a great deal of the coach, s/he responds quickly to them, helping the members of the group accept their own feelings and those of others.

When the student responds in the third category of behaviours, the psychomotor or acting category, the learner uses his/her new skills by conducting interviews, demonstrating new behaviours to others, or participating in role playing situations. These responses often provide the most obvious evidence of the learner's full participation in the activities of the lesson. Cognitive, or knowing manipulation of the content provides the student with a necessary "factual" base: the learner's affective, or feeling, response to content expresses one's will to face the consequences of the new knowledge and its effect on oneself. Psychomotor response represents commitment to action.

Clarification of these three dimensions of education were articulated by Bloom (1956) and others in widely respected taxonomies of educational objectives. Counselling theory incorporated three dimensions to develop the learners behavioural, attitudinal and cognitive repertoire. (see also Krathwohl, Bloom and Masia, 1964).

2. The Student Use of Group Dimension

The second dimension describes the purpose of the learning group. The student uses the group in the following four ways: practices new behaviours; uses feedback and criticism from the group, to modify new behaviours; studies individuals in the group as models for new behaviours; uses the group setting to develop skills of self-expression. The group affects its members most when they have developed a strong sense of mutual trust and an interest in helping one another through the lessons. The group seeks to provide an essential balance between acceptance and challenge. All acceptance stunts improvement in skills and development of problem-solving capabilities: all challenge makes people react defensively and become more set in ineffective behaviours.

There are three levels of activity in the learning group: safe group use; careful group use; risky group use. Each level is built one upon another in this order.

Students respond at three distinct levels on this dimension:

1. The student continues interpersonal behaviours which in the past have met his/her needs; such as withdrawing, bullying, or harmonizing activities. ('safe group use')
2. At the level of careful group use, the student ventures into practicing new behaviours modelling those of the coach and other group members. Initially, seeking support and acknowledgment for those new behaviours from other group members; eventually trying the behaviours with strangers.

3. At the level of risky group use, the learner asks directly for criticism, using it to refine and make the new behaviours more effective; begins to give feedback to others; ventures opinions which may be startling to other members; expresses strong feelings; or objects to some procedures the coach has used. These group activities extend the range and increase the effectiveness of the student's interpersonal skills.

The autoletic flexibility (or safe learning environment) enables the student to use the group, at all three activity levels, to practice newly learned skills. Also, the more effective learner uses all the responses named in the "response to content dimension", and more of the behavioural categories named in the "use of group" dimension.

3. The Problem-Solving Dimension

The learner could use both of the content group dimensions to their fullest, and still achieve none of the objectives of the Life Skills course. The complete Life Skills process/content model requires a third dimension. The Life Skill student uses a whole array of problem-solving behaviours: 1) recognizes a problem situation, 2) defines a problem, 3) chooses an alternative solution, 4) implements it, 5) evaluates the result.

As the student matures in the course, the array of problem solving behaviours increases until, ideally, the participant uses them as the situation requires. This array of behaviour provides the third dimension.

The need for this dimension became apparent after follow up studies of graduates of the early courses revealed that while their human relations skills had improved they were still encountering and creating many of the same problems that they had before. Therefore some form of problem solving process must be taught - not only as a topic but also embedded in every lesson, and in the developing process of the course, to reinforce the application of the problem-solving method to everyday living situations.

APPLICATION IN ABE

Youth

In 1984, the Futures/Youth Start Program was developed and placed in Community Colleges by the Ontario Ministry of Skills Development during the Year of Youth.

The Futures Pre-Employment Program (PEP) is mandated to meet the educational and career planning needs of youth 14-24 years of age who have dropped out of school and/or left home, or who are not succeeding in the regular school system. The course is comprised of a large life skills component, academic upgrading (mathematics, communications), computer literacy, career planning (includes interest and aptitude tests), and work placement components. Students attend for 16 weeks on a full time basis during which the development of self-awareness and self-confidence are stressed to enable the individuals to develop a realistic picture of themselves as persons, as well as their skills and abilities in the area of employment. The provision of reliable information about resources helps the students to support themselves more effectively emotionally and financially in the community.

Following the in-class portion of the program students may choose to complete a full time work placement in the community, up to 52 weeks in duration. Three work placements of four months each are organized, based on the students' occupational goals and needs for supportive employment.

The Futures Program addresses the issues of: youth employment (dealing with a surplus of unemployed young people); re-directing of young people back into the workforce; acquisition of effective coping skills needed for responsible citizenship; and the development of effective and appropriate skills and resources to enable young people to participate more fully in the adult society of today.

Natives and Life Skills

Fifty percent of the learners enrolled in the courses conducted by Saskatchewan NewStart were Natives and as a consequence the course had to serve their needs as well as meet the needs of the non-Indian students. Markus (1974) wrote a Life Skills program specifically for Natives living on rather isolated reserves. Currently courses are being offered in such places as the Regina Plains Community College, but no package of lesson plans has as yet derived from these programs.

Native students in the Saskatchewan NewStart Program generally considered Life Skills training as a course in coping successfully in a second culture, with which they had to come to terms. Approximately one half of the Life Skills coaches were Natives and some eventually took leadership roles in the growingNative Movements of western Canada.

Presently in Ontario, Native Life Skills groups are offered on reserves or in Native communities in Northern and South Western Ontario, generally during the winter months, and on an as-needed basis in urban community colleges. Native students continue to attend life skills programs to enhance their adjustment to urban life. The northern groups focus on the needs and issues which arise in coping with life in isolated northern communities or on reserves.

One important aspect has been the development of training programs for Native addictions counsellors based on the life skills philosophy and incorporating the life skills coach training model in the counselling program. Native coaches are being trained on an on-going basis (in such centres as Sudbury, Elliott Lake, London and others) through courses given by Native coaches and educators.

Women

The development of special interest group Life Skills Courses has been most completely undertaken for women, with funding from the Counselling Foundation of Canada, and the Ontario Ministry of Community and Social Services.

The Metropolitan Toronto YWCA implemented the Life Skills course for women initially in a variety of low rental housing projects, and subsequently in correctional institutions, mental health centres, and for sole support mothers on social assistance, older women on social assistance, ex-psychiatric women, high risk women, and women who are physically handicapped, in pre-employment programs, and re-entering the labour market. As a result Life Skills manuals were developed: Discovering Life Skills for Women (Volume 1&2).

Subsequent books dealt with additional areas such as values clarification, assertiveness training, and handling anger. By this time the YW was also working with ex-psychiatric patients and material on self-esteem, loneliness and stress management was developed to meet their needs.

The YWCA's Life Skills program expanded to include pre-employment women, young adults on probation and parole, and physically disabled women.

The YWCA team undertook a multicultural program in which it endeavored to make its programs and services more available to women from other cultures and to sensitize the staff of the YWCA to their needs. As part of this project the Life Skills manuals were revised to eliminate cultural bias and a section of multicultural lessons was added to *Volume II of Discovering Life Skills with Women*.

Finally, work with these students indicated a need for simpler, more specific materials to use with these groups. *Discovering Life Skills with Special Needs Groups* (Volume 4) was written.

Basic Job Readiness Training

The original Life Skills program in ABE, in Ontario, was Basic Job Readiness Training (BJRT), (began in 1975 at Durham, Loyalist, & George Brown Colleges), which saw the first application of the Saskatchewan NewStart Life Skills technology in Ontario. The program was designed to meet the literacy and pre-employment needs of chronically unemployed adults. Indeed, BJRT is the model on which the following ABE Life Skills programs were based: Basic Employment Training; Focus For Change; Rehabilitation Through Education; Training The Handicapped Adult in Transition; Headstart For the   Hearing Impaired.

During the twelve week course some issues addressed are: personal growth through the increase of self-awareness and self-esteem; the development of the individual's skills through direct skills teaching and group practice in a low risk environment; the development of a "support network" among the students to provide encouragement to remain in the program through the development of mutual respect and trust; awareness of personal skills and abilities which can be transferred from the home to the work environment; the development of an image of "employee" where none existed or was incomplete before.

These students are hampered by a "failure" image developed over years of fragmented work experience resulting from psychiatric difficulties, incarceration, medical problems, low education levels, developmental delays, arrival unprepared for life in a new country and society, years of isolated child rearing at home, involuntary lay-offs, business failures and many other factors.

The BJRT program components are Life Skills (60%), academic upgrading (30%), career planning and work placement (10%). (Algonquin College, course outlines 1988). The course specifically addresses attitudes toward employment, employer expectations and needed behavioural changes necessary to enable students to become permanently employed. Techniques used include "direct skills" teaching and group practice, job search techniques, community resource exploration, and transferability of skills from one occupation to another. Students are taught problem-solving behaviours applied to develop realistic concrete plans regarding education, skill training, on the job training programs and setting occupational goals. Career planning narrows the occupational choices to about three possibilities or areas of interest.

The work placement component allows the student to experience the work environment and assess his/her own abilities and limitations with respect to these types of jobs. Students practice job search techniques through locating their own work placements and attending interviews in order to finalize the arrangements.

A training allowance is provided (through CEIC) to establish a financial basis for those students who are supporting themselves or to help support their families. The program is open to men and women participants, (18 years of age and older) who read at grade six level or higher, who have experienced continuing difficulty in obtaining employment and in maintaining steady employment. (Algonquin College, course outlines, 1988).

Basic Employment Training

Basic Employment Training (George Brown, Mohawk, Northern, & St. Clair Colleges, 1980) is a program designed for adult students, (18 years of age or older) who read at less than the grade six level. It is 26 weeks in duration and three work placement sessions are included. The program components are literacy and numeracy (60%), Life Skills and career planning (30%), and work placement (10%). (Algonquin College, course outlines, 1988).

In BET the primary focus is on literacy skills which will enable the students to attain a functional literacy level, often the main barrier to participation in society, and the work force specifically, for these individuals.

The main intent of the program is to prepare students for entry level employment opportunities. There is less emphasis on further educational upgrading or skills training. The experiential learning model is effective in teaching productive coping strategies through role-play, modeling, direct skills teaching and group practice, all of which work regardless of low reading levels to ensure increases in skill functioning.

Focus For Change

Simultaneously, the Canada Employment and Immigration Commission (CEIC) recognized the need for programs which would facilitate the entry of women into the labour market. In Ontario 16 week programs such as Focus for Change (Mohawk College, 1978) were developed which address the specific concerns of women returning to or entering the labour force such as day care, financial support, poorly defined employment goals, low self-confidence, lack of employment opportunities and information, and low education levels. Special consideration was given to the needs of single mothers or women in low-income situations. The program design ensured the development of a community-based environment in which these students could learn and grow effectively and safely.

These women must also receive support and guidance in handling the challenges on the homefront, such as organization of personal time, and the work-load at home, negotiating study time with family members, acquiring reliable day care/baby sitting services (if applicable), compromising the values of a homemaker and housekeeper with those of student and employee.

Special Needs Groups

Adult educators responded to the concern regarding the education and employment of special needs groups through the development of programs to meet their specific needs.

Rehabilitation Through Education (1973) now Redirection Through Education, George Brown College was developed to provide life skills programming to ex-psychiatric clients in the community. This program includes the life skills, academic upgrading components in conjunction with career exploration and work experience. In one program students work, in their own "tea room" restaurant where they receive hands-on work experience in the operation of a small business. During the program students are helped to develop realistic employment goals and plan the steps to reach these goals. (RTE Report, 1981).

The focus of the program is to enable post-psychiatric patients to learn new coping behaviours which will result in increased community tenure (fewer and shorter periods of hospitalization). Participation in an adult education program allows the development of a new positive image as a student to replace the old negative image of a patient. Also students benefit greatly from participation in the educational milieu as full-fledged members of the adult learning community.

A second special needs group whose education and employment concerns are addressed through specific programming is the physically disabled student. *Training The Handicapped Adult in Transition* (THAT, 1980, Mohawk College) began during the Year of the Disabled, as a full time life skills program whose curriculum directly addressed the problems and resource needs of physically disabled adults entering the work force or life in the community. Emphasis is placed on the skill development of students, and the resource development of adapted learning tools in the classroom (i.e. computer terminals, Bliss boards, adjustable work tables), as well as technical aids for use in the work place. Special topics discussed are reactions to disabled workers in the work environment, management of personal income (possibly for the first time), use of community based transportation systems, use of technical aids in the work place, and coping with "normal" employees. The development of realistic education and training goals emphasizes an awareness of students' personal abilities and limitations as factors in developing attainable occupational goals.

Recently, *Headstart for the Hearing Impaired* (Fanshawe 1984, Algonquin 1986, George Brown 1977) was developed to meet the education and employment needs of hearing impaired and deaf adults. These special needs students are among the most frequently underemployed workers in our society. Also a large number of these students do not complete secondary education beyond the grade 10 level. They face unique problems in coping with the "hearing world", the greatest of which is lack of commuication with the hearing population and all the social norms which form part of participation in community life, or making use of community-based resources which might be able to meet their needs.

Again, the life skills, academic and career planning components help these students to understand the work place and employer expectations, to determine realistic occupational goals and hopefully to increase their participation in the life of the community.

Many of these special needs students continue to participate in regular life skills programs, as well. However, these specialized programs help them meet their unique needs for learning new coping skills directly related to their skill deficits and provide coping strategies which help equalize their learning and working potential in the community.

CONCLUSION

In conclusion, the Life Skills programs offered through adult education departments stress greater participation in the community and in the work force, for adult learners. There is an emphasis on upgrading academic of literacy skills to decrease barriers to employment and use of community resources. The experimential learning techniques which include direct skills teaching and group practice, roleplay, and modeling result in improved coping skills, interpersonal relationships, changed behaviours and attitudes. The techniques support the development of concrete and realistic plans for attainable occupational goals. Students report increased self-awareness and self-confidence of themselves and knowledge of their abilities and potential. For many, increased community tenure is an additional benefit. Improved problem-solving behaviours are reflected in the areas of success for students.

The initial development of the Life Skills course took place within an ABE environment. Saskatchewan NewStart had been created to develop new methods of training and counselling adults who were disadvantaged as to their educational/employment attainment. It focused on the creation of new methods and materials of literacy and upgrading but saw Life Skills as an essential component of an ABE program.

The regulations of the then Canada Manpower Training Program required that students apply themselves full time at academic studies until they had acquired the academic credits to enter occupational training. Saskatchewan NewStart, with its freedom to experiment, developed individualized academic upgrading programs which the students studied for half-days, the remainder devoted to Life Skills training. A comparison of the two programs found that the NewStart students progressed as quickly as the other students.

REFERENCES

Adkins, Winthrop, and Rosenberg, Sydney, (1966). *Training Resources for Youth*, Bedford-Stuyvesant, YMCA.

Alberta Education, (1986). Career and Life Management, Curriculum Guide.

Algonquin College, (1988) Basic Job Readiness Training, Basic Employment Training, Focus For Change, Headstart for the Hearing Impaired, Course Descriptions and Eligibility Brochures, documents available from Algonquin College, Ottawa, Ontario.

Bennett, et al., (1976). *Discovering Life Skills With Women*, Volume I Toronto, YWCA, 274 pages.

Bloom, B. S., (Ed.), (1956). *Taxonomy of Educational Objectives: Cognitive Domain*, New York, McKay.

Carkhuff, R. (1969). *Helping and Human Relations*, (Vols 1 and 2) New York, Holt, Rinehart and Winston.

George Brown College, Rehabilitation Through Education, Course Description and Eligibility Brochures, George Brown College, Toronto, Ontario, (RTE Report) (1981).

Gryba, Eugene S., (1974). *Life Skills for Northern Adolescents*, Prince Albert, Training Research and Development Station, 427 pp.

Himsl, Ralph, (1973). Life Skills Coaching Manual, 580 pp.

Ivey, A. (1971). *Microcounselling: Innovations in Interviewing Training*, Springfield, Thomas.

Krathwohl, D.R., Bloom, B.S. and Masia, B. B. (1964). *Taxonomy of Education Objectives: Affective Domain*, New York, McKay.

Markus, Hank, et al., (1974) *Life skills for Northern Saskatchewan*, Laronge, Department of Northern Saskatchewan.

Melling, Geoffrey, (1980). *Developing Social and Life Skills*. London, Further Education Curriculum Review and Development Unit, Secretary of State for Education and Science.

Ministry of Colleges and Universities, Queen's Park, Mowat Block, Program Records, Toronto, Ontario.

Mohawk College, (1985) Training the Handicapped Adult in Transition, (THAT) Course Brochures and Faculty Interviews, (documents available from) Mohawk College, Hamilton, Ontario.

Moore, O.K., and Anderson, A.R., "Some principles for the design of clarifying educational environments"; in Goslin, D. A. (ed.) *Handbook of Socialization Theory and Research*, N.Y.: Rand McNally. 1969, 571-613.

CHAPTER 5

The Role of Literacy in Methods of Teaching English as a Second Language

Ḅarbara Burnaby
Jill Bell

Is English' as a second language (ESL) teaching to adults really adult basic education (ABE)? ESL teaching in Canada to adults *is* basic education in that most ESL learners urgently need English language skills as a basis for critical aspects of their participation in the communities in which they are living.

Although some learners are Francophones or Native Canadians, the majority are non-English-speaking immigrants. In most cases, these learners have moved from non-English-speaking communities in which they were able to live and work well as skilled and active members of society. By moving to an English-speaking community in Canada, they have placed themselves in a situation in which their participation in most aspects of community life is restricted by their lack of proficiency in the predominant language of communication. What they need is a knowledge of English — oral and written — to permit them to get beyond the language barrier and to re-establish their normal adult lives.

The main position taken in this paper, however, is that ESL for most learners is essentially *different* from adult basic education for English-speaking Canadians in that ESL learners need to learn basic and advanced English language skills and cultural information about how English language and literacy operate in Anglophone Canada but *not* basic literacy and life skills *per se*. While they must learn some cultural information about the way oral language and literacy operate in (English) Canada, it is generally the case that they already have sophisticated life skills strategies and literacy skills many of which they can readily transfer to the (English) Canadian context. However, some ESL learners also lack skills in the areas of literacy in any language and/or have difficulty integrating themselves into the cultural patterns of urban, North American, industrialized societies. Many of the latter need help of the type that adult basic education offers, and more, since they do not speak the language of community communication either.

It is argued here that such learners need a special combination of adult basic education and ESL learning. This paper is organized so as to discuss first the characteristics and needs of the majority, well-educated ESL population along with the methods normally used to teach them. Following that, the characteristics and needs of those ESL learners who have special problems with respect to literacy in English will be considered.

ESL FOR THE MAJORITY OF NON-ENGLISH-SPEAKING LEARNERS

As basic as English language learning needs might be in the lives of ESL learners, it was pointed out above that the majority of them cannot be approached in education programs in the same way as English-speaking Canadian candidates for adult basic adult education in that most of the former are well educated, literate, and skilled in viable occupations. As a clumsy but interesting measure of the relationship between the literacy and life skills needs of the ESL learner population and those of the English-speaking ABE population, the following table shows education levels of the total Ontario population taken from the 1981 Census (Bourne et al, 1985: Tables 3 and 7). It concerns the population fifteen years or older and out of school with respect to the level of their highest education attainment, analysed on the basis of those who were born in Canada and those who were not. Figures represent rounded percentages of total on each column.

Ontario Population 15 Plus, Not in School, by Birthplace

Education	Total	Canada	Outside
Less than Grade 5	3.6	1.9	7.8
Grades 5 to 8	13.8	12	18.3
Grades 9 & 10	15.8	17.8	10.7
Grades 11–13	30	32.4	25.2
Post-secondary	19.4	19.1	20.3
University	16.8	16.6	17.6

Note that while immigrants are more strongly represented at the low end of the educational attainment scale they are also stronger at the high end as well. While British and French ethnic origin immigrants represent a significant proportion of this population, their educational distribution is not different enough from those with non-English-speaking countries to skew the data to a great extent. Portuguese immigrants represent the greatest percentages of their population at the lowest levels of education and Indo-Pakistani at the highest.

The key concept in understanding the difference between adult basic education and ESL is that of transfer. Learners can be expected to transfer skills and knowledge from one context to another. In the case of educated ESL learners, it can be expected that they will transfer to their English language learning in Anglophone Canada a great deal of what they already know about oral language communication, literacy, and life skills, as well as transferring to the ESL classroom what they know about how to learn in formal educational situations.

What they need to learn, then, is the particulars of English language vocabulary, grammatical patterns, idioms, specifically English-Canadian cultural patterns in the use of language and literacy, and other cultural information about life in Anglophone Canadian society. What they do not need to be taught is how language and literacy generally work.

Teaching ESL to most non-English-speaking adults is, therefore, unlike teaching language or literacy skills to people who speak the target language as a mother tongue. Most native speakers of English have learned most of the grammar, vocabulary, and basic cultural patterns or oral and written English language use before they are ten years old and take them for granted in their daily lives. At ten years old they may not yet be sophisticated users of specialized vocabulary or knowledgeable about the more complex facets of specialized literacy use, but normal English-speaking Canadian pre-adolescents are experienced speakers of an almost adult level of English grammar and are in command of a large oral and written vocabulary. Native English-speaking learners in adult basic education bring with them to the classroom mature knowledge of English grammar, vocabulary, and social patterns of language use. They may not speak a standard dialect or have confidence in using the language in ways which more educated speakers use it, but they have a substantial, implicit understanding of how the system works.

As examples of aspects of English which most ESL learners need to acquire but which native speakers know well, the following details are given. The difference between a 'jar' and a 'bottle' is that a bottle is generally taller and thinner and usually holds more liquid than solid contents. The difference between 'Mrs.' and 'Miss' relates to marital status, but the use of 'Ms.' as unmarked for marital status has sensitive cultural connotations related to changing gender roles in Canadian society. 'Get up' usually means to get out of bed and 'get over' means to recover from an illness or problem. In clauses which have two verbs, after verbs such as 'hope' the infinitive 'to . . .' (hope to go) is used, but after verbs such as 'enjoy' the gerund '. . . ing' (enjoy going) is used. English distinguishes between nouns which normally take plurals (two apples) and those which do not (water). English speakers use standard comparisons such as 'pretty as a picture' as opposed to standard expressions in other languages such as 'pretty as a heart' in French.

In Canada it is now somewhat old-fashioned to send a thank-you letter to a hostess or a gift giver since we use the telephone so much, but thank-you letters for the most formal occasions such as wedding gifts are still expected. In western countries, peoples' names are written with the surname last. Titles (Mr., Ms., etc.) are only used with the surname (i.e. 'Mrs. Mary' is not usually used). In Canada when one is invited to dinner, one is expected to arrive within about a half an hour of the time given: arriving early or more than half an hour late is not usually appreciated.

These examples are given because they typify the kinds of learning content that ESL learners say they need. Basic grammar and vocabulary are critically important and learners want explanations and examples of how Canadians use language in all sorts of everyday relationships. It is expected that such learning will help them to attain a status in Canadian society comparable to that which they held before in other cultures. By contrast, adult basic education learners who are native English-speaking Canadians are in total command of the language points illustrated here, and they have usually had more than enough explanations and examples of how educated Canadians behave. What they generally want is the literacy and basic 'schooling' tools to gain the power to control the status they want in their own society.

In sum, then, the content and context for most ESL learning is different from that for Canadian ABE learners. In ESL, the content focus is on the extensive area of English language learning which most native speakers of English have mastered early in life. It also concerns sociolinguistic and cultural information which people from one culture must learn when they are beginning life in another culture. Further, most ESL learners can be expected to be experienced in learning in formal educational settings and to have the knowledge and skills that are generally assumed to be the result of elementary and, even, secondary schooling. Canadian English-speaking ABE learners, on the other hand, need a focus on developing their role as learners in whatever situation will facilitate their learning, and they need to work on literacy and other kinds of content usually provided in elementary and secondary education. Basic English grammar and vocabulary patterns, of the sort illustrated above, are not a problem for them.

ESL Methodology

Second language teaching has a long history and a vast academic and practically-oriented literature. A paper of this length and in this context is not a suitable forum for a discussion of the field in all its linguistic and social facets. The accompanying bibliography gives references to current theoretical and practical works which can provide initial access to the field. Here, we will give a brief overview of trends in second language teaching in Canada in this century, highlighting the approach currently accepted most widely. It must be kept in mind that the following descriptions are broad generalizations, and that there has been and continues to be a great deal of eclectic use of the approaches sketched here.

In the early part of this century, the prevalent approach to second language teaching was what we now call 'grammar-translation'. In other words, teaching was mainly through the medium of the language of the learner with an emphasis on learning the rules of grammar of the language to be learned. Grammar rules and vocabulary lists were introduced in the learners' first language, and practice was mainly provided through written exercises and reading of written passages. Detailed analysis of written texts in the target language was also used. The teacher controlled the agenda and the class activities.

For various reasons, after the Second World War the approach to second language teaching changed focus on the learning of oral language', sometimes almost to the exclusion of written language. The language of instruction was more often the target language rather than the mother tongue of the learners. Learners were drilled in patterns of sentences in the second language until these patterns became automatic oral habits. Curricula based on contrasts between the grammar of the learners' first language and that of the second were sometimes used where a student group was all from the same first language background. Grammar rules would not necessarily be indicated explicitly by the teacher, but they would form the backbone of the curriculum — arranged from simple to more complex structures from a grammatical point of view. The content and activities of such classes were generally teacher directed.

Since the early 1970's, another focus has gained the ascendency in second language teaching. This approach, called the 'communicative approach', assumes that learners need to be exposed to learning opportunities which match their communicative needs and that they can be expected to transfer literacy and spoken language skills from their first language to their communication in the second language. One effect of this approach is needs-based curricula in which the learners' actual short and long term communicative needs are taken into account. A second effect is that vocabulary and grammar teaching are combined with teaching about how sentences are put together in oral and written discourse to make coherent text suitable for real and communicative purposes. A third effect is that culturally sensitive communicative situations, such as changing the date of an appointment or making an excuse, form the core of the curriculum rather than grammar points such as the use of the indefinite article. Finally, depending on the literacy skills of the members of the class, literacy is usually addressed early in the program, and the specific uses of literacy in the target society are explored in comparison with uses of literacy which might be the norm in the home communities of the learners.

In a class based on the communicative approach, one might find the teacher introducing a communicative situation such as explaining why one was absent from some event. Some activity would be set up by the teacher to show the learners, in as realistic a way as possible, what English speakers would say and do in such situations. For this, role play, film or audio tape, or teaching pictures might be used. The teacher would model various likely expressions which would be used in the situation. Important grammatical patterns and vocabulary that came up in the models would be discussed and practised. Differences of application of the situation in speech and writing might be modeled, for example, a student explaining to a friend over the telephone why she didn't go to a class party compared with a parent writing a note to a child's teacher explaining why the child was absent from school. Learners would probably practise by working in pairs and small groups in addition to whole class activities. Reading skills such as skimming text to get the gist quickly and scanning to find individual pieces of information in a complex text would be practised using the kinds of materials learners encounter daily such as signs, labels, application forms, advertising, and so on. Writing activities might include how banking forms are used, taking messages on the telephone, and other types of writing depending on the learners' needs.

Given the focus on learners' needs in this approach, ESL programs using the communicative approach are designed as far as possible for group learners according to their purposes for learning English. Although the majority of classes in Canada still, of necessity, teach general English skills to groups of learners who have varied purposes and life situations, there is a growing number of classes aimed, for example, at university students in scientific programs, or doctors preparing to pass Canadian professional examinations, or workers in one factory. In some classes, oral language is the focus while in others most of the work is on written language depending on the purpose.

In sum, this approach aims to address a number of learners' needs: the need to gain access to basic information about the target language and culture; the need to negotiate learning styles and activities with the teacher; the need for opportunities to try out what is being presented to them so that they can integrate what is presented into their own lives appropriately; the need for learning materials relevant to their personal life situations; and the need for opportunities for practice which will promote accuracy and fluency. The balance between written and oral focusses depends on the needs expressed by the learners. The result of this combination of factors is a highly learner centred program based on what can be practically accommodated given the learners' needs.

ESL WITH SPECIFIC LITERACY NEEDS

Up to this point, the discussion has been on ESL teaching for learners who are at least functionally literate in their first language, who are comfortable learning in a formal classroom situation, and who have experience with the ways in which language and literacy operate in large urban industrialized communities. However, a number of ESL learners have specific needs relating to the learning of literacy in English. While this group is in the minority among ESL learners, as suggested in the statistics given above, the needs of this ESL literacy group are given considerable attention here because their situations match most closely those of Canadian, English-speaking ABE learners.

We wish to note here that, given the scope and constraints of this paper, the discussion below is necessarily highly simplified. Ethnographic research suggests that literacy is in fact culturally specific and must be understood in a cultural context. Heath (1983) has demonstrated the variations in literate behaviour which are found even between communities which are geographically close, while other writers (Schiefflin and Cochrane Smith 1984; Scollon and Scollon 1981; Street 1984; Anderson and Stokes 1984) suggest that differences are stronger yet across linguistic and ethnic groups. These writers suggest that we learn to interact with print not in any pattern predetermined by the demands of the print itself, but according to the ways in which we see print used around us. Thus, we ask readers to keep in mind this critical aspect of literacy learning as cultural learning. To a considerable extent, what is said below also applies to well educated learners as well as to those with special problems in learning literacy in English.

Non-Roman Alphabetics

One component of the ESL literacy group is called non-roman alphabetics. This group is comprised of people who are literate in a language which has a writing system that does not use the roman alphabet — languages such as Chinese, Japanese, Korean, Thai, Urdu, Arabic, Hebrew, and so on. Learners who are familiar with syllabic writing systems such as Hebrew may encounter problems different from those who are used to a logographic system such as Chinese. Many of these learners have already studied English or other roman alphabet languages in their home countries and are familiar with the way roman systems work. However, others experience a considerable amount of difficulty learning to read and write in English, especially with our complex spelling system. While these learners may need some specific help in the early stages of their ESL learning, they usually are able to get quickly beyond their initial problems. Once they have gained some understanding of and experience with the way in which English uses letters to represent sounds and words, they are usually able to operate in regular ESL classes, transferring other skills they have from their mother tongue literacy experience to literacy in English.

Mother Tongue Non-Literates

Problems encountered by ESL learners who are not literate or have gained limited literacy skills in their first language are even greater than those of non-roman alphabetics. Even within the non-literate category, we distinguish two groups: (1) those who have been brought up in a society which has a rich literacy in the main language of the community (e.g. Portuguese in the Azores) even though some members of that society have not become literate personally; and (2) those who have been brought up in a society (e.g. some of the tribal areas of Cambodia) in which literacy has not played a significant part in local communications. In the first sub-group, learners can be expected to have observed a great deal about how literacy and schooling function even if they were not skilled or experienced in it themselves, whereas, in the second sub-group, it is to be expected that learners will know little of the potential functions of literacy or schooling.

Many non-literate learners attend regular ESL classes when they first arrive in English Canada, but they commonly drop out after only a few classes. The problem is that, while regular ESL classes teach literacy skills such as spelling, reading for meaning in a second language, and forms and functions of literacy that are culturally specific to Canada, it is generally assumed that the ESL learners will transfer the bulk of their literacy skills directly from literacy in their first language. Such skills include being able to recognize and write roman letters, to understand the concepts of word and sentence, to predict the content of written text in contexts like labels, posters, or newspapers, and so on. These skills are not taught in regular ESL classes, so non-literate learners are not able to keep up with the literacy aspects of the ESL teaching. more significant, however, is the fact that most ESL teachers use literacy as a tool to teach oral language as well. Examples and diagrams are written on the blackboard, written materials are used as the basis for exercises, and reading or writing assignments may be given as homework. Thus, non-literate learners soon realize that they cannot follow even the oral language teaching being offered.

A more profound factor in this situation is the likelihood that non-literate ESL learners have had little or no experience with formal schooling, particularly with schooling in the cultural form found in North America. Those learners who have had some schooling may have experienced it as unpleasant and frustrating. When they arrive in a regular ESL classroom they may be intimidated by the crowd of strangers they find there; they may not understand the rules of turn-taking in communication between the learners and the teacher; they may not know how to get help when they are having difficulty. Most importantly, the classroom may represent to them either bad experiences they have had in the past or opportunities that they deeply regret not having had earlier in their lives. Whatever the reason, they are likely to lose confidence either in themselves or the teacher and to drop out of the class.

It is important to emphasize here that while literacy learning for English-speaking ABE learners is usually an enormous task, the task of learning English literacy for non-literate, non-schooled immigrants, who control neither the English language skills nor Canadian 'street smarts' of Canadian ABE learners, is infinitely greater.

Forms of ESL Literacy Teaching

Successful teaching of ESL to non-literate learners can take several forms. Some learners are reached by one-to-one tutoring arrangements in which the learner does not have to face the formal classroom situation and the tutor can tailor learning experiences to accommodate the learner's needs for both oral language and literacy skills. The problem with this approach currently in Canada is that most individual tutors are volunteers who have not received much training. Usually, these tutors are trained in methods which are appropriate for teaching literacy to English speakers, but which do not take into account the special needs of non-native speakers. This concern aside, the one-to-one tutoring situation has the great advantage of the possibility of creating learning situations which suit precisely the needs, interests, and skill levels of the learner, a luxury not enjoyed by most teachers in either ESL or literacy group teaching situations.

As a second form, it is becoming more common now for ESL literacy teaching to be offered to groups of learners in community agencies, in English in the workplace programs, and even in special classes in large regular ESL programs in community colleges and schools. Oral language taught in these classes is chosen to be closely related to the learners' day to day experiences and needs. Literacy skills are introduced using a variety of approaches, several of which are sketched out here.

One is that written language used in class is based on words and language patterns that the learners already know. The language experience approach (Rigg, 1977) is used in which the teacher or another scribe writes down a passage dictated by an individual student or the whole group *in exactly the words used by the learners*. Then, various types of reading and writing activities are used to practice and extend the vocabulary and sentence patterns contained in it. Such activities might include reading over the passage as a group, identifying individual words, finding several words which begin with the same letter, finding word which are spelled with the same pattern ('come' and 'some'), copying words or patterns from sentence strips based on the original pattern, arranging individual words on cards to form one of the original sentences, and making different sentences by substituting other words for ones in the original sentence.

Another common basis for choosing literacy content to be taught in ESL literacy classes is the immediate needs and experiences of the learners outside of class. Learners may come to class with questions about the meaning of signs and symbols they see around them at home, on the subway, in stores, and so on. On the basis of what the teacher knows about the learners' daily lives or what they say about their literacy needs, the teacher often chooses to focus on certain aspects of literacy. Such aspects might be symbols and other kinds of printed information on food packaging, filling out government forms, recognizing the different types of unsolicited mail that learners receive in their homes, recognizing street and transportation signs, reading and writing for basic banking, and so on. Numeracy as well as literacy skills are likely to be involved.

Because the learners are not likely to know the oral language or even the functions behind their observed uses of literacy, the introduction of these topics must be preceded by discussion of the use of literacy in these contexts and the language associated with it. Where possible, actual experiences with the use of the literacy items, such as a group trip on public transportation or cooking in class following a recipe on a package, are useful demonstrations of the functions and meanings involved. Reinforcement of oral language as well as reading and writing is needed as the group works on activities designed to help them recognize written items in context, in scanning text to find what they want, in comparing similar items such as packages for important differences, in finding directions they recognize on forms, and so on. These various approaches to selection and exploitation of content for ESL literacy classes are not all incompatible.

Since it is common in ESL literacy classes to have learners whose skills in oral English and first language literacy are varied, teachers usually arrange small group practice activities so that at some times learners are grouped according to similarities in their oral English or literacy skills and at others according to their differences. For example, in paired practice of an oral English pattern, it might be best to put their learners together who have about the same level of English skills. On the other hand, in an exercise on filling out a cheque, it might be best to group students so that some know the numbers well orally while others have better skills in writing and spelling to write the numbers down. It is common in ESL literacy classes for the entire class to undertake class projects such as a photo story in which tasks are divided so as to make use of the strengths and learning needs of each member of the class.

One final point with respect to the teaching of ESL to non-literate learners is that the learning of literacy skills in the learners' first language can sometimes be the most effective point of entry into both English oral language and literacy learning. Individuals and entire ethnic groups tend to have different perceptions about the relationship between literacy and the mother tongue and that of English. Some are inclined to see the exercise of learning literacy in the mother tongue as useless to their needs in Canada and are motivated to attempt to learn literacy right away in English. Others consider it valuable to learn literacy in their mother tongue first and to tackle English later. Of course, the needs of the latter group can only be met if facilities are made available to them to learn in their first language. The context of a mother tongue literacy group can also be a valuable place in which learners discuss in their first language various concerns they have about their life in Canada, and, if the teacher is bilingual or some of the learners speak English quite well, it can be an opportunity for a lot of oral English language learning as well.

IMPLICATIONS

It is clear from this discussion that there is a great deal of potential and need for communication and collaboration among those involved in the fields of ESL and literacy. These two fields have developed in Canada in relative isolation from each other. However, in recent years several forces have combined to bring them closer together. One factor is the ever-increasing pressure on all adults to develop their literacy skills to meet the growing demands in our urban, industrialized society. This pressure has forced native English and non-English speaking people alike to seek help with their literacy skills. The result is that many providers of literacy learning opportunities are finding many non-native speakers of English on their doorsteps. Also, in the past decade or so,

Canada has received a number of immigrants and refugees who have low literacy skills in their first languages because of conditions in their home countries. Thus, ESL teachers are finding increasing numbers of non-literates in their classes. The high profile of both ESL and ABE, as indicated in the recent publication of the Ontario Ministry of Colleges and Universities (1986) document, *Project Report: For Adults Only*, serves to strengthen the movement for convergence of these two educational concerns about learner populations which they have in common.

There is every good reason for people in the fields of ESL and literacy to enhance their cooperation through the development of methods, approaches, materials, and programming which will better meet the needs of ESL learners, English speaking non-literates, and especially ESL literacy learners. Increased flow of information between the two groups can be expected to have a beneficial effect not only on the training of literacy tutors who have ESL learners, but also on ESL classroom teachers who have non-literates in their classes.

NOTES

1. What is said here with respect to English as a second language in English-speaking Canada holds true for French as a second language in Francophone Canada given that such factors as the following are taken into consideration: French is under more social pressure than English in English-dominated North America; the sociolinguistics of communication in French Canada are not the same as those in English Canada; and the relationship between speech and writing in French, and particularly in French Canada, is not the same as that for English.

2. Jim Cummins and others have found evidence that minority language group children generally do better in learning their *second* language as well as their first if their first language is used as the medium of instruction and language of initial literacy in the early years of schooling. See J. Cummins, *Bilingualism and Minority Language Children* (Toronto: OISE Press, 1981) for a review of the literature. There is little research to indicate if such effects are typical in adult literacy learners as well. However, recent studies of Hmong refugees learning English in camps in Southeast Asia and in the United States suggest that learning mother tongue literacy has beneficial effects on ESL learning among these adults. See Barbara Robson, "Alternatives in ESL and literacy: Ban Vinai." (Washington, D.C.: Center for Applied Linguistics, 1981 (mimeo) and R. K. Green and S. Reder, "Factors in individual acquisition of English: A longitudinal study of Hmong adults." (paper presented at the Hmong Research Conference II: The Hmong in Transition, Southeast Asian Refugee Studies, Minneapolis, Minnesota, University of Minnesota, November, 1983).

REFERENCES AND SUGGESTED READINGS

Anderson, A. B. and S. J. Stokes, (1984). "Social and institutional influences on the development and practice of literacy." In H. Goelman, A. Oberg, and F. Smith (eds.) *Awakening to Literacy*. Exeter, NH: Heinemann.

Bell, Jill and Barbara Burnaby, (1984). *A Handbook for ESL Literacy*. Toronto: OISE Press/Hodder and Stoughton.

_____, Barbara Burnaby and Jane Love, (1984). *English as a Second Language Professional Development Modules*. Toronto: OISE Press.

_____, (1988). *Teaching Multilevel Classes*. Toronto: Dominie Press.

Bourne, L. S., A. M. Baker, and W. Kalbach et al, (1985). *Ontario's Ethnocultural Population, 1981: Socio-Economic Characteristics and Geographical Distributions*, Ethnocultural Data Base Materials, Series III, Special Report Number 3. Toronto: Ontario Ministry of Citizenship and Culture.

Bowen, J. Donald, Harold Madsen and Ann Hilferty, (1985). *TESOL: Techniques and Procedures*. Rowley, Massachusetts: Newbury House.

Center for Applied Linguistics, (1983). *From the Classroom to the Workplace: Teaching ESL to Adults*. Washington, D.C.: Center for Applied Linguistics.

Cummins, J., (1981). *Bilingual Education and Minority Language Children*. Toronto: OISE Press.

Elson, Nicholas (ed.), (1983). *Teaching English as a Second Language to Adults: Methodology*. Toronto: Ontario Ministry of Citizenship and Culture.

Gower, Roger and Steve Walters, (1983). *Teaching Practice Handbook: A Reference Book for ESL Teachers in Training*. London: Heinemann Educational Books.

Haverson, Wayne W. and Judith Haynes, (1982). *Literacy Training for ESL Adult Learners*. Washington, D.C.: Center for Applied Linguistics.

Heath, S. B., (1982). *Ways with Words*. Cambridge: Cambridge University Press.

Rigg, P., (Fall 1977). "Beginning to read in English: The L.E.A. way." *SPEAQ Journal* 1:3 pp. 60-70.

Rivers, Wilga M. and Mary S. Temperley, (1978). *A Practical Guide to the Teaching of English as a Second Language*. New York: Oxford University Press.

Schieffelin, B. and M. Cochrane Smith, (1984). "Learning to read culturally: Literacy before schooling." In H. Goelman, A. Oberg, and F. Smith (eds.) *Awakening to Literacy*. Exeter, NH: Heinemann.

Scollon, R. and S. Scollon, (1981). *Advances in Discourse Processes*: Vol. VII. *Narrative, Literacy and Face in Interethnic Communication*. Norwood, NJ: Ablex.

Scribner, S. and M. Cole, (1981). *The Psychology of Literacy*. Cambridge, Mass: Harvard University Press.

Street, B. V., (1984). *Literacy in Theory and Practice*. Cambridge: Cambridge University Press.

CHAPTER 6:
Literacy for Participation

Reprinted with permission: VIEWPOINTS: A SERIES OF OCCASIONAL PAPERS on Basic Education, ISSUE NO. 4, ALBSU (Adult Literary & Basic Ed Unit) 1987, p. 17-20. (U.K.)

In this article, I propose a core literacy provision of three elements (functional literacy, mastery of English and writing) as a framework which would enable students to fulfil chosen purposes or find starting points of various kinds; and I question whether they are currently in balance in staff and curriculum development. I suggest that sociological and historically based research could make a valuable contribution to the theory and practice of adult literacy education and that if practitioners generally were in touch with such theory, and related innovative practice, and able to generate new skills from this, we would be able to offer a better student centred service and argue the case for "Literacy for a participatory democracy" in wider debates and dialogues about the contexts, methods, purposes and effects of literacy learning in the twentieth century post industrial society.

My starting point has been a process of trying to understand the obvious differences between what different people say, think and write about the uses of literacy, and of trying to find my own rationale for the work that I do. Differences in ideas and assumptions are often manifest in staff training events, governments pronouncements, media interviews, contact with schools, casual conversations with friends, acquaintances or in public places, and in interviews with students. Where there is no shared language or knowledge that can be drawn on, such differences create gaps in communication; and while it is sometimes prudent not to air issues which may cause dissension and repression, there is also a danger in constantly resorting to woolly terms like "missing out" and an important sense in which the purposes of literacy and students' previous experiences of literacy learning ought to be the basis on which the literacy curriculum is built. If this were so, I believe there would be a ripple effect which would enable dialogue to take place with and about schools, with people in general via the media (in a way that could get beyond the shock/horror approach and our purely defensive reaction to it) and with "the authorities". I am not suggesting that one limiting, unified view of the purpose of literacy learning would or should emerge; I am suggesting that we could and should talk about the issues more freely and honestly than we sometimes do. This article tries to outline (very sketchily) some of the thinking and practice I am trying to learn about in order to be able to do this.

In thinking of a literacy curriculum that would consist of three strands, I include also the mechanisms by which students find themselves in one or the other, and ways in which they might influence each other to create a dynamic process within which students can work towards chosen goals (which, incidentally, we need to record), or find starting points of various kinds.

I suspect, however, that the notion of adult literacy provision as a multistrand curriculum, of which I've chosen to write about the three I see as key, is something I've thought myself into while preparing this article. My (limited) observation tells me that, in practice, the content of literacy programs is a mixture of some kind or kinds of functional work with fairly traditional skills based work (spelling, "grammar"), for students whose orientation is "mastery of English" (Kenneth Levine's phrase). This, I contend, comes about because a functional approach is the received wisdom of Adult Literacy and yet very many students express aims to do with mastery of English, or no aims at all ("they come for social reasons really") to which tutors respond with traditional reading, writing and English teaching plus perhaps the end-of-term relaxation of writing a piece for the scheme magazine.

I feel that there are huge gaps here, where there ought to be dialogue, but isn't. The gaps have to do with the different assumptions about literacy and literacy learning, or lack of any useful knowledge at all. I'm aware of this in my own practice and have tried to use my own experience as a basis to explore theory and learn about innovative practice in order to discover what I need to be able to do and say after I've said "hello" to a student or group of students. It seems to me that these resources ought to be part of every practitioner's repertoire, and that we need to develop them in order to get past dominant notions of "maintaining confidence", "individual attention" and limited interpretations of student centred learning. I believe that much of the practice which would help both students and staff of literacy schemes to understand better what literacy could be FOR exists only on the radical and innovative fringes of literacy work, and much of the theory goes unread. References in this article are to writers and practitioners whose work I have found helpful in sorting out my ideas so far. By putting them down on paper in this way, I feel I've made a commitment to study them further.

If asked what principle guides them in the development of adult literacy courses and programs, most practitioners would mention Student Centred Learning and it is to this concept that I now turn.

STUDENT-CENTRED LEARNING

Functional Literacy

For ten years, student-centred learning has been the corner-stone of curriculum development in adult literacy and adult basic education. In practice, this has meant the development of materials and strategies ("Themes and Skills") with a functional emphasis — on shopping, travelling, work, leisure, dealing with organisations etc. Functional literacy has included work with limited aims like signing a cheque, or preparing for a job or course entry test and would also be said to cover developments like "Literacy and Dressmaking"/ "Car Maintenance"/"Adult Basic Education and Local History" courses. In training, we examine our own everyday uses of literacy and we plan literacy work to meet the needs of students who are described in case studies. Perhaps it is partly this case study approach which has given rise to too much "planning for" (it's difficult to have a dialogue with a case study) and the vacuum I perceive in the negotiation of alternative approaches. I remember the shock I felt when I was made aware that functional literacy need not be student-centred at all, partly because content and methodology could still easily be tutor dominated and partly because, although relevant to the real needs of adults in a general sense, and capable of being developed in a participatory way, a functional topic might not be genuinely relevant to a learner or group of learners at a particular time and could not in any case be guaranteed to secure success at work or in other transactions.

I found corroboration for my unease about the functional approach coming from two sources, one from research and one — implied — from innovative practice. Firstly, Kenneth Levine (University of Nottingham, 1980) points to the vagueness of definition and economic relativity which diminishes the usefulness of functional literacy as a concept or guiding principle: as soon as a given set of literacy skills become generally acquired, the acceptable level in the society as a whole will rise again, leaving those previously behind, behind again. It is easy to see that this has happened (with regard to the possession of a general level of literacy) in the job market in this country in recent times.

However, Levine does accept that the new thinking regarding literacy (he is talking about the mid-1960s) was adult, selective, developmental and participative even if it fell short of these ideals in practice. He acknowledges that functionality has persisted as a useful concept and offers a new definition which gives equal weight to the getting *and* giving of information via the written word.

It is this contrast between passive, individualized activities and active, participatory activities which are emphasized in the Takeaway Project at Reading in Berkshire. The Takeaway Project concerned numeracy, but the parallel literacy activities could be easily inserted into the list below which was produced to help clarify the innovatory nature of the project.

Role	Passive/Individualized Activities	Active/Participatory Activities
Worker	learns technical maths needed on job as defined by employer	learns the maths needed for trade union bargaining
	learns how to check wages slip	works on maths involved in reorganizing workplace and work structures
	learns how to check dole money, and how to check entitlement to other benefits	learns about the financial world and big business generally
	learns how to operate fiddles on the job	finds out how much the government spends on social security, and how much is left unclaimed
		finds out about different kinds of fiscal policy

Role	Passive/Individualized Activities	Active/Participatory Activities
Consumer	works out best buy in shops	finds out how much profit firms made on different sized packets
	works out from bus/train timetables how to get to "x" on time	finds out how much firms spend on advertising and marketing
	checks bills	finds out how retailing the same product under trade names maximizes profit
	works out how much to tip	
	works out best deals in financial affairs eg hire purchase v bank loan v moneylender	starts up co-operative bulk-buying group
	learns how to measure for DIY	
	plans holiday expenses	
Citizen	works out how to handle budget	finds out how local and national government collects money and spend it
	checks bills for rent, rates, fuel	
		gets involved in campaigns to lobby government on spending policy
		finds out how much money the maths scheme has, how it spends it, and how/where to get more.

Brian Street, in "Literacy in Theory and Practice", 1984, claims that the ALBSU approaches (as described in "Working Together: An Approach to Functional Literacy") go beyond the limitations of functional ideas about literacy in that they emphasize that literacy is an essential practical activity with real social purpose. Street argues that this makes the ALBSU approach an example of an "ideological" model of literacy and contrasts this favourably with the "autonomous" model still prevalent in schools.

Contact with innovators and academics like these reminds me that I have a lot to learn about collaboration with students in functional curriculum areas and that the ideas underlying a functional approach — which might themselves comprise part of the literacy curriculum or dialogue with students — are more complicated than I supposed. I also suspect that rolling back the edges of functional literacy — at least in my own mind — will reveal the cobwebs that festoon the resources on offer to students who are aiming for mastery of technical English and the rusty nature of the equipment available for installing writing as a central activity.

MASTERY OF ENGLISH

I sense that tutors are often defensive about pursuing an overtly skill-based program, but that much of it goes on, partly because students ask for it and partly because it's the easiest thing to fall back on when other approaches don't seem to work. Perhaps if "mastery" aims were fully recognised as OK approaches in literacy, there would be more innovation in methodology bubbling up from the grass roots rather than, as now I suspect, emerging only occasionally as the product of a limited number of training courses. For even where "Catch Up English" or the like are respectable (ie named as such in the publicity) parts of a literacy scheme curriculum, there may be little dialogue about methodology or reflection on students' earlier learning experiences. Whether in 1:1 partnerships or in groups, it is likely that the teaching of the techniques of English will be at its most traditional — a diet of exercises. It is almost as if everyone involved is colluding in a deliberately reactionary stance, rather in the way that the Ward Lock series of "Old Fashioned" . . . books do. Perhaps tutors are unwilling to initiate and sustain dialogue on these points because they accept the traditional model of literacy which they encountered (and "succeeded" with at school) and would feel insecure about abandoning a familiar structure and taking students' experiences as a starting point.

However, alternatives to a traditional approach (which after all have not worked first time round) *are* found and perhaps we need to encourage tutors to try some new methods and examine the basis of their traditional approach. It is, for example, entirely consistent with a student-centred philosophy for students to go to a text investigation of their strategies for punctuation, as one ILEA tutor has been doing, assessing the relative success of the different strategies. It is entirely consistent with a student centred philosophy for students to go to a text seeking answers to questions which they pose (having first decided if it's a text worth bothering with) rather than being subjected to the humiliating charade that is the traditional form of comprehension exercise. Our experience with spelling, which has received a great deal of attention, tells us that, even in an area of skills where alternative, adult, participatory approaches have been widely disseminated and are now part of established practice, tutors still hanker after a magic formula which will release them from needing to mediate between historically determined conventions, accepted notions of correctness and the student's learning orientation.

WRITING

I would guess that the writing group is often thought of in literacy schemes as a minority interest only, where little of the real work goes on. So, if few students express a desire "to be writers", does writing deserve to occupy a central place in the literacy curriculum, and if so, how does this come about?

By "writing", I mean the kind of activities that have been developed through the "Write First Time Movement", the kind of writing that includes composition and production, and I believe these are important because once you get involved in writing — the *active* literacy mode — you come face to face with all the practical questions about what literacy is for, about how to convey meaning in print, about who is to read it. You have the raw material in the form of ideas and you have raw material in the form of drafts (to work on) and texts where what people say and think is set down for all to see. This is clearly shown in the poster which is part of the Write First Time/ALBSU pack "Conversation with Strangers" by Sue Shrapnel Gardener. Students say:

> "The hardest thing about writing is to put the first word down."
>
> "Do I want someone to read it. Will it interest anyone else?"
>
> "I was quite surprised that you could cut the type up and move it around, until the writing and the pictures seemed to fit."
>
> "Whatever I write, I want to share it with the world."
>
> "I was glad I remembered all that, I was so proud of it. It didn't have to be a good piece, it was as it was."

It is good news that Sue and the people she worked with have set down some of their experiences as classroom material and that the learning from the first ten years of writing development in adult literacy will go on and be shared. I hope that these materials will be widely used and seen as relevant to all literacy practitioners.

In my experience, it is mainly from writing groups that students are becoming actively involved in schemes and it is in writing groups (where so far the content is mainly the recording of experience) that students are able to work at relevant forms for written language in a participatory way. Therefore I do think that writing groups should occupy a central place in the literacy curriculum — the productive side might well service the literacy scheme as a whole in a variety of ways — and perhaps it is not entirely fanciful to hope that a preoccupation with voluntary tutor training which for me as a support worker provided the main dynamic of literacy work in the early days should now give way to a preoccupation with the support of writing groups. For too long, I believe, writing has been seen as merely a classroom or "homework" exercise (writing for teacher), with occasional or even regular opportunities to contribute to magazines or take part in writing events. But unless there is real learning from these developments and from the innovators who are extending their and our knowledge of the writing process, these events and magazines will continue to have the status of end of term activities only and may actually devalue the skills, effort and participation involved. Even the built-in opportunities for extending writing that we now have, for example the project section of the RSA Certificate of Continuing Education, seem, in my experience, to have few if any links with the writing movement, and too many of the projects submitted are like the worst kind of school topic work: derivative, sterile and of no real interest to writer or reader. Again, I feel that through lack of contact with innovation and research, support for candidates submitting these projects has been too narrowly based.

Writing — and active reading — will undoubtedly become a more central literacy activity if the outcome of Robert Merry's Student Activities Project and the Writing Development Project get taken up. I should also be interested to know if the practice of groups taking it in turns to produce the scheme magazine can bring about change. I should like to work on developing a dialogue as part of the initial interview/assessment procedure which would encourage students to give the Writing Workshop a try. I feel sure that many more would become actively involved in literacy, through writing and that there would be fewer students in "ordinary" groups or one to one partnerships coming "just for social reasons really." I also think there would be some mileage, in centres where there is enough literacy activity to sustain two or three strands, to put on every now and again quite carefully structured "conferences", aimed at developing dialogue and cross-fertilization between students in the "mastery" group, the writing group and the function group and hoping for ideas for new activities to be generated from this dialogue. I think it would be worth exploring whether it would be helpful to establish the practice of inviting CCE students to spend, say, a month in the writing group before embarking on a project. And new staff and voluntary tutors could spend a probationary period in the writing group learning to listen, to transcribe (as Sue Shrapnel Gardener describes) and to be a resource and a support rather than a "teacher".

LITERACY LEARNING IN SCHOOLS
Where in schools can we find practice or research which connects with what we are beginning to understand about literacy learning? I don't know what has happened to "Breakthrough to Literacy" or the Bullock Report's Language Across the Curriculum, but I do know that there are two books (as well as the corpus of publications describing the work of James Britton, Harold Rosen, Douglas Barnes and many others), records of the authors' exploratory work with inexperienced teenage readers which ought to have a radical impact on the system: *Achieving Literacy* by Margaret Meek and *Finding a Language* by Peter Medway. How many adult literacy practitioners know of this work and feel a sense of solidarity with it?

What these innovators share is a desire to understand and value the learner's own language and experience in learning, and to help learners build on this. What interested me particularly about Peter Medway's approach was that he was able to make himself, for a short time, a real resource for the pupils he was working with, through the medium of a written log. The writing in the log was initiated by students, was addressed to a real reader and had a purpose — to help the pupils learn independently and actively — which had been agreed between writer and reader. It was a mode of expression in which some writers became confident and fluent. How many of us are trying to move towards this, in our "marking" of students' writing. Could similar techniques (? distance learning) replace concerns we sometimes feel and express in incredibly school-sounding terms such as "irregular attendance", "the importance of home-work" and even "disruptive students".

Peter Medway was clear that the communication and learning that his students engaged in must be congruent with a culture and purposes that made sense to them and about which they were able to make choices; and it's clear from his narrative, as it is from Margaret Meek's account, how radically different that was from the kinds of learning usually promoted in schools. Since most school learning is expected to take place through the medium of reading and writing, we can return here to the two models of literacy described by Brian Street. If we accept the distinction he draws between the concept of literacy as an "autonomous", neutral set of skills whose acquisition can be erroneously thought to confer various economic and intellectual benefits and the concept of an "ideological" model of literacy which is much more closely related to actual social practices, we can gain glimpses from writers like Margaret Meek and Peter Medway of what a more ideological model of school based literacy learning might be like. We can also say that in the responses Peter Medway made to his pupils through the log, he was being more functionally literate in Kenneth Levine's terms than any teacher operating in the autonomous mode.

THE SYSTEM

The literacies that have coalesced and become fossilized into the idea of an autonomous neutral set of skills now taught discretely in schools have derived from forms of written expression which grew up to fulfil particular social functions in the church, the professions, commerce and so on. The original model was Latin and it would be interesting to examine the case for and against the existence of this heavily classical lingua franca of standard English in the light of Brian Street's sociological analysis.

The trouble is that access to this lingua franca has been and is by means of an education system which is preoccupied with sorting and grading people, a process which was once closely related to firm ideas about class and station in life and is still more about the achievement of predetermined standards than about learning. It was first thought that the poor would benefit from being able to read the scriptures, then that workers needed to be literate to contribute to the industrial society and this made common cause with the democratic argument that everyone had a right to be educated. Proponents of a lofty liberal/humanist view exerted a pernicious influence by forcing a distinction between education and training which, when allied to the class distinctions embodied in the organization of the education system, made it possible not to accept the need to redefine the purposes of education in accord with democratic principles. What we've had has been a system of mass education to serve the needs of an industrial society and it was assumed that universal literacy would be an automatic by-product of this. In the context of an article on "Literacy — What For?" it can be suggested that the failure of that expectation by a factor of perhaps 40 per cent invalidates the model of literacy used and the purposes it was assumed to fulfil.

Many people would argue that it has been the mass element itself, the need to teach children in large numbers which has created a neutral literacy and alienated large numbers of children from learning it. If this is so, we need to look at ways of modifying the model as the ineffectiveness of traditional ways of teaching it become recognised as it becomes possible to use alternative methods of supporting and resourcing learning. If we think, for example, of the involvement of parents in helping children to read, it would be important for this to be a two way process, or rather a three way process, a genuine exercise in creating knowledge rather than an extension of teacher determined instructional modes.

The common radical element in all this is that schools and learning (and thus literacy) ought to be *for* participation and we in adult literacy can help show that student centred learning, by which we mean collaborative learning according to students' choices and purposes is the right educational model for a participatory democracy and will contribute towards new literacies.

REFERENCES

Gardener, Sue Shrapnel, (1985). *Conversations with Strangers,* WFT/ALBSU.

Levine, Kenneth, (1986). *(PAPER) Functional Literacy: Fond Illusions and False Economies,* Dept. Sociology, University of Nottingham.

Meek, Margaret and others, (1983). Routledge & Kegan Paul, *Achieving Literacy.*

Medway, Peter, (1981). *Finding a Language,* Chameleon/Writers & Readers.

Street, Brian, (1985). *Literacy in Theory and Practice,* Cambridge.

Williams, Raymond, (1984). *The Long Revolution,* Pelican.

CHAPTER 7:
The Rubic Cube: A Model for Job Skills Upgrading

Susan Lafleur

"It is a built-in fact that people are the real resource of any enterprise, and that those people have to be given every chance to optimize their abilities and knowledge and skills. If you don't give people the chance to achieve you'll seriously diminish the results of their combined efforts" (Galagan, 1988:20)

Today's employment market is vastly different from the job scenario our fathers and grandfathers (or mothers and grandmothers, for that matter) experienced. Just one generation ago, our antecedents were part of a relatively static tableau. Unemployment was at a very low level and job security was a certainty. One could reasonably expect to work for the same company, or in the same job for 25 to 30 years — one's entire career in fact. When job changes did occur, it was probably because the incumbent had made the decision to move rather than an organizational decision to downsize by cutting staff.

Technological and educational changes in the past twenty-five years have brought about a significant transformation of the work place. Expectations have changed. Perspectives of both employers and employees have polarized. The growing importance of on the job training/upgrading has been greatly influenced by the attitudinal changes of these two groups.

Twenty-five years ago on the job, skills training was largely synonymous with the apprenticable trades. Today employers are taking a more active if somewhat slow[1] part in job skills training and upgrading. In fact the terms training and upgrading are applicable to the entire spectrum of jobs from management, to professional to blue collar worker.

Companies these days, have little choice but to provide job training to give the required knowledge base and skill sets to enable all ranks of employees to be productive. Indeed some businesses now discuss the potential of "a career path" and together with the employee, establish a series of clearly identified steps leading to growth, career positions. "The perfect career path is a logical pattern of experience that progressively fulfills both the individual's and the organization's goals" (Mirabele, 1986:64)

One could engage in lively debate as to whose best interests are being served, however the intent of this article is to wrestle with the problem of job training in the work place and how to establish a company training profile reflecting all the requirements for professional upgrading through the latitude of jobs within the organization.[2] (see appendix A)

WHAT IS REQUIRED

WANTED: DIRECTOR,
ORGANIZATIONAL TRAINING & DEVELOPMENT

The ideal candidate for this highly responsible position is adept at identifying organizational issues, assessing training requirements and developing strategies to respond to all levels of technical and management training.

You will have demonstrated abilities and quality experience in job needs analysis, instructional design, course development, and excellent presentation skills. You have at least 7 years experience as a professional adult educator.[3]

The above is a fictitious example of the type of want ad that one sees increasingly in the career section for professional employment. It illustrates the growing awareness of and interest in the range and complexity of on the job adult education/training.

The demand for training to fit into the organizational structure, the requirement for undertaking an in depth training needs analysis and the matching of job skill requirements with training performance objectives is receiving more than just lip service. The ideal candidate for this job will be expected to accomplish all of the above with a limited training budget and to demonstrate the cost-benefit of each training initiative. To top off the job requisites the aspirant will also be an excellent communicator with superior problem solving and decision making skills!

Tongue in cheek aside, let us assume that this director will be required to plan and establish an in-house training department. Forgetting for a moment the overall magnitude of the mandate, let us focus on the process to identify, organize and continually update the company training profile. There are several fundamental questions to be considered:

1. What levels of employees must be trained?
2. What specific skills must be learned?
3. How will training requirements be identified?
4. Does courseware exist to meet the identified training need? Must in-house courses be developed?
5. What are the time constraints necessitated by the training? How many people? How many courses?
6. Can a process be developed by which, once skills training requirements have been identified, they can be effortlessly up dated as jobs change and expand, demanding new skills but not altering the fundamental nature of the work?

Although there is not one simple answer to these questions, the RUBIC cube concept provides an important matrix for bringing together the formulation of a comprehensive training needs profile:

1) identifying job skill sets to be acquired
2) establishing the level of competency demanded by the work
3) matching terminal performance objectives of the job with the course objectives
4) updating this information quickly and easily as necessary

The focus of this short essay will be to concentrate on the organizational approach to structuring a company wide training profile using the RUBIC cube as a matrix model.

ESTABLISHING THE MATRIX

There are in all probably no more than perhaps 150-200 actual job skills required to meet the range of all jobs. Many of these skills, moreover, are common to a number of job positions at different levels of authority within the organization. For example, keyboarding skills[4] are central to clerical-secretarial jobs. However, it is also a skill needed by administrative, financial, technical, other professional and sales/marketing positions. What distinguishes keyboarding skills in any one of these positions is the complexity, level of competency required and the level of the position at which the job must be adroitly performed.

Using another example, such as inventory control in a manufacturing environment, the same principle can be applied. Inventory control as Materials Resources Planning (MRP), is an automated process to track all inventory coming into a plant, all parts and pieces used in the manufacturing process, and all finished goods shipped out. The Shipping and Receiving Clerk must know how to accurately input to the system all information re: incoming stock (size and part numbers, quantity, cost quality of goods received). This very same automated system is also used by the finance department to plot global, and track specific, costs; by the assembly department to flag depleting stock; by bench technicians for repair and maintenance requirements; by production and quality control managers for re-order and production scheduling; by sales and marketing professionals for determining product delivery dates; and by the CEO and senior management to make crucial decisions on planning and forecasting. All, need to know how the system functions, all, use it in a different way for a different purpose.

The lynch pin in the process, is the Stock Clerk who does the first check of incoming inventory and the entry data. The consequences of the accuracy of this initial step and the subsequent application of the data within the data base, used by so many, is paramount. Identifying the skills central to each user level and then, integrating them into a company wide training profile may become the Human Resources Manager's nightmare.

A further example of a non-technical skill requirement that also impacts throughout an organization, at any level, is communication skills both oral and written. Obviously sound inter-personal communication skills facilitate harmonious working relationships. These same skills are important to the expression of analytical and problem solving tasks related to team/group work projects. Indeed at the individual personal level concise communication skills are central to any reporting situation (verbal or written) to both colleagues and superiors.

Writing skills are receiving growing recognition as being vital to a diversity of jobs. Obviously, the writing skills demonstrated by the technician/technologist who must be competent in thorough documentation procedures, will not demand the same level or focus, as the middle manager who is obliged to write proposals for, and make recommendations to, a higher administration level. The difference in skill ability between these jobs is the emphasis of the written communication. Therefore, applying the above idea to a panoply of jobs, it is the depth and significance of perhaps no more than 159-200 job skills, which when woven together in a specific format, determine the scope of any job description.

THE RUBIC CUBE MODEL

When starting to organize a systematic approach to undertaking a company wide, training needs analysis, generic skills should be grouped together. These generic skills can then be broken down into sub-sets as required to flesh out a job description. To continue the example cited earlier of an Inventory and Stock Control Clerk, a profile of skills might look like this:

Must be able to:

. read and verify bills of inventory, lading, shipping etc.
. fill out/complete bills of inventory, lading shipping etc.
. use a calculator and be able to carry out simple mathematical functions.
. verify prices, figures, quantities, price per quantity etc.
. demonstrate stock room control procedures — principles of organization and management.
. apply knowledge of computer skills — data entry, data retrieval, report generation (for statistical purposes), send messages.
. demonstrate a knowledge of and ability to apply customs and excise duties.

The same computer literacy skills required to execute an automated MRP program will be similar for other occupations using the same data base. The level of responsibility implied by each job skill is also recorded. Using a chart such as the one shown in appendix A, the data on job tasks can be organized into a manageable format.

This initial data collection is gathered using a questionnaire or personal interview with all supervisors and managers. The quality assurance of the information assembled in this way should be followed up with a questionnaire to a sample population of incumbents actually doing the job.

Once specific job skills have been identified according to the rank/position of employees within the organization, they can be overlaid to build a clear and accurate job description. As skills are identified it might become apparent that the Stock Clerk is in need of some basic literacy training, necessary to the job functions. This skill will now be added to the Clerk's individualized training program.

Putting these two concepts together to begin to build the matrix, we find that we have three sides already in place. It now becomes a straightforward exercise to append the three remaining sides of the matrix — level of competency (5) required by the job, courseware to meet the skills and competencies, and follow-up test and evaluation.

fig. 1

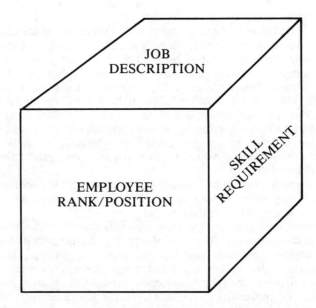

The Rubic Cube provides a useful matrix model for developing an approach to a company wide training program that interconnects job descriptions, skill requirements, available courseware and evaluation of competencies. Each cube represents a skill, or a level of competency, or a job task or a training objective etc. The cubes can be rotated to display the interrelationship of any of the job skills, competencies, training required and courses available for all employees throughout an organization.

fig. 2

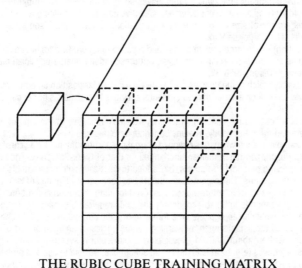

THE RUBIC CUBE TRAINING MATRIX

CONCLUSIONS

In the long term the model will be much more than a tool at the disposal of the human resources department to identify job skills, training needs and update job descriptions. It can also be used as a planning tool to aid the department manager and his or her subordinates to develop and plan career path opportunities. "Instead of assuming the employee is a one dimensional set of skills and abilities, the manager . . . (with the Rubic Cube matrix) . . . can help the employee explore and apply a whole composite of skills he or she may never have thought about previously." (Liebowitz, 1988:77) It would not be a sweeping generalization to say that employees who take an active role in defining and planning their own career growth are more productive, more committed to their jobs.

The matrix which has now been established, becomes the foundation of an in depth, company wide training profile. The implementation should be a smooth process which can be readily up-dated.

As each side of the cube is part of an intersecting matrix it is an easy task to change any module, on any side without destroying the integrity of the whole. Even the emerging work place issues of today, such as human rights/equal rights, multiculturalism, AIDS, aging in the workforce, are topics for skills development which can be readily incorporated into the matrix model. As identified skills are mastered, or as certain job skills become obsolete, they can be deleted from the demonstrated list of job requirements and new ones added.

The Rubic Cube, once a toy for intellectuals, has become child's play in its application to a training and development environment. (Brozeit, 1986).

NOTES

1) Some employers do have a progressive attitude to offering on the job training, both at the work site and on company time. However, job training/retraining is an expensive undertaking in terms of paid wages lost production/productivity time, which often leaves small companies (75 employees or less) at a disadvantage. Identifying and then implementing an active approach to training is an equally complex undertaking regardless of size or focus of the organization. As Lawrence Olson states in his article "Training Trends: The Corporate View"
". . . training (often) exists largely as an ad hoc and reactive function. One training director of a large company said he is more like a pharmacist filling out prescriptions, than a physician diagnosing and treating problems." (Olson, 1986:33)
2) "By knowing exactly which competencies are needed in a particular position an employee . . . (and an employer) could embark on a series of developmental activities to expand his or her capabilities for the job." . . . Ibid. P.64.
3) Although this is a fictitious job description it is nevertheless indicative of the type of advertisement appearing more and more frequently, in many Canadian newspapers.
4) The obvious example of a job which has changed dramatically within the past 7-8 years, but for which the general job description has remained unchanged, is that of Clerk-Secretary. The introduction of wordprocessing, using personal computers, has added to the basic skill requirements but the overall nature of the job is the same. The impact of computers has been equally significant for many other jobs (e.g. CAD for drafting and architectural specialists; CAM for manufacturing and robotics). The critical point for any organization is to be able to identify the skills required by changing technology, and to implement training within an appropriate time frame so that the competitive edge will not be lost.
5) I have not discussed the establishment of learning competencies as an integral part of job skill sets. Much has been written about DACUM (Developing a Curriculum) system of determining learning competencies/objectives (e.g. be able to define, be able to use, be able to use and problem solve) and analytical and psychomotor skills as the basis for course development/selection. The DACUM system

proposes that terminal performance objectives (TPO) be established to set goals of what the learner should "be able to do" upon completion of training. These objectives are measurable or quantifiable, and lead logically to evaluation and follow up at the completion of training.

6) The efficacy of the matrix model depends on whether it is a functional one. I believe it is, and that it can be integrated into any delivery mode of training — classroom, interactive video, computer based or distance education.

REFERENCES

Adams, R. E., (1975). *DACUM Approach to Curriculum Learning and Evaluation in Occupational Training*, Department of Regional and Economic Expansion, Ottawa.

Briscoe, Dennis R., (Aug. 1987). "The 10 Commandments of Development" in *Training and Development Journal*, Vol. 41, No. 8, P.54-59.

Brozeit, Richard K., (Oct. 1986). "If I Had My Druthers (a career development program)" in *Personnel Journal*, P.83-90.

Galagan, Patricia, (Aug. 1988). "Donald E. Petersen, Chairman of Ford and Champion of Its People" in *Training and Development Journal*, Vol. 42, No. 8, P.20-24.

Kaufman, Roger, (Oct. 1987). "A Needs Assessment Primer" in *Training and Development Journal*, Vol. 41, No. 10, P.78-83.

Liebowitz, Zandy, Beverly Kaye, and Caela Farren, (Oct. 1986). "Overcoming Management Resistance to Career Development Programs" in *Training and Development Journal*, Vol. 40, No. 10, P.77-81.

Mirabele, Richard, David Caldwell and Charles O'Reilly, (Sept. 1986). "Designing and Linking Human Resource Programs" in *Training and Development Journal*, Vol. 40, No. 9, P.61-65.

Olson, Lawrence, (Sept. 1986). "Training Trends: The Corporate View" in *Training and Development Journal*, Vol. 40, No. 9, P.33-37.

Shear, Arthur E, (1985). "Occupational Analysis and Training" in *Journal of European Industrial Training*, Vol. 9, No. 7, P.23-27.

Washing, Harry A. and Kurt W. Bovington, (May 1986). "Keeping Account of Employees' Skills" in *Supervisory Management*, American Management Association, Vol. 31, No. 5, P.21-24.

APPENDIX A

	PERSONAL COMPUTING	COMPUTER LITERACY	MRP MATERIALS RESOURCES PLANNING	SPREAD SHEET CALCULATIONS	WORD PROCESSING	DATA BASE MANAGEMENT	COMPUTER GRAPHICS
EXECUTIVE							
DIRECTOR/ MANAGERIAL							
CLERICAL/ ADMINISTRATIVE							
PROFESSIONAL (Sales & Mktg., Software Specialist, Design Engineers)							
TECHNICIAN/ TECHNOLOGIST							
ASSEMBLY/ QA/QC							
CLERK, SHIPPING & RECEIVING							

PART IV
ASSESSMENT IN ADULT BASIC EDUCATION

Most instructors feel uneasy about selecting tests for basic learners. Jones identifies a number of assessment tools that have been used in adult literacy and basic education programs and discusses their use as instruments of andragogy rather than instruments of certification. He argues that instructors need to find the test that is most appropriate to the needs of the learner. The author classifies various tests according to the assumptions made about the goals of literacy instruction. A discussion is presented under each of the following test categories: achievement, skills, functional inventory, and profile.

Prior assessment of adult knowledge and skills as well as measurement of final outcomes are important components of training and upgrading strategies. Taylor emphasizes that instructors must be aware of the purposes of adult assessment, the various methods of testing and the different considerations in choosing a test or measure. In addition, instrument readability is highlighted. He points out that readability formulas can be classified into simple and complex computations and describes the application of such formulas to a standardized instrument used in a basic education population.

Because illiteracy is a hidden and obscure reality, the assessment of a community is an extremely important first step in planning a program. As Wagner points out, many literacy facilitators are often under the impression that they know the community in which they are living and working. He draws attention to the need and importance of a field study or community assessment and presents a methodological framework for the preparatory phase of a literacy program. A recurring message throughout the chapter is that the framework allows for the translation of problems and needs into terms of andragogical activities or organizational decisions, and involves the community members.

Evaluation is a process of making personalised judgements and decisions about achievements and about the effectiveness of what we are doing. It also can be used to improve a learning activity. Fellenz suggests that formative evaluation is a very useful tool in basic education and that naturalistic approaches are well suited to carrying out such practices. The author offers practical suggestions for implementing naturalistic evaluations for the purpose of improving adult learning situations.

CHAPTER 1:

Tests for Adult Basic Education and Adult Literacy

Stan Jones

Most students attending adult basic education (ABE) and adult literacy (AL) programs dislike taking tests as much as anyone. ABE/AL students may have more justification for this attitude, since many have been poorly served by the tests they have been given. As part of the certification process that schools perform, many school tests are used to classify students as successes or failures. And many ABE/AL students are in these programs because they have been classified as failures by such tests at one time or another. Because of student sensitivity, some programs administrators are reluctant to use tests, fearing they will keep away students that might be served.

Yet tests need not be used only to classify students and mark failure. As Bloom, Madaus, and Hastings (1971) point out, tests can serve to help students find their way through the system, to help them set goals and to mark their progress. In this chapter, I want to identify a number of tests that have been used in ABE/AL programs and discuss their use as instruments of instruction rather than instruments of certification. Because most programs want to provide education that is appropriate for each student, it is necessary to evaluate a new student's ability in some way. During a course, some measure of progress is invaluable for demonstrating to the student that learning has taken place and for identifying new goals. For tests to be used in these ways, they must be consistent with the andragogical assumptions of the program.

As we will see, there are a variety of tests designed for these programs, just as there are a variety of programs. Indeed, there are too many tests for this chapter to review each in detail. Nafziger, Thompson, Hiscox, and Owen (1975) have the most comprehensive review of ABE/AL tests, but much of the information has been superseded by newer editions of tests they discuss[1]. Readers seeking detailed test reviews are urged to examine the *Ninth Mental Measurement Yearbook* (Mitchell, 1985). What this chapter will try to do is to identify several kinds of tests, review the assumptions underlying each type, and, briefly, point out tests representative of each type.

It is not the thrust of this chapter to suggest that some types of tests are better than others. Rather it is to argue that test-users, students and teachers, need to find the test that is most appropriate to their needs. Educational tests exist because they can provide useful information to both students and teachers. Students can use the information to help them understand what they know and what they need to know, enabling them to set appropriate goals. Teachers, of course, use the information to counsel the student and to guide the student into appropriate learning activities. Often, however, both find the information they get not as useful as it should be because they have used the wrong test or because they do not know how to interpret the information the test provides. Frequently, they then decide that the test is a bad test or that all tests are bad tests. Instead of finding a test that is more appropriate for the situation or finding out how to interpret the test, the teacher and the student launch their joint educational enterprise without all the information they could have.

We will not be able to provide a detailed set of procedures for selecting tests for a particular program. Anderson (1981) presents a set of criteria that can be used to match test characteristics to program needs; test-users are urged to consider the discussion in Anderson and to examine the model analysis she provides.

Nafziger, et al, (1975) group the tests they review into three types, based on the means by which scores are derived: criterion-referenced (scores are determined by comparing examinees' performance to an external standard), standardized (scores are determined by comparing examinees to each other), and informal (scores are not compared to a specific standard). While we will note which of these categories each of the various tests fit, we have found it more useful to classify tests by the assumptions we think they make about the goals of ABE/AL instruction:

Achievement These tests attempt to replicate for adult students the achievement measures typically used with school-age children.

Skills These tests measure skills that are thought to underly competent reading and arithmetic performance.

Functional These tests attempt to relate the examinee's performance to that of a typical adult in the society, using everyday material.

Inventory These tests undertake to measure the examinee's self-assessment in typical literacy/numeracy settings.

Profile These measures are less tests than criteria that can be used to evaluate a student's performance on a range of literacy/numeracy tasks.

SCORING

We will discuss each type in turn, but it is useful to first say a few words about scoring. While most in-class, teacher-made tests are scored simply by counting the number correct, with some items having different weights, this is seldom the case with standardized tests. Instead the raw score, the number correct, is converted to a scale that provides for the comparison of the raw score to some criterion. For norm-referenced tests, this criterion is the performance of others who have taken the test. One commonly used normed score is the percentile score, which indicates the proportion of all examinees that a particular examinee out-performed. For example, a student who answered 24 vocabulary and 30 reading comprehension items on the Test of Adult Basic Education, Level M, is at the 42nd percentile (the examinee scored higher than 42% of the other examinees).

Norm-referenced scores may also be represented by measures of how well a particular examinee did relative to the 'typical' examinee. The most common of these is a z-score, or standard score, which is a measure of how far from the average score a particular score is. For example, the average, or mean, score on vocabulary on Level M, Form 5, of TABE is 21.28 and the standard deviation is 6.46. The z-score for our student who answered 24 correctly is 0.42 (24-21.28 / 6.46), indicating that this student did slightly better than the average student. On the other hand, the mean score on reading comprehension is 30.24 with a standard deviation of 8.42. A raw score of 30 becomes a z-score of -0.03 (30-30.24 / 8.46). The z-score is negative because the raw score is lower than the average.

Because raw scores lower than the average have negative z-scores, and because we have trouble thinking about negative numbers, z-scores are often converted to mathematically equivalent positive numbers. A typical conversion would be to multiply each z-score by 50 and add 250; a version of this is used by the National Assessment of Educational Progress who conducted the Young Adult Literacy Study in the United States. A z-score of -1.5, for example, is equivalent in this system to a scale score of 175; the average score is 250. Because z-scores typically run from -3 to + 3, most of these scaled scores would lie between 100 and 400. Other scale conversion systems are in use. American College Testing, for example, multiplies the z-score by 5 and adds 20 so that a z-score of -1.5 is an ACT score of 11.25. The College Board tests (SAT and GRE) convert z-scores by multiplying by 100 and adding 500; a -1.5 z-score becomes 350.[2]

A common, and controversial, norm-referenced scoring of adult tests is grade equivalent scoring. Here, the adult's performance on the test is compared to that of a typical student in a particular school grade. Grade equivalent scores are not derived mathematically from the raw score, as are the scale scores discussed above. Rather they are empirically determined by having students, usually secondary school students, take both a school achievement test, which already has grade norms, and an adult achievement test and relating the scores on the two. The grade equivalent for a particular raw score must then be looked up in a table. The student who scored 24 on TABE vocabulary and 30 on TABE reading, for example, is said to be at grade 6.2. Grade equivalent scoring is problematic, even for school-children (Brown, 1983), and much caution must be taken in interpreting such scores for adults.

It is also possible to compare scores on a test to some other criteria. On an adult literacy test, one could, for example, identify items that all competent adults might be expected to succeed with and score the examinees by how many of these they are able to do. The Southam Literacy Survey (1987), for example, tested adults on a number of key items that had been identified as central to competent adult performance.

Participants in the survey had to correctly answer 80% of theseitems to be classified as fuller literates. Other criterion-referenced schemes will be discussed below.[3]

ACHIEVEMENT TESTS
Undoubtedly the most familiar ABE/AL tests are the Adult Basic Learning Examination (ABLE)[4] and the Test of Adult Basic Education (TABE). A

Canadian test derived from the ABLE, the Canadian Adult Achievement Test (CAAT) has been recently introduced and a French language test, related to CAAT, is under development.[5] While each of these tests reflects a somewhat different approach to measuring achievement and each has a slightly different set of components, they all purport to provide a measure of school achievement for adults that is comparable to that provided by achievement tests for school children. To that end, they all provide test scores in terms of grade equivalents and all have a range of reading and arithmetic items thought to be typical of school curricula.

The tests typically consist of a number of sub-tests, such as spelling, vocabulary, reading comprehension, number operations (simple arithmetic), and numerical problem solving (word problems). These sub-tests are often grouped to provide skills area scores, so the first three might form a language score and the latter two may be combined into a mathematics score. Each has a series of tests at different levels of difficulty and ABLE and TABE have several equivalent forms at each level.

The tests may also have other sub-tests. For example, the TABE has a section on language mechanics, as does ABLE at the highest level. CAAT includes a mechanical reasoning section, taken from the Differential Aptitude Test at the middle and highest levels and science and language mechanics tests at the top level.

In order to provide grade equivalent scores these tests have been equated to standardized school achievement tests. For example, ABLE is equated to the Stanford Achievement test (SAT) and TABE to the California Achievement Test (CAT). Indeed, the first version of TABE was composed of items taken from the CAT and slightly modified for an adult audience; the second edition, and all editions of ABLE and CAAT, have items written especially for the test, but which have been written to provide comparability to school test items.

Test users are cautioned, both by me and by the creators of TABE, ABLE, and CAAT, that the 'score' a student achieves on the test is not very precise. Since the score an examinee gets on a single administration of a test is affected by many things in addition to the examinee's ability (attention that day, particular disturbances during the administration, the reliability and validity of the test), that score is only an estimate of the examinee's 'true' score. Because of this test analysts prefer to report a band of scores within which the examinee's true score is most likely to lie. This range is determined by the standard error of measurement (SEM). Our examinee who answered 30 TABE reading comprehension items correctly, attained a reading comprehension score, for example, which is equivalent to grade 6.0, but his/her true score could range from 5.4 to 6.4, because the test is not that precise. In fact, this is a relatively small range for an adult achievement test, because this score is in the range where the test is most precise. An examinee whose attained score on the same test is directly equivalent to grade 9.1, could have a true score any where between grade 7.1 and 12.9. This has important implications for measuring and reporting student gains. A student whose score appears to have changed from 9.1 to 10.5, for example, may have made no gains at all since the results are within the range of scores expected simply from random fluctuations in performance from one day to another.

Nonetheless, these tests are useful when students are in programs designed to prepare them for further academic study. Because they are based on school curricula, they measure the kind of literacy and numeracy skills normally expected in academic programs. These tests may be especially useful for the many ABE programs, particularly in the United States, which prepare students for the GED Test. Both ABLE and TABE provide tables that estimate GED scores from the ABLE or TABE score. Users should note, however, that such estimates are inexact; scores on the GED science test, for example, are estimated from reading scores on TABE.

Since research has clearly shown that those skills that serve students well in academic study are not always the skills needed in everyday life or in jobs, these tests may be less appropriate for measuring such skills for everyday or job purposes.[6]

SKILLS

The reading comprehension sections of adult achievement tests provide a single measure of the complex task of reading. Skills tests attempt to measure parts of that complex process. In many ways they are like achievement tests: scores are norm-referenced, grade-equivalent scores are provided, the literacy measured is school-oriented literacy. But they do not measure ability to read if we understand that to mean the ability to comprehend meaning from a text, because they provide no texts to be comprehended.

The most widely used of these is the Wide-range Achievement Test (WRAT). The version used with adults has three components, an arithmetic section, a spelling section, and a word pronunciation section (called reading by WRAT). WRAT is relatively easy to administer, though individual administration is required. Yet it is difficult to know what information about reading, other than relatively elementary word recognition information, is obtained from WRAT. The developers of WRAT have not shown that it predicts scores on tests, such as TABE or CAAT, that more obviously do measure reading. Since it does not require the examinee to understand even a complete sentence, it can hardly be said to be a test of reading.

A test that is primarily a skills test, but is not standardized, is the Reading Evaluation - Adult Diagnosis (READ) test from Literacy Volunteers of America (LVA). The test is designed to fit the LVA curriculum, which begins with letter recognition and proceeds to individual words before moving on to brief texts. Because the test is skills oriented we have included it here, even though its scoring is not norm-referenced. Typically the test is administered until the examinee misses a fixed number of items; at that point the test ends and the examinee's score is calculated. The score's only meaning is that it is related to particular points in the LVA teaching material. In effect, teaching starts at the point in the curriculum where the testing ended.

READ clearly reflects LVA's view that reading is a bottom-up phenomenon, that one has to understand letters before one can understand words, and words before one can understand sentences. While this view, one shared with the Laubach curricula, was once dominant, it no longer has much research support. For this reason, READ should be used only by those who share LVA'S, or Laubach's, philosophy of adult literacy education. Since WRAT shares this bottom-up approach to reading, it, too, is inconsistent with modern theories of reading and reading instruction.

FUNCTIONAL TESTS

Because the achievement and skills tests have often seemed somewhat removed from the everyday uses of literacy and numeracy several tests that attempt to more directly measure the latter kind of skill have been developed. The most well-known of these is probably the APL test developed as part of the Adult Performance Level project (Northcutt, Selz, Shelton, Nyer, Hickok, & Humble, 1975), but others do exist such as the Reading/Everyday Activities in Life (R/EAL) and the Ontario Test of Adult Functional Literacy (OTAFL) and its French counterpart Test ontarien d'alphabétisation fonctionnelle des adultes (TOAFA).[7] These tests all score examinees, not against each other as achievement and skills tests do, but against a hypothetical 'competent' adult. Typically items are chosen to represent a range of texts encountered in everyday life, such as school notices, classified ads, instructions, and grocery lists. Questions are then devised that require examinees' to process these texts much as they would when they encounter them in everyday life. For example, examinees may be asked to find all the apartments in a set of classified ads that meet a particular set of requirements (cost less than $600, allow pets, etc.).

It is in choosing the texts that the tests have encountered the greatest criticisms. The APL identified over 60 competencies which characterized adult functioning in the United States. Test items were developed to measure each of these. The validity of the competencies, and the items, was measured by the ability of successful adults to answer them. Unfortunately, the measure of adult success was simply income and the APL project has been properly criticized on these grounds (Cervero, 1980, 1981; Griffith & Cervero, 1977). The criticisms of APL have been extended to other functional tests even though they have used different criteria for selecting the functional items (Litchman, 1974; Jones & Déry, 1988; Jones & Librande, 1988).

Items for the OTAFL and TOAFA tests were selected in consultation with students in adult literacy programs, who reviewed all the items considered for the test. These students were asked if the texts were important, if the questions asked about the texts seemed realistic, and if they had encountered these texts outside school. Some responses were contrary to expectation; for example, the students rated questions on TV program guides as of little importance, though these often show up on various functional literacy tests. They rated health and school items of greatest importance (and this is reflected in the test).

Scores on functional tests are often more difficult for instructors to interpret than scores on achievement test because they are not designed for comparing students with each other. Rather they reflect the ability of the student to deal with a range of reading and numeracy tasks outside the instructional setting. Because much teaching material is designed to fit the model of school literacy which is reflected in achievement tests, but not in these functional tests, (none have grade equivalent scores, for example) it is not always apparent how to use functional test information for traditional school-oriented ABE programs.

One of the strongest arguments, however, for using these tests, at least in conjunction with a more traditional achievement test, is that many students will be able to demonstrate their real abilities on them because they have had more experience with this kind of literacy. In these tests they have a chance to show, to the teacher and to themselves, that they can successfully complete some literacy tasks, giving them confidence to proceed and the teacher a better insight into the students' strengths. As ABE and AL programs develop their own curricula and move away from using exclusively school-based approaches to teaching adults literacy and numeracy, functional tests will be an important tool in assessing out-of-school literacy abilities.

INVENTORY TESTS

To some extent scores on functional tests are related to the examinee's experience with similar texts (another reason they are often criticized). There is no doubt that experience with and attitude toward reading is an important characteristic of ABE/AL students. Several procedures have been developed that attempt to measure this experience.

The most systematic of these is Baseline, a computer moderated assessment developed by the Adult Literacy and Basic Skills Unit in the United Kingdom. The assessment asks the student how well she can deal with a variety of reading tasks. The tasks are presented in a manual, not on the computer, and resemble many of the tasks on functional literacy tests. Instead of asking the examinee to do the task, however, and then seeing if it was done properly, the inventory simply asks the examinee to say how easily he could do it. Examinees are also asked whether they regularly do certain kinds of reading, such as magazines, store coupons, and maps. Similar assessments are made of writing and numeracy. The computer uses the student's responses to generate a series of statements about the student's attitudes to reading, such as:

You are not very confident about reading.
Confidence often develops with more practice.

How useful students would find this information depends, I would think, on how counselors use it to guide the students.

There is, in fact, no reason why the assessment could not be delivered by a teacher rather than the computer and several good reasons why a teacher would be better. Lytle's informal assessment procedure (Lytle, Marmor & Penner, 1986; Lytle, 1988) works in much the same way, though without, apparently, the systematic presentation of texts that Baseline uses. The opportunity for the assessor to get information about the student through discussing reading with the student, is a promising new approach to literacy assessment. What needs to be done is to study experienced and insightful assessors who use such interviews in order to develop training procedures. Counselling interviews are not a completely novel procedure, but we have not worked out their use in assessing cognitive skills. Work, such as Lytle's, promises to provide us with new insights into how such interviews, conducted by trained assessors, can serve ABE/AL students.

Some intake assessors have been using a combination of inventory interviews and functional tests. The students take the test, as a regular test, so that standard information is available for all students in the program, but then the counselor interviews the student about the test and her performance on it. The interview provides additional information that can be used by the teacher and counselor to guide the student to appropriate learning experiences.

PROFILES

A somewhat independent development, but similar in intent to both inventory and functional approaches is the use of profiles for assessing achievement, Several profile schemes exist, but the most elaborate one for ABE/AL is the Practical Skills Profile scheme of the Royal Society of Arts. A profile scheme consists of a number of profile sentences or goals that a student might attempt; for example, one of the RSA Practical Skills is D7, *Read a variety of digital and non-digital displays*. Accompanying each sentence is a list of criteria that a student must meet in order to have demonstrated competence in that skill. For D7 they include:

> Correctly read data from these sources
> Use the data in practical ways, e.g. read an electric meter and record the data,
> set up a video to record a time programme.

As such, the profile sentences might be seen as specifications for a test and we might expect that RSA would provide test items for each profile sentence. The emphasis, however, is on the practical, and the evidence for having achieved a particular skill is not the passing of a test but the demonstration of that skill in everyday contexts. For example, evidence for profile sentence D26, *Carry out everyday financial transactions,* is the presentation to an assessor of cheques, deposit, and withdrawal slips actually used in the individual's life.

Because there are over one hundred profile sentences in the practical skills scheme, it is not expected that every student will attempt every sentence.[8] Counselling, and goal-setting, as to which skills to attempt are an essential element of the program. This may, in fact, be one of the most important parts of the system. Because the students can set rather clearly defined goals, with explicit criteria for assessment which can be achieved in a reasonable time, they can see progress. RSA issues a certificate which lists the profile sentences completed so that a record of the student's achievement is available. Because the certificate is designed to be added to as the student completes new profile sentences, the certificate offers early, official, recognition of the student's accomplishments and progress.

SUMMARY

Adult educators are often under pressure to report the progress of students in their programs. Because grade equivalent scores are a widely recognized, but not widely understood measure, educators often choose a test because it provides such a score, even though the test may not be appropriate for the program. Other tests provide ways of measuring progress and educators should use the type of measure most appropriate to their program. One measure of student progress, for example, might be the number of profile sentences completed, or the increased confidence to undertake more difficult literacy and numeracy tasks. Students are not well served if inappropriate tests are used. Their real progress may be disguised and their sense of accomplishment diminished if the test measures skills they have not been learning or are not interested in learning.

When a test is chosen because it provides a particular kind of score, there is a real danger that the teaching will be designed for the test, even when that teaching is not what is most appropriate. Tests should not guide instruction, instruction should guide tests. The test types discussed in this chapter indicate that there are a variety of approaches to assessing adult literacy and numeracy; programs should be using a test that is consistent with the kind of instruction they want to provide.

NOTES

1. At the time of writing of this chapter Sue Waugh and Lucie Déry were preparing English and French guides, respectively, to adult literacy tests for the Ontario Ministry of Basic Skills. Review of drafts of these guides suggest they will be helpful to those seeking more details about each test.
2. A full discussion of various schemes for norm-referenced test-scoring can be found in Brown (1983), chapter 8.
3. Brown (1983), chapter 9, discusses a variety of criterion-referenced procedures.
4. A list of all tests discussed and their publishers is provided at the end of the chapter.
5. In the early stages of development this French test was known as Épreuve canadienne de rendement pour adultes, but at the time of writing no final name had been determined.
6. Hill and Perry (1988) discuss in detail the assumptions about reading that underlie the TABE. Most of their arguments apply to all the tests discussed in this section.
7. The Basic English Skills Test (BEST) has a functional literacy component, but this is rather short compared to the ones we discuss and is intended primarily for an ESL audience.
8. In a related profile scheme, the Continuing Education scheme, students are expected to complete each of the 21 skills.

Tests Discussed

Adult Basic Learning Examination (ABLE). 3 levels, 2 forms at each level. San Antonio: The Psychological Corporation.
Adult Performance Level. Orlando, FL: Media Systems.
Baseline. London: Adult Literacy and Basic Skills Unit.
Canadian Adult Achievement Test (CAAT). 3 levels. Toronto: The Psychological Corporation, Canada.
Practical Skills Profile. London: Royal Society of Arts.
Reading/Everyday Activities in Life. 2 forms. New York: Westwood Press.
Ontario Test of Adult Functional Literacy (OTAFL). 3 levels. Ottawa: Centre for the Study of Adult Literacy, Carleton University.
Reading Evaluation – Adult Diagnosis (READ). Syracuse: Literacy Volunteers of America.
Test of Adult Basic Education (TABE). 4 levels, 2 forms at each level. Monterey, CA: CTB/McGraw-Hill.
Test ontarien d'alphabétisation fonctionnelle des adultes (TOAFA). 3 niveaux. Ottawa: Centre d'études en alphabétisation des adultes, université Carleton.
Wide-Range Achievement Test. 1 level for adults. Jastak Associates.

REFERENCES

Anderson, B. L., (1981). *Guide to adult functional literacy assessment using existing tests.* Portland, OR: Functional Literacy Project, Northwest Regional Educational Laboratory.

Bloom, B. S., Madaus, G. F., & Hastings, J. T., (1971). *Handbook on Formative and Summative Evaluation of Student Learning.* New York: McGraw-Hill.

Brown, F. G., (1983). *Principles of educational and psychological testing* (3rd edition). New York: Holt, Rinehart & Winston.

Cervero, R. M., (1980). Does the Texas Adult Performance Level Test measure functional competence? *Adult Education, 30,* 152-165.

Cervero, R. M., (1981). Assessment in adult basic education: a comparison of the APL and GED tests. *Adult Education, 31,* 67-84.

Griffith, W. S., & Cervero, R. M., (1977). The adult performance level program: a serious and deliberate examination. *Adult Education, 27,* 209-224.

Hill, C., & Perry, K., (1988). *Reading assessment: autonomous and pragmatic models of literacy* (LC Report 88-2). New York: Literacy Center, Teachers' College, Columbia University.

Jones, S., & Déry, L., (1988). *Test ontarien d'alphabétisation fonctionnelle des adultes,* (rapport de projet). Ottawa: Centre d'études en alphabétisation des adultes, université Carleton.

Jones, S., & Librande, L., (1988). *Ontario test of adult functional literacy* (Final report). Ottawa: Centre for the Study of Adult Literacy, Carleton University.

Litchman, M., (1974). The development and validation of R/EAL, an instrument to assess functional literacy. *Journal of Reading Behaviour, 6,* 167-182.

Lytle, S. L.,, Marmor, T. W.,, & Penner, F. H., (1986). *Literacy theory in practice: assessing reading and writing of low-literate adults.* Paper presented at the annual meeting of the American Education Research Association, San Francisco.

Lytle, S., (1988). From the inside out: reinventing assessment. *Focus on Basics, 2*(1), 1-12.

Nafziger, D. H., Thompson, R. B., Hiscox, M. D., & Owen, T. R., (1975). *Tests of adult functional literacy: an evaluation of currently available instruments.* Portland, OR: Northwest Regional Educational Laboratory.

Northcutt, N., Selz, N., Shelton, E., Nyer, L., Hockok, D., & Humble, M., (1975). Adult functional competency: a summary. Austin, TX: The University of Texas, Division of Extension.

Southam Literacy Survey, (1987). *Literacy in Canada.* Toronto: Creative Research Group.

CHAPTER 2:

Assessment of the Basic Dimensions and the Concept of Instrument Readability

Maurice C. Taylor

Adult education and training in both business and industrial environments have encouraged the growth of programs and courses which require some form of prior assessment of adult knowledge and skills coupled with the measurement of final outcomes. A recent federal government report entitled *A Review of the Canadian Jobs Strategy* (1988) has sparked a new interest in establishing valid instruments for adult selection into academic, job-training, upgrading and work place literacy programs.

In both Canada and the United States numerous publications such as *Competing in the New Global Economy* (1988), the *Quarterly Labour Market & Productivity Review* (1988), *Basic Skills in the Workplace* (1988), and *Workforce 2000* (1987) attest to the fact that the knowledge explosion is creating new information so rapidly that job skills and knowledge are becoming obsolete in an ever shorter period of time. Less than 2 years ago more than 100,000 jobs were lost and hundreds of thousands of Canadians were severely affected by technological change. To cope with change, workers and employers must be equipped with new skills and in turn a mechanism for assessment of these new skills.

Individuals will increasingly need to be trained and retrained or upgraded so that they may participate fully in this new economy. There is no indication that this demand will abate or that any sector, occupation or vocation will be exempt. (For Adults Only, 1986, p. 6) Attached to this strategy of re-skilling is the requirement of some form of adult assessment.

Many provinces are now putting in place contemporary skills training systems as part of a balanced economic policy. For example, Ontario's Training Strategy through the Ontario Basic Skills and Ontario Basic Skills in the Workplace are equipping workers with the job entry and basic literacy and numeracy skills essential to gaining employment, further training or becoming a more effective worker. Prior assessment of adult knowledge and skills as well as measurement of final outcomes take on an integral part in this new training system.

Investment in people is a key strategy in our economic renewal. Utilizing the human resources of both working and non-working people to overcome barriers to participation in the labour market is a part of a balanced economic policy. Adult assessment therefore plays a vital role in this strategy. Assessment of the basic dimensions can be viewed as a mechanism in the decision making process. Adult educators must be aware of the different purposes of adult assessment, the different methods of testing and the considerations in choosing a test or measure.

ASSESSMENT OF THE BASIC DIMENSIONS

Researchers have attempted to categorize the major dimensions of human behaviour. These dimensions represent the diversity and complexity of adult behaviour and include intelligence, aptitude, achievement, cognitive style, personality, motivation and interest inventories.

Aptitude and achievement tests are considered to be on a single continuum from general skills measurement at the aptitude level to very specific knowledge measurement at the achievement level. The aptitude test's primary function is to assess broad intellectual factors and wide ranges of knowledge. The objective of achievement tests is the assessment of specific knowledge typically learned in a school or training program.

Personality and motivation inventories refer to the broad assessment of an individual's characteristics as contrasted with capabilities or achievements. Interest inventories determine the theme and occupational orientation of an adult. Some instruments go as far as identifying an individual's interest with regard to a wide arc of occupation orientations while other forms are geared toward specific occupations.

Andrulis (1978) has proposed a classification system for the specific categories of aptitudes and achievement and personality tests. This scheme is useful in better understanding the purpose of tests and measures for adults. Aptitude and achievement tests can be divided into three groups. The first group describes general intelligence and provides a global measure on inherent capabilities of an individual. Aptitude measures tend to focus on verbal and quantitative skills without necessarily yielding an IQ value. Although the practical difference between intelligence and aptitude measures is slight, both have a common goal of assessing the native capabilities of an individual.

The second group are devices which assess the individual's level of achievement. Andrulis (1978) defines achievement as a manifestation of the individual's knowledge, after having engaged in numerous educational, training or environmental experiences. A third group is cognitive style measures. These devices measure more precisely a skill or capability that the individual might possess such as spatial orientation.

Personality measures can also be categorized into three groupings: general pesonality measures which yield two or more personality dimensions, specific personality measures which focus in on one trait and individual adjustment measures.

Of utmost importance in the assessment of adults is the need to focus upon testing objectives. Typical objectives appear to be based on the four dimensions of diagnosis, prescription, monitoring and evaluation. Diagnosis is used to search out and identify those characteristics which either inhibit or foster certain types of performance or behaviour. In using the diagnostic approach we ask what is the cause or reason for the learner's behaviour.

Prescription allows one to make recommendations regarding the educational or remedial direction an individual should take given the adult's meaured assets and liabilities. In recommending an appropriate prescription, we must ask what is the current level of the individual's knowledge or skill. The relationship between diagnosis and prescription is very close.

Monitoring provides a measure of the ongoing development and change in the adult as the individual fulfills a prescribed course of action such as academic upgrading, therapy or a remedial process. Monitoring objectives demand that selected tests be administered to determine if the goals set for the individual are being met in terms of expected level and frequency. This is usually done over short time periods.

The main focus in evaluative testing is to determine whether or not the adult's goals and objectives have been attained. These mechanisms help answer broad-based questions appropriate for individual and group evaluation. Evaluation is the final step in testing as it flows from the first three steps of diagnosis, prescription and monitoring.

The selection of a particular assessment device is determined not only by the testing objectives but also by other characteristics of the instrument. Some characteristics which aid in the selection process are the logistical considerations, confidentiality, norms, test interpretation and readability of the instrument.

Most assessment devices are classified by levels of security which designate the various instruments' availability either to a selected group of trained examiners or to a wider variety of individuals with minimal experience in the field of assessment. Another logistical consideration deals with the administrative responsibility for presentation of the instrument. The logistics of cost per individual must include not only those involved in securing the instrument, but also the administrator's time in setting up environmental conditions, scoring, handling and processing the completed instrument.

Confidentiality of results is another area of concern. Adrulis (1978) states that a controversy stems from the rights of adult subjects to be aware of their responses to the various assessment mechanisms that may have been utilized in either an academic or industrial setting. From an ethical point of view, it is difficult to justify the release of test results to counsellors, teachers and trainers while withholding the results from an adult, especially when the subject evidences maturity and knowledge to use the information properly.

The availability of norms on a national, provincial and regional level is another consideration in the selection of assessment devices. Interpretation of results will be more valuable and realistic if the norms are specific. But norms rise and fall in importance depending on the purpose for which an instrument is being used. Norms when strictly interpreted are examples of typical performance by individuals and are not necessarily indicative of how all subjects will respond on a particular instrument. Andrulis (1978) claims that if only limited norms exist, it does not necessarily require searching for a better instrument, but rather reconsidering the use of the instrument in light of the absence of appropriate norms or, developing norms specific to one's needs.

The validity and reliability are also two essential characteristics of a sound test. Although the purpose of this investigation is not to address the types, definitions and typical psychometric problems encountered in a testing environment, it should be stressed that anyone who chooses tests, interprets scores or makes decisions based on test scores should have a thorough understanding of the concept of reliability and validity.

Another category of information which aids in the selection and administration of tests concerns the adult's prior education. Is the individual able to read the test items?

A report entitled *Learning for Life: Overcoming the Separation of Work and Learning* (1984) presents a number of strategies and recommendations to promote a Canada wide debate on the issue of educational leave. The report states that the old cycle of schooling, training and work is likely to be replaced by a sequence of retraining and re-education. In recognition of this, arrangements for lifelong skill development must be investigated carefully.

Special attention and priority are given to the educationally disadvantaged adult group. Immediate action is proposed to establish a ten-year program to combat adult illiteracy in Canada. The implications of these recommendations in terms of adult assessment means that as educationally disadvantaged adults achieve their highest potential level of literacy competency through paid time off selection and assessment of final outcomes must be based on instruments that are readable by this adult group.

THE CONCEPT OF READABILITY

Over the past four decades one of the problems in adult education has been the assessment of readability — how to tell whether a piece of writing is likely to be readable to a particular group of adult readers. In examining the phenomena of a test, scale or measure being difficult for adult learners to read in a business, industrial or research environment invokes the concept of readability once again.

Readability, in the broadest sense, is the sum total (including interactions) of all those elements within a given piece of printed material that affect the success which a group of readers have with it. The success is the extent to which they understand it, read it at optimum speed and find it interesting. As Harvey (1987) states it is not a replacement for teacher judgement, as teacher judgement is a vital part of assessing readability.

This definition of readability considers three major aspects of the reading process: comprehension, fluency and interest. Comprehension refers to the understanding of words and phrases, and the relating of ideas in the passage to our own experience. Fluency is the extent to which a person can read a given text at optimum speed. This element emphasizes the perceptual aspects of reading. The third component refers to the motivational factors which will affect interest. These three elements are not separate but interact with each other to affect readability.

Various researchers have defined readability as the degree to which a given class of people find certain reading matter compelling and comprehensible. Such a definition stresses both the characteristics of the reader as well as the degree of "compellingness" of the text. It argues that a definition of readability must be based on the characteristics of the readers, as it can be assumed that people will tend to continue to read only that which they understand. Alternatively, readability refers to the ease of understanding of written materials due to the style of writing used (Klare, 1975). The style of writing (or how the content of the writing is stated) can be measured in such a way that a numerical value can be assigned to each writing style. These values are assigned through the use of readability formulae where the numerical value that results from the measurement of style quantifies the ease or difficulty of the writing. With most formulae this numerical value has been translated into an educational skill level associated with the material.

A readability formulae or index "is like a yardstick that helps us measure certain qualities in the writing so we can make objective judgements about reading level" (Lauback & Koschnick, 1977, p. 12). Many readability formulae have been developed as a result of research into factors within writing that correlated highly with style difficulty. Most readability formula values are calculated by measuring sentence and word familiarity or word length.

Copley et al (1982, p. 157) suggest that readability formulae may classified into two major categories:

1. Simple Computation Formulae

The Reading Ease Formula (Flesch) — One hundred running words are selected. The number of syllables are counted. The average length of the sentences is found (# words ÷ # sentences). The results are then subtracted from constants to determine the readability level (any grade levels)

The Fog Index (Gunning) — One hundred running words are selected. Determine the average length of the sentences. Count the number of difficult words (three syllables or more). Add the two figures together and multiply by .4 to determine the readability level (any grade levels).

2. Complex Computation Formulae

Spache Readability Formula — One hundred running words are selected. The average sentence length is computed. The percent of difficult words is determined by matching the words in the selection against those on Stone's Revision of the Dale List which accompanies the formula. The average sentence length and percent of difficult words are added to a constant. The sum represents the grade equivalent (for use with materials between 1.3 and 4.0 grade levels).

A Formula for Predicting Readability (Dale-Chall) — This formula is the same as Spache's except that the Dale List of 3,000 words is used to determine the familiar words (for use with materials between 4.0 and 16.0 grade levels). The reader is cautioned to use the conversion chart to determine the ranges of readability.

The Dale-Chall formula can be simplified by using Layton's chart which also eliminates the need for computation and allows writers to determine the percent of unfamiliar words and sentence length to use when composing materials at a specific grade level.

Although the concept of readability has been widely studied, a review of literature indicated that only recently has there been an application of readability formulae to standardize instruments.

INSTRUMENT READABILITY

Taylor and Wahlstrom (1985) conducted a study to examine the procedure for applying readability formulae to a standardized assessment instrument

(Levenson's Internal, Powerful Others and Chance Scales (IPC) and to modify the instrument for use in an ABE program. The Fog, Flesch and Fry readability formulae were selected to examine the readability of the scales for an ABE population. Application of the formulae indicated that the scales needed to be modified to a lower reading level. Item writing procedures, quality comparisons, application of the formulae and a Q-sort were used to develop a modified IPC suitable for an ABE learner with reading skills of the fourth- and fifth-grade range. Although the procedures used to modify the instrument to assure a low readability has desired merit, the authors recommend that a more comprehensive adult readability formula be derived which incorporates additional characteristics beyond word difficulty and sentence length. Bruce (1981) argues that current readability formulae ignore or violate current knowledge about the reading process.

Most formulae affect only the sentence length and word difficulty while ignoring factors that influence text comprehensibility, such as cohesion, the number of inferences required, the number of items to remember, the complexity of ideas, rhetorical structure, dialect, required schemata, punctuations, clauses and double phrases. Nor do they account for reader-specific factors such as interest and the purpose of reading. Another limitation in the use of readability formulae is their failure to assess the meaning or comprehension of text. Marshall (1979) states that comprehension is the process of dealing with meaning and from this perspective readability and comprehensibility are not interchangeable terms.

Further development and research on readability and comprehension is needed to examine new variables and to test their performance especially in the area of grade level estimates for technical reports and documents. Within the adult education community it is desirable to have procedures and instruments relevant for use with the ABE learner. A new test assessment formula should include the following factors: sentence length, vocabulary difficulty, personal interest and comprehension.

It is increasingly apparent that instruments used in an ABE population are difficult for adult learners to read. As prior assessment, selection criteria and accountability of adult performance become issues in business, industrial and educational environments and as we attempt to utilize the human resources of both working and non-working people, the concept of test readability takes on a new importance.

REFERENCES

Andrulis, R. (1978). *Adult Assessment: A Source Book of Tests and Measures of Human Behaviour.* Springfield Illinois: C. C. Thomas.

Bruce, B. (1981). "Why Readability Formulas Fail?" *Reading Education Report No. 28.* Center for the Study of Reading, University of Illinois, Urbana.

Canadian Association of Adult Education (1985). *A New Direction for Canada: An Agenda for Economic Renewal.*

Canadian Labour Market and Productivity Centre (1988). *Quarterly Labour Market and Productivity Review.* Ottawa, Canada.

Copley, P., Roubinek, D., Layton, J., Range, D. (1982). "Implementing and Evaluating Reading." In Klevins, C. (Ed.) *Materials and Methods in Adult and Continuing Education.* Los Angeles: Klevens Publications Inc.

Harvey, R. (1987). "Write, Rewrite and Evaluate Adult Materials." In Klevins, C. (Ed.) *Materials and Methods in Adult and Continuing Education.* Los Angeles: Klevins Publications Inc.

House of Commons. (1988). *A Review of the Canadian Jobs Strategy.* Second Report of the Standing Committee on Labour, Employment and Immigration. Ottawa, Canada.

Johnson, W. (1987). *Workplace 2000:* Word and Workers for the 21st Century. Indiana: Hudson Institute, Indianapolis.

Klare, G. (1975). "Assessing Readability." *Reading Research Quarterly. 10* (1). 62-102.

Laubach, R. & Koschnick, K. (1977). *Using Readability.* Syracuse, New York: Reader's Press.

Marshall, N., (1979). "Readability and Comprehensibility." *Journal of Reading, 22* (6), 542-544.

Ministry of Colleges and Universities (1986). *For Adults Only.* Toronto.

Ministry of Skills Development (1986). *Breaking New Ground.* Toronto.

Premier's Council (1988). *Competing in the New Global Economy.* Report of the Premier's Council. Queens Park, Toronto.

Taylor, M. & Wahlstrom, M. (1985). Application of Readability Formulas to an Adult Basic Education Test. *Adult Literacy and Basic Education, 10* (3), 155-170.

United States Department of Education and Department of Labour (1988). *Basic Skills in the Workplace.* Superintendent of Documents, Washington, D.C.

CHAPTER 3:
Field Study of Community Literacy Methodical Questions

Serge Wagner

In 1987, within the framework of the Community Literacy program in Ontario, I wrote a methodological and didactic document entitled "Étude du milieu et analyse des besoins en alphabétisation des adultes" (Field Study and Analysis of Literacy Needs of Adults). This guide, which dealt with the preparatory phase of a community literacy program, was intended for practitioners, and had been designed for the Franco-Ontarian sector. Only the general methodological framework and didactic style of that guide have been retained in this text. In pre-literacy, the practitioners require a methodological model, the presentation of which is relatively simple. On the one hand, they need methodological information and on the other hand, they need a guide which is effective because it is easy to understand and follow, all of which obliges the writer to carry out some didactic research.

It is this double objective which the following article will attempt to attain. For this reason, the article is aimed primarily at practitioners.

ESTABLISHING AN OVERALL PLAN

In the pre-literacy phase, the field study and analysis of needs are not to be reduced to a speedy operation during which a few sparse statistics are recorded. Neither does it imply a university-style survey which would require resources and a lengthy duration, which are not within the reach of community literacy groups.

First and foremost, the practitioner should draw up an overall plan for herself. Methodologically speaking, this is the first aspect of the procedure.

The facilitator should understand that it is important to plan the operation well, and to determine in a precise and realistic manner those objectives which are to be pursued, the data to be studied, and the phases which will be required. The data which will be obtained and analyzed should provide very specific and useful information. For example, the study should yield information for the following operations or activities: the search for financing, ways to sensitize the general public, recruitment methods, the potential pool of illiterate persons, identification of possible collaborators, determination of a plan of establishment, selection of priority areas for intervention, pedagogical content, organizational development.

This entire operation should permit the translation of problems and needs into terms of pedagogical activities or organizational decision.

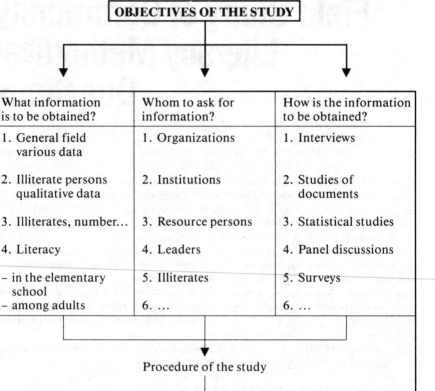

Figure 1: Objectives and Planning of a Field Study

Type of Data
Two principal types of data are obtained through a study of this kind.

Quantitative Data. These are statistical data the figures. For example, it is necessary to know the number and localization of the illiterate persons. It is equally important to know their distribution according to age, sex, professional activity, etc. However, these data are worthless unless they are analyzed and interpreted. The practical consequences for literacy must be extracted from them.

Qualitative Data. For example, these are statements, accounts of interviews, reflections. These data pertain to attitudes, perceptions, behaviour. They also relate to the problems in the field, those problems experienced by illiterate persons. These data are as essential as the quantitative data. However, they must be treated cautiously: they often reflect prejudices and personal opinions. These data must also be analyzed, "relativised". The data in question may be demographic, geographic, economic, socio-cultural, linguistic, behavioural.

THE SOURCES OF INFORMATION

On the Quantitative Data

The quantitative data are important. First of all, they lend credibility to the project — particularly if the statistics presented are drawn from a reliable source (moreover, the potential number of illiterate persons often constitutes one of the criteria for financing where funding organizations are concerned).

Above all, the statistics are useful. They lead to identification of the potential pool of people, its localization, and its principal characteristics. At the present time, the most reliable source for statistics is in the federal census data produced by Statistics Canada. We should state right away that all data pertaining to literacy on an international scale are always based on the population 15 years and over. The main drawback of the Statistics Canada data on illiteracy is that there are no data on illiteracy as such. Information on the degree of education is, however, available. Therefore, these data must be used cautiously, and the necessary reservations should be applied. In the industrialized nations, two criteria are usually considered in establishing two thresholds of literacy:

- **complete illiterates:** since it is generally accepted that at least four years of study are required in order that a person may be able to read and write adequately, those persons with less than 5 years of education are very likely to experience serious difficulties in the area of reading and/or writing.
- **functional illiterates:** in the industrialized countries in general, it is estimated that those persons with less than 9 years of education must be regarded as functional illiterates. This is the basic threshold in order to be able to function minimally in an industrialized society (for example, at least Grade 9 is usually required in order to obtain a large number of jobs, and everyday printed texts generally assume an educational level of about ten years).

Statistics Canada data on illiteracy enable us to establish "correlations". For example, we may find out where under-educated persons are distributed throughout a given territory; we may know their distribution according to sex, age, ethnic origin, employment, etc. These correlations, as already mentioned, are extremely useful because they enable us to get a more dynamic picture of illiteracy, and to better target the priorities (sex, locality, age ...). Once the recruitment is completed, they will also enable us to ascertain whether those groups which were targeted have been reached in a significant manner.

Federal census data are available to the public. Some are published by Statistics Canada (in the Bulletins). Other data are available only through direct consultation with the services of Statistics Canada. Some libraries carry all Statistics Canada publications. Certain statistical data are not published by Statistics Canada, but have been the subject of "special orders" on the part of certain organizations. Furthermore, it is even possible to place orders with Statistics Canada (costs are incurred) for more precise data concerning your locality or region (it is then necessary to apply to the Statistics Canada Reference Centres).

Concerning Qualitative Data

The field study affords a privileged opportunity to forge links with the local organizations and people in the field. These initial contacts will be useful in order to collect the qualitative data. Great care must be taken to identify those persons and/or organizations likely to know the targeted population.

In each region, and in each locality, the situation is special. However, what is a good source of information in one place is not necessarily so in another. For example, as possible sources of information in one area, we should mention: the princpals of elementary and secondary schools, adult education in community colleges, the local clergy, Employment and Immigration Canada (local office), the office of social and community services in the municipalities, the regional office of the Ministry of Social and Community Services, distress centres and shelters for battered women, local and charitable organizations, social clubs, the local libraries, the staff of local bookstores, local unions, the Workmen's Compensation Board, associations for the handicapped, local businesses (grocer, servicemen, etc.) and the personnel (hiring) offices of companies.

Within these organizations, there are persons who have had a prolonged contact with the local community, and who know illiterate individuals personally. It is these persons who must be sought out for the identification (and recruitment) of illiterates. Other persons who may have been contacted, even if they do not know the illiterate population very well, could be useful in the publicity-recruitment campaign.

These different people could provide pertinent information on the problems of the locality, and on the needs of illliterate and under-educated individuals. These various pieces of information will be used in the drawing up of the more specific literacy project, and in the preparation of didactic material. Lastly, the illiterates themselves are an important source of information. We should not limit ourselves to statistical data, nor to what "other people" think about illiterates. It is also necessary to make direct contact with these people and their surroundings, and to listen to them.

Even during the field study phase, it should be possible to meet a certain number of illiterate people and discuss their individual and collective situations with them, as well as their interest in literacy activities. These exchanges (in the form of an interview) will permit us to gain a better understanding of the reality of life for illiterate people, their needs, their interests, etc. and enable us to identify some "leaders", those individuals who could be involved in recruitment, development and organization pertaining to the literacy project.

Illiterate persons should not be regarded as mere consumers of literacy activities thought out by "others". The very notion of community literacy implies that these people are actively involved in the literacy project!

THE SURVEY TECHNIQUES

There are several methods of collecting the data required for the field study. The principal methods are identified herein. It is not necessary to retain all of them. However, since each method has its limitations, it will be necessary to combine some for the purposes of a study on illiteracy and literacy. Therefore, a single survey among illiterates will be insufficient: other data (e.g. statistics, workers in the field) will be necessary in order to set the literacy project in motion.

- Interviews with the "experts" and "leaders" in the field. In every community, there are some individuals who have privileged information on the subject that the facilitator wishes to obtain information; the situation of that community in general, and the problems and needs of its illiterates. These interviewees could just as easily also be social workers or the parish priest as an activist from a socio-political or cultural movement. The method consists of identifying such potential participants, meeting them, questioning them, and thus being in a position to draw some benefit from their experiences and from their skills.

  A preliminary list of possible participants should also be drawn up, and questions should be prepared for submissions to them. Often the the process unfolds like a "chain reaction": an initial interviewee suggests meeting other individuals.
- The study of existing documents. The experience of others has often been consigned to works and studies. It is necessary to utilize these data, since they will often help avoid repeating a study which has already been carried out. Studies on a region or a community may be found in various places: the public library, social agencies, school boards, etc.

  Whenever local participants are questioned, one should not forget to ask them which documents would be useful for the "field study/analysis of needs" operation (some of these documents could even be used or adapted in literacy workshops. For example, a booklet on the history of the francophones in the area.
- Study of statistics. It is essential to obtain objective quantitative data. For example, it is necessary to know the total number of francophones and the number of illiterate francophones in order to be in a position to determine the potential pool of literacy candidates. It is also useful to know how these persons are distributed throughout the area covered in order to determine the implementation procedures for literacy activities, and to identify sites which are suitable for local literacy projects.

  Statistical data are important because they convey reliable information, and often lend credibility to a funding application. This question will be developed under 'Organizational Aspects'.
- Personal observation. This method seems so obvious that it is often overlooked. While passing through the area, one should observe it closely and attempt to discern significant facts. One's observations, perceptions and hypotheses should also be noted.
- Panel discussion with informants. Employees and activists from organizations, as well as leaders in the field, are invited to exchange their views on all or some of the questions raised in the field study. This may seem like a variation on the individual interview with participants, but this method has some advantages. Such meetings are only organized after a certain amount of data has been collected. In the course of the survey, one is quickly confronted with contradictory perceptions (for example: "there are no illiterates", "illiterates are not interested in becoming literate", etc.). The panel discussion formula win therefore permit an exchange of views on these different perceptions. It will also provide an opportunity to obtain the opinion of others on certain matters: for example, on certain needs already

identified, on the hypotheses of services to be offered to illiterates, etc. It will thus be possible to question the perceptions and prejudices, to validate the hypotheses of service, etc.

- Direct survey among the people concerned. We suggest making contact with illiterates in order to initiate interviews. However, a group may decide to lead a detailed survey among a large sample of illiterate individuals, or even among the local population as a whole. This is the 'sampling' technique, and three methods may be considered for the accomplishment of this type of survey: the written questionnaire, the telephone survey, and the personal interview.
- The mail survey has to be eliminated for illiterate people. However, this method could be retained during the research phase with social workers. Nevertheless, one should realize that this is a method in which the rate of non-response is high.
- The telephone survey is less costly than the personal interview, since the interviewer does not have to travel. Even though it is carried out by telephone, this is a direct interview (at the level of oral communication). The questions should not be too long. Furthermore, the responses are not always reliable: some respondents refuse to give out the personal information about themselves over the telephone.
- The direct interview. This is the best method for obtaining detailed, reliable information. The interviewer is in the physical presence of the person being interviewed; contact is direct. This is the survey technique which yields the best rate of response. However, it is also a costly method, particularly when the population is scattered, which is always the case in a rural area. This technique could be utilized (by going door-to-door) in small localities, or in neighbourhoods where the percentage of illiterates is very high.

THE QUESTIONNAIRES, THE QUESTIONS ... THE INTERVIEWERS

In order to carry out this investigative work, we must not allow ourselves to improvise. We should not present ourselves to anyone unless we have in hand the list of those questions which we feel should be put to people with the aid of a tape recorder:

The Questionnaire

There are various types of interviews and questionnaires. A structured interview is one in which a precise list of specific questions is asked. In a non-structured interview, the list of questions is shorter, and the nature of the questions is more open. The questionnaires always comprise a precise number of pre-determined questions.

In all cases, the questions which one wishes to ask are drawn up in advance, in writing, and the same questions are put to the same types of people. Thus, a series of common questions must be prepared for social workers, and another series for illiterate persons (and there is no reason why there should not be common questions for both these categories of people). It is by having these analogous questions that it is possible to compare and analyse the results obtained.

The Questions

The questions must be prepared in terms of the particular population which is being addressed. A social worker and an illiterate person are not questioned in the same manner.

For illiterate persons in particular, one must ensure that the questionnaire is understandable. When the questions are clear and simple, the chances of obtaining clear and precise replies are better. The terms used must be checked (for example, with regard to the francophones, the majority do not know the meaning of the term ... illiterate!). It is a good idea to test the questionnaire with a few people in order to see whether they understand the questions, and whether meaningful replies are obtained.

One should also be careful not to be too abrupt with people. A certain progression should be allowed in the order of the questions: begin with questions of a more personal nature.

A good questionnaire should not be too long. Otherwise, people being questioned will become tired, and the replies will no longer be meaningful.

The Interviewers

For various reasons, it is necessary to prepare the interviewers. For example, they must be made to understand that comparable responses will only be obtained if the questions have been asked in an analogous manner.

It is necessary to select people who are able to set the interviwees at ease, and who are capable of communicating effectively with them. Contact with illiterate people is not necessarily a straightforward matter. These people are often living on the fringe of the social institutions. At first contact, they may be uneasy. The person interviewing them must be able to build up a climate of confidence gradually.

There should also be an understanding on the method of recording responses, so that the notes from interviews or completed questionnaires may be compiled without difficulty.

THE FUNCTIONAL ANALYSIS OF DATA

The survey does not end with the collection of data. Regardless of the techniques used, a considerable amount of information will have been collected, and will have to be rendered useful and functional for the project.

In the first place, it is necessary to collect and regroup these diverse pieces of information. An attempt must then be made to understand them, to grasp their significance. Links could also be forged between those different data which become complementary. This procedure must be carried out both for the quantitative and the qualitative data.

In analysing the data, it is important to extract the practical aspects from it for the literary project. For example, if it is noted that the illiterate people are fairly concentrated in a certain place (quantitative data) on the one hand and, on the other hand, several people or organizations in that place are inclined to become involved in a community literacy project (qualitative data), one may conclude as a possible proposal that the first experiment be carried out in that place.

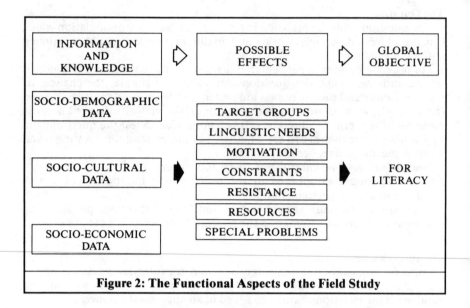

Figure 2: The Functional Aspects of the Field Study

The practitioner should make decisions which are logically derived from the data which he has collected. One might say that all the failures in community literacy occur either because of the lack of a good field study, or due to choices which do not conform with the data collected. There are those who collect the information, but fail to do the work of functional analysis. However, this is the most important task of all!

ORGANIZATIONAL ASPECTS

Each group may determine the importance which will be given to the field study phase and the analysis of needs. It is also up to each group to determine the methods which it intends to follow in order to attain its objectives. Regardless of the type of survey selected, however, the entire process must be carefully prepared, and each stage must be planned in minute detail.

An overall view of the tasks to be carried out has already been presented in Figure 1. In Figure 3, the three major chronological phases of each survey identified, and the actions to be set at each phase are specified. Each of the tasks identified must be itemized, the responsibilities shared, and deadlines fixed.

Such a list of activities remains very general. Each phase must be itemized and subdivided. Furthermore, the plan should be detailed in terms of the survey methods selected, because each survey method or technique requires specific procedures.

Phases/Tasks	Content	Who?	When?

1. **Establishment of a preliminary work plan**
  – functional definition of the objectives of the survey
  – list of information to be obtained
  – selection of data gathering methods (depending on financial and human resources)
  – preliminary list of people/organizations to contact
  – sharing of tasks according to a pre-established schedule
  – readjustment of plan (where applicable)
  – identification of complementary procedures			

2. **Process of the Survey**
  – interviews
  – study of documentation, statistical data
  – exchange of views on data obtained
  – identification of complementary procedures			

3. **Compiling of Data/Production of Report**
  – pooling of different data obtained
  – analysis
  – writing of the report
  – typing, typesetting, printing, distribution			

Figure 3: Phases and Tasks of the Survey			

LEVELS OF STUDY

In order to give a picture of illiteracy and literacy in an area, there must be a "survey" on two levels: that of the community in general, and that of the areas of illiteracy.

The Community in General

First of all, this means having a good knowledge of the locality or region in which the literacy project is to be developed. That region has its own general characteristics (which will influence the literacy project). For example: the extent of the territory, the socio-economic activity, the socio-economic features, population dispersion or distribution, the major problems, and the particular cultural expectations.

In each region, there are also networks of social workers, community organizations, and public institutions which intervene on the socio-cultural level. A good knowledge of this network will be essential to the development of the literacy project. An inventory of the facilitators and community resources should be drawn up. For example, a knowledge of the following facts must be ensured: local infrastructures, social organizations, means of communication, the local mass media, material resources, and local sources of funding.

It is particularly important to study the socio-economic characteristics of the area where intervention is anticipated, since the economic question lies at the very heart of the phenomenon of illiteracy.

In fact, illiteracy is not a mere chance occurrence. Neither is it a simple technical problem of not knowing how to read and write. Illiteracy seldom proves to be an isolated, individual phenomenon.

Those who are experiencing difficulties in reading, writing and arithmetic are not experiencing only these difficulties. They are often under-educated people on a low income. They are usually concentrated in areas of poverty. They are generally labourers, seasonal workers, etc. There are of course exceptions, those for whom illiteracy is a limited, circumscribed, isolated and exceptional problem. The majority of illiterates, however, find themselves "on the bottom rung of the ladder".

The person conducting the survey should be especially attentive to this, and know how to detect these areas of poverty which are not always visible, and in which it is extremely likely that many illiterate people are concentrated.

The Illiterate Areas

This is definitely the most important phase in the analysis of the field and the study of needs. We have already seen that illiteracy was a reality which was not usually restricted to difficulties in the mastery of reading, writing and arithmetic, and we also saw that literacy should not be reduced to the mere "technical" learning of these skills.

Illiteracy is not only the "lack of schooling". Illiterate people have a culture (based mainly on oral communication, and the values and lifestyle of those people in their community). Socio-cultural institutions do not generally know the "illiterate" world very well. Those who are illiterate or under-educated usually tend to live on the fringe of the social institutions and conceal their difficulties. The cultural world remains to be discovered, because an "illiterate culture" does exist.

The Study of the Illiterate Area Comprises Several Tasks:

- It is necessary to identify, pinpoint as closely as possible and know the illiterate and under-educated population which would probably be interested in literacy activities. Those concerned should be identified as accurately as possible: age, sex, job, locality, lifestyle, daily habits, meeting places, leisure, etc.
- One should ask whether any special, identifiable categories are to be found among them. Perhaps we could, if necessary, arrange for certain target groups to be given priority in literacy activities. For examples: the handicapped, young unemployed people, mothers, the elderly, workers, etc.
- Special attention will be given to the situation of women. A considerable proportion of them are living in conditions of poverty. For the most part, these are women who find themselves heading single-parent families. Equal attention is to be given to the situation of women in rural, semi-rural and suburban areas. They are often living isolated lives, and often experience travel problems (it is the husband who uses the car).
- An initial table of linguistic and cultural needs will be prepared: levels of illiteracy, difficulties in the areas of reading and writing; difficulties with regard to oral communication, attitude with respect to the mother tongue.
- There will also be testing to ascertain whether any needs exist in the area of arithmetic. The needs in this area are sometimes experienced at a general level (basic operations, decimals, fractions), at other times at a functional

level (be able to add up purchases, write cheques, control one's cheque or cash book, handle one's budget, etc.).

• The motivations and expectations of illiterate persons are noted. These may be very diverse in nature. Here, then, is how some people express their motivation to learn to read and write: "for the children's education", "to use the telephone book", "for a promotion in the job field", "for correspondence with the family who lives far away", "to understand automobile terms", "to fill out forms".

Furthermore, the practitioner should attempt to know the literacy situation in his/her region, both at the youth and adult levels: data on the student population, rate of school attendance and drop-out rate, data on "special education", experiences in adult education, basic training projects, etc.

CONCLUSIONS

The aim of the preceding elements of methodology was to draw attention to the need and importance of the field study, particularly in community literacy. In doing this, we wanted to counteract the excessively empirical tendency of numerous practitioners who detest any form of systematic work. Many of these facilitators are under the impression that they know the area in which they are living and working. Most of the time it is an illusion. Illiteracy is a hidden and obscure reality; the secret of developing a good method is to cultivate doubt in oneself and one's own convictions.

Doubt is what produces and develops the method!

REFERENCES

Conseil international d'éducation des adultes, (1973). *Le monde de l'alphabétisation. Politiques, recherche et action* (The World of Literacy. Politics, Research and Action), Ottawa, CRDI.

Hamadache, A. and Martin, D., (1986). *Theory and Practice of Literacy Work, Policies Strategies and Examples*, Paris and Ottawa, UNESCO and CODE.

Pothier, N. and Vermétte, M., (1982). *La pré-alphabétisation et l'utilisation des bénévoles en alphabétisation: le point de vue de la pédagogie* (Pre-Literacy and the Use of Volunteers in Literacy: the Pedagogical Point of View), Quebec, Ministry of Education.

Thiagarjan, S., (1976). *Programmes Instruction for Literacy Workers*, Teheran: Hulton Educational Publications.

UNESCO, (1973). *La formation du personnel de a'lphabétisation fontionnelle* (The Training of Personnel for Functional Literacy), Paris UNESCO.

Wagner, S., (1987). *Étude du milieu et analyse des besoins en alphabétisation des adultes* (Study of the Field and Analysis of the Literacy Needs of Adults), Toronto: Queens Printers.

CHAPTER 4:

Applying Naturalistic Evaluation in Basic Education

Robert A. Fellenz

Evaluation can be used for two distinct purposes. One is to place a summary judgement on a performance, activity, or object. As teachers and students we are quite familiar with this approach especially as it relates to grades. As teachers we try to be objective, fair, and comprehensive in the assignment of grades; yet there always seems to be a great deal of subjectivity that enters into even the norm referenced or competency based exam. As adult learners we are frequently torn between shrugging off grades as some outsider's assessment of progress made on their standards and at their time line and being troubled exceedingly by any estimate of our mental ability as less than perfect.

The second approach to evaluation is less concerned with assessing the value of a performance or a person and more directed toward the improvement of the learning experience. It is often called *formative evaluation* for its purpose is to reform or improve the learning activity. It leads not to the awarding of a grade or a certificate but to suggestions for improving the teaching/learning interaction.

Formative evaluation can be done in many ways. A diagnostic test or need assessment, for example, can be used to establish the needs of an adult learner so that instruction can begin at an appropriate level. Text books or teaching materials can be reviewed to determine which are most appropriate for a local situation. Students can be interviewed to discover specific areas with which they are having difficulty. Actual tasks performed on a job can be observed and compared to competencies taught in a training program. Case studies can be reviewed to determine how well programs in an area are meeting the needs of local citizens. All of these are examples of formative evaluation, that is, the gathering of information in order to make decisions which will improve an instructional program.

The purpose of this article is to suggest that formative evaluation is a very useful tool in adult basic education and that naturalistic approaches are well suited to carrying out such formative evaluations. Practical suggestions for implementing naturalistic evaluations for the purpose of improving adult learning situations will be offered.

NATURALISTIC INQUIRY

Much of our assessment in basic education is grounded in scientific or rationalistic theories of measurement. Such approaches are very careful to determine exactly what is to be measured and then to measure that component as exactly as possible so that we can be absolutely sure about something. All students to be measured are treated the same. Exceptions are not allowed or at least kept to a minimum. Results are summed and averaged and often treated with more sophisticated statistical procedures. Caution is used in drawing conclusions so that they will apply to all situations everywhere.

Such exactness of measurement is good but often it does not fit the needs of the classroom. The reason for this is that such evaluation is based on the goal of good measurement rather than good teaching. Rationalistic approaches presume that there is certainty or one right way of doing things and that, if we are careful enough, we can discover it. A naturalistic approach, on the other hand, questions whether all people are the same and whether there is one right way of teaching anyone or anything. Instead, it tries to discover the best way to teach this person at this time. It approaches measurement more like a sponge than a ruler. All information that is available is gathered in and examined for possible usefulness. Rather than reject material because it appears to be too subjective, naturalistic approaches presume that there is some subjectivity to all measurement and concentrate on the relevance and the supportive nature of the data in general to reach conclusions. While the rationalistic evaluator asks: "Is it accurate?" the naturalistic inquirer questions; "Is it useful?"

The degree to which a teacher uses naturalistic evaluation in the classroom should correlate with that teacher's philosophy of education. Basic education can be viewed primarily as an academic program teaching fundamental language arts and math skills and providing the foundation for entry into a productive job market. It can be seen as a means of socializing individuals into the main stream of society. Or, it can be described as a human enterprise in which individuals who are both teachers and learners interact to encourage human growth and learning. The countless studies and classroom experiences that this author has encountered say that disadvantaged students cannot learn until they gain some confidence in themselves and that the teacher's major role is to help these adult learners realize that they can learn. This leaves him or her with no choice but to treat this teaching/learning transaction as a human enterprise.

AN EXAMPLE OF A NATURALISTIC EVALUATION

The following section provides some insights derived from an evaluation performed on a large state-wide adult basic education program (Fellenz & Conti, 1984). There is a twofold purpose in this: one is to provide examples of the kind of information that can be gathered through a naturalistic approach to evaluation; the other, to share meaningful ideas that were discovered regarding the teaching of less educated adults.

The design of this evaluation rested on the presumption that education is a human enterprise. As such it is a process that deeply affects people both in the cognitive and affective domains. Therefore, the data that were gathered and the analyses that were made examined especially the affect that the various elements within the program were having on the people involved. Because the evaluative data were also to be used to satisfy a number of federal and state reporting requirements, a variety of quantitative data were also gathered through various surveys and record reviews. However, this report will focus on qualitative aspects of the study.

Texas covers a large geographical area with much of its population centered in several urban areas. The adult basic education program was administered through fifty-some local cooperatives ("co-ops") centered in school districts, community colleges, or regional service centers. Each co-op is quite independent and distinctive in the type of program in place. A large part of the population speaks a native language other than English. Usually this is Spanish but in some areas there are significant numbers speaking Asian or European languages. GED, high school completion, and competency-based high school degree programs serve large numbers of young high school drop-outs as well as older adults. In addition, there are a number of citizens, mostly older, who never gained more than the most basic of literacy skills. Vocational training usually is separate from basic education programs.

The evaluation team decided to visit 10 of these area co-ops and to interview students, teachers, administrators, and other local personnel who had insight into the operation of the program. Semi-structured interview schedules were developed that focussed on background information, planning, management, recruitment, instructional staff, linkages with other agencies, and the instructional program. Teacher and student interviews also asked about instructional facilities, materials, and staffs as well as reasons for participation and gains achieved through the program. Approximately 100 students, 65 teachers, and 40 administrators were interviewed in sessions that averaged an hour in length. In addition, classes were observed, out-reach centers were visited, and program records were reviewed.

RESULTS OF A NATURALISTIC EVALUATION

The major purpose of this section is to demonstrate the type of results that are likely to result from a naturalistic evaluation. To a large degree, of course, that depends on what the interview schedule is designed to discover. However, good interviews by their very nature allow those being questioned to discuss issues they believe vital to the topic under consideration. Thus, important variables may arise even though they were not foreseen at the time the interview schedule was designed.

One category of findings that emerged from this evaluation (Fellenz & Conti, 1984) that would not likely have come from a more quantitative approach related to the distinctness and differences among equally successful programs. For example, several learning centers visited used diametrically opposed approaches to the organization of their program. In one center almost all instruction was done in groups and was so well organized that students missing a morning class could cover that same material in an evening session or could change levels of instruction when switching from one content area to another simply by changing rooms. Another center was completely individualized. However, both centers seemed to be serving well the needs of local adult learners. The point to be made here is such differences between successful programs – or teachers, administrators, or methods—would tend to be blurred in evaluations looking at averages or similarities, and the "recommended program" – the average of successful programs – might not be successful anywhere.

The issue of linkages between the adult basic education program and other community agencies provides another example of how the conclusions of a naturalistic approach might differ from a rationalistic study. "Linkages" is the term used by officials to describe such cooperative arrangements; it is not the term used by practitioners. When asked about linkages, both administrators and teachers said none existed; however, later in the interview they would begin speaking of "cooperative arrangements" and of "working with" other groups. The interviewers, of course, adjusted their vocabulary to ask about cooperation rather than linkages; a survey may or may not have been so adjusted during a field test.

The examination of several case studies in this area of interagency cooperation produced a valuable suggestion for practice. Several co-op directors had developed excellent rapport with other agencies in the area. However there was an observable degree of difference between the actual amount of program cooperation in the various communities. In discussing this with the directors, the evaluation team concluded that the more successful directors did one thing that the others did not do. They formalized their agreements with other agencies through a simple letter signed by the local director of the basic education program and by the director of the cooperating agency. Such agreements seemed to stimulate other personnel within the agency to increased cooperative efforts.

Another finding had implications for staff hiring and training practices. Interviews with teachers, students, and administrators soon convinced the evaluators that successful ABE teachers are marked more by their "human" skills than by their content expertise. In their hiring practices, the more successful administrators checked applicants for content knowledge and specific teaching skills but only after they had convinced themselves that these potential teachers could relate to the adult learners. Students certainly supported this for their highest acclamations went to teachers who listen, who explain things clearly, who are supportive and encouraging, and who care.

The disturbing drop-out rate that had been accepted as common to many programs was a problem that the evaluation team had been requested specifically to examine. Local records supported the common assumption: large percentages of learners dropped out of basic education programs. However, the search for reasons for this (a search that the open-ended interview approach allowed) revealed a startling phenomenon. Many of the students recorded as "drop-outs" were really only "stop-outs." The meeting of immediate goals, the demands of job or family, or physical relocation caused *temporary* withdrawals from organized learning programs, but perhaps as many as half of these "drop-outs" reenrolled in a few months or a few years. Realization of the extent of the "stop-out" phenomenon lead insightful local administrators to maintain contact with former students and to keep their records on file.

But the most rewarding finding of the total evaluation was that the basic assumption of the evaluators was indeed true; adult basic education is essentially a human enterprise. The response to the question, "What is the prime need of basic education students?" was so unanimous it was like a roar: *Increased self-confidence.* "What was the greatest gain of students?" Like an echo the roar came back: *Increased self-confidence.* The essence of successful programs is the relationship among the individuals involved in the programs.

The undereducated adult learner is usually in such a state of stress that a strong supportive relationship with an understanding teacher is vital if learning is to occur. It is not that content learned and tests passed allow the individual to reached desired goals; rather *it is that growth in self confidence frees the learner to be and to do.* Human growth is not a happy side effect of basic education programs; it is the main effect that makes other objectives possible.

MAKING NATURALISTIC EVALUATION EFFECTIVE

There is no such thing as an effective step-by-step manual for naturalistic evaluation. Such a manual is an impossibility for an approach based on taking an inside look at a local situation must be designed according to local conditions. Insight into the issues being examined together with good common sense and an understanding of people are essential though. Thus, the following suggestions are offered more in the manner of reminders of how to learn than of how to evaluate for that is what the evaluator must do when using a naturalistic approach— learn through listening to and observing others.

A naturalistic evaluation can be structured or unstructured. In the first approach, the evaluator defines the reality to be examined ahead of time. In education this means the aspects of the program to be investigated are carefully thought through and questions are posed that will get at all the areas the evaluator considers important. The unstructured approach begins with the premise that the designers of the evaluation might not know the total reality out there or that others involved in the situation may have a different viewpoint on what is occurring. This approach relies on the participants both to identify the essential ingredients and to describe them. Either approach demands an evaluator who is sufficiently insightful in the area being examined to make sense of what people are saying and doing.

Guba and Lincoln (1982), who have produced the most comprehensive work on naturalistic evaluation to date, maintain that: "Of all the means of exchanging information or gathering data known to man, perhaps the oldest and most respected is the conversation (p. 153)." Good interviewing allows one to see a situation from another's viewpoint and to interpret what is happening from that individual's experiential and value framework. But to be a good interviewer, one must respect the person being interviewed and be convinced that that person can teach one something valuable. Conveying that impression to the one being interviewed, i.e., that you really believe that he or she can teach you something that you are eager to learn, is probably the best key to successful interviewing.

Preparation for an interview goes beyond deciding what you want to find out and who you intend to interview. The better you understand the setting of the evaluation and the backgrounds of the interviewees the more efficient use can be made of the time available for dialogue. Rehearsals of interviews are also helpful whether they be with another person in a simulated situation or simply done mentally trying to imagine various ways certain questions might be interpreted. However, preparation for an interview should also include preparing the interviewee. Before sitting down to a face-to-face encounter, the interviewee should know the purpose of the evaluation, the general content of the questions, and the benefit that the interview will have for him or her. Most students and teachers are quite willing to share if they are convinced that what they share will actually be used to improve the program.

Such prior sharing of goals of the interview usually makes it easier to establish that feeling of rapport so essential to good dialogue. An interview really is a dialogue in which both individuals must share with each other if effective communication is to happen. Guba and Lincoln suggest "Value neutral, but encouraging cues allow the interviewee to be expansive without subtly influencing him to alter behaviour or opinions in deference to the interviewer (175)". This is not meant to imply that the time of the interview be shared equally; the effectiveness of most interviews is directly proportional to the amount of time the interviewee uses for sharing beliefs and insights.

Questions asked during an interview must be clear and unambiguous. But most importantly they must be questions that the interviewees can answer. There are many things we would like to know about learning or programming, but it does not do any good to ask students, teachers, or administrators about these issues if they do not know the answers. In fact, this can be misleading for sometimes people will be so anxious to help that they will make up information. A good rule of thumb here is to ask general questions to get at specific behaviour. Once some concrete example of behaviour has been shared, the interviewer can follow up with penetrating questions about the cause, result, or implications of this behaviour. This follow-up is the strength of the interview process for it provides opportunities not only for clarifying answers but also for pursuing reasons. Surveys can tell us what happened; interviews, why things happened.

Evaluators who use naturalistic approaches must realize that compiling and analyzing the data they gather can consume a great deal of time. Data management systems for the microcomputer have made this process so much simpler, but writing a report based on quotations rather than statistics can be a more challenging and time-consuming process. However, it can produce a much more revealing and interesting document – especially when dealing with a human enterprise such as education. Of special value here, but also throughout the interview process, is the team approach to naturalistic inquiry. A team is not as easily fooled as an individual; a team more frequently spots nuances and follows up on useful clues; a team is more likely to produce a broad and valid report.

In summary, evaluations can be done because they are supposed to be done; that is, educators are expected to give grades, to say how well learners, teachers, materials, or programs have done. But evaluations can also be done to improve the teaching/learning interaction. To do so they must be useful, for as Guba and Lincoln say, "If evaluation results are rarely used, it is because those results are rarely relevant to local needs (38)". The purpose of this article has been to suggest an approach that can make evaluation in adult basic education relevant and useful to local needs.

REFERENCES

Fellenz, Robert A. and Conti, Gary J. (1984). *Comprehensive Evaluation of the Statewide Texas Adult Basic Education Program: Evaluating a Human Enterprise*. College Station, TX: Interdisciplinary Education, Texas A&M University. (ERIC Document Reproduction Service No. ED 260 213)
Guba, Egon G. and Lincoln, Yvonna S. (1982). *Effective Evaluation*. San Francisco: Jossey-Bass.

PART V
REMEDIAL APPROACHES IN
BASIC EDUCATION

Adult educators are becoming more adept at applying principles of andragogy to remedial learning situations, various authors in this section point out. It is apparent that some adult learners have unique individual characteristics that require special learning conditions. As a result, attempts at remediation have increased considerably over the past few years. Specific reading procedures, diagnostic-instructional strategies and the integration of mathematical learning principles are a few of the topics discussed in this section. These techniques are providing instructors and learners with different approaches for developing knowledge and practical skills. Also presented are examples of successful methods for meeting the learning needs of the unconventional student. These include individualized microcomputer programs, experiential learning and addressing student beliefs about literacy instruction.

How often have we observed, in our classrooms and groups, people experiencing the familiar fears of failure because of the learning demands and conditions of the main-stream program. Many researchers would agree that if we begin with the assumption that everyone can learn and will learn under the right conditions, then the first place for explanation of learning failure is in errors in the instruction, not faults in the learner. The purpose of this section is to provide suggestions for instructional improvements and to better understand the uniqueness of some adult learners.

*The first chapter by **Singh and Singh** begins with a description of remedial reading procedures which have been used effectively to increase accuracy and comprehension among adult learners. These procedures are outlined under antecedent and consequent categories. As well, a number of multi-component remedial packages are described that have been used to increase the reading proficiency of young and adult learners. The authors conclude with a commentary on effective research designs for investigating instructional procedures.*

*When discussing the beginning adult reader, several factors emerge such as diagnostic techniques, teaching strategies and instructional materials. **Thistlethwaite** addresses each of these concerns with a focus on the diagnostic-instructional strategies used to teach the adult reader. Both whole text level strategies that exemplify real reading experiences and word level activities are illustrated for the instructor or tutor. The author provides an overview of assessment tools and referenced adult oriented reading materials.*

*As a helpful guide to the adult literacy and basic education instructor, **Chapline** and **Newman** explain the different learning principles that have been applied to a successful remedial mathematics program.*

Methods of integrating affective and cognitive elements in the learning environment and suggestions for introducing interesting mathematical content are presented. In addition, the authors point out that learners should be given the opportunities to become involved in the problem solving process and help formulate generalizations.

*In her chapter, **Vacc** depicts a practical microcomputer core program for use in adult basic and remedial education. Programming considerations such as coping with syntax errors, changing directions and including new questions are explained to enable instructors to modify the core program to meet the individual needs of the remedial adult learner. As she states, the number of new programs that can be developed from the core is limited only by an instructor's creative ability to modify the DATA statements.*

***Lohnes** outlines the different considerations required to develop an experiental remedial program for adult learners. Such topics as creating a learning environment, monitoring procedures, the role of administration and program methodology, provide a framework for organizing a meaningful remedial program. Practical examples and lessons for spelling, phonics, and mathematics are provided. She also underlines the importance of developing a curriculum that reflects learner needs.*

*Often students enter literacy programs with misconceptions that interfere with progress. In a case study format, **O'Brien** documents a learner's beliefs about reading and writing and literacy instruction. She describes the negative role that these misconceptions played in the early stages of a remedial program and the positive outcomes which resulted when the program addressed those concepts and beliefs. Also highlighted are various learner encounters with literacy and their influence on the acquisition of reading and writing skills.*

CHAPTER 1

Remedial Reading Procedures for Adult Learners

Judy Singh
Nirbhay N. Singh

If functional literacy is taken to mean a person's ability to use literacy skills in order to function effectively in an adult community, then the number of functionally illiterate adults continues to grow despite intensive efforts to reverse the trend. These are people who have difficulty in applying literacy skills in daily life, such as shopping, writing cheques, and occupation-related tasks. Estimates of the number of adult illiterates vary, depending on the population surveyed, the definition of literacy, and methods used to collect the data. For example, in both the professional (e.g., Wangberg, 1986) and popular press (e.g., Bowen, 1986; Gorman, 1988), current estimates of adult illiterates in the U.S. ranges from about 17 to 27 million, at least one in every eight Americans.

There have been numerous attempts to provide comprehensive adult literacy programs in several countries (see Singh, Singh & Blampied, 1985), with most of them concentrating on reading as a basic skill. These programs vary in the approach they take, ranging in scope from individualized remedial instruction for reading accuracy to comprehensive reading activities which incorporate listening, writing, and discussion. This chapter reviews procedures which have been found effective in increasing reading accuracy and comprehension. Since evaluative studies of remedial procedures with adults is very limited, a number of procedures typically used with younger readers have been included because they are considered to be equally applicable to adults.

READING MATERIALS

When teaching adult learners to read, teachers are sometimes uncertain whether they should use reading material which is at the reading-level of the student or at a level appropriate to the age or interest of the learner. We think that while there is nothing inherently wrong with using reading materials at the learner's reading-level rather than interest- or age- level, it may create a number of problems. For example, it may be uninteresting and reduce the learner's motivation to learn to read fluently. In addition, the learner may think that reading "kid's stuff" is demeaning to him. However, there are good arguments for using material that is age- appropriate and of interest to the learner. Often the adult learner has some specific material that he or she has to learn to read. – For example, some adult learners may wish to take and pass a given examination in order to gain further promotion in their job or to obtain a driver's license. For them, the most appropriate reading materials would be those that are related to the examinations that the learners have to take. Even for those who do not have to take examinations, appropriate reading materials would include books, magazines, and newspapers.

ORAL AND SILENT READING

Most proficient younger readers and adults read silently. However, to adequately assess, diagnose, and provide remediation for reading problems requires the reader, child or adult, to read orally. While some aspects of reading (e.g., comprehension) can be assessed without recourse to oral reading, it is only through oral reading that the teacher is able to identify the kinds of reading errors made by the reader. Since there appears to be a strong correlation between speed and accuracy during oral reading and comprehension (see Jenkins, 1979), we feel that oral reading provides an effective medium for detecting and remediating reading deficits in adult learners.

REMEDIAL READING PROCEDURES

Remedial reading instruction can be categorized in a number of ways. For example, they can be categorized as either antecedent or consequent remediation procedures. Antecedent procedures are those which precede and facilitate accurate reading. Prompts represent a group of antecedent procedures (e.g., verbal cues, instructions, previewing, models) which can be used to facilitate subsequent reading. Consequent procedures are those used to consequate the reader, with some being used to consequate accurate reading (e.g., descriptive praise) and others for errors (e.g., attention, drift, overcorrection). Of course, a number of these procedures can be combined to form a remediation package, utilizing either antecedent or consequent procedures or both (see Singh & Singh, 1986).

Antecedent Procedures

A number of antecedent remediation procedures can be used to enhance the reading of the adult learner, including previewing, word analysis, and modeling,

1. Previewing. This requires the teacher to provide a brief synopsis of the content of the material to be read before the student attempts to read it (Singh & Singh, 1984). Previewing the text provides the reader with contextual cues during actual reading thereby reducing errors and increasing comprehension. A good example of the use of previewing is in the Language Experience Approach (LEA) which has been used with adult learners for about 50 years (Brouse, 1939; McNinch, Shaffer, & Layton, 1976). The LEA assumes that adults will learn to read stories that are of personal interest to them and written in a language with which they are familiar. In this approach the adult learner dictates a story to the teacher who writes it down and then uses it for remedial instruction. The learner usually has little difficulty reading the dictated story because it has been discussed with the teacher beforehand and then written in a style and language familiar to the reader.

Another example of the use of previewing is the organic primer approach which uses stories written by the teacher for instructional purposes but is based on discussions with adult learners about their interests and experiences (Amoroso, 1985). The teacher uses an illustration to initiate discussion about the story and encourages the learners to discuss how they feel and what they think about the topic. These discussions introduce the adult learners to the vocabulary used in the text and facilitates later reading. The LEA and organic primer approach use previewing to stimulate the learner's thinking about the material to be read and to introduce new words that are likely to appear in the text, thus enhancing reading accuracy.

2. Word Analysis. The teacher may use word analysis as an antecedent instructional procedure if it is clear that the learner has deficits in word recognition skills. There are several components of word analysis including phonic analysis, structural analysis, syllabication, and blending. Phonic analysis deals with the sounds letters represent. Structural analysis takes the learner a step further by providing instruction on the segmentation of words by meaning rather than solely by letter-sound relationships. This is followed by instruction in syllabication, that is a word or word part that can stand alone. Finally the learner is taught how to blend word parts to make a recognizable whole word. However, since this procedure is usually included in the early part of reading instruction to young children, it is likely that adult learners would have had problems in mastering it if they still had reading problems during their school years. Thus, it may not be the best possible strategy to use with adults since this method would have been associated with reading failure at school.

3. Modeling. Modeling can be used in two ways as an antecedent procedure. If the teacher is aware of the word recognition problems of the learner, a list of difficult words can be drawn up from the text that is to be read. The other approach is to provide instruction through oral modeling, that is, the teacher reads to the learner for a short period of time to demonstrate what reading should be like. Usually oral modeling is carried out for 5 or 10 minutes per session then the learner is required to read the same text. Oral modeling is often included in multi-procedure remediation packages.

Consequent Procedures.

Adult learners' reading can be facilitated by manipulating the consequences of their reading through a number of consequent procedures.

1. Praise. A simple consequent procedure is to provide praise or reinforcement following accurate reading or good comprehension. Praise not only provides positive feedback in terms of accuracy of performance but also increases the learner's self-esteem and confidence in reading.

2. Prompts. Another simple procedure is to prompt the learner that an error has been made without the teacher providing the correct word. This enables the learner to stop, make another attempt at decoding the word through either word analysis or contextual cues, and then continue reading. If the learner is not able to identify the error or is unable to self-correct it, other types of teacher prompts may be necessary, e.g., verbal cues or word analysis cues.

3. Modeling. Modeling can be used as a consequent as well as an antecedent procedure. Consequent modeling requires the teacher to prompt the learner that an error has been made and in the absence of a self-correction, the teacher models the correct word.

4. Word Analysis. Word analysis can also be used as a consequent error correction procedure (Singh & Singh, 1988). Typically, the learner reads a text and when an error is made, the teacher may use a word analysis cue to prompt the correct word. The teacher can use all or some of the components of word analysis as outlined earlier. Word analysis has been used as a consequent remedial instruction procedure in the LEA approach by McNinch et al (1976). For example, once the class has dictated a story the students are required to find all words that begin with specific letters. In addition, students may complete individual work sheets made up of exercises in word analysis if they express an interest in such activities (Amoroso, 1985, p. 400). Word analysis skills are important because they enable the adult learner to become an independent reader.

5. Overcorrection. Overcorrection procedures were originally designed to reduce the maladaptive behaviour of behaviourally-disordered individuals (Foxx & Bechtel, 1983). However, recent studies extended its application to educational areas, including reading (Singh, 1985). In the first application of this procedure to oral reading, Singh, Singh and Winton (1984) found that students decreased their oral reading errors and increased self-correction of errors with this procedure. In this study, following an oral reading error, the student was required to repeat the correct word five times and then reread the sentence in which the error word occurred before continuing with the rest of the text. In addition to punishment for errors, it is likely that overcorrection is effective because the reader's errors are corrected in context during reading rather than in isolation once reading has been completed (see Singh & Singh, 1988).

6. Delayed Attention to Errors. Research has shown that teacher's immediate attention to oral reading errors reduces the number of errors made by children. However, recent research has shown that the reduction in oral reading errors is greater and increases in self-correction is larger when teachers delay their attention to children's reading errors (McNaughton & Glynn, 1981; Singh, Winton & Singh, 1985). Delayed teacher attention requires the teacher to delay attention to the reader's error until the end of the sentence in which the error occurred. If the reader pauses after making an error, delayed attention is provided between 10 and 15 seconds later and the correct word supplied by the teacher. Delayed attention is effective because it prevents teachers from pre-empting the opportunities of the reader to self-correct his or her errors. When given the opportunity, readers will often self-correct a substantial number of their errors.

7. Repeated Reading. Singh, Singh and Blampied (1984) have suggested that repeated reading may be a useful procedure for the adult learner. Repeated reading involves selecting a short reading passage of 50 to 200 words, depending on the reading ability of the reader, and having the reader reread it several times until a criterion rate of reading is reached. With each rereading the words become more familiar and fewer errors are made. As errors decrease and word recognition becomes automatic, the speed of reading increases and enhances oral reading fluency.

Variants of the repeated reading procedure have been used in a number of studies with adults. For example, Moyer (1979) used this procedure with an adult whose reading ability had been severely impaired as a result of brain damage. The patient's reading rate increased by 40 to 50% in 12 weeks, with the improvement being maintained over several years. More recently, Lopardo and Sadow (1982) used this procedure with college students enrolled in a corrective reading course. This procedure is particularly suitable for adult learners since repeated reading can be used during silent as well as oral reading.

MULTICOMPONENT REMEDIAL PACKAGES

A number of multicomponent instructional packages have been used to increase the reading proficiency of young and adult learners. These packages capitalize on different aspects of training procedures that have been used individually. For example, it is intuitively appealing to use procedures that not only prepare the learner about what he or she will be reading (e.g., through previewing, discussion) but also to include praise for accuracy, and error-correction procedures for remediating reading deficits. Similarly, a number of programs use listening, writing and discussion with the hope that a more comprehensive approach to reading will increase the learner's reading proficiency and self-confidence in reading.

1. Language Experience Approach. The language experience approach to reading relies heavily on the experiences of the adult learner. Initially only the dictated stories of the learners are used for instruction but later, job-related material or reading materials that they are familiar with are also used. Instructional components include discussing a topic, writing about the topic, reading the text to a criterion level of performance, and analyzing the text for sentences, phrases, and separate words (Brouse, 1939; McNinch et al., 1976; Singh et al., 1985).

One of the strengths of the language experience approach is that it can use the diverse backgrounds of the learners as a source of instructional material and the teacher can employ a variety of strategies in either a group or one-on-one format. Furthermore, the initial reading materials are dictated by the adult learners themselves and therefore use a vocabulary and a style that closely resemble their spoken language. One of the claims of people using this approach is that it is successful because it is based on the interests and goals of the adult learner and allows the student to participate actively in the learning situation. However, it must be noted that descriptions of current programs are inadequate in terms of providing detailed instructions about the instructional strategies used. Thus, the teacher's ability to diagnose reading deficits and prescribe appropriate remediation may be a crucial variable in determining the success of this approach.

2. Behavioural Remediation Programs. Recently, Singh and Singh (1986) used a number of behavioural procedures to increase reading proficiency in children. The remediation program included previewing of the text, delayed attention to oral reading errors, overcorrection of errors, and positive reinforcement for self-corrections. Results showed that the remediation program was effective in reducing oral reading errors and, during the course of the study, increasing comprehension. Although this program has not been used with adult learners, it appears suitable for this population as well.

3. Assisted Reading. This procedure involves the teacher and learner reading simultaneously until the student feels confident to continue reading on his or her own at which point teacher assistance is faded out. However, if at any stage

the reader begins to experience difficulty additional teacher support is provided. The teacher can incorporate the use of oral modeling by reading the text, first with the learner following along silently and then reading it together. When the learner reads the text, it is usually less difficult because the teacher has already modeled new or difficult words. Initially much of the reading is done simultaneously but as the learner progresses he becomes more and more independent.

Assisted reading is based on a number of behavioural principles including modeling, prompting, feedback, and reinforcement. In essence, simultaneous reading can be seen as participant modeling where the teacher acts as a model and provides a continuous prompt for correct reading. The learner's attempts at independent reading is reinforced as is his or her accuracy in reading. If the learner makes an error or has problems in decoding a new or difficult word, the teacher models the correct word and gets the learner to repeat it. Assisted reading emphasizes contextual cues rather than word analysis for decoding words. This may be an appropriate approach to take with adult learners because they tend to have a better facility for using contextual cues than word analysis cues.

There are several features of this procedure which make it suitable for adult learners. Since the learner has access to a model who simultaneously reads the text, he or she may choose any reading material that is of interest. That is, the learner is not bound by materials designed for beginning readers which an adult will undoubtedly find boring and unmotivating. Another feature of assisted reading is that it is a form of errorless learning because with the teacher modeling correct reading, the probability of the learner making errors is drastically reduced. If an error is made, it is corrected within the context of the text material by the teacher. This aspect of assisted reading would appeal to the adult learner who as a child may have experienced a great deal of frustration because reading was dominated more by errors than accuracy. Finally, since assisted reading encourages and reinforces independent reading adult learners may feel more confident in trying to read independently knowing that the teacher is close at hand to assist, if necessary.

Thistlethwaite (1983) has suggested that in assisted reading the text material can be tape-recorded so that adults can read in private. They can listen to the tape several times and follow the material in their own texts. When they feel confident enough they can read along with the tape recorded version and fade out external assistance by gradually lowering the volume of the tape-recorder. This variation of assisted reading would be most appropriate for adult learners who have already gained a certain degree of independence through working with a teacher.

Other Approaches

A number of other remedial instruction approaches are available for teaching the adult learner. One example is the Basic Learning Skills System (Caldwell & Rizza, 1979), a computer-assisted literacy program. This program is designed to improve the reading, math, and language skills of those adults whose current skills are between the third- and eighth-grade level through computer-assisted tutorials, drills, tests, printed materials, and video presentations. The reading component is divided into five subcategories, with increasing levels of competence in reading: word analysis, word meaning, literal comprehension, interpretive comprehension, and evaluation of the text material in terms of content and style. One of the drawbacks of this program is that it does not cater for those who have not reached a third-grade reading level. Although evaluative data are limited, at least one study has shown that adult learners gained an average of a grade in reading achievement after about 13 hours of instruction (Rizza & Walker-Hunter, 1978). Further details of computer assisted instruction in adult basic education can be found in the chapter by Vacc in this book.

Another approach is through the use of television and radio as the instructional medium. For example, Operation Alphabet was initiated in Philadelphia in 1961 (Cook, 1977) as a television literacy program. Operation Alphabet consisted of 100 half-hour programs designed to introduce basic reading and writing skills to the third-grade level. While a number of television and radio programs have been used with adult learners (see Singh et al., 1985), there is little evaluative data to show that this is a cost-effective method of instruction. In addition, most of these programs suffered from design, presentation. and material distribution problems (Hargreaves, 1977).

CONCLUSIONS

While the problem of adult illiteracy has been acknowledged and some effort has been made to overcome it, there is little in the research literature that provides us with guidelines for choosing effective instructional methods. This chapter has attempted to highlight a number of remedial procedures that may be useful for teaching or improving the reading ability of adult learners. Even though most of these procedures have been used with adults, there is a dearth of methodologically rigorous studies which have evaluated their efficacy in this population. While group-design studies would be appropriate for such evaluations, we firmly believe that studies using single-subject research designs (Barlow & Hersen, 1984) will provide valuable data on instructional procedures. Indeed, since adults usually feel more at ease when working in a one-on-one teaching situation, especially during reading remediation sessions, a single-subject methodology appears to be ideal for such research.

A number of procedures that could be used for reading remediation (e.g., drill, sentence repeat) have not been included because they are deemed inappropriate for use with adults. However, that is not to say these procedures are not or will not be found to be effective with adults. These procedures are typically used with children and appear to be best suited for use with that age group.

REFERENCES

Amoroso, H. C., (1985). "Organic Primers for Basic Literacy Instruction". *Journal of Reading*, 28, no. 5, 398-40 1.

Bowen, E., (1986). "Education: Losing the War of Letters". *Time*, 127, no. 18, 46.

Brouse, H. T., (1939). "Experiment in Adult Elementary Reading". *Adult Education Bulletin*, 15-18.

Barlow, D. and Hersen, M., (1984). *Single Case Experimental Designs*, New York: Pergamon Press.

Caldwell, R. M. and Rizza, P. J., (1979). "A Computer-Based System of Reading Instruction for Adult Nonreaders". *Association for Educational Data Systems*, 12, 155-162.

Cook, W. D., (1977). *Adult Literacy Education in the United States*, Newark, Delware: International Reading Association.

Foxx, R. M. and Bechtel, D. R., (1982). "Overcorrection." In *Progress in Behaviour Modification*, Vol. 13. Edited by M. Hersen, R. M. Eisler, and P. M. Miller. New York: Academic Press, pp. 227-288.

Gorman,C., (1988). "The Literacy Gap." *Time*, 132, no. 25, 56-57.

Hargreaves, D., (1977). "The BBC Adult Literacy Project." *In Adult Literacy Handbook*. Edited by C. Langley. London: British Broadcasting Corporation, pp. 73-74.

Jenkins, J. R., (1979). "Oral reading." In *Communications Research in Learning Disabilities and Mental Retardation*. Edited by J. E. Button, T. C. Lovitt, and R. D. Rowlands. Baltimore: University Park Press, pp. 67-9 1.

Lopardo, G. and Sadow, M. W., (1982). "Criteria and Procedures for the Method of Repeated Readings". *Journal of Reading*, 26, no. 2, 156-160.

McNaughton, S. and Glynn, T., (1981). "Delayed versus Immediate Attention to Oral Reading Errors: Effects on Accuracy and Self-Corrections". *Educational Psychology*, 1, 57-65.

McNinch, J., Shaffer, G. L., and Layton, J. R., (1976). "Language Experience: Reading." In *Methods and Materials in Continuing Education*. Edited by C. Klevins. Los Angeles: Klevins, pp. 305-315.

Moyer, S., (1979). "Rehabilitation of Alexia: A Case Study". *Cortex*, 15, 139-144.

Rizza, Jr. P. J. and Walker-Hunter, P., (1978). *The Basic Skills Learning System*, Minneapolis, Minnesota: Control Data Corporation.

Singh, J., Singh, N. N., and Blampied, N. M., (1984). "Using Repeated Reading to Increase the Reading Proficiency of Adult Learners". *Lifelong Learning*,9, 8-11.

Singh, J., Singh, N. N., and Blampied, N.M.,(1985). "Reading Programs for Adult Illiterates: A Review of Instructional Methods and Materials". *Human Learning*, 4, 143-155.

Singh, N. N., (1985). "Overcorrection of Academic Behaviour." In *Proceedings of the Eighth Conference of the Australian Behaviour Modification Association*. Edited by C. Sharpley, A. Hudson, and C. Lee. Melbourne, Australia: ABMA, pp. 382-391.

Singh, N. N., and Singh, J., (1984). "Antecedent control of oral reading errors and self-corrections by mentally retarded children". *Journal of Applied Behaviour Analysis*, 17, 111-119.

Singh, N. N. and Singh, J., (1986). "A Behavioural Remediation Program for Oral Reading: Efffects on Errors and Comprehension". *Educational Psychology*, 6, no.2, 105-114.

Singh, N. N., and Singh. J., (1988). "Increasing Oral Reading Proficiency through Overcorrection and Phonic Analysis". *American Journal of Mental Retardation*, 93, no. 3, 312-319.

Singh, N. N., Singh, J., and Winton, A. S. W., (1984). "Positive Practice Overcorrection of Oral Reading Errors". *Behaviour Modification*, 8, no. 1, 23-37.

Singh, N. N., Winton, A. S. W., & Singh, J., (1985). Effects of delayed versus immediate attention to oral reading errors on the reading proficiency of mentally retarded children. *Applied Research in Mental Retardation*, 6. 295-305.

Thistlethwaite, L., (1983). "Teaching Reading to the ABE Student Who Cannot Read". *Lifelong Learning*, 7, no. 1, 5-7, 21.

Wangberg, E.G., (1986). "An Interactive Language Experience Based Microcomputer Approach to Reduce Adult Illiteracy". *Lifelong Learning*, 9, no. 5, 8-12.

CHAPTER 2:
The Adult Disabled Reader

Linda Thistlethwaite

When discussing teaching the beginning adult reader, instructors and tutors frequently ask themselves several questions. Which tests should I use to determine reading level? What materials can I use for instruction? Which teaching strategies are most effective to use with adults? A discussion of each of these concerns (assessment; materials; strategies) follows. Materials will be discussed as they relate to specific strategies rather than in a separate section. The description of strategies will focus on those that are text-based and those that are word-based.

ASSESSMENT

Word list tests, written reading tests, informal reading inventories, vision and hearing checks, and non-traditional assessment measures are five types of assessment that might be given. The *Slosson Oral Reading Test* (SORT) (Slosson, 1982) and the *Wide Range Achievement Test* (WRAT) (Jastak & Jastak, 1978) are two of the frequently used word list tests. Each simply requires the adult to read a list of words at various levels of difficulty and purports to establish reading ability based on this isolated word task. Results do not indicate the level at which the adult can comprehend written text. They might be used to determine the general level at which to begin more in-depth assessment.

The following written reading tests are examples of those presently being used to assess reading ability for adult beginning readers: (1) *Tests of Adult Basic Education* (TABE) (1987), (2) *Adult Basic Learnings Examination* (ABLE) (1986) and (3) *Adult English as a Second Language Diagnostic Reading Test* (AESLDRT) (Reyes, et al, 1981). Both the TABE and ABLE present the reader with a series of passages to read; however, the TABE uses only literature or content area selections while the ABLE includes functional selections (advertisement, weather forecast, etc.) as well. Following the reading, the adult answers written multiple-choice comprehension questions. The AESLDRT has a maze format for which the reader is directed to choose the word that syntactically and semantically fits the context.

The third type of reading assessment, the informal reading inventory, contains sets of passages at increasing levels of difficulty and is administered individually, either orally or silently. Following the reading, the adult retells what has been remembered and/or orally answers comprehension questions regarding the text. The *Bader Reading and Language Inventory* (Bader, 1983) contains a set of graded passages based on adult interests.

Having the adult learner's hearing and vision checked is a vital part of the assessment procedures. Neglecting the obvious will lead to wasted time for both the learner and the instructor or tutor.

Non-traditional assessment procedures, the last category of reading assessment measures, might more properly be called diagnostic-instructional strategies. They can easily be related to real-world reading tasks. The same strategy may be used either diagnostically or instructionally. If used instructionally, the teacher will model, share insights into how to approach the reading problem, give examples, break the text and/or the procedure into small, manageable steps, and give frequent feedback so that the student is aware of his progress. Diagnosis using the same basic strategy will not have these components. Many of the instructional strategies discussed in the next section could be used as non-traditional assessment procedures.

INSTRUCTIONAL STRATEGIES
The General Approach

Before a discussion of effective instructional strategies, a word about the general approach to teaching the beginning adult reader is in order. Many adult basic education programs today emphasize a phonics approach to teaching reading. Others offer a language experience approach. There are benefits to both approaches. If the adult has never had instruction in phonics, a phonics approach that offers many opportunities for real reading (even at the beginning level) may be very efficient. Many of the phonic materials are almost self-teaching and therefore are appealing to volunteer tutors and instructors who do not have a background in teaching reading.

However, the language experience approach based on a whole-language/psycholinguistic view of the reading process (Hall, 1976; Smith, 1979; Padak & Padak, 1987) may be more effective in teaching beginning adult readers, especially those who have previously met failure with a phonics-oriented approach. In this language-based approach, the emphasis is on the reader's own language patterns and content that is familiar to the reader. In essence, it is the reader's speech (thoughts on a topic, conversation with the tutor, creative story, retelling of an event, or summary/interpretation of local or national news) written by the tutor/instructor. The adult can continue to provide his own reading material by dictating his autobiography or by dictating a letter to a friend or relative (Kennedy & Roeder, 1975; Padak & Padak, 1987).

One important guideline in selecting an approach is to determine what will be most effective for the adult that you are working with. Find out about the adult's early reading experiences. Are there negative memories associated with phonics instruction and the completion of workbook pages? Ask the adult what he does when he comes to something that he doesn't know while reading. If his only strategy is to sound it out, you must be careful that by using a phonics approach that you don't further emphasize the decoding aspect of reading rather than the meaning-getting aspect. *Phonics in Proper Prospective* (Heilman, 1981) is a good review of the phonics approach to teaching and is recommended for those using either a phonics or a language experience approach.

No matter what approach you choose, take time to get to know the adult learner. Rather than wasted time, this sharing provides an opportunity for assessment of oral language abilities and will provide numerous directions for instruction (Meyer, 1987).

The following diagnostic-instructional strategies include both text-level and word-level activities. Although the adult should never be asked to read something that is less than a complete text, it is appropriate to weave in word-level activities. Also included will be specific texts that are good to use with beginning adult readers. Sometimes it is not possible to differentiate between the instructional strategy and the material used.

Text and Text-Level Activities

(1) Language Experience Text Modifications: Sometimes the adult dictates a language experience story that is too complex for the adult to later read The tutor can re-write the language experience story to a more appropriate level. Or the tutor can try the organic primer approach (Amoroso, 1985), with the tutor writing selections for reading practice with the experiences and interests of the adult in mind. Books from the library's general adult collection, such as a photography book or cookbook, can be used as a catalyst for language experience (Crowley-Weibel, 1983) and allow the adult to interact with actual adult materials.

(2) Reading of Texts Found in the Reader's Environment: Signs on a walk taken around the neighbourhood or a song that the reader knows by heart are good sources of environmental reading material. Even adults who consider themselves to be non-readers will see that they can read something and will begin to view themselves as readers. A cookbook or menu, an application form, a letter from a friend or relative, the TV Guide, or a children's book that might later be read to the adult's own children as other sources of real-life reading materials.

(3) Writing Activities: Since reading and writing are mutually supportive activities, beginning adult readers should be encouraged to write. Writing for five minutes in a journal, creating a new verse for a song or poem as either an individual or small group writing experience, a community newssheet published by the adult literacy class, and letters written to family members and friends are four writing activities that might be used (Kazamek, 1984). The adult beginning reader could also write short notes and phone messages. Any of the ideas presented above when discussing dictated language experience stories could also be avenues for personal writing.

(4) Types of Assisted Reading: Assisted reading can be used effectively if both the adult beginning reader and the tutor bring something to the reading situation. For example, the adult beginning reader might bring an understanding of a topic such as auto-racing (which the tutor knows nothing about) while the tutor brings expertise with the written word. The tutor and beginning reader read together, perhaps with the tutor "fading out" when the adult feels comfortable with the text (Watson, 1982). Additionally, assisted reading can be done with those materials that the adult wants to read but is not yet ready to read independently. Taping selections the adult learner will be interested in allows the adult to participate in an assisted reading activity without direct assistance by the tutor.

Or the tutor and adult can read echoically with the adult reading a sentence after the tutor has read it. Following sentence-by-sentence reading, the adult reads the entire paragraph independently. (Gillet & Temple, 1986). A simpler type of assisted reading is for the tutor and reader to take turns reading. This helps the beginning reader to keep the general train of thought of the selection and provides opportunities for the tutor to model fluent reading. Use of predictable print, selections which contain repeated phrases or a predictable pattern of events, is useful for assisted reading. Other possible materials are language experience stories and texts found in the reader's environment.

(5) Miscue Analysis: With the beginning adult reader, it is helpful to analyze the types of miscues that are being made. Are they graphically similar but meaningless? Or is it obvious that the student has retained the meaning of the text despite substituting a word that is graphically and phonically dissimilar to the text word. Miscue analysis can be done with any text that the student can read instructionally (Goodman, 1974). Strategy lessons can be designed to focus on the particular types of miscues the reader is making.

(6) Use of Context: When the reader comes to a word that he doesn't know, saying "blank" and reading to the end of the sentence often provides the reader with hints regarding what the word might be. A modification of the cloze strategy (Taylor, 1953), the deletion predictable but perhaps difficult words, forces the reader to use context and may be used with those readers who are word-bound and have difficulty saying "blank" and leaving the word unpronounced. Used diagnostically, the cloze activity gives evidence of the beginning adult reader's ability to predict, an important strategy not only for using context but also for comprehending text in the larger sense.

You may give choices for the deleted word or ask the reader to hypothesize words that would fit the sentence and are consistent with the entire text. The cloze strategy should be used first as a listening activity and later as a reading activity. Teacher modeling of the thought processes is necessary if the reader is to be successful with this strategy. Collaboration, several adult beginning readers working together, often heightens the benefits of using cloze.

(7) Reader-selected Miscues: One characteristics of adults is that they seek to be independent in their learning (Knowles, 1980). Even adult beginning readers can be independent and taught to monitor their own comprehension. The adult should continually be asking "Does this make sense?" while reading. Placing a checkmark in the margin and going on allows the adult to keep from getting bogged down with details. After finishing the selection (paragraph, story), the reader goes back to those points where miscues had been self-selected to see if the text now makes sense. If it does not, teacher assistance is needed (Watson, 1978).

(8) Use of Prior Knowledge: Using background experience and the experience of the selection read thus far are aids to reading. The tutor can elicit what the reader already knows about the content of the text to be read via brainstorming about the topic. Misconceptions can be cleared up and the reader will have a "set" for reading the selection. Langer's PREP strategy (1981) gives an excellent description of a method to elicit prior knowledge.

Or you might present the reader with 5-10 concepts from the selection and have the reader arrange them into a "tree diagram" format (Thelen, 1982). The amount of difficulty that the reader has with the task will be an indication of how easy or difficult the reading of the text will be. Or the tutor can present the student with these concepts already arranged in hierarchical order. The reader can refer to this structured overview of the text while reading.

Taking time to have the reader survey the text and predict is also useful. Reading the first paragraph and hypothesizing what questions might be answered in the selection is also an effective activity (Valeri-Gold, 1987). With fictional material, use the DR-TA, the Directed Reading-Thinking Activity (Stauffer, 1975; Haggard, 1988). Have the reader read the first paragraph or first page and predict what will happen next. Stopping periodically to predict and substantiate predictions with background experiences plus the text read thus far encourages the reader to monitor comprehension while reading. Thinking about the text in terms of "What I knew before I read," "What I learned from the reading" and "What I still don't know," (Heller, 1986) encourages the reader to use prior knowledge as well as monitor comprehension.

A number of adult-oriented materials can be used when encouraging adult beginning readers to assess their prior knowledge before reading: *Adult Reading: Comprehension* (Malone, 1981); *Mastering Basic Reading Skills* (Swinburne, et. al., 1985); *America's Story* (Bernstein, 1985); *Family Development Series* (Udvari, 1978); *Modern Reading Skilltext Series* (Johnson, 1983); *Practicing Occupational Reading Skills* Stewart & Taylor, 1982); *Reading Comprehension in Varied Subject Matter* (Ervin, 1980). Also useful are weekly news magazines written for beginning and intermediate readers: *Extra* by Xerox, *NewsScan* (teen-oriented) by News Readers Press, and *News for You* (adult-oriented) by New Reader's Press. Some metropolitan newspapers now have sections or monthly news reviews for adult beginning readers.

(9) Independent Reading: Adult beginning readers need a great deal of time for independent reading. One of the best ways to improve one's reading is to read, read, read. Help the adult to obtain a library card so that books and magazines can be checked out. Reading easy material allows the reader to turn words that once had to be "attacked" into sight words that are recognized immediately. Additionally, this independent reading practice puts the responsibility for learning on the shoulders of the adult reader. Recently, more and more novelettes have been written with the older beginning reader in mind, i.e., *The Crisis Series* (1982), *The Fastback/Double Fastback Series* (1985-88), *Life-Times* (1979), *Adult Readers Library* (1981), *Sundown Reading Series,* and *Spotlight on Literature* (Goodman, 1980). Old language experience stories provide additional texts for independent reading.

(10) Questioning: Although asking direct questions regarding material being read is the most often used method of assessing comprehension, it is useful to precede questioning with a simple retelling. Asking the reader to retell the passage will allow the tutor to determine the general level of comprehension, the rememberance of the organization of the text, and whether the reader focuses on the main ideas or the lesser important details.

One type of self-questioning has been referred to in the reader-selected miscue activity (Do I understand this?) Another type of self-questioning is ReQuest, reciprocal questioning (Manzo, 1969). Readers decide how far they can read before they need to stop and check their comprehension. Following the reading, the reader asks the tutor questions about the material read. Following this, the tutor questions the reader. In addition to the independent learning aspect of this questioning strategy, reciprocal questioning also allows the tutor to model higher-level comprehension questions for the adult beginning reader. The goal is for this higher-level questioning behavior to become automatic for the reader. Direct teaching of literal, inferential, and extra-textual relationships may be necessary.

When the adult begins working with more difficult content materials, the tutor may want to use a guide-o-rama (Cunningham & Shablak, 1975), a type of study guide that shows the student "how" to read the text, i.e. pointing out sections that should be read carefully or skimmed, pointing out the organiza-tion of paragraph or selection, noting that a troublesome word is actually defined in the context, and encouraging the reader to relate information just read to information previously read or learned.

Before using this as a guided reading procedure, the tutor should model the reading of a somewhat difficult text, thinking aloud the strategies used to comprehend the text (Davey, 1983; Heller, 1986) and allowing the adult begin-ning reader to "see" into the mind of a good reader. The tutor reads a selection to illustrate personal use of prediction and imagery to help focus comprehen-sion. Also modeled are being on the lookout for text that doesn't make sense and using fix-up strategies when comprehension breaks down, i.e., re-reading, using context, resorting to the dictionary, or deciding to consult another text.

(11) Reading to the Adult Beginning Reader: Don't forget the obvious: reading to the adult learner affords the opportunity for enjoyment of literature beyond the learner's reading ability or, if the newspaper is read, to keep up on current events. The reading sessions may be very stressful for the beginning adult learner. Thus, the "reading to" period is a wind-down time that provides a few minutes of relaxation.

Word Level Activities

Although it is important to emphasize whole text activities, it is also appro-priate to work at the word level if the isolated word study is followed by reading the studied words in whole text situations. Sometimes individual words, such as those commonly found on signs, are themselves complete texts.

(1) Functional Vocabulary: Sorting labels into piles of known and unknown is a particularly non-threatening activity. The adult learners themselves are responsible for deciding whether or not they can or cannot read a given label. A similar activity is to have the adult sort words encountered on signs or from advertisements into piles of known and unknown. You can find various word lists of everyday terms that adults meet daily in their environment or compile your own list.

Examples of essential vocabulary terms/phrases from Wilson's Essential Adult Vocabulary List (1963) are *beware, closed, dentist, own, help, men, out, pedestrians prohibited, use other door,* and *women.* The *Bader Reading and Language Inventory* (Bader, 1983) contains two lists of functional words. Sets of word lists, pre-primer through at least eighth grade, containing basic and general words deemed appropriate for the given grade levels can be found in informal reading inventories such as the ones by Bader (1983) and Johns (1985). More recently, Wangberg, Thompson, and Levitov (1984) developed a list of frequently used words by beginning adult readers as they participated in a series of interactive language experience lessons using microcomputers.

(2) Voice-Pointing: For adults who are truly non-readers, try a voice-point-

ing exercise (Gillet & Temple, 1986: 90-94). Eight words from a previously memorized four-line text, i.e., a verse from a popular song, are presented as a pre-test. Then the adult reads the memorized text. In random order the adult is asked to point to the eight pre-test words. Finally, the pre-test words are again shown in isolation. Pronouncing 75% of them correctly would indicate that the adult has a stable concept of word, can match speech to text, and has the ability to remember words presented in a visual/aural manner.

(3) Word Families: Learning word families (i.e., *cake, rake, make, lake*) is a good way to increase a reader's sight word knowledge via using a familiar phonogram and initial consonant substitution. Cunningham's compare-contrast strategy (1979) is based on the phonogram concept as readers are urged to compare parts of an unknown word to known words. For example, a reader's knowledge of bad and man assists in figuring out the pronunciation of *sadden* as the reader compares *sad* (unknown) to *mad* (known) and *den* (unknown) to *men* (known). Older readers may find that this compare-contrast method of analyzing words is more productive than sounding and blending isolated word elements. Rather than learning word families in an isolated way, teach them as key phonograms appear in the reader's language experience stories or in environmental texts.

(4) Word Sorts: Have adult beginning readers complete various word sort activities. For example, you may want to see if the adult can see similarities and differences among words by categorizing them into various word families. Present the following words on individual notecards: *book, look, bake, cake, took,* and *rake*. Does the adult see that *book, look,* and *took,* end the same and that *bake, take,* and *cake* end the same? You can make the activity as easy or as difficult as you want by having the words more or less similar. Word sorts can also emphasize semantic relationships with the reader categorizing words according to meaning-based comparisons. Words sorts can be *closed* with the teacher/tutor providing the category labels or *open* with the reader determining the basis on which a given set of words might be grouped (Gillet & Temple, 1986; 202-206).

(5) Vocabulary Knowledge: Evaluate the adult's vocabulary and concept knowledge. Prepare a passage by underlining several important vocabulary terms. After listening to (or reading) the passage, ask the adult to give synonyms for the underlined terms. Ask for antonyms for additional insights into the adult's conceptual knowledge. Or present the adult with incomplete analogies, such as engine is to truck as _____ is to sailboat. The ability to handle analogies will provide insights into the adult's reasoning abilities. Responses to semantic word sort activities noted earlier will also given insights into the adult's vocabulary knowledge.

SUMMARY

When working with adult beginning reader or the adult intermediate reader, emphasizing text level strategies that exemplify real reading experiences is important. Word level activities can also be used for instruction, but they should be incorporated into textual reading. Reading should always begin and end with whole texts rather than isolated words or sentences. And when used diagnostically, many of these instructional strategies provide information that cannot be obtained from the more traditional, norm-referenced tests typically used.

REFERENCES

Adult Basic Learning Examination (1986). (2nd edition). San Antonio, TX: The Psychological Corporation/Harcourt Brace Jovanovich.

Adult Reader's Library (1981). Glenview, IL: Scott-Foresman.

Amoroso, H. C., Jr. (1985). Organic primers for basic literacy instruction, *Journal of Reading*, 28, 398-401.

Bader, L. (1983). *Bader Reading and Language Inventory.* New York: Macmillan.

Bernstein, V. (1985). *America's Story.* Austin, TX: Steck Vaughn.

The crisis series (1982). Belmont, CA: Fearon/Pitman Learning.

Crowley-Weibel, M. (1983). "Use the public library with adult literacy students," *Journal of Reading*, 27, 62-65.

Cunningham, D., & Shablak, S. L. (1975). "Selective reading guide-o-rama," *Journal of Reading*, 18, 380-382.

Cunningham, P. (1979). "A compare-contrast system of mediated word identification," *Reading Teacher*, 32, 774-778.

Davey, B. (1983). "Think aloud-modeling the cognitive process," *Journal of Reading*, 27, 44-47.

Ervin, J. (1980). *Reading comprehension in varied subject matter.* Toronto: Educators Publishing Service.

Fastback/double fastback series (1985-1988). Belmont, CA: Fearon/Pitman Learning.

Gillet, J. W., & Temple, C. (1986). *Understanding Reading Problems* (2nd edition). Boston: Little, Brown.

Goodman, B. (Ed.). (1980, 1988). *Spotlight on Literature.* NY: Random House.

Goodman, Y. (1974). "I never read such a long story before," *English Journal*, 63, 67-71.

Haggard, M. (1986). "Developing critical thinking with the directed reading-thinking activity," *The Reading Teacher*, 41, 526-533.

Hall, M. A. (1981) *Teaching Reading as a Language Experience.* Columbus, OH: Charles E. Merrill.

Heilman, A. (1981). *Phonics in Proper Perspective.* (2nd ed.). Columbus, OH: Charles E. Merrill.

Heller, M. (1986). "How do you know what you know? Metacognitive modeling in the content areas," *Journal of Reading*, 29, 415-422.

Jastak, J., & Jastak, S. (1978). *Wide Range Achievement Test.* Los Angeles, CA: Western Psychological Service/Manson Western Corporation.

Johns, J. (1988). *Basic reading inventory* (4th edition). Dubuque, IA: Kendall/Hunt.

Johnson, E. (1983). *Modern reading skilltext.* Columbus, OH: Charles E. Merrill.

Kazamek, F. (1984). "I wanted to be a tencra to help pemp to 1_____: Writing for adult beginning readers," *Journal of Reading*, 27, 614-619.

Kennedy, K., & Roeder, S. (1975). *Using Language Experience with Adults.* Syracuse, NY: New Readers Press.

Know Your World Extra. Columbus, OH: Xerox.

Knowles, M. (1980). *The Modern Practice of Adult Education.* Chicago: Follett.

Langer, J. (1981). "From theory to practice: A pre-reading plan," *Journal of Reading*, 25, 152-156.

LifeTimes (1979). Belmont, CA: Fearon/Pitman Learning.

Malone, V. (Ed.). (1981). *Adult Reading: Comprehension.* Glenview, IL: Scott-Foresman.

Manzo, A. (1969). "The request procedure," *Journal of Reading*, 13, 123-126, 163.

Meyer, V. (1987). "Lingering feelings of failure: An adult who didn't learn to read," *Journal of Reading*, 31, 218-221.

NewsScan. Syracuse, NY: New Readers Press.

News for You. Syracuse, NY: New Readers Press.

Padak, G. and Padak, N. (1987). "Guidelines and a holistic method for adult basic reading programs," *Journal of reading*, 30, 490-496.

Raphael, T., & Pearson, P. D. (1985). "Increasing students' awareness of sources of information for answering questions," *American Education Research Journal*, 22, 217-235.

Reyes, E., Lindberg, M., Messmer, E., Lee, A., & Reyes, R. (1981). *Adult English as a Second Language Diagnostic Reading Test.* Burlingame, CA: ACSA Foundation for Educational Administration – California State Department of Education.

Slosson, R. (1982). *Slosson Oral Reading Test* (2nd edition). East Aurora, NY: Slosson Educational Publishers.

Smith, F. (1979). *Reading Without Nonsense.* Chicago: Holt, Rinehart & Winston.

Stauffer, R. (1975). *Directing the Reading-Thinking Process.* New York: Harper & Row.

Stewart, C., & Taylor, E. (1982). *Practicing Occupational Reading Skills.* NY: Random House.

Sundown reading series. Syracuse, NY: New Readers Press.

Swinburne, L., Warner, J., & Warner, M. (1985). *Mastering Basic Reading Skills.* Austin, TX: Steck-Vaughn.

Tests of Adult Basic Education (1987). Manchester, MO: CTB/McGraw-Hill.

Taylor, W. (1953). "Cloze procedure: A new tool for measuring readabiliiy," *Journalism Quarterly, 30,* 415-433.

Thelen, J. (1982). "Preparing students for content reading assignments," *Journal of Reading, 26,* 544-549.

Udari, S. (1978). *Family Development Series* (rev. ed.). Austin, TX: Steck-Vaughn.

Valeri-Gold, M. (1987). "Previewing: A directed reading-thinking activity," *Reading Horizons, 27,* 123-126.

Wangberg, E., Thompson, B. & Levitov, J. (1984). "First steps toward an adult basic word list," *Journal of Reading, 28,* 244-247.

Watson, D. (1982). "In college and in trouble-with reading," *Journal of Reading, 25,* 640-645.

Watson, D. (1978). "Reader selected miscues: Getting more from silent reading," *English Education, 10,* 75-85.

Wilson, C. (1963). "An essential vocabulary," *The Reading Teacher, 17,* 94-96.

CHAPTER 3

Remediation in Mathematics: New Approaches for Old Ideas

Elaine B. Chapline
Claire M. Newman

Adult students often have negative attitudes toward mathematics. Tension related to math learning is a realistic, not a pathological, response in adults who haven't mastered math sufficiently when they last studied it and who have established a math avoidance pattern. When working with a group of such students who have developed anxieties about their ability to deal with or to learn mathematics, new approaches are necessary to help students get past these feelings leaving them freer to attend to and focus their energies on learning, to acquire confidence along with competence and to become independent math learners.

As the instructor works with students to develop math knowledge and skills, concurrent attention needs to be directed to affective learning. Just as cognitive and affective learning should be integrated when working with adults, the mathematics content and the strategies and materials used for solving problems are interrelated and grow from one another.

LEARNING ENVIRONMENT

A non-threatening learning environment, essential for adult studies, provides both support and challenge. Students need to be encouraged to "think aloud" and to feel that their ideas are worth consideration. A student need not be constrained by having to state only a fully developed or "correct" idea. Emphasize instead, the processes with which the students are working and see alternate routes in problem solving rather than a single approach to obtaining a right answer. By providing practice and support for seeking out alternatives, the instructor implicitly recognizes that students differ in learning styles, approach to subject, and background experiences.

To provide this environment, an instructor needs to refrain from quickly responding to a student's ideas with a statement of its "rightness" or "wrongness." Such concern for maintaining openness while ideas are being considered, needs to be balanced with the concern for students' having clear knowledge of the correctness, efficiency and merit of the various ideas which may be considered. This balance is difficult to achieve and to maintain. One strategy an instructor may use is to empathize with students' needs and struggles to master the math materials. This empathy can exemplify an attitude toward students that facilitates supportive, non-threatening, yet task-oriented instructor behaviour.

Teacher attitudes are communicated in both gross and subtle ways. Instructors may feel they are being helpful when they say, "it's easy." Students, on hearing this and accepting the instructor's judgment, tend to blame themselves when they don't understand an idea. Their old sense of failure can thus be reactivated. It is helpful when the instructor recognizes that a mathematics concept is difficult. The most supportive message is given when difficulties are acknowledged and faith in the learner's ability to master the materials is communicated.

Students should be made aware of the steps that usually take place during problem solving. Since tension is often experienced while one is searching for a solution strategy that will work, students should become aware that some tension is to be expected and even prized. This sort of tension, rather than having a debilitating effect, can be experienced as stimulating.

MATHEMATICAL CONTENT

It is important to select mathematics that sparks student interest and enthusiasm since students who have been unsuccessful with mathematics often find it difficult to pay attention to material they found dull and uninteresting in the past. Include new and different materials where possible so that learners do not feel that they are reworking old, perhaps distasteful, content. The goal is to enable students to perceive mathematics as interesting, purposeful and relevant to life experiences.

Pattern discernment is a fruitful component of mathematical reasoning. A unit of work dealing with patterns involves students in explaining number relationships. Sequences of odd and even numbers, squares, the binary sequence, are only some of the topics that can be used to show the importance of patterns.

As an example, explore the sequence of odd numbers: 1, 3, 5, 7, 9, ... Consider the sum of the first ten (or twenty, or hundred) odd numbers. Rewrite the number in reverse order and add.

$$1 + \ \ 3 + \ \ 5 + \ \ 7 + \ \ 9 + 11 + 13 + 15 + 17 + 19$$

$$19 + 17 + 15 + 13 + 11 + \ \ 9 + \ \ 7 + \ \ 5 + \ \ 3 + \ \ 1$$

$$\overline{20 + 20 + 20 + 20 + 20 + 20 + 20 + 20 + 20 + 20}$$

Notice that each vertical sum is 20. How many such sums are there? (1). What is the sum of the first ten odd numbers? Since the first ten odd numbers have been added twice, the sum of the first ten odd numbers is $1/2 \cdot 10 \cdot 20$ or 100.

So far so good! But how can we use this to find a general rule for calculating the sum of as many odd numbers as we choose?

The proposed problem lends itself to several problem-solving techniques that assist in its solution. Instead of finding the sum of the first hundred, find the sum of the first four, or five. That is, show students how to start with related problems that are easier to solve. Show them how to record data systematically so that they can look for a pattern. Is there a pattern to the sum?

ODD NUMBERS	
Numbers (n)	Sum
2	1 + 3 = 4
3	1 + 3 + 5 = 9
4	1 + 3 + 5 + 7 = 16

Help them experience the "Aha!" feeling.
$4 = 2^2$, $9 = 3^2$ and $100 = 10^2$

Additional discussion of the sequence of square numbers leads to the generalization: the sum of the first n odd numbers is n^2.

A geometric model of the numbers provides the learner with a concrete visual approach that leads to or verifies the above generalization.

1

$1 + 3 = 2^2$

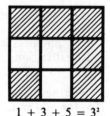

$1 + 3 + 5 = 3^2$

The preceding activity may arouse students' interest in other number sums. How about adding consecutive whole numbers!? Start with a few — say the first four:

$1 + 2 + 3 + 4$. See if reversing the order works this time. That is,

$$1 + 2 + 3 + 4$$
Reverse: $4 + 3 + 2 + 1$
Add: $5 + 5 + 5 + 5 = 4.5$

So, $1 + 2 + 3 + 4 = 1/2 \cdot 4 \cdot 3 \cdot 5$ or 10

There are four numbers to be added — four vertical sums, each one more than the largest number, 4. This yields $4 \cdot 5$ or 20. But, since this ios twice the required sum, the answer is $1/2 \cdot 20$ or 10. Try another! To calculate the sum of the first five numbers, write:

Reverse: $\underline{5 + 4 + 3 + 2 + 1}$

Add: $6 + 6 + 6 + 6 + 6 = 5.6$

Therefore, $1 + 2 + 3 + 4 + 5 = 1/2 \cdot 5 \cdot 6$ or 15.

Summarize these explorations and look for a pattern.

WHOLE NUMBERS	
Number (n)	Sum
2	$1 + 2 = 1/2 \cdot 2 \cdot 3$ or 3
3	$1 + 2 + 3 = 1/2 \cdot 3 \cdot 4$ or 6
4	$1 + 2 + 3 + 4 = 1/2 \cdot 4 \cdot 5$ or 10
5	$1 + 2 + 3 + 4 + 5 = 1/2 \cdot 5 \cdot 6$ or 15

Is the sum of the first six numbers $1/2 \cdot 6 \cdot 7$? Try it and see! Now generalize! The sum of the first n consecutive numbers is $1/2n(n + 1)$. The sum of the first twenty numbers is $1/2 \cdot 20 \cdot 21$; the sum of the first hundred numbers is $1/2 \cdot 100 \cdot 101$; and the sum of the first thirty-five numbers is $1/2 \cdot 35 \cdot 36$.

Take the opportunity to look at the numbers n and $(n + 1)$ and to observe that if n is an odd number, the next whole number, $(n + 1)$ must be odd. This helps in the arithmetic. For instance, to calculate $1/2 \cdot 35 \cdot 36$, rearrange the numbers. That is, $1/2 \cdot 35 \cdot 36 = (1/2 \cdot 36) \cdot 35$ or $18 \cdot 35$.

For further reinforcement, use a geometric model.

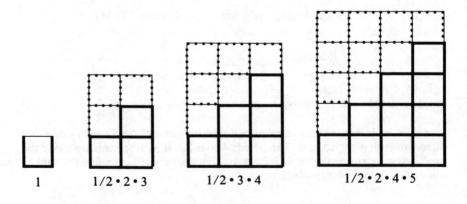

1        $1/2 \cdot 2 \cdot 3$ $1/2 \cdot 3 \cdot 4$ $1/2 \cdot 2 \cdot 4 \cdot 5$

Now try the generalization what is the sum of the first 38 whole numbers? It should be $1/2 \cdot 38 \cdot 39$ or 741. Use a calculator to verify the answer or speed up the calculation process.

Are your students ready to think about sums of even numbers? First compare consecutive even numbers with the corresponding whole numbers.

	1st,	2nd,	3rd,	4th,	5th,...
Whole Numbers	1,	2,	3,	4,	5,...
Even Numbers	2,	4,	6,	8,	10,...

Help them to see that the even numbers can be written $2 \cdot 1, 2 \cdot 2, 2 \cdot 3, 2 \cdot 4, \cdot 5$... so that the nth even number is in the *form* $2n$. (What is the 13th even number? _____ the 42nd even number?) Now about the sum, say, of the first five even numbers. It is convenient to observe that

$$2 \cdot 1 + 2 \cdot 2 + 2 \cdot 3 + 2 \cdot 4 + 2 \cdot 5 = 2(1 + 2 + 3 + 4 + 5)$$

and that

$$1 + 2 + 3 + 4 + 5 = 1/2 \cdot 5 \cdot 6.$$

This means

$$2 + 4 + 6 + 8 + 10 = 2(1/2 \cdot 5 \cdot 6) \text{ or } 5.6$$

It seems that the sum of the first five even numbers is just twice the sum of the first five whole numbers. Will this work for other sums of even numbers? It is true that the sum of the first six even numbers

$$2 + 4 + 6 + 8 + 10 + 12 = 2 \cdot 1/2 \cdot 6 \cdot 7 \text{ or } 42?$$

Is it true that the sum of the first seven even numbers

$$2 + 4 + 6 + 8 + 10 + 12 + 14 = 7 \cdot 8 \text{ or } 56?$$

If the sum of the first n whole numbers is $1/2n(n + 1)$, is the sum of the first n even numbers $n(n + 1)$?

Try it and see.

Adults in today's world need to be number literate. To be number literate is to know the meaning and magnitude of the numbers one encounters in the real world. To be number literate is to be comfortable and confident with numbers — to be able to interpret numbers in ways that make them manageable and understandable. Approximation and estimation, perhaps more than any other basic skills, can open up a new view of the world of numbers to the adult who wants to develop number know-how.

Although approximation and estimation have always been important, they have become critical now that inexpensive calculators are available to the general public. Pressing a wrong key or placing a decimal point in the wrong position can create havoc. The person who uses a calculator should be in control. One must be able to judge the reasonableness of a result.

Traditionally, most of the work with approximation and estimation has been taught through the topic of rounding numbers. Unfortunately many adults complete their schooling with a poor understanding of "rounding" *and* the impression that "rounding" and "estimating" are synonymous. Adult students need to clarify their understanding of "rounding" and to explore other helpful ways of looking at numbers.

The number line is a useful visual device for rounding numbers. Consider 83. To round to the nearest ten, the number is associated with a point between 8 tens (80) and 9 tens (90).

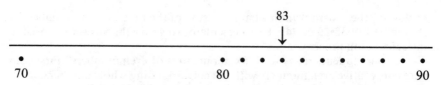

Since the point is closer to the point named 80 (than it is to 90), 83 becomes 80, correct to the *nearest ten*.

Take 837! The number lies between 83 tens (830) and 84 tens (840) and

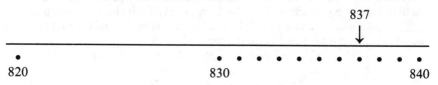

is seen to be closer to 840 than to 830. Therefore, it becomes 840 to the *nearest ten*.

However, to correct 837 to the *nearest hundred*, the number must be placed between consecutive hundreds. That is, 800 and 900.

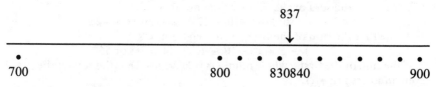

Now it is important to notice that 837 lies between 830 and 840 as would be the case with 831, 835, 839.463, or any number having "8" in hundreds place and "3" in tens place. It is the "3" that places 837 closer to 800 than to 900. Therefore, 837 becomes 800 correct to the *nearest hundred*.

Many more such visual activities will give students an image of a number line, an image that can be recalled whenever the need arises.

There are other techniques for estimating numbers. One such method might be called "front end arithmetic." It requires the ability to handle one-digit arithmetic and the powers of 10. For example, to estimate a product such as 863 × 4162 use 800 × 4000. The product is approximately "32 followed by 5 zeroes" or 3 200 000 — about 3 million.

Consider the product 8.63 × 4.162. One should see this as a number between 8 × 4 (32) and 9 × 5 (45). The number literate adult knows where the decimal point belongs in such a product without needing a rule.

Suppose one needs some idea of the magnitude of the quotient 854 ÷ 21. Front end arithmetic gives 800 ÷ 20 or 40, but notice that rounding yields 900 ÷ 20 or 45, a different estimate. Estimates need not be the same. Another estimator might observe that since 84 = 4 × 21, 840 ÷ 21 = 40. In this case 834 has been expressed as 840, a number convenient for the task at hand. Estimation is a creative endeavour. Adults should be encouraged to use a variety of methods. They should feel free to invent their own methods as long as they make number sense.

LEARNING STATISTICS

Problem solving, use of the inductive learning process, and mathematical models are interrelated strategies which contribute to creating a supportive learning environment.

Problem solving and inductive reasoning aid students in becoming independent learners. The problems selected and any directed learning activities should be designed specifically to develop students' ability to identify and use problem-solving processes. Among the key processes to consider are:

(1) looking for a pattern, (numeric, geometric or algebraic);

(2) using an orderly, systematic approach to the information given;

(3) recording information systematically, so that a pattern can be perceived;

(4) referring to one's existing skills in problem-solving based on prior experience;

(5) working on a smaller or easier problem that is a prototype or part of a larger problem;

(6) transferring a successful method from the context of a simple problem to that of a more complex one; and

(7) accepting mistakes and profiting from them. "Brainstorming" sessions in which a variety of ideas are generated before they are evaluated may help students to "free up" their flow of ideas.

Consider the following problem: There are 12 people in a room. If each person shakes the hand of each of the others, how many handshakes will there be? One student suggests the answer 12 × 11. The instructor asks her to think about the result further while other members of the group continue the problem-solving process. In another part of the room students are shaking hands. One hears: "You shook my hand before!" And from the first student: "Oh!" Of course! If each person shakes the hand of each of the others, each handshake will be counted twice. Thus we must take one-half of each product. The generalization becomes a formula: If there are *n* persons, there are 1/2(n-1) handshakes. In the original question, n = 12. Thus there are 1/2(12)(11) or 66 handshakes. Students who actually counted handshakes verify that the formula works. They have moved from specific examples to a generalization — a formula that gives them the power to solve an entire class of problems of the same kind.

Hold on, now! Other students are solving this differently. Given 3 people, A, B and C, A shakes the hand of B and C (2 shakes) and then B shakes C's hand (1 shake). A diagram illustrates the situation.

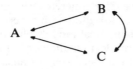

Thus for 3 people there are 2 + 1 handshakes. Try 4 people: A, B, C, and D. A shakes the hand of B, C, and D (3 shakes), B shakes the hand of C and D (2 shakes) and C shakes only D's hand (1 shake). this 4-person situation can be depicted this way:

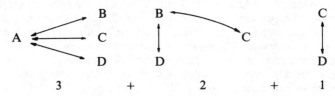

$$3 \quad + \quad 2 \quad + \quad 1$$

When 5 people participate in acting out the problem the result becomes 4 + 3 + 2 + 1. A record of these results reveals a pattern.

Number of People (n)	Number of Handshakes
3	2 + 1 = 3
4	3 + 2 + 1 = 6
5	4 + 3 + 2 + 1 = 10

To count the handshakes for 5 people, add the first 4 whole numbers. The sum of the first four whole numbers (from the earlier discussion) is $1/2 \cdot 4 \cdot 5$ or 10. If there were 12 people, there would be

$$11 + 10 + 9 + 8 + 7 + 6 + 5 + 4 + 3 + 2 + 1 = 1/2 \cdot 11 \cdot 12$$

handshakes. Notice that this result is the same as the one obtained by thinking about the problem in another way.

Students should know that there is no single best way to solve a problem. The instructor who encourages students to use a variety of methods and strategies helps students develop confidence in their ability to choose a problem-solving strategy and to discard it in favor of another one when that decision is appropriate. Students learn to stick with a problem-solving task without becoming discouraged by a strategy that has not worked.

Mathematical models play an important role in all mathematical learning. Geometric models were illustrated in the discussion of number sums. Unfortunately, some educators consider concrete representations of abstract ideas an inappropriate learning tool for adults. To accept this view is to disregard the significant part that mathematical models play in the adult's real world. For example, a floor plan is a model that allows one to plan furniture arrangement before moving the furniture into a room or house.

As another example, consider a model for the handshake problem discussed above. Let points represent people and segments represent handshakes. Then two persons-one handshake is represented by

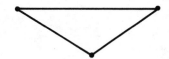

Three persons-three handshakes by

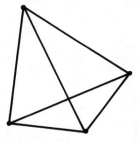

Four persons-six handshakes is represented by

One can move from the reality situation to the mathematical model and back again once they are seen as equivalent.

SUMMARY

This article has illustrated several principles for adult remedial learning that the authors have found successful. First, because adults in need of remediation in mathematics usually experience a high degree of math anxiety, it is important to integrate affective with cognitive elements in the learning environment. Second, so that these adults can become independent learners, they should be given many opportunities to engage in the problem-solving process, use inductive reasoning, discern patterns, and formulate generalizations. Third, the mathematical content presented should seem new, different, and interesting. Finally, instructional strategies should include concrete models whenever possible so that learning can proceed from the concrete to the abstract.

---

* This chapter is based on the authors' work with adult students during a federally-funded materials development project.

REFERENCE

Chapline, E., Newman, C., Denker, E., & Tittle, C. K. (1980). *Final report: Teacher education and mathematics project* (WEEA Grant No. G-007801145). New York: Queens College, City University of New York.

CHAPTER 4

Remediation in Adult Education Using an Individualized Microcomputer Program

Nancy N. Vacc

Whether one is aligned with those who view the current interest in computer-assisted instruction (CAI) as one more educational fad or with those who see CAI as a panacea for all educational problems, the growing impact of this new technology on programs in our educational institutions today cannot be ignored. Likewise, the role and potential value of using microcomputers in adult education cannot be overlooked as members of our younger generation (i.e., current users of microcomputers in elementary and secondary schools) become adult learners.

As Meierhenry (1982) and Vacc (1984) indicated, the microcomputer has great potential for improving and enriching adult education, particularly in the area of remedial education. Thompson (1980) reported that the computer is a multimedia resource that can serve as a text, test, or tutor, while Benderson (1983) suggested that the computer could be used as a tutee; four instructional techniques that are already being used in adult education. The difference is that the microcomputer would supplement the traditional presentation of course content in formal learning situations and supplement or replace the human resource used in informal learning. The concept of CAI is further enhanced by the consideration that students spend more time on task when using a microcomputer (Vacc, 1987), microcomputers appear to have a significant effect on raising achievement levels through drill-and-practice programs (Bass, Ries, & Sharpe, 1986; Howell, Sidorenko, & Jurica, 1987; Roblyer, 1985), and the time required to learn subject matter is substantially less with microcomputers (Kulik, Bangert, & Williams, 1983.) The latter element is of particular interest in adult education because of the additional time needed by many adults to learn new information as age increases (Cross, 1982), and the short-term learning situations desired by many adults.

An additional strength of using CAI in adult education appears to be the active engagement of the learner when working with the microcomputer. As Wray (1983) indicated, microcomputers are capable of interacting rather than simply reacting, a style of teaching that is relevant to the humanistic approach in adult education. CAI also provides a supportive system because it offers privacy to the user, spares individuals from having to reveal to others how much they may not know, and contributes to positive attitudes. These provisions are important for adult learners who may feel inadequate and need experiences that will help build self-confidence and/or permit them to progress at their own rate.

In general, microcomputers appear to have a place in adult education with potential benefits, particularly in the area of remedial instruction. Those who learn best through visual stimulation will benefit from the text and graphics modes of the computer. Speech synthesizers can be used to facilitate individuals who have visual impairments or who learn more readily through auditory channels, while the use of the keyboard and/or touch-sensitive screens or light pens will aid those who need tactile (touch) and kinesthetic (movement) stimulation to supplement the traditional auditory and visual approaches to learning.

A major problem, however, is the limited amount of software that has been developed for use in adult developmental or remedial education. While microcomputer programs that focus on areas such as career planning and interest inventories are available, "drill and practice" type programs which are suitable to the wide-ranging individual needs of adult learners have not been produced. This dilemma may be partially solved if instructors are able to develop their own microcomputer programs as needed to meet the individual requirements of adult learners.

The intent of this chapter is to present a "core" microcomputer program from which a variety of programs can be created as needed to supplement lessons in different content areas and provide developmental or remedial drill and practice activities for adult learners. The program has been developed for the Apple microcomputer, but can be adapted for other microcomputers with minor changes.

USE OF THE CORE PROGRAM

The function of the core program, which is presented in Figure 1, is to provide the user with completion questions that have only one acceptable answer. After the user's name is requested and directions are printed (if needed), a question is presented to the user who has two opportunities to type the correct answer. Immediate feedback is provided during the program through responses for correct answers, responses for incorrect answers, the correct answer after a second incorrect response, continuous information on the number of problems correct out of total number attempted, and a summary statement concerning the percent of correctly answered problems.

Figure 1. Core program that presents questions with only one acceptable answer.

```
10  HOME:SPEED = 175
20  VTAB 6:HTAB 9:FOR D = 1 TO 25:PRINT " "; :NEXT
30  FOR D = 1 TO 12:HTAB 9:PRINT " "; :NEXT
40  HTAB 9:FOR D = 1 TO 25:PRINT " "; :NEXT
50  FOR D = 18 TO 6 STEP -1:VTAB (D):HTAB 34:PRINT " "; :NEXT
60  VTAB 12:INVERSE:HTAB 12:PRINT "COMPLETION QUESTIONS"
70  FOR C = 1 TO 3000:NEXT:NORMAL:SPEED = 255:HOME
```

```
 80  PRINT "LET'S GET ACQUAINTED.:PRINT:INPUT "WHAT IS YOUR NA-
     ME?";N$
 90  HOME:VTAB 3:PRINT "HI, ":N$;". DO YOU NEED DIRECTIONS?"
100  PRINT:INPUT " (TYPE YES OR NO): ";D$
110  IF D$ [   ] "YES" AND D$ [   ] "NO" GOTO 100
120  IF D$ = "YES" GOTO 500
130  HOME:VTAB 12:PRINT "CHECK THAT THE CAPS LOCK KEY IS DOWN."
140  FOR C = 1 TO 2000:NEXT
150  HOME:N = 0:R = 0
160  READ Q$,A$:WA = 0:N = N + 1
170  IF Q$ = "***" GOTO 440
180  PRINT Q$:PRINT
190  PRINT:PRINT:INPUT G$
200  IF G$ = A$ GOTO 320
210  S = -16336:FOR X = 1 TO 60
220  SOUND = PEEK(S)-PEEK(S) + PEEK(S)-PEEK(S):NEXT
230  WA = WA ← 1:IF WA]1 GOTO 410
240  W = INT[RND[1]*3] ← 1
250  ON W GOTO 260,290,300
260  HTAB 6:VTAB 12:PRINT "PLEASE TRY AGAIN."
270  VTAB 21:HTAB 4:PRINT "PRESS ANY KEY FOR ANOTHER TRY."
280  WAIT -16384,128:POKE -16368,0:HOME:GOTO 180
290  VTAB 13:HTAB 7:PRINT "INCORRECT. HOW ABOUT ANOTHER TRY-
     ?":GOTO 270
300  VTAB 13:PRINT "WHOOPS!! HERE IT IS AGAIN."
310  GOTO 270
320  K = INT[RND[1]*3] ← 1:R = R ← 1:PRINT:PRINT
330  ON K GOTO 340,380,390
340  VTAB 13:HTAB 4:PRINT "FANTASTIC JOB!!"
350  PRINT:PRINT:HTAB 4:PRINT "THAT'S ";R;" RIGHT OUT OF ";N;""."
360  VTAB 21:HTAB 4:PRINT "PRESS ANY KEY TO CONTINUE."
370  WAIT -16384,128:POKE -16368,0:HOME:GOTO 160
380  VTAB 13:HTAB 4:PRINT "WAY TO GO, ";N$;"!":GOTO 350
390  VTAB 13:HTAB 4:PRINT "YOU REALLY DO KNOW THIS MATERIAL!!"
400  GOTO 350
410  VTAB 14:HTAB 5:PRINT "THE CORRECT ANSWER IS. . ."
420  INVERSE:PRINT:PRINT:HTAB 10:PRINT A$;:NORMAL:PRINT "."
430  VTAB 21:HTAB 2:PRINT "PRESS ANY KEY FOR A NEW PROBLEM."
435  WAIT -16384,128:POKE -16368,0:HOME:GOTO 160
440  VTAB 5:PRINT "OKAY, ";N$;", HERE ARE YOUR RESULTS:"
450  PRINT:HTAB 6:PRINT "YOU COMPLETED ";INT [R/[N-1]*100];"% OF
     THE"
460  PRINT:HTAB 10:PRINT "PROBLEMS CORRECTLY."
```

```
470  VTAB 19:HTAB 6:PRINT "I LIKED THE WAY YOU WORKED."
480  PRINT:PRINT:HTAB  4:PRINT  "KEEP  ON  PRACTICING  AND
     LEARNING!":END
500  HOME:VTAB 4:PRINT "YOU WILL BE GIVEN A PROBLEM THAT HAS"
510  PRINT:PRINT "ONLY ONE ACCEPTABLE ANSWER. IF YOU DO"
520  PRINT:PRINT "NOT GET THE ANSWER THE FIRST TIME, YOU"
530  PRINT:PRINT "WILL BE GIVEN A SECOND CHANCE. THE"
540  PRINT:PRINT "CORRECT ANSWER WILL BE PROVIDED AFTER"
550  PRINT:PRINT "THE SECOND INCORRECT ANSWER.
560  VTAB 20:HTAB 6:PRINT "PRESS ANY KEY TO CONTINUE."
570  WAIT -16384,128:POKE -16368,0
580  HOME:GOTO 130
600  DATA HOW MANY SYLLABLES IN THE WORD EDUCATION?,4
610  DATA "EAT" IS WHAT PART OF SPEECH?,VERB
620  DATA 2 4 8 _____ 32, 16
630  DATA 4 * 8 + 6 = _____,38
640  DATA WHAT IS THE VALUE OF Y IN THE EQUATION 9Y-4 = 23?,3
650  DATA TYPE THE NUMBER WORD FOR 8.,EIGHT
660  DATA 4 YARDS = _____ INCHES,144
670  DATA AN _____ IS A FERTILE PLACE IN A DESERT.,OASIS
680  DATA THE ORGANIC REMAINS OF ANIMALS FOUND IN ROCKS ARE
     _____.,FOSSILS
690  DATA DIDN'T IS THE CONTRACTION FOR _____ _____.,DID NOT
700  DATA THE CORRECT SPELLING IS WENESDAY/WEDESDAY/WEDNES-
     DAY?,WEDNESDAY
710  DATA THE HIGHEST OFFICE IN OUR GOVERNMENT IS HELD BY THE
     _____.,PRESIDENT
900  DATA ***,***
```

Newman (1980) indicated that adults learn more quickly when instruction is related to the learner's personal activities. Accordingly, the microcomputer core program and its modifications provide the ABE instructor or tutor with a technique for personalizing remedial education through the use of drill-and-practice questions that (a) focus directly upon the respective learner's immediate needs, interests, and personal situations, (b) can easily be modified in accordance with the learner's progress, (c) can be used repeatedly for reinforcing newly acquired skills, and (d) include immediate, nonjudgmental feedback concerning the learner's performance.

The ABE/ASE teacher can use the microcomputer as a means of providing individualized practice in reading and/or mathematics skills as a supplement to the traditional worksheets or workbooks. For example, individual drill-and-practice lessons can be developed through modifications of the core program to aid the learner who might be having difficulty with identifying certain suffixes, prefixes, or correctly spelled words. A program requiring the user to provide the number of syllables in a series of words can be developed for a learner experiencing syllabication problems. Identifying compound words, synonyms, homonyms, or parts of speech; forming contractions; practice with alphabetical order; and cloze exercises (i.e., filling in blanks with the words that are missing) are examples of other reading skills for which microcomputer programs can be developed based on the core program. Or, the core program can be most appropriate for drill-and-practice exercises with the mathematics processes. In addition to problems in addition, subtraction, multiplication, and division, practice and reinforcement of mathematics skills can be provided through programs on number sequence, number words, equalities and inequalities, percents, decimals, fractions, exponents, measurement, and solving equations. Again, these programs can be developed according to the needs of individuals or groups of learners.

Use of the core program is not limited to literacy learning. It can be incorporated within a basic job-training program in a business, industry, or community-college setting as a means of providing reinforcement of skill development and/or drill and practice concerning a given task, or to help an individual be more effective. For example, as part of a job-training program, an employee's general understanding and comprehension of the operation of industrial equipment can be reinforced through use of adaptations of the core program.

Using the core program is also appropriate for adult learning environments such as church-sponsored educational programs, hospital adult-education programs, classes offered by health and welfare agencies for learning special skills or health and welfare knowledge, and remedial and regular education programs in correctional institutions. In each situation, programs can be developed to meet the individual needs of learners with regard to vocational, educational, and/or rehabilitation training. Use of the core program is limited only by the innovativeness of the ABE instructor.

Users of the core program have found it to be most helpful in their job situations. Following a series of training sessions focusing on the model program, two groups of professional educators (including adult basic education instructors) evaluated its overall usefulness as 4.6 based on a five-point scale in which "1" was poor and "5" was superior.

MAKING A COPY OF THE CORE PROGRAM

The following discussion is based on the assumption that the reader has little knowledge of the microcomputer except how to start (i.e., "boot") the system, insert a disk(ette), run a program, and turn off the system.

To use the core program, the system is booted and the disk on which the core program is to be stored is inserted in the disk drive. The user types NEW (followed by the "return" key) to clear the microcomputer's memory of any existing program and to indicate that a new program is to be entered. The system's "prompt" (i.e.,]) will appear on the screen when the microcomputer is ready and the core program can be typed exactly as presented in Figure 1, commencing with statement 10 and ending with statement 900. The return key is used only at the *end* of a statement. If the content of a statement goes beyond 40 spaces, the text is automatically moved to the next line on the screen.

The program, when typed, will be entered in the microcomputer's memory and can be RUN, but it is not stored or saved on the disk until the user types SAVE followed by a filename (e.g., SAVE CORE PROGRAM, whereby CORE

PROGRAM is the name of the program or file stored on the disk.) To check that CORE PROGRAM has been saved on the disk, type CATALOG which lists all the filenames or programs "stored" on that disk.

If no typing errors have been made, all statements in the program will be completed when the program is RUN. The user is requested to type his or her name, respond yes or no to the request for directions, and respond to 12 questions that address a variety of content areas. The 12 questions for the core program are included in the data statements (i.e., lines 600-900). These questions, which represent a variety of content areas, demonstrate the types of items that can be asked using the given item format. When the 12 questions have been answered, a summary of the user's performance is provided.

COPING WITH ERRORS MADE WHEN TYPING THE CORE PROGRAM

If an error was made when typing the core program, the microcomputer will respond with a message indicating that a "syntax error" exists in a given statement. For example, if an error was made when typing statement 120 the message would read ?SYNTAX ERROR IN 120. To determine what the error in statement 120 is, that line can be listed by typing "LIST 120". The computer will then provide the statement as typed (e.g., 120 IF D$ = "YES" GO TO 500).

At this point, it should be mentioned that the spacing used to type a statement in the program, may be different than that shown when the statement is "listed". For example, statement 120 in the core program contains spaces after IF, "YES", and GO TO, for ease of reading. However, when statement 120 is listed in response to the LIST command, it more than likely will contain additional spaces after the D$ and the equal sign (i.e., IF D$ = "YES" GOTO 500). The microcomputer operates on a set format for listing statements in a program, but it will accept different spacing when a program is "entered" into its memory. The spacing in command statements is usually of little concern except within PRINT statements which are discussed later. Additional spaces or no spaces between commands or before and after colons are tolerated.

Returning to the example of the syntax error in statement 120 (i.e., IF D$ = "YES" GOTO 500), the problem is the space in the command GOTO. To make the needed correction, begin with the number and retype the statement as presented in Figure 1, with the correct typing of GOTO. After making the needed change, the program will need to be saved again so the program stored on the disk will contain the correction.

Hard-to-Determine Errors

The above procedure would be followed for any error encountered during the "running" of the program. Sometimes, however, errors are difficult to locate and usually involve typing errors such as the following.

Zero and Letter O Confusion — one possible error may be the use of capital letter O for the zero. The zero is distinguished from the letter O by a diagonal line (i.e., 0) so check all numerals to insure that a zero was typed rather than an O.

Spacing in Statement Number — an error can occur if a space has been included in a statement number. For example, if statement 310 was typed as "3 10 GOTO 270", it would be interpreted as statement 3, resulting in a syntax error because the 10, which is viewed as a command, it not an interpretable operation. Correcting this error involves two steps; retype statement 310 without error, and then delete statement 3. The latter is easily achieved by typing the number 3 followed by the return key (i.e., to delete a statement, type the statement number followed by the return key). This procedure is interpreted as entering a statement 3 which contains no operations to be performed. Therefore, it will not be listed as one of the statements in the program.

Undetectable error — if the syntax error in a given statement cannot be located, and the error message continues, retype the statement and again run the program. The error may have involved a hard-to-detect error such as striking the control key in conjunction with another key. Retyping the statement as it appears in Figure 1 should take care of the problem. As final "words of wisdom", always re-save the program after making a needed correction.

MODIFYING THE CORE PROGRAM
Once the core program has been saved on a disk, it is available for unlimited use as is, or it can be altered in unlimited directions to form new programs.

Adding New Questions
The data statements (i.e., lines 600 to 900 in the core program) consist of the DATA command, the question to be asked, a comma, and the correct answer immediately following the comma. Keeping this same format, additional questions can be added between statements 721 and 899 or between other sets of statements (e.g., 601 and 609). Statement 900 is a built-in check for regulating when the last question has been read by the computer. It should not be altered in any way or an "out of data" error will be encountered and the summary of the user's performance will not be provided.

To increase the number of questions to 20, data statements might be added as follows:

720   DATA NAME THE SMALLEST PARTICLE OF MATTER.,ATOM
730   DATE OBSTRUCTING THE PASSAGE OF LEGISLATIVE BILLS BY ENDLESS SPEECH-MAKING IS _____.,FILIBUS-TERING
740   DATA ABSOLUTE MONARCHY CRUELLY ADMINISTERED-?DICTATORSHIP/TYRANNY/PLUTOCRACY?,TYRANNY
750   DATA NAME THE LARGEST MOUNTAIN IN NO. AMERICA?, MOUNT MCKINLEY
751   DATA ANSWER WITH TRUE OR FALSE — AN OPERA IS A DRAMA SET TO MUSIC.,TRUE
752   DATA $1/8$ + ;6/8 = ?,$7/8$
753   DATA THE AREA OF A RECTANGLE THAT IS 6" LONG AND 10" WIDE IS _____ SQUARE INCHES.,60
754   DATA WE ARE GOING TO (THERE OR THEIR) HOUSE.,THEIR
] SAVE CORE PROGRAM 2
] CATALOG

Notice that the statement numbers in the above illustration are initially sequenced by tens but change to ones after statement 750. Numbering by tens rather than ones leaves "free" space to add statements. The data statements are read beginning with the smallest numbered line and progressing sequentially until the end-of-data statement is encountered (e.g., statement 900 in the core program). If questions are to be presented in a certain order, they must be included in the DATA statements in that order. For example, if the question contained in statement 752 is to be presented before the question in statement 730, then the statement number for that question should be a number between 720 and 730 rather than 752.

A second item of importance in the above illustration concerns the symbols used for the different mathematical processes. The asterisk (i.e., *) is used for multiplication, and the slash (i.e., /) is used for division.

A final point concerns the SAVE command. The core program was initially saved on the disk with the filename of CORE PROGRAM. With a change of questions in the original program, two options are available. The new questions can be included as part of the original program (e.g., SAVE CORE PROGRAM), or the modification can be saved using a different name (e.g., SAVE CORE PROGRAM 2) so that both versions of the program are stored on the disk.

Changing Questions in the Program

If a new set of questions is desired, *each* DATA statement in the core program will need to be changed. The LIST statement introduced earlier is used in this task. Typing LIST without a statement number after it results in a listing of all the statements in the program. In contrast, typing LIST and a statement number in the program *followed by a comma* provides a listing of all the statements in the program from that number to the end of the program. Thus, typing LIST 600, provides a listing of all the DATA statements so those that need to be retyped can be identified. Unchanged DATA statements will appear in the modification; if a question is not wanted, the data statement containing it needs to be changed or deleted.

As long as the same format for the DATA statements included in the core program is followed (i.e., the DATA command followed by the question, comma, and answer immediately after the comma), statements 600 through 720 can be easily changed and more DATA statements can be added to include any question that requires completion with only one acceptable answer.

Modifications of the core program are limited only by the format of the item, and questions can range from simple to complex problems. An important requirement is that the question be void of commas because they are interpreted as a signal for the end of a question or answer. To illustrate, suppose the data statement was entered as DATA WHO WROTE HAMLET, MACBETH, AND JULIUS CAESER?,SHAKESPEARE. Although the intended question is "Who wrote Hamlet, Macbeth, and Julius Caesar?", the question printed on the screen will be "Who wrote Hamlet" and the expected answer is "Macbeth". To summarize, the data statement is read until a comma or end of statement is encountered with the information read prior to the comma being stored in memory as the question. Reading the data statement that continues until another comma or end of statement is encountered and this information becomes the answer. In the above illustration, "Julius Caesar?" becomes the next question and "Shakespeare" is the expected answer.

Directions For Using the Program

To make the core program usable with a minimum of changes, generic directions have been included within quotation marks after the PRINT command in statements 500 through 550. The first command in statement 500 (i.e., HOME) clears the screen of all text. The second command, VTAB 4 (i.e., vertical tab) indicates that the text to be printed should start on line 4; dimensions for the monitor screen are 40 spaces by 24 lines. As it implies, the PRINT command controls the text "outputted" to the screen or the printer. Text to be printed is enclosed in quotation marks following the PRINT command. Statement 500, therefore, indicates that the screen is to be cleared of all text and the words, YOU WILL BE GIVEN A PROBLEM THAT HAS, are to be printed on the screen beginning with line four. PRINT used by itself indicates that a line should be skipped; an "empty" line is printed since there is nothing in quotation marks following the command.

Text will be printed exactly as it is listed within quotation marks with no regard to the 40 spaces across the screen or hyphenation. If a sentence contains more than 40 characters, the 41st character will be printed on the next line even though it might be the second letter in a word. Therefore, spacing must be given careful consideration if the words to be printed extend beyond 40 characters. The same requirement needs to be considered when entering information in data statements.

Responses for Answers Provided by User

The core program was developed to allow for a random selection of three responses to correct answers and three responses to incorrect answers. Correct responses are included in statements 340, 380, and 390. To change one of these responses, retype the respective statement substituting the new response within the quotation marks. Likewise, changes can be made in the responses to incorrect answers which are contained in statements 260, 290, and 300. Changes in the responses to correct and incorrect answers are limited only by the imagination of the instructor. The variable N$, included in statement 380, for example, adds a pleasant personal touch. It is a location in the random-access memory that contains the name entered by the user in response to the question, "What is your name?", which is asked at the beginning of the program.

Although the core program is confined to one type of question format, the reader is directed to Vacc (1985) for alterations to the core program to include questions with more than one acceptable response (e.g., DATA THE 16TH PRESIDENT OF THE UNITED STATES WHO WAS ASSASSINATED WAS _____.,LINCOLN,ABRAHAM LINCOLN,ABE LINCOLN). This reference also presents an explanation of the BASIC language commands used in the core program.

SUMMARY

A microcomputer core program that permits the provision of only one acceptable response to a given question has been presented. Considerations in using the program were also addressed as follows: coping with syntax errors, adding questions to the set included in the core program, including new questions, changing directions, and changing responses.

The number of new programs that can be developed from the core program is limited only by an instructor's creative ability to modify the DATA statements to meet the individual needs of adult learners. The unlimited variations that can be made in the core program should provide partial fulfillment of the void in software suitable for use in adult basic and remedial education.

REFERENCES

Bass, G., Ries, R., & Sharpe, W. (1986). Teaching basic skills through microcomputer assisted instruction. *Journal of Educational Computing Research, 2*, 207-218.

Benderson, A. (Ed.). (1983). *Focus: Computer literacy.* Princeton, NJ: Educational Testing Service.

Cross, K. P. (1982). *Adults as learners.* San Francisco: Jossey-Bass.

Howell, R., Sidorenko, E., & Jurica, J. (1987). The effects of computer use on the acquisition of multiplication facts by a student with learning disabilities. *Journal of Learning Disabilities, 20*, 336-341.

Kulik, J., Bangert, R., & Williams, G. (1983). Effects of computer-based teaching on secondary school students. *Journal of Education Psychology, 75*, 19-26.

Meierhenry, W. C. (1982). Microcomputers and Adult Learning. In D.C. Gueulett (Ed.), *Adult Learning.* Chicago: Follett.

Newman, A. P. (1980). *Adult basic education: Reading.* Boston: Allyn & Bacon.

Roblyer, M. D. (1985). *Measuring the impact of computers in instruction.* Washing, DC: Association for Educational Data Systems.

Thompson, B. J. (1980). Computers in reading: A review of applications and implications. *Educational Technology, 20*, 38-41.

Vacc, N. N. (1987). Microcomputer word processor versus handwriting: A comparative study of writing samples produced by mildly mentally handicapped students. *Exceptional Children, 54*, 156-165.

Vacc, N. N. (1985). Using microcomputers in teaching English: Developing your own computer programs. *Journal of Educational Technology Systems, 14*, 35-46.

Vacc, N. N. (1984). Computers in adult education: Writing and Reading. *Lifelong Learning, 7*, 26-28.

Wray, D. (1983). Computer-assisted learning in language and reading. *Reading, 17*, 31-36.

CHAPTER 5:

Remedial Learning: An Experiential Approach

Diana M. Lohnes

A remedial program must be a vibrant, valuable and varied program. In partnership and co-operation, the learner is integrated to the group collectivity and acquires the necessary skills to effectively and efficiently assume a differentiation of roles in a demanding world. To the classroom come the learners and teachers who bring to the group their total selves, the emotion as well as the intellectual.

A remedial classroom is the professional home where student involvement must be ensured in the learning program and process. It is not merely a room in which remedial classes and lessons are presented. Certainly the core program can focus on improving the literacy and numeracy skills of the learners. However, the communication of academic information is a complex activity that must account for the unique characteristics of both students and teachers.

The remedial teacher is a resource person whom learners access to assist in achieving their academic and personal goals. This individual must develop the insight to recognize and understand how each student is unique. Knowing that a man is particularly proud of being able to repair his own vehicle may be the key to unlock the world of mathematics for that same learner. So, the remedial instructor must be curious about the students. A system has to be created to identify the learner's strengths, weaknesses, needs and goals. Information from student surveys, interviews, informal/formal testing and group discussion can be compiled to create learner-generated/learner-centered objectives. The student's experiences, goals and knowledge must be respected and included in all aspects of a co-operative, learner-specific program. On the other hand, the teacher must exercise not only the professional skills to interpret the collected information but the discretion to use this responsibly. Information that is disclosed informally or formally can become public only with the expressed permission of the participants.

The remedial teacher must acknowledge his or her own strengths and weaknesses. To have adequate personal academic resources, or access to such resources either within the educational institution or the community, is only the beginning. The remedial instructor must be innovative and creative, and must value his or her own learner role in order to enter into active involvement in the student's learning process. Classroom activities that support established program objectives must also concur with the needs of the participants. Principles and intents must be clearly identified and upheld so that the participants will not lose the focus of the program.

Education has to be an involved activity that includes all participants. Practical application of life skills techniques and methodology can secure learner co-operation in the academic program. Discussion of academic goals and identification of "learner contracts" and weekly timetables will ensure the maintenance and achievement of academic goals. Negotiation skills and organizational skills must be developed and utilized continuously in the remedial class to establish a viable, flexible program.

Administrative support of the remedial program presupposes a full awareness of the course objectives and the practical application of these objectives. To better understand the nature of the student group, an administrator can be invited to participate in class activities. Recognition of this individual as a resource person can highlight the program manager as one person who cooperates in the achievement of program objectives.

The program administrator must allow an adequate budget for the maintenance and continuation of a remedial course. The acquisition of adequate and updated teaching materials is a costly but necessary venture. Some texts require workbooks in which, indeed, students do write. Video and film equipment are expensive. Cassette tapes and machines need constant servicing or replacement. Transportation expenses and insurance coverage for class adventures can be expected. The program budget needs to accommodate these and other requirements.

Also important is the need for teacher development in the specialized field. Professional resource books and materials are necessary to facilitate the sharing and mixing of educational expertise. Adequate coverage for instructors who visit other institutions or attend conferences must be included in the departmental budget. Yet, these are worthwhile expenditures that maximize individual and departmental accountability within the remedial program. In summary, the teacher must have the professional skills and institutional support to enable the students to assume greater initiative and responsibility for their own learning.

Remedial learning demands a particular physical set-up in the classroom. Round tables, larger rectangular tables and an area for group meetings or discussions are some requirements. Adequate blackboards, display areas and flip charts allow the communication of classwork and related activities. In addition, study carrolls and single desk/chair structures enable instruction to occur in a more traditional style. Provision must be made for independent learning, one-to-one instruction, small and large group sessions. The choice of methodologies and teaching curriculum are reflective of the student-generated/student-centered goals and needs.

Any remedial classroom needs to have a "quiet" area, an area for use by those seeking privacy. Let the students arrange the classroom furniture and encourage the rearrangement of furniture periodically, particularly if the intake of students to the program is on a continuous basis. The learning environment must foster an awareness of co-operation as a tool of learning.

Some learners are more territorial than others. Consequently, the "decoration" of their individual learning areas can be their responsibility. The visual attractiveness of class walls and display areas is enhanced by both learner and teacher involvement. Pictures, posters and teacher-aids must be updated continuously and this can be the responsibility of all, of a group, or of one individual.

No classroom would be complete without a file cabinet or cupboard to house student files, supplementary exercises, resource texts, picture files. In other words, valuable possessions that would be difficult to replace are locked up. If students do not have access to their own lockers or to those of friends, an identified area in the classroom can be available for them to secure valued possessions.

The learning environment must be orderly and tidy since it is the outward reflection of an organized, directed remedial program. The joy of learning is reflected in the uncluttered, colourful display of the learning software and hardware. The learning area or classroom is a professional home and those who access it are responsible for its maintenance and appearance.

THE INTERDEPENDENCE OF THE PARTS OF A LEARNING SYSTEM

All parts of a learning system are interdependent: definition of objectives an methods of assessment, choice of methodologies and teaching curriculum. Underlying any remedial program are defined, structured outlines of core objectives that must be achieved if a student is to successfully complete the program. Standards are dictated by the educational institution itself and/or defined by the instructor. The instructor must design a clear, concise reporting system to reflect the learner's progress toward the successful completion of the objectives which he or she identifies and selects. The monitoring procedure reflects the degree of which established standards are met. Student-teacher monitor meetings must be held at regular, scheduled intervals throughout the student's duration of attendance in the program. Furthermore, the meetings must be held privately, since this is one of the few occasions in a remedial program when both instructor and learner can receive private feedback in trust and in confidence. A written report of the proceedings of this meeting can be given to the learner and also kept on file for future reference. Student evaluation is a serious matter; create time to accomplish it meaningfully and effectively.

In addition, the remedial instructor may be required to report learner success and program success not only interdepartmentally but also to the institution or to an outside agency. This demand on time and energy necessitates the creation and establishment of an organized record-keeping system. As the student must understand his or her criteria for evaluation, so must the teacher know the criteria for the program's evaluation. This will ensure an adequate reporting system is established and maintained.

After a time, a student can expect to mainstream into the regular program. The moment of "letting go" can be critical for the learner and the instructor. The transferee must have achieved academic skills and coping skills to confront a new world of different methodologies and expectations. In short, the student must now act independently of the remedial environment and must utilize skills to integrate to the regular group collectively. Meanwhile the remedial teacher experiences both a sense of loss and a sense of pride. The period of readjustment is a time of private reflection for all.

THE NATURE OF THE REMEDIAL PROGRAM

The exciting nature of the remedial program is such that we can move from the subject of Spelling to Reading to Consumer Awareness to History . . . to life. We can learn a simple concept in class an at the same time learn about ourselves as social beings and our role in the social hierarchy. The remedial program must provide the learner with the necessary skills and resources for dealing at a personal and social level with social issues. The development of positive interpersonal relationships is strongly linked to the development of self-esteem, confidence and motivation.

Remedial learning is adventurous! It is also learning specific: the composing process, vocabulary development, reading comprehension, grammar, numeracy, problem-solving . . . Class discussions can lead into yet-to-be-explored topics through questioning. Consider the following:

> If a baby pig is a piggy, then where do we get "Piglet" from? Who is Winnie-the-Pooh anyway?
>
> If a piggy bank is a coin bank in the shape of a pig, then why do we call coin banks not in that shape "piggy banks"?
>
> If a baby chicken is a chick, then why do we not call it a chicky (like piggy)? And why do we not spell Chiclet "Chicklet"?

These examples are taken from a spelling lesson when students were learning to add the letter Y to a base word. The simple creation of words like 'piggy' can also lead to the subject of children's literature. Now, children's storybooks in the remedial classroom may not seem like adult reading material. On the other hand, they reflect culture and social values. With practice, the remedial learner can acquire the skills to read a bedtime story to his or her child for the first time.

Remedial learning is creative! In phonics we can learn the sound system, not as letters that are presented in the order of the alphabet, but as they are articulated. By increasing the vibration of the vocal chords, we change the sound of P to B. Add the nasal quality and B changes to M. Add the vowels of A or O and generate a variety of words: pop, bob; pan, ban; nap. To simplify the instruction, call the letters of P, B, M . . . the Labial family, members who are related because of their means of articulation (lips and air). Next introduce the notion of vowels at regular intervals. This process will ensure that students discover the creation of words by utilizing their own ability to articulate sounds. Other sound families are outlined as follows. (See Table 1.) Accept the challenge to generate a multitude of new words that become surprisingly easy to sound and to spell!

TABLE 1

Articulation Family	Not Vibrated	Vibrated	Nasal	Relatives
Labial family	p	b	m	w
Labial/Dental family	f	v	r	
Dental family	s	z		
Palatal/Dental family	t	d	n	l
Palatal family	ch	j		
Glottal family	k	g		

Those who prefer a more traditional approach to vocabulary development or spelling can expect to recite "rules" and take dictation. But, can they analyze their errors? The following form effectively identifies spelling error patterns of each learner. In this way the learner becomes actively involved in his or her own evaluation of assignments.

ANALYSIS OF MY SPELLING ERRORS

Correct Spelling	How I spelled the word (incorrectly)	Handwriting not clear	I didn't say the word correctly	I substituted one letter for another	I changed the order of the letters	I left out some letters	I confused the word	I left off a word ending
interest	intrest		X			X		
respect	rispect	X	X	X				
feet	feat			X			X	
climbed	climd					X		
want	wont	X		X				

Journal writing is another method to encourage the learner's growth through supportive communication. A journal is not a catalogue of daily events, but rather an exercise in creativity. Free of the threat of making mechanical or grammatical errors, the student becomes more confident and able to write for personal pleasure or need. The journal is the medium to communicate messages of feelings — hopes, fears, aspirations. Beware. No teacher should ask a student to maintain a journal (eg. write four times a week for ten-minute intervals) unless that same teacher has actual experiential knowledge of the exercise. Eventually, entries in the journal will evolve from reportive to thought-provoking issues and, at times, lack specificity and clarity of expression. The journal promotes selected written messages activating memories and allowing the creator to scan the totality of his or her innermost thoughts. The instructor needs to be prepared for this type of communication.

Furthermore, the teacher is responsible to respond, in writing, to student-selected journal entries and must be prepared for his or her own self-disclosure. Because the exercise becomes increasingly time-consuming, it should not be continued over a long period, unless both participants are prepared to assume responsibility for this energy-demanding activity.

Less demanding but still effective is SWISH (an acronym for Silent Writing Intensive Sustained Habit). During this activity, both students and teacher (with the teacher acting as the model) write continuously for 5 to 10 minutes at a time, without worrying about spelling, grammar, etc. SWISH effectively allows high intensity practice in writing immediately, continuously and freely. Students gain self-confidence in their writing skills and abilities. They ask for more feedback concerning their writing (since the work is corrected only at the learner's request). Finally, students are better able to accept suggestions for improvement. Like Journal writing, SWISH becomes a source for learner-generated vocabulary for spelling groups. It gives diagnostic information for teacher purposes and offers insights to students' experiences, families and feelings. Also, articles from SWISH or from journals can be collected and published in a class Newsletter which enable students to further display their writing and share stories with peers.

In mathematics we can discover fractions used in the world of cooking and in other aspects of life.

One egg is $1/12$ of a carton.	(cooking)
One dime is $1/10$ of a dollar bill.	(finance)
One day is $1/7$ of a week.	(time measure)

Examples and illustrations solicited from the learner often result in more variety. The application of the knowledge is highlighted such activities as designing a budget or a circle graph, to name a few. Watch for and collect other examples in magazines and from billboards. Always be on the lookout to gather material that could possibly be incorporated into class activities.

The use of graph paper to add, subtract, multiply and divide whole numbers and decimals can help the student organize and complete mathematics course objectives. It is a simple, yet effective, technique.

Complete programs such as the "BLADE Mathematics Library" (and the "BLADE Communications Library") have merit in the remedial classroom. Different levels of mathematics are presented in specific texts with their corresponding audio tapes. Exercises, end tests, and booklets . . . all included. Such a program requires that each student use and retain exercises and unit end tests as a record of his or her progress. Consequently, students achieve mastery over specific mathematical (or communication) skills and learn organizational skills at the same time. Programs like this are a teacher resource that allows independent or peer learning, and enables more freedom to focus on specific class needs or learner needs which require the teacher's immediate assistance.

And, no remedial classroom is complete without the daily newspaper:

40% off winter coats!
10% off gas barbecues!
$9^1/4$ interest on Canada Savings Bonds!

The learner can glean much information from printed media coverage (Retail Sales, Local News, World Reports, Entertainment). This knowledge can be applied to school, social and personal activities.

Local newspapers often offer excellent, low cost materials on how to use the newspaper. Put a sign on the door:

"Quiet Please. Do Not Enter. We Are Reading."

And, have everyone read including the teacher! Ask students to look for all those items in the newspaper that reflect an identified topic like mathematics. Cut out the selected pieces and display them on a bulletin board. This activity will initiate small and large group activities and subjects for discussion during "Rap" groups or class meetings! Ensure that specific skills practice and instruction are integrated in communication, mathematics, etc. within themes that are of relevance and importance to the learner. Packaged kits are available for such topics as Drivers' Manuals, Citizenship and Career Orientation. However, even more energy must be directed other software, based on a variety of themes. Such available and accessible resources encourage the learner to identify and set realistic goals within alloted time frames.

Most importantly, the opinions and comments of the learner must be continuously solicited and incorporated to develop and evaluate an organized curriculum reflecting the needs of the learner to achieve realistic goals: academic, personal and employment-oriented.

ADDING "MEANINGFUL" TO A REMEDIAL PROGRAM

The development of trust that evolves between student and teacher is a necessary factor in the creation of a meaningful remedial program. Course objectives must be learner-specific and learner-directed if the educational experience is to be a rewarding one. Ultimately, both students and teachers become equipped to transform everyday situations into real and meaningful learning experiences. Emphasis must be on process rather than product since processes have no precise definition. They change and are re-created with each unique group.

The remedial program is successful when the learners' negotiated goals have been met and when the students can develop and practice the skills and behaviours to take direction for their own future in an increasingly demanding society.

REFERENCES

Blade, (1988). Training and Development Resources, Pointe-Claire, Quebec.
Booth, Susan and Brooks, Carol, (1988). *Adult Learning Strategies, An Instructor's Toolkit by Ontario Adult Educators,* Toronto, The Ontario Ministry of Skills Development.
Brundage, Donald H. and Mackeracher, D., (1980). *Adult Learning Principles and Their Application to Program Planning.* Ottawa: The Ministry of Education.
Carr, Jacqueline B., (1984). *Communicating and Relating,* 2nd Edition, Iowa, Wm, C. Brown Publishers.
Hamadache, Ali and Martin Daniel, (1986). *Theory and Practice of Literacy Work, Policies, Strategies and Examples,* Ottawa, UNESCO.
Hubbard, Francis A., (1988). *How Writing Works, Learning and Using the Processes,* New York, St. Martin's Press.
Klevens, Chester, (1987). *Materials and Methods in Adult and Continuing Education, International — Illiteracy.* Los Angeles, Klevens Publications Inc.
Shane, Sandford A., (1983). *Generative Phonology (Foundations of Modern Linguistics).* New Jersey: Prentice-Hall Inc.
Thomas, Ves., (1979). *Teaching Spelling, Canadian Word Lists and Instructional Techniques,* Toronto, Gage Education Publishing Company.

Student Concepts of Literacy Learning: The Neglected Factor in Remediation

Margaret A. O'Brien

Adult students enter literacy programs with concepts about how one reads and writes, and with beliefs about how one should be taught how to read and write. For some students these concepts and beliefs are misconceptions which, in the past, have hindered the acquisition of literacy skill, and which, if ignored, will interfere with progress in the new literacy program. While this statement seems intuitively obvious, explanations of reading disability frequently overlook the role played by the student's own belief system. The case study of the adult literacy student presented in this paper provides support for the inclusion, in a model of remediation, of the factors of concepts of reading and writing, and beliefs about literacy instruction. The case study documents the negative role which the student's concepts and beliefs played in the early stages of the remedial program, and the positive outcomes which resulted when the program addressed directly those concept and beliefs. The case study also demonstrates the powerful role that a student's independent encounters with literacy can play in learning to read and write.

BACKGROUND LITERATURE

The role which misconceptions of the reading process can play in reading disability has, until recently, been ignored in the literature (Johnston, 1985; Taylor, Harris and Pearson, 1988). Neurological and processing deficit models predominate. Johnston (1985) argues for an alternative model of reading disability, one which gives a significant role to strategies. Through three case studies of adult illiterates, he demonstrates how misconceptions and missing conceptions of the reading process can contribute to the development of ineffective reading strategies, which in turn inhibit the acquisition of reading skill.

Several authors stress the need to identify, prior to the commencement of a literacy program, the student's personal expectations for outcomes of the program (Charnley and Jones, 1979; Cook, 1977; Mezirow, Darkenwald and Knox, 1975; Newman, 1980). This case study highlights the need to identify, as well, student expectations for the form which literacy instruction will take.

Studies of adult literacy students also suggest that the majority of students are satisfied with their literacy programs, and believe that the instructor or tutor is the expert who knows what is best for them (Jones and Charnley, 1978;

Davis and O'Brien, 1985). This case study and my observations of other adult literacy students suggest that, what is true for the majority of students is not true for all students: some students do have definite views of how they should be instructed. Further, mismatches between an instructor's and a student's model of literacy instruction can create serious problems in literacy programs, problems which can impede student progress.

Studies of young beginning readers conducted by Clay (1979) highlight the role that independent reading practice plays in the acquisition of reading skill. Clay concludes that practice does more than improve automatic recognition of words and fluency, it actually raises the child's level of reading ability. She argues that significant learning occurs in these independent reading experiences: the child learns about the patterns and relationships of the code, about the role of meaning in reading, about the effectiveness of various reading strategies. An interruption in the tutoring program of the adult subject of this case study afforded an opportunity to observe this positive role that independent attempts to cope with reading and writing can play in the acquisition of literacy skill.

THE STUDENT AND HIS INSTRUCTIONAL HISTORY

In the fall of 1984 Jim, a 37 year old dock yard worker enrolled in the tutoring program which serves as a practicum for students enrolled in the Masters degree program in Reading. Following an assessment, he received tutoring twice weekly for fourteen weeks.

Jim grew up in rural Nova Scotia. His parents sent him to school sporadically, just often enough to keep the truant officer at bay. By the age of nine he stopped attending completely; at 11 he was working on a farm; at 13 he went to sea as a cook's helper.

When he was in his late twenties, he participated in a Canada Manpower literacy program, but, as he explained, it wasn't designed for true beginners like himself. Failure and frustration resulted.

In the two years prior to coming to our program, Jim participated in a program which Davis and O'Brien (1985) call a skills program i.e. a program based on the underlying assumption that "there is a sequence of component skills which must be mastered in order to become a competent reader and writer" (p 18.). In this program he received one year of one-one tutoring followed by one year of small group instruction.

Jim's program emphasized the systematic acquisition of phonic skills. The program consists of five levels (approximating grades one to five) of workbooks and controlled vocabulary reading materials based on phonic relationships e.g. long vowels.

Writing instruction, in this program, supports the reading skill instruction. In the first three levels of the program, writing consists of dictation, in isolation and in sentences, of the word patterns and high frequency words under study, and a small amount of functional writing, e.g. cheque writing. Some composition is introduced at levels four and five. Accuracy in both writing and reading is stressed.

A research project (Davis and O'Brien, 1985) included observation of Jim's class and an interview with his teacher. Both the observation and the interview with the teacher indicated that she followed the prescribed program carefully.

Jim's certificate indicated that he had spent 100 hours in this group program. Jim reported that he had also spent approximately 100 hours in the one-one tutoring program.

Jim's teacher was pleased that we were taking him into the program. She described him as seemingly intelligent, highly motivated, a regular attender and a hard worker. She noted, however, that he was making little progress in the program: he had extreme difficulty remembering sounds and the spellings of words. She had concluded that he must be learning disabled.

Influence of Prior Instruction on Jim's Concept of Reading and Writing

Jim's concept of reading reflected the focus of his recent program: you read by sounding out the words. When he read a grade one level passage from a Reader's Digest Skill Builder, he spelled and sounded letter by letter 85 of the 385 words, e.g. for the word 'went' he would first say the letters (w-e-n-t), then try to sound each letter individually and finally try to blend those letters into the word. This was his only strategy for words which he did not recognize immediately. Sometimes, he used the strategy to check words which he had read correctly. It was almost as if the word had 'popped out' too fast and he didn't trust that it was right.

We obtained no writing sample in the assessment sessions, for he insisted that he couldn't write because he couldn't spell yet. Comments in later sessions indicated that he believed that spelling was the key to writing competence; once you knew how to spell all the words, writing long pieces would follow effortlessly. His previous program had shaped this simplistic view of writing as transcription; in that program writing instruction in the first three levels consisted solely of spelling instruction and dictation exercises.

Influence of Prior Instruction on Jim's Beliefs About Literacy Instruction

When we began our work with Jim we did not realize the importance of taking into account a student's perceptions of how one learns to read and write. We assumed, for example, that, because he had been unsuccessful in his previous program, he would welcome a new approach.

The reading program which we developed for Jim emphasized the use of context strategies. The program had no component of direct instruction in phonics rules, although the application of phonics was discussed in the context of his attempts to read and write.

Much to our surprise, Jim, who seemed so eager to come to our program, responded negatively. The tutor's initial attempts to deemphasize sounding out strategies and to emphasize use of context strategies, met with resistance. When she suggested that he leave out a difficult word and go on, he would balk and say "But how is that going to help?". When she suggested that he think about "what would make sense there", he steadfastly persisted in his spell/sound strategy. And when she tried using read-along tapes with him, he responded angrily that his very first literacy program, the Manpower program, had used tapes and he certainly hadn't learned to read in that program. Attempts to get him to write met with outright refusal: what was the point of writing when you couldn't spell all the words.

After four lessons tension was high; we reevaluated. We had made a serious error in developing Jim's program: we had not taken into account his beliefs about literacy learning and his expectations for the tutoring program. We assumed that because Jim had been unsuccessful in his previous program he would welcome a new approach, each one which represented a radically different approach to literacy instruction. If we had explored his beliefs about literacy instruction, as I did two years later, we would have learned that he didn't believe that he needed a different approach; rather, he believed that we would have "a better way to get this (sounds) into his head". He believed that learning all the sound/symbol relationships was the key to learning to read and write, a belief shaped by his previous instruction.

In short, there was a mismatch between Jim's model of literacy instruction and our model. We had treated Jim as a young beginning reader with no instructional history. We had embarked on delivering a literacy program without considering his views of literacy learning, nor explaining our views. In medical terms, we had not kept the patient informed.

Other studies have reported that many literacy students accept unquestioningly that tutors knew best how to teach them to read (Charnley and Jones, 1979; Davis and O'Brien, 1985). Jim, however, taught us that we cannot assume that is true for all students, particularly student who have had recent literacy instruction. That instruction sets expectations for how one is supposed to be taught.

Working With His Perceptions and Beliefs

Jim brought many misconceptions about literacy and literacy learning to the tutoring situation. Dialogue between Jim and the tutor played a key role in dispelling those misconceptions, and in the development of more effective reading and writing strategies.

To develop a wider repertoire of word identification strategies, the tutor talked with Jim about strategies before, during, and following reading activities. Prior to the reading of a selection, the tutor reviewed with him the various strategies he could use in addition to sounding; during the reading, she often suggested a specific strategy or invited him to think of an alternative strategy; following the reading, together, the tutor and Jim evaluated the effectiveness of the new strategies.

Jim was also encouraged to monitor the effectiveness of the new strategies in his independent reading outside of the tutoring situation. He was encouraged to keep lists of words which gave him problems in his home reading. In the tutoring session Jim and the tutor then discussed what strategies he had tried, how effective they had been, and what other strategies he could have tried.

To overcome his strong belief that English is a phonetically regular language, and that, therefore, once you have learned the code, you can read anything, the tutor took opportunities to point out when phonetic sounding did not work on a word, that context must be used as well. It took much effort to dispel this theory, but gradually Jim began to recognize such words himself and would remark before the tutor could respond, "I know, that's one of those words that doesn't follow the rule".

The choice of reading material was also an important factor in changing his misconceptions about reading strategies. Selection of material which matched his background and interests maximized the possibility for successful use of the context (meaning) to decode unknown words, thus demonstrating to him the value of the strategy.

The choice of reading material also made possible successful independent reading experiences. Jim entered the program believing that he should not, and could not, read independently; he needed the support of a tutor or friend to correct his errors and supply unknown words. He thus avoided print in his environment, shutting out daily opportunities to learn how to read. After six sessions Jim felt confident enough to try reading some material at home; soon he was an avid home reader, completing two forty page high interest/low vocabulary books per week. As well, he began to attempt to read the print in his environment, newspaper headlines and captions, advertising flyers.

The successful experiences with new reading materials and strategies did more than change his concept of reading and his perception of himself as a reader, they gave him confidence in our approach to teaching literacy. The success in reading opened the door to work in writing.

In the beginning of the tutoring program Jim clung to his belief that the key to writing was spelling, and resisted writing. It was only after he achieved some success with reading that he was willing to try to write. Again, dialogue with the tutor was essential. The tutor repeatedly drew parallels between the reading approach, which he now believed worked, and the approach which we wished to use for writing, one which, like the reading approach, emphasized his role in the process, the role of much practice with real writing.

Ultimately, it was the growing evidence of increased skill with reading and writing which turned Jim into a believer in our approach to literacy instruction. Initially, the tutor helped Jim to see his gains. She pointed out improvements: increased fluency in reading, a growing repertoire of high frequency words spelled correctly. Quickly, however, Jim developed his own personal benchmarks: total number of pages read independently in a week, length of time he was able to sustain reading, first time he got lost in a book until two in the morning.

These benchmarks of progress are important to literacy students, as has been noted in previous studies (Mezirow et al., 1975; O'Brien, 1981). Student-centred, holistic approaches to literacy instruction do not have the benchmarks which students typically equate with school learning: worksheets completed successfully, workbook levels and readers completed, unit tests passed. Within such approaches, the tutor plays an important role in identifying for the student new ways of measuring progress, ways which focus on self-evaluation by the student rather than external evaluation by a teacher. Techniques such as taping of earlier and later readings for comparison of fluency and strategies, comparison of difficulty levels of earlier and later reading materials, and the keeping of all writing dated in a file folder help the student to evaluate progress. Students will gradually develop their own benchmarks, benchmarks which have the most personal meaning for them.

Influence of Literacy Experiences Outside of the Instructional Setting

A forced interruption in the tutoring program afforded the opportunity to observe the influence of literacy experiences outside of the instructional setting. In 1985-86, Jim did not participate in a literacy program. During the winter he worked on an oil rig. Life on a rig can be boring, and so, Jim turned to reading "anything (he could) get a hold of". He read signs, newspaper headlines, picture captions and advertisements, and participated in the group recreational pastime of reading the personal columns. As well, he discovered he could read, with little assistance, the letters he received.

Jim also wrote letters. He established a productive pattern with a friend: Jim drafted the letter, the friend edited the spelling, Jim recopied the letter. Through this modelling, he learned the spelling of many frequently used words.

In summer, Jim returned to work at the shipyard. He was assigned to the receiving department, which meant that he had to pick up items from local companies. The job required that he keep a work log.

Jim developed a strategy for filling in the names of companies on the work log: he copied them from the signs on the fronts of buildings. But as he put it, he gradually realized that after several visits, he no longer needed to use this crutch, he could spell the words without checking.

In the fall of 1986, Jim returned to the Learning Centre. It was clear to both Jim and I that ,his reading skill had improved, not diminished as one might predict. He could read material more difficult than the material he was reading when he left the program; his reading, although still halting was more fluent; and he had abstracted new knowledge about the code, e.g. common prefixes and suffixes. As well, he could now spell many commonly used words as well as words which he had encountered in his print environment in both work situations.

Jim had gained more from these independent encounters with literacy than self-confidence and increased skill. His beliefs about how one learns to read and write had changed, particularly his beliefs about his role, the student's role, in the learning process. When Jim came to the program he believed that teachers taught you how to read, that somehow, they put that skill into your head, a metaphor he used frequently. His successful experiences with reading and writing on his own demonstrated to him the role that he could play in his learning. He began to perceive of himself as a learner, not someone who is taught. He began to change his view of teacher, from imparter of knowledge and skill, to learning partner.

I do not wish to leave the impression that practice alone is sufficient for literacy learning. I am, however, arguing, like Clay (1979), that a student's independent literacy activities can make a significant contribution to the development of literacy skill, and that a literacy student's progress will be greatly aided if he/she can be convinced of the value of that contribution.

Need for Constant Monitoring of Student Perceptions

Perceptions and beliefs should be a major factor in the development of any literacy program, as demonstrated above; they also should be monitored throughout the program. Our last year of work with Jim highlighted the importance of monitoring perceptions throughout a program.

During the winter of 1986-87 a tutor worked with Jim for one 90 minute session per week. At Jim's request, writing was the major focus of the sessions. The tutor used a process approach to writing instruction. For the first six sessions, they followed the same pattern with each piece of writing. At the first session, the tutor and Jim discussed a possible writing topic, with the tutor asking questions to help Jim to elaborate and clarify his thoughts. Jim then wrote a draft at home. At the next session, the tutor entered on the computer Jim's text, unedited and double spaced. Jim then revised this computer print-out with the assistance of the tutor. The tutor raised questions about content, and used the piece as a starting point for mini lessons on mechanics such as punctuation.

Jim learned quickly; he was soon able to make minor revisions for content clarity, and to provide basic punctuation, periods and question marks. As well, he no longer required a computer copy; he could revise from his own text. One day the tutor suggested that Jim do a revision at home, before coming to the session. Jim's response was quick and negative: he couldn't revise something on his own; he needed a teacher beside him. In fact, he was now making most of the essential basic revisions spontaneously, yet he believed that the teacher was somehow doing it.

Smith (1981) notes: "Teachers may not teach what they think they are teaching." Instructors, program materials and instructional activities continually give messages to students about what reading and writing is, how one learns to read and write, and about the student's capabilities. Clearly, in this instance, the tutor's physical presence gave the student the message that he could not do it on his own.

One-one tutoring can do much to bolster the confidence of the scared learner, and give them the confidence to enter group programs. They can, however, also lead to tutor dependency, a problem identified by Jones and Charnley (1978). The tutor who is sensitive to the potential for dependency can avoid the problem by providing opportunities for independent work in the tutoring situation. In this case, the tutor disappeared while Jim worked on a first revision of a piece; soon he had the confidence to revise independently at home.

CONCLUSION

Jim came a long way in 46 hours of instruction and many more hours of practice on his own. He did not reach the grade eight level considered necessary to function in our society. He could read material at a grade four level and could write simple one page pieces about personal experiences, with most high frequency words spelled correctly, reasonable attempts at unfamiliar words, and accurate basic punctuation.

He had, however, made gains which I consider more important, for they will contribute to continued literacy learning. Jim now sees himself as a reader, staying up until two in the morning to finish an interesting book. His last sessions suggested that he is also beginning to see himself as a writer. He still thinks he should be able to make sense of the code through rules, but this is more wistful thinking than a fastly held belief. Most importantly, he sees himself as a learner, not someone who is taught.

Jim was not the only one to gain from this experience. We had learned a major lesson: programs, teachers and personal experiences all shape perceptions of reading writing and literacy learning; instruction must take into account those perceptions.

Postscript

Jim has continued his literacy learning. He's determined, as he puts it, to keep going as long as is necessary. He enrolled in a group adult literacy class this past year, and is making good progress. As part of a special literacy day, he was asked to speak to his fellow students and instructors about his struggle to learn to read and write. His self-selected main message was, in his words: you can't learn to read and write if the only time you read and write is when you come to literacy class. He's come a long way from his long search for the right teacher to put 'it' into his head.

REFERENCES

Charnley, A. H. & Jones, H. A. (1979). *The Concept of Success in Adult Literacy.* Cambridge: Huntington Publishers Ltd.

Clay, Marie (1979). *Reading: the Patterning of Complex Behaviour.* Exeter, New Hampshire: Heinemann Educational Books.

Cook, Wanda Dauksza (1977). *Adult Literacy Education in the United States.* Newark: International Reading Association.

Davis, Nanciellen & O'Brien, Margaret (1985). "Literacy programs and their participants in the Halifax-Metro area." Final report prepared for the Social Sciences and Humanities Research Council of Canada. Halfax, Scotia: Mount Saint Vincent University.

Johnston, Peter H. (1985). "Understanding reading disability: a case study approach." *Harvard Educational Review,* 55, 153-177.

Jones, H. A. & Charnley, A. H. (1978). *Adult literacy: a Study of Its Impact.* Gloucestershire, England: F. Bailey & Son.

Mezirow, J., Darkenwald, G. & Knox, A. (1975). *Last Gamble on Education: Dynamics of Adult Basic Education.* Washington, D.C.: Adult Education Association of the U.S.A.

Newman, Anabel (1980) *Adult Basic Education: Reading.* Boston: Allyn and Bacon.

O'Brien, Margaret (1981). "Four Adults Learning to Read." Unpublished doctoral dissertation. Edmonton: University of Alberta.

O'Brien, Margaret (1985). The methodology of adult literacy instruction in Canada: some concerns. *Reading-Canada-Lecture.* 3, 21-28.

Smith, Frank (1981). "Demonstrations, Engagement and Sensitivity: the choice between people and programs." *Language Arts,* 58, 634-642.

Taylor, Barbara, Harris, Larry & Pearson, P. David (1988). *Reading Difficulties: Instruction and Assessment,* New York: Random House.

PART VI
TRAINING AND
PROFESSIONAL DEVELOPMENT

Training and professional development is a core activity in any educational program. Through these activities we reflect on the integration of the content we are teaching and the values being expressed. It is this reflection that helps us make sense out of the teaching/learning process — all within the framework of what constitutes being professional and being competent in one's role. In the same context, many people reinforce their own role as a learner, perceiving themselves as students. Hence, the relationship of teacher and learner becomes interchangeable. The purpose of this section is to examine the many issues related to improving one's role in the adult literacy and basic education field. Classroom concerns such as teaching styles and participation of volunteers are addressed. As well, the impact of research on training functions, the importance of understanding the nature of learning and the new roles facing colleges and universities are raised.

*Each teacher has a specific teaching style. As **Conti** points out they can be divided into two major approaches: learner centred and teacher centred. He argues that these are very different and cites research evidence to support the notion that teaching style does make a difference in how well students learn. In addition, he discusses the transactional encounter between learner and teacher and how motivational factors influence the effectiveness of various teaching styles. **Conti** concludes that literacy instructors can use teaching styles information to plan and conduct effective learning activities.*

*The role of volunteers is not to be underestimated since most practitioners and professionals also have experiences as volunteers. **Moore** and **Westell** outline some of the strengths and limitations of using volunteers and examine new ways of enhancing their participation in the literacy movement. Much of the volunteers' activity in literacy takes place in community based settings where they often act as community facilitators.*

***Burton** emphasizes the role of the universities and colleges, not only in supporting research, but also, the effect of technological change and the influence of this on training. In the chapter, she mentions that the educational void is being filled by other than traditionally publicly-supported institutions such as colleges and universities. She stresses that institutions need to take on a new role in order to be current within society and to meet the influencing challenges of technology.*

*The place of research is essential to training and professional development, since its main purpose is to create and understand knowledge. **Draper** emphasizes that research is a way of learning in itself as well as a* *way of solving problems. In the chapter, he dispels a number of myths about research, illustrating that it is an activity in which each person is involved, whether intentionally or not. Research including those done through theses, has a place within pre- and post-service training.*

Barer-Stein calls our attention to the importance of understanding the Universal Learning Process that emerged from her own recent research. Using the phases of the Process as a framework, she suggests ways of coordinating teacher interventions with the behaviours of the learner as s/ he progresses. For both teacher and student to have a grasp of this process, and even the fact that learning is a process rather than an act, provides choice points for decision and action. Some classic questions such as those concerning adult motivation and program planning are re-examined against this learning framework.

Of the three chapters which especially focus on research within this section, special attention is drawn to the importance of seeking and practicing alternative approaches, such as experiential and learner-centred research. Theoretical background for this is provided by Draper and Barer-Stein and an application of this is presented by Horsman, who attempts to document the ways in which learners express feelings about learning. Her chapter also outlines some barriers that people face in participating in literacy and other forms of educational programs. She makes the point that social context is especially relevant to literacy and influences one's personal meaning of it.

CHAPTER 1:

Teaching Styles and the Adult Basic Educator

Gary J. Conti

Unlike classrooms for children or formal credit courses in a university, the format for adult basic education (ABE) classes varies greatly. Some classes meet on a regular schedule and focus on a specific topic: others are open-entry, open-exit learning centres. They meet at all hours of the day. Most programs have classes for non-native speaking students, basic literacy skills, and advanced high school equivalency skills. With such diversity, the roles of ABE teachers are often different. In such complexity, the question arises as to whether the type of teacher in the classroom actually makes a difference.

Each teacher has a specific teaching style. This style is composed of the teaching behaviours that are consistent over time and that do not change regardless of the content being taught. While teachers may differ in their degree of acceptance of various styles, teaching style can be divided into two major approaches. In the learner-centred approach, teachers emphasize activities such as encouraging students to take responsibility for their own learning, personalizing instruction, relating new learning to prior experiences, assessing student needs, involving the student in the learning process, and fostering flexibility In the classroom to stimulate the student's personal development. In the teacher-centred approach, teachers function as managers of the classroom conditions which they have determined as necessary to bring about the desired behavioural change in the student. Both approaches are practiced in current ABE programs, and both approaches to teaching have firm roots in different philosophical schools of educational thought.

These two styles of teaching are drastically different. Are they equally effective for all learners in ABE, or does teaching style make a difference in student achievement? Since recent research in adult education has began to focus on what happens with the learners In the teaching-learning transaction, it is possible to begin to answer these questions. Initial research evidence seems to indicate that teaching style does make a difference in how well students learn.

RECENT RESEARCH FINDINGS

Two studies have investigated the relationship of teaching style to student learning in ABE. In southern Texas, the teaching style of 29 part-time teachers was assessed with the Principles of Adult Learning Scale, and the achievement of their 837 students was analyzed.[1] Analysis of covariance indicated that the teacher's style had a significant influence on the amount of student academic gain. However, the gain differed with the different types of classes in the program. In the classes preparing students to take the General Educational Development (GED) test, the teacher-centred approach was most effective. In the English as a Second Language (ESL) and the basic level classes, the learner-centred approach facilitated the most learning.

These differences were attributed to the difference in the goals of the learners. In GED classes, learners are externally motivated to pass the GED test. The lack of a high school diploma poses a barrier in their lives, and the GED class offers an opportunity to alleviate this burden. Since the teacher should be familiar with the GED exam and since the testing conditions are totally beyond the students' control, a teacher-centred approach is the most effective for them in obtaining their goal.

On the other hand, the motivation for students in the basic level and in ESL classes is very different. Here the students have the intrinsic desire to improve skills related to reading, mathematics, and English proficiency. These skills are not merely needed for certification but rather are necessary to overcome deficiencies which affect the students everyday in numerous aspects of life. Moreover, they are related to the learner's self-concept. The risk taking inherent in this process of personal exploration and development requires a supportive environment with acceptance by the teacher. A. learner-centred approach, which establishes a strong personal bond between the teacher and the learner, provides a means for the students to resolve interpersonal concerns while developing academic skills.

In a second study, it was found that teaching style affects other aspects of student learning in addition to academic achievement. The relationship of teaching style to the moral development of inmates enrolled in ABE classes in the Texas prison system was examined.[2] Statistically significant findings indicated that the learner-centred approach was generally the most effective for stimulating higher levels of moral development among the students. One element that was extremely influential in fostering this growth was allowing students to collaboratively participate in decisions about the learning process once the broad parameters for the curriculum had been determined.

Two similar studies which were conducted with students in college-credit allied health courses further support these teaching-style findings. The relationship of teaching style to academic achievement was explored for allied health professionals taking credit classes in a nontraditional format such as evening courses, week-end courses, or off-campus courses.[3] Once again teaching style was found to be significantly related to student achievement. Students of teachers practicing a learner-centred approach learned above the average for the total group. However, students in the classes of instructors firmly implementing a teacher-centred approach also achieved above the average. Student achievement was significantly lower for students where instructors moderately employed teacher-centred techniques.

A second study expanded this allied health study. The follow-up study compared these nontraditional continuing education professionals to the students in the traditional, on-campus, and daytime program.[4] Similar results were found. Among the significant differences, the greatest learning gain was by students of teachers using the learner-centred approach; the high teacher-centred approach resulted in slightly above average gains while the moderate teacher-centred approach produced the least student achievement. This study also explored the interaction of teaching style to the learner's status as either a nontraditional or traditional student. The nontraditional group, which included more adults and those who were not going to school to satisfy basic certification requirements, achieved more than the traditional group under all variations of teaching style except for the moderately teacher-centred approach.

IMPLICATIONS

Studies such as these indicate that teaching style has a significant effect on student actions. This is not a surprising finding if education is viewed as a transactional encounter

> in which learners and teachers are engaged in a continual process of negotiations of priorities, methods, and evaluative criteria. Viewing teaching-learning encounters as transactional means that the sole responsibility for determining curricula or for selecting appropriate methods does not rest either with the educator or with the participants.[5]

Both the teacher and the learner enter the transaction with an established set of values, experiences, and ideas. As they interact, each is affected by the other. As an external source to the student's existing situation, the teacher can present to the learner new and diverse alternatives for ways of thinking, of interpreting their experiences, and of critically examining their values. While some of these alternatives might be exhilarating and others may produce anxiety,[6] the exact nature of this exchange is influenced by elements that both the teacher and student bring to the encounter.

Teachers enter this encounter with distinctive teaching styles. Yet, where do these styles come from? Teachers do not simply decide to have a certain kind of style. Instead, their styles are actual behaviours which operationalize their beliefs and values concerning teaching and learning. These actions in turn can be related to various philosophical schools of educational thought. It has been suggested that a knowledge of one's educational philosophy is a crucial criterion for distinguishing between professionals and practitioners in teaching.[7] "It has been further posited that in adopting a philosophy an educator may (1) adopt a currently elaborated philosophy and consistently practice it, (2) adopt an eclectic approach from different theories, or (3) select one specific theory as a framework upon which to construct a personal educational philosophy.[8] Regardless of the approach used, the ABE teacher should realize that each philosophy is built upon a set of assumptions.

"These assumptions are interrelated, and some assumptions from one philosophy are not compatible with those of another philosophy. In addition, the teaching-style research indicates that the actions generated from various combinations of these assumptions produce different results with learners. In order to analyze critically their own actions in the classroom and to relate this behaviour to the teaching-style findings, teachers need to be aware of these assumptions. Furthermore since an educational philosophy is a subset of one's overall life philosophy, teachers should ask themselves which of these assumptions most comfortably fits their approach to life, teaching, and learning. Inconsistencies among the basic assumptions which a teacher favors can indicate areas for further rigorous analysis and potential areas for change.

Philosophy is concerned with what beliefs people hold important and what they value. An educational philosophy should address such questions as (1) what are the teacher's goals in the classroom, (2) what does the teacher want to happen in the learning process, (3) how does the teacher view the learner, (4) how does the teacher define learning, and (5) how does the teacher know that learning is occurring. Answers to questions such as these will uncover the fundamental beliefs and values undergirding a teacher's educational philosophy.

Although several possible philosophies exist, much current educational practice can be categorized as either teacher-centred or learner-centred. The teacher-centred approach is currently the dominant approach throughout all levels of education in North America and is closely related to the ideas of B. F. Skinner. This approach to learning assumes that learners are passive and become active by reacting to stimuli in the environment. Elements that exist in this environment are viewed as reality. Motivation arises from basic organic drives and emotions or from a tendency to respond in accordance with prior conditioning. Since humans are controlled by their environment, schools have the responsibility of determining and reinforcing the fundamental values necessary for the survival of the individual and the society.[9]

"In this teacher-centred approach,

> the role of the teacher is to design an environment which elicits desired behaviour toward meeting these goals and to extinguish behaviour which is not desirable. The teacher, then, is a contingency manager, an environmental controller, or behavioural engineer who plans in detail the conditions necessary to bring about desired behaviour.[10]

A teacher-centred approach is implemented in the classroom in several ways. Learning is defined as a change in behaviour. Therefore, acceptable forms of the desired behaviour are defined in overt and measurable terms in behavioural objectives. Outcomes are often described as competencies which the student must display after completing the educational activity. The attainment of the competencies is determined by evaluating the learner with either a criterion-referenced or a norm-referenced test. Through such a method, both the teacher and learner are accountable for the classroom activities.

Although a teacher-centred approach is widely practiced in adult education, the tenets of a learner-centred approach are strongly supported in the field's literature. This approach is closely associated with the writings of Abraham Maslow and Carl Rogers. A learner-centred approach assumes that people are naturally good and that the potential for individual growth is unlimited. Reality is relative to the interpretations that individuals give to their surroundings as they interact with them. Consequently, behaviour is the result of personal perceptions. Experiences, which are viewed as events in which a person acts purposefully with the anticipation of probable consequences, play an important role in learning. Motivation results from people's attempts to achieve and maintain order in their lives. In this process, they are proactive and are capable of taking responsibility for their actions.[11]

In the classroom, the whole focus of learner-centred education is upon the individual learner rather than a body of information.[12] Here the teacher strives to present subject matter in a manner conducive to student's needs and to help students develop a critical awareness of their feelings and values. The central element in a learner-centred approach is trust; while the teacher is always available to help, the teacher trusts students to take responsibility for their own learning. Learning episodes are often group activities that stress the acquisition of problem-solving skills, that focus on the enhancement of the self-concept, or that foster the development of interpersonal skills. Learning is a highly personal act. It is best measured by self-evaluation and constructive feedback from the teacher and co-learners.

MOTIVATIONAL INFLUENCES

Learners are the teacher's partners in the teaching-learning transaction. The current findings from the teaching-style research indicate that factors which the learners bring to the exchange influence the effectiveness of various teaching styles. Thus, a major learner variable appears to be motivation. Two types of motivation exist. Intrinsic motivation stems from the learner and is associated with the inherent value of an activity. Extrinsic motivation is stimulated by a force external to the learner and consequently may be associated with the value of the outcome of an activity. Learners come to the ABE classrooms with different motivations. While learners are responsible for their own motivation and while teachers cannot directly motivate learners, the instructor can create a stimulating environment and thereby influence learners.[13] However, each teacher must ask, "Is the student motivated to learn with me?"

Although none of the teaching-style research has explicitly measured motivation, motivational factors which commonly exist in many educational situations have been used to explain teaching-style findings. In situations with extrinsically motivated learners who were concerned with satisfying external criteria, the teacher-centred approach to instruction was most effective. This was found among GED students preparing for the high school equivalency examination and traditional college students seeking a degree to satisfy entry requirements into the allied health field. In contrast to these task-oriented situations, the learner-centred approach was most effective in conditions involving intrinsically motivated learners and learning in the affective domain. Basic education and ESL students and those involved in continuing professional education are participating in the process of lifelong learning. A discussion of issues relating to such things as moral judgement require a trusting environment before a learner can critically explore, reflect upon, and share experiences and ideas. Thus, as ABE teachers examine their personal philosophy, they should also assess the motivational factors influencing their students. The combination of teacher and student factors can then be compared to the available research findings.

STYLE AND EVALUATION

Teaching style is also related to evaluation methods because teachers have different views of what constitutes learning and different methods for determining if and when learning took place. Evaluation may be categorized as either summative or formative. Summative evaluations are conducted at the end of an activity and serve as a summary of what occurred during the learning process. While summative evaluation results may be used to diagnose the learning needs for the next activity, they are not useful for modifying events related to the current activity. Formative evaluations, on the other hand, are conducted while the learning activity is in process. Information from the evaluation is used to reformulate the ongoing activity in order to achieve the greatest possible success. Each type of evaluation has its own strengths and is useful when employed in an appropriate situation.

Each type of evaluation is utilized to a different degree with the various teaching styles. The teacher-centred approach has a need for measuring the success of the student in learning the curricular materials presented during the planned activities of the teacher. The learner-centred approach depends on numerous formative evaluations to monitor a student's continuous progress and uses this evaluation information to modify the learning situation to fit the student's needs.

ABE teachers are under strong pressures to use summative evaluations. The requirements of funding agencies and local administrators to document student progress encourage the use of summative evaluations. The dominance of summative evaluation techniques at all levels of education in North America further fosters its use. Nevertheless, ABE teachers should realize that an alternate type of evaluation exists. The actual evaluation techniques that they use should be dependent upon their view of learning as implemented through their teaching style and indicated by the needs of their students.

CONCLUSION

Much recent research and interest in education has focused on teaching style. Several studies in adult education indicate that teaching style does influence student outcomes. Although caution must be exercised in interpreting the results of these studies because they isolate only one of the many variables in the complicated human interaction that is occurring in the classroom, the results suggest that teachers do make a difference. This is true in the academic area as well as in areas of personal development. The nature of these differences supports the view of education as a transactional encounter between the teacher and the learner. As teachers look at their own teaching style and the philosophical assumptions upon which it is based, they must also examine that other crucial element in the exchange — the learner. Equipped with a knowledge of their own classroom tendencies and of how these influence their interpretation of student's motivational needs, ABE teachers can use the information on teaching style to plan and conduct effective learning activities which both utilize their strengths and facilitate adult learning.

NOTES

1. Gary J. Conti, "The Relationship Between Teaching Style and Adult Student Learning." *Adult Education Quarterly*, 35, no. 4. 1985, 220-228.
2. Linda J. Wiley (1986), *The Effect of Teaching Style on the Development of Moral Judgement in Prison Inmates*. Unpublished doctoral dissertation, Texas A&M University, College Station, TX.
3. Gary J. Conti and Ruth B. Welborn, "Teaching-Learning Styles and the Adult Learner" *Lifelong Learning*, 9, no. 8, 1986, 20-24.
4. Gary J. Conti and Ruth B. Welborn. "The Influence of Teaching Style and Learning Style on Both Traditional and Nontraditional Learners." *Proceedings of the 27th Annual Adult Education Research Conference*, in press.
5. Stephen D. Brookfield (1986), *Understanding and Facilitating Adult Learning*, San Francisco, Jossey-Bass Publishers, 1986, pp. 21-22.
6. Ibid., pp. 21-23.
7. John L. Elias and Sharan Merriam (1980), *Philosophical Foundations of Adult Education*, New York, Robert E. Krieger Publishing Company, p. 9.
8. Ibid., p. 206.
9. Burrhus F. Skinner (1971), *Beyond Freedom and Dignity*, New York, Alfred A. Knopf.
10. John L. Elias and Sharan Merriam, op cit., pp. 87-88.
11. Ibid., pp. 115-121.
12. Ibid., p. 122.
13. Raymond J. Wlodkowski (1985), *Enhancing Adult Motivation to Learn*. San Francisco, Jossey-Bass Publishers, pp. 12-13.

REFERENCES

Brookfield, Stephen D. (1986), *Understanding and Facilitating Adult Learning*, San Francisco, Jossey-Bass Publishers.

Conti , Gary J. (1985),"The Relationship Between Teaching Style and Adult Student Learning," *Adult Education Quarterly, 35, no. 4. 220-228.*

Conti, Gary J. and Welborn, Ruth B. (1986), *"Teaching-Learning Styles and the Adult Learner," Lifelong Learning, 9*, no. 8, 20-24.

Conti, Gary J. and Welborn, Ruth B. "The Influence of Teaching Style and Learning Style on Both Traditional and Nontraditional Learners," *Proceedings of the 27th Annual Adult Education Research Conference*, in press.

Elias, John L. and Merriam, Sharan (1980). *Philosophical Foundations of Adult Education*, New York, Robert E. Krieger Publishing Company.

Skinner, Burrhus F. (1971), *Beyond Freedom and Dignity, New York, Alfred A. Knopf.*

Wiley, Linda J. (1986), *The Effect of Teaching Style on the Development of Moral Judgement in Prison Inmates,* Unpublished doctoral dissertation. Texas A&M University, College Station, TX.

Wlodkowski, Raymond J. (1985), *Enhancing Adult Motivation to Learn. San Francisco, Jossey-Bass Publishers.*

CHAPTER 2:

Voluntarism in Community Based Literacy

Anne Moore
Tracy Westell

Volunteers have been central to the literacy movement in most community literacy programs in Canada, and yet the issues surrounding their involvement remain largely unexplored and unchallenged. We, as literacy workers, rarely get the chance to reflect on issues of concern to us. This paper provided us with a wonderful opportunity to reflect on and challenge some of our assumptions about how we use volunteers in community based literacy. It is not meant to be the last word on voluntarism but the first word that will hopefully generate more discussion amongst literacy practitioners.

This article will attempt to outline some of the strengths and limitations of the use of volunteers, as well as to examine new ways of enhancing the participation of volunteers in the literacy movement.

HOW WE PRESENTLY USE VOLUNTEERS

There are two ways in which literacy programs presently use volunteers: as tutors and as board or committee members. All tutors in community based literacy programs go through a tutor training. Although the design of the training is different for each program, generally programs try to familiarize new volunteers with the structure and philosophy of the program, the community, their role as a literacy tutor, teaching methodology, adult basic literacy materials, and the polities of education. Tutor workshops are usually 12 to 20 hours in length, and spread over a series of two to eight sessions.

The goals of the tutor training are to ensure that the tutor understands the community based and learner based philosophies. It tries to give volunteers a sense of membership in the program, and helps them to develop a feeling that they can be equal partners with staff and learners in the running of the program (hopefully that feeling becomes a reality for tutors). The expressed goal of the tutors is usually to understand the teaching methodology and feel more self confident about their skills.

Most programs try to interview each new volunteer before or after the tutor training depending on the availability of staff time. Not everyone makes a good tutor, but some programs are more selective than others, depending on their waiting lists and on their definition of what makes a good tutor. The interview covers things which pertain immediately to the role of the tutor; the motivation of the volunteers, their work and educational background, as well as the practical aspects of time, availability and commitment. This interview process enables the staff to get a personal sense of each new tutor and whether or not they will be able to fit into the program. It is also a time to allay the fears or apprehensions of the volunteers. Depending on the results of the interview the tutors are invited to partake in all aspects of the program, and are given the choice of working one-to-one, or in small groups.

STRENGTHS OF OUR PRESENT USE OF VOLUNTEERS

Over the last five to ten years literacy programs across Canada have maintained satisfactory literacy programming with a great deal of dependence on the volunteer tutor. From this experience we have found that volunteers offer some real benefits.

For a community based program the most obvious advantage of using volunteers is having a constant flow of people into the program who represent the community and its voice. This model ensures that the community plays an active role in creating and directing a program that can more readily come to know and respond to the needs of the community, whether this be done as learners, tutors or board members. Also when tutors and learners come from the same area it ensures at least a minimum sharing of common interests and understanding in commutilty issues. Where the literacy organization is well integrated in the community, it transforms its role from social service to a community development model of organization. Volunteers help this to become a reality.

In a time when literacy programs were receiving little or no funding, volunteers were the obvious means of serving the literacy needs of the community. Even with increased funding it is still true that without volunteers many literacy programs could not continue to operate, or to be as responsive to the community's needs.

The learning needs of educationally disadvantaged adults are unique and individual and may require individualized learning strategies. Adult learners are frequently coming to literacy after years of being out of the main stream school system. It is important that we can offer a non-formal, relaxed situation in which a learner may gain confidence. The use of volunteers, who are not usually formally trained as teachers, and who feel at ease with the learner-based methodology, suit these needs of adult learners. Volunteers enable programs to offer one-to-one tutoring offering a dynamic learning partnership, which can be especially suited to the individual's needs.

Volunteers enable a program to be flexible in the timing and location of tutoring. Learner and tutor pairs are able to decide between themselves when and where they choose to meet, depending on their individual schedules and needs. The one-to-one tutoring situation, which only volunteers can provide on a large scale, is a good solution for those who may be experiencing physical and situational barriers to participation caused by poverty and/or lack of support services. Volunteers increase the accessibility of literacy education.

Learners, on first entering a program, often feel isolated by their lack of education and by a lack of opportunity to express themselves in a trusting environment. This feeling of isolation often makes them feel intimidated by a group learning situation. The one-to-one tutoring experience can be a good transition from total isolation to a collective learning experience.

LIMITATIONS

Without negating the strengths of using volunteer tutors, there are many ways in which the use of volunteers hinders rather than helps adult learners and creates problems for literacy program staff.

A common perception of volunteer based literacy programs is that they are charitable organizations doing charitable work. In this context, literacy work retains the image of a superfluous service and remains unrecognized and frequently underfunded. This perception perpetuates the idea that the illiterate adult has fallen through a crack in the education system and requires saving by the work of charitable do-gooders. Lost in this perception is our conviction that education is a right for everyone in society and that there are political and systemic reasons for illiteracy. This conviction is central to the community based literacy movement.

Our use of volunteers often limits the vision that funders and the general public have of community literacy. Their limited vision brings into question our credibility as an educational organization and our potential to acquire long range stable funding. Only organizations that use paid staff (or 'teaching professionals') are deemed credible and deserving of core funding and support. Almost by definition volunteers are limited by the time, commitment and skills that they can offer to tutoring. Most of the complaints that learners have about tutors have to do with not enough time, and the tutor not being able to meet the needs of the learner due to the tutor's lack of skills, training or inspiration.

Volunteers require a lot of training and supervision by staff, which is both time consuming and constantly undermined by the ongoing demands of running an organization. There can be a high turn over rate among tutors which further increases the work of the staff. Not being able to supervise and provide adequate support to the learning partnerships diminishes the quality of the learning experience, and can alienate the learner from the program. The idea of education as an empowering process cannot be ensured with learning partnerships meeting outside of the program, and only occasionally making contact with the staff.

Although many adult learners initially prefer one-to-one learning situations, they often discover that the experience does not lead them out of their isolation and may often foster feelings of dependency. It must be recognized that the education of adult learners may be limited by simply providing one-to-one tutoring: learners can and do flourish in small group learning situations where they are able to benefit from interaction with other learners. Adults can often learn more about getting support and confidence in attaining their goals from other learners or from staff who are aware of earlier support services. While volunteers have conventionally been associated with offering one-to-one tutoring, it is time for literacy programs to find new ways of training and using volunteers without perpetuating the isolation of the learner.

Many of the volunteers attracted to literacy programs are frequently university educated and middle class. The disparity between the experience of the tutor and the learner is often great. This disparity creates inequality in the learning partnership which may show itself in a lack of understanding and empathy or, at its worst patronizing or condescending attitudes in the tutor. Also it is not uncommon to find the learner showing deference and exaggerated gratefulness towards the tutor because they are aware that the tutor is not being paid for their time. These attitudes put a strain on and sometimes destroy the learning arrangement and erode learners' self-confidence and independence.

One of the problems that programs have in their use of volunteers, is the question of accountability: because volunteers are unpaid their relation to the program functions on the level of trust and not for example, on the level of contracts or job guidelines that must be followed. It is difficult to ask a volunteer to account for their progress on the job. Because of this dynamic, evaluation and assessment both at a program and an individual level is difficult to carry out. Programs encourage an ongoing evaluation by the learner and tutor of their work, but this type of ad hoc evaluation does not always satisfy the program or funders.

As the level of funding from different levels of government increases, so will the demands for more effectively training and evaluation techniques increase. Already the demands of government funders have forced programs to more closely scrutinize the progress of learning partnerships. Again this places time demands on staff, that could possibly be avoided by changing the emphasis from volunteers to paid workers.

RETHINKING VOLUNTARISM

Up until now we have talked about the strengths and limitations of using volunteers in literacy programs. At this point we would like to offer some ideas that might initiate futher discussion and action in addressing our concerns about the use of volunteers.

It is important that volunteers be retained in the literacy movement, but we must shift our emphasis from volunteer tutors to paid workers. This means that volunteers would be adjunct to the program, not the primary tutoring resource. We must have more paid staff, so that we can increase the number of learning hours that programs offer, and provide consistency in the quality and type of tutoring offered. It is important that we can continue to offer one-to-one tutoring by staff or volunteers for learners who are intimidated by a group situation.

If we move towards having staff become more involved in the process of tutoring, we can decrease the number of tutors needed and impose a more stringent selection process on volunteers. Programs organizers have been reticent about imposing strict criteria on the volunteer selection process mainly because of our dependence on them and because of their unpaid status. The consequences of a bad tutor can be so devastating on a learner that program organizers must see it as their job to be highly selective of those who volunteer. This would result in a more consistent and quality learning, and less staff time would be required to supervise and train tutors. The selection process might include using applications, references and in depth interviews for screening potential tutors. We might consider using a process similar to that of many agencies who place volunteers in developing countries.

Involvement in a community based literacy program is often as much a learning experience for the tutor as for the learner. To give some shape to the tutors learning experience, we must provide ongoing support and workshops for the tutor. Hopefully this will give them a forum for their concerns, a format for ongoing evaluation of their input, an affirmation of the importance of their contribution, as well as supporting the further development of their tutoring skills.

The role of the volunteer should not be limited to one-to-one tutoring. There are a number of ways of using volunteers which would minimize the potential isolation of the one-to-one experience: a) encouraging tutors to meet with their learner at the program centre; b) providing enough learning groups so that a learner could have their own tutor as well as belonging to a group (these groups could be formed around particular issues or needs); c) create a group of tutors and learners who would take the training together and continue on as a learning and support group who would meet regularly; d) ensure that volunteers have a sense of membership in the program so that they can communicate this to the learner and encourage them to participate more fully in the program.

Incorporating the use of learning groups more fully in literacy programming would not only deal with the problem of isolation but would also facilitate our own understanding of community development. Successful groups are empowering, especially for people who have been isolated in their community. One of the ideas that we tend to forget is that the community development process in literacy is not only empowering for learners but can also be empowering for volunteers.

Community literacy programs might consider developing along the lines of a learning centre. The learning centre model can address the needs of the educationally disadvantaged by providing programming which responds to a wide variety of adult learning needs (ie. courses/workshops on health issues, parenting, inter-cultural communications, computers etc.). This model also offers more room for innovation in utilizing volunteers on a short term basis as resource people (whether they be tutors, learners or other members of the community). In this way we could take advantage of the skills that they bring with them (ie. a nurse could help us develop health materials or give a workshop on health issues).

These are just a few ideas to consider, and there are many other ways in which we can more effectively include volunteers in literacy programs.

WHAT WE ARE ENVISIONING

Up until now our dependence on volunteers has been due to a shortage of staff and money and our narrow vision of what community literacy could be. The way in which volunteers are presently used in literacy programs has been developed more out of neccessity than out of a serious reflection of what is best for adult learners. At present most programs probably spend a greater amount of time educating tutors than they do learners. After several years in the community one cannot help but wonder if we have been trapped into a dependence on volunteers that is perpetuating the isolation of learners and ignoring their needs.

On the other hand volunteers offer a way of drawing the community into the program and vice versa. They offer new insights and fresh ideas and a flexible and informal learning environment for learners who have had negative experiences with the traditional school system. Clearly we do not want to eradicate the use of volunteers from the community based literacy context.

What we are envisioning is a program model that is not completely dependent on volunteers: where staff and volunteers could initiate small groups so that learners would have more choice of how and when they learn; where they could have the benefit of both small groups and one-to-one; where staff could devote more time to learners and less time supporting tutors; where there would be a more consistent method for referring learners to other educational organizations or community agencies; and where the environment would be more conducive to hearing and acting on feedback from learners.

CHAPTER 3:

Basic Job Retraining and Paid Educational Leave

Lynn Burton

* "The future of work will consist of learning a living".

Technology will not only affect the kinds of jobs available in the future economy, it will also affect the total number of jobs available and the skills requirements of all jobs. These other two effects have equally important implications.

Consider the impact on the level of employment. It is quite clear that technology creates new jobs and destroys others. Will the net impact of these changes sustain, increase, or reduce employment levels? At least some evidence suggests that more jobs will be destroyed than created by technological change. A recent study of robotics suggests that robots will eliminate 100,000 to 200,000 jobs by 1990 in the United States and create 32,000 to 64,000 jobs. The increased movement of production jobs, even in high-tech electronics, to overseas locations also threatens the level of domestic employment.

Technology will also have a widespread effect on the skill requirements of future jobs. It is commonly assumed that as more and more workers use computers and other sophisticated technical devices in their jobs, they will need computer programming and other sophisticated skills. Yet a variety of evidence suggests just the opposite: as machines become more sophisticated, with expanded memories, more computational ability, and sensory capabilities, the knowledge required to use the devices declines. (Levin and Rumberger, 1984).

New technologies for the "Smart Machines of Tomorrow" (Cornish, 1985:5) and technology to revitalize existing industry are shaking the foundations of North American society. Old jobs will disappear and new jobs will emerge. (Centron, 1983:15) Who will do the work? What work will they do? Who will provide? No matter how many jobs may be created in a strong economy the problem will remain unsolved if the jobs and skills of those who will do the work are not brought together. In order to respond to the emerging challenges the rudiments of basic reading, writing and arithmetic are required. The shaky foundation, caused by the functional illiteracy of one out of every five Canadians, threatens. How can we respond to new workplace challenges without a firm adult basic education base?

Crises can be the precursor of positive change. We are seeing a radical restructuring of work as current skills are devalued and new ones are created at an ever-increasing rate. At the same time, we are seeing tomorrow's workers graduating from education programs that no longer equip them with the skills

325

required for meaningful employment in a changed world. What are our alternatives and how do we implement them?

This section will attempt to determine some of the more significant societal directions impacting on basic skills development through a literature review; to draw out the major implications of the review; to position Canada within this changing skills requirement context; to examine contemporary patterns of public policy on basic skill development and post-secondary institutional response to changing skill requirements; and, throughout to project alternative options for the future.

THE CHANGING ENVIRONMENT IN CANADA

Who Will Do the Work?

Within the framework of the changing economic situation, labour force growth has been determined by changes in the labour force working age population, labour force participation rates, and levels of net immigration. On that basis, it is expected that in the 1980s and 1990s the rate of labour force change will rejoin the historical tendency in the two per cent range, after having gone through a period of substantial increase in the 1970s. Immigration no longer holds the ever-flowing potential for ready labour force entrants, partially because of global demands for highly skilled and qualified workers.

The rise and now the dramatic fall in the proportion of the population under twenty-two years of age has taken place with rapidity and impact on the educational institutions. Recently educated young people have been relied on in the past to bring up-to-date and specialized skills to the work force. An expected decline of this group by nearly twenty-five per cent over the next ten years means adult training and retraining takes on new importance.

The post Second World War baby 'boom generation', has impacted with great force on the educational systems. leaving in its wake empty classrooms.

> "Our aging population gives us an opportunity for productivity improvement. By 1995, more than 50% of the work force will be 25-44 years of age, the group most adaptable and most inclined to invest in retraining and continuing education. By the time most workers reach age 40, they have had eight jobs. (Ontario Ministry of Skills Development, 1986).

While the 1980s can be referred to as the era of the young adult, the 1990s will experience a middle age bulge and in about 2015, the post-war baby boom generation will reach the present retirement age of sixty-five.

As the youth share of the labour market decreases and fewer youth are available, there will probably be less competition for entry level jobs. Although fewer young people entering the labour force may bring the unemployment rate down, it will also reduce the number of young people ready to go on to further education because of the immediacy of a job offer. The pool of highly qualified and highly skilled youth is expected to decline in a strong economy.

A need for further education of the existing labour force becomes obvious. Fundamental improvements are required in training processes so that shortages can be alleviated by domestic means in the medium and longer term. In addition, those young people who enter the labour force will need to retrain, upgrade and update their skills throughout life. Special initiatives and short-term projects to meet the immediate employment and training needs of this group should be considered as modules within a continuum of lifelong learning and employment.

Population structure is seen as a major influence on adult education in the 80s (Apps, 1980:4). By 1990, projections for Canada imply that over 75 per cent of women, aged 24 to 54 will be in the labour force. There will be a need over the next decade increasingly to educate and integrate women into industries in which they have not traditionally been employed in large numbers. Relatively static demands for clerical and office workers and for workers in health, education, and public administration will mean decreased opportunities for women in those traditional female occupations. For example, jobs such as that of motel clerk are being automated for ease of guest registration and checkout. A break with the past will be necessary and women will need to be employed in a broader, more diverse set of occupations in the future. New and flexible work arrangements, such as benefit protected job sharing, may support the involvement of women in the workplace. In order to facilitate this integration, a process will be required that is partly related to training and education systems; partly to dissemination of information; partly to societal expectations and the elimination of systemic barriers; and, partly to revisions of obsolete or discriminatory hiring and pay-fixing practices, and also to the internal promotion procedures of employers. (Skills Development Leave Taskforce, 1983:15)

Recent trends toward early retirement may change increasing the work force participation of seniors. Extended longevity, slowing in functional aging, along with increased inflation and lessening real income may increase the desire for older people to remain in the work force. In conjunction with new human rights legislation and the removal of mandatory retirement, these factors may slow the withdrawal of older workers from the labour force and create an environment for flexible work arrangements. Additionally, the "greying" of the work force will deplete the stock of current highly qualified and skilled manpower and inhibit the mobility of the work force. The aging of faculty, guidance counselors, researchers, and teachers will impact on the educational delivery systems.

What Work Will They Do?

The impact of computers and robots on our economy, the world of work, and our personal lives will be phenomenal. New technologies create new business and adaptive technologies restructure and make productive existing workplaces. Many workers will be required to perform new duties which require different skills levels. There is considerable speculation on new hybrid balances between work. learning, and home life. (Best, 1984:61). Consider the potential work force impact of voice-activated word processors, networked desktop terminals, and fifth generation thinking computers. (Russel, 1986:174).

Manufacturing, although not disappearing, is losing ground to "clean, white-collar industries' that do things, move things and manage things. (Wright, 1983:21). Retraining the people displaced by workplace change is the major challenge in the coming decade. (Zemke, 1983:19) The growth in part-time jobs may indicate that new work, leisure and learning flexibility is being introduced merely as an unplanned function of workplace requirements rather than a deliberate public policy initiative.

"The traditional 3Rs – reading, writing, and 'rithmetic, must be enhanced with the 3Rs for modern times – reading, relating, and reasoning," (Smith, 1986). Learning to learn becomes the basis for existence in the rapidly changing world. "Highly trained technical illiterates" will need to broaden their technical skills to include management, communications, effective and generally more generic skills levels in response to change. (Surich, 1986). While job specific skills are necessary, these will change throughout life. Adaptability, flexibility, and the capacity to learn become critical.

Who Will Provide?

The greying of the work force; new work force participation for women and other groups; and, the proclivity of profound workplace and societal change challenge both educators and managers in business and industry. (Wright, 1983:21)

Conventional wisdom and historical myth have found colleges and universities perched atop geographical and philosophical hills. (Butler, 1983:6). Perhaps partially in response to the collegial aloofness, industry provides for its own educational needs. The Carnegie Foundation in *Corporate Classrooms: The Learning Business* refers to training for the workplace as the parallel system. They say that spending on training in the workplace ranges upward from a low of $40 billion a year. (Carnegie Foundation, 1985:6)

At the same time as this private sector training boom becomes reality, colleges are asking themselves if they can help to bridge the gap between school and work and even if they should. (Butler, 1983:6). As this debate about responding to both the part-time student and workplace training needs rages in the post-secondary institutions, potential declining enrollments and uncertain government funding threatens the survival of even more colleges and universities. (Dunn, 1983:30).

"The change environment promises a new and vital role for higher education. The relationship between higher education and industry is no longer sequential and it will become increasingly interactive and lifelong." (Hollander, 1983:18)

Where We Stand

The European Management Forum (EMF), an independent non-profit foundation based in Geneva stated the following in its 1986 report on competitiveness for the twenty-two OECD countries. The perceived strength of Canada's natural and human resources placed Canada in sixth ranked position, well behind Japan, the United States, and Switzerland, and clustered with Germany and Denmark.

One of the ten critical factors in the EMF assessment of competitive position is human resources. "A highly educated and well-motivated work force is an essential ingredient in national competitiveness." (D'Cruz & Fleck, 1986:82). Canada scored relatively well on criteria related to the structure and dynamics of its population – growth rates. age distribution, and female participation in the labour force. The Canadian educational system also received good marks from the EMF. Canada is among the world leaders in per capita public expenditures on public education and has a good record in terms of the population that accesses higher education. It is estimated that Canada spends in excess of $30 billion annually on the formal educational systems. This amount dwarfs substantially that $20 billion that goes into both defense and foreign aid. When the educational endeavours of business, the voluntary sector, trade unions, and professional associations is included, Canadian educational spending is staggering. Even with this, a large portion of the more than $1 billion Canada's thirty largest companies spend annually on educational programs is devoted to upgrading the skills in mathematics and communications of high school and university graduates.

Ironically, with Canada's high per capita spending on education, it has one of the least literate populations among the OECD nations in the EMF study. Up to sixty million Americans and more than four million Canadians are functionally illiterate, a term that designates those adults with grade eight education or less. (Collins, 1986:13). The capacity of the Canadian work force to adjust to change was also questioned in the EMF assessment. It is not easy to acquire new skills when one does not even have basic reading and computational skills on which to build.

The availability of skilled labour was not seen as a problem, however, the quality of those skills was rated poorer than those in fourteen other OECD countries. Apprenticeable trades training in Canada is fragmented and the quality is inconsistent. (Construction Sector Committee, 1986). Although the Interprovincial Standards Committee on Apprenticeable Trades (Red Seal) has certainly begun to address quality. standards, and consistency issues, there is still much to be done. Canada Employment and Immigration Commission is currently working with some provincial governments via training agreements to further assess this area.

At the same time as Canadian educational investment burgeons, research and development initiatives wane in comparison to other countries. While Canada seems able to attract highly qualified researchers. (Gilmour, 1986:A4). Canada's commitment to these highly qualified people and to the rhetoric of increased emphasis on research and development is questioned. Canada seriously lags behind the leading countries in the rate of introduction of robotized manufacturing and factory automation. Given the strong potential of our existing labour force structure identified in the EMF analysis, the efficient deployment of our work force was questioned.

If it is estimated that Canada has one of the highest per capita spending on education of the OECD member countries, one must ask why Canada is not ranked first on the human resource factor. Why do Japan and the United States maintain a towering lead over all other countries? Are they more efficient, or are they merely benefitting from the emigration of skilled talent from the more mature developed economies? Does it have something to do with the 65 hours of on-the-job training in Japan. For every 35 hours in the United States, for every 25 hours in Canada? (Labour Canada Task Force, 1982:65). Is the perception of the strong influence of a well trained and motivated management in the United States a valid one? Did the ongoing Japanese commitment to long-term planning, continuous learning, research and development, and leading edge innovation help to regain its number one overall competitive position, and its number two slot on the human resource contributing factor? Some believe that countercyclical training (Task Force on Labour Market Development, 1982:65) and the commitment to research and development and to lifelong learning contribute substantially to Japan's leading edge technological positioning. Are there lessons that Canada can learn from these major competitors?

PUBLIC POLICY ON BASIC SKILL DEVELOPMENT

"Education is a peculiar process. You aim at one thing and you hit another."
(Leacock, 1986:3)

With close to the highest per capita investment in formal education systems of the twenty-two countries studied in the EMF analysis and with Canada Employment and Immigration Commission investing close to $2 billion a year on training, are we missing the target?

In an effort to bring together the skill requirements of jobs with the available skills of people and to combat long-term unemployment, the federal government created the Canadian Jobs Strategy. This six pronged program replaced the National Training Act (1982) which in turn had replaced the Adult Occupational Training Act (1966). According to the Canada Employment and Immigration Commission, (E.I.C.) material on the Canadian Jobs Strategy (C.J.Ş.), (Canada Employment & Immigration Commission, 1985:6), the six programs have been created to:

1. meet immediate needs of employers and workers; and,
2. address specific problems with assistance to those who need help urgently.

E.I.C. promotional material on the Canadian Jobs Strategy describes the programs as follows.

The Skill Investment program helps workers before they lose their jobs because of technological or economic change. It coordinates the efforts of employers and workers to give people a chance to learn new skills before they are laid off, or their existing skills become redundant. It has special features that make it practical for small businesses and self-employed individuals to participate.

The Skill Shortages program acknowledges that, even in times of high unemployment, some skills are in short supply. This program allows employers to hire and train workers to meet their firms, skill needs.

The Innovations program encourages just that – new ideas and innovations. It encourages dynamism, new ways of tackling labour-management problems, and creativity. According to the promotional literature, "the doors are open for fresh thinking."

The Job Entry program helps new entrants to the labour force, especially school drop-outs or women re-entering the labour force after a long absence to get established. It provides help for workers to find that "first job" – and for employers takes some of the risk out of the hiring process.

The Job Development program offers assistance to long-term unemployed individuals who need special assistance to get back to work. The program's

goal is to get away from short-term "make-work" projects – instead, providing workers with lasting skills to ensure permanent employment.
The Community Futures program is designed for areas, especially single-industry communities, hard hit by economic downturns. It offers a wide-ranging package of incentives and benefits for both businesses and workers.

While the verdict is still out on the effectiveness of the Canadian Jobs Strategy, groups such as the Canadian Association for Adult Education and its provincial affiliates are surveying its effectiveness from the perspectives of their constituencies. Preliminary findings challenge the move away from funding the community colleges as providers to funding private consultants; the neutrality of advisory councils appointed by member of parliament nomination; the capacity of EIC to finely predict critical skills shortages; and, the efficacy and actual spending on the programs. While the rhetoric for the programs sounds very promising, the government's commitment to the Canadian Jobs Strategy is questioned. In 1986, innovations program billed as "the program that looks to the future" had its budget cut from $75 million to $27.8 million. (Beauchesne, 1986)

The Skill Investment Program of CJS does include an extended training leave option for individuals threatened with lay-off. However, the recommendations of the major sector National Advisory Panel on Skill Development Leave (Ahenakew et al, 1984) the Minister of Employment and Immigration appear to have largely gone unheeded. These recommendations included action to be undertaken immediately and action to be undertaken by 1986.

The actions proposed to be undertaken immediately (1984) included:

1. Endorsing the two principles identified under the goal of "Canada as a Learning Society". These principles include:

'A Right to Learn' throughout life so as to acquire and maintain the skills, knowledge and ability to make a contribution to society and to pursue a life of fulfillment and good citizenship; and,
'An Earned Right' to time and adequate income to engage in learning of their choice for all who have made a contribution to Canadian society.

2. Initiating a ten-year program to combat adult illiteracy.
3. Initiating a program for those threatened with job loss or skill obsolescence.
4. Establishing education delegates in workplaces.
5. Accelerating action on barriers to educational leave.
6. Establishing the federal government as model for other employers.
7. Initiating a national process of planning and consensus-building for the remainder of measures through
  a) the establishment of a council on educational leave, to
  b) the more detailed descriptions and analysis of the proposed programs.
The actions proposed to be undertaken by 1986 included:
  1. Developing a universal program of educational leave.
2. Developing additional local and regional mechanisms to connect learners, needs, and opportunities including:
  a) local training councils;
  b) changes to Canada Employment Centres; and
  c) experimental community Employment Centres.

In addition to the emphasis on basic skills development at the national level, each of the provinces maintains a major focus in this area. The focus on skill development, continuing education, and/or human capital development in response to technological change is being increasingly segmented out as new ministries in the provinces. For example in Ontario a new Skills Development Ministry was recently established.

One critical area that often falls through the jurisdictional slats is that of illiteracy. While the federal, provincial, and municipal governments argue over who has the responsibility, the non-profit groups such as Frontier College, the Canadian Labour Congress, and Laubach Literacy often must step in to bridge the void.

The 1987 Industry Committee Report of the National Advisory Board on Science and Technology (NABST) to the Prime Minister called for major new initiatives to eradicate illiteracy. Recognizing the deadweight costs associated with the many of our citizens, lacking even the basic skills required to acquire new skills, the NABST called for urgent action on illiteracy. At the 1988 National Conference on Technology and Innovation in Toronto, the Prime minister boldly took the lead when he said "we cannot afford to waste one single mind". The National Literacy Secretariat at the Department of the Secretary of State was also established and funded.

Clearly, literacy and human resource development, from the lower end of the scale to the university level, emerge as central to Canadian economic development and our competitive future. Unemployment in Canada stubbornly persists, as critical shortages of skilled personnel emerge. Technological, market, and workplace change precipitate job loss at the same time as new jobs are created.

According to the 1988 NABST Private Sector Challenge Committee Report to the Prime Minister, Canada must shift from reactive agency and employer centred temporary adjustment and patch-work skill development programs. The emerging model to anticipate and manage transitions should encourage individual self-choice, initiative, entrepreneurism, and life-long learning. Employees should not be the unemployed, low self-concept victims of change. Rather, the reality of career and job change should be recognized and positive transitional educational, entrepreneurial, and job change transitional programs should become normal for all people wanting a productive role in Canada's labour force.

WHAT CAN THE COLLEGES AND UNIVERSITIES DO?

Institutions must develop balanced education portfolios to allow them to shift focus to suit educational, social, and economic needs. While some schools continue to ask if higher education has a role to play in or for the workplace, many people believe that there is a substantial requirement for post-secondary institutions to help meet the labour market needs. At the same time as a number of Chief Executive Officers call for employees with the developed capacity to learn, to communicate, and to think creatively; personnel officers are hiring the candidates whose skills will likely be most directly applied to immediate tasks to enhance the company's short-term economic position. Since an individual is likely to change careers throughout life, a good generic skill base on which to build job specific skills is required. (Choate, 1986)

In order to respond rapidly to external needs, new work and learning arrangements in cooperation with business and labour people will be required. These new links potentially expand university and college resources and provide interchange and work experience opportunities for university students and faculty. State-of-the-art equipment and facilities are shared. Joint research parks, telecommuting new distance education models, and flexible recognition of both academic and experiential learning are examples of mechanisms designed to foster these new linkages.

The cooperative education model that alternates work experience and academic semesters provides the student with on-the-job experience and gives the employer the opportunity to assess potential long term employee candidates. Are other types of cooperative arrangements possible?

What is the potential for academic and workplace faculty and employee interchanges? Are there unique master/mentor, new employee on-the-job work, and learning possibilities? A bill before the Congress in the United States at the moment looks at the establishment of tax-sheltered individual employee training accounts and learning vouchers for those threatened with lay-off due to technological change. (Fever, 1986:26)

Will paid educational leave and individual training accounts build new flexibility into the workplace? A number of school systems with an oversupply of teachers have introduced the four in five plan. This plan permits the employee to work four years at 4/5 salary and take the fifth year on sabbatical leave at 4/5 salary. Employee/employer training accounts and centres now are part of collective agreements for the United Auto Workers with General Motors and some telephone companies. What antecedent measures are necessary in order to move society into a recurrent learning mode? The National Advisory Panel on Skill Development Leave proposed that one day of educational leave be granted for every thirty worked. What impact would one day of continuous learning for every thirty worked have on the readiness of our work force and/or introducing flexibility into the labour market?

Are educational institutions prepared to meet the needs of these new clientele groups? Do they have the capacity to respond? Do they have the willingness to respond and to create the new relationships with business and the community at large? At the same time, if fewer hours are worked, how can the educational institutions best respond to society's increased leisure time learning needs?

Not only does the post-secondary institution need to respond to new community/corporate sponsors, but the part-time, working student population is emerging as the new majority. Demographic trends indicate that this will likely continue. New student groups will require more appropriate institutional responses. For example, bookstores, libraries, and other support services need to be open at times convenient to new clientele groups. As telecommuting becomes an increasingly acceptable workplace alternative, flexible learning opportunities at the institution, at work, and at home emerge.

Continuing education in the post-secondary institution must respond or the proprietary schools and industry itself will, and are, filling the educational void. This means new and responsive organizational models for continuing education service. New balances between generic and job specific skills acquisition are needed.

Change requires new learning modes of operation and response. Futures visioning and alternative scenarios planning should become normal. Collaborative arrangements that recognize the input from all interested parties should be utilized in program planning. A movement towards a lifelong learning strategy must build in new optimism and flexibility. Educational episodes should give way to long-term educational strategies. The lockstep arrangements which boxed life into school, work, and retirement will need to flow into the more flexible model.

The demographic impact of declining enrollments of traditional college-aged students and the evolution of the new majority – the part-time learner – has put stress on post-secondary institutions to become more responsive. The rise of the parallel corporate education system further treatens the unresponsive institution.

Institutional survival pressures the university and/or college to change. Linkages through work and learning, higher education, and industry cooperation hold promise for new understanding and the sharing of resources and expertise. Industry-university research parks for the transfer of technology and the sharing of state-of-the-art equipment and expert people are one such example of the new cooperation.

Just as the matrix organizational model for the educational institution encourages new, appropriate, and worthwhile communication between the academic and continuing education divisions, so new mechanisms to encourage industry, trade union, academic, and government discussion and involvement must occur. one such mechanism, the advisory council, not only helps the post-secondary institution become more responsive to workplace and community change, but it also provides the school with access to, and understanding of, new markets.

CONCLUSION

Change is not new; what is new in the 1980s is its speed and pervasiveness. The question of how best to manage this change challenges our collective spirit with both skill development problems and opportunities. According to John Naisbitt in *Megatrends,* "As our school systems fail us, corporations will become the universities of the future." (Carnevale, 1983). If this is not to happen, educational institutions will need to evolve a new role in shaping national economic structure and the development of its human potential. This cannot be done from the lofty tower.

The expense of not helping citizens learn throughout life is implicit in the needs as defined. Not learning is not an option.

"The responsibility for change lies with us. We should begin by teaching ourselves not to close our minds prematurely to the novel, the surprising or perhaps the seemingly radical. This means fighting off the idea-assassins who rush forward to kill any suggestion on the basis of its impracticability, while defending whatever now exists as practical no matter how outdated, absurd, unworkable or oppressive it may be. (Toffler, 1980)

REFERENCES

Ahenakew, Ray; Booker, Clair; Bourgeault, Guy; Eady, Mary: Ironside, Anne: Rogers, Lenore; Smith, Stuart; Walda. Carolynn. National Advisory Panel on Skill Development Leave (1984). *Learning for Life.* Canada Employment and Immigration Commission, March 4.

Apps, Herold W. "Six Influences on Adult Education in the 1980's." *Lifelong Learning,* June 1980, p. 4.

Beauchesne, Eric. "Job Strategy Program Cut in Bid to Reduce Spending." *The Ottawa Citizen,* November 19, 1986

Best, Fred. "Technology and the Changing World of Work." *The Futurist,* April 1984, p. 61.

Butler, Erik Payne. "Higher Education's Role in the American Economy." *Educational Record,* Fall 1983. p. 6.

Canada Employment and Immigration Commission. "The Canadian Jobs Strategy . . . Working Opportunities for People." *How it Benefits Employers,* November 1985, p.

The Carnegie Foundation for Advancement of Teaching (1985). *Corporate Classrooms: The Learning Business.* Princeton, N.J., P. 6.

Carnevale, Anthony Patrick. "Higher Education's Role in the American Economy." *Educational Record,* Fall 1983.

Cetron. Marvin J. "Getting Ready for the Jobs of the Future." *The Futurist,* June 1983, p. 15. Choate, Pat. (on) "Lifelong Learning: The Proactive Economic Response." Future Focus, The Next Fifteen Years conference. World Future Society. New York, NY, July 16, 1986.

Collins, Winston, ed. *Royal Bank Reporter.* Royal Bank of Canada. Fall 1986, p. 13.

Construction Sector Committee. Canadian Labour Market and Productivity Centre, 1986.

Cornish, Edward. "The Smart Machines of Tomorrow, Implications for Society." The Futurist, August 1983. p. 5.

D'Cruz, Joseph R., and Fleck, James D. "The 1986 EMF Scorecard on Canada: Mixed, but Encouraging." *Business. Quarterly.* Summer 1986, p. 82.

Dunn, Samuel A. "The Changing University – Survival in the Information Society." *The Futurist.* June 1983. p. 30.

Feuer, Dale. "Tax Breaks for Training." *Training,* April 1986, p. 26.

Gardner. John W. "Responsibility Networks." *Community Education Journal,* July 1981, p. 6.

Gavert, Roy V. "Business-Academe, An Emerging Partnership." *Change,* April 1983, p. 23.

Gilmour, James (as referenced in) "No Brain Drain from Canada, Research Finds", *The Globe and Mail,* November 13, 1986, p. 24.

Hollander, T. Edward. "The Partnership of Higher Education and Industry, Some Fundamental Changes." *Adult Education.* Clearing House Newsletter, June 1983. p. 18.

Labour Canada Task Force on Micro-Electronics and Employment. *In the Chips: Opportunities, People, Partnerships.* Labour Canada, 1982, p. 65.

Leacock, Stephen. (as quoted in) *Royal Bank Reporter,* Royal Bank of Canada. Winston Collins, ed., Fall 1986. p. 3.

Levin, Henry M. and Rumberger, Russell W. *Forecasting the Impact of New Technologies on the Future Job Market.* Institute for Research on Educational Finance and Governance. School of Education. Stanford University. Project Report No. 84-4A, February 1984.

National Advisory Panel on Skill Development Leave. *Learning for Life.* Canada Employment and Immigration Commission, March 5, 1984, p. 11.

Ontario Ministry of Skills Development. *Breaking New Ground.* Ontario's Training Strategy, September 1986. p. 4.

Russel, Robert Arnold (1986). *Winning the Future.* Carroll and Graf Publishers, Inc. New York, NY, p. 174

Skill Development Leave Task Force. *Learning a Living in Canada.* Canada Employment and Immigration Commission, 1983, vol. 1, p. 15.

Smith, Stuart. (on) "The Changing Educational Milieu." Career Education for the 1990s: The Role of Liberal Studies conference. Ryerson Polytechnical Institute. Toronto, Ontario, October 24, 1986.

Surich, Joe. (on) "The Changing Educational Milieu." Career Education for the 1990s: The Role of Liberal Studies conference. Ryerson Polytechnical Institute. Toronto, Ontario, October 24, 1986.

Task Force on Labour Market Development. *Labour Market Development in the 1980s.* Canada Employment and Immigration Commission. Ottawa-Hull. July 1981.

Toffler. Alvin (1980). *The Third Wave.* William Morrow and Company. Inc. New York, NY.

Wright. James E. "Retraining the Adult Workforce." *Lifelong Learning.* October 1983, P. 21.

Zemke. Ron. "The Robots are Coming! Training Tomorrow's High-Tech Workers." *Training,* June 1983. p. 19.

CHAPTER 4:

Learning through Research

James A. Draper

Research is a systematic way of examining a problem or answering a question. The research process has three components: systematically collecting information; organizing and analyzing it in the light of common sense and previous knowledge; and drawing conclusions. The term "research" is used here to refer to evaluative as well as to other kinds of research. Evaluation is a specific form of research in which learning is assessed according to predetermined criteria. Research is a process of reflective thinking, extending what is already known, and learning.

Research and evaluation can make an important contribution to personal and professional development. Because the purpose of research is learning, and because learning is highly personal and individual, the most meaningful kind of research is a personal quest for knowledge. Research and good practice in literacy education go hand in hand. Everyone is involved, in one way or another, with research and evaluation.

There are, however, a number of myths about research and evaluation that impede their use. One such myth is that evaluation and research are best left to specialized researchers. On the contrary, practitioners are quite capable of undertaking a program of research and evaluation. Other mythologies about research are that it requires highly technical skills; that the information collected needs to be quantified, computerized, and statistically manipulated; and that research is a costly frill only to be undertaken if an agency has the time and money. Research is also considered to be depersonalizing, threatening, and shrouded in academic jargon — a time-consuming distraction from the real task of educating. However, much research is just the opposite. It is highly personal, subjective, descriptive, inexpensive, and it can be simply expressed.

Literacy and adult basic education programs lend themselves to a variety of research methods. In participatory research, for example, the research subjects who are to benefit from the findings are involved in all stages of the process. "Common people" become the researchers. The participatory approach involves planning from the grass roots and encourages program commitment.

Research decisions should be part of the initial planning of a literacy program, not a possible option or an afterthought, "if there is time left over". Research is as integral as teaching is to planning an educational program. Ideally, formative evaluation is an ongoing process, enabling continuous program improvement. Summative evaluation — to assess program outcomes or to decide on program continuation — is done towards the end of a program. (The References cite many publications relating to evaluation in adult basic education.)

The selection of the research approach is crucial. A design ill-suited to the instructional program can be as detrimental as the choice of the wrong teaching method. Each approach has its own set of "rules", underlying values, and resource requirements (Merriam and Simpson, 1984).

THE RESEARCH SPECTRUM IN LITERACY EDUCATION

Like other educational activities, literacy education includes the following components: program planning; selection and training of resource persons, tutors, teachers, administrators, and counselors; classroom teaching and learning; production of materials; recruitment of learners; organization and administration of the program; and follow-up to ensure the retention of the newly acquired skills. Research should be integrated with all these functions.

Literacy research informs government policy formulation and funding decisions. Research findings also influence program planning and development patterns for government, community- based agencies, universities, and other organizations. Socially-oriented research topics might include: the factors in learner motivation; the prevention of relapse; the relationships between literacy and employment, health, poverty, and crime; literacy and community development (Nelson and Dymock, 1986) or a profile of adult learners — their perspectives, aspirations, or life-styles. Studies might examine: the role models that are most beneficial to learners; the resources that enhance literacy programs; the creation of the optimum climate for learning; or alternatives for management, accountability, or the allocation of resources. In short, the topics for research are limitless.

PRINCIPLES AND OUTCOMES OF RESEARCH

Research findings help to create knowledge. If knowledge is power, then withholding information is the manipulation of power. When used unethically, research can be a form of control and exploitation. Since the purpose of educational research is to maximize learning, involving as many people as possible can extend its outcomes. From the early planning stages of the research, making decisions about who controls research and how its findings will be used are crucial.

Needs assessment is a particular research process. Like all research, it begins with a question: What do I want to know? The questions asked often determine the answers received, for example, the question, What courses would you like to take? will generate information different from What would you like to learn? The learning derived from the research process is sometimes more beneficial than the final product or written report of the findings.

The purpose of the research determines the degree of internal/external control. There are pros and cons for having an insider or an outsider involved in agency-related research and evaluation. Who is involved in research should depend upon how the findings are to be used. Although insiders may have the expertise, outsiders have more credibility. Sometimes too, funding agencies impose inappropriate evaluation criteria for literacy education programs.

EXAMPLES OF LITERACY RESEARCH

Research on adult literacy is relatively recent compared to other areas of education (Lind, 1986). Nevertheless, developing nations have done considerable research relating to their various literacy and non-formal education programs. Innovative ways of documenting and interpreting learning have resulted from this work. Some international studies are comparative or cross-cultural.

A study undertaken for UNESCO on "The Causes and Consequences of the Relapse into Illiteracy Among Young People in the Federal Republic of Germany", (Geise, 1986) highlights relapse as a concern to all adult educators, not only to those in developing nations. This study deals with such questions as: What reading and writing is acquired in school? How does one develop a 'writing culture'?, What are the living conditions of illiterates?, Why do young adults leave school?, and What do early school-leavers do?

More research is needed on early school-leaving. A number of related questions arise — Are we justified in assuming that the completion of less than 12 years of schooling is a bad thing? Should we be considering economic advantages or quality of life? and On what criteria do we base judgement? The interpretation of research findings sometimes neglects another important question, From whose point of view do we plan and interpret research?

Educational perspectives are shifting, and the onus of learning is moving from the teacher to the student. The implications of these changing roles are discussed by a number of researchers, including Harris and Bell (1986).

Literacy is assumed to be an element essential to individual and societal development. And yet "educational practitioners and researchers are far from a consensus in their analysis of the role of literacy in the social, economic, and civic integration of individuals in the development of their country" (Rainey and Creative Associates, 1980). They examine the economic improvements resulting from literacy gains and the effectiveness of various instructional methodologies. Their report adopts the philosophical position that research must be undertaken in full collaboration with local researchers and literacy specialists. They conclude that the economic value of literacy skills is related to the available employment opportunities. Charnley and Associates (1982) deal with the relations of illiteracy to under- and unemployment.

Research has also addressed literacy education from an international perspective. The UNESCO Experimental World Literacy Project report (1976) presents case studies of literacy programs in a number of different countries. This report identifies the common principles in planning and implementation and compares the differences in outcome from one cultural setting to another. Duke (1985) provides basic data about countries utilizing adult education to combat poverty, a hostile political climate, and social oppression. Additional comparative literature is provided by Bhola (1983), Dave et. al. (1986), Fordham (1985), and King (1979).

The Canadian literacy experience has been studied by a number of researchers. A Government of Quebec statement (1982) discusses the role of the state in adult education, the cost of literacy campaigns, and inequities of access. In 1983, an Adult Basic Education Committee in Saskatchewan produced an extensive document examining various funding mechanisms and programs for literacy education. A comparable statement from the Ministry of Colleges and Universities in Ontario, *For Adults Only* (1986), discusses issues in adult basic education and the priorities for government funding support. The Canadian Survey, *One in Every Five* (1985) by Devereaux, raises the question of why a sizeable proportion of those classified as functionally illiterate do not choose to participate in literacy programs. Participation and non-participation are two sides of the same coin. This study, however, adopts the questionable definition of functional literacy as the completion of nine years of formal schooling, demonstrating the importance of selecting criteria for the interpretation of statistical data.

Literacy research has also addressed the interaction of educators and the provision of service within communities. One study documented the development of a model for school boards in establishing adult basic education (ABE) programs. This model was the result of educators reflecting on educational innovation in adult basic education (Draper and Herman: 1982). Another study adapted the social services model of adult basic education to rural and urban settings (Herman et. al., 1984).

Research has examined the interaction of literacy with other aspects of learners' experience. One study found that most ABE students who dropped out of school did so because of conditions prevailing outside the classroom, beyond the teachers' control (Russell, 1982). Murray (1981) studied the importance of reading in the lives of two groups of older adults — those in institutions and those living independently — to conclude that the "assumed passivity" of older institutionalized adults was a learned behavior. It appeared that the lack of reading materials in many institutions perpetuated the passive attitude, in turn reinforcing the policy of not providing reading materials. Other examples could be given of assumptions that are 'self-prophesied' by teachers, administrators, social workers, and others. Further research needs to be done to test the various assumptions we make about the people we work with.

Other studies have questioned assumed relationships, with similar findings, for example, the assumed relationship between illiteracy and occupational health and safety. A recent study (Draper, 1985) assessed the level of reading comprehension required to understand various government produced material, concluding that it was well beyond the reading ability of "the average citizen" for whom it was intended. The report recommended that ministries consider literacy levels when communicating their activities and messages to the public. The *Plain Writing Project* in Canada is an initiative supporting this goal.

A body of research addresses the relationship between literacy and culture. The work of Northcutt and Associates (n.d.) at the University of Texas describes adult functional literacy in pragmatic terms and develops devices for the assessment of literacy at several operational levels. Within this theoretical framework, the study observes that literacy is bound to a specific cultural context and level of technological development. Literacy does not consist in a single skill or set of skills: it is more accurately defined as the functional application of skills to such general knowledge as an occupation or consumer behavior. These general knowledge areas are integrated within the specific culture and society.

There is research into the research process itself. Mezirow and Irish (1974) found that local directors of Adult Basic Education programs ranked evaluation as their least important literacy activity. Apart from the likely absence of evaluation from these programs, this attitude prevents productive agency-university research partnerships. The lack of such partnerships prevents the kind of evaluation which would enable agencies to improve their programs and which would allow university members to enrich the body of theoretical literacy knowledge.

Some practitioners appear uninformed about the research process, the likely benefits to their professional development, and the improvements to their program which could result. For example, when two university faculty members in Toronto approached a field-based literacy agency to arrange a collaborative research project, the agency responded abruptly that there was not time for research and the learners wouldn't be interested in participating anyway. It is unlikely that the learners were consulted about the request, or that they realized how much they could give to and receive from their involvement in research.

DISSEMINATION OF RESEARCH FINDINGS

Research has only limited value if it is not shared with others. Darkenwald and Associates (1974) describe problems in the dissemination of research findings and the sharing of innovations in adult basic education. The dissemination process may involve translating jargon or specialized terms into language that is understood by practitioners. One of the reasons for the formation of the Canadian Association for the Study of Adult Education was to encourage dialogue between the producers and the implementers of research findings. Similarly, the Association for Recurrent Education in the United Kingdom published *Research and Practice in Adult Literacy* (Hamilton: 1985) to promote debate on literacy education and to foster theoretical, empirical, and practical work in the field and to link research with practice in literacy education.

SUPPORT OF RESEARCH: FOCUS ON UNIVERSITIES

Studies show that the universities can best support literacy education through research, evaluation, training practitioners, providing senior managers, and advising (Draper, 1987; Draper and Clark, 1980). Universities are well equipped to draft suitable research questions; develop innovative, alternative research methods; and review critically literacy research.

The Canadian Commission for UNESCO (1985) advocated cooperation among local, provincial, national, and international agencies. An initiative to implement this cooperation could comprise a consortium of university graduate programs and community-based literacy education agencies. Such a consortium would promote synergy between practitioners and researchers.

Universities in Canada can encourage dialogue with developing countries. One study (Kidd, 1967) assessed the Canadian capability to assist with the world literacy campaign. Another study by the British Committee on Literacy (1976) examined the role of universities in promoting literacy education in developing countries. This role includes documentation, production and distribution of materials, consultation, financial support, and joint submissions of proposals to government and other funding agencies.

A prevalent misconception about university-based research is that it is theoretical, abstract, and remote from the practicalities of experience. In fact, the reverse is true. Such research is more frequently based on a personal commitment to the topic and is grounded in experience. University masters and doctoral theses are typical examples of practitioner research (Draper, 1981; Dobson, 1986).

CONCLUDING REMARKS

Research and evaluation are components essential to literacy programming and to understanding and improving practice. Learning and research are as integral to each other as learning and teaching. In Rethinking Adult Literacy, Draper (1987) points out that the microcosm of literacy education is linked to larger issues. Each research study, each addition to knowledge, each insight, illuminates and clarifies the larger whole. The philosophies and values implicit in the processes of teaching and learning require reflection and refining. Not all research is quantifiable; qualitative studies may address such aspects as learners' esteem and personal growth. The research process is beneficial to practitioners as well, clarifying the relationships among stated intentions, values, and actual practice.

Research does not always focus on the product or outcome of a program. The process of research is a journey that has value in itself. Through researching our present, we are likely to be better prepared for the future. There are a number of interrelating benefits to undertaking research. On one hand, one can conduct research to: defend one's program, satisfy one's funding agency, solve a problem, clarify goals, improve teaching and program effectiveness, or to make comparisons. On the other hand, becoming involved in research can help build self-confidence, strengthen community and self-growth, or build group commitment and cohesiveness — "Now we know!" or "We did it, together!".

REFERENCES

Adult Basic Education Review Committee (1983), *Final Report*, Regina, Saskatchewan: Continuing Education.

Bhola, H. S., Muller, J., and Kijkstra, P. (1983), *The Promise of Literacy* (Campaigns, Programs and Projects), Report of the International Seminar on Campaigning for Literacy, Udaipur, India, Jan. 4-11, 1982, Baden-Baden, Germany: Nomos Verlagsgesellschaft.

British Committee on Literacy (1976), *Illiteracy in the Developing World*, London, U.K.: The Secretary to the British Committee on Literacy.

Canadian Commission for UNESCO (1985), *Learning in Society: Towards a New Paradigm*, Occasional Paper No. 51, Ottawa.

Charnley, A., Osborn, M., and Withnall, A. (1982), *Review of Existing Research in Adult and Continuing Education*, Vol, IX, "Adult Education and Unemployment", N.I.A.C.E. (U.K.).

Dave, R. H., Quance, A., Perera, D. A. (eds.) (1986), *Learning Strategies for Post-Literacy and Continuing Education in China, India, Indonesia, Nepal, Thailand, and Vietnam*, Hamburg: UNESCO Institute of Education, #4.

Darkenwald, G. G., Beder, H. W., and Adelman, A. K. (1974), *Problems of Dissemination and Use of Innovations in Adult Basic Education: Selected Research Findings and Recommendations* (Summary of Volume II of Planning for Innovation in Adult Basic Education, Study Directed by Jack Mezirow), New York: Center for Adult Education, Teachers College, Columbia University.

Devereaux M. S. (1985), *One in Every Five*, Ottawa: Statistics Canada and Department of the Secretary of State.

Dobson, John (1986), *Adult Education Theses in Canada: 1980-1985*, Antigonish, Nova Scotia: Department of Adult Education, St. Francis Xavier University.

Draper, James A. and Clark, Ralph J. (1980), *Adult Basic and Literacy Education: Teaching and Support Programs Within Selected Colleges and Universities in Canada*, Toronto: Department of Adult Education, The Ontario Institute for Studies in Education.

Draper, James A. (1981), *Adult Education Theses : Canada* (to 1980), Toronto: Department of Adult Education, The Ontario Institute for Studies in Education.

Draper, James A. and Herman, Reg (1982), *Towards a Model of Adult Basic Education*, Toronto: The Ontario Institute for Studies in Education.

Draper, James A.,(Chairman) (1985), *Concerning Policies and Priorities for Dealing with Literacy and Occupational Health and Safety*, Toronto: Advisory Council on Occupational Health and Occupational Safety, Ministry of Labour, Seventh Annual Report.

Draper, James A., "Universities and the Challenge of Illiteracy", *Indian Journal of Adult Education*, Vol. 48, No 1, Jan.-March, 1987.

Draper, James A. (1987), *Re-Thinking Adult Literacy*, Toronto: World Literacy of Canada.

Duke, Chris (ed.) (1985), *Combatting Poverty Through Adult Education: National Development Strategies*, London: Croom Helm.

Fordham, Paul (ed.) (1985), *One Billion Illiterates: One Billion Reasons for Action* (Report on the International Seminar: "Cooperating for Literacy", Berlin (West), October, 1983) Toronto: International Council for Adult Education (and DSE).

Geise, Heinze W. (1986), *Causes and Consequences of the Relapse into Illiteracy Among Young People in Federal Republic of Germany*, A Study for UNESCO (Paris), Oldenburg University.

Government du Québec (1982), *Learning: A Voluntary and Responsible Action* (Statement of a Comprehensive Policy for Adult Education), Québec: Commission d'Étude sur la Formation des Adultes, Ministère des Communications.

Hamilton, Mary (ed.) (1985), *Research and Practice in Adult Literacy*, Nottingham: Association for Recurrent Education.

Harris, Duncan and Bell, Chris (1986), *Evaluating and Assessing for Learning*, N.Y.: Nichols Pub, Co.

Herman, Reg, Moore, Linda, and Ryan, Fred (1984), A *Social Services Model for Adult Basic Education* (A.B.E.), Toronto: The Department of Adult Education, The Ontario Institute for Studies in Education.

Kidd, J. Roby (Project Director) (1967), *Functional Literacy and International Development* (A Study of Canadian Capability to Assist with the World Campaign to Eradicate Illiteracy), Ottawa: Overseas Institute of Canada.

King, Kenneth (ed.) (1979), *Literacy Research in Developing Countries* (Report of the Bellagio IV Workshop on Educational Research with Special Reference to Research on Literacy, Geneva, Switzerland), Ottawa: International Development Research Centre, Canada, and German Foundation for International Development, Centre for Education, Science and Documentation.

Lind, Agneta and Johnston, Anton (1986), *Adult Literacy in the Third World* (A Review of Objectives and Strategies), Stockholm: University and Institute of International Education.

Merriam, S. B., and Simpson, E. L. (1984), A *Guide to Research for Educators and Trainers of Adults*, Malabar, Florida: Robert E. Krieger Publishing Co.

Mezirow, Jack (Project Director), *An Evaluation Guide for Adult Basic Education Programs*, New York: Center for Adult Education, Teachers College, Columbia University (no date).

Mezirow, Jack, and Irish, Gladys (1974), *Priorities for Experimentation and Development in Adult Basic Education*, New York: Center for Adult Education, Teachers College, Columbia University.

Ministry of Colleges and Universities (1986), Continuing Education Preview Project, *Project Report: For Adults Only*, Toronto: Ministry of Colleges and Universities.

Murray, Martha S. (Jan. 1981), "Older Adults and Reading: The Effect of Residential Lifestyles", *Lifelong Learning: The Adult Years*.

Nelson, A. J. A., and Dymock, D. R. (1986), *Adult Literacy and Community Development* (Report of a Workshop, August 19-25, 1985), Armidale, Australia: Department of Continuing Education, University of New England.

Northcutt, Norville, *Functional Literacy for Adults: A Status Report of the Adult Performance Level Study*, Austin: University of Texas, (no date).

Popham, James W. (1972), *An Evaluation Guidebook: A Set of Practical Guidelines for the Educational Evaluator*, California: The Institutional Objectives Exchange.

Rainey, C. Mary and Creative Associates (1980), *Economic Incentives and Literacy Motivation: A Preliminary State-of-the-art Review*, Washington, D. C.

Russell, E. E., "Use of CLER in Promoting Recruitment into an Adult Basic Education Program", *Viewpoints in Teaching and Learning*, Vol. 58, No. 4, Fall 1982.

Rutman, Leonard (1980), *Planning Useful Evaluations*, California: Sage Publications.

Steele, Sara M. and Brack, Robert E. (1973), *Evaluating the Attainment of Objectives in Adult Education: Process, Properties, Problems, Prospects*, Syracuse, New York: University.

Training, Research and Development Station (1974), *Evaluations of Life Skills Training*, Prince Albert, Saskatchewan: Manpower and Immigration.

UNESCO, UNDP (1976), The Experimental World Literacy Program: A Critical Assessment, Paris: The UNESCO Press.

CHAPTER 5:

Reflections on Literacy and The Universal Learning Process

Thelma Barer-Stein

It should be impossible to think about literacy without thinking about the process of learning. But we often do. There are so many other concerns that take priority like teacher recruitment and training, production of curricular materials, effective assessments and of course funding. But there are signs that interest in learning is increasing. Conti (1989) among others, acknowledges success in applying learner-centred approaches to literacy teaching; there is serious discussion that an understanding of learning itself may be more important than a focus on 'education' (Cross & McCarten, 1981; Osborne, Charnley & Withnall, 1982); and there is strong acknowledgement that a teacher's underlying philosophy has an effect on learning outcomes for the learners (Elias & Merriam, 1984).

But it is not enough just to focus on this matter of learning. In most discussions, the careful distinction of 'student' and 'teacher' most often defines only one as the learner. We must recognise that both are learners. We assume that teachers and tutors already understand what learning is all about, and so we, as teachers do not usually question how we learned the knowledge and skills that we possess, or what factors have influenced that learning, or even how it is that the process of learning is glossed over. Yet, on reflection we likely will acknowledge that the most effective teachers are also effective learners.

In other words, common practice in education is to focus on the *content* of what is to be taught, rather than on the *process* through which one learns that content, whether as teacher or as student.

It may be that this common focus on education instead of on learning has been a stumbling block, preventing success in the hoped-for eradication of illiteracy. For a while we thought that widespread illiteracy could be alleviated by pushing adults to 'participate' or by trying to 'increase access' with more informal approaches.[1] We thought that more education would be better education; it just seemed a matter of 'mobilizing our forces', spreading out and reaching more people. But the response to these carefully planned projects, programs and campaigns did not result in immediate and unanimous literacy for all. The results of those efforts leaves gaps as well as questions. Adult illiteracy, however deviously defined (Thomas, 1989), could not be eradicated by collaring adults and giving them the education that experts thought they needed.

Why doesn't this work?

It seems there are some elusive factors in what makes people want to learn and want to go on learning. Even where education is available and accessible, youths and adults 'drop out' (Soljan, Golubovic, & Krajnc, 1985:68-73; Rogers, 1986:163; Bhola, 1985:80). Learners may engage in a program of literacy or basic skills and begin to develop a semblance of interest and confidence but this is tenuous. Such newfound confidence may be abruptly shattered on encountering a job interview, receiving a document that requires interpretation, or becoming involved in a work procedure that demands innovative thinking. For others, the path to literacy may be pursued only so long as there is a teacher to approve and offer guidance. Once left alone, the individual's fragile self-esteem may not withstand threatening spouses or jealous peers (Mackeracher, 1989). Taking part in a program of any learning may well set one aside from others as being different. Learning may cause subtle shifts in how one views daily life, future plans, even one's own family and one's own past behaviour.

Learning can cause change. That change may be immediate and startling arising from sudden insights, or it may be very gradual and scarcely apparent. The changes may develop inwardly with slight shifts in values, beliefs or attitudes rather than in immediate overt behaviours. There is no one pattern of change.

The feelings, perceptions and attitudes that are part of the learning process intertwine together within each individual with a complexity and lack of predictability that can only be equalled by the complexity that makes each individual unique.

Learning courses and programs may be readily available, but whether or not the individual learns or even how much is learned, or how long the supposed learning is retained, are factors that defy prediction. We need to understand learning itself.

Despite the elusiveness and the complexity of learning, and even despite a vague sense of discontent with our results, we, as educators, still go on planning and evaluating in much the same old way, and we still puzzle over classic questions:

"How can we motivate adults to learn?"

"How can we reach the people we designed our programs for?"

And Hamilton and Barton (1985) add these:

"How can we develop procedures for learning better as students and teachers?"

"How can we help the redefinition of teacher/learner roles that are locked in school memories?"

It is significant that each of these classic questions begins with *How can we* . . .? The underlying assumption seems to be that we as teachers, tutors, administrators, policy makers and funders obviously hold all the cards of expertise. Having all the knowledge and all the skills, we simply have to keep shuffling these around until we come up with the winning hand that really works. Educators are not alone in this elitist thinking; it is still shared by many health professionals and managers and administrators of industry and business, not to mention governments.

But there are important signs of cracks in such polarised thinking that dichotomizes the professional and the client, the manager and the worker, the teacher and the student (Labonté & Penfold, 1981; Hancock, 1982; Peters & Waterman, 1982; Miller, 1976; Daloz, 1987). The "cracks" really depict the gnawing presence of doubt in one's previously accepted belief of infallible expertise. Together with this doubt, there is a growing awareness of the advantages of shared responsibility, cooperation and collaboration . There is also a growing acknowledgement of the power of dialogue. The notion of "we" is changing. It is changing with the recognition that others have something of value to contribute to the puzzle of human complexity and unpredictability.

Acknowledging that such a view may be plausible is not quite the same as putting it into practice. It demands changed behaviour from the expert. It implies learning to relinquish such things as control, power, authority in favour of cooperation and collaboration. Changed behaviour and learning cannot be imposed, they must develop from individual volition in order to be effective, sincere, and lasting.

As educators, we rarely question the assumptions upon which our own educative approaches rest, nor how congruent these may be with the ideals we outwardly profess. What is different right now, this very moment, is that we have paused in the usual flow of familiar things to question what we have always assumed to have understood. Perhaps in this halt to examine ordinary assumptions, we may discover some connecting links to fill those elusive gaps.

To flesh out these reflections, let's look briefly at the two dominant teaching approaches and review some universal things that we already know about learning. Then I would like to introduce you to a Universal Learning Process that emerged from my recent research. With these providing common background, we'll take another look at those nagging questions we noted at the outset. Perhaps together we can blow away some of the dust and clarify the concepts of 'learning' and 'education'.

THE TWO DOMINANT TEACHING APPROACHES

One must approach all generalizations warily. This is true of the statement that 'teacher-centred' and 'learner-centred' represent the two dominant teaching approaches. There are many situations where both approaches are intertwined, or where one may dominate, as well as situations where one or the other are used exclusively. The point here is just to highlight some of their characteristics and differences for both the teacher and the learner.

It is important to distinguish immediately that 'education' represents the *provision* of learning opportunities while 'learning' may be distinguished as the *partaking* of those opportunities (Barer-Stein, 1985a). While both learning and education may be associated with institutions, they also occur in daily life experience and may not always be planned or even anticipated, but may emerge spontaneously.

Teacher-centred approaches to education focus on the content of what is to be taught, with the teacher as arbiter of curricular materials, and the controller of the teaching environment. The teacher as representative of the educational institute is authority, arbiter, resource and evaluator. It is assumed that the student is there to 'learn' the subject matter selected and to a level deemed adequate by the educators. The student is seen as passive recipient, with only token participation usually in the form of questioning or the preparation of projects. The predominant teaching style is lecturing.

While learner-centred approaches to education acknowledge the role of teachers and administrators, there is more focus not only on the needs of the learner, but also on engaging the student in increasingly responsible participation within that learning. This may include group discussions to plan the curriculum, to prepare and to search out resources, to give class presentations and even to contribute or share in evaluations of the learning. The teacher is seen as collaborator, resource and support. All of this implies that the student must step beyond mere memorization and rote reporting and move into the realm of thoughtful planning and responsible participation. Frequently it also implies the mutual contribution of knowledge and skills from life experience, and the direct involvement and enhancement of those skills.

The awareness of these two distinct approaches to teaching has surfaced research and questions regarding *how* teachers do in fact teach, and *how* learners do in fact learn (Martin, Hounsell & Entwhistle, 1984; Boud & Griffin, 1987).

The advantages of teacher-centred approaches rest in their accountability, credibility and peer consensus of content and evaluation. The application of Skinnerian behaviour-modification and Pavlovian stimulus-response as well as other applications of cognitive psychology research are intended to provide predictability of results and uniformity of behaviours. This has yet to be achieved. Years of schooling completed or lists of courses studied still do not serve to define either literacy or basic skills (Thomas, 1989.). As Thomas states, the notion of completed years of formal schooling as a means of defining literacy simply "made no sense at all when applied to a particular individual".

The traditional grip that teacher-centred approaches have on most educational approaches (in health promotion and business management as well as literacy), is not difficult to justify. Deciding in advance 'behavioural objectives', 'competencies to be achieved' and 'numerical outcomes' makes for tidy administration and evaluation. All that is required is a consensus of peers. The standardization of initial assessments, literacy and skills courses, teaching methodologies are all believed to contribute to predictable learning outcomes, that is, to programs that work.

Having prepared all of these educational panaceas, educators then embark on marketing programs . The educational programs seem great, but the 'consumer' adult is not always eager to participate. What seems to be overlooked, as it certainly was in the work of Frederick M. Taylor and his "scientific management" (Drucker, 1974), is that elusive, confounding and unpredictable *human factor*.

Although the teacher is dominant in most educative situations, the failure of the student is not usually attributed either to the teacher or to the school or institution, but rather is attributed to the *student's failure to conform* with prescribed standards of expectations and outcomes. It may even be construed as a potential failure to conform to later societal expectations. The label of school failure leaves a deep imprint. On the other hand, the label of success may be applied most frequently to the individual with the greatest accumulation of diplomas or degrees and few may bother to discover just how much meaning was accumulated or even if thinking occurs on a regular basis.

The fact that early education may be mandatory for children and later education may be mandatory for youths and adults to achieve careers, professions or to get a job, has made some degree of educational imposition accepted. We learn what we have to learn. Repeated use makes the learning entrenched. When previous learning is no longer useful, it gradually sinks from conscious memory. Dewey (1933) decried such superficial learning, and his words make me wonder how much of our own schooling was really learning?[2]

> Learning is not learning things, but the *meaning* of things. *Learning is learning to think*. (1933: 78,236)   (emphasis is mine)

In the two dominant teaching approaches, then, there resides arguments of philosophy and thus of values and meaning. Values of control and predictability struggle with values acknowledging human development and autonomy. Perhaps a deeper examination of learning itself will help us to find a more comfortable resting place in this dilemma and even to grasp what makes people want to learn and want to go on learning.

SOME UNIVERSAL ASPECTS OF LEARNING

It is interesting how traditional scientific research is seen by many as the only source of knowledge, despite the fact that quantitative research by its very nature is unable to explain unobservable human characteristics and is more adept at answering questions of 'why' than of 'how'. Since only a very small part of human experience is amenable to research by observation, scientists attempt to overcome this constraint by placing humans in contrived situations and controlling the possible variables for ease in studying behaviour. The results, like those from animal (Pavlov) and chicken studies (Skinner) are then extrapolated to the behaviour of unique individuals in the complexity of daily life situations.

The answers discovered from any research are primarily directed by the type(s) of questions asked. It is typical of quantitative research methodologies that experiments with controlled variables necessitate the limitation of aspects of real life. (For example, Taylor was interested only in the production aspects of factory work, not in the workers themselves.) Quantitative research can at best then, only deal with fragments of reality. One wonders what might be discovered if it were possible to study real life experiences?

There is skepticism about such a possibility. Merriam (1987) has noted: ". . . one theory to explain all of adult learning may never emerge." Similarly Brookfield (1986:25) in acknowledging the immense diversity of people and cultures remarks, ". . . a general theory of adult learning . . . holds little promise for successful completion".

Yet we must acknowledge that there are some qualities and characteristics of learning possessed in common by individuals everywhere. These require only reflection to expose their commonness. Thomas (1983) has listed some of these as "universal facts of learning":

- that learning is common to everyone at every age
- that learning is voluntary, a matter of personal choice
- that learning is cumulative
- that learning is what an individual does
- that learning is associated with most human activities & characteristics
- that learning outcomes cannot be predicted

From my own recent research, I would add two more (Barer-Stein, 1985):

- that we do not learn what we already know
- that learning is a sequential process of experiencing the unfamiliar

In later writing Thomas (1988:24) notes: "Current research into styles of learning is somewhat primitive, for the most part tending to be dominated by concerns for teaching."

The anthropologist, Kroeber, is cited by Montagu (1968:202) as describing the essence of culture as "learned behaviour socially transmitted over time as the paramount determinant of human behaviour." Montagu himself (1968:239) confirms learning as the essence of all cultures and suggests that the human ability to transcend what was learned is the basis for the uniquely human "potentiality for innovation, creativity, reorganization and change."

When we examine closely the thirty-six adult learning principles meticulously detailed by Brundage & Mackeracher (1980) we recognize most of these too, as being universal and probably applicable as well to youths and children with the greatest differences being caused by degree of life experience.

Griffin (1988) draws attention to universal human capabilities that are rarely considered by educators and which should be considered as enriching to any learning situation: the human relational capabilities, metaphorical or intuitive capabilities, as well as the spiritual and emotional ones, are often neglected in favor of emphasis on one's rational capabilities.

There are then, many universal aspects, qualities and capabilities common to all people everywhere that are associated with learning.

The importance of each of these and the use to which they will be put will be determined in large part by each person's 'cultural matrix' (Barer-Stein, 1987a; 1989). The 'cultural matrix' is that social origin which gives birth to the fundamental philosophies, values, beliefs, attitudes that direct our behaviours and colour our perceptions and feelings. We each view our own world through the framework of our own culture . Culture is the stuff of daily living.

INTRODUCING THE UNIVERSAL LEARNING PROCESS

Things become ordinary and habitual because they are assumed to be well-known and well-used. In fact, we usually overlook just *how* it is that something or someone came to be so familiar. We had to learn that familiarity. And it is only by peeling away the layers of accumulated familiarities and continually questioning how it is that something came to be what it is — that an underlying structure or process can be revealed.

In just such a reflective stance, I sought to understand more deeply the concept of culture itself and serendipitously discovered the emerging process of how an individual learns (Barer-Stein, 1985, 1989). Perhaps I should not have been so surprised, for we all know that each person inherits their racial tendencies and *learns* their culture (Montagu, 1968:339). The English Second Language (ESL) teacher who became the focus of my phenomenological[3] work had at one point in our dialogue remarked:

> I think there is a special quality about the mind, a willingness to move into a
> different way of seeing, a willingness to understand another point of view, at
> least to entertain it, to LISTEN. . .   (Barer-Stein, 1985)

MODEL OF THE UNIVERSAL LEARNING PROCESS*
FIGURE NO. 1: (EXPERIENCING THE UNFAMILIAR)

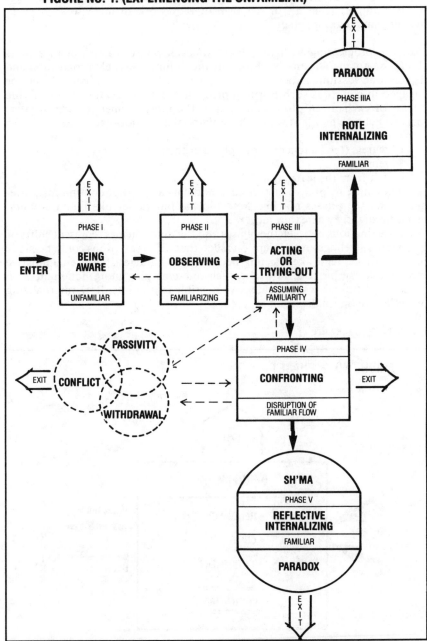

*© BARER-STEIN 1989

It is this "special quality of the mind" that I wish to appeal to now in describing the aspects of the learning process and hoping that each reader will insert examples from his or her own literacy work to increase its relevant meaning and make it personal.

Before progressing with the details of each phase, some overall aspects should be noted. This model shows the individual's possible progression and depicts one learning process. At any given moment an individual may be engaged in countless such learning processes and conceivably be in varying phases of each. Each phase and each of the inner themes (described later) represent choice points at which the individual may choose to:

1. progress
2. regress (return to a previous phase or theme)
3. remain
4. exit from the learning

It may even be helpful to picture this model as a spiral of continuous movement, and the phases not like solid blocks, but rather like liquid colours, blending slightly where they meet.

The distinctions between the phases and the inner themes represent shifts of behaviours, feelings and perceptions such that differentiations could be made between them. And like learning itself, these characteristics are cumulative throughout the process, now and then one emerging more dominant than others. The full process indicates two possible end-points: Rote Internalizing or Reflective Internalizing.

Phase I: Being Aware

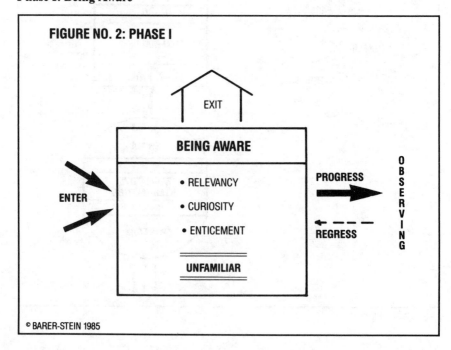

© BARER-STEIN 1985

Being Aware embodies a certain expectant stillness of anticipation. That cautious flicker of attention, no matter how brief or prolonged, is the opening door to a learning process. It signals that attention has been caught by something *unfamiliar*. Familiar things elicit only the nod of confirmation of their well-worn smoothness of familiarity, but the unfamiliar is a bump in that previous smoothness. One has to be aware of something first in order to note whether or not it is familiar, and this is accomplished by a superficial mode of thinking I have named as the *Reflective Pause* which includes:

- *collecting* of information
- *questioning* of what was collected
- *comparing* with previous knowledge
- *selecting*

That initial attentive flicker was lit from within the individual by three intertwining inner themes:

Relevancy: purpose and connectedness to the person

Curiosity: the individual's desire or need to know

Enticement: the bait: what the individual thinks s/he wants and
hopes to get, but without getting 'caught' or committed.

These intertwining themes of the first phase represent the individual's intertwining feelings. Relevancy and Curiosity emerge from within, but Enticement can be both internally or externally stimulated.

This means that no educator can demand or command these feelings. Nor does any person of any age learn to read and write merely for the sake of reading and writing: literacy and numeracy take on relevancy and importance to the degree that the individual can use them as tools to achieve other goals deemed personally important or valuable. Hence the success of literacy programs that embrace the stated needs either of individuals or of communities such as health care, running a business, developing and maintaining safe water supplies or the uniquely personal needs of letter writing, children's story reading and so on. People do not learn in groups, they learn as individuals, but that individual learning may be enhanced through group synergy. It is therefore pertinent to discover not only communal needs and desires, but also individual ones.

Attention is driven by Relevancy, Curiosity and Enticement, but it is also fuelled by identity and belonging. If 'everyone is doing it', it suddenly becomes important for the individual to do it too. This suggests then, that literacy goals need to be seen as valuable by a community's leaders and role models, and each person needs to perceive its value for themselves.

Phase II: Observing

The phase of observing generally represents an attitude of "just looking", with the willingness to extend attention. The two inner themes here are *sequential*:

1. *Spectator:* attentiveness, watchfulness
2. *Sightseer:* attentive focussing on a particular aspect

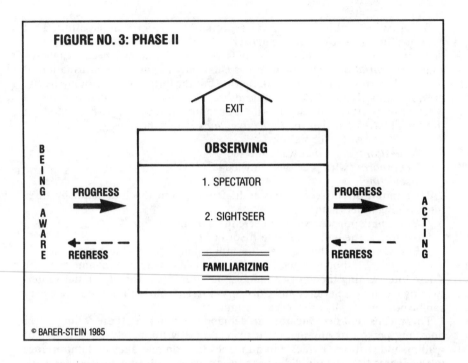

The individual shifting into the Observing phase still retains some distance from the interest, is non-committal, and is only 'participating' by offering attention.

The importance of this Observing phase in the learning process should not be overlooked. Recognizing that Awareness and Observing *must* precede taking part or trying out, will provide incentive for the teacher or tutor to provide many examples and aspects to be observed, and patience when individuals are reticent to take part. Stimulation to the Observers can be provided by openly encouraging *their collecting* of information, by soliciting *their questions* and concerns and by helping them to make *comparisons* with previous ways of knowing and doing. All of this requires time for reflection; the teacher must support and offer such reflective time.

Phase III: Acting or Trying Out

This phase now depicts the individual not only moving closer to the matter at hand, but also willingly taking part in it. Every feeling from the previous two phases intensifies, including more frequent and intensified application of the Reflective Pause. In this phase there are four *sequential* inner themes that depict feelings and behaviours:

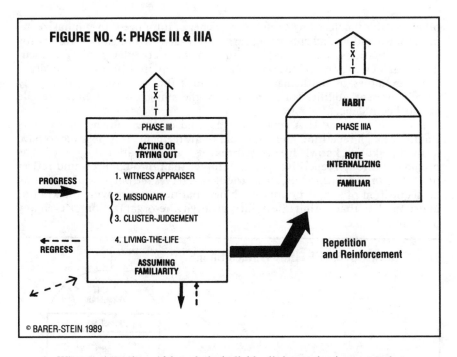

FIGURE NO. 4: PHASE III & IIIA

© BARER-STEIN 1989

1. *Witness-Appraiser:* Although the individual's increasing interest and confidence is still grounded in superficiality, (the Reflective Pause mode of
   thinking) the ability to observe and to do, breeds an inflated assuredness
   and the individual seems to glide into the energetic
2. *Missionary:* Emblazoned with the zeal to-do and to-give and above all to let
   everyone know about this newfound interest and/or skill
3. *Cluster-Judgement:* This is a perception closely associated with the Missionary behaviour and feelings that divides the world into the we-they:
   those who have or can do this thing and those who don't or can't. It is a
   judgemental sweeping up of individual differences into one indistinguish-
   able mass, with 'they' being somewhat inferior to 'we'
4. *Living-the-Life:* The feelings of Relevancy and Curiosity may now be
   shunted aside in favor of self-imagined Enticements and visions of skill
   and beliefs of knowledge that heighten still further the individual's participation and confidence.

Acting or Trying Out displays the willingness to take part, and an increasing
confidence and sense of belonging. The well-used Reflective Pause continues
to provide hasty and handy generalizations. The individual's sense of identity
and belonging is derived more from superficial acceptance than from any
rootedness in the past, responsibility for the present, or genuine commitment
for the future of this skill or knowledge.

This is a critical point for the literacy learner, unaware that the inevitable
facing of the difficulties and realities of reading, writing and numeracy await in
the unforseen real-life circumstances. Having learned so far to copy, to imitate
and to recite with teacher or peer support, the esteem shattering confrontation
of real-life situations may affirm earlier personal insecurities or the jeers of

others outside the 'learning circle'. The teacher or tutor needs to emphasize the need for expanding and enhancing current skills in order to gain flexibility for varying situations. Occasional exposure to more complex readings, documents, as well as ways of speaking and questioning in differing social situations, examples of mathematical calculations that are useful but slightly beyond present abilities all help to allay the smugness that may precede deflated confidence.

The shift to phase IIIA represents the kind of Internalizing that occurs simply through repetition and continual reinforcement. It is possible to have learned a skill or knowledge so well that it becomes habitual — but it has become so through repetitive imitation rather than through profound reflection. *Rote Internalization* requires little effort, serves the purpose of providing an acquisition of simplistic routine things, but does not provide the kind of understanding that permits flexibility, creativity, re-organization or even any profound change.

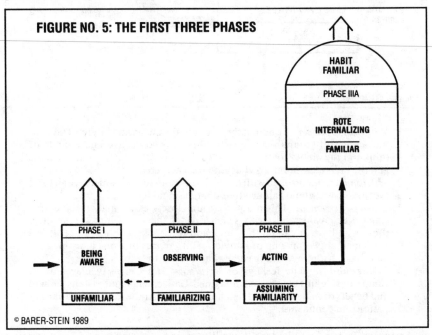

FIGURE NO. 5: THE FIRST THREE PHASES

© BARER-STEIN 1989

The first three phases are commonplace steps in any learning process and may well provide an aura of accomplishment for both educator and learner. What is crucial here is to recognise the superficiality of such learning derived from memory without any concern for meaning, implications, or possibilities. Those who are satisfied solely with *Rote Internalization* are satisfied with a mechanical way of thinking and doing. Throughout the teacher will hear phrases like: Is this how you want me to do it? Is this what you wanted me to say? There is a willingness to be told and shown and a willingness to copy, to fit in with others and to expect external support, guidance, approval and appraisal. There is little drive to exceed beyond what is expected, no wish to excel beyond one's peers. This is not to say that Rote Internalization does not serve a useful goal for some things — but not for all learning.

Phase IV: Confronting

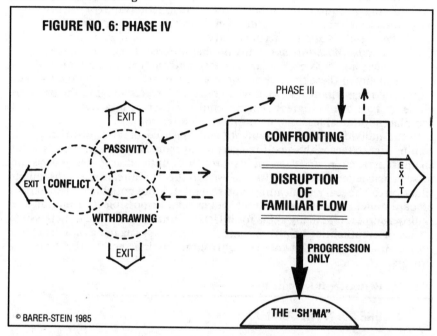

FIGURE NO. 6: PHASE IV

PHASE III

EXIT

PASSIVITY

EXIT | CONFLICT

WITHDRAWING

EXIT

CONFRONTING

DISRUPTION
OF
FAMILIAR FLOW

EXIT

PROGRESSION
ONLY

THE "SH'MA"

© BARER-STEIN 1985

It is unfortunate that the term 'confronting' so often has a negative connotation when in fact it really means coming face to face. Does its common negative connotation depict something of the discomfort we may feel on being really close to something and seeing it differently? We must keep in mind that the reaction to Confronting, whether negative or positive, depicts more about the person than it does about the object of confrontation.

If this looks like the most confusing part of the Learning Process, it is also the most confusing for the learner. The assumption of knowledge or skill now must give way to doubt. There may be a collision of value or belief systems, old assumptions may seem to be disproved, shock or trauma may force a re-evaluation of what had formerly been accepted or even commonplace. This *Disruption of the Familiar Flow* may occur for any of these reasons or simply because something or someone doesn't make sense.

Throughout this process, each movement indicates a choice and a decision. What do you do when the tools that worked before suddenly don't work anymore? The Reflective Pause is not profound enough, you thought you knew and now you don't, the skills don't even work. As the arrows in the model indicate, the individual can return to Phase II, can Exit from the Process altogether or can shift laterally into one of these three possibilities of behaviour and feelings or even an interplay of all three:

- to choose *Passivity* is to attempt to ignore the Confronting, or to meet and pass in such a way that expresses no apparent reaction, no overt change in behaviour;

- to choose to engage in *Conflict:* engaging in verbal or physical battle, including the subterfuges of distraction and/or surprise attacks in the hope of winning one's way through strategy to prove there really is *not* a differing reality;
- to choose *Withdrawal* usually implies a retreat from the source of anxiety and possibly fear, into oneself and one's past familiar world

In the end any of these three choices serve only to act as delaying tactics. The individual must still decide whether to retreat by regressing into the previous phase, to Exit or to progress. The unfamiliar closeness to a vivid reality jars complacency and at least momentarily rivets attention.

If the individual feels uncomfortable, confused or even disoriented on coming face to face with something perplexing, some assurance that this is not an unusual reaction, and that doubts, problems, unfamiliar things or ways can be seen as challenges are helpful, at least in theory. In reality, an unfamiliar situation can be scary, demeaning, and fearful. It is not possible for teachers to prepare students for all eventualities, but explaining possible information and skills resources, practicing skills for differing situations and creating possible scenes or eventualities help to initiate the learner in engaging in a reflective stance. It is also helpful to see Confronting as inherent to the Learning Process.

Phase V: Reflective Internalizing

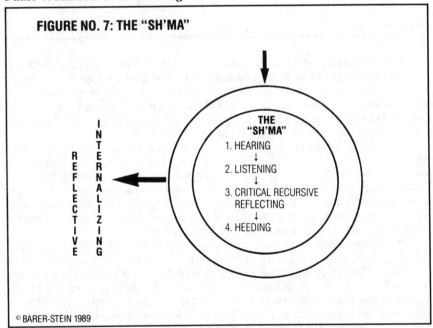

FIGURE NO. 7: THE "SH'MA"

THE "SH'MA"
1. HEARING
2. LISTENING
3. CRITICAL RECURSIVE REFLECTING
4. HEEDING

REFLECTIVE INTERNALIZING

© BARER-STEIN 1989

This final phase of the Learning Process also represents another choice possible to the individual in the Confronting phase. The movement directly from Confronting to Reflective Internalizing without the delaying of Passivity, Withdrawal or Conflict is characteristic of someone who:

— likely has had previous experience with the Sh'ma

— cannot be seen or described as 'average'

— recognizes that Understanding, Involving and Emphathizing, even when yielding disturbing or undesired knowledge, is nonetheless an *enhancement or expansion of what was previously understood*

But what is this Sh'ma? To move from phase four into Reflective Internalizing can only be achieved with the individual's asking: "How did this come to be? What is its meaning for me?" (Barer-Stein, 1988:83) Derived from the Hebrew word *shema* meaning 'to hear', this word is used here to encompass *four-fold sequential steps*: Hearing, Listening, Critical Recursive Reflecting, and Heeding:

1. *Hearing* represents the awareness and immediate recognition of what is heard. This is pressed forward by the intensity of Curiosity and Relevancy as well as the Enticement that resides in learning for the sake of learning

2. *Listening* represents the close attentiveness to a *dialogue* with the thing or individual, an opening of oneself to accept and consider and a willingness to 'see differently'

3. *Critical Recursive Reflecting* represents the analyzing and interpreting of possibilities and their possible meaning and place. This may involve imagining, visualizing, inferring, projecting and collecting and arranging of both Surface and Submerged Knowledge[4] in order to make sense and find meaning, returning again and again in reflection

4. *Heeding* represents the effortless embracing of the thing as a part of oneself and one's identity and behaviour.

Language has its limitations. In common psychology parlance, the notion of Internalizing connotes "the deepest and most personal level of social influence" (Musson & Rosenzweig, 1973:69) but I intend this term to include not only the personal derived from the social, but also *the profoundest critical and recursive reflecting on the meaning of these*. Such continual looping back of reflections probes deeper into sedimented layers of knowledge. The resulting Familiarity is directly derived from this personal effort that often involves also creativity, reorganization and ultimate change.

Finally, the *Paradox of Internalizing* (refers to both Rote and Reflective Internalizing), whether as a result of rote learning or of reflective learning, represents the familiarity defined in the truism: the better you know something, the less you are aware of knowing it. Such eventual familiarity is a necessary and useful part of the Learning Process. Imagine attempting to retain in consciousness every detail of what you learned in order to read and to write as well as you now do — and having to repeat these details! On the other hand, retaining some level of vigilance regarding past learning experiences enhances empathy for our own present and future learning and for that of others. Distinguishing which aspects can be productively submerged and which should be deliberately retained is important but very personal for each learner.

The trouble with this whole matter of learning is its familiarity. We assume that we understand what is familiar and we overlook the changes that occur over time, often with a subtlety that escapes notice. Each learner must maintain not only a vigilant awareness of the fact that learning is a process and not an act, but also that it is important to deliberately and persistently reapply the Learning Process to question presuppositions and well-worn assumptions.

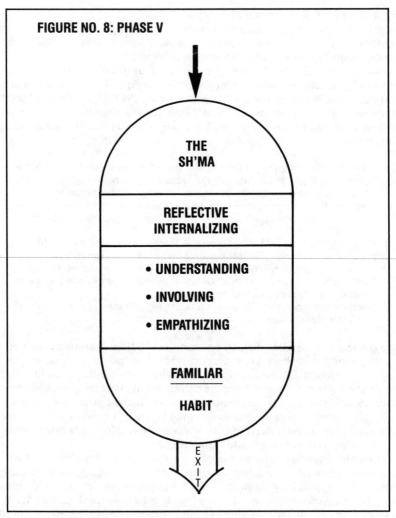

FIGURE NO. 8: PHASE V

THE
SH'MA

REFLECTIVE
INTERNALIZING

• UNDERSTANDING

• INVOLVING

• EMPATHIZING

FAMILIAR

HABIT

EXIT

The literacy and basic skills teacher can help to provide the impetus for further learning by provocative questioning that opens other doors of learning — but only a crack. Learning is not something that someone can either do *to* you or *for* you. Recognition that each individual shifts into sequential learning phases within their own personal time frames is important. Further, not everything is relevant to everyone. Providing opportunities for choices and encouraging suggestions from the learners enhances interest and participation. Just as the learner should be encouraged to question and to reflect on possibilities, so should the teacher. Finally, teacher as well as student must consciously practice yet another truism: that mistakes and problems are really just opportunities for imaginative creativity, The Sh'ma.

FURTHER IMPLICATIONS FOR LITERACY

Understanding a little more about how learning happens is important for the teacher and for the student because both are learners. It is not that learning is anything new, for we each have a lifetime of learning experiences; but a re-examination of assumptions often proves rewarding.

In the light of this refreshed understanding of the Process of Learning, let us re-examine those earlier nagging questions.

Illiteracy and innumeracy (Paulos, 1988) are global problems that will not disappear with the imposition of more programs or more intensive campaigns. Attempts to demystify words and numbers and bring them to the level of a mechanical function to be mastered or memorized is to deny the value of words and phrases as aesthetic literature (Eyford, 1975) and as depicting personal meaning and responsibility (Fulford, 1989). Words and numbers are more than mere things, they represent what each of us are as human beings. The learning of literacy and numeracy must envelop something of the wonder and excitement of what words and numbers can represent, encompass, and unfold — as well as communicate. UNESCO's Right to Learn (1985) cites the act of reading and writing as only one out of six rights. These other rights express the enhancement of the quality of humanness that develops from basic knowledge and skills: the questioning and analyzing, the imagining and creating, the reading about one's own world and participating in writing its history, the pursuit of further learning through access to educational resources and the ongoing development of these individual skills into collective ones. Are these the goals practically applied by each literacy tutor and each student?

Collaring adults and giving them the education that 'we' think they need may work if we are satisfied with mechanistic reactions and dependency relationships, the result of Rote Internalizing. At least some of the factors that encourages ongoing learning include a sense of achievement and relevancy, a curiosity satisfied and a growing confidence. We already know, for example, that adults who enjoy taking courses and classes are likely those who had such earlier enjoyable experiences. While learning is an individual process, it is always socially embedded. A learning process that helps to engage an individual towards and into Reflective Internalizing is satisfying if only because the individual has been consciously engaged in process as well as content. Content may vary, but recognizing that the Learning Process is universal provides some sense of predictability, familiarity and even a means of self assessment. Both routes to Internalization, whether Rote or Reflective, melt into well-worn habituation, except that the Reflective individual may be more likely to maintain a vigilance of the process and hence be more willing to learn again. One knows what to expect.

The rhetoric of 'empowerment' and 'self-directed learning' needs to be matched by an attitudinal shift by both teachers and students. The notion of learning expressed by UNESCO and the progression of learning implied in the Universal Learning Process requires not only a progression of attitudes, feelings and behaviours, but also the individual acceptance of increasing commitment and responsibility as well as interdependence and collaboration rather than dependence upon singular authority. Many teachers and tutors will have *to learn how to share* knowledge and skills and eventual understanding. This is very different from either imposing or simply providing knowledge and skills.

'Sharing' implies mutuality, reciprocation and dialogue. It also implies a sense of trust and equality that may not have existed in a learning situation previously.

Illiteracy and innumeracy are not really constrained within specific cultures or specific social classes. Much more is implied than can ever be stated within the limitations of literacy definition. Illiteracy is so insidious that it cannot be contained by either socioeconomic or cultural stratas. In a world where indigenous literature and arts studies are shunted in favour of the practicality of schooling for jobs; where politicians read speeches crafted by others and executives sign letters composed by more literate assistants; where factory technicians stumble over instruction manuals and workers cannot fill out forms or documents — *quantity* of programs and teachers for literacy and basic skills education will be meaningless unless relevancy and quality are considered a priority. But neither relevancy nor quality will be able to emerge until experts and professionals themselves are willing to learn how to relinquish their tenacious grasp on domination and the penchant for control.

A new frankness must emerge. When we talk about "motivating adults" are we really speaking about provoking them to learn what they want or need, or are we speaking (yet again) about imposing what we assume they need? Can we really insist on believing that the average person is content to be an object for manipulation or a victim of circumstances seemingly beyond control? (Labonte & Penfold, 1981) Responsibility for learning must be shared, beginning with the assumption that individuals are capable of exercising choice, decision and judgement as well as responsibility and commitment. Have we, as experts and professionals really tried to offer ourselves as resources and collaborators rather than authorities, judges and controllers? Instead of attempting *to act upon* others, can we gear our educational machinery *to acting with* others? People will already have been "reached" when we willingly share in designing projects, programs and campaigns for literacy or anything else.

"Better learning" can only occur when together with students, we redefine teacher/learner roles within the understanding of how frequently these roles may be interchanged in any learning process. "School memories" of teacher-dominated classes, anxiety-ridden assessments and tests and lock-step progression can only be submerged from memory by beginning with a shared approach and a sensitivity to the process of learning.

Which brings us to the most important point: we each must learn to make learning itself a conscious process so that we are aware of the possibility of progression and just exactly what that progression may entail. With every teacher and tutor, every administrator and planner and every student consciously aware of the Universal Learning Process, it will be impossible to think about literacy without thinking about learning.

*The author wishes to acknowledge the critical comments and suggestions of the following: James A. Draper, Om Shrivastava (India), Lorisa Stein, and Benja Chanpaibool (Thailand).

NOTES

1. Throughout this reflective discussion I will use single quotes to denote commonly-used words or phrases in the education field (jargon). In part, this is to draw attention to our mutual assumptions of understanding — and the need to re-examine them.
2. For a detailed comparison of Dewey's "educative process" and the Universal Learning Process, please see Barer-Stein, 1987.
3. In a work in progress, I am attempting to more clearly differentiate phenomenological research work from qualitative of which it is frequently considered to be a part. Essentially I do so by equating quantitative research with the Observing phase, qualitative with the Acting phase and phenomenological work with the final learning phase of Reflective Internalizing.
4. "Submerged Knowledge" is discussed in detail in Barer-Stein (1985) and compared with Polanyi (1974) notion of knowledge; Gadamer's (1975) "nothing disappears but everything is preserved"(p.12); Schutz's (1973:176) "restorable knowledge" and Berger & Luckman's (1967:67) "sedimented experiences" and "stock of knowledge".
5. See also Daloz (1987:140-150) for an exciting discussion on "Dialectic, the Dynamic for Transformation" which links closely with the Sh'ma.

REFERENCES

Readers familiar with my work will note an evolution and refinement in both expressions and diagrams from the 1985 works.

Barer-Stein, Thelma (1985a). "Partaking & Providing: Towards Understanding Lifelong Learning in the 80's" *Continuing Education Review Project*, Ontario Ministry of Education Colleges & Universities, Toronto.

Barer-Stein, Thelma (1985). "Learning as a Process of Experiencing Difference, unpublished doctoral (Ph.D.) thesis, University of Toronto, Ontario Institute for Studies in Education.

Barer-Stein, Thelma (1987). "On the Meaning of Learning Reflections with Dewey", in *The Canadian Journal for the Study of Adult Education*, Vol 1, No. 1, May

Barer-Stein, Thelma (1987a). "Learning as a Process of Experiencing the Unfamiliar" in *Studies in the Education of Adults*, (U.K.) Vol 19, No. 2.

Barer-Stein, Thelma (1989). "Experiencing the Unfamiliar: Matrix for Learning" in Beverly Cassara (ed) *Adult Education in Multicultural America*, N.Y.: Routledge (forthcoming).

Barer-Stein, Thelma (1988). "Experiencing the Unfamiliar: Culture Adaptation & Culture Shock as Aspects of a Process of Learning", in *Canadian Ethnic Studies*, Vol. 22, No. 2.

Berger, Peter & Luckman, Thomas (1966). The *Social Construction of Reality*, Garden City: Doubleday.

Bhola, Harlans (1985). "Without Literacy, Development Limps on One Leg", in *Adult Education & Development*, Bonn Germany: German Adult Education Association, No. 24.

Brookfield, Stephen (1986). *Understanding & Facilitating Adult Learning*. San Francisco: Jossey-Bass.

Brundage, Donald & Mackeracher, Dorothy (1980). *Adult Learning Principles and Their Application to Program Planning*, Toronto: Ministry of Education.

Boud, David & Griffin, Virginia (eds) (1987). *Appreciating Adults Learning*: From the Learner's Perspective, U.K.: Biddles Ltd.

Conti, Gary (1989). "Teaching Styles and the Adult Basic Educator" in Taylor and Draper (eds) *Adult Literacy Perspectives*, Toronto: Culture Concepts Inc.

Cross, K.P. & McCarten, A. (1981). *Adults as Learners*, San Francisco: Jossey-Bass.

Daloz, Laurent A (1987). *Effective Teaching & Mentoring: Realizing the Transformational Power of Adult Learning Experiences*, San-Francisco: Jossey-Bass.

Dewey, John (1933). *How We Think: A Restatement of the Relation of Reflective Thinking to the Educative Process*, Boston: D.C. Heath.

Drucker, Peter (1974). *Management: Tasks, Responsibilities & Practices*. NY: Harper & Row.

Elias, John & Merriam, Sharon (1984). *Philosophical Foundations of Adult Education*, Malabar Florida: Krieger.

Eyford, Glen (1975). "Artist as Educator: A Philosophical Examination of the Communicative Function in the Arts", Ph.D. thesis, University of Toronto, Ontario Institute for Studies in Education.

Fflug, Bernd (1985). "Now I have Learned the Sudanese word "MUSHARAKA" (= "participation") in *Adult Education & Development*, Bonn Germany: German Adult Education Association, No. 24.

Fulford, Robert (1989). In an address for the Jackson Memorial Lecture Series,Ontario Institute for Studies in Education, April 4.

Gadamer, Hans-George (1975). *Truth and Method*, N.Y.: The Seabury Press.

Griffin, Virginia (1988). "Holistic Learning & Teaching in Adult Education: Would you Play a One-String Guitar?" in Barer-Stein and Draper (eds) *The Craft of Teaching Adults*, Toronto: Culture Concepts Inc.

Hamilton, Mary & Barton, David (eds.) (1985). *Papers of the Association for Recurrent Education: Research & Practices in Adult Literacy*, Sheffield U.K.: Sheffield Polytechnic Department of Educational Management.

Hampden-Turner, Charles (1970). *Radical Man: The Process of Psycho-Social Development*, Cambridge Mass.: Schenkman.

Hancock, Trevor (1982). "Beyond Health Care: Creating a Healthy Future", *The Futurist*, Aug.

Labonté, Richard & Penfold, Susan (1981). "Canadian Perspectives in Health Promotion: a Critique", *Health Education*, April.

Mackeracher, Dorothy (1989). "Women & Basic Education", in Taylor and Draper (eds). *Adult Literacy Perspectives*, Toronto: Culture Concepts Inc.

Marton, Ference, Hounsell, Dai & Entwhistle, Noel (eds.) (1984). *The Experience of Learning*, Edinburgh: The Scottish Academic Press.

Merriam, Sharon (1987). "Adult Learning & Theory Building: A Review" in *Adult Education Quarterly* (U.S.A.) Vol. 37, No. 4.

Miller, John P. (1976). *Humanizing the Classroom*, N.Y.: Praeger Publishers.

Montagu, Ashley M. (1968). *Culture: Man's Adaptive Dimension*, N.Y.: Oxford University Press.

Musson, Paul & Rosenzweig, Mark R. (1973). *Psychology: An Introduction*, Toronto: D.C. Heath.

Osborne, M., Charnley, A. & Withnall, A. (1982). "Review of Existing Literature in Adult & Continuing Education, Vol. XI, *The Psychology of Adult Learning and Development*, Leicester U.K.: National Institute for Adult Continuing Education (NIACE).

Paulo, John Allne (1988). *Innumeracy: Mathematical Illiteracy & its Consequences*, N.Y.: Hill & Wang.

Peters, T.J. & Waterman, R.H. Jr. (1981). *In Search of Excellence: Lessons from America's Best Run Companies*, N.Y.: Warner Books.

Polanyi, Michael (1974). *Personal Knowledge*, Chicago: University of Chicago Press.

Rogers, Alan (1986). *Teaching Adults*, Milton Keynes, U.K.: Open University Press.

Schutz, Alfred & Luckman, Thomas (1961). *The Structure of the Life-World*, Tr. by Zaner & Englehard Jr. Evanston: Northwestern University Press.

Soljan, N.N., Golubovic, M. & Krajnc, A. (1985). *Adult Education in Yugoslav Society*, Zagreb, Yugoslavia: Andragogical Centre. (see especially pp. 68-73)

Thomas, Alan M. (1983). *Learning in Society: A Discussion Paper*, Canadian Commission for UNESCO, Occasional Paper No. 41.

Thomas, Alan M. (1988). *Principia Mathetica: A Study of the Politics of Learning*, Toronto: Department of Adult Education, Ontario Institute for Studies in Education. (Quoted with author's permission)

Thomas, Audrey (1989). "Definitions & Evolutions of the Literacy Concepts" in Taylor & Draper (eds) *Adult Literacy Perspectives*, Toronto: Culture Concepts Inc.

UNESCO (1985), The Right to Learn, Declaration of the Fourth UNESCO Conference on Adult Education, Paris, March 19-29.

CHAPTER 6:

From the Learners' Voice: Women's Experience of IL/Literacy

Jenny Horsman

When I listen to women in the Maritimes talk about their lives, I see a world not captured by the usual discourse on literacy. The traditional focus on the importance of motivation as the key to participation in literacy programs, and the assumption that literacy is a unitary set of "functional" skills, does not reveal the experience of literacy which people have in their daily lives. The specific experience of women and the way in which their lives interrelate with others is lost in these models. Women's lives are structured by and around men, children and societal institutions.

"WOMEN — THEIR LIVES AS THEY SEE THEM"

In 1986, I interviewed twenty Maritime women who were learners in literacy or upgrading programs to explore their experience of literacy. I also interviewed staff of these programs. The interviews were open ended because I wanted the women to talk about their lives as they saw them: how they perceived their literacy skills and the need of literacy; how they came to be in their program and what they sought by their involvement[1].

Most of the women I interviewed did not make a conscious choice to attend a literacy or upgrading program. Pressure from the social service agencies led them to become involved in upgrading. The women believed that if they did not take part in the literacy program they might become ineligible for benefits. As Marion said:

> they asked me if I wanted to further my education in case they ever stopped (welfare payments) . . . and I'd have to get a job . . . I'm glad I did take it, but I said (to them) you can't really cut (assistance) off, what would you do with the kids? But they made it sound like that. They should have put it another way, instead of trying to (pressure me) . . .

The women felt they had no 'choice' other than to attend the program, but they were glad to have learned of its existence and to be able to participate. For example Susan said: . . . "school was the last thing on my mind" . . . but once she had met the coordinator and begun to participate in the program she became interested and enthusiastic.

"REALITY vs 'ATTITUDE' and 'MOTIVATION' "

Some social service personnel expected undereducated women to willingly participate in these programs. Nevertheless, they also spoke about the need to 'motivate' them. The staff in the literacy programs appeared to be more aware of the constraints in the women's lives. They often described barriers to participation such as unemployment, poor housing, poor food, and lack of childcare. For many rural women the cost of fuel to drive to town to a class or the cost of childcare, if it can be found, make participation impossible. When tutors go to the learner's homes, children create distractions making it hard for the women to concentrate on the lesson. Although program staff appeared to recognize these realities they still spoke of women having a 'poor attitude' and 'lacking motivation.'

Women in relationships with men often experienced an additional barrier to upgrading. For these women their decision to participate in upgrading was strongly affected by their spouse, because of his hostility or support. Their participation did not just 'happen' because they became motivated and 'chose' to participate. As the coordinator of one program reported:

> Our women aren't married but the men in their lives aren't happy about them coming in here two or three times a week, and they'll use everything they possibly can (to stop them) . . .

I heard a horrifying number of accounts of violence, but many examples of pressure were far more subtle. Women were sometimes physically attacked by their husbands, men tampered with or would not allow use of the car. In some cases husbands refused to babysit to prevent women from getting to classes. Jill described her husband as saying:

> I really didn't want you to go on this course . . . but I didn't want to say no because then that would be pushing my ideas on you so I thought I'd let you try it and find out how hard it is.

The impact of this man's attitude is that he does not go out of his way to help with the childcare or household tasks in order to make taking the course easier.

Some women were cautious of challenging their partners' hostile attitudes to their learning. When they continued school in spite of the hostility it often threatened the relationship. One program coordinator described her own experience:

> . . . it was a major, major problem in my marriage that I wanted to be involved in Home and School. It was another major problem that I wanted to learn to sew and devote one evening a week to sewing classes . . . and then the big crunch I think was my wanting to write my GEDs,[2] that was one of the real bad things.

When she first planned to participate in these things her dream was:

> . . . for my husband to accompany me to a Home and School meeting, for my husband to have been willing to participate in the community club . . . I would have been in seventh heaven if . . . that could have been shared. . . .

Instead it became the disagreement around which her marriage broke down. As Rockhill has also observed, it is the very possibility of change through literacy, and education more broadly, that makes it such a threat for women, and makes some partners so hostile.[3]

A few men did of course encourage their partners to take part in classes. Some couples even took part in tutoring together, but few women had such supportive husbands as Pat:

> . . . that guy loved me and believed in me and see I was very lucky and blessed to have that man come in my life and he's the one that encouraged me to go to that school . . . 'You can do it', and am I ever glad he pushed me because I found that I can do it.

I did not include men in the study. But discussions with program workers suggest that the importance of the partner's support or opposition to participation in programs is unique to women.

DEFINING AND ASSESSING LITERACY LEVELS

Most of the women were enthusiastic about attending literacy class; their reasons for this were unexpected. When they spoke about their literacy skills there was little clarity about what they could not read or write or why they felt the need to go to an upgrading or literacy program. They did not report having trouble 'functioning' even when they were assessed as illiterate.

"Educators claim that it is possible to define those who are literate or 'functionally' illiterate and assess their literacy level. The achievement of grade eight in schooling or its equivalent, a measure set by UNESCO, is seen as the level below which a person is functionally illiterate. However, it is used to indicate more than a person's grade attainment. It is used to imply that people with less than grade eight have insufficient literacy to be able to function adequately in society. Each woman I interviewed tried to explain their grade level, saying that she had such and such a grade level, but was really at another grade level, or maybe not quite at that level in reading. It soon became clear that even identifying a grade level does not produce the clarity the definition promises.

Women who were identified as grade two or three reported a surprising breadth of items that they were able to read. Alternatively, women who were identified as grade eight or nine sometimes had difficulty reading basic material. There seemed to be a lack of fit between the way others described the women and their own reports of what they could and could not do. After each interviewee had spoken about the things she could and could not read I was unable to define whether she was 'literate' or 'functional.'

Mary was diagnosed as almost totally illiterate and described as being at grade two level. She gave the impression that she was able to read most things she needed to in her life. She told me she read the local newspaper regularly and had no trouble doing this. Mary reported that she had no trouble reading the guarantee when she a new steam iron and figuring out her rights about replacement, or reading the agreement for the purchase of her new fridge. When I asked her whether she had read the small print in the purchase agreement she assured me she had, and when I said that it sounded as if her reading was pretty good she resorted to her tutor for corroboration: "Like S--- told you . . . my reading's pretty good" . . . This contrasts with the coordinator's report of her reading level and the tutor's report of her work on the Laubach books'.

Her tutor implied that working from this elementary course book was not easy for Mary:

> We never do more than one lesson, sometimes we don't (even) do one lesson, if it's kind of difficult we sort of will stop half way and leave it 'til the next day.

Mary reported finding the books easy, and that she read them quickly.

The issue of Mary's true reading abilities is complicated by the contrast between what Mary feels she needs to read and write and what other people believe her needs to be. Although Mary tried very hard to oblige me by thinking of things she had trouble reading and things she might want to read when she improved her skills, she was unable to think of anything. She did not seem reluctant to be honest about the limits of her skills nor did she downplay her literacy need because of embarrassment. For anything I suggested that she might want to read she either said she could read it or did not want to read it.

From my discussion with Mary I did not sense that she felt any absence of literacy skill in her life. This may have been because her skills were objectively better than others judged them to be. It may have been that she as not identifying how improved literacy skills could affect her present life situation or contribute to long-term change. There appeared to be a gap between what others saw as 'functional' for her and what she identified as serving no purpose for her.

During our discussion about how she might use the skills she was learning, her tutor frequently mentioned 'functional' skills they had studied. Mary clearly did not identify them as useful to her, but the tutor continued to imply that they were functional for Mary. I am not criticizing the tutor for failing to identify what was 'functional' in Mary's life. I am suggesting that her approach is framed by the materials she has been taught to use and the language of literacy work.

> Interviewer: "So you read everything else and you can read all of that (the newspaper)? So there's not really many things that you've wanted to read and couldn't that has made you do this?
>
> Mary: No
>
> Int.: Nothing really that you've wished you read better, to able to read?
>
> Tutor: You learned to write a cheque
>
> Mary: Right
>
> Int.: You hadn't written a cheque before?
>
> Mary: No I never

When I asked Mary whether there were other things that she 'had to learn' or 'wanted to write' her tutor replied:

In these (Laubach books) there's a lot of things about day to day living, today's lesson, even though we didn't finish it, had a grocery list and different things like that, what else? We learned to write thank you notes.

But when I asked Mary if she wrote any of those things or had a bank account she said:

No, we have a bank account but it's not cheques, it's more or less a savings account.

Her tutor also seemed to think that letter writing at least might be a useful skill, but I didn't get that impression from Mary herself:

Tutor: When S--- was in Ontario he used to call

Mary: Right yes

Tutor: Then he came home too quickly. Do you remember when we were doing the letter and where you put the name and I said oh good now S--- gone you can write a letter, but he came home?

Int.: You would've written to him, would that be useful, or would you call him normally?

Mary: No like I told D--- he used to call me.

Int.: So you didn't really need the writing?

But before Mary could reply, her tutor said:

If he had stayed away longer . . . but he came home quicker than you thought.

Mary is seen by others as 'functionally' illiterate, but her reason for attending literacy class does not seem to carry out any 'functional' tasks. Labelling Mary as illiterate says little about how literacy skills operate in her life. Mary's case illustrates Rockhill's assertion that fixing literacy as a set of technical skills makes literacy as experienced in women's lives inaccessible to us[5]. The depiction of a dichotomy between literacy and illiteracy does not contribute to understanding the way in which different skills become important for different purposes at different times in ones' life.

When I asked women why they had chosen to participate in a literacy program, by asking about the skills they felt they lacked or hoped to acquire, their answers did not reveal the reasons, nor what difference improved literacy skills could make in their lives. For example, Mary's response to the question was:

I don't know . . . 'cos like people said, it's been a long time since I'm out of school . . .

and when I said:

But it doesn't sound like there's much you can't read that you need to?

She said there wasn't. When I tried to continue to probe, asking:

There's nothing you have to write, do you write things occasionally?

She replied:

No, not really Jenny.

"MEANING WAS MISSING FROM THEIR LIVES"
As the women talked, it was clear that they felt that meaning was missing from their lives. They talked in various ways about a 'lack' much more indefinable than literacy skills. They looked to participation in educational programs to alter their lives in some way, to provide meaning. As Susan said:

I don't know what I'm doing, my life has no meaning, other than getting up, looking after . . . (my child), going to school . . .

Jane also saw literacy class as a way of bringing some meaning into her life:

I was tired of just being in the house all the time, I'd lock my door, I was afraid of people, I was in the house for six years, I'd stay in the house all the time.

Even when she got work she still felt there was something missing:

You're shut off from the world if you're just bringing up a child and working and nothing else.

For Jane, the literacy class seems to have been important for the feeling of connection with others it offered her. She described the course as being 'like one family'.

Mary identified something lacking in her life, and even though it didn't seem to equate with lack of literacy, she was enthusiastic about the class because it did go some way towards addressing this 'need'. When I first asked what her life had been like she offered just one word: "boring." Later when I asked her what she did when she had finished her work she said "nothing." And when I tried to get her to expand on that "nothing" with the details of her every day tasks she said very slowly and resignedly: "Oh, not too much." Her only outing seemed to be a weekly walk to the store to do her food shopping, and her only visiters were members of her family. Life seemed to be concerned mainly with providing food and care for her family. It is not surprising that the literacy class was a high spot. Her tutor came two afternoons a week and they always stopped for tea and pie or cake and spent a lot of time chatting about their lives and their families. When I asked her what she got out of the lesson she commented on having "somebody to chat with, to talk to. . . "

I thought perhaps that what Mary really wanted was a social get together and that she liked the literacy class because this was the only way in which she had been offered any chance to interact outside the confines of her family life. When I asked this however, Mary was adamant that she would not have wanted a social gathering instead of literacy. When I asked her if she would have liked something that involved getting out and meeting people she said she would. When I asked her whether she would have preferred that she said very firmly:

> I wouldn't mind doing both as far as that goes.

I had a strong sense that for Mary, literacy class may be the only thing available to her to fill a 'gap' in her life. It is important that it fills the time:

> 'Well' I said 'it might give me something to do to occupy some time'

and provides social contact with another woman. Mary does not identify what she would use literacy for, and she does not appear to feel inadequate for not completing her schooling. But for her it seems studying literacy is significant.

Most of the women I interviewed had children, many of them were single parents. For many of the women, their only daily contact with another human being was with their child. Several of them spoke of their child as their own friend, and important in their lives. In spite of this, the women spoke often of wanting some free time away from their children. When they finally got it however they often had nothing to do. Marion described how impatiently she waited for the children's bedtime:

> I can't wait 'til bedtime, and then I'm bored. I usually just sit there . . . wishing there was something to do.

The children often provided a reason for participating in a course. In reply to my question: "If it weren't for the kids what would you do?" Marion said: "Work at a factory or somewhere."

Because of her children she might return to school: "If it wasn't for the kids I wouldn't, if I had to go to school I'd just say no."

For these women, education was of primary importance for the sake of obtaining qualifications in order to get a job. As Betsy said:

> I'll have a fighting chance against all these other people who have their grade 12 and college at least . . . I'm getting so that this GED course seems to be the only way out for a better job, you know a job period, I don't care if its a better job I just want a job.

Betsy has a husband, so although she would like a job paying a decent wage, even minimum wage will at least supplement the family income:

> It's just more or less to help me find a job, like a better paying job than $4 an hour. You know I'd settle for $5 an hour if I could get it. Like, well I know how to cook, I'm a cook and a waitress and they just pay minimum wage if you're lucky, and you know that can't support a family or anything . . .

Women who were single parents knew that without a job that paid more than minimum wage they knew they were trapped on welfare. Marion for example was clear that her alternatives were remaining on welfare "for the rest of my life", or achieving a "career" as no job paying minimum wage would allow her to support her two children alone. She has to believe that a career is attainable even though the barriers to this achievement and the general lack of jobs in the area make it unlikely.

One woman saw children as providing a break from the pattern of the work the women were engaged in and would otherwise have continued. After describing how she had to stop waitressing when her pregnancy became too obvious to avoid having some male clientele making fun of her, Linda said:

> I was glad though in a way to get out of waitressing. My Mum has been a waitress, seventeen or eighteen years, and its been hard on her. There's not much she can do now. If I can get a chance to better myself and do something I really want to do I'm going to take the chance.

Literacy was not taken on only for the sake of the children. There seemed to be a complicated interrelationship for some of the women between participating in education to improve themselves and thereby helping their children. Frieda said:

> I've got to have a grade 12 certificate, I'm going to do something I've always wanted to do . . . nursing, or nurse's aid, or assistant . . . but I want to be a nurse . . . I'm doing it for my children as well (as for myself).

Susan also said:

> I explain to her that I'm taking my reading, my upgrading for her, to help to improve myself for her and for myself too . . .

When I asked if she would want to take the course if it wasn't for her daughter, she said:

> No, not as much, cause I'd just say if you don't like me the way I am that's tough.

Some women also saw literacy as necessary to do things with their children, such as going to the zoo and reading the signs, or going to the museum. In this way the women saw themselves as able to help with their children's education:

> It would help me with her a lot more because if I could read stuff to her she'd understand it. I could bring it down to her level, it would be easier . . . (When we went to the zoo before) there were some words I didn't understand so how could I explain it to her? We could go to the park, we could get books and sit outside and read. Reading I think has a lot to do with life. If you can read and understand what you're reading I think you can do a lot with it.
> (Susan)

Susan wanted to be able to read to her child:

> There's an every day need for it. I read to my little girl and there's words that I don't understand and I put in a make believe word and she's going to catch on now.

Many of the mothers felt it was important to be able to read, not only to help their children to learn to read, but also because they felt they needed a role model to make them think reading is important.

The children become part of the women's dreams for the future, both because the women's own pursuit of literacy skills are focussed around how to help the child, and also the children themselves become the 'dream.' Their lives will be 'better', free of the pressures of survival, they will have the careers that the women themselves hope for but do not expect to achieve:

> . . . hoping they'll go through college and make something of their lives . . . I hope they can get a career . . . I'd encourage them if they want to go . . . if she says well I want to get married I'll say yes, but you can get married and have a career . . .

"INADEQUACIES OF TRADITIONAL FRAMEWORKS FOR LITERACY"

I have illustrated, with reference to the lives of a selected sample of Maritime women involved in literacy and upgrading classes, some of the inadequacies of traditional frameworks for literacy.

The complexity of literacy and illiteracy in women's lives is lost in frameworks for literacy which concentrate on motivation, and see illiteracy as a simple set of skills a woman needs to acquire in order to function adequately in society.

For the women I spoke with, attending a literacy program was not simply a matter of motivation. Whether they were able to attend or wished to attend was bound up with the relationships in their lives: social agencies required it of them; men were opposed to their attendance or supported them; and the needs of children might either provide a barrier to attendance or be the main focus for their desire to improve their literacy skills. The women did not attend literacy classes to learn 'functional' skills but sought to find meaning in their lives and often, to pursue a dream for their children's lives.

NOTES

1. The research was carried out for a doctoral thesis and is written up in full in Horsman (1988).
2. General Education Development, a set of examinations which offers a high school equivalency diploma.
3. This entire paper owes much to many discussions with Kathleen Rockhill and in particular to her article (1987).
4. Laubach Literacy of Canada is the Canadian affiliate of a U.S. based literacy organization oriented to eradicating illiteracy through the use of volunteers working on a one to one basis with a student. The volunteers are trained in the use of the programmed reading scheme produced by the organization. This organization is unusually strong in the Maritimes where the voluntary scheme has been integrated in to government initiatives on literacy.
5. Ibid.

REFERENCES

Horsman, J. M. (1988). *"Something in my mind besides the everyday": Il/literacy in the context of women's lives in Nova Scotia".* Unpublished doctoral dissertation, University of Toronto, Toronto.
Rockhill, K. (1987) Literacy as threat/desire: Longing to be SOMEBODY. In J. Gaskell & A. McLaren (Eds.), *Women and education. A Canadian perspective.* Calgary: Detselig.

PART VII
VARIABLES AND SETTINGS IN BASIC EDUCATION

The facilitation of learning is a highly complex activity involving individual personalities, the prevailing political and economic climate and various settings for the educational exchange. Little attention has been given to the importance of these variables in the field of adult literacy and basic education. This section traces the crucial influence of these various elements on practice and brings into focus strategies for increasing the effectiveness of learning. Issues such as the emergence and modification of women's basic educational programs, the role of basic skills in a changing economy and administrative concerns are highlighted. Also discussed in this section are examples of diverse practice settings such as prisons, the workplace, non-traditional institutions and the community at large. Together these variables and settings help to influence the nature and form of basic education.

One of the major impacts on adult education in the 80's has been the status of women. MacKeracher provides the reader with a transformative solution to the problems faced by under-educated women. She examines the relationship between women and basic education from the perspective of dilemmas inherent in the definitions of literacy and the functions of related educational opportunities. As well she focuses on the relationship of women and girls to the formal education system and the meaning of literacy in their day-to-day lives. Threaded through her chapter is the message that there is a difference between 'more' and 'better' basic education for women.

Rubenson provides an analytical framework as a vehicle for examining the role of basic education in a changing economy. His analysis begins with a discussion of the conflicting perspectives on the relationship between education and the economy. He then focuses on the educational implications of new technology and alternative employment strategies and further examines basic education and public policy in the framework of social justice. Rubenson concludes that remedial education could be regarded as a fundamental right based on a democratic interpretation of equality.

Most adult educators would agree that institutional basic education programs could benefit from administrative and organizational improvements. Rachlis describes three issues of administrative concern for adult literacy and basic education programs: resources and staff, clientele and content. His discussion focuses on accessibility, interagency co-operation, curriculum support, and evaluation. He makes the point that improvements in these areas will increase the growth of basic education and help ensure that the field of practice is viewed as a professional activity.

*Adult education and related literacy programs have a firm foundation in prisons throughout Canada as **Isabelle** points out. In correctional institutions adult education is no longer defined only in terms of basic literacy. Programs such as distance learning and life skills are helping inmates to become more employable and acquire acceptable social skills. **Isabelle** mentions the importance of individualization and self-paced learner programs, providing some interesting accounts of inmates who have become literacy tutors.*

*Recently the hidden problem of adult illiteracy in the workplace has come to the public's attention. **Chang** examines three basic perspectives in workplace literacy. She describes the relationship between illiteracy and unemployment, and between education and employment, as well as the necessity to incorporate occupational literacy skills instruction in ABE curriculum. Through a comprehensive treatment of the literature **Chang** argues that workplace literacy instruction must be tailored to individuals or to occupational groupings.*

***Pearpoint** discusses the various shifts that are effecting the present form and nature of literacy education. He describes new partnerships with delivery agencies, changes in terminology, and new frontiers for basic learning such as the home and industry. In addition, successful and innovative programs like HELP, Independent Studies, Beat the Street and Learning in the Workplace are presented with a focus towards differing needs of learners.*

*Another setting for the educational exchange is the community. **Shuttleworth** describes a successful community development process that has provided learning opportunities enhancing the growth of citizens of all ages. He provides an integrated model of action consisting of research, planning and development. He focuses on the different services and corporate partnerships that have responded to a variety of community needs. Highlighted are citizens' needs for basic literacy and numeracy, English language instruction, skill training and employment opportunities.*

CHAPTER 1:

Women and Literacy

Dorothy MacKeracher

This essay examines the relationship between women and basic education from the perspective of dilemmas inherent in the definitions of basic education (especially literacy) and the functions of related educational opportunities, the relationship of women and girls to the formal education system, and the meaning of literacy in the day-to-day lives of women. The terms "literacy" and "basic education" are used interchangeably throughout the essay although basic education is acknowledged to include skills in computing, learning, earning, and managing the basic tasks of living, as well as skills in literacy.

WOMEN AND THE DEFINITION OF LITERACY

Any definition of basic education should include, or at least imply, a description of the functions of literacy. The nature of any definition will affect how literacy is assessed and reported, and what public policies and educational programs are developed to address literacy concerns. Many definitions are possible; not all are used. We will consider three types of definitions in relation to women.

School-related Literacy

Definitions which equate literacy with the completion of a minimum number of years of schooling are the most commonly used by those in authority. The relevant data are easy to obtain and report. In Canada, individuals are defined as basically literate if they have completed more than grade 4 in school and as functionally literate if they have completed more than grade 8. Using these definitions, men and women are equally likely to be defined as being not literate: approximately 1 per cent of men and women between 20 and 34 years and 7 per cent of those 35 years and over have not completed more than grade 4 in school; and approximately 7 per cent of men and women 20 to 34 years and 32 per cent of those 35 years and over have not completed more than grade 8 (Statistics Canada, 1984).

The functions of literacy implied in a school-related definition are unclear. By the end of grade 4, individuals may have learned some basic skills, and by the end of grade 8, may have consolidated these skills; but without constant use, such skills are likely to deteriorate over time (Stock, 1981). This definition implies that the non-literate are under-schooled and that literacy problems can be solved by the extensive and intensive application of more (i.e., remedial) schooling.

Occupation-related Literacy

A related definition of literacy, one which is equally easy to describe statistically, is to equate functional literacy with the completion of the requisite educational background for entry into occupational training programs. Using this definition, literacy is differentiated and specified by occupation. Training programs for some blue-collar occupations, which are traditionally male-dominated, can be entered with a grade 8 education; training for some occupations in health and clerical sectors, which are traditionally female-dominated, require a minimum of grade 10. Among men, 7 per cent of those 20 to 34 years and 32 per cent of those 35 years and over would be defined as being not literate using this definition; among women, 17 per cent of those 20 to 34 years and 48 per cent of those 35 years and over would be similarly defined (Statistics Canada, 1984). Most men and women are trained and employed in occupations which require grade 12 or higher as a minimum entry level. However, the problems for women are exacerbated by:

- women continue to seek entry to, and girls to aspire to, traditional female-dominated occupations (Ellis & Sayer, 1986; Boothby, 1986);
- blue-collar workers, mostly men, tend to be advanced to higher skill levels through on-the-job training programs, paid for by employers, which require no prior educational achievement (Boothby, 1986; Devereaux, 1985);
- health and clerical workers, mostly women, tend to be advanced through promotion to supervisory roles rather than through training programs designed to increase skill levels (Boothby, 1986); and
- women attempting to enter male-dominated occupations are often harassed by employers, employees, other trainees and unions, and do not benefit from employer-paid, on-the-job training to the same extent as men (Boothby, 1986; Deereaux, 1985).

The use of an occupation-related definition of literacy poses a major problem. The use of educational prerequisites for occupational training appears to be somewhat arbitrary. There are no clearly discernible reasons for accepting grade 8 for some occupations but requiring grade 10 or 12 for others. Specific occupational groups rarely define the general knowledge and skills an entrant should have learned as background education. Such definitions might help elementary and secondary schools modify their curricula to prepare both girls and boys for entry into occupational training programs as early as possible.

Behaviour-related Literacy

A behavioural definition of literacy would describe the tasks an individual must perform competently and independently on a regular basis as an adult. For example, the U.S. Office of Education has defined literacy as "the ability to hold a decent job, to support self and family, and to lead a life of dignity and pride" (MacKeracher, 1979, p. 3). To fully understand the extent of literacy using this definition, we would need to test the capabilities of a representative sample of the population. The Southam literacy survey assessed the extent to which Canadians are able to read (Southam News, 1987) but not their ability to hold a job or support a family. Data on employment, annual income, and poverty levels could be used in combination with educational levels to predict the level of non-literacy. Using any combination of such factors, women are more likely than men to be defined as non-literate.

Women with less than grade 9 education earn an average income equivalent to 59 per cent of the average income of men at the same educational level. In fact, women have to complete a postsecondary certificate to earn as much as men with less than grade 9 education (Statistics Canada, 1985). Approximately 45 per cent of families headed by a woman, but only 10 per cent of families headed by a man, have incomes below the poverty line. Twenty per cent of families headed by an under-educated adult were living below the poverty line (Statistics Canada, 1985; National Council of Welfare, 1985). Participation in the labour force is increasing for all groups of women but most slowly for the women with the least education. Less than 27 per cent of women, but 58 per cent of men, with less than grade 9 education participate in the labour force. Assessments of literacy using a behavioural definition indicate that women must have considerably more than grade 8 to be able to find and hold a decent job which will provide enough income to support self and family.

A redefinition of literacy as the ability to lead a life of dignity and pride in spite of chronic unemployment, discrimination in training and employment policies and practices, reduced earning power, and differential wages might change the nature of remedial basic education programs. Our definitions of literacy, and hence of non-literacy, are inadequate. We have not fully defined the functions and purposes of basic education in terms suitable to our post-industrial, technological society. Defining literacy as an abstract quality attained through participation in some quantity of schooling will no longer do. We need to be able to define literacy in terms of how one uses the skills of basic education and what purposes can be achieved through their use. In home and work settings, literacy skills are not necessarily engaged in for their own sake, as frequently happens in schools, but to accomplish goals related to daily living.

WOMEN AND THE EDUCATION SYSTEM

The education system appears to be designed to hold girls and women, boys and men in different retention patterns. Girls are often allowed to "pass through" the system unchallenged by the need to learn the skills required in a rapidly changing society (deCoito, 1984, Ellis & Sayer, 1986). Ellis and Sayer (1986) also indicate that girls are more likely than boys to aspire to careers which do not require advanced education.

At the other end of the system, when individuals re-enter educational institutions for occupational training, women are more likely than men to be directed toward non-skill, general education programs (academic equivalency, language skills, job readiness, work adjustment, or occupational orientation programs), while men are more likely to be directed toward skill training programs (occupational preparation and apprenticeship programs).

Boothby (1986), Herring and LaFountaine (1986), and deCoito (1984) all report that women are less likely than men to be admitted to industrial and institutional training programs in general, and to skill training and apprenticeship programs in particular. A disproportionate number of women at all levels of educational attainment, are registered in non-skill institutional programs (Boothby, 1986).

There are a number of factors which affect this distribution. First, women tend to request admission to female-dominated occupations which require higher levels of general, preparatory education. Of the female-dominated occupational courses to which women seek admission, only five have large concentrations of trainees with less than grade 9 education: hairdressing, power sewing, garment making/repairing, merchandising, and commercial cooking. Of the male-dominated occupational courses to which men seek admission, fifteen have large concentrations of trainees with less than grade 9 education. These courses are in machining, construction trades, fabricating, assembling and repairing, transport equipment operation, horticulture, agriculture, and processing occupations (Boothby, 1986; MacKeracher, 1979).

Another factor stems from the fact that, among those 25 years and over, women are less likely than men to have completed some postsecondary education or a vocational certificate (Statistics Canada, 1984). In the past, women have tended to complete the basic education programs which provided general background rather than specific occupational preparation and to not go on to postsecondary education. This trend is disappearing fortunately (Statistics Canada, 1984), but even among the young women registered in institutional training programs, a disproportionate number are in non-skill, general education programs (Boothby, 1986).

There appears to be a set of forces acting within the total education system which encourages, even directs, women to complete more general education than men, to not seek careers which require advanced education, and to begin occupational specialization at a later stage in their development. We need more information about these forces if we are to change programs for women.

WOMEN AND THE MEANING OF LITERACY

Definitions of literacy rarely describe the meaning of literacy in terms of either the social meanings assigned to it by society or the personal meanings derived from the experience of being literate. Three metaphors have recently been proposed to describe the meaning of literacy: as adaptation, as power, and as a state of grace (Scribner, 1984). This section will examine the relationship between women and literacy using these three metaphors and two more: as the use of written language and as the ability to create and share meanings derived from personal experience.

Literacy as the Use of Written Language

In the literacy-as-the-use-of-written-language metaphor, the literate person has skills in reading, writing, spelling, grammar, punctuation, vocabulary, composition, and comprehension. Composition includes reproductive activities such as paraphrasing and summarizing, and productive activities such as creative writing; comprehension, the reproductive activities of analysis and the productive activities of synthesis. When postsecondary educators complain about the "illiteracy of students", they are referring to this metaphor.

Virginia Woolf, in *A Room of One's Own* (1929), discusses some of the reasons why women are more likely than men to need remedial help in learning these skills, particularly in composition. Her discussion traces the development of women as the topic discussed in, and the creators of, literary works. She concludes that, for too long, women were kept in a state of penury and subservience to their husbands and fathers, without full access to the world beyond their homes. The ideas they dared to express in public were ridiculed, not because of the quality of the ideas, because the ideas came from women. As a result, women did not write much, and when they did, they often altered their values in deference to the opinions of existing authority figures. Woolf writes convincingly that the freedom to write and publish is the beginning of "the freedom of the mind" (Woolf, 1929, p.61). Her conclusion is that, with full access to educational opportunities and exposure to life in all its variations, with financial independence and the locked privacy of one's own room, women would gradually learn the literacy skills required to use written language creatively, with each generation building on the work of those who had gone before.

> Intellectual freedom depends upon material things. Poetry depends upon intellectual freedom. And women have always been poor, not for two hundred years merely, but from the beginning of time. Women have had less intellectual freedom than the sons of Athenian slaves. Women, then have not had a dog's chance of writing poetry (Woolf, 1929, pp.101).

Literacy as Adaptation

In the literacy-as-adaptation metaphor, literacy skills are viewed as essential components in the survival, maintenance, and growth of the individual both alone and within various social roles and groups. In the previous metaphor, we see that women need reading and writing skills. The literacy-as-adaptation metaphor implies that women need survival skills in such areas as communicating (giving and receiving information), problem solving (inquiring into the conditions which affect living), and decision making (choosing between available alternatives); plus skills in performing traditional roles as nurturer and maintainer of the family unit such as preventing accidents and disease, purchasing and using food, clothing and equipment, parenting, exercising legal and moral rights and responsibilities, creating and maintaining formal and informal interpersonal relationships, and so on. Further, an increasing number of women also need skills in performing not-so-traditional roles as providers and protectors of the family unit including specialized skills for working in a selected occupational field and general skills related to the work ethic, managing time and money, and so on; and survival skills in balancing all tasks, roles and groups while maintaining optimal stress and work overload levels.

If literacy is a function of schooling, then we should find the skills of this metaphor, and the previous one, included in the school curriculum either explicitly or implicitly. An examination of the elementary curriculum indicates that written language and basic survival skills (communicating, problem solving, decision making) form the bulk of the compulsory curriculum and that traditional role-related skills (both female and male) are given cursory attention in some schools (cf., MacKeracher & Jantzi, 1985). The secondary curriculum continues to provide opportunities to learn written language and basic survival skills while some role-related and specific work skills may be learned in elective courses. Through its policies and practices, the secondary school also teaches general work-related skills and attitudes such as promptness, obedience to authority, acceptance of extrinsic rewards, and the ethic that hard work is necessary for success.

One can conclude that the school system places a high value on written language skills, basic survival skills and some general skills related to labour force participation, and a low value on the skills related to nurturing and maintaining families and to working in specific occupations. That is, schools are generally preparing girls for survival and the non-traditional roles of providing for the family unit through work, but not for the traditional roles of women in the home.

Within society, there is an unspoken assumption that women do not need to be taught the skills of wife, mother and homemaker through the formal education system (MacKeracher, 1979). These skills are non-productive in the sense that they do not result in products for consumption outside the family unit (Cebotarev, 1986). They are learned largely through role-modelling, a process which does not require the use of written literacy.

The literacy-as-adaptation metaphor presents women with a basic conflict. The compulsory formal school curriculum rarely includes preparation for adaptive roles which are traditionally female, but does include preparation for some aspects of adaptive roles which are traditionally male. Women who remain in, or re-enter, the education system are being prepared to enter and succeed in the world of work; but that world, through discriminatory practices, may not encourage women's participation or success. Men do not experience the same conflict: the education system prepares them for traditionally male roles and the world of work offers them encouragement and opportunities to participate and succeed.

Given current trends toward more single-parent families and women's increasing participation in the labour force, girls and women should receive training in all adaptation skills. Under such a scheme, women would need to receive twice as much educational preparation as men, thus increasing the probability that they would be held even longer in preparatory education.

Literacy as Power

The literacy-as-power metaphor encompasses at least three different interpretations. First, literacy skills help individuals develop feelings of autonomy in the sense that literate persons have better alternatives for finding the information they need without having to rely on others. Those who cannot read or write usually find they cannot function alone and require others to read to them or write for them. If the persons on whom they depend are not available, they may feel helpless or powerless. Those who are not literate often express the desire to never have to feel humiliated or dependent again (MacKeracher, 1979). At the same time, they may be very adept at using oral literacy skills and at hiding their lack of written literacy skills from others (Bernstein, 1980). They may experience excessive stress in trying to maintain this facade and, in addition to feeling powerless, may draw back from others to avoid discovery.

Second, literacy skills empower individuals in the management of information. Persons who cannot read or write may be dependent on others to tell them what selected information means. They may express the desire to never be deceived again, to never be placed in a position in which someone can take advantage of them (Watson, 1985).

Third, in a largely literate society, a person who cannot read or write may not be able to participate in communal activities on the same basis as others. They may not have the vocabulary to share and discuss their own thoughts and feelings. They may feel alienated from the larger community because they cannot share equally in cultural, social and political activities; they may feel like second-class, powerless citizens (Watson, 1985).

To survive in a literate society, non-literate persons usually develop a network of contacts who can provide the support necessary to live without written language — children to read formal notices from those in authority, neighbours to provide information about daily life, a spouse to share the mail (Bernstein, 1980). Women have a tendency to be more skilled than men in developing such networks. The non-literate woman, therefore, is more likely than her male counterpart to be able to function without literacy skills and less likely to enroll in literacy programs; but also more likely to become powerless if her support network fails. A woman who cannot read or write may survive many years without needing to become literate; but life's unavoidable transitions — children growing up and leaving home, neighbours moving away, a spouse dying — may eventually lead to unmanageable situations. A non-literate woman may become increasingly isolated at she ages; and as more women leave the home to participate in the labour force, non-literate young women still in the home may have fewer persons available to provide literacy support on a daily basis. For these reasons, non-literacy among women of all age groups should never be dismissed as negligible.

The literacy-as-power metaphor also provides women with a dilemma. If the woman does enter a literacy program, her increasing skills in using written language may lead to inevitable changes in her support network (Bernstein, 1980). Relationships based on dependency may change as the newly-literate woman strikes out on her own. The woman may experience more stress in the face of her changing relationships than she ever experienced as a non-literate. Further, literacy for women is counter-productive if it simply reinforces traditional roles at a time when women are seeking to participate in their communities and share in the power through both paid employment and leadership roles (Fordham, 1983).

Literacy as a State of Grace

In the literacy-as-a-state-of-grace metaphor, literacy skills confer on individuals special virtues through their knowledge about the content and methods of the arts, sciences and humanities. As with the other metaphors, this one presents women with a two-edged sword.

In traditional society, a woman who was in a "state of grace" was skilled in using non-verbal and oral traditions to nurture and maintain her family unit and to express herself through symbolic modes of communicating such as art, myth, ritual, and crafts (Callaway, 1981). The essential knowledge relevant to this state of grace was passed on from woman to woman, mother to daughter, in close-knit social networks or learned through role-modelling. Neither of these processes requires written literacy. To maintain a state of grace in a changing society, a woman was often called on to develop skills using written literacy to provide for and protect her family unit and to express herself through literate modes of communicating such as letters, reports, policies, and certificates. In modern society, a woman is expected to be able to use both forms of literacy, an extra burden for women who do not read or write at all. In addition, women will need to learn to communicate through computerized modes to keep pace with technological advances.

The change from a traditional to a modern society began in the nineteenth century when women entered those areas of paid work which were considered suitable for them: the care and nurturing of sick persons through nursing, the training and guidance of young persons through teaching, the maintenance of the home through domestic science, and the recording of socioeconomic information through clerical work. As women became more skilled in this paid work and the literate forms of communicating, they began to write "how-to" books about these activities so that all women could become more skilled in similar, but voluntary, work at home. As a result, women were called on to maintain their state of grace within society by becoming literate enough to read what was being written for their betterment (Ehrenreich & English, 1979) and by training in occupations in nursing, teaching, homemaking (service), and clerical sectors. As these areas of endeavour acquired legitimacy, men gradually took over the writing of some of these books, thereby rendering the advice given largely irrelevant to women.

If the schools were to promote the literacy-as-a-state-of-grace metaphor, we should find girls and women learning to communicate through symbolic and computerized models, oral and literate traditions. Few schools have a curriculum to routinely do this.

Literacy as the Creation of Personal Meaning
In the literacy-as-the-creation-of-personal-meaning metaphor, literacy skills allow the individual to go beyond passive reading and reproductive writing to actively producing and sharing meanings derived from personal experiences. The skills required for this type of literacy are rarely taught, directly or indirectly in schools. To be able to create meanings from personal experiences, individuals must be able to think reflectively about their own life experiences, to ask questions about these experiences which will lead to the discovery of patterns in action and thought, and to conceptualize and name these patterns. To be able to share the meanings thus created, individuals must be able to disclose their ideas through dialogue with others or creative writing.

This metaphor not only provides a dilemma for women, it also discloses a fundamental problem. Traditional divisions of power and labour have resulted in the creation of a widely-accepted world view based on the experiences of men (Smith, 1978; Sherman & Beck, 1979). Being a receiver of knowledge is more congruent with the traditional roles of women than being a producer of knowledge, and the knowledge women have traditionally received has been grounded in a male-defined world view. "Women constitute an enormous, historically submerged group of people, deprived of the power to conceptualize, to name, and to categorize [their own] reality" (Sherman & Beck, 1979, p.4). The right to say and write about "how it is" is a characteristic of the male world. This world defines and gives meaning to the behaviour of both men and women; women judge and are judged by criteria created by and for men (Callaway, 1981). Throughout history, women have acquiesced to this version of reality through silence (Belenky et al., 1986) Woolf (1929), writing about the history of women, states:

> All these infinitely obscure lives [of women] remain unrecorded. . . . [I] went on in thought through the streets of London feeling in imagination the pressure of dumbness, the accumulation of unrecorded life, whether from the women at the street corners. . . or from the violet-sellers and match-sellers and old crones stationed under doorways (Woolf, 1929, p.85).

The reliability and validity of male-created meanings is legitimized through written modes of communicating which form the basis of acknowledged literacy. If a woman cannot read, understand or agree with writings grounded in the male-defined reality, then she may be judged to be illiterate, ignorant (dumb), incompetent, or silly. The lack of this form of literacy may be a major cause of women's excessive presence in academic equivalency programs.

It is not just that women have failed to "speak their minds", but that they have tended to use male-created meanings to define their reality before they spoke. As a result they often conveyed a sense of uncertainty, a lack of conviction about what they said. Women who have learned to re-examine and re-name the meanings within their own experience find they are able to give voice to their ideas with certainty about the reliability and validity of those ideas.

Literacy programs which assist the "muted minorities", including women, to reclaim and name their personal and collective experiences have been very successful. Such programs owe much to the work of Freire (1973). Exemplary programs for women are described by Corkery (1986), Barndt (n.d.), Arnold and Burke (1983), deChungara (1979), and Mezirow (1978), among others. As participants in programs of this type, women who were previously silent find they have something to talk and write about. Women who are not literate find they have something to learn which is grounded in their own reality, and through their own writings, something to read which is relevant to them.

In the male-dominant world view, procedures for governing are based on methods which bring order to the concerns of citizens by organizing those concerns into public issues for administrative purposes. "Issues are not identified as they become significant in the experience of those who live them but, rather, as they become relevant to administrators" (Callaway, 1981, p.40). In a CBC radio program in 1986, Flora Macdonald, then Minister responsible for the Employment and Immigration, commented that if literacy was not a *public* issue, then it was not an issue and nothing could be done about it.

Women who are not literate need to develop the literacy skills related to the literacy-as-the-creation-of-personal-meaning metaphor in order to make their concerns public issues. The paradox and dilemma are that, in so doing, they will become literate and negate the need for literacy programs. The programs, therefore, should focus, not on literacy as such, but primarily on the developmental concerns of women. The literacy skills related to this metaphor are both a means and an end: as the means for generating the issues relevant to women for public discussion and further action, and in the end, the generation of literate (and more literate) women.

CONCLUSION

Academic equivalency programs, which essentially provide for the remedial application of *more* basic education, may prepare women for occupational training and participation in the male-dominant world of work but do not solve the problem of "literacy for women". Programs which allow women to explore their own experience, make sense of that experience, and promote this "sense" into personal concerns and public issues can be best understood, not as remedial education, but as *transformative participation in better basic education*. Participation in such programs leads to personal, family and community development.

A further examination of the meanings of literacy which arise from the literacy-as-the-creation-of-personal-meaning metaphor might provide us with a more coherent definition of literacy and, by implication, of the functions and goals of basic education; and might offer a means for examining the relationship between girls and women and the education system. Clearly this metaphor can be extended to all women, not just those who cannot read or write, and can form the basis for learning programs throughout life.

REFERENCES

Arnold, R. & Burke, B. (1983). *A popular education handbook.* Toronto: OISE Press and CUSO-Development Education.

Barndt, D. (n.d.) *Just getting there.* Toronto: International Council for Adult Education.

Belenky, M. F., Clinchy, B. M., Goldberger, N. R. & Tarule, J. M. (1986). *Women's ways of knowing.* New York: Basic Books, Inc.

Bell, J. & Burnaby B. (1984). *A handbook for ESL literacy.* Toronto: OISE Press.

Bernstein, J. (1980). *People, words and change: Literacy volunteer handbook.* Ottawa, Algonquin College of Applied Arts and Technology, Continuing Education Division.

Boothby, D. (1986). *Women re-entering the labour force and training programs: Evidence from Canada.* A study prepared for the Economic Council of Canada. Ottawa: Supply and Services Canada.

Callaway, H. (1981). Women's perspectives: Research as re-vision. *Convergence, XIV* (4), pp.34-42.

Cebotarev, E. A. (1986). Women, work and employment: Some attainments of the International Women's Decade. In A. Thomson (Ed.), *The decade of women.* Toronto: Canadian Congress on Learning Opportunities for Women (CCLOW), pp.63-74.

Corkery, M. (1986). Subversion: Chilean women learning for change. In A. Thomson (Ed.), *The decade of women.* Toronto: CCLOW, pp.133-140.

deChungara, D. B. with M. Viezzer. (1979). *Let me speak! Testimony of Domitila, a woman of the Bolivian mines.* New York: Monthly Review Press.

deCoito, P. (1984). *Women and adult basic education in Canada: An exploratory study.* Toronto: CCLOW.

Devereaux, M. S. (1985). One in every five: *A survey of adult education in Canada.* Ottawa: Supply and Services Canada.

Ehrenreich, B. & English, D. (1979). *For her own good: 150 years of experts' advice to women.* New York: Anchor Books.

Ellis, D. & Sayer, L. (1986). *When I grow up . . . Career expectations and aspirations of Canadian schoolchildren.* Report of a study for the Women's Bureau, Labour Canada. Ottawa: Supply and Services Canada.

Fordham, P. (1983). *Co-operating for literacy.* Toronto: International Council for Adult Education.

Freire, P. (1973). *Education for critical consciousness.* New York: Seabury Press.

Herring, B. & LaFountaine H. (1986). *Women in the labour force: 1985-86 edition.* Ottawa: Supply and Services Canada.

MacKeracher, D. & Jantzi, D. (1985). Policies and practices in science education. In F. M. Connelly, R. K. Crocker & H. Kass (Eds.), *Science education in Canada: Policies, practices and perceptions.* Toronto: OISE Press, pp.130-149.

MacKeracher, D. et al. (1979). *Adult basic education for women: A model for policy development.* Toronto: CCLOW.

Mezirow, J. (1978). *Education for perspective transformation: Women's re-entry programs in community colleges.* New York: Columbia University, Teachers College, Centre for Adult Education.

National Council of Welfare. (1985). *Poverty lines: Estimates by the National Council for Welfare.* Ottawa: National Council of Welfare.

Scribner, S. (1984). "Literacy in three metaphors." *American Journal of Education, 93* (1), pp.6-21.

Sherman, J. A. & Beck, E. T. (Eds.) (1979). *The prism of sex: Essays on the sociology of knowledge.* Madison, WI: University of Wisconsin Press.

Smith, D. E. (1978). A peculiar eclipsing: Women's exclusion from man's culture. *Women's Studies International Quarterly, 1* (4).

Southam News (1987). *Southam literacy survey.* Ottawa: Southam News.

Statistics Canada. (1985). *Women in Canada: A statistical report.* Ottawa: Supply and Services Canada.

_____ . (1984). *Census of Canada. Population: School attendance.* Ottawa: Supply and Services Canada.

Stock, A. (1981). Post-literacy educational strategies: The United Kingdom experience. *Convergence, XIV* (4). pp.44-51.

Thomas, A. M. (1981). Functional literacy for inmates. *Learning, III* (3), pp.8-10.

Watson, G. (1985). The right to learn — A development priority. *Canadian Library Journal, 42* (40), pp.197-201.

Woolf, V. (1929). *A room of one's own.* London: The Hogarth Press.

CHAPTER 2:

The Economics of Adult Basic Education

Kjell Rubenson

Why address an issue like "The Economics of Adult Basic Education?" Educators working in Adult Basic Education (ABE) find the frequent reference to economic output not only foreign but also repulsive. Firstly, they claim education is something good in itself. It develops civilization and provides the means through which individuals can reach their full potentials. Secondly, they argue that remedial education should be looked upon as a right, not a privilege that needs to be justified on economic terms. These are convincing arguments. However, whether one likes it or not, educational policies have and have always had (see for example Adam Smith, The Wealth of Nations) a close link to the economy. Presently, there are two main forces in society that tend to reinforce the connection between economic and educational policies.

The first force concerns government's changed philosophy on public expenditure. The "new economics" of the 1980's has guided policy making in a large part of the Western World, particularly in Great Britain and the U.S.A. It is based on a skeptical view of the ability of the government to do public good and on a belief in the free play of the market forces (Seldon, 1983). The effort to reduce public spending has not only been promoted on ideological grounds. Serious budget deficits have also forced countries governed by traditional Keynesian values to reduce public spending on, among other things, education.

The other major social force that reinforces the economic and educational policies connection has a more direct link to the labour market. The combined effects of recent technological breakthroughs in microelectronics and telecommunications have had profound structural impact on the economy and pushed it towards an information economy. Consequently, human resource investments are being viewed as critical to the whole process of economic development. A nation's competitiveness on the world market is to a large degree expected to depend on its resources in terms of knowledge, learning, information and skilled intelligence.

A good example of this trend is the Organization for Economic Co-operation and Development's (OECD) major study on "education and effective economic performance," which examines how education helps improve the performance of the economy and resolve some major economic problems. It is somewhat ironic that education, after first being embraced as the solution to all problems in the 1960's, then depreciated during the cynical 1970's, is now, once again, being presented as the cure for social problems. The crisis in education in the 1970's was partly a reaction to unrealistic expectations for the reforms of the 1950's and '60's to accomplish social and educational equality and economic growth. As a result of that crisis, there occurred a paradigmatic shift in the social sciences. Underlying assumptions of relationships between education and economic performance, and of education as an instrument to equalize the available goods and services of society, were questioned. Thus, today there is some scepticism among social scientists towards recent policy documents in which education is proclaimed as the solution to achieve economic competitiveness and decreased unemployment. The link between education and employment has especially been questioned.

In the face of these queries, statistics of the kind shown in Table 1 have been used to argue for more education for the disadvantaged.

Table 1
Unemployment Percentage Rate Ratio by Education for Canada
(Source: Statistics Canada, *The Labour Force*, April, 1986 "71-001")

Education	Unemployment Rate
0–8 years	13.6
High School	12.2
Some Public School	8.6
Public School Diploma	7.2
Undergraduate Degree	7.3
Total	10.2

It is evident that the unemployment rate is higher among those with less education. However, as is often stated, unemployment will not disappear due to education as unemployment itself is caused by economic conditions and not by educational gaps (Harman, 1987).

In fact during the recent recession, the worst since the great depression, a certain cynicism regarding the role of education has surfaced, as evidenced in statements like, "The main purpose of ABE and other forms of adult education for disadvantaged groups is to keep the unemployment figures down."

Departing from the above discourse on the role of education in economic development, the purpose of this article is to examine the role of adult basic education in a changing economy. The analysis starts with a brief discussion of paradigms with conflicting perspectives on the relationship between education and the economy. The article then turns to the educational implications of the new technology, and is followed by a discussion of alternative employment strategies. The article concludes with some remarks concerning adult basic education and public policy, which are discussed in the framework of social justice.

THE DISCOURSE ON ECONOMIC RETURNS FROM EDUCATION

The increased expansion in public spending on education in the 1960's was partly based on the human capital theory. Proponents of this theory maintained that there exists a strong link between investment in education and economic growth (Denison, 1962; Schultz, 1960), and that more equal distribution of investment in education would equalize individual earnings (Schultz, 1961). When, during the 1970's, it became more and more evident that education was not generating the expected economic growth and that there was little change in income equality, the human capital theory was questioned (see e.g. Blaug, 1976; Dean, 1984; Sobel, 1982a, b). The screening theory was put forward as an alternative (Arrow, 1973; Doeringer and Piore, 1971; Thurow, 1975). This theory seeks to explain what the human capital theory cannot — that is, why there is such a persistent preference of employers for workers with ever higher levels of education (Blaug, 1976: 46). The screening theory states that most jobs do not require special distinguishable skills or amounts of education. What employers are looking for are personal attributes like cognitive skills, personality traits such as self-reliance, achievement, drive, compliance with organizational rules and trainability. The theory postulates that employers faced with a selection problem treat educational qualifications as a screening device to distinguish among new workers in terms of personal attributes (Blaug, 1976; Sobel, 1982a, b). According to "the strong form" of the screening theory, initial education is important not only for getting a job but for receiving subsequent training and promotion (Blaug, 1976; Sobel, 1982a).

Advocates of the human capital school have rebutted and questioned the validity of the screening theory, especially the strong version (Psacharopoulos, 1980). Further, they maintain that even if total real output per person declined over the years 1973-81, increased average levels of education of the workforce still made a positive contribution to output per person (Denison, 1979 ref. in Wilkinson, 1986: 544).

Wilkinson (1986: 546), reviewing the research on the returns from or benefits of education concludes:

> In summary, whether one accepts the function of additional expenditures on education to be an investment in skills which add to productivity, or as a means to gain credentials for jobs, it is quite conceivable that the benefits expected by individuals or society may not be as great as anticipated.

According to the screening theory, remedial education may or may not be necessary for the individual to handle a specific job, but it is definitely of great importance for getting the job. Several objections could be raised against this conclusion. Most of the studies are based on short-term longitudinal research or, more often, cross-sectional data which do not allow the examination of the impact of education over the life cycle (Fagerlind, 1975). Further, using years of schooling as measurement masks differences between different forms of education of similar length. Thus, low and high status education of the same length yield very different returns (Gesser, 1985). Finally, the statistical techniques used to study outcome (commonly some form of regression analysis) can be questioned on the grounds that they presuppose a much more specific theory than the ones available (Klees, 1986).

However, my main objection to Wilkinson's conclusion is not to the theoretical and/or methodological issues — crucial as they are — but to the fact that he fails to address the present changes that the economy is undergoing. Has the relationship between education and the economy changed as a result of a move towards an information economy where lifelong education is becoming more of a norm than an exception; and, if so, how? It should be pointed out that my criticism does not imply that Wilkinson's conclusions may not be true. However, one must be careful in drawing conclusions regarding the present and future relationship between education and the economy based on studies which do not account for changes that occur in working life.

THE CHANGING WORLD OF WORK

It is widely anticipated that the information technology will affect all aspects of life and raise serious economic, social, cultural, and political issues. This is as far as the consensus goes. While some have presented the technology as a new Jerusalem which promises a better world of work, others have warned of increased unemployment and deskilling. A few years into the new era the picture is getting somewhat more clear, although social scientists still differ in their assessment of the effects. In this section I shall briefly address two issues over which researchers fail to agree: employment effects, and changes in job content and skill requirement.

Employment Effects

In the early 1980's there were many alarming reports, especially from Western Europe, that the micro-chip revolution would bring about dramatic changes for large proportions of the presently employed workforce. That discussion has continued to focus on the unemployment situation and has dealt more with future predictions than with present trends. Looking at the employment situation at large, OECD recently concluded that four years into the present economic recovery, OECD unemployment is about three times as large as it was in 1973 (31 versus 10 million) and 12 million higher than in 1979 (OECD, 1986a). When the OECD analyzes these high unemployment figures, it does so more in terms of GNP growth, labour, productivity, inflation and nominal wages than in terms of effects of the new technology. While it is well established that the new technology increases productivity and therefore has a labour-saving effect, long-term predictions are difficult to make. Shorter and longer term impacts tend to be confused, and the extent to which new jobs created by the technology can be predicted is problematic. OECD (1983) sums up a number of studies that have tried to assess the employment effects of robotization within manufacturing. According to their figures the number of workplaces suppressed per robot is between 0.8 and 6.2, depending on the type of application. However, these predictions are very uncertain and there is not much hard evidence upon which to base a long-term prediction.

There is evidence that the new technology may have greater impact on some sectors than others and that women will be more affected than men. Women are primarily concentrated in a very narrow range of occupations and industries, such as office work and the information industry, which may be hard hit by the technological revolution (OTA, 1985; Reskin and Hartman, 1986). Those who continue to choose traditionally women's occupations during the coming 5–15 years will carry a disproportionately large burden of the adjustment to the technological revolution. Potential unemployment among women in Sweden is estimated to be in the range of 2–37 percent, depending on productivity, the expansion of office production, the proportion of women in gainful employment and women's choice of careers (Drambo and Bark).

It is important to stress that the vulnerable unemployment situation for women is not only a problem of the new technology but is ultimately a reflection of sex-bound career selection. Unless women can acquire skills in other career areas, they will not be able to capitalize on any employment compensation effects that the technology will have, since the employment created will not match their skills.

Another aspect of the employment effect has to do with structural changes in the labour market, i.e. where are the jobs going to be. Judging from the general discussion the impact of the new technology, one can easily get the impression that all new jobs created are in the high technology sector. However, as Levin and Rumberger (1983) pointed out in their analysis of the U.S. situation, while it is true that high technology jobs will be the fastest growing occupations, their relative number in the labour market is very small. A similar view is presented by the Canadian government:

> "Many of the growth occupations have, however, little impact on training volumes. For many of them, there are numbers of unemployed people who can take the jobs without major training. Others involve low skill levels."
> (Minister of Employment and Immigration, 1984: 6)

Instead, the Canadian report concludes, the pressure for training will come from rapidly growing occupations, which are unlikely to create large numbers of jobs but which will be critical to the successful introduction of technological change and to the overall competitiveness of Canada. Recent labour market statistics support this assumption. The increase in jobs in the U.S. during the last years of recovery are mainly low-paid and full-time jobs in the service section (OECD, 1986a). A large number of these have been temporary jobs. For many, this represents a form of underemployment (OECD, 1986a: 20). Between 1979 and 1985, 44 percent of the net new jobs paid poverty-level wages (*The New York Times*, Feb 1, 1987). Accepting the above data, I would like to suggest a small warning against relying solely on occupational classifications as used in labour market forecasts since this kind of data partly mask the impact of the new technology. Thus, according to the Swedish Bureau of Statistics (SOU, 1984: 20), four out of five jobs related indirectly to the use of computers would not be identified as such if the estimation were based on occupational groupings.

To sum up the employment effects:
- the net employment effects of the new technology are very difficult to estimate;
- studies show that women, over the next 5–15 years, may be extremely hard hit by office automation;
- there will be a rapid expansion of high-technology jobs but the absolute number of these jobs is not as high as is commonly believed;
- the labour market forecasts predict that the majority of the jobs in the next 10 years will be in low-skill areas; and
- the classification system used in labour forecasts masks the full effect of the new technology.

Changes in Job Content and Skill Requirement

There is no agreement among experts whether or not the new technology will require a more skilled workforce. One camp argues that the application of technology is part of the process of dividing work tasks into simplified operations that require few skills to perform (Levin and Rumberger, 1983). Further, they maintain, there is an apparent risk that the development will create new "class barriers" within the blue collar sector as well as among salaried employers. The possibilities to develop personally in the job or to advance to more qualified jobs will depend on which side of the "barrier" one happens to be (Schuetze, 1987). In the literature, this notion of "polarization" has gained much support. The concept is based more on studies of what happened in industry during the 1960's and general social theory than on inquiries into what presently occurs in the world of work. In recent years some findings have been presented that question this predominant view. Kern and Schumann, who once coined the concept polarization, in a recent study found changes that contradicted their earlier conclusion (Kern and Schumann, 1984). Instead of the expected dequalification and a further division of labour resulting from the new technology, they found that the development was going in the opposite direction. Thus there were far reaching attempts to get rid of the division of labour. Their findings are reflected in the name of their book, "The End of the Division of Labour?"† Instead of management trying to become more independent of the workers' qualifications through division of labour, they found that a great effort was made to make better use of the skills possessed by the work force. Employer sponsored education occurred more widely than they had found in the earlier study, which used a broader definition of what constituted "employer sponsored" education. Kern's and Schumann's interpretation was that in a time when the human productive function to a larger extent is replaced by technology, polarization is no longer functional. Instead, employers are more conscious about the importance of the quality of the human production and the limits that a polarized workforce set. They therefore see the necessity to pay closer attention to human resources for the productivity and ultimately the competitiveness in a world markert.

In spite of the positive developments outlined above, the new concept of production had one devastating effect — segmentation — which in one way is worse than polarization. What distinguishes winners and losers is no longer a good job or a bad job, but having a job or not. Thus, while the sector of the labour market Kern and Schumann surveyed showed increased demand and appreciation for skills as a consequence of introduction of new technology, the difficulty to get into the labour market escalated.

---

†Das Ende der Arbeitsteilung?

Conclusions Regarding ABE

What does the above discussion tell us with regard to the economics of Adult Basic Education? A few emergent trends can be detected.

Looking first at the broad structural development of the labour market, there seem to be two contradictory messages. The Kern and Schumann study reveals a changed concept of production in which human skills are awarded increased importance. The North American data, on the other hand, show that most jobs will not be created in what traditionally have been regarded as educationally demanding jobs.

The difference could be less sharp than it appears to be. The position that most of the occupations with the largest projected absolute growth have little impact on the training value as they involve low skill levels, is based on the assumption that no redefinition of these jobs will occur. The new production concept founded by Kern and Schumann originated from their observation of car and machine manufacturing and the chemical process industry. The change was a direct response to the introduction of new technology and linked to a new philosophy on work organization.

Thus, whether or not other jobs will change will depend on whether or not the introduction of new technology or any other force will make the new concept of production seem economically advantageous. Since "janitors and sextons," according to the U.S. forecast, will experience the largest growth in employment, it could be of interest that a large Swedish furniture chain, when advertising for janitors, demanded that the applicants have an education that corresponded to a university entrance requirement. Whether or not the Swedish example is a reflection of the new production concept, and whether or not the screening function of education is getting even more pronounced, are impossible to tell at the present point.

One interpretation, however, would be what has been called the "japanization" of the world of work. What this implies is that the internal labour market within a company will become more important. In this respect, the janitor's position could be seen as an entry position, the first step in a "career line." The emphasis on level of education at the time of employment assures the employee of one characteristic — that in a changeable world of work, trainability is becoming increasingly valuable.

In the discussions on the need of the labour market to adjust to the information economy and to the changing patterns of international trade and unemployment, one issue stands out — flexibility. A recent report by a high-level group of experts to the Secretary-General of OECD concluded:

> We therefore recommend new initiatives in the field of education and training at a number of points. The most important among them are: Initial schooling has to provide people with basic knowledge and skills: it also has to prepare them for a vocational world of rapidly changing requirements: it therefore has to be broad education rather than narrow training.
>
> Not only is it necessary to create new opportunities for education and training by public or private action, but many people have to be made aware of the consequences of insufficient or once-for-all training. (OECD, 1986b:16)

In a time when the only certainty is that the future of the labour market will undergo rapid change, the key to flexibility is seen as peoples' ability to cope with changes and to turn them to their advantage in the future. In this scenario the ability of the workforce to learn becomes crucial. The example above, in which janitors need "university entrance qualification," can be seen as an enterprise wanting to assure maximum future flexibility of its employees.

Kern's and Schumann's new concept of production can be seen as a response to the demand for flexibility, where the catchwords are "efficiency through flexibility." The consequence with regard to ABE is that there will be a demand for non-Tayloristic patterns of organization which require broader and more educationally oriented skills.

A survey comissioned by the European Community and based on responses from industry lists the following general qualities as required from the workforce involved with computer-based systems or equipment (after Schuetze, 1987: 104).
• the capability for analytical thinking applied to different processes of work;
• a sense of quantitative appreciation of different processes;
• the ability to conduct dialogue with equipment;
• a sense of responsibility and capability for autonomous work;
• the ability to link technical economic and social considerations in the appreciation of equipment and working methods; and
• a planned and methodical approach to work.

Further, according to Kern and Schumann, team work is stressed. The crucial question that the new concept of production raises is whether or not the present work force and/or those unemployed have the necessary capacity to learn.

Adult educators have fought hard to destroy the myth that the capacity to learn starts to deteriorate at an early age and have rightly pointed to methodological flaws in earlier research designs. However, in the eagerness to do this they have neglected to consider existing individual differences. People's abilities to learn after having left school is partly related to the kind of environment in which they live. The initial differences in ability widen with age and a deterioration in school-related abilities has been observed among those who enter jobs that do not require the acquisition of new knowledge (Harnqvist, 1977; Stoikov, 1975). Thus there has been a deterioration in the human capital or, using the terminology of the screening perspective, the trainability has decreased. This is not to say that there has occurred any biological or physiological changes that have resulted in loss of capacity.

These declines in school-related abilities are serious, since the introduction of the information technology may very well result in the work process becoming less concrete. The trend is increasingly towards presenting and communicating the production process through the use of symbols. Thus there will occur an abstraction of the knowledge through which people command their work situations. This would require a work force that has general theoretical knowledge as well as knowledge specific to the actual work process. As well, there would be an increased demand for abstract thinking, information seeking and probability calculation (SOU 1984: 20).

Accepting for awhile the argument that most new jobs will not be very skill-demanding, the issue becomes: should poorly qualified people in traditionally low-skilled, low-paid jobs be helped to acquire the competencies they need to move into other sectors of the economy. According to some (see OECD, 1986a), such a move would help expand the economic capacity.

CONCLUDING REMARKS
In this article I have approached the question of the economics of ABE, drawing on some of the core issues in the economics of education, with special emphasis on the consequences of a changing economy. Looking at the broad societal developments, it is clearly evident that the move towards an information economy has brought the educational issue into the centre of the eco-

nomic sphere, forcing a closer relationship between education and economic policies.

The discussions so far have, to a large extent, focused on how to strengthen the private sector-university research partnership, and the universities' and colleges' roles in human resource development. Much less attention has been given to what happens with the human capital at the lower levels of the work hierarchy. Thus the issue of economic competitiveness could be interpreted as being equivalent to the standards of excellence basic research and the transfer of this knowledge into the private sector. However, I would like to offer the suggestion that it is as important in an information economy to stop the decline of human capital that presently occurs in low-skill areas. The constant benefits of training/educating the groups that traditionally receive little employer-sponsored or other forms of education should be re-examined, based on the changed concept of production as presented by Kern and Schumann. This focusses the discussion on responsibility for this kind of training/education — or, stated differently, who should pay for what?

Commonly, remedial education has been seen as an equality issue and regarded as the responsibility of the state. The main function of employer-sponsored programmes has traditionally been to adapt previously acquired general knowledge and skills to the needs of the job and to compensate for the deficiencies of both general and vocational education. The education and training offered is almost totally determined by the employer's perception of what measures could increase productivity, and equity concerns seldom enter the discussion (Smith, 1983). If we accept that the perception that what presently constitutes skills is changing, this ought to have consequences for who should pay for what kind of education. A development along the line that Kern and Schumann presents implies that the distinction between manual and intellectual labour is getting blurred. Consequently the division between what is thought of as general and/or remedial education, and company-specific education, will be more difficult to maintain.

From a human capital perspective Kern's and Schumann's results, like general policy comments of a similar nature, can be indirectly interpreted as a recommendation that investment in education for the broad work force is justified on economic terms. If this is accepted, then it ought to be in the interest of employers to support education that guarantees the trainability of the work force. Further it suggests that governments ought to look upon remedial education not solely from the point of equity, but that there is also economic justification for this kind of education. Thus there is reason to review the financial responsibility for remedial education.

In this connection I would like to draw attention to the recently established "Renewal funds" in Sweden. Companies with a profit of $80,000 U.S. have to set aside 10 percent of the profit to a "renewal account." The money for this account is supposed to be used for education of the employees and research of vital importance to the long-term goals of the company. The labour unions have the final say for the use of the money. The intention as expressed in the bill from the Riksdag is that special attention should be given to the needs of those with few years of schooling. These funds have generated a substantial amount of money. For example, Volvo has $125 million U.S. to spend during 1986.

The interesting thing with regard to what is discussed in this article is that, in several companies, both employers and labour have as a first priority to give general education to those with short education. This strategy could be seen as another indication of the new concept of production. The Swedish example has to be understood in light of the special relationship that exists there among government, labour and industry. However, it also underlines the very fact that developments regarding remedial education will be linked to a large extent to developments in working life. The economic justification as stated here could be said to be embedded in the broad framework of the human capital theory as outlined above.

To return to the previous discussion on the discourse on the economic return from education, this conclusion does not imply a stand with regard to the respective merit of the human capital and screening theories. It merely alludes to the fact that looking at some sectors of the economy, a claim for education can be made on human capital grounds. The interesting thing with regard to the present developments, however, is that both theories seem to apply to different segments of the economy.

As was so clearly revealed in the anecdotal example from the Swedish furniture company, the role of education as a screening device is certain to become even more marked in an information economy. In view of the recent trend to lower-paying jobs, what O'Toole (1977: 64) stated ten years ago may become even more true in the time to come:

> Paradoxically, as the investment value of education slumps, the importance of its credentialling function soars.

If one accepts the screening theory, what are the consequences for ABE? It could be argued that there is no economic justification for remedial education. Instead the major reason for its existence would be to achieve equality. If we accept this line of argument, it implies that certain groups are "doomed" to stay in low-skills areas, unable to compete in or enter the labour market.

Having stayed away from the social aspects of ABE in this article, I would now like to end with some reference to Rawls' theory of justice (Rawls, 1971). According to Rawls, the primary goods at the disposition of society are liberties, power, opportunities, income and wealth, and self-respect. "Rawlsian" justice can be stated as the just distribution of social primary goods.

> All social primary goods — liberty and opportunity, income and wealth and the bases of self-respect — are to be distributed equally, unless an unequal distribution of any or all of these goods is to the advantage of the least favored. (Rawls, 1971: 303)

Rawls presents three interpretations of equal opportunity which he calls "the system of natural liberty," "liberal interpretation of equal opportunity" and "democratic interpretation of equal opportunity" (Rawls, 1971). The first interpretation is the nineteenth-century ideal of careers open to talents (Martin, 1985: 101). The principles involved here are that there are no official restrictions on the taking of opportunities and that nothing should be done to disturb the outcomes, whatever they might be, that result from the free market in opportunities.

The liberal position is that fair equality of opportunity demands going beyond mere formal equality of the system of natural liberty. This can be achieved by rearranging the social contingencies so as to mitigate advantages or disadvantages secured from social circumstances. However, beyond this, the liberal interpretation ascribes to the basic laissez-faire approach of the "natural" interpretation which accepts the resultant distribution of positions, income and wealth as correct. According to the democratic interpretation of equality, the laissez-faire approach has to be abandoned. Martin (1985: 75) points out that the democratic interpretation differs from the liberal interpretation in two respects. It recognizes that considerations must be given not only to social starting points but also to natural endowments; and further, it does not stop after the initial attempt has been made to reduce the gap in initial advantage, but continuously acts to achieve what Rawls calls reasonable equality of opportunity.

Thus, with respect to Rawls' notion of justice, remedial education could, from an economic point of view, be regarded as a fundamental right based on a democratic interpretation of equality.

REFERENCES

Arrow, K. (1980). Higher education as a filler. *Journal of Public Economics*, 2: 3, p. 193-216.
Blaug, M. (1976). Human capital theory—A slightly jaundiced survey. *Journal of Economic Literature*, September, p. 827-855.
Dean, E. (1984). *Education and economic productivity*. Cambridge, MA: Ballinger.
Denison, E. F. (1962). *The source of economic growth and alternatives before us*. New York: Committee for Economic Development.
Denison, E. F. (1979). *Accounting for slower economic growth: The United States in the 1970's*. Washington, DC: Brookings.
Doeringer, P. B. and Piore, M. J. (1971). *Internal labour markets and manpower analysis*. Lexington, Mass.: D. C. Heath and Company.
Drambo, L. and Bark, A. (1983). *Kontorsautomation och Kvinnors Framtida Arbetsmarknad*. Stockholm: Data-effektutredningen Ds A.: 9.
Fagerlind, I. (1975). *Formal education and adult earnings*. Stockholm: Almquist and Wicksell.
Gesser, B. (1985). *Utbildning, jamlikhet, arbetsdelning*. Lund: Student Litteratur.
Harman, D. (1987). *Illiteracy: A national dilemma*. Cambridge, MA: The Adult Education Company.
Harnquist, K. (1977). *Enduring effects of schooling—A neglected area in educational research. Educational Researcher*, 6: 10, p. 5-11.
Kern, H. and Schumann, N. (1984). *Das ende der arbeitsteilung? Rationalisierung in der industriellen produktion*. Munich: Verlag C. H. Beck.
Klees, S. J. (1986). Planning and policy analysis in education: What can economics tell us? *Comparative Education Review*, 30: 4, p. 574-607.
Levin, H. and Rumberger, R. (1983). *The educational implications of high technology*. Palo Alto: IFG Stanford University.
Martin, R. M. (1985). *Rawls and rights*. Lawrence, Kansas: University Press of Kansas. New York Times, *Forum*, Sunday, February 1, 1987.
OECD (1983). *Industrial robots*. Paris: OECD.
OECD (1986a). *Employment outlook*. Paris: OECD.
OECD (1986b). *Labour market flexibility*. Paris: OECD.
OTA (1985). *Automation of America's offices*. Washington, DC: Office of Technology Assessment, Congress of the United States.

O'Toole, J. (1977). *Work, learning and the American future.* London: Jossey-Bass.

Psacharopoulos, G. (1980). On the weak versus the strong version of the screening hypothesis. *Economic Letters.*

Rawls, J. (1971). *A theory of justice.* Cambridge, MA: Harvard University Press.

Reskin, B. F. and Hartmann, H. I. (eds.) (1986). *Women's work men's work.* Washington, DC: National Academy Press.

Schuetze, H. (1987). Adult education and the changing workplace. In Duke, C. (ed.), *Adult education: Perspectives from China.* London: Croom Helm.

Schultz, T. (1960). Capital formation by education. *Journal of Political Economy.* 67: 4, p. 1026-1039.

Schultz, T. (1961). Investment in human capital. *The American Economic Review,* 1: 2, p. 1-17.

Seldon, A. (1983). The new economics. *Journal of Social, Political and Economic Studies,* 8: 1, p. 3-40.

Smith, A. (1963). *An inquiry into the nature and causes of the wealth of nations.* Homewood, IL: Richard Irwin.

Sobel, I. (1982a). The human capital revolution in economic development. In P. Altbach, R. Arnove and G. Kelly (eds.), *Comparative education.* New York: Macmillan Publishing Company.

Sobel, I. (1982b). Human capital and institutional theories of the labour market: Rivals or complements? *Journal of Economic Issues,* XVI: 1, p. 255-272

SOU (1984). *Datorer och arbetslivets forandring:* 20.

Statistics Canada (1986). *The labour force, April, 1986.* (71-001), 1986.

Stoikov, V. (1975). The economics of recurrent education and training. Geneva: ILO.

Thurow, L. C. (1975). *Generating inequality—mechanisms of distribution in the U.S. economy.* New York: Basic Books.

Wilkinson, B. W. (1986). Elementary and secondary education policy in Canada: A survey. *Canadian Public Policy,* 12: 4, p. 505-572.

CHAPTER 3:

Administration of Adult Basic Education Programs

Lorne Rachlis

Adult Basic Education programs are the orphans of education institutions. The head office may not even know how they got started, it keeps them undernourished, and usually tolerates their existence. The programs are sometimes staffed by well-meaning, but untrained adult educators, receive little physical resource or curriculum support, and must cope with an amorphous mandate and a peripatetic clientele, while having to "keep the numbers up" in order to justify their continued operation.

The following issues are of particular administrative concern for Adult Basic Education programs:[1]
  (i) Clientele — access, behaviour, assessment, needs, interagency cooperation
 (ii) Content & Resources — curriculum, student evaluation, standards, learning materials, locations, curriculum support
(iii) Staff — credentials, role, staff evaluation, pre- and in-service training.

CLIENTELE

Using any common definition for undereducation in Canada today, there is a vast potential market for Adult Basic Education.[2] And yet, only a small percentage of this total market actually enrols in programs designed to alleviate this undereducation and only a fraction of these people complete the program or continue to more advanced upgrading or retraining. One might wonder what we are doing wrong, or even if what we are doing is what is needed/wanted.[3]

Administrators must let the clients know what programs are available and relevant to them and try to entice them in.[4] This is done by encouraging word of mouth promotion by satisfied students and by "second-hand word of mouth" done by informing the professionals (social workers, medical workers, employment and vocational counsellors, etc.) who deal directly with the clients. Of course there is advertising in the traditional sense, mostly through the freebies of media community announcements and notices in school board publications. In cooperation with a variety of other agencies, there are inducements or barrier reducers (subsidized child care and transportation, and work placements). And there must be a welcoming, friendly, supportive environment. Despite all this, enrolment remains small compared to the target group. And then those who *do* enrol seldom stay long enough in any program to achieve the top level of academic prowess offered and often leave before achieving their own original goals.[5]

As with many adolescent potential drop-outs, many Adult Basic Education students do not come to class on time, do not attend regularly, and do not make significant (to us) academic gain before leaving.[6] They usually arrive with good intentions but they do not have the formal learning skills needed for traditional academic success. What they often carry with them into the classroom setting are a host of self-defeating coping mechanisms and the burden of family or work responsibilities and personal problems. Practising punctuality and regular attendance and commitment and perseverence must be part of the learning situation promoted by a patient staff.

In order to be near the clients (thus reducing one access barrier) locate programs in public libraries, in elementary schools, in churches, in factories. Keep the programs small and personal in order to alleviate school or authority phobia and to allow each student to receive individual attention and individualized instruction.[7] Phone them when they are absent, promote buddying up for mutual support and for note-taking when one is absent, and allow each student the opportunity to experience some success each day. Place school and social work counsellors in each program in order to head off small problems before they become big ones, to help the students set goals and plan strategies to reach these goals, and to help them build self-awareness and self-confidence. This is important at all levels starting with the non-readers through to the high school readiness level.

Adult Basic Education students have a broad range of needs, only some of which can be addressed through schooling or upgrading. Many publicly-funded support systems must be coordinated in order to address these needs. The teachers must deal with the students' life-styles and habits and expectations, as well as with their mastery of academic content.

A final service to the students is "exiting" or alternatives counselling. Adult Basic Education students might sometimes be better served in another type of program or setting or may need support in other ways than those offered by the Adult Basic Education program. Inter-agency cooperation (a data bank of other services available, networking by front-line personnel in the agencies which serve the clientel in Adult Basic Education classes) is crucial in order to bring to bear appropriate and timely assistance with a minimum of red tape and duplication.

CONTENT & RESOURCES

What should an Adult Basic Education instructor teach? What standard of achievement should be set? How can accomplishment or progress be determined and reported?

Conventional andragogy tells us that adults should participate in designing their curriculum content, should participate in determining the methods of presentation so as to recognize their individual learning styles, and should participate in the evaluation of the content and of their own performance (if this is done at all).[8] Conventional education tells us that the appropriate government agency determines course content, sets training standards for teachers, and, increasingly influences performance standards for students. Adult Basic Education students have weak academic backgrounds and poor learning skills, and often cannot identify or articulate their educational needs. They are unable or unwilling to determine content or standards. In addition, there are no compulsory curriculum guidelines in Adult Basic Education, there are no formal requirements for instructor qualifications, and there are no achievement standards.

In Adult Basic Education the instructor should build on what the students know, recognizing the value of their life experience. But how to do this, and with what content, has become an art practised by sequestered instructors. Most Adult Basic Education instructors scramble constantly for materials which are at an appropriate level of difficulty and of interest to the current class. In many ways, this is good. It encourages the instructors to be involved in shaping a responsive curriculum. However, it is inefficient (many people constantly re-invent the wheel), and some instructors are better at this than others.

To meet the need for curriculum development, subject expertise, and methodology and evaluation upgrading, administrators should encourage inter-program visitations and meetings (both among the instructors themselves and with subject and methodology experts). Book publishers have not been responsive, seeing only a small potential market. Until this is shown to be otherwise, form curriculum writing teams of instructors and have instructors share files of materials with each other.

The appropriate content for a given group of Adult Basic Education students at a given time is often different from that of another. Thus the need for flexibility in means of presentation and of what is presented. The spread of abilities and backgrounds in a typical elementary school class, where the children are all the same age, is wide. Add one or two or more decades to each student's age and vary the countries of origins and the life experiences to get the mix of an Adult Basic Education class. The students may have little in common except a desire to improve their lives. This does not mean there can be no commonality in subject matter. It does mean that the content must be flexible. One approach to determining what should be taught is to help the students set their academic goal in keeping with their abilities and interests, and to structure the content to help them reach the goal.' Adult Basic Education programs traditionally teach English (reading and writing, vocabulary and grammar) and mathematics (arithmetic and simple word problems). These are the basic tools needed to upgrade academically or to retrain. But these must be presented in some context. It is important to broaden the content base wherever possible, especially as the students approach the secondary level. Life and study skills should be a vital part of every program and can be delivered by the instructor and school and social work counsellors working together. Civics gives the students a broader perspective and a starting point for articulating and pressing their concerns. Current events, field trips, adult student conferences and other "social" activities can all be part of the curriculum giving students structural practice in communication and organization skills. Expand their horizons and understanding and give them opportunities to grow with more than vocabulary, grammar and arithmetic exercises. The Adult Basic Education program thus becomes a relevant compelling part of the student's life. It is not easy to do this, and left quietly alone in an isolated setting, essentially divorced form mainstream education, the Adult Basic Education instructor cannot do this. Commitment and involvement and real support for Adult Basic Education are required form the administrative level.

The curriculum content is remarkably similar from one Adult Basic Education program to another, considering that each has grown so independently. Local arrangements for presenting the content do differ. If there are two instructors at one site, they usually divide the students into a low group and a high group. Three instructors form three groups (non-readers, intermediate and high school readiness). Another arrangement is for a pair of teachers to divide their students so that one teaches half of them math for the first half of the session, while the second teaches English to the remaining students. After coffee break, they trade students and teach their own subject again to the students they had not seen yet that day. But in all cases, because of the diversity of abilities and levels of the students, much of the instruction should be done on an individual basis and not in lock step. The major resource cost is for duplicating paper.

Because of the need to ease the students into the life of the class and to make them feel welcome, little formal testing is usually done in the Adult Basic Education program, either initially or later. The instructors get a sense of the students' level by seeing them work, and experience tells them what to do with them next. This is part of the "art" of being an Adult Basic Education instructor. Some better organization or process may be needed here: some application of theory and some practical borrowing form the regular school system.

There is a role for a central government agency to provide curriculum advice and guidance, for suggestions or recommendations on appropriate resources, for sample unit outlines.[10] Guidelines could suggest subject matter of importance, the order of presentation of topics, the order of development within a topic. Guidelines could give advice on methodology (what works well and under what circumstances) and suggest optional enrichment and remedial materials. The agency could promote the exchange of ideas and the development of materials by establishing a clearing house and by encouraging educational instructors to promote curriculum writing. Through the incentive of volume sales, publishers might co-operate in such an endeavour.

Standards and content in Adult Basic Education should depend on what the student needs and wants to do next and not on an artificial and imposed standard. Responsiveness and flexibility have always been the watchwords of Adult Basic Education. A resource book on content, methodology and assessment will help justify the use of public funds, energies and resources directed to Adult Basic Education. The resource book could recommend the competencies to be demonstrated for a particular Adult Basic Education goal. For example, "An Adult Basic Education student who wishes to proceed to secondary level education should be able to . . ." Different competencies would be necessary for different goals.

Standardization of the paper work associated with Adult Basic Education would be helpful. For example, registration information and a record of competencies achieved, if standardized, would facilitate the moving of a student from one program to another and from one institution to another. This would simplify communication to social agencies and to employers. Accountability and responsibility, review and response, are needed in Adult Basic Education as much as in any other part of the school system.

STAFF

Teaching Adult Basic Education has been a calling more than a profession.[11] Most Adult Basic Education instructors are women. Most Adult Basic Education teaching positions are part-time (usually in the morning). Classes are often not held on school breaks. Thus, these positions have been attractive to women with young children or women re-entering the work force. Adult Basic Education instructors are employed in a variety of ways, but usually without a contract or benefits or seniority, and thus subject to removal with no recourse. Adult Basic Education has not had a high profile with education institutions or administrators. Since Adult Basic Education is "pre-credit" and is usually taught by staff employed through Continuing Education, teacher certification is not required. Typical instructor credentials are:

— non-credit adult teaching experience
— no teacher certification but a Master's Degree in Adult Education
— no teacher certification but a Master's Degree in English
— social work training
— elementary school teaching experience, and
— secondary school teaching experience.

What counts is qualification, not certification. The stamina, patience and desire to help and to motivate others, the ability to project genuine interest in and concern for others, the ability to work without supervision, the confidence to be flexible and responsive and innovative, these are all valuable characteristics of an Adult Basic Education instructor.[12]

Other than Master's level courses in adult education and the usual teacher certification courses there is no pre-service training available for teachers of adults, and in particular, for Adult Basic Education instructors. In most institutions, there is little or no in-service training available either. It's sink or swim for the new Adult Basic Education instructor who may have the good fortune of working with experienced colleagues. Professional preparation and development for Adult Basic Educators is just as vital as that for any other educators. But because of the nature of the literacy student, it should not determine eligibility for teaching Adult Basic Education. Again, what should count is qualification, not certification. The lack of professional training opportunities can be addressed in several ways. Prospective staff can serve "apprenticeships" before being hired, as volunteers or as teacher aides, or as supply teachers, or on a short-term basis (during peak intake times or to replace teachers who are ill or on maternity absence). They thus get to know the program and its philosophy of adult education, and the expectations on staff members; and the administrator gets to know them before seniority becomes commitment.

In addition, new staff and even some returning staff, can participate in orientation workshops prior to a new term. They can become familiar with course materials, with expectations of the next (high school credit) academic level, with methodology and with the nature of the students who come to the program. In-house professional development seminars, usually with a curriculum flavour (including multiculturalism) and regular swap sessions can be held five or six times each year, bringing together instructors from different locations and institutions in the region. Teachers may wish to formalize these meetings and their interrelations through formation of an association. Administrators should encourage visits by Adult Basic Education instructors to other programs and to the social agencies with which the students deal, for a mutual awareness-raising.

Keeping Adult Basic Education programs small to meet student needs may result in isolation of the instructor. Sometimes instructors may spend 10 or more years in one site, either as the only staff person or with the same teaching partner. With minimal curriculum and other resource back-up, such isolation is not in the best interests of the instructors or of the students. It may be necessary to re-assign instructors to new program sites periodically, emphasizing to them that the skills and knowledge they have acquired will be of great value at their new location, and that they will benefit personally and professionally through the renewal process.

We (the providers of Adult Basic Education), are the experts and, among ourselves, are the answers to many questions. We can identify issues needing research and areas needing resources, but we often do not have the ability or mandate to follow through. The institutions and government agencies must be encouraged to give leadership in designing and in facilitating participation in pre-service and in-service training for adult educators. This training could include: knowing the clientele, identifying and responding to needs, marketing, curriculum writing, methodology, determining appropriate content, and knowing where to look for help or answers. They must fund needs assessments and other research studies on such topics as adult learning styles and how to meet them.

Some Adult Basic Education instructors have not seen their supervisor or administrator except in social situations since they were hired. A quick "How's it going" or a curt "Explain your attendance drop-off" may be all the communication that the instructor receives, and "I'm running out of paper" may be all the communication that the instructor sends. How, then, are typical Adult Basic Education instructors, isolated from the usual collegial contact of the staff room or faculty lounge to know how they are doing, or where to go for advice? Staff evaluation by the responsible administrator is as essential to the growth and improvement of an Adult Basic Education instructor as it is for any other teacher. The evaluation process should be a positive, growth-oriented one, which provides the opportunity for a dialogue. The instructor can explain the philosophy of education being used (or can be guided to develop one) and can demonstrate content mastery and methodology and show the students in action. The evaluator can give specific positive reinforcement for things done well and make specific positive suggestions for the improvement of instruction and for personal or professional growth.

The administrator of Adult Basic Education programs must visit each location regularly, to have a coffee, or to deliver a parcel, etc. Thus, whenever you come to visit, you are not a stranger and do not disturb the students. Each instructor should receive a more formal classroom visit every year. This part of the evaluation process can begin one day with a 10 or 15-minute chat during which the instructor suggests the time of the formal visit, and outlines the topics to be taught and the context of the topic in the curriculum, including the purpose and objectives for the day. Spend the whole session with the class, mingling at coffee-break and sometimes helping with assigned work. As soon as possible after the class, preferably immediately after, the instructor and you then spend an hour going over what was seen. Ask questions, praise good things and give the instructor time to expound and question you. Where necessary, suggest a direction in which greater effort or changes would be beneficial.

This co-operative approach to the evaluation process is successful in that it is a positive growth experience for both the instructors and the administrator. The instructors know where they stand and there are performance reports available for references and for documentation. You get to know each other better, and involvement and commitment is generated for both. Hopefully, instruction, and the learning situation for the student, and the work situation for the instructor, are all improved.

And finally, the administrator of Adult Basic Education must be aware of, and participate as is practicable, in the environmental political realities. To raise the profile of Adult Basic Education so that adequate resources are available and reasonable access is provided, the host institution (or whatever group supports the program) must be aware of its value and the format being used. An advisory committee to the host organization on Adult Basic Education, with community, staff and institutional decision-makers on it is one way of generating broad-based understanding and commitment, as well as providing in-put to the program. Open-houses, newspaper human interest stories, networking within the organization and without, are not likely to increase enrolment directly, but will solidify the image of the program and hence the substance.

From an administrative perspective, there is much to be done to improve the delivery of Adult Basic Education and encourage its growth.[13] Inter-agency co-operation is vital in order to meet the needs of the students — the students' needs not being neatly packaged to meet agency mandates. Some standardization, some direction is needed in the topics appropriate to Adult Basic Education programs and in the development and presentation of material within the topics, all based on the goals to which the students are working. Counselling by qualified education and social work personnel is crucial to the students, who may need assistance in assessing their own strengths, setting realistic goals and developing strategies to help reach those goals. The funding or research in adult education, a clearing house for information, and development of pre- and in-service training programs in adult education and the facilitating of staff participation in such programs is important, as is regular growth-oriented staff evaluation. Some formal recognition of Adult Basic Education as a professional activity is necessary in order to ensure the quality of Adult Basic Education.

NOTES and REFERENCES

1. Continuing Education Review Project (1986). *Project Report: For Adults Only*. Toronto: Ministry of Colleges and Universities.
Draper, James A. and Barer-Stein, Thelma (1980). Plain Talk for Administrators of Teachers and Adults, in Knox, Alan B. (ed.), *Teaching Adults Effectively*. San Francisco: Jossey-Bass.
Mezirow, Jack, Darkenwald, Gordon G. and Knox, Alan B. (1975). *Last Gamble on Education*. Washington: Adult Education Association of the U.S.A.
Work Group on Adult Literacy (1985). *The Right to Learn*. Toronto: The Board of Education for the City of Toronto.
2. Cervero, Ronald M. (1985). Is a Common Definition of Adult Literacy Possible?, in *Adult Education Quarterly*. Vol. 36, No. 1.
Devereaux, M. S. (1985). *One in Every Five: A Survey of Adult Education in Canada*. Ottawa: Statistics Canada and Department of the Secretary of State.
Thomas, Audrey M. and Cairns (1983). *Adult Illiteracy in Canada: A Challenge*. Ottawa: Canadian Commission for UNESCO.
3. Cassara, Beverly B. (1980). Needs Assessment for the Educationally Underprivileged, in Pennington, Floyd C. (ed.), *Assessing Educational Needs of Adults*. San Francisco: Jossey-Bass.
4. Fitzgerald, Gisela G. (1984). Can the Hard-to-Reach Adults Become Literate?, in *Lifelong Learning*. Vol. 7, No. 5.
Irish, Glady H. (1980). Reaching the Least Educated Adult, in Darkenwald, Gordon G. and Larson, Gordon A. (eds.), *Reaching Hard-to-Reach Adults*. San Francisco: Jossey-Bass.
5. Long, Jerry (1983). Recruiting and Retaining the Prospective Adult Basic and Secondary Education Student, in *Lifelong Learning*. Vol. 7 No. 2.
6. Darkenwald, Gordon G. and Valentine, Thomas (1985). Outcomes of Participation in Adult Basic Skills Education, in *Lifelong Learning*. Vol. 8, No. 5.
7. Baker, George A. (1983). Serving Undereducated Adults: Community as Learning Center, in Kasworm, C. E. (ed.), *Educational Outreach to Select Adult Populations*. San Francisco: Jossey-Bass.
8. Knowles, Malcolm (1984). *The Adult Learner: A Neglected Species*. Houston: Gulf.
9. Davison, C. V. (1972). Programme Planning with Disadvantaged Adults, in Brooke, Michael W. (ed.), *Adult Basic Education*. Toronto: New Press.
Zimmerman, H. (1972). Task Reduction: A Basis for Curriculum Planning and Development for A.B.E., in Brooke, Michael (ed.), *Adult Basic Education*. Toronto: New Press.
10. National Advisory Panel on Skill Development Leave (1984). *Learning for Life*. Canada: House of Commons.
11. Mezirow, Jack, Darkenwald, Gordon G. and Knox, Alan B. (1975). *Last Gamble on Education*. Washington: Adult Education Association in the U.S.A.
12. Knox, Alan B. (ed.) (1979). *Enhancing Proficiencies of Continuing Educators*. San Francisco: Jossey-Bass.
13. Continuing Education Review Project (1986). *Project Report: For Adults Only*. Toronto: Ministry of Colleges and Universities.
Work Group on Adult Literacy (1985). *The Right to Learn*. Toronto: The Board of Education for the City of Toronto.

CHAPTER 4:

Adult Basic Education in the Prisons

Laurent Isabelle

Why should anyone be interested in the basic education of adults who are now inmates in either federal or provincial prisons'? Are prisons a suitable environment for basic education, and are inmates really interested and motivated to seek knowledge and to develop marketable occupational skills as well as acceptable social skills?

As a reader of this first paragraph, you might well ask: What are the issues? Why are so many inmates illiterate? Is there a connection between illiteracy and criminality? What are the causes, the cures? What programs, if any, are successful at mediating? Why is it that most illiterates (or uneducated) who are inmates are much like other illiterates out of prison in that they tend *not to* enroll in our society's multiple educational programs designed and offered for them? Why is it that success rates are very high among those who come forward, yet this does not seem to entice the others to enroll?

A lot has been written and published on these contentious topics in Canada and in other countries but I have no intention of reviewing that vast literature in the traditional ways. Issues such as the link between illiteracy and crime, the origins of illiteracy among offenders, and an analysis of the most effective literacy programs for offenders cannot be dealt with in this abbreviated treatment. As a point of interest to those who may like more details, a recent search of automated data bases by Griffin and Glasgow (1987), educators of the federal penitentiary system, has resulted in the identification of 403 articles on literacy in prisons! We know that a search of the writings on education of inmates, in general, on education of inmates in vocational/trade programs, on education of inmates at the college/university levels, etc. will yield a list of articles, treatises, books, conference proceedings, etc. in the several hundreds more.

Clearly, education of prison inmates is not a neglected area. Simply allow me to single out two books, published in the early 1980's, which are perhaps the most recent and comprehensive, and which in my value system, are virtually exhaustive reviews of the literature: one, Ross and Fabiano *Time to Think* (1985), a thorough analytical treatise well worth the reading and it is very exciting for most persons involved in the rehabilitation of inmates; two, *On Prison Education*, Morin (1983), a compendium of Canadian writings, published in both French and English, which still is an excellent source of information on issues and trends in the education of prison inmates. Although the authors of these two books do not provide a focus on literacy as adult basic literacy (A.B.E.) *per se*, they do scrutinize the kinds of learning they think are required to reduce criminality.

407

Several articles in various journals have touched upon the why, the how and the results of education of adult inmates in very special ways. Just to single out the best in my view, consider Ayers (1981), *L'Education en prison*, Cosman's (1979, 1980), *Penitentiary Education in Prison*, Duguid (1981), who has published several articles, but especially *Moral development, justice and democracy in the prison*, Gendreau and Ross (1983), *Success in Corrections: Programs nd Principles*. You might be interested to read Griffin and me, in a bilingual (not a translated text) article published in the Journal of the Canadian Vocational Association (1984) entitled *The Education of Inmates dans les pénitenciers fédéraux du Canada* and/or *Objectives of the Education of Inmates – Principles and Priorities* (1986), which I wrote for the fall issue of the Journal of the CVA. But then, given all of the above writings, why would I accept to write this section of this chapter?

Perhaps because there are well over 25,000 Canadians in prison right now: 12,500 in federal penitentiaries, the other half in provincial institutions, and that is still tragic. From the point of view of costs alone, you and I must be concerned (to say the least) because we are spending over one billion dollars annually housing, feeding, entertaining — not forgetting providing education, health care and guarding — these adults in prison, most of whom are men.[2]

Perhaps because recidivism ("qui retombent dans la même faute", dit Larousse, toujours) remains very high: close to 80 per cent of present federal inmates are in prison for a second, third or fourth time. It is difficult to imagine persons behaving in such ways, time after time, that for us "out there" in Canadian society prison is or becomes the only solution.[3]

Perhaps because life in prison is not really life as most of us know it. Life in prison is near hell, really. It's the cell, 2 m by 4 m, steel bed, steel toilet bowl and steel basin in some special cells, porcelain in others, securely bolted to the floor; it's the cement: floors, walls, and ceilings; it's the noise — of loud radios or TV's, of shouts and screams, of banging steel doors, of locking mechanisms; it's the drab olive green colour of nearly all the clothes; it's the food, which is quite well prepared, well-balanced and nourishing, really, but yuk; it's the bells in the early morning, it's the bells to call (or send) the inmate to work, it's the bells at security-check time, it's the bells at lunch time, it's the bells after lunch break, it's the bells, bells, bells! It's the sad, mournful, cynical, anguished, bitter, angry or frequently vacuous faces — all over the place — except perhaps the teachers', the chaplains', the nurses', the psychologists', the psychiatrists'. . .; it's the sky that you can never see without its prison base, the electrified fence. How can an inmate learn, grow, change, improve here?

Because education, among all opportunities "offered" or "available" in prison, is *the* one where the inmate can be fully in charge of his/her destiny. Yes, because the inmate student "at" or "in" school, is like all students, in full charge of his or her learning. No one, no teacher, no guard, no inmate friends, can learn for the inmate. Here, the inmate is alone and free. The inmate student in the school is the master/mistress of his/her self-discovery in the only place where he or she has no harsher boss than him/herself.

The school[4] is the only place where the inmate can freely share his/her strengths and fully reveal his/her weaknesses without any fear of reprisal. Ridicule? Maybe. But the inmate in school who ridicules others usually does not enjoy a long 'school-life' . . . and so the risks are minimal — at least on the long haul. The school is *the* place where the inmate can really try to be "me" who yearns, who seeks, who tries, who succeeds, who sometimes fails — but who need not abandon the struggle — because all around are others going through the very same struggles.

Adult basic education in prison starts right there and it is really sad to see so few enroll. Once those first steps have been made, then can one learn the alphabet. The alphabet? Yes, the first nation-wide analyses of the educational levels of inmates in federal penitentiaries were carried out between 1983 and 1985 and they revealed that 20 per cent of the inmates (in either federal or provincial prisons) are functionally illiterate on the basis of the United Nations standard which is Grade 5. That means 2400 out of 12,000 in federal prisons and 2400 out of 12,000 in provincial prisons. If you prefer the Canadian Association for Adult Education criterion, which is roughly the Grade 9 level, then the percentage of functional illiteracy in prison rises to at least 60 per cent according to the same 1983-85 data; that means 7200 out of the same 12,000 base. (Double that to include provincial systems.)

Once those steps to enter school where the inmate can really say "I can be me" have been made, then the inmate can take on tasks leading to literacy and numeracy. Statistics on numeracy in prison populations, by the way are quite like those on literacy. So how many illiterates have enrolled? Well, in March 1985, the number was only one-tenth what it could have been according to the results of standardized tests administered to inmates over the previous four years. In that year, only 248 inmates participated in adult literacy programs below the grade 5 level.

Adult basic education in prison inmate populations starts with literacy and numeracy and I will present my views later on why high school completion and some college-level work should be considered "basic" education for all Canadians today. Then, it's elementary and secondary level schooling on to Grades 10, 11 and 12 for literature, mathematics, history, social studies, science, normally following provincial curricula and standards. Then and then only, by the way, should the inmate in search of vocational skills be encouraged to enter vocational shops. *Inability to read and count should not be pathways to admission to vocational programs.*

Yet we continue (*in* and *out* of prison it seems) to admit some profoundly handicapped students to our occupational classes and shops. Incidentally, 168 of the 322 teachers (March '85 historical data base) are teachers from a local school bord, community college or university on contract between the CSC and their employer; the remaining 154 are qualified teachers, employees of the federal government, and most of them are employed in the trade or vocational programs. As these teachers leave, or retire, they are being replaced by teachers on contract. The policy aiming to offer inmates accredited educational programs of the highest possible quality is, in the view and experience of the writer, best met by contracts between the CSC and the various institutions identified earlier, specifically public school boards, community colleges and universities.

Adult basic education in Canadian federal prisons must be an individualized and self-paced approach because no two inmates have exactly the same levels of aptitude, interest, motivation, knowledge and experience, or have exactly the same work assignment. Although inmates whose work assignment is "school", might appear on the surface to be similar individuals with similar needs, they are nevertheless unique individuals who respond best to individualized approaches.

In an article entitled *Bea in the SHU* (1986), I have described in considerable detail how Bea Fisher approaches adult basic education of inmates whose characteristics and behaviour are such that they are confined in a Special Handling Unit (the SHU! as it was called in my days in Corrections. . .). In this environment the inmate is in his cell virtually all the time, some 23 or 24 hours a day. In this unit of the Saskatchewan Penitentiary in Prince Albert, where there were then 80 inmates, there were 25 residents enrolled in courses ranging up to Grade 10, each of whom was a student in his cell and to whom Bea had access through closed-circuit T.V. At the time of writing (1988), there were 50 residents in the unit. Of these, 27 were enrolled in courses up to the grade 10 level, and ten others enrolled in other courses, for a total of 37 out of 50 residents. Bea's "classes" are via TV and she is the teacher, the TV technician (camera-"man", sound"man", projectionist, recorder and conserver), the advisor/counsellor — not to mention all the other roles she fulfills such as librarian, paymistress, etc. All her students are enrolled in an individualized self-paced program, but all self-directed learning is enhanced by Bea's well planned and executed "classes". It may interest you to know that so far, four inmates have earned basic literacy certificates (grade 5), 10 have attained grade 8 equivalency, and 6 have earned grade 10 ABE certificates.

Adult basic education in prison includes Life Skills programs. Why? Because inmate standings on Life Skills scales are generally very low . . . as they are on literacy, numeracy or vocational scales really. There are no firm statistics, here, but, there are hundreds who do not know how to prepare a c.v., how to complete an application form, how to read and understand an apartmental rental agreement, how to open and maintain a bank account . . . and some of my former colleagues could go on and on to further illustrate the point.

Inmates enrolled in Life Skills programs may be inmates who have chosen or who have been assigned to go to school; they may be inmates who have been assigned to other "work stations" and who are strongly encouraged to attend daytime or night-time Life Skills classes, or they may be inmates on the verge of release. Exposure to a Life Skills program for the latter may be a sort of last ditch effort to prepare them for 'life on the street'.

Adult basic education in federal prisons may mean, for a select few, involvement as tutors of fellow inmates at any level of the elementary and secondary school programs. I met two of them on one of my visits to the penitentiary in Springhill, Nova Scotia. The CSC welcomes volunteers from the external community to help out in nearly innumerable ways; some are literacy tutors as are these two inmates. One, a post-graduate in the Social Sciences, from a university in the southern United States, in prison because he was convicted of drug trafficking; the other a Grade 12 high school graduate from Newfoundland in prison for theft, I think he told me. They were tutors in the school's A.B.E. programs, helping prison colleagues to learn how to read and write. Tutoring was their paid employment while in prison and from the A.W.E.T. (Assistant Warden, Education and Training), I discovered that they were superb instructors in the Laubach or Frontier College's S.C.I.L. approaches. Both said that they each had regular school enrollees (and for this work they were paid) as well as other inmates who would not have enrolled at the school let alone admit that they were functionally illiterate (in this instance they were like all other volunteers, unpaid).

It was fascinating to hear them describe how they "taught", or "tutored" in those "unknown" circumstances, to whom and where they "taught or tutored". There are really no bounds to human imagination! For some inmates the reading instruction was the outside — the yard; for others, the chapel, for others the corner of the carpentry shop; for some the gymnasium, for some the greenhouse! And it was obvious to me that they alone could have access to those fearful, timid, shy, withdrawn inmates.

At first, I was shocked but then I grew to understand; then I knew that I had to promote teaching, tutoring as a job for inmates. For these inmates, learning to tutor is quite often the very first experience at doing something for someone else. I consider this basic education for that adult. Am I wrong?

Adult basic education *in prison*, for me, also means enrolment in college level courses or undergraduate university level courses or programs — albeit for a relatively small number of talented adults — very few of whom have ever had a rewarding school experience. In March 1985, for example, there were 409 inmates enrolled in college level courses and 328 enrolled in university level courses. Is that Adult Basic Education? Not for those educators who limit A.B.E. to a literacy program, nor for others who maintain that A.B.E. is only elementary and secondary level education of adults. It is A.B.E. for those educators who hold that a *first* experience at the post-secondary level, for talented and highly motivated adults, is basic for Canadians living in the last decades of the twentieth century. For most of these incarcerated post-secondary students, the basic college or university level exposure will be a distance learning experience by virtue of contractual agreements between the CSC and Athabasca University, Télé-Université or the Open Learning Institute. For others, it will be enrolment in traditional college or university courses given on "prison campus" or through correspondence.

What do I mean by distance learning? In the context of my three-year involvement as Director of Education, it meant enrolment at Athabasca or O.L.I. for English language courses, at Télé-Université for those seeking French language courses — as if one were a student by correspondence — except that it is enhanced learning through tutoring by a qualified university instructor or teacher (or professor!) who travels to the penitentiary to meet with his/her students on a pre-arranged basis.

A.B.E. in federal prisons is basic education of an adult to enable him/her to become a responsible law-abiding, self-respecting and self-directing adult. A.B.E. in prison spans the spectrum from elementary to post-secondary education at the college/university levels. For the profoundly disadvantaged person who is a prison inmate A.B.E. must be nothing less.

Note: The author thanks D. Griffin, Ph.D., formerly Chief of elementary and secondary (including A.B.E. and Life Skills) programs of the CSC for his assistance in presentation of data and editorial comment.

NOTES

1. The Correctional Service of Canada, *soit dit en passant*, calls prisons "établissements" (en français), "institutions" (in English) or "pénitenciers", which are prisons according to Larousse, subject to a penitentiary regime". . .
2. As a matter of fact — of 12,500 inmates in federal prisons — 143 are women. Equal opportunities, you ask?
3. I will not get involved in the debates on capital punishment.
4. Some might argue that what I write about the school is also applicable to the church or chapel; others might say that it's also true of their group therapy sessions aimed at addressing alcohol and drug abuse, etc. . . but, forgive me, I will not change my text.
5. Student Centered Individualized Learning.

REFERENCES

Ayers, Douglas (1981). "L'Education en prison", *Revue canadienne de l'education*, Vol. 6, No. 2.

Cosman, J. W. (1979). "Penitentiary Education in Canada", *Learning*, summer issue.

Duguid, Stephen (1981). "Moral Development, Justice and Democracy in the Prison", *Canadian Journal of Criminology*, Vol. 23, No. 2.

Gendreau, Paul and Robert Ross (1983). "Success in Corrections: Programs and Principles", *Juvenile Justice*.

Isabelle, Laurent et Douglas Griffin (1984). "The Education of Inmates dans les pénitenciers fédéraux du Canada", *Journal de l'Association canadienne de la formation professionnelles*, Vol. 20, No. 2, août.

Isabelle, Laurent (1986). "Objectives of the Education of Inmates — Principles and Priorities", *Journal of the Canadian Vocational Association*, Vol. 22, Nos. 2 and 3, fall.

Isabelle, Laurent (1986). "Bea in the SHU", *Guidance and Counselling Journal*, Vol. 2, No. 2, Nov., pp. 74–77.

Morin, Lucien (1981). "On Prison Education", Canadian Government Publishing Centre, Supply and Services Canada, 332p.

Ross, Robert and Elizabeth Fabiano (1985). "Time to Think", Institute of Social Sciences and Arts, Johnson City, Tennessee.

CHAPTER 5:

Literacy and Illiteracy in the Workplace

Kathryn L. Chang

- An insurance company employee pays a policyholder $2,200.00 on a $100.00 claim instead of the $22.00 authorized because she doesn't understand decimals.
- A train motorman, on trial for negligence in a fatal accident, admits that he has trouble reading his service manual, as do many of his co-workers.
- A feed-lot laborer accidentally kills a herd of cattle when he misreads a package label and feeds them poison instead of food.
- A computer company executive who makes $75,000.00 a year reads at a fourth grade level and has his wife help him write sales reports. He once ran up a $200.00 phone bill when he called her from Brussels to help him prepare a speech.

These are brief examples of problems with literacy in the workplace, taken from the newsletter of the Business Council for Effective Literacy. They illustrate the role of basic reading and writing in an employment enviroment, ie. whether or not a person needs to be able to read and write, and what happens if s/he can't. This is the simplest view of literacy in the workplace, a multi-facetted field of study. At its most complex, it involves all levels and types of literacy skills demanded by the job. The term "occupational literacy" encompasses this complex description; occupational literacy involves all levels of communication, computation and logic skill from the basics to such specialized areas as graphical literacy, technical literacy and computer literacy. An examination of each separately, and of the interrelationships, reveals implications for adult education programming.

LITERACY IN THE WORKPLACE

There are various perspectives on the role of literacy in the workplace. One is that illiteracy in the workplace is a problem, and this is closely related to the relationship between illiteracy and unemployment. A second perspective involves the relationship between education and employment, which includes the preparation that is, or is not, provided for literacy in the marketplace and for occupational literacy. A third perspective is the necessity for incorporation of occupational literacy skills instruction in Adult Basic Education and adult vocational education curricula. Each perspective merits examation, as they are interrelated.

Although literacy in the workplace may be examined from different positions, one thing remains constant. Research demonstrates that the ability to read job-related materials is a major occupational/functional skill. The Adult Functional Reading study (Murphy, 1975), sponsored by the Educational

Testing Service, determined that "reading materials at work is a critical part of the domain (of functional reading activities). A relatively large number of people perform such tasks for a relatively long time and consider them highly important." Sharon (1973), in a major study for the Educational Testing Service involving 5,067 adults, reported that 33% of the sample read at work (out of 38% of adults working on a typical day), that job-related reading was viewed as highly important, and that the people who read at work tended to be from a higher socio-econcmic level. Diehl (1980) noted that reading at work appears to be an ubiquitous activity; close to 99% of the subjects interviewed for one hundred different occupations representative of the total American employment scene reported doing some reading at work each day. Adams (1979) related reading ability to occupational health and safety. The negative implications of illiteracy for health and safety in the workplace are outlined extensively in a report prepared by the Task Force on Literacy and Occupational Health and Safety (1985), an advisory council to the Ontario Minister of Labor.

Reading, in most cases, is essential to job entry, survival and upward mobility. Just as the ability to read promotes independent learning, so it promotes independent working; the ratio of supervisor to worker is generally insufficient to allow for constant interpretation of reading materials for the worker (Thornton, 1977). Bricknell (1975) summarized by stating that reading is the fundamental vocational skill in our society because a person has to be able to read to find out about available jobs, to get a job, to keep a job, to get ahead in a job and to change to another job.

ILLITERACY IN THE WORKPLACE
Literacy in the workplace is linked integrally to the enormous problem of adult functional illiteracy. It is estimated that as many as 20% of the adult population cannot read and write well enough to function in contemporary society (Thomas, 1976), and this spills over to become illiteracy in the workplace. The cost of illiteracy is measured both in human terms and in financial terms. In brief, illiteracy in the workplace costs millions of dollars in low productivity, workplace accidents, absenteeism, poor product quality, and lost management and supervisory time (BCEL, 1986).

Closely related to this is the connection between functional illiteracy and unemployment which also results in expense for individuals and for society. The Business Council for Effective Literacy has determined that up to 7% of the currently unemployed are functionally illiterate. The Chicago-based Coalition for Literacy has calculated the annual costs in America to be $237 billion in lost earnings, $6 billion in social assistance payments, and $8 billion in diminished tax revenues. For society and for individuals, unemployment has far-reaching negative consequences, psychologically, financially and politically. The inability to read and write at a functional level, therefore, can prevent individuals from working safely and efficiently, and from getting and keeping jobs.

PREPARATION FOR LITERACY IN THE WORKPLACE
The skills and knowledge needed by individuals to live and work in our society are supposed to be imparted through the educational system. However, many informed and influential people question the adequacy of current educational endeavors to provide training for functional literacy in general (Kozol,

1980; Hunter & Harman, 1979), and, specifically, for occupational literacy (Mikulecky, 1982, 1984). The relationship between education and employment has become tenuous; there are increasing complaints from business, industry, the military and the general public that growing numbers of workers are inadequately prepared for work. There are further complaints that significant numbers of adults do not have sufficient reading skills to function in occupational settings. Two educational systems are involved in this failure to provide preparation for literacy in the workplace.

GENERAL EDUCATION AND LITERACY

Most adults have had the opportunity to go through the general education system, and many are still functionally illiterate. In designing and implementing ABE and workplace literacy programs, it is essential to examine how the need for both has arisen, and to avoid re-creating the same problems. Literacy-related problems within the general education system may be posed by the teachers, the students, the reading and writing materials, and/or combinations thereof.

Too many teachers know very little about the reading and writing processes (Lee, 1981; Thornton, 1979). They ignore the vital relationship between reading and learning; as a tool to facilitate learning, reading is a unique and predominant mode of preserving and conveying information (Goodman, 1970). Most teachers simply assume that students can read (Herber, 1978), an assumption with no basis in fact (Duke & Powers, 1973). Some commonly held misconceptions are that:

- reading is learned at the primary level and attention to reading beyond that level is unnecessary;
- reading is not a responsibility of the content area teachers;
- teaching reading is a specialized area, beyond the capability of the subject area teacher;
- classroom reading can be circumvented by the use of descriptive handouts and oral presentations (Thorton, 1979).

Lack of knowledge and a negative attitude towards reading cause many teachers to contribute unknowingly to the adult illiteracy problem. Literacy-related problems may also result from the lack of skills and knowledge on the part of the students. Such problems, such as inadequate concept development, insufficient language proficiency, and deficient textbook and study skills, can prevent individuals from functioning in phases of the educational system. In addition, a student may experience deficiencies in subject-specific reading skills; each subject area inherently contains a predominance of certain skill requirements (Cheek & Cheek, 1981), and a student may be weak in only one. Finally, students may simply not be reading at the prerequisite level for the course or grade in question.

Just as literacy-related problems can centre with the teacher and/or the students, so they can with the reading and writing materials. Reading materials such as blackboard notes, exam questions, teacher-made handouts, and textbooks may either be too difficult or too easy to read. According to Abram (1981), the readability of materials should be less than or equal to the reading skills of the reader. However, assuming that the students have the prerequisite reading skiHs levels, research indicates that textbooks used are often too difficult for the intended users (Schulteis & Napoli, 1975; Thornton, 1977). It should be noted that readability includes more than what formula can measure: legibility of print, illustration and color, vocabulary, charts and graphs, conceptual difficulty, syntax, organization, structural and stylistic elements, use of redundancy, types of inferences, abstract terminology, and concept development and reading ability of the users. Readability may be best used synonymously with suitability, understandability and learnability (Irwin & Davis, 1980). Curran (1976) hypothesized that readability is a necessary but not sufficient condition for comprehensibility, and that both are necessary but not sufficient for useability. All to often the "readability" of the materials used for courses causes problems that negatively affect learning in all areas of general education, as do reading-related difficulties presented by teachers and by students.

OCCUPATIONAL EDUCATION AND LITERACY

The literacy-related problems that exist in general education exist, and are even magnified, in the systems providing education for employment. In addition to problems caused by instructors, students and reading materials, there are further difficulties.

To begin with, reading is treated as a prerequisite to entry to occupational programs; students are supposed to function at a specified grade level as a minimum entrance requirement. It is assumed that trainees are able to read the texts, notes, exams and other curricular materials. Perhaps for this reason, the majority of American technical and vocational institutions make no provision for either general reading and study skills or occupation-specific reading skills (Thornton, 1980). In a thorough examination of the literature in the Dialog Data Bases concerning reading in post-secondary occupational education, Thornton (1980) found that there was practically no reference to occupation-specific reading skill development, and that, if reading was treated at all, it was a curricular issue.

Occupational education programs are rife with potential literacy-related problem areas. To begin with, the technical language peculiar to a trade or profession may be complex and difficult to learn (Lee, 1981). For example, trade-related literature may be of a wide range of difficulty according to the task; the amount of technical language, trades language, and lay description; the use of diagram and illustration; and the attendant language-to-diagram ratio (Thornton, 1979). Textbooks and technical manuals often have a very high reading level due to the technical language and the necessity for accuracy before readability (Thornton, 1979).

Then there are the problems that examinations can present. Hunt and Lindley (1977) made the claim that pre-employment tests are often too hard to read; applicants must contend with unnecessary and irrelevant reading demands before they can meet and solve the problems on the job (Mikulecky & Diehl, 1979). As well, tests are usually given in settings which deprive the student of access to other cues or sources of information that s/he might consult on the job in accomplishing job tasks (Jacob & Crandall, 1979). Too, job-training achievement is measured by different tasks and strategies than is actual job performance (Sticht, 1978).

Further complications arise from the fact that most occupation educators lack the background to deal with reading either as a curricular issue or as an occupational skill (Lee, 1981). Many occupational educators emerge from their specialty area, often have less academic and teacher education background, and are hired because of the ability to translate a specialty into job skills (Thornton, 1979).

The most significant problem seems to be that not enough is known about the specific reading demands of most occupations to prepare individuals while in the training process (Sticht, 1978; Thornton, 1979).

Many of these problems can be solved, thereby obviating the need for ABE and workplace literacy programs over time. Until then, the responsibility falls on literacy and basic education administrators. It is they who must ensure that the ABE instructors possess the following:

1. a thorough knowledge of the reading and writing processes, regardless of their subject area;
2. the ability to assess student's ability and interest, and to individualize instruction;
3. an awareness of the complexity of the "readability" of materials, commercially prepared and their own;
4. knowledge of the differences between reading at school and reading on the job.

Those educators responsible for curriculum development may find direction in the research and practice pertaining to occupational literacy.

OCCUPATIONAL LITERACY

Most research in the field of occupational literacy is based on the monumental work of Sticht and his various colleagues at the Human Resources Research Organization. Within the military environment, the research of Sticht et al. (1971-1978) focused on determining the literacy demands of jobs, determining the relationship between literacy-ability and job-ability, developing reliable and valid testing procedures for matching individuals with jobs, and developing ways of restructuring materials to reduce the literacy demands. Among the numerous contributions to current research were the FORCAST readability formula (Caylor et al, 1973) designed to be used with job-related reading materials, and the categories for literacy strategies (reading-to-do and reading-to-learn) which Diehl (1980) expanded upon. Three important conclusions drawn by Sticht (1975) were:

1. a substantial portion of job trainees are deficient in job reading skills:
2. six weeks of focused job reading training improved job reading skills at least two reading grade level years specific to job reading skills; and
3. programs of integrated job reading and job skills training are feasible.

Much occupational-literacy research has been conducted by the military; however, it is difficult to obtain, and may not be generalizable to the civilian environment.

Most research into occupational literacy has been directed at identifying literacy demands for specific jobs. Research in the civilian sector has tended to minimal; it appears that most research being conducted on testing and establishing literacy requirements is done within companies and is not published. Smith (1976) researched generic skills for occupational training. Heinemann (1979) analyzed the performance of secretaries in job-related reading tasks. Ross (1980) conducted an analysis of the nature and difficulty of reading tasks associated with beginning office workers' jobs. Spicer (1975) attempted to identify the communications competencies required by future businesspersons. Moe, Rush and Storlie (1979) described the literacy requirements necessary to hold a job in ten occupations and the corresponding requirements necessary to succeed in vocational training programs which prepare individuals for each of those occupations. Chang (1983) researched the curricular and occupational reading demands of the plumbing trade. Diehl and Mikulecky (1980) interviewed workers in one hundred occupations and examined the general nature of on-the-job literacy tasks, the difficulty of job materials, the relationship between that difficulty and an individual's reading ability, the relationship between literacy and job success, and the characteristics of component and non-competent readers. This means that ABE curriculum developers can find some specific information about the literacy of a limited number of occupations in research reports.

The generalizability and usability of much of the above effort is affected by natural limitations and by questionable methodologies. As a result of criticisms, current research has taken two different tacks. In an attempt to narrow and clarify the field, researchers are examining the differences between the literacy demands while on the job and while training for the job. There are major differences between curricular reading demands in the school/training setting and occupational reading demands in terms of cognitive demands, the availability of extra-linguistic cues, the uses of information gained, and the nature and frequency of tasks encountered. Data gathered by Mikulecky (1981) suggests that workers face far more stringent literacy demands on the job than students currently face in school; on the average, students from both technical and high schools read less in school than they will be expected to on the job. Sticht (1978) found that reading for job preparation was more demanding than reading for job performance; curricular reading demands involve reading to form and retain new concepts, ie. reading-to-learn, as opposed to occupational reading to look up specific information for relatively immediate use, ie. reading-to-do.

This is closely related to the second direction of current research, ie. the way information gained through reading is processed to enhance occupational effectiveness. According to Mikulecky (1985), evidence suggests that job performance may be more closely related to metacognitive aspects of literacy than to the basic literacy abilities of achieving literal comprehension or communicating simple messages. Guthrie et al. (1984) demonstrated that people can and do acquire competencies to meet their occupational reading needs. Kirsch & Guthrie (1982) emphasized the importance of studying reading and literacy as a system of culturally organized skills and values that are acquired in particular contexts to satisfy particular needs.

Other studies in occupational literacy have had different focuses. Projects have been directed at occupational/vocational curriculum development (Farning & Boyce, 1976; Howell, 1976; Horne, 1979). The needs of non-English speakers, ie. ESL-literacy in the workplace, were the focus of projects sponsored by the Experiment in International Living ("Shifting Gears 2. Hands-on Activities for Learning Workplace Skills and English as a Second Language," 1984), and the Centre for Applied Linguistics ("From the Classroom to the Workplace: Teaching ESL to Adults," 1983). Special occupational literacy strategies for learning disabled adults were outlined by Seitz and Scheerer (1983) and by Davis and Woodruff (1985). Some projects have been commissioned to develop literacy programs for specific corporations (Pagurek & Fitzgerald, 1984), while others investigate literacy programs offered in-house by business and industry (Baar-Kessler, 1984; Kirsch & Guthrie, 1982, 1983; Mark, 1984). Other studies are directed at specific types of occupational literacy, such as graphical literacy (Sofo, 1985), technical literacy (Conklin & Reder, 1985; and computer literacy (Goodard, 1983; Hill, 1985; Hunter & Aiken, 1984).

Most of these studies are available from ERIC and can provide the specifics needed for specialized programs. Basically this means that ABE instructors and curriculum developers need not begin by conducting their own intense research, especially when each student may present a different occupational goal.

WORKPLACE LITERACY AND ABE

Why is it a good idea to incorporate instruction in employment-related reading into ABE programs? Theory in the field of adult education suggests that adult students desire and benefit most from tasks that have immediate application and personal relevance. Employment is a vital interest of very many ABE students. The use of occupational reading materials is therefore highly motivating to many students. There is an additional aspect of social responsibility that enters as well; ABE programs must help adult students to become actively involved in the life and work of their communities. It would be highly irresponsible to ignore employment-related literacy.

The incorporation of workplace literacy skills into ABE curriculum seem both desirable and possible. As with all adult education endeavors, instruction in work-related reading and writing should be relevant to the individual in terms of need and timing, ie. what the student needs when it is needed for success in employment. It is therefore impossible to totally generalize workplace literacy instruction. The specific types of materials, the levels of difficulty and the necessary strategies vary according to the job and must be determined either through accessing research findings or intensive investigation on the part of instructors.

Although workplace literacy instruction must be tailored to individuals or to occupational groupings, there are some generalizations that research substantiates. Rush (1985) recommends that instructors prepare ABE students for success in work roles by:

– developing reading lessons around specific work topics and with real work materials;
– teaching the meaning and recognition of essential work-related vocabulary;

– stressing instruction in reading graphic information; emphasizing the application of reading-to-do skills by involving such tasks as following directions;
– teaching reading-to-learn skills to students going on to occupational training programs;
– allowing for the repetitive nature of reading on the job; and
– encouraging the use of alternative sources of information as an aide to comprehension.

In summation, it is imperative that the situation which has lead to the crisis in adult and occupational illiteracy not be duplicated in ABE programs. Curriculum developers can look to research for knowledge of the competencies required in specific job and training settings. Instructors can focus on the use of the principles of adult learning and content area reading. Adults can be better prepared for literacy in the workplace.

REFERENCES

Abram, M. J. (1981) Readability: Its use in adult education. *Lifelong Learning,* 4, pp. 8-9, 30-31.

Adams Report. (1979) *Education and Working Canadians.* Ottawa, ON: Commission of Inquiry on Educational Leave and Productivity.

Baar-Kessler, M. (1984) *An Analysis of the Concept of "Literacy" and Investigation of the Fortune 500 Companies in Literacy Training.* M. Ed. thesis, Rutgers University.

Bricknell, H. M. (1975) National Perspectives on Career Education. In Nielsen & Hjelm (Eds.), *Reading and Career Education.* Newark, DE: International Reading Association.

Business Council for Effective Literacy. (1986) *Newsletter,* 1, 8, pp. 3.

Caylor, J. S., Sticht, T. G., Fox, L. C., & Ford, J. P. (1973) *Methodologies for Determining Reading Requirements of Military Occupational Specialties.* Alexandra, VA: Human Resources Research Organization.

Chang, Kathryn L. (1983) *Reading Demands of the Plumbing Trade.* Unpublished master's thesis, University of Calgary, Calgary, AB, 1983.

Cheek, M. C., & Cheek, E. H. (1981, April) Tips for administrators on content area reading. *NASSP Bulletin,* pp. 81-85.

Conklin, N. F. & Reder, S. (1985) *Changing Channels: A Guide to Functional Literacy for the Automated Workplace.* Portland, OR: Northwest Regional Educational Lab.

Curran, T. E. Readability Research in the Navy. (1976) In Sticht & Zapf (Eds.), *Reading and Readability Research in the Armed Services.* Alexandria, VA: Human Resources Research Organization.

Davis, B. & Woodruff, N. (1985) *Trade Related Reading Packets for Disabled Readers.* Sewell, NJ: Gloucester County Vocational-Technical School.

Diehl, W. A. (1980) *Functional Literacy as a Variable Construct: An Examination of Attitudes, Behaviours and Strategies Related to Occupational Literacy.* Unpublished doctoral dissertation, Bloomington, IN.

Diehl, W.A. & Mikulecky, L. (1980) The Nature of Reading at Work. *Journal of Reading,* 24, 3, pp. 221-227.

Duke, C., & Powers, A. (1973) Reading in the content area. *Clearing House,* 47, pp. 221-226.

Farning, M. & Boyce, E. (1976) *Developing and Verifying a List of Competencies for the Communication Skills Area in Vocational/Technical Post-Secondary Education.* Wisconsin Rapids, WI: Mid-State Vocational, and Adult Education District.

Goodman, K. (1970) Behind the eye: What happens in reading. *Reading-Process and Programs.* Urbana, IL: National Council of Teachers of English.

Guthrie, J. et al. (1984) *Relationships Among Competencies and Practices of Reading.* Newark, DE: International Reading Association.

Hawkins, J. A. Jr. (1977) How should reading and study skills test scores correlate? *Journal of Reading,* 20, pp. 570-572.

Heinemann, S. T. (1979) Can Job-Related Performance Tasks be Used to Diagnose Secretaries Reading and Writing Skills? *Journal of Reading*, 23, 3, pp. 239-243.

Herber, H. L. (1978) *Teaching reading in the content areas*. New York: Prentice-Hall.

Hill, K. H. J. (1985) *Adult Computer Literacy*. Paper submitted to an Advanced Seminar in Adult and Continuing Education, Kansas

Horne, G. P. (1979) *Functional Job Literacy: Implications for Instruction*. Wellesley, MA: the Commnwealth Centre for High Technology/Education.

Howell, J. D. (1976) *An Identification of the Competence in English Needed by Vocational Students in the Community Colleges and Technical Institutes in North Carolina*. Unpublished doctoral dissertation, North Carolina State University at Raleigh.

Hunt T. & Lindley, C. T. (1977) Documentation of Selection and Promotion Test Questions: Are Your Records Sagging? *Public Personnel Management*, Octcber - November, pp. 415-421.

Hunter, B. & Aiken, R. (1984) *Computer Literacy in Vocational Education: Perspectives and Directions*. Knoxville, TN: Tennessee University.

Hunter, C. & Hannan, D. (1979) *Adult Illiteracy in the United States*. New York: NY: McGraw-Hill.

Irwin, J. W., & Davis, C. A. (1980) Assessing readability: The checklist approach. *Journal of Reading*, 24, pp. 124-130.

Jacob, E. & Crandall, J. (1979) *Job-Related Literacy: A Look at Current and Needed Research*. Bloomington, IN: Centre for Applied Linguistics.

Kirsch, I. & Guthrie, J. T. (1980) *The Concept and Measurement of Functional Literacy*. (1977-1978) In Karnes, Ginn and Maddox (Eds.), Issues and Trends in ABE. Jackson, MS: University of Mississippi Press.

Kirsch, I. & Guthrie, J. (1982). *Prose Comprehension and Text Search as a Function of Reading Volume*. Newark, DE: International Reading Association.

Kirsch, I. & Guthrie, J. (1982) *Case Studies of Reading in a High Technology Corporation*. Newark, DE: International Reading Association.

Kozol, J. (1980) *Prisoners of Silence*. New York, NY: Continuum Publishing Co.

Lee, H. D. (1981) Dealing with reading in industrial arts. *Journal of Reading*, 24, pp. 663-668.

Mark, J. L. (1984) *Private Sector Providers of Basic Skills Training in the Workplace*. Washington, DC: American Association for Adult and Continuing Education.

Mikulecky, L. (December 1981) School Training and Job Literacy Demands. *The Vocational Guidance Quarterly*, pp. 174-180.

Mikulecky, L. (1982) Job Literacy: The Relationship Between School Preparation and Workplace Actuality. *Reading Research Quarterly*, 17, pp. 400-419.

Mikulecky, L. (1984) Preparing Students for Workplace Literacy Demands. *Journal of Reading*, 282, 3, pp. 253-257.

Mikulecky, L. (1985) *Literacy Task Analysis: Defining and Measuring Occupational Literacy Demands*. Paper presented at the National Adult Educational Research Association, Chicago.

Mikulecky, L. & Diehl, W. (1979) *Literacy Requirements in Business and Industry*. Paper commissioned for the National Institute of Education. Bloomington, IN: Reading Research Centre.

Moe, A. J., Rush, R. T. & Storlie, R. L. (1979) *The Literacy Requirements of a Licenses Practical Nurse on the Job and in a Vocational Training Program*. West Lafayette, IN: Department of Education, Purdue University.

Murphy, R. T. (1975) *Adult Functional Reading. Study; Project 1: Targeted Research and Development Reading Program Objectives Subparts 1, 2 and 3*. Princeton, NJ: Educational Testing Service.

Pagurek, J. & Fitzgerald, B. (1984) English in the Workplace: McDonald's Executive English. In *Carlton Papers in Applied Language Studies*. Ottawa, ON: Carlton University.

Ross, N. (April, 1980) *An Analysis of the Nature and Difficulty of Reading Tasks Associated With Beginning Office Workers Jobs in the Columbus, Ohio Metropolitan Area*. Paper presented at the Annual Meeting of the American Educational Research Association, Boston, MA.

Schulteis, R. A., & Napoli, K. (1975) Strategies for helping poor readers in business subjects. *Business Education Form*, 30, pp. 5-11.

Seitz, S. & Scheerer, J. (1983) *Learning Disabilities: Introduction and Strategies for College Teaching*. Massachusetts.

Sharon, A. (1973) What Do Adults Read? *Reading Research Quarterly*, 9 pp. 148-169.

Smith, A. D. (1976) Reading Skills – What Reading Skills? In Merritt, J. E. (Eds.), *New Horizons in Reading*. Newark, DE: International Reading Association.

Sofo, F. (1985) A Difference Approach to Literacy: Graphics. *Australian Journal of Adult Education,* 25, 20, pp. 27-34.

Spicer, C. (April, 1975) *The Identification of Communication Competencies Required by Future Businesspersons: An Application of the Delphi Method.* Paper presented at the International Communication Association annual meeting, Chicago.

Sticht, T. G. (Ed.) (1975) *Reading for Working: A Functional Literacy Anthology.* Alexandria, VA: Human Resources Research Organization.

Sticht, T. G. (April, 1978) *Literacy and Vocational Competence.* Occasional Paper No. 39, Columbus, OH: The National Centre for Research in Vocational Education.

Thomas, A. M. (1976) *Adult Basic Education and Literacy Activities in Canada 1975-76.* Toronto, ON: World Literacy of Canada.

Thornton, L. J. (1977) *Relationship of Carpentry Material Installation Instructions and Carpentry Textbooks to Reading Ability of High School Carpentry Textbooks to Reading Ability of High School Carpentry Students.* Unpublished masters thesis, Suny College of Technology, Utica, NY.

Thornton, L. J. (1979) Reading Sensitivity in Post-Secondary Occupational Education. *Lifelong Learning: The Adult Years,* 3, 4, pp. 12-15, 19.

Thornton, L. J. (April, 1980) *Review and Synthesis of Reading in Post-Secondary Occupational Education.* Pennsylvania State University.

CHAPTER 6:

Issues, Trends and Implications in Adult Basic Education "New Frontiers in Literacy Education"

Jack C. Pearpoint

Most of us, who have been waiting for the literacy train to pull into the station — with money and job security, etc. — have just recently seen some light in the tunnel. Two throne speeches in 1986: Ontario and Ottawa made short references to illiteracy. A secretariat was created in Ontario Ministry of Skills Development and some new monies began to flow. But on Sept. 8, 1988, International Literacy Day, we reached a milestone. Prime Minister Mulroney spent the morning at Frontier College with his family, read to children and adults, then proceeded to a luncheon where he announced a five year $110,000,000 commitment of the Federal Government to literacy.

The significance of the day was not the budget commitment (which is a substantial beginning), but rather that this was a major policy statement by the Prime Minister that literacy is officially on the agenda. Mr. Turner and Mr. Broadbent affirmed support for the initiative within hours confirming that the literacy issue may be one of the few genuinely non-partisan issues which will receive continued support regardless of party affiliation. Now the next stage of literacy work begins.

Bureaucrats at all levels are suddenly consulting on "literacy" to rush policies and perhaps even some funds into the newly found issue. It's a long overdue beginning — but a beginning none the less. However, these speeches are far from the fundamental change or substantial support that is needed to guarantee effective literacy skills for all citizens. They are important and welcome developments, but they are not "the future" of literacy education.

Literacy has been on the margins of adult education, which has equally been on the fringe of the mainstream education systems for recent decades. Not surprisingly, since the need is urgent for hundreds of thousands of Canadian adults, "new frontiers" of literacy education are emerging. Few are in the education mainstream — and, in many cases, barely in the literacy network.

Let's let our minds wander to what will be in the year 2000. My prognosis is for major shifts.

TRENDS FOR THE FUTURE

A few of the elements of the educational shift are already visible, but they are only just the beginning. My predictions of trends include changes in terminology; locations for learning; jurisdictional shifts; more conferences and research; dramatic impacts from technology; acknowledgement that literacy is an essential foundation; and educational restructuring that will include shifting the role of the teacher to "learning facilitator".

Terminology

Literacy will be dropped as a term. New positive individualized terms will emerge, and the new androgogy will not be constrained by buildings or course limitations. "Literacy" is one of the places where "new frontiers" in education will be created because there is so little "establishment" to retrain.

Location: From School to Work!

School-based programs will diminish dramatically. Since there are only very few school-based literacy programs now, this may seem outrageous, particularly since "new money is coming on stream"; and, in the sort term, there will be rash of new school board and community college classroom-based programs. But these programs will lose their allure the minute the funding formula shifts, and they will be on to new and better financed priorities — whatever they are. This is not a critique, but rather a prediction.

However, even in the short term, some of what will happen with the new literacy monies is distressing. What is wrong is that many of these programs will repeat the techniques that we already know will fail. Few will have the courage, the time or the curiosity to delve a little deeper and ask what can we do to avoid repeating what we already know does not work. And so, many if not most, will set up "new" programs which will not be new, and thus repeat the inadequacies of the past — and ultimately repeat the failures. Most will conclude that the students could not cope with the programs, so they must unfortunately be dumped for better "investment" returns. I do not consider this cynical, even though it is depressing.

Workplace Training

The new frontiers will be based in industry and in the home . . . not in schools or community colleges. This trend has already begun, and is being resisted by most established institutions whose financial security is at risk. The trend is only the leading edge, but the direction is clear. One of the reasons is the growing dissatisfaction with the existing school system. While in many cases the "blame" is misappropriated, the school system is an easy target. It is expensive, and the end product from an industrial perspective simply isn't adequate. The trend is NOT to work with the schools to "make it better", but as is already happening in several precedent setting union contracts, to create an education fund, and design or purchase the programs of choice . . . at the plant or in the union hall. While this is not yet common, it is a major shift. Industry is saying we will do it ourselves and, if necessary, we will contract out to the best supplier rather than simply accept the education system's standard packages.

Jurisdiction & Bureaucracy

Since literacy has been a tiny piece of turf with few benefits and enormous liabilities until now, the short term will be characterized by "turf" battles with the various potential players racing to garner credit with minimum cost. Since bureaucratic guidelines and systems are only just being developed, competing systems will be established that have little to do with teaching reading and writing, and an enormous amount to do with finding things that can be "counted" and audited, and most important, that look good in the press. Consultants will have a field day. A well established pattern will be repeated. Enormous sums will be spent to study and publicize "good projects", but the support will be substantially less than the study and promotions budget.

Research

After dealing with virtually no substantial research base for years (no money — no interest), Southam Inc., in frustration, undertook the first significant literacy survey in Canada in a decade. Their effort has been rewarded by a medal from UNESCO for their contribution to literacy. In parallel, computer firms and developers of all shapes and sizes are trying to jam "literacy" into a marketable package that will "fix" the literacy problem. There is also a rash rush for academic "research" in the field. Unfortunately, because many of the most experienced practitioners and theorists have not been part of the educational mainstream, they will be overlooked and ignored. The new "bandwagon" topic will be adopted by "experts" of all types who will squeeze literacy into the comfortable formats and forms of other topics, and thus produce volumes of inappropriate and largely irrelevant material. This of course will be funded generously because it can be accounted for in tidy binders and manuscripts without any of the discomforts and inconveniences of dealing with the real needs of people who do not conform, occasionally eat garlic, and don't follow WASP guidelines for how to be a better employee. This does not deny the need for genuine research, but rather predicts how funding allocations will be administered.

Conferences

And there will be conferences — dozens of conferences. While necessary, most will be "about" "people with problems", and will be closer to the model of "hunger" conferences discussing malnutrition over chateaubriand. But some of these meetings will allow new actors to inject some realism into developing options.

Technology: Manage or be Managed!

That is the challenge of the computer. And it has only just begun. It is frightening, but also fascinating because of the genuinely new opportunities it presents for real and relevant education. Most of us do not even have conceptual frameworks that will allow us to comprehend the enormity of the irrevocable change that has begun. But the new technology will control us, or give us more control than we have ever dreamed possible. Educationally, it is already technically possible that the most up-to-date knowledge on virtually any topic can be delivered at low cost to your office or home — virtually instantly — in electronic print, including the entire Library of Congress, scientific articles, weather data, a course on 747-engine maintenance, the stock market trends, and the who's who of philatelists interested in stamps from Burma. In short, the computer is already at the point where access to information surpasses our capacity to understand.

Practically, this alters the very notion of what most educators consider to be their role. Most teachers — regardless of level — think that they "deliver information". What educators have not yet come to terms with is the fact that many of today's youth have been exposed to more information about more issues than most earlier generations knew existed. Thus, "giving information" is fundamentally redundant. Teaching people to "manage information" . . . there is the challenge for the future.

Presently, most people do not understand the information that is available to them, thus it does not "empower" them in any way. We need to develop skills to sort, organize, edit out drivel, and genuinely utilize the information at our fingertips. That is the new task of education.

Literacy: Foundation or Frill?

Literacy is now non-negotiable. It is the prerequisite to give citizens the power to manage their lives. And there is no point in teaching "horse and buggy" technology in the space age. I am not talking about whether people can read Proust or Chaucer. I am talking about managing information that affects people's daily lives.

The availability of electronic information is going to have an enormous impact on educational systems. Since the information can be delivered any place, many are going to ask "why schools"? Some of them will "take their learning elsewhere". Some of these trends are already visible. For example, industry has for many years complained that "graduates" from various programs were not meeting their needs. While some of their criticisms are less than fair, the next decade will see government, labour and industry supporting training in the workplace. And this will create enormous pressure on post-secondary training institutions.

Recent reports on drop out rates are creating a fundamental shakedown in the education system. Teachers are being slammed and are angry and afraid of their futures. Meanwhile parents and economists (often for very different reasons) are protesting loudly about the quality of our education systems. The concerns are being raised by "bleeding hearts" "hard nosed" types who agree that it is bad economics to spend enormous amounts of money on educating youth and adults only to have them "drop out" and join the ranks of the unemployed for length periods. Hard questions will be asked . . . and answers will be demanded like never before. Experimental programs will evolve to deal with incorrigible kids because the expense of giving up is too high. The next logical institution, the prison system, is dramatically more costly, long-term and disastrous.

Educational Restructuring — Back to the Student!

There is a need for a radical rethinking and restructuring of education. It should not be just cosmetic. We need to develop a system that is genuinely responsive to the needs of students — and not just with rhetoric.

A senior educator just told me that now that he is out of the education system he realizes that it is the only industry where the customer is always wrong. The customer has to come, take whatever is offered — and be grateful. He told me about an exercise he gave his graduate students. "Pretend you are school principals — and make recommendations to improve education in your school." The responses were invariably lists with demands for more equipment, better facilities, small classrooms, etc. Part two of the exercise was identical, but "your school" was now private where parents pay. The suggestions were very different — usually beginning with more parent involvement, curriculum concerns, learning styles, etc. It is fascinating that the same students consistently repeated the pattern. Clearly the suggestion of accountability to parents produces a very different result.

More Accountability: More Partnerships

I am not suggesting that we "privatize" all schools, but rather that we introduce new kinds of community accountability so that new partnerships of teachers, parents, business and others are encouraged to be creative and responsible to some of the more complex educational challenges we face. If we already know that some things don't work for students, it is responsible and correct to experiment with some creative options. That needs to be encouraged. It will make our system MUCH more responsive. It will also make it educationally exciting again.

Learning Facilitators — Information Managers

In the new era that will evolve where we focus on building life-long learners, teachers will become "learning facilitators" or "information management consultants". People will go to them, and they will go to people, when they are needed, and where they are wanted. It will be exciting and challenging teaching in that atmosphere — because the students will be there to learn. It will be dynamic — not passive. The new generation of students will be demanding consumers — and that will re-inject quality and vitality into our educational systems.

It might even progress to live up to the educational vision that the founder of Frontier College, Alfred Fitzpatrick, wrote about at the turn of the century:

> "Whenever and wherever people shall meet, then should be the time, place and means of their education."

THE NEW FRONTIERS IN LITERACY
HOW CAN WE MAKE IT WORK?

The answer is "with the consumers". That is why I am excited. Many people are depressed because when they look for educational innovation, they look to "educators". Wrong direction! Try looking to the literacy consumers — the people who experienced failure in the system. After all, the most logical place to look for new literacy initiatives is among the people who need it. It is their priority, and things are happening.

The Problem is the Answer

Consumers who have been on the fringe of our society are evolving as the leadership of the next stage of development. And I don't mean simply token leadership. Aboriginal Canadians are a case in point. Statistically, they should have given up and collected their treaty money forever. Objectively, they face tremendous difficulties. A decade ago, who could have imagined — in their wildest dreams — that Canadian Indian leaders would sit at a meeting with all the First Ministers of Canada. These new leaders performed with pride, integrity and an eloquence that was stunning to all Canadians, including the politicians around the table. Against all odds, a new leadership cadre is evolving that will restore the self-esteem of Aboriginal Canadians, and thus build a new and constructive future — from the ashes of a welfare sink-hole. In this struggle "literacy" is a fundamental issue and, in partnership with selected professionals and friends, aboriginal Canadians will develop new "literacy education" options that some of us may find useful.

Already, Native Survival Schools are springing up from coast to coast, and their graduates do not have the 30% + dropout rate prevalent in the rest of our schools. These graduates are competing and succeeding on all fronts — even though critics charged that in sustaining culture and tradition, there was no content. It simply is not true. New leadership and new interdependent systems will emerge.

The Partnership Theme

Education — including literacy education — is going to shift to "Partnerships". We have proved that throwing money at complex problems without appropriate support, all in the name of supporting "local" initiatives, does not work. Similarly, bureaucratic paternalism, no matter how well-intentioned, is now unacceptable, and more important, unworkable and uneconomic. The next logical stage is "partnerships". The experts on any problem are the people on the front line. They have more information that anyone else. However, they may not be able to organize and manage that information in their own interests. Thus, Partnerships. Supportive professionals can work with local groups to assist them to manage the information they have and translate it into forms that are required for funding, reporting, training, etc. The key is that "consumers" must have genuine involvement and control. It is a tough regime to work in . . . but it works! And that is more than can be said for many of the earlier models. Partnerships build on strengths and can deliver.

Tough Road Ahead!

For all the apparent optimism, I am not going to wait for the gravy train to arrive with the answers. It is going to be a tremendous amount of work, and there will be many disappointments. Although literacy may be "motherhood" to some of us, we must observe that our society has a habit of institutionalizing many of our mothers. Rather than living with them and appreciating the fullness of life, we write a cheque and allow them to vegetate until "death do us part". Shocking but true! By the same measure, I do not expect any literacy miracles. Literacy is essential for justice in our society. But for many, our society is far from just. It is a matter of will, and collectively, we have not responded to the need. The response of the Federal and Provincial governments to acknowledge and begin funding literacy is excellent — but it is only the beginning.

If it were a perfect world, most of our literacy programs, especially those like Beat The Street (a program utilizing the talents of street people to teach street people) would not be required at all. But they are. This country needs hundreds of new programs to meet the needs of hundreds of thousands of learners who have been missed. And if all was just, it would simply be a matter of pointing out the slippage in the system, and educators and policy-makers would rush to repair the oversight. Such is not the case.

Individuals make extraordinary efforts, and some officials bend rules and close their eyes to facilitate support — we all know how it works. But officials and practitioners should not have to look away and battle for crumbs — but they do, and we do too! I do not expect it to change that much. Instead, we scrabble over crumbs, fight with large and bureaucratic systems, and, most debilitating, are under constant attack by our colleagues.

I think the best conclusion is to be specific. I want to give a short case history of incredible success — fraught with incredible frustration. I could use many different programs to make the point. HELP uses ex-offenders to find jobs for ex-offenders; Independent Studies involves people with handicaps in creating new visions for people with handicaps; Native people are tutoring native people; workers are teaching other workers, immigrant parents working with other parents. We have also initiated a program to encourage parents and peers to read to each other — to put reading back into our culture. These and many more are examples of partnerships which I think are the pattern for the future. But the case history I have selected is Beat The Street: street-people tutoring street-people — another Frontier partnership. It points out the operational frustrations, the need for supportive partnerships, and the dilemma of dealing with success. Lastly, I reveal my survival techniques . . . the five minute solution.

BEAT THE STREET — A PATTERN FOR THE FUTURE?
Over the past three years, Beat The Street has been featured dozens of times on national (CBC's Journal, and CTV's W5), TV Ontario and local television. Newspaper articles are everywhere, and speaking invitations range from House of Commons committees, to conferences, schools and street gatherings. More recently, the Federal Minister of Youth, Jean Charest approved three year funding to expand Beat the Street to Regina and Winnipeg. Other cities need it. And yet, cynics search for a way to prove that it cannot succeed. Extensive records are kept of student writings, and many students have opted to take correspondence courses to get "formal" upgrading. Their A grades aren't enough. Criticism remains. The founders (Tracy and Rick) aren't "trained professionals"; there are no standardized measures of improvement, etc. The evidence is there . . . but some people can't afford to risk seeing success. Because the actual "hours" studied exceed many other more formal programs, many Board of Education officials are worried — it looks too good. They should rejoice that lost learners are returning to the fold and thriving. Administrators are making choices about how they see the world, and when they reject these students again, they confirm all the biases that such students bring about "schools" and teachers. It need not be so.

And perhaps more fundamental, programs like this go beyond just challenging the lack of success of other "professionals". They demand a very basic value shift — to say and *mean* that street-people are people too. That sounds rash, but most people are quite willing to give to charity to be sure that street-kids don't freeze to death and occasionally get a decent meal. But we don't want to admit that they are no different than us. "There, but for the grace of God, go I". And perhaps as serious, charity is fine, but you wouldn't want to have "one of them" next door.

Fortunately, some professionals look at the remarkable transition of individuals and ask how they can be of help. Others are threatened. They are terrified they will be blamed. After all, if "project directors" and instructors with no professional training can succeed, they must have failed. Their reaction is to discount, attack, challenge and undermine. The techniques tend to be bureaucratic and/or coated with paternalistic professionalism: "Are we sure this is in their best interests?" Their real concern is personal job security at a time of cutbacks, therefore, they do not want anyone, especially low-cost nonprofessionals to succeed.

Many are traumatized by the fear of change. This fear recycles because if something different or new works, then someone (they) might be blamed for earlier failures, and change might occur. Thus, it is easier to decry and deny than to change, adjust or adapt.

Support is Essential

Projects like Beat The Street need very special kinds of support. They are not neat and tidy. They are poor fits in rigid organizational structures. The people who have the street-smarts to make the program work on the street are unlikely to have solid organizational skills, bureaucratic competence, etc. Their "degrees" were earned on the street — not in a school of management. Thus, a "partnership" is needed. And the partnership must have the time, skill, patience and will to work through the thousand problems that will occur. How does one account for a pair of boots, a jacket and a meal purchased without receipts for a kid who "needed them". The "obsession" to help is right, but is nearly impossible to control and categorize into tidy budget formulas that can be marked, reported and audited.

The Problem of Success — Can You Measure It?

What is success? The new "accountability" phobia requires that everything be assessed, evaluated, tested and reported on, in triplicate. The principle of accountability is not in question. The reporting methodology is! Most people in Frontier College programs will not and cannot "register" in full-time upgrading programs with a class register and exams. Thus, our critics say that all we really provide is "bleeding-heart, adult day-care". We say important learning is taking place. We cannot bow to the temptation to have pre and post tests for our programs. We would de facto frighten away 95% of our students. At this stage, they cannot cope with that kind of supervision., Instead, we solicit their interests — work on their agendas — at their speed and for as long as they choose. If they identify a formal Grade 10 exam, a driver's licence, or reading to their child as a priority, that is our curriculum. Thus, students come and go, set the goals and determine when they have succeeded. We collect student writings over time and thus document dramatic shifts in skills and attitudes. We collect stories — the anecdotes of "where I was" vs "where I am now", and "where I am going". The positive evidence is overwhelming, but it is not standardized. It is qualitative rather than quantitative data.

We cannot "prove" that a student moved from Grade 3 to Grade 7 in 6 months. Or that on a standardized test the score moved from x% to y%. For our detractors, this is adequate to claim that "There is not proof". They say literacy is marginal, and that even if it works it could not be done on a scale that would have any impact. Even more disturbing than these "jabs" is the fact that funding formulas (if available) are virtually locked in to these traditional definitions.

Regardless, we have measures of success. It is just that many of them are beyond academic measure. For example, at Beat The Street, what percentage rating do you assign for getting a woman who spoke only through "Charlie", her pet rat, to talk directly to people, and get off the street into a room after 7 years? What mark do you give for getting over hundreds of kids back home? What mark do you give for teaching a street-person to read her medical prescriptions correctly so she was able to emerge from a drugged stupor after several years? Many have jobs now — what is that worth?

SUCCESS IS FIVE MINUTES — CHARLIE TOLD ME!

I watch the incredible struggles of people at HELP, Independent Studies, and Beat The Street and Learning in the Workplace. I know that today's "all star" may well be gone tomorrow. When you work with people who have been "wounded" that deeply, seldom do things occur without interruption. This makes me reflect on the meaning of "success". All too many think it means Grade 10, or having a degree, or owning a house. But on the street, success is 5 minutes. That's what I have learned.

I learned it before Beat The Street and HELP, from Charlie Tann — a man who wanted to work with "throwaway" kids after spending 25 years in jail. Charlie had a unique approach. He simply found destitute youth and announced that he had appointed himself to be their friend . . . and they were stuck with him. He salvaged dozens and dozens of kids who were waiting out a death wish. But once, when I was visiting Charlie, he had just organized yet another funeral for one of his adopted friends who had no family. I asked how he could be so hopeful as he faced the despair of so many young and wasted lives. Charlie said — "Five minutes".

He explained that many of his kids had never been wanted, and had never had unqualified love and warmth even for five minutes. Charlie gave that love. The first round was; often only five minutes; than an hour, a day and maybe a week. Some made it for life . . . but not all.

Charlie's point was that everyone should have five minutes, and he didn't want anyone to face death, or life, without that. Charlie postponed his death long beyond medical predictions, because he always had another kid that needed those five minutes. I see Charlie's spirit at work all the time, because I have the privilege of seeing some of the very same kids he salvaged on a regular basis. No monument could pay greater tribute than these living testimonials to faith and the determination never to give up.

When I grow frustrated with yet another budget crisis, or the unquenchable bureaucratic thirst for truisms laced with the "buzz words" of the month, I take five minutes. I think of Charlie and the Tony's, Angie's, Tom's, Tracy's and Rick's, and the "five minutes" that they have been able to give a thousand-fold to lonely people who have been overlooked so many times before. Then I feel renewed. Because my role, and the role of Frontier College is not to dole out happiness or welfare to the "disadvantaged", but rather to work with a few people, a few projects, that will build leadership through dignity — by spreading self-respect.

This is not a commodity one can buy — and you cannot even give it to another person. But, in special partnerships between people, it can be created in each of us, and shared. That is what Frontier College is all about, whether it be delivered by a sweating labourer-teacher on a rail gang, through a con finding a former cell-mate a job, or via Beat The Street, where street-people restore self-esteem and dignity to the "throwaway" people of our society.

OUR FUTURE: HUMAN RESOURCES

Some will argue that these programs are not really literacy programs. I think this is precisely the point. The literacy programs of the future — will not be "literacy centres". Literacy is essential to full participation for citizens, thus the appropriate technology solutions to the literacy issue of the 90s will be to take education to the people — on issues that deem to be important — wherever they are. Hopefully by then, they will be called management communications, and other names that are not demeaning like "illiteracy". We hope that reading will soon be central to our culture. And hopefully, there will be more organizations forming partnerships between "consumers" and professionals so that self-esteem can be restored to more of the most valuable of all the world's resources — the human being.

Two brief poems summarize both the technique and my plea for the future. The first is a Chinese proverb; the second, the first poem by a young man (Tracy LeQuyere) who just learned to read.

First the technique:

Tell me, I'll forget.
Show me, I may remember.
Involve me, and I'll understand.

And then, my plea for the future:

DON'T PASS ME BY!

I'm a man at thirty-three
Who just learned to read.

I was there all the time
But people just passed me by.

One day a woman said I will
Show you a lie.

I know you can read with
a little time

I won't pass you by.

So she gave me a little time,
And I gave her a little time.

See this writing,
I will have more in time.
Don't pass me by!

CHAPTER 7:

Adult Basic Education and Community Development
Corporate Partnerships in the City of York

Dale E. Shuttleworth

The city of York, a municipality of 134,000 within metropolitan Toronto, has the lowest levels of income and highest rates of unemployment and functional literacy in the region. Forty-two percent of its residents speak a language other than English in the home and the largest proportion of newcomers in recent years has been from the West Indies and Asia. About 60 percent of the students do not complete high school. York also has had a chronic shortage of day care accommodation, as well as the second largest proportion of senior citizens in metro Toronto. Although York is located several miles from the central business district, it has become the "inner city" of metropolitan Toronto in the past decade (Census data, 1981).

The Community Services Office of the Board of education for the City of York is committed to providing learning opportunities that enhance the growth and development of citizens of all ages. Its mandate includes adult and continuing education, multicultural programs, community education, community economic development and school and community relations (Hands on the Future, 1986). Although each of these functions is interrelated, this article will focus on adult basic education experience in the context of a community development process.

Adult and continuing education programs in the city of York are offered in three ways: (a) through the Adult Day School, which is organized as a secondary school under the collective agreement with the Ontario Secondary School Teachers' Federation; (b) as community and continuing education classes initiated by the Board of Education through provisions of continuing education funding; and (c) as a result of corporate partnerships with other community organizations and groups. These programs are interdependent in that those offered through continuing education funding and corporate partnerships often help to identify areas of need that are later incorporated into the Adult Day School. This integrated model of action research/planning/development has continued to evolve to serve the citizens of York.

ADULT DAY SCHOOL

The first adult basic education class was organized in 1979 in a public library as a continuing education program to serve the 27.2 percent of residents with less than a ninth grade education. In June 1982, the Board approved the establishment of the Adult Day School (ADS) as a department of York Humber High School with teachers provided under the collective agreement with the Ontario Secondary School Teachers' Federation. Although projected at 168, the program enrolled 265 students by the end of September. In January 1983, ADS became a regular secondary school with continuous intake to expand its services in response to community needs. As of October, 1988, the enrollment reached 1600 with a teacher staff of 123.5.

All teachers at ADS are required to complete the Ministry of Education Qualifications Course in Adult Education. This course was originally developed by ADS and is now offered by faculties of education in universities across the province.

Since its inception, ADS has not occupied its own building but utilizes vacant space in elementary and secondary schools and other community locations to emphasize an informal, individualized, easily accessible, neighbourhood-based operation. ADS programs have been divided into the following five departments.

Basic education and Upgrading. As a re-entry program, ADS provides academic instruction, remedial assistance, and life skills up to the tenth grade level as well as college preparation. Most students wish to improve their literacy and numeracy skills, either to be better prepared for employment or to gain access to a skill development program at a community college. In addition, the Adult Individual Development Program offers basic education and life skills to the developmentally handicapped.

English as a Second Language. English as a Second Language (ESL) classes are provided at the basic, intermediate, and advanced levels in several locations. All ESL students receive life skills as an integral part of their program.

Tutorial Outreach. In September, 1984, the Action for Literacy in York (ALY) tutorial outreach program was incorporated into the Adult Day School. ALY, originally sponsored by the Learning Enrichment Foundation, is an individualized program for homebound persons and those unable to participate in regular ADS classes because of physical, emotional, or cultural disabilities. Thirty teacher-tutors serve approximately 500 students in private homes and other community settings.

Education in the Workplace. Ten teachers have been assigned to entry-level employment and training programs offered in a variety of business, industrial, and service settings. These teachers provide basic education and upgrading, ESL, and life skills to employees in the workplace on a withdrawal basis. Industries have included renovations and construction, office services, maintenance and caretaking, health care services, day care, retail sales, industrial sewing, furniture manufacturing, courier and light delivery, food services and catering, bus driving, waste wood recycling, electronic assembly and machine technologies (Adult Day School Progress Report, 1986).

The **Business Skills Department** prepares students for careers in offices or in business related areas. Courses in word and numerical processing and office services are provided at the introductory, senior and refresher levels.

CONTINUING EDUCATION
In 1988 more than 21,000 students were enrolled in community and continuing education classes (as compared to 16,044 students enrolled in the regular

day school program). These classes are offered through provisions of the continuing education budget formula in the following areas:

Evening and Summer School. Secondary school credits, as well as general interest courses, are offered in six Community Education Centres. During the summer, both elementary and secondary classes are provided during the day and in the evening.

Multicultural Programs. A variety of community education classes are offered in elementary schools and other community settings that respond to the needs of recent immigrants and reflect York's cultural diversity. Parent and Pre-School Programs provide ESL day and evening classes for mothers and their children. Older adults attend ESL classes in their apartment building. Heritage preservation programs in 16 languages and cultures are provided for elementary school children. Preparation for Citizenship classes are also available in several locations.

Community Education Programs. These general interest classes are offered in eight community schools, other elementary schools, apartment buildings, and a variety of other locations in response to expressed needs of children, parents, and senior citizens. Examples include arts enrichment, parenting, before and after school care, and leisure activities for older adults.

ADS Hybrid Programs. Students enrolling in the Adult Day School after the regular contract staff have been assigned are served through continuing education provisions. These include basic literacy and ESL classes, a Tutorial Outreach evening program, education in the workplace and a summer program to extend ADS to a 12-month year.

CORPORATE PARTNERSHIPS

The Community Services Office continues to co-operate with community organizations and agencies, as well as business and industry, to extend learning opportunities through continuing education provisions and the Adult Day School. The most notable examples are as follows:

In 1979, the *Learning Enrichment Foundation (LEF)* was established with assistance from the York Board of Education, as a non-profit community development corporation devoted to multicultural arts enrichment, child care services, and employment/training, particularly for youth and redundant workers. The Board of Directors includes representatives from the City of York, the York Board of Education and Humber College, as well as citizens from the community at large. LEF has been a partner in the development of the Adult Day School by providing child care for children of ADS students through sponsorship of 18 parent-run day care centres located in elementary and secondary schools. In addition, LEF is a major source of employment and training opportunities for the education in the workplace component.

The Foundation also operates *A + Employment Services*, which finds full- and part-time employment for ADS students, as well as the *Job Opportunities for Youth (JOY) Employment Centre*. The JOY Centre is a co-operative venture with academic and clerical skills provided by ADS; employment counselling, placement and child-care by LEF and staff training by Humber College. Matching funds to operate the Centre are provided by the Ontario Ministry of Skills Development.

The *Entrepreneurial Training Centre* is a training facility to encourage entrepreneurial and small business development.

The *York Business Opportunities Centre (YBOC)* is a small business incubator (28,000 sq.ft.) operated by LEF which provides consultative assistance, start-up space and child-care for workers in the entrepreneurial ventures and skill training program. Clerical and computer services, ESL, basic education and upgrading are provided by ADS while courses in small business development are offered through continuing education provisions. Since its inception YBOC has assisted in the establishment of at least 40 businesses employing more than 160 workers. (Learning Enrichment Foundation, 1987-88).

The *Small Business Owner Development Program* is an outreach program of YBOC which has provided business consultation and a support network for 90 small businesses in the local area.

Humber College. The Humber College/York Board of Education Liaison Committee has been established to share information and encourage complementarity between the two systems. The Adult Day School provides a basic education and upgrading to prepare students to enter certificate and diploma programs at the college.

MacTECH is a training program for unemployed workers in machine technologies established at George Harvey Collegiate Institute and Standard-Modern Technologies. It was jointly sponsored by the York Board of Education, Humber College, Standard-Modern Technologies, Weston Machine and Tool and Magna International. This program provides a new source of trained personnel in response to the direct needs of high-technology employers.

MICROTRON Centre is a training facility for microcomputer skills, word and numerical processing, computer-assisted design, graphics and styling, and electronic assembly and repair located in five rooms at Vaughan Road Collegiate. The project is jointly sponsored by the York Board of Education, Commodore Business Machines, Comspec Communications, LEF, York Business Opportunities Centre and Humber College. The facility is available to serve the training needs of local employers, municipal government, voluntary organizations and the community at large.

MICROTRON Bus is a refurbished school bus, originally obtained from Humber College, which accommodates a sample of equipment from the MICROTRON Centre. It visits business and industry, other employers and organizations on a scheduled basis to provide training in information technology, robotics, computer-assisted design and desk-top publishing. This project was jointly sponsored by the York Board of Education, the Learning Enrichment Foundation, Commodore Business Machines, Comspec Communications, Corel Systems, the York Business Opportunities Centre and the York Lions Club.

COSTI-IIAS. The Community Services Office co-operates with COSTI-IIAS Immigrant Services in sponsoring evening classes in upgrading for immigrant workers. COSTI-IIAS also assists the Board in offering classes for persons preparing for citizenship.

The York Community Economic Development Committee. In 1984, the York Community Economic Development Committee was established as a joint undertaking of the City of York, York Board of Education, York Association of Industry, the United Steelworkers of America, the Learning Enrichment Foundation, and the federal and provincial governments to encourage industrial, commercial, and institutional employment training in the city.

As a result of the work of this Committee, training programs have been established in the areas of machine technology, industrial sewing, upholstered furniture, renovation and construction and day care services. Each program has an Advisory Committee to allow local employers to "drive" training and recruitment programs.

Workers' Educational Association. The Community Services Office co-operated with this non-profit adult education organization to establish the EdINFO Booth as an educational information facility utilizing space donated by the West Side Mall. Other partners included Humber College, the Learning Enrichment Foundation and the York Interagency Network.

Distance Education. "Return to Learn", a television literacy series for adults was undertaken as a joint venture of the Adult Day School, Graham Cable and York Public Libraries. The format of the weekly series shown on the cable system combines basic education, ESL and life skills to reach homebound individuals.

The venture was expanded in 1987 as "LWL-TV", a television version of the "Learning Without Limits" magazine which is published by the Community Services Office. Programming includes literacy and numeracy skills, English as a Second Language and preparation for citizenship, technical and business education and leisure-learn activities. The project reaches 90,000 cable subscribers and includes an advertising opportunity for local business and industry.

Sole-Support Mothers. The Adult Day School has co-operated with the YWCA to co-sponsor the Focus on Change Program for sole-support mothers providing academic upgrading and life skills. A similar program is also operated by the Opportunities for Advancement organization under continuing education provisions.

Older Adults Project. The Older Adults Project Committee surveyed agencies, organizations, and schools that work with seniors to identify needs and available resources to better serve the educational, social, cultural, and health care needs of these citizens. A variety of community education programs are offered in seniors' residences, recreational centres, churches and schools.

Caribbean Re-entry Program. The Community Services Office has worked with a group of concerned parents and community organizations to establish a re-entry program for school-leavers who have come originally from the West Indies The program stresses academic skills in the context of the history and cultures of the Caribbean region.

COMMUNITY DEVELOPMENT PROCESS

Community development has been defined as a process of social action in which the people of a community organize themselves for planning and action; define their common and individual needs and problems, execute these plans with a maximum reliance on community resources; and supplement these resources when necessary with services and materials from governmental and non-governmental agencies outside the community. (International Co-operation Administration, 1956, p.1).

As a major resource within the city of York, the Community Services Office has focused on the needs of citizens for basic literacy and numeracy, English language instruction, skill training, and employment opportunities. Five Community Liaison Officers work directly with citizens in identifying needs and resources and developing problem-solving skills. The Adult Day School has assumed a flexible, non-institutional mode of operation, which creates an informal, responsive environment that respects the rights of the learner as an individual.

Through working co-operatively with such partners as the Learning Enrichment Foundation and Humber College, as well as the governmental and commercial sectors, a new sense of synergy has emerged in which vital resources have combined to make the enterprise stronger. While York is a relatively small municipality, it retains a real sense of community and a will to survive that have been definite assets in the community development process. As community educators, we must be proactive partners in this process.

REFERENCES

Adult Day School Progress Report (1986), Toronto, Canada: City of York Board of Education
Census data (1981), Ottawa, Canada
Learning Enrichment Foundation Annual Report (1987-88), Toronto, Canada: Learning Enrichment Foundation
Hands on the Future (Report of the Community Services Office) (1986), Toronto, Canada: City of York Board of Education.
International Co-operation Administration (1956), *Community Development Review*, No. 3.1.

PART VIII
THE INTERNATIONAL PERSPECTIVE

It is helpful for literacy workers to relate their classroom work to a larger international and world perspective. Close linkages between these activities, whether in urban or rural areas or in developing or industrialized countries offer valuable learning opportunities. The purpose of this section is to highlight the importance of maintaining a global view of the literacy issue. In doing so, practitioners enhance the cross-cultural exchange of ideas and experiences. Certainly, there are many rich and innovative experiences emerging from new nations that have relevance to literacy education programs in the more industrialized countries.

*Within the international framework, **Bhola** presents a theory of literacy relating to practice and policy. He suggests that a theoretical framework is important as a way of understanding the practice of literacy. This theory focuses on two different levels: individual and societal. He also comments on the most significant international declarations on literacy and learning which have occurred, especially since 1965. Comments of this nature, as well as an interpretation of these events, are also referred to by **Draper** in Section One of this book.*

***Draper** attempts to link literacy and development, emphasizing that literacy must be seen within the broader meaning of communication. One of the responsibilities of donor governments to literacy activities is to understand the purpose of educational programs as they relate to individual, regional and national development. Development involves a qualitative learning process and therefore quantitative approaches to assessing the outcomes of these activities are not adequate. He also describes the role of the non-government organizations in various countries. The experience of World Literacy of Canada is especially noted. As a non-government organization, it works primarily with counterpart NGO's in other countries. Such arrangements can maximize the utilization of resources, and encourage the development of nonformal educational programs.*

***Clarke** describes a number of responses to adult literacy needs in many parts of the world such as China, Cuba, Brazil and the United Kingdom. He shows various factors that have accounted for their success. Underlying these factors are the four basic principles of functionability, participation, integration and diversification. **Clarke** suggests that these principles are a good foundation for analyzing the Canadian initiatives. He also observes that a shift from the traditional to an emerging paradigm in adult literacy and basic education is presently occurring. Bridging these paradigms are the activities of co-operative education and work placement programs.*

The Canadian Commission for UNESCO is very active in examining the various issues relating to education, including adult literacy and basic education. The Commission helps link the experience in Canada to the international scene. It was the Canadian Commission which introduced the Right To Read *statement at the last meeting of the UNESCO International Conference on Adult Education.* **Bélanger** *discusses several of the contributions made by UNESCO in the struggle against illiteracy. These include the role of raising public awareness, the normative role, multilateral co-operation and the exchange of ideas and experiences in the field of literacy work. As* **Bélanger** *points out, working through its Commission, Canada is able to co-operate as well as to participate in overcoming various worldwide problems.*

*   **Gillette** *describes the range of ways young people participate in literacy activities. He explains a typology of patterns of participation based on key variables such as number of organized schemes in the world, age, education and nature of youth participation. These variables are analyzed under three categories of patterns: project, program and campaign. In addition the author discusses some drawbacks of the program pattern and offers guidance for overcoming these limitations.*

CHAPTER 1:

Adult Literacy in the Development of Nations: An International Perspective

H. S. Bhola

Fears about the future of literacy in the new information age has proved to be unfounded. In both the developed and the developing world, literacy remains *central* to the processes of education and socialization (1984a). While illiteracy is essentially a burden of the Third World where 98 per cent of the world's illiterates live, the industrialized world has now discovered its own functional illiterates (Giere, 1987). The moral burden of illiteracy today is a burden of the whole world community as evidenced in the United Nations General Assembly Resolution No. 42/104 of December 7, 1987 proclaiming 1990 as the International Literacy Year and asking UNESCO to lead the world community in mobilizing for universal literacy by the year 2000 (UNESCO, 1987).

A FRAMEWORK FOR DISCUSSION: DEFINITIONS AND ASSUMPTIONS

During the last two decades literacy has been studied by historians, anthropologists, linguists, sociologists, political scientists, students of literature, psychologists, and pedagogues. Scholars and practitioners have talked of cultural literacy, public literacy, critical literacy, dominant literacy, liberatory literacy, emergent literacy, differentiated literacy, and several other literacies (1). Such uses of the term literacy have not promoted definitional clarity. While it is impossible to separate the skill of reading from the content and function of reading, a definition of literacy will have to deal with the skill of codifying and decodifying written symbols.

A UNESCO document published in 1958 suggested that "a person is *illiterate* who cannot with understanding both read and write a short, simple statement on his everyday life." Later, in 1978, UNESCO proposed a newer definition: "A person is *functionally illiterate* who cannot engage in all those activities in which literacy is required for effective functioning of his group and community and also for enabling him to continue to use reading, writing and calculation for his own and the community's development" (UNESCO, 1983). More recently, Bhola has talked of "the literacy of marks" rather than "the literacy of alphabets" (or of ideograms). This new literacy of marks, has been defined as: the ability of a person smoothly and effortlessly to code and decode a living and growing system of marks — words, numbers, notations, schematas, and diagramatic representations — all of which have become part of the visual language of the people, and thus have come to be collectively and democratically shared by both the specialist and the non-specialist (Bhola, 1984a). Universally applicable, absolute definitions of literacy are thus quite impossible. What is possible are contextual definitions of literacy particular to languages, cultures, and historical moments.

It is also important to separate literacy taught to children in the school setting from literacy taught to adults in out-of-school settings. Of course, those who learn to read in schools become literate, and those who are taught literacy in out-of-school settings, learn to read. However, the teaching of reading to children and the teaching of literacy to adults are phenomenologically different enterprises with their own special psychological, social, economic, linguistic, and cultural parameters.

An important assumption is made in discussion of literacy that is not always clear to the non-specialist. Definitions of literacy assume the ability to read and write in the mother tongue. In the real world, however, this norm is often compromised. That is so because many mother tongues are still unwritten. Other mother tongues while already committed to writing have no written history or literature to speak of. Some of these languages are spoken by so few that they are unlikely ever to have even a marginal role in national politics and economy. Often, therefore, a language other than the mother tongue may be selected as the language of literacy. It might even be a metropolitan language such as English, French or Portuguese.

LITERACY AND THE INDIVIDUAL

The theory of literacy has been focussed on two different levels: individual and societal. Jack Goody had hypothesised that literacy brought a change in the "technology of intellect" as the newly literate used new modes of describing, and categorizing the world (Goody, 1968). Scribner and Cole (1981) suggested that the influence of literacy may not be general as claimed by Goody, but specific to the range of literacy practices in particular contexts. More recently attention has shifted from the psycological effects to social consequences of literacy. Literacy is seen as adding new potential to the literate individual as transactions are made with the physical and social environment. In Freire's colorful words, the literate by learning to read the word learns to read the world as well (Freire and Macedo, 1987).

LITERACY AND SOCIETY: A POLITICAL THEORY OF LITERACY

The theoretical relationships between literacy and society have also become clearer during the 1980s. No one claims a deterministic role for literacy in bringing about modernization and democratization. Nor do people dismiss literacy as a myth. A beneficial dialectical relationship between literacy and society is considered possible and probable if the leadership would articulate and sustain the political will to put literacy to work in the service of development (Bhola, 1984a).

The role of adult literacy in the development of nations can be best understood as a political process within a policy-making context. Analyses of literacy initiatives in the varied ideological contexts of Iraq and Sudan in the Middle East; of Botswana, Ethiopia, Kenya, Nigeria, Sierra Leone and Zambia in Africa; of Bangladesh, India and Thailand in Asia; and of Nicaragua in South America on the one hand (Bhola, 1983); and of nation-wide literacy campaigns of the USSR, Viet Nam, the People's Republic of China, Cuba, Burma, Brazil, Tanzania and Somalia on the other hand (Bhola, 1984b) have provided elements for a theory of literacy for development (Bhola, 1988):

Figure No. 1 — A political theory of literacy for development.

Motivational – Developmental Model	Planned Development Model	Structural – Developmental Model
Gradualist	Reformist	Revolutionary
< > _____	< > _____	< >
Organic Growth	Growth with Efficiency	Growth with Equity
Project Approach to Literacy	Program Approach to Literacy	Campaign Approach to Literacy

Depending on its development ideology, a nation will show affinity for one of the three ideal-type development models placed on a continuum in the figure above. These are: (i) the motivational-developmental model, (ii) the planned development model, and (iii) the structural-developmental model. Each model admits of a particular calendar of social change, using change strategies that could be best described as the gradualist, the reformist or the revolutionary. Each model will be pre-occupied with the so-called organic growth with efficiency or growth with equity. Again, each model will find the project, the program or the campaign approach to literacy more or less congenial than others.

The figure above should not suggest a one-to-one relationship between the development ideology of a country and its choice of the model, on the one hand; and between the development model and its choice of the literacy strategy, on the other hand. These relationships are confounded by many complexities and contradictions. First, development ideologies, development models, and literacy strategies do not exist in pure forms: as concepts with complex internal structures they include both the apposite and the opposite within themselves. Marxists practice state capitalism. Capitalists make laws to promote equity that are the envy of socialists. The motivational model cannot avoid the structural. Planning time-frames are relative to historical contexts; and it is not always possible to separate the gradualists from the reformists. Campaigns can be built upon a multiplicity of projects. Again, campaigns often peter out into mere programs and programs sometimes heat up into campaigns.

Second, what is in the manifesto, does not always manifest itself intoactions, sometimes for lack of honest intentions on the part of leadership, sometimes for lack of control of circumstances both endogenous and exogenous. In most cases, rhetoric is ahead of reality, while in some instances, social processes breakout of the limitation imposed by the prevailing ideology or the interests of the power elite.

The Motivational-Developmental Model

The motivational-developmental model is rooted in the assumption that individual motivations are, first, the engine of individual development and, consequently, of the development of human collectivities. In its ideal form, this model considers existing structures to be benign, and quite responsive to the new demands put on them by the newly emerging constituencies. The motivational-developmental model is built on the assumption, not of conflict, but of cooperation among castes, classes and racial groups who are seen as ready and willing to work together for the greater good of all. Motivations must be learned. People must acquire higher aspirations and must work to deserve the new social and economic rewards. Education is central to all these processes. Since education is typically a slow process, the motivational-developmental model is a gradualist model of development. Things take time. Change has to be organic and may be spread over many generations.

The Structural-Developmental Model

The structural-developmental model considers structures as the primary determinants of development. To bring development to an underdeveloped society, there must be structural reform. In other words, the rules of the game must be changed to give the poor and the excluded a fair chance. It is within just and progressive structures that individuals can be motivated to learn new aspirations and to work to fulfil their own individual potential. The structural-developmental model assumes conflict of interests among castes, classes and races; and assumes further that the privileged will not surrender their privileges without a struggle. The structural-developmental model is a revolutionary model of development and is impatient in regard to the calendar of change. The implementers of this model do not want to wait but are anxious to overthrow, what they consider, are structures of exploitation and oppression. On the other hand, they would compromise efficiency if equity is jeopardized.

Planned Development Model

Mid-way between the two models of development just described, we can place the planned development model. The planned development model seeks to use a coordinated strategy of structural change and individual motivations. It purports to be a social-scientific model — above politics and somehow free of ideology. What is sought is growth with efficiency. Planned development model accepts the existence of conflict but works on the assumption that cooperation among different interest groups can be established. The language of discourse in this model is that of conflict resolution, institution building, manpower development, education and entrepreneurship. The planned development model is a reformist model. It seeks to give people time to reason, to negotiate, to invent and to create so that the future is moulded out of the present and not built upon its debris.

THE CHOICE OF THE LITERACY APPROACH:
PROJECTS, PROGRAMS AND CAMPAIGNS

As the graphic presentation of the theory of literacy for development above indicates, different development models are congenial to different policy and strategy combinations for literacy promotion. Within the context of the motivational-developmental model, the approach to literacy promotion chosen is, typically, the project approach. Literacy is offered to those who ostensibly can make immediate use of literacy skills in their lives. This often means no more than the professionalization of select groups of workers within particular sectors of the economy, in the hope of enabling participants to become more productive both for their own good and for the benefit of their society. The majority of adult population is, however, abandoned to the long historical process of literacy by attrition of illiteracy, through the process of formal schooling.

Societies following the planned development model vary considerably in regard to their political cultures. Those leaning towards conservatism will be satisfied with the project approach, promising to expand projects incrementally into nation-wide literacy programs. Other, committed to bringing about egalitarian social systems may actually launch large-scale literacy program to cover a whole country.

As we move away from the center towards the structural-developmental model, there is a radicalization of the social visions as well as of the approach to literacy promotion chosen by nations. The favorite approach selected for the eradication of illiteracy is the campaign approach. The literacy campaign is born out of a high level of commitment on the part of the society. It is business *un*usual. Illiteracy is sought to be eradicated from the whole society and all possible resources of the society are focused on the task. It should be pointed out here that a *political* definition of the campaign makes much more sense than a merely temporal definition. A campaign is not just something that is enthusiastic and intense, and lasts only a few months. A campaign may indeed last for years, covering one region after another, proceeding sector by sector, and establishing new agendas and objectives as old ones are met. Political commitment and organizational style are the essence of the campaign strategy, not the length of time period of a campaign. It should also be pointed out that literacy campaigns undertaken by revolutionary societies over a period of years will begin to look more and more like what we have called literacy programs. After the achievement of initial tasks of literacy, new targets will have been set, and the temporary logistical and infrastructural arrangements will have become institutionalized.

SOME SIGNIFICANT POLICY DECLARATIONS ON LITERACY

A flavor of the policy aspirations of nations can be presented through a review of international policy declarations made during the two decades of 1965 to 1985. These declarations have not always been fully embraced, yet their influence on national policies has been wide-spread. These declarations do show an increasing understanding of the politics of literacy and a preference for the campaign approach if our actions have to be commensurate with the size and scope of the task ahead.

The Teheran Conference, 1965

The World Conference of Ministers of Education on the Eradication of Illiteracy held in Teheran during 1965 has been quite influential in literacy work all the world over. It accepted adult literacy as "an essential element in overall development. . . .closely linked to economic and social priorities and to present and future manpower needs." The conference thereby tied adult literacy too closely to economic purpose and indeed showed preference for literacy to be given in the context of "projects designed to further economic and social development" and "in particular, employment and training problems." The Teheran conference is well known for equating functional literacy with work-oriented literacy, thus providing what is now referred to as *technical literacy* (UNESCO, 1965).

The Declaration of Persepolis, 1975

The International Symposium for Literacy in Persepolis rejected the narrow work-oriented conception of literacy. Instead of a *technical literacy,* it proposed a *humanist literacy.* It demanded that literacy be "a contribution to the liberation of man and to his full development." It demanded that literacy teach "critical consciousness" making people capable of "acting upon the world, of transforming it" and thus making "authentic human development" possible. It demanded, concomitantly, structural changes in the political, social, and economic institutions of developing nations (Bataille, 1976).

The Udaipur Declaration, 1982

The Udaipur Declaration was adopted in the spirit of Persepolis, but it is significant for its support of an international strategy for literacy promotion based on the campaign approach. "Recognizing that literacy is a decisive factor in the liberation of individuals for ignorance and exploitation and in the development of society," the Udaipur Seminar suggested the literacy campaign as the strategy commensurate with the size and scope of the tasks ahead. It was suggested that while these campaigns may have to be nationally-planned initiatives, they must provide "avenues for popular support in all phases" and pay special heed to the "participation of disadvantaged groups that historically have remained subjugated and marginal, especially, women" (Bhola, 1984b).

Declaration of the Paris Conference, 1985

The Fourth International Conference on Adult Education held in Paris in 1985 established a new human right: The Right to Learn. "The right to learn is: the right to read and write; the right to question and analyse; the right to imagine and create; the right to read one's own world and to write history; the right to have access to educational resources; the right to develop individual and collective skills. . . . The right to learn is not a cultural luxury to be saved for some future date. . . . It is not the next step to be taken once basic needs have been satisfied." The time is now to exercise this right for all humanity (UNESCO, 1985a).

The International Literacy Year — 1990

The culmination of literacy policy development world wide, is found in the declaration of the Year 1990 as the International Literacy Year (ILY) by the United Nations, with UNESCO as the lead agency. The objectives of the ILY, briefly, are: increasing action by the governments of Member States afflicted by illiteracy; increasing public awareness of the scope, nature and implications of illiteracy; increasing popular participation, within and among countries; increasing co-operation and solidarity among Member States in the struggle against illiteracy; and using ILY as a summons for action for eradicating illiteracy by the Year 2000 (UNESCO, 1987).

THE PRACTICE OF LITERACY

The latest available UNESCO statistics on illiteracy in the various world regions are presented in Table 1 below:

**Table 1: Number of illiterates and illiteracy rates in 1985
for the adult population aged 15 and over**

	Absolute number of illiterates 15 and over (in millions)	Illiteracy rates aged 15 and over (in percents)		
		Men	Women	Both
World total	888.7	20.5	34.9	27.7
Developing countries	868.9	27.9	48.9	38.2
Least developed countries	120.8	56.9	78.4	67.6
'Developed' countries	19.8	1.7	2.6	2.1
Africa	161.9	43.3	64.5	54.0
Latin America	43.6	15.3	19.2	17.3
Asia	665.7	25.6	47.4	36.3
Oceania	1.6	7.6	10.2	8.9
Europe (including USSR)	13.9	1.6	3.0	2.3

Source: UNESCO Office of Statistics, *The Current Literacy Situation in the World* (UNESCO, July 1985).

As the table indicates, there were 889 million illiterates living in the world in 1985 among those 15 years and older which translated into 27.7 per cent of the total adult population — 20.5 per cent Male and 34.9 per cent Female. Fully 98 per cent of these adult illiterates lived in developing countries. To make matters worse, 100 million children between the ages of six and eleven years in the developing countries were not enrolled in schools. In the developed industrialized countries, there were 20 million illiterates, but the problems of functional illiteracy, the inability to use literacy at a level high enough to deal independently with the demands of the economy, society, and politics, were far more extensive (UNESCO, 1985b).

THE HISTORY OF HISTORIES

The bright side of the coin is that literacy has become an issue all over the world. No nation is *against* literacy, even though in some countries it may not be a national priority yet. While numbers of illiterates in the world have increased because of the population bulge, the percentages of illiteracy have indeed increased. "In the 35 years between 1950 and 1985, the rate of illiteracy in the adult population has declined from an estimated 44.5 per cent to 27.7 per cent — and this despite unprecedented population growth. This is proof that illiteracy can be vanquished" (UNESCO, 1987b).

Thus, it can be said that transcending the time-frames of literacy projects, programs and campaigns and above the individual histories of nations, there is the history of histories, the larger history of all the peoples of the world, leading finally to the universalization of literacy. Literacy is, as Bhola has pointed out, the destiny of the human species. Universal literacy is inevitable. The challenge is to make the inevitable, as immediate as possible, within the particular contexts of nations and cultures and bring both hope and power to the people, now (Bhola, 1987).

NOTES

1. These, and many other, descriptors were used at a recent conference, "The right to Literacy" organized jointly by the Modern Language Association of America, the Ohio State University and the Federation of State Humanities Councils, Columbus, Ohio, September 16-18, 1988.

REFERENCES

Bataille, L. (Ed.). (1976). *A Turning Point for Literacy: Proceedings of the International Symposium for Literacy, Persepolis, Iran.* Oxford, UK: Pergamon Press.

Bhola, H. S. (in collaboration with Josef Muller and Piet Dijkstra). (1983). *The Promise of Literacy: Campaigns, Programs and Projects.* Baden-Baden, West Germany: Nomos Verlagsgesellschaft.

Bhola, H. S. (1984a). "A Policy Analysis of Adult Literacy Promotion in the Third World: An Accounting of Promises Made and Promises Fulfilled," *International Review of Education,* 30 (3): 249-264.

Bhola, H. S. (1984b) *Campaigning for Literacy: Eight National Experiences of the Twentieth Century, with a Memorandum to Decision-Makers.* Paris, France: UNESCO.

Bhola, H. S. (1987). "Destined for Literacy," *Educational Horizon,* 66(1):9-12.

Bhola, H. S. (1988). "The Politics of Adult Literacy Promotion: An International Perspective," *Journal of Reading,* 31 (7): 667-671.

Freire, P. & Macedo, D. (1987). *Literacy: Reading the Word and the World.* South Hadley, MA: Bergin and Garvey.

Giere, U. (1987). *Functional Illiteracy in Industrialized Countries: An Annotated Bibliography.* Hamburg: UNESCO Institute for Education.

Goody, J. (Ed.). (1968). *Literacy in Traditional Societies.* Cambridge: Cambridge University Press.

Scribner, S. & Cole, M. (1981). *The Psychology of Literacy.* Cambridge, MA: The Harvard University Press.

UNESCO. (1965). *World Conference of Ministers of Education on the Eradication of Illiteracy, Teheran, 8-19 September 1965. Final Report.* Paris: UNESCO.

UNESCO. (1983). *Backgrounder: Literacy Education,* Paris: UNESCO.

UNESCO. (1985a). *Fourth International Conference on Adult Education, Paris, 19-29, 1985. Final Report.* Paris, UNESCO.

UNESCO. (1985b, July). *The Current Literacy Situation in the World.* Paris: UNESCO Office of Statistics.

UNESCO. (1987, September). *Report of the Director-General on the Draft Programme for International Literacy Year and the Results of the Work Carried out for its Preparation.* Item, 16.7 of the provisional agenda for General Conference Twenty-fourth Session, Paris 1987, 24 C/67. Paris: UNESCO.

CHAPTER 2:

International Communication and National Development: The Vital Role of Literacy

James A. Draper

The major purposes of this chapter are to examine the role of non-governmental organizations (NGOs) in international literacy and development work; to emphasize the value to literacy work in Canada that can come from the experiences of other countries; and finally, to show the connection between international development and Canadian support of development programs overseas. Examples are given from the experiences of World Literacy of Canada (WLC), although the experiences of other NGOs in Canada could also have been given.

A view of one's world begins with an individual perspective and our teaching begins at that point as well. Our goal as educators is to expand the "world" of learners beyond the culture of silence that frequently characterizes the plight of the socially and educationally disadvantaged, the poor, and the oppressed. One's world is determined by what one has touched and experienced. It is an integral part of our living and learning. our "world" is inseparable from our existence. Furthermore, bringing about change is a process of reflecting and exploring the realm of new possibilities such that literacy makes a difference to the daily life of the individual.

To focus on the word 'difference' begs one to ask: Different from whose point of view? Whether literacy makes a difference or not can only be determined by an individual perspective. Since the goal of literacy education, primarily, is to improve the quality of human life and to make things different than they are, then personal experience, again, must be the basis of final judgement. Key questions are: Am I and my community beneficiaries of our learning experiences? How can we, together, sustain and grow as continuous learners?

THE CONTRIBUTION OF INDIGENOUS
INTERNATIONAL AGENCIES

Voluntary, non-profit and non-government organizations in Canada have always been at the forefront in dealing with social and educational issues. One such organization is World Literacy of Canada, which was established in 1954 to work in the international field of literacy and development, primarily in India, Africa and the Caribbean, and to a lesser extent, in Canada. Because of its experiences in various countries, working in the field of non-formal adult education, it was able to see the link between illiteracy, poverty, and the relationship of these to individual, community, and national development. Sensitivities that grew out of this international experience led it to become aware of illiteracy/functional illiteracy in Canada. It was this organization that undertook the first systematic study of adult illiteracy in Canada, and in 1976, released the findings of this study at the first national conference on adult basic education in Canada.

The first step to action is awareness of a problem, just as a critical examination of the issues is a first step to collective action. It was the WLC that initiated the founding of The Movement for Canadian Literacy. World Literacy of Canada was also one of the supporters of the Canadian Right to Read Declaration and has, in numerous other ways, supported the work and the development of a network of adult literacy agencies in Canada.

The point that arises from the experiences of WLC is the importance of tapping the experiences of international organizations that are doing literacy and development work overseas, including involving those of its members who return from overseas assignments. Such organizations and individuals can be important allies in literacy work. It is an acceptable fact that illiteracy is not an isolated world issue. It cuts across all cultural, political and geographical boundaries. The efforts of literacy education are strengthened if local, regional, national, and international literacy and development programs are seen to have generic purposes that focus on improving the quality of life for all people.

INTERNATIONAL SHARING:
WHAT WE HAVE LEARNED FROM OTHER COUNTRIES

We in Canada have learned much from the experiences of Third World, developing nations, including the Nicaragua Literacy Crusade approach to development and Thailand's Khit Pen humanistic and participatory approach to learning and teaching. Our learning from other countries and from our own experiences can be discussed under two general categories. The first is the development of a new vocabulary to describe the work we are doing in literacy education. The second are the alternative ways of describing the process of literacy and poverty.

In recent years, educators have acquired a different vocabulary which more accurately describes what we are doing. Many of these descriptors we had not used before in Canada, for example: literacy as a step toward liberation; literacy and non-formal education which is aimed at bringing about social change and developing self-reliance; empowerment; authentic development; literacy as a means for forming and transforming the world; and the right to literacy, perceived as a human right, which was one of the stated outcomes, internationally endorsed, at the fourth UNESCO International Decade Conference on Adult Education, held in Paris in 1985.

It is also recognized that the right to learn also parallels the right to question; that being illiterate is often an indicator of someone, or some group, who was likely to be disadvantaged in other areas, including unemployment, poor health and housing, all of which describes the broader concept of poverty. Literacy is a contruct which is meaningful only in a specific cultural context determined by the technological state of a particular culture or nation, thus emphasizes the relative meaning of the term "functional literacy". We now perceive what we are doing in the broader context of non-formal education, a term widely used in newly developing nations. In fact, we have come to humbly recognize that, in many ways, Canada is a developing nation with its Third World regions.

The second area of new learning for educators is the different way in which we now describe the process of literacy, from the adult learner's point of view. For example, that the goal of literacy education results in changing the self-concept of the learners; literacy invariably leads to changes in life-styles, and in improving the quality of life; literacy as a way of reordering power relationships between people and institutions; literacy as a way of reexamining values; education as a form of transition; and literacy education that is perceived in the broader context of communication, with the purpose of improving communication skills. As we all know, literacy education is more than the act of becoming literate. Being illiterate reflects a lack of opportunity to learn, and our goal is to break the deadlock of the illiterate's marginality. Illiteracy, then, is a kind of blindness, and becoming literate is comparable to improving one's sight.

. . . .

The remaining portion of this paper is a *Brief*, delivered by World Literacy of Canada to *The Special Joint Committee on Canada's International Relations, Toronto, 1986*. The Brief was written and presented by James A. Draper. The purpose for including it here is to illustrate the rationale for linking the work of international NGOs to government international relations and policy. NGOs have an important role to perform in the development of world communication and peace. At the same time, through cross-cultural sharing, NGOs in Canada have much to learn from the experiences of colleagues in other countries, and in return, have much to offer. (Draper, 1974)

The *Brief* is divided into three parts. The first identifies some of the philosophical assumptions and principles which guide literacy and development programs, both in Canada and elsewhere. These assumptions are based on cultural values and are highly selective. The second part outlines some implications for action, based on the stated assumptions. Lastly, the *Brief* discusses some the consequences and areas of support required for literacy education programs in Canada and in other geographical regions.

THE BRIEF

First, WLC wishes to go on record as being supportive of statements of belief and policy which are essential to world peace, development, and international cooperation. Statements that are worthy of note include:

- reemphasizing the effectiveness of Non-Governmental Organizations (NGOs) in relation to costs, involvement of local people in development, and interagency cooperation in the field, in undertaking literacy and development programs;
- the interrelationship between democratic and development principles; and
- the use of appropriate technology in community development.

WLC is also fully in agreement with redirecting more military resources for development; the need to reduce tied aid; and the need for aid that meets the basic needs of people, such as health, food production and drinking water, thus laying the foundations of improved economic and social life for the poorest in society.

I. **Assumptions And Principles**
1. Human beings are characterized by their *ability to communicate*. While an oral tradition and non-verbal communication have characterized human evolution, communication through an alphabet and through print is a recent phenomenon. For the masses of societies throughout the world, the opportunity to learn the skills of reading and writing are even more recent.
2. Literacy must be considered in the *broader context of communication*. Becoming literate extends one's potential opportunities for sharing and receiving information upon which decisions are made. However, the skills of reading, writing, and numeracy, are really only meaningful when they can be applied to daily living. We speak then, not of literacy per se, but of *functional literacy*.
3. Literacy education which, for most adults, occurs in *non-formal,* out-of-school settings is a continuing process that goes beyond the learning of basic literacy skills. It involves the acquisition and the *transformation of knowledge and critical thinking.* The process and outcomes of literacy education are intended to lead to an improvement in the understanding and appreciation of oneself and of others. *Becoming literate is a process of self-discovery.*
4. Those who do not have a formal education are not to be thought of as being unlearned. Learning is part of being human. People learn how to survive, to cope, to create, and to manage their environment. They learn ways to express their feelings and to perceive themselves as learners, as workers, and as participants in society.

   Generally speaking, however, those who *lack the equivalent of a basic and elementary education,* especially in a culture which relates to itself primarily through the medium of print, are likely to be *disadvantaged.* That is, they are unlikely to be able to function effectively or efficiently in their society. What constitutes effectiveness will be determined by one's local community, as well as by social, economic and citizenship expectations, and the availability of resources and services.
5. The *process* of literacy and of non-formal education includes more than the act of teaching and being taught. The larger context of literacy education also includes the training of teachers, as well as counsellors, administrators, and planners, as well as the research and evaluation that supports these programs. Any program of aid must perceive education in its *broader context of individual and community development*.
6. WLC supports the work and statements of UNESCO. At the UNESCO General Conference held in Sofia in 1985, references were made to: *the democratization of education,* the promotion of general access to education, and an intensification of the struggle against illiteracy.

   UNESCO's Major Program II, "Education For All", outlined a number of priorities for education as background to the Canadian-sponsored statement entitled, "The Right To Learn". Program II specifically endorses the need to establish closer links between education and the world of work; the need to intensify literacy and civics programs; the need for research aimed at a clearer identification of illiterate adults, and a better knowledge of the causes of illiteracy; and the need for greater support for adult education.

Finally, UNESCO speaks of the *right to education*; the right to take part in cultural life; the right to enjoy the benefits of scientific progress; the related matters of employment, protection of the family, and the right to an adequate standard of living; and the right to health. WLC believes, as UNESCO does, that adult literacy/basic education is a *universal necessity* and not merely a disability suffered by the populations of Third World countries. *Literacy is not a luxury, but a necessity.*

7. Similarly, the 1980 World Bank Sector Policy Paper on Education is important since it endorses, more than ever before, the relationship between *education and development* and the relationship between *education and work*. Recently, the World Bank provided hard research data to confirm and substantiate the common-sense arguments for basic education.[1]

    The 1976 Conference on Adult Education and Development, held in Nairobi, and organized by the International Council for Adult Education, also emphasized the essential component of *non-formal education in the development process.*

8. Adult illiteracy is acclaimed as a world-wide issue. This is not so much because adult men and women are unable to read and write, but that without functional literacy, they are potentially *unfulfilled as human beings*. They are limited in their abilities to communicate because they only marginally participated in society and because they have limited knowledge to improve the quality of their lives. *Illiteracy is linked to the broader issue of poverty.* "Illiteracy in rural areas is very closely related to poverty, which poses the problem of motivation to become literate."[2]

    A 1984 meeting in Paris emphasized "the intersectoral nature of the problem of illiteracy that includes social, cultural, civic, health, and educational dimensions must be understood". [3]

    The President of the Canadian International Development Agency (CIDA) points out that "the pursuit of universal literacy is not an idealistic dream, but probably the smartest move a developing country can make". She goes on to say that "education, literacy, the upgrading of human resources, is of decisive importance in the struggle for world development". [4]

9. In two ways, Canada shares the problems of illiteracy with other countries. First, because of its concerns about the human conditions of poverty and illiteracy and the underdeveloped potential of individuals, communities and nations. Second, because *Canada itself has an unusually large percentage (about 24%) of illiterate/functionally illiterate adults in its population*. (Thomas, 1983). Canada now stands with others as a country which has personal concerns about an undereducated adult population and about the implications of this to underdevelopment.

    At the UNESCO Second Collective Consultation of International Non-Governmental Organizations on Literacy, the participants were urged that "in International Literacy Year, the problem of functional illiteracy in industrialized countries not be underestimated and that special efforts be made with regard to the least privileged". (UNESCO, 1985)

II. **Implications For Action**

1. From the above, it is clear that an investment in learning, and in education that is relevant to learners, is an *investment in human and community growth*. Key concepts include functionality, self-help, participation, process and self-reliance.

2. The *growth of individuals and the growth of societies are interconnected* and one can hinder or enhance the growth of the other. People must have the opportunity and *the will to participate*. Having limited or no skills of reading and writing can be a barrier to participation.

3. Currently, many countries are reassessing the utility and productivity of formal educational programs, and seeking *alternative forms of "schooling"*. Non-formal education is seen as a viable alternative, especially when this is linked to regional and national development goals.

4. There is no government ministry or division of government that does not, directly or indirectly, attempt to influence, educate, and inform sectors of the public. Hence, one can argue that *all government ministries should be concerned about, and responsible for, adult learning and education,* including literacy and basic education. This is a concern that transcends provincial and international boundaries.

5. *Most world issues are interconnected:* peace and disarmament, human rights, telecommunications and culture, international cooperation, food aid, women's contribution to development and environmental issues. Overcoming these and other issues requires *intentional learning* and changes in attitudes and behaviour.

   Development assistance requires self-help and educational programs *aimed at economic self-reliance*. Environmental issues are now becoming an integral part of adult basic education programs, which lead to social action, for example, the social forestry program which World Literacy of Canada supports in India. There are long-term benefits to carrying out projects *with* people, rather than for them; for example, people being taught to grow better crops rather than only being given food.

6. *Dialogue is a two-way process*. We have much to learn from development and literacy/basic education programs in other countries. Programs of self-help and aid should carry with them an openness for dialogue; an openness to exchanging ideas and experiences; and an openness to interchanging the roles of learning and teaching.

   Basic education programs in *Canada could benefit from knowing more of the experiences in other countries* in the areas of development and literacy. This potential needs to be acknowledged and systematic attempts to study and analyze such programs should become legitimate parts of Canadian funded projects. On the other hand, experiences from Canada have the potential of being useful to others.

7. Non-governmental organizations, such as World Literacy of Canada, have a vital role to perform in implementing development programs and improving international relations. WLC's practice is to connect with NGOs in other countries, believing that such agencies are best able to identify and priorize local needs, as well as plan and implement programs that are relevant to meeting these needs. Ways need to be found to

overcome obstacles that would prevent WLC and other NGOs from expanding this *cooperative and supportive relationship* with development agencies elsewhere.

8. Statements about the functions and purposes of literacy and adult basic education are based upon particular *views of human nature*, a belief in the ability of adults to learn, perceptions of what constitutes an "illiterate person", and knowing the character and profile of the undereducated adult. In order to deal with the problem of illiteracy in society, it is important to understand illiterate adults in terms of their personal context and the environment in which they live, their life-styles, values, and aspirations. Development and educational programs, and programs aimed at international cooperation, are built upon a philosophy, upon a system of values.

III. Consequences And Areas Of Support

A greater government commitment to supporting NGO *literacy and non-formal adult education programs can be seen to be beneficial* in at least two ways: one that focuses on *international cooperation and assistance*; the other that focuses on specific *programs in Canada*. Both orientations are interconnected. Supporting effective international development programs is dependent on an informed and sympathetic electorate in Canada and NGOs can help in bringing this about.

A. International Focus

An underlying assumption is that international relations can be improved if Canada supports development and aid programs that are perceived by the recipient partner as *relevant*, based on the *needs of the recipient*, and are genuinely intended to increase the recipient's choices, self-reliance, and independence. Most developing nations put a clear priority on *literacy programs linked to development*. WLC and the broader community of NGOs are committed to such programs. Canadian commitment should be encouraged to support the following kinds of programs, as examples only.

1. We suggest that literacy education be incorporated more fully into programs that are primarily aimed at increasing food production, health care, family nutrition, reforestation, cottage industries, and so on. That is, *literacy becomes functional when it is linked to daily living. Literacy education includes more than the learning of content*, but also the learning of *values* and *attitudes* which are intended to humanize daily living.

2. Some international programs may not always be seen to relate directly to production and development. It is important to acknowledge that learning is an integral part of development programs. As a process, one must also be aware that the changing of values and behaviour takes *time* and is often implicit. Programs of evaluation need to take these realities into account. Clearly, understanding the goals of such programs and being open to accepting alternative and innovative ways to achieve these goals is important to agencies that support literacy and development programs.

3. *Research, evaluation*, and the *recording* of what and how learning is carried out are also essential parts of the process. Reference has already been made to the potential for a *cross-sharing of experiences* and the

benefit to Canada if there is an openness to learning from others.

4. Canadian NGO presence in other countries is an extension of *the image others have of Canada*. Adequate funding and carefully selected programs can greatly add to the positive images others have of Canada. World Literacy of Canada has a network and good working relationship with NGOs in other countries, linking NGOs to other NGOs, and is conscious of the fact that it is an envoy of Canada.

B. Canadian Focus

Programs in Canada might include the following, as examples only.

1. Supporting basic literacy education programs in Canada is an essential prerequisite for an *informed citizenship*. Some of the content of functional literacy programs in Canada could include discussions on, and an understanding of, *international issues*. Because they are under-schooled, and lack literacy skills, *almost one-quarter of Canada's adult population may be excluded from a dialogue on international, social and political issues. Access to information* is the basis for having an informed public.

2. In Canada, as elsewhere, it is important that:
   - *print materials* developed in Canada be written at *appropriate reading levels*, including materials intended for public development education, i.e., at grade 6 to 8 levels (the "plain writing" programs supported by World Literacy of Canada and other Canadian NGOs could be a model for accomplishing this goal);
   - ways be found for communicating through other than print media;
   - ways be explored for undereducated citizens to express their viewpoints to government through means other than written submissions.

3. The community of NGOs provides a valuable means of promoting *public education and development education* about international issues to which we are committed and to which we feel we can make some contribution, including illiteracy, social development, human rights, development and peace. Their international work provides good examples of Canada's contribution in dealing with world problems. In fact, the *sharing* is two-way. NGO experiences in other countries can be applied to development and literacy work in Canada, and the reverse is true as well. Both endeavors are guided by such principles as developing independent/interdependent individuals and communities.

4. The Canadian Commission for UNESCO is one NGO with which WLC works closely in Canada. WLC is pleased that Canada continues to support the United Nations and UNESCO, and hopes that this support will continue. The Canadian Commission for UNESCO has performed a significant role in supporting literacy work in Canada and in advancing international discussion on the *connections between literacy and all other areas of human endeavor.*

NOTES

1. A point made by M. Catley-Carlson, President of the Canadian International Development Agency (CIDA), in a speech to the annual meeting of the Canadian Association of Graduate Schools, November 1, 1984.
2. First Collective Consultation of International Non-Governmental Organizations on Literacy, Paris, 1984, p. 6.
3. Statement by M. Catley-Carlson, Ottawa, January, 1984.
4. Same as 3. above.

REFERENCES

Draper, James A., "A Commitment to Development and International Education: Some Examples from Canada", in *Literacy Discussion,* Vol. 4, No. 4, Winter, 1974.
See the Canadian Commission for UNESCO publication, *Adult Illiteracy in Canada: A Challenge,* prepared by Audrey Thomas, 1983.
UNESCO, "Second Collective Consultation of International Non-Governmental Organizations on Literacy", Czechoslovakia, November, 1985.

CHAPTER 3:

International Sharing: Learning from the Experience of Others

Alan Clarke

When I was asked to write this essay I thought about how my interests in, and knowledge of, literacy programs in other countries had been helpful to me in analyzing the situation facing adult education in Canada. The opportunity to find a different perspective for reflecting on what is happening can be very useful in ensuring appropriate action. I have found that time and effort invested in learning about what happens in other countries can be very beneficial.

For almost two decades we have had a paucity of leadership in Canada at all levels of education and particularly in the field of adult education. With many others in Canada, and in other countries of the developed world, I see activities in adult education being very much on the fringe of the educational structures in our society. I am reminded of the Chinese proverb;

If you are thinking one year ahead,

plant rice;

If you are thinking ten years ahead,

plant trees;

If you are thinking a hundred years ahead,

educate the people.   *(Source unknown)*

In Canada, and in much of western society, we do not make the necessary commitment to ensure full participation and involvement in the life of the community by the economically and educationally disadvantaged adult. We constantly seem to be seeking the "quick fix"; the policy or program that will serve immediate political needs. A decade ago some politicians were usually the only ones seeking the solution that would bring results within their term of office. Today many bureaucrats seem even more anxious than many politicians to push for the policy and program options which promise the least risk regardless of the financial and social cost. In many instances we can not even claim to be "planting rice".

John C. Cairns, formerly Director of the Centre for International Programmes at the University of Guelph, who was also the head of UNESCO's Literacy Program for more than a decade, stated recently:

> When one sees the fumbling, the confusion and the lack of professionalism with which we in Canada have faced our relatively modest problems of functional illiteracy, one can only weep.[1]

As one of the founders of the Movement for Canadian Literacy, more than a decade ago, I share the frustration and anger reflected in that statement. I also see some hope.

The responses to adult literacy needs in many other parts of the world have been quite different and for various reasons. As noted by Ali Hamadache and Daniel Martin in *Theory and Practice of Literacy Work* (1986:14)

> Until the end of the first quarter of the 20th century, literacy was almost always brought about gradually through school attendance by children while adult education was far from being a major concern of national leaders and educators.

This useful publication is a rich resource for those interested in the policies, strategies and examples of literacy programming. For my purposes let me acknowledge that, although there were some attempts at adult literacy programs prior to the Second World War, most national literacy campaigns have been a post-war phenomena.

THE EXPERIENCE IN CHINA

We were only slightly aware in Canada during the 1950's of the attempts of Chairman Mao to reduce the adult illiteracy rate of the population in the Peoples Republic of China. This remarkable revolutionary who, while teaching in a technical college, began evening classes for workers in the community is one of the few educators ever to succeed to a national leadership role. It was perhaps inevitable that in concert with a program of industrialization and agricultural co-operatives, he would launch a national campaign for the eradication of literacy in 1955.

By 1982 it was announced that the adult illiteracy rate in China had dropped from close to 80% to 23.5%. The campaign was deemed to be successful for three reasons: the first is the linking of education and learning with production at all levels, the second a great flexibility of approach to local needs and conditions and the third, teaching adapted, as far as possible, to the student's specific aptitudes.

> China applies the "walking-on-two-legs" policy whereby the state and the people co-operate to run a wide variety of schools in order to develop literacy, post-literacy and continuing education. In addition to those set up at the provincial, prefectural and county levels, schools are also run by industrial and commercial enterprises, communications and transport services, trade unions, and agricultural forestry and fishing institutes. Still others are operated by women's organizations the Communist Youth League, the people's militia, etc. (UNESCO, 1987)

THE EXPERIENCE IN CUBA

Canadians generally became aware of national literacy campaigns when Cuba introduced its program in 1961. This campaign was conducted in a country which has a single language and had a moderate rate of illiteracy, only 23.6%. What was phenomenal about it was that Cuba completed its campaign in nine months from April to December 1961. In a campaign marked by eagerness and enthusiasm, schools were closed, teachers and students became tutors with a teacher learner ratio of one tutor to two, or sometimes, three learners.

Other Experiences

Although literacy program activites in other parts of the world built on these experiences throughout the sixties and seventies, most Canadians remained unaware of the problem except perhaps for the many mass campaigns in other countries.

Two are particularly significant in terms of scale and community involvement. The giant Mobral program in Brazil concentrated on literacy and functional training involving four to five million adult learners at any given time. The program had branches in almost every community in Brazil and it was planned and implemented by the leading sociologists, educators, economists and other professionals in the country.

The United Kingdom's Adult Literacy Campaign which began in the mid 70's engaged the British Broadcasting Corporation (the BBC) as well as Local Education Authorities (LEA's) supported by the Adult Literacy Resource Agency, an autonomous body under the National Institute for Adult Continuing Education. Probably for the first time in a developed country, major resources in a variety of sectors were committed to a literacy campaign. The unique contribution of the BBC was a major factor here. Their three year plan to co-ordinate radio and television with supporting publications had the following characteristics:

(1) there would be a dual thrust to contact potential students and potential volunteer tutors;
(2) the most effective use of television would be to reduce anxiety rather than to provide instruction;
(3) the television programs would be transmitted during peak viewing time and would have to be acceptable to the mass literate audience among whom the non-readers would be concealed;
(4) there would be efforts to persuade other BBC program producers to make common cause with the literacy program to ensure widespread distribution of the "message".(Thomas, 1983:39)

FACTORS OF SUCCESS

Hamadache and Martin (1986) recount the factors in the success of literacy campaigns and emphasize that "each country must find its own solution to its own problems". They identify some common elements; two political factors; national commitment and the political and socioeconomic framework; and three technical factors; public awareness, mobilization and planning. Other common elements they identify are four basic principles: functionability, participation, integration and diversification. While they are somewhat uncomfortable about these categories they note that:

such a distinction has the advantage of drawing a line between those elements which are primarily the concern of government (political factors), those which are primarily the responsibility of administrators and planners (technical factors) and those which are ultimately the concern of all (basic principles). (Thomas, 1983:29)

Functionality

Literacy programs must be based on objectives that learning to read and to write are not ends in themselves. The Declaration of Persepolis extended the concept of functionality by pointing out that in most cases,

> successes were achieved when literacy was linked to man's fundamental requirements, ranging from his immediate vital needs to effective participation in social change.(Persepolis, 1975)

Participation

Closely linked to functionality, the principle of participation is best expressed in the statement that the learner "should not be the object but the subject of the process whereby he becomes literate". Paolo Freire linked literacy and liberation from the oppression of others. Engaging adults in the process of learning requires that they see the investment of their time and efforts leading to results which are beneficial and important to them.

Integration

Literacy programs must be integrated not only into the process of lifelong learning but into a whole body of economic and social reforms.

Co-ordination of national and provincial levels of funding and planning, and at the level of delivery in local communities, is essential to the integration of literacy and learning programs with other social, economic and cultural development activities.

Diversification

Hamadache and Martin (1986) note that "there is no such thing as a simple model for literacy programmes". They go on to quote Amadou-Mahtar M'Bow then Director-General of UNESCO that programmes:

> must adapt themselves to circumstances, individuals, socio-economic and cultural contexts and living conditions and draw their inspiration from them. The diversification of methodologies and approaches is therefore essential for success. (Persepolis, 1985:33)

These four principles are neither surprising nor new. In one form or another they are part of the rhetoric in many, if not most, discussions in the various Federal sources of funding, the various Provincial ministries where policies are set and the various institutions in the community with responsibility for implementation and delivery. The problem is that by the time the teacher and learner come into contact with each other, these principles are not reflected in the level of support they receive or the context in which they will both work and learn.

How many teachers and administrators have been concerned and involved in ensuring that the basic needs of their students are being met? How often are cheques late, support services inadequate, teaching support services removed?

How serious have efforts been at any level, either Federal, Provincial or local to ensure that educational resources are available to those in greatest need?

How often are tax dollars spent on promotional activities to compete for the registration fees of those often already well educated and capable of paying the increasingly higher fees being charged for adult education programs?

What serious co-operative mechanisms exist at the local community level for the development of policies, strategies, programs and delivery of resources for literacy or other adult basic education programs? How well do those that have the money and resources co-operate with each other?

My experience, and I wish it was otherwise, is that policies, strategies and programmes in most jurisdictions, except in some small ways in Quebec, do not reflect these basic principles. One could argue, perhaps because of its "fringe" nature, most adult basic education policies, strategies and programmes are characterized by fragmentation, powerlessness, disintegration, and competitiveness. These four principles are reflected not only in the courses but also in the support that the adult student receives. The context in which the adult educator, both the teacher and the administrator works are also characterized by these principles. This is where the concept of a paradigm may be useful. One definition of how change occurs is that a number of "fringe" activities with particular values and energies came together to create an "emerging paradigm", which is more appropriate and relevant than existing "mainstream" values and energies. The "emerging" paradigm succeeds the "dominant" paradigm and the process continues.

The concept of "paradigm shift" is important to my thesis because of the energy for change that derives from shared values. My experience in the mid sixties with the Company of Young Canadians helped me to realize the deep emotional hold existing values have on most of us. The anger, then, about anti-Vietnam war activists, and volunteers engaged in solar energy and organic gardening experiments seems long ago and strangely out of context with the late 1980's. When I hear some of the defensiveness and antagonism expressed by mainstream educators about different approaches, such as community based learning opportunities for adults, I remember the sixties.

If, as I believe, fragmentation, powerlessness, disintegration and competition characterize much of the current activities of the "dominant" paradigm perhaps we can begin to espouse the four principles of functionality, participation, integration and diversification as a basis for encouraging the"emerging" paradigm.

Apart from identifying principles which can help adult educators and learners to begin to shape their future it is important to have a vision of that future. Miguel Angel Escotet,(1986:425) writing in *Prospects*, UNESCO's Quarterly Review of Education, has his analysis of the present situation:

> education has come to be regarded ... as a supplier of "human resources"; it has been twisted into a formal institution concerned in practice with the immediate provision of trained skills and aptitudes, in which human beings are perceived as agents of production, their social, cultural and civic roles being relegated to the background.

Escotet calls for immediate recognition of education, "creating in men and women a sense of critical awareness and responsibility in respect of both themselves and their physical and social environment, so that they can work together to build their own future."(Escotet, 1986:430)

The urgency is not only for more appropriate approaches and methods to ensure participation in society. Given global population growth a different approach to adult education may be essential for our survival. Escotet describes how our time-scale shortens with the speed of technological invention and the unprecedented global population figures:

> It took some 5 million years up to AD 1800 for the total world population to reach the one billion mark. In barely 130 years, by 1930, the population had grown to 2 billion and by 1960 it had reached a total of 3 billion. By 1975 we had outstripped the 4 billion mark, and in the year 2000 there will be 6 billion human beings on earth. In the same year, the developing countries will be inhabited by 80 percent of the world's population. (Escotet, 1986:431)

There is little question that our dominant paradigm is inadequate to the challenge of the present and the future.

I wonder sometimes whether mainstream educators at the policy and administrative level are even aware of the challenge. Most adult educators though, do have some freedom to provide a more appropriate and relevant opportunity for adults to learn. The time may well be now for finding ways to do this within institutions, and particularly within communities.

Mainstream education from a variety of perspectives has not adapted to advances in science and technology. Escotet notes:

> Educational institutions and their teaching systems lag far behind when it comes to new forms of knowledge and learning. While the education system shapes some of the components of society, it is also conditioned by society, and has, therefore, to adapt to society's many and increasingly varied changes. The requirements of changing ways of thought, scientific discoveries, new technologies, the steady turnover of the school population and the emergence of parallel education in the form of television and radio are only some of the factors which formal education has difficulty in assimilating. The education system itself is reluctant to accept new teaching techniques and aids. In the age of the satellite, schools are using blackboard and chalk. This is not even realistic planning, it is enslavement to the past. (1986:434)

How will change come about? Who will initiate the changes needed and where will they occur?

My thesis is that change is already occurring. It is being initiated and helped along by creative administrators, teachers and learners and it is happening in many settings, some supportive and others decidedly reactionary.

Not all share the same vision or espouse the same values. However as a significant number have become so disenchanted with present policies and practices, some organizing for and encouraging of, the emerging paradigm is worth a try.

While it is comforting to assess the situation in such a way that one sees oneself as an agent for change, let me suggest *you are not supporting the emerging paradigm if*:

- you are an administrator and have served in your present position for more than five years.
- you are a teacher and have not consciously and systematically sought to ensure that what you are teaching is relevant to your students.

- you are either an administrator or teacher and use your position in the hierarchy to end dialogue or to impose a decision.
- you are either a teacher or an administrator and are not actively involved in the cultural, social or political life in your community.
- you are an administrator or teacher and are unfamiliar with the social and economic conditions of your students.
- you are an administrator and teacher and do not, at least every three months, actively pursue a professional development activity.
- you are an administrator or teacher and are not reading professional journals or books related to your field on a regular basis.
- you are a teacher or administrator and regard your "professional role" as what you do while you are "at work".
- you are a teacher or administrator and you realize something is seriously wrong with education or society but that it is someone else's responsibility.

I could go on although these of course reflect my own biases. If you agree with my analysis you should be able to draw up your own list.

Activities that often act as a bridge between the "emerging" and the "traditional" paradigms are co-operative education and similar work placement programs. These programs are best when they are designed to provide the student with an opportunity to make practical use of what is being learned. Again, their usefulness depends on the degree of commitment to the program by the institution and particularly the faculty. To be relevant to the adult student the programs that seek to provide learning opportunities in a work setting must have teaching, counselling and other support services readily available where and when required. Unfortunately in my experience far too many co-operative education and work placement programs are not only kept on the fringe of an institution's activities but are underfunded, understaffed and otherwise undersupported.

I am of course influenced by my own experience where I have encountered too many educational policy makers and administrators, and even some teachers, who have played the hierarchical game, and done what was necessary to do to get ahead. I still remember the shock some years ago when, in a management seminar for high school principals, the participants readily admitted working a kind of crisis management each week "to survive until Friday". The weekend provided a break before the week began again on Monday and the strategy for survival was to hold on again until Friday. For some reason I then asked "how many hope that the world out there, as well as the world of education won't change too much before you retire?" Almost everyone in the room agreed. My shock was that most of them were in their late 30's.

Escotet writes:

> What the world really needs is educated people capable of understanding the contemporary driving forces in the world and who can adapt to them and transform them. (1986:434)

Whether the present education system is going to contribute to this capacity will, in large part, be determined by those teachers and administrators who begin to do their own analysis, to take some risks and to do what they can to encourage a more appropriate and relevant "paradigm" for their work.

They have some reason to be optimistic. An international year to combat illiteracy has been proposed (International Literary Year 1990). Public awareness of the situation facing illiterates in Canada will increase as well as public knowledge of the extensive experience with literacy campaigns elsewhere.

My only hesitation is the sense I have that many Canadian educators believe that the way it is done in Canada is the best way, regardless of the results achieved.

Experience, however, has convinced me that much is to be gained by learning how things are done elsewhere; if only to get a different perspective on what we are doing here.

AUTHORS NOTE

This essay was written in early 1987 in advance of the Southam Survey, the announcement of a Literacy Secretariat by the Federal Government and the release of a Report on Illiteracy in Canada by the Council of Ministers of Education. My anxieties about, and hopes for, literacy programs remains the same.

NOTES

1. John C. Cairns in his acceptance of the Lewis Perinbam Award on September 30, 1986.

REFERENCES

Declaration of Persepolis (1975), The International Symposium for Literacy, Persepolis, September 3-8.
Escotet, Miguel Angel (1986)."Utopian Planning of Education & Development, Prospects, UNESCO" *Quarterly Review of Education*, Vol. 16, No. 4.
Hamadache, Ali & Martin, Daniel (1986). *Theory & Practice of Literacy Work, Policies, Startegies & Examples*, UNESCO, Paris & Canadian organisation for Development Through Education, Ottawa.
Mahrendroo, Vaiju. From an article in UNESCO special No. 3 (1987) where much of the information is from a chapter on China by Li Jiyuan in the study 'Learning Startegies for Post-Literacy & Continuing Education in China, India, Indonesia, Nepal, Thailand and Vietnam', UNESCO Institute for Education (Hamburg) in collaboration with UNESCO National Commission of Federal Republic of Germany.
Thomas, Audrey (1983). *Adult Illiteracy in Canada : A Challenge*, Occasional Paper No. 42, Canadian Commission for UNESCO.

The Final Eradication of Illiteracy: A Mission Given to UNESCO by the International Community

Paul Bélanger

Public opinion, world over, knows about the United Nations Educational, Scientific and Cultural Organization because, among other activities, UNESCO is conspicuously involved in the promotion of literacy.

Indeed, during the last decades, literacy has become one of the key symbols of the United Nations' commitment to human rights. The most crucial contribution of UNESCO to the development of literacy is certainly the emergence of a global vision pertaining to this issue. Global in the sense of an international perspective encompassing, on an equal basis, all and each of the five thousand million women and men living on the small spacial vessel called earth. Global also as an ecological project in which literacy is not only a right, and not only a demand of the dispossessed masses of the world, but is also an instrument needed to solve the crucial problems facing humanity today. In his address on the occasion of the award of the International Literacy Prizes for 1985, the Director General of UNESCO, Mr. Amadou Mahtar M'Bow, stressed these dimensions. "Its global dimensions and its social and human implication," said the Director General, "make literacy a radical challenge for the international community."

From its inception, forty years ago, UNESCO has undertaken many initiatives to promote literacy and to cooperate in field projects which aimed at the eradication of illiteracy by the year 2000. The most concrete contribution of UNESCO to reach this goal is its persistent campaign to remind the international community that illiteracy is "one of the great social problems of our time and a major challenge" to the world.

I shall firstly give the picture of the present situation as seen by UNESCO and indicate the major issues this United Nations Organization has raised in the fight against illiteracy. Secondly, I shall describe in broad terms what UNESCO has done and is doing in this field, what are the issues raised by these actions as well as the impact of such undertakings.

THE ISSUE OF LITERACY AS SEEN BY UNESCO: THE SCOPE AND NATURE OF THE PROBLEM

In 1985, according to the data provided by UNESCO for the 1986 literacy day, there were in the world an estimated 889,000,000 people over the age of fifteen who could not read and write. 60% of these illiterates are women. Indeed, 20% of the male adult population are illiterate in comparison to 32% of the female adult population.

Africa and Asia are the most affected regions: 162 million African people and 666 million Asian people are presently illiterate. This means an illiteracy rate of 54% for Africa and 36.3% for Asia. The illiteracy rate is approximately 55% in the Arab states and 17% in Latin America and the Caribbeans.

Since the beginning of the present decade, we are also discovering the hidden illiterates in the industrial countries. Illiteracy is no more a problem confined to the South. It is now very concretely a world problem.

UNESCO data show that the absolute number of literate adults is increasing. During the period 1975-1985 the number of adults in the world (15 years and above), who have received literacy training, rose from 1,708,000 to 2,314,000. As a consequence, the rate of illiteracy fell from 32.9% in 1970 to 27.7% in 1985. These figures show an important progress at the world level, if one takes into account the rapid growth in the world population.

Nevertheless, UNESCO insists in reminding world opinion that the absolute number of illiterate adults is still increasing. At the present moment, more than 27% of adults world over are illiterate, and, among them, as stated above, 60% are women. The last estimate given by UNESCO suggests that, without any new action being taken, the absolute number of illiterate people will go significantly beyond the level of 900,000,000 by the year 2000.

The UNESCO vision on this issue is not a pessimistic one, but one of hope and responsibility. UNESCO documents repeat again and again that, without a firm determination of member-states, the problem will find no real solution. During the last fifteen years, the international community has learned a lot about the most efficient strategies to deal with the problem. Many countries, like for example Birmania, China, Cuba, India, Nicaragua, Tanzania and Thailand, have achieved very significant results through different approaches. UNESCO itself, through its own experience of the Experimental World Literacy Program (EWLP) has learned much about what to do and not to do.

Indeed, the debate on literacy is shifting more and more from the feasibility aspect to the political and technical dimensions of the problem. Within UNESCO meetings we now hear less about the possibility of literacy and more about the need to define priorities. The debates revolve around the best strategies to train educators, to develop adapted programs to specific contexts, to evaluate the impact of the different programs, to create new approaches for post-literacy programs, etc. It is certainly one of the great achievements of UNESCO to have been able to make literacy an international issue, to have awakened world public opinion on this crucial problem, and, yet, to have developed this issue, through practical and diversified approaches, in a positive perspective. The eradication of illiteracy is no more an impossible target, though it is one that needs profound changes in priorities.

THE ROLE OF UNESCO IN THE STRUGGLE AGAINST ILLITERACY

Within the United Nations system it is UNESCO that has the statutory and moral mandate to carry the responsibility for the struggle against illiteracy.

The Role of Raising Public Awareness

The first role of UNESCO within this mandate is to raise public awareness and to mobilize all governmental and nongovernmental efforts towards this task. UNESCO has taken many initiatives to continuously remind the world public opinion that "illiteracy is one of the great social problems of our time". Literacy is one of the major concerns of the UNESCO delegates at all general conferences held every two years since 1946.

However, it is only in 1960, at the Montreal Second International Conference on Adult Education, that a concrete recommendation was made to launch a vast campaign for the eradication of illiteracy. This recommendation gained more and more momentum in the 1960s. In 1964 for example, the general conference decided to undertake an international experimental program to prepare the campaign. This program, the Experimental World Literacy Program (EWLP), was prepared by a special conference held in Teheran in 1965 and was implemented between 1967 and 1973. Furthermore, in 1966, UNESCO, in collaboration with the United Nations General Conference, proclaimed the 8th September of every year as the international literacy day. Every year since then, UNESCO and a growing number of member states have taken the opportunity of this day to release new data on the situation of illiteracy and to make appeals for the intensification of all necessary action.

It is within this same perspective of educating public opinion and promoting literacy that UNESCO is awarding on the 8th September of every year four International Prizes to recognize the achievements made by governmental and nongovernmental organizations in the campaign against illiteracy. These four prizes are: the N. K. Krupskaya Prize donated by the USSR in 1979, the International Reading Association Prize (USA) donated in 1979, the Noma Prize given in 1980 by a Japanese publisher, and the Iraq Prize given in 1981 by the Government of Iraq. In August 1986, these four prizes were given to the National Literacy Centre of Angola, the National Literacy Plan of Argentina, the Allama Iqbal Open University in Pakistan and the Ministry of Social Affairs of Morocco.

This goal of mobilizing public opinion has also led UNESCO to produce several studies on literacy and to publish special issues of UNESCO periodicals like, for example, the UNESCO Courier in 1980 and 1984. Every occasion is being used to raise the issue of illiteracy and to mobilize effort against it, as it was done, for example, during the International Youth Year in 1985.

The project of the United Nations, in collaboration with UNESCO, to declare the year 1990 the International Literacy Year (ILY) is a very crucial activity, as it will permit a significant step further in the campaign of public awareness concerning the issue of illiteracy. Indeed, at the Sofia General Conference in 1985, the Director General was requested to prepare a draft program for an international literacy year in order to "contribute to greater understanding by world public opinion of the various aspects of this problem and to intensify efforts to spread literacy and to launch a possible world literacy campaign" under the hospices of the United Nations and UNESCO.

The objectives of the ILY were approved by the 24th Session of the UNESCO General Conference in the autumn of 1987. These objectives are:

— increasing action by the governments of Member states . . .,
— increasing public awareness . . .,
— increasing popular participation . . .,
— increasing co-operation and solidarity among Member States in the struggle against illiteracy,
— increasing co-operation within the United Nations system . . .,
— using International Literacy Year for launching the Plan of Action for the eradication of illiteracy by the year 2000 . . . .

A special Secretariat was created by the Director General, along with an intersectorial taskforce, to prepare and implement the United Nations ILY program. Furthermore, the NGO community brought its support and dynamism by setting up an international taskforce on literacy under the initiative and with the support of the International Council for Adult Education.

The Normative Role

The second main contribution of UNESCO in the struggle against illiteracy is of a juridical nature. The United Nations system and UNESCO have developed many normative instruments to recognize and legitimize the universal human right to read and write. Already in 1944, Article 26 of the Universal Declaration of Human Rights was referring to this right to provide education for all. Following the recommendation of the Montreal International Conference in 1960, a UNESCO meeting held in Iran in 1972 issued an international declaration called the "Declaration of Persepolis". This declaration states that "literacy is not just the process of learning the skill of reading, writing and arithmetic, but a contribution to the liberation of man and to his full development". Two years later in Nairobi the UNESCO General Conference adopted a recommendation concerning the development of adult education, which puts literacy as an integral part of the educational task recommended to the member states. This recommendation asks the member states to recognize more concretely the role played by adult educators and literacy workers, and to give them the needed conditions for an efficient implementation of their task. Always in the same perspective of pressuring governments and nongovernmental organisations, the General Conference of 1980 recommended that the 1981-1983 program of UNESCO give a new impulse to the existing efforts of UNESCO and its member states. A similar stand was taken in 1983 for the second medium-term plan.

Finally, the last, and probably the most significant, normative tool adopted by UNESCO is the declaration of "The Right to Learn" adopted in 1985 at the UNESCO 4th International Conference on Adult Education. The right to read and write is the first point stressed in this declaration. "Recognition of the right to learn is now more than ever a major challenge for humanity. The right to learn is: the right to read and write; the right to question and analyze; the right to imagine and create; the right to read about one's own world and to write history; the right to have access to educational resources; the right to develop individual and collective skills."

This declaration, published world over and in all United Nations official languages, has become now a reference for literacy workers in order to have their task recognized and to obtain the needed resources. More important, the declaration has become an instrument to help people assert their right to learn, and to learn in the integral sense of the term, that is to be able to read the reality and to master the environment. Indeed, as the declaration states: "the act of learning, lying as it does at the heart of all educational activity, changes human beings from objects at the mercy of events to subjects creating their own history".

Multilateral Cooperation

The third main contribution of UNESCO is the concrete work done in the field of multilateral cooperation. It is impossible within the limits of this short paper to summarize all the projects initiated and supported partially or totally by UNESCO since 1960 in the field of literacy. Literacy has become a high priority in UNESCO programs since 1966, and we have already referred to the important decade of the Experimental World Literacy Program. Another example is the second medium-term plan of 1984-1989 which proposes an intensification of UNESCO and member states' efforts in this field.

Multilateral cooperation has taken many forms: expert missions, complementary financial support, studies and action research, pilot projects, planning of literacy and post-literacy programs, gathering of data, training of educators, building of exchange networks, promotion of interregional cooperation, collaboration with nongovernmental organizations on all continents, creation of a special network of voluntary contribution for world literacy work, etc. An indicator of UNESCO strong involvement in the struggle for literacy is the list of publications, studies and documents published by the section of literacy at the UNESCO office in Paris, and this by a very small team in the division of primary education, literacy and adult education (such a list is available from UNESCO, 7 Place Fontenois, 75700 Paris).

Since 1979, UNESCO has also made special efforts in helping member states and their ministry of education to define interregional plans for the struggle against illiteracy. Concerning Latin America and the Caribbean, for example, a regional conference of ministers of education was called in Mexico City in 1979 and was followed by three intergovernmental regional meetings, at the end of which a plan of action for that region was adopted. In Africa in 1982, two conferences were held, one in Harare and the other in Bamako, to develop a regional program for the eradication of illiteracy. In the Arab community, a meeting of specialists was held in Morocco in 1984 at the initiative of the UNESCO Regional Education Bureau for the Arab States. This meeting called for the fostering of pedagogical training of literacy workers within the Arab societies. The same year the Arab Literacy and Adult Education Organization (ARLO) held the 4th Alexandria Conference in Tunis to study the development of literacy within the framework of life long education.

Exchange of Ideas

The fourth contribution of UNESCO in the struggle against illiteracy are its diversified activities (conferences, seminars, meetings, publications) which increased the exchange of ideas and experiences in the field of literacy work on a horizontal basis. It is within this sphere of activities that debates on key problems were started and developed: the discussion of the language issue in literacy, the debate on macro-approaches like national campaigns versus functional strategies, the comparative analysis of illiteracy in industrial countries and that in the third-world, the relation between literacy and post-literacy and between primary education and adult literacy, the reversal of perspectives looking at illiterates as passive targets rather than active participants, etc.

One of the most important issues that UNESCO has raised and developed is the one relating literacy and integral development, that is, one stressing the intimate relation between illiteracy and poverty and between literacy and rural development.

It is within the thousand of small, medium and large meetings, held on all continents by UNESCO international offices or regional bureaus, that, slowly, new approaches and new attitudes for the diversification of strategies and for the evaluation of past experiments and shifting of priorities were developed. These meetings gathered together, on an equal basis, planners, governmental and nongovernmental leaders, literacy workers and representatives of grassroots people. And in these meetings, without much noise, several momentums were created which made UNESCO capable of convincing the United Nations Assembly to declare an international literacy year and of stating without fear of cynical criticisms that the eradication of illiteracy is a goal attainable before the end of this century. Such a goal is in the process of being achieved, but it is a goal that needs a new impetus, which we can develop, and a new choice of priorities, a choice we can make within the limits of today's realities.

UNESCO's EXPECTED ROLE

However, despite all these achievements, UNESCO will have to deal with a difficult issue in order to play its expected role in the struggle for the eradication of illiteracy. In the second half of the 1980s, UNESCO has been facing a serious organizational and financial crisis which put pressure on the decision-makers. While the 1984-1989 medium-term plan did propose an intensification of efforts in the field of illiteracy, at the same time, due to a lack of financial resources, it has recommended a closer integration of the sections on primary education and adult literacy.

It becomes clear that we cannot decide, neither at the national nor at the international level, to develop further programs of literacy and freeze the allocation of resources for literacy at the same time.

The tendency of questioning the specificity of adult literacy and of integrating young and adult basic education runs, on the one hand, the risk of decreasing our ability to tackle the challenge of school enrollment for the 100 million children, who still today have no access to primary education. On the other hand, it runs also the risk of separating adult literacy and post-literacy from the imperatives of rural development, from primary health care and from the community context, all areas in which adult literacy has shown to be most efficient.

One can only hope that this new trend is a temporary one. The meeting of UNESCO experts, held in Hamburg in December 1985, proposed that the

1990-1995 medium-term plan includes a large life-long learning plan with two distinct and complementary programs, one on the primary education of children and the other on literacy and adult education.

Indeed, adult literacy, as a tool for development, was historically one of the landmarks of UNESCO. Instead of being a **problem** for the organization, the campaign for the eradication of illiteracy must become one of the **solutions**, helping UNESCO to find a second breath, a surplus of legitimacy and a stronger support from the world public opinion, a support UNESCO needs to go through this critical phase of its recent history.

CHAPTER 5:

Youth's Participation in Literacy Work

Arthur Gillette

"Increasing popular participation, within and between countries, in efforts to combat illiteracy...," is one of the avowed objectives adopted for' international literacy work. It is an ambitious goal. To bring it down to earth and make it realistic in terms of tangible activities requires an analysis of present forms of popular participation in literacy work, and a projection into the immediate future of guidelines emerging from that analysis. To attempt such analysis and projection with regard to participation in literacy by one still insufficiently tapped segment of the population — youth — is the task of this chapter.

Young people already do play an important part in literacy work. Indeed, there are few if any literacy efforts in the world that do not depend in some measure upon the energies and skills (and sometimes the ideas) of the younger generation.

Youth's roles in literacy work are varied, and include, for example, direct teaching functions; dissemination of information and promotion of awareness; construction and repair of premises; fund raising; the generation of resources in kind; and a variety of miscellaneous tasks such as distribution of eyeglasses, publication of post-literacy reading material and running village reading centres.

Since youth participate in literacy activities in a wide and changing variety of ways, it seems useful to attempt a typology of patterns of participation based on certain key variables: e.g., the number of organized schemes in the world; percentage of potentially 'mobilizable' young people actually mobilized; criteria for selection of sites and target groups for literacy action; nature of the sponsoring body; minimum age and education requirements for participation; intensity of participants' involvement (length and schedule); and nature of of youth participation (on a continuum between voluntary and obigatory).

The term 'schemes' is used broadly in the previous paragraph to designate organized activities enabling the participation of youth in the provision of literacy. It seems possible to structure our description and analysis around an examination of the above-outlined key variables by referring successively to three patterns, defined for the purposes of a working hypothesis only: the *project pattern* (generally small-scale on-off schemes in terms of youth participation as an expectation); the *program pattern* (more systematic, with participation as an expectation); and the *campaign pattern* (massive). For the sake of timeliness and comparability, this examination will limit itself to schemes organized in the last dozen years.

THE PROJECT PATTERN

Before looking systematically at the evidence available, it is perhaps well to illustrate this approach with a concrete example. In 1981, the Voluntary Workcamps Association of Ghana (VOLU) decided to move beyond its previous traditional workcamping and take Part in the Ghana Government's new policy of reviving mass literacy work. (Atta, 1985)

At the outset, VOLU organized two training courses for 114 mostly young volunteer literacy instructors. Then a first-phase target was set for 26 literacy classes with 280 pupils. This had to be scaled down to five villages and towns in two regions, with ten learners (illiterate farmers and youngsters who had not had the opportunity to attend school) in each class. In most cases, the literacy classes were organized as a complement to regular workcamp construction projects.

Evidence for the following systematic analysis is drawn from the publication *Volunteering in Literacy Work: A Guide to National and International Opportunities,* (1985) which presents basic information on 59 organizations in 44 countries covering all regions of the world and including 12 industrialized countries (socialist and market economy), collected by the use of questionnaires.

Activities under the project pattern were reported in just over one-quarter of UNESCO's member states, although work undertaken by regional and international organizations almost certainly takes place in other countries as well. On the whole, the activities are focused on a relatively limited number of fairly small projects, each involving tens (rather than hundreds) of young people, and thus barely scratching the surface of the potentially 'mobilizable' pool, i.e., educated youth.

In synthesis, youth participation in the provision of literacy under the project pattern seems to have the following salient characteristics:
- it is carried out in a relatively large number of countries (more than a quarter of UNESCO's member states) but only a few potentially 'mobilizable' young people are actually mobilized;
- these activities tend to be limited and selective in terms of site and size (often working with a few localities or a single locality only) and of target groups (having in their overwhelming majority singled out a very few) — hence the name 'project' pattern;
- by and large, the activities are undertaken on the initative of and sponsored by non-governmental groups, which may however seek government cooperation for their execution on an ad hoc basis and sometimes co-operate with other NGOs;
- minimum age and education requirements in the vast majority of project-type activities aim chiefly to attract older teenagers and young adults with at least a secondary school level (probably making them largely the preserve of middle- to upper-class young people, especially in developing countries);
- a relatively intense involvement is required of participants, with a medium-to long-term (e.g., 6- to 24-month) stint and a heavy schedule (half-time-plus to time-and-a-half) prevailing;
- youth's participation in project pattern literacy work is strictly voluntary and usually requires self-sacrifice which often expresses the dedication typical for various forms of social action undertaken by committed minorities.

THE PROGRAM PATTERN

Study-service schemes undertaking literacy work seem an appropriate kind of activity to illustrate the program pattern. Information on 21 countries' study-service programs, gathered between 1978 and 1982, is presented and analyzed in a recent UNESCO report, *Study Service: A Tool of Innovation in Higher Education*. (1984) Reference will only be made, in this section, to schemes which refer explicitly to literacy work undertaken by student participants. 'Study service' is defined in the UNESCO report as 'activities carried out by (university) students for the benefit of the community which are regarded as part of their vocational and civic training. (UNESCO, 1984:1)

Looking at study service in a systematic fashion, we find that of the 21 countries covered by the UNESCO report, which may be considered to operate the major study-service schemes in the world since all member states were polled in preparing the report, six make explicit mention of ongoing literacy work among activities of their students. This is equivalent to just under four percent of UNESCO's member states, a rather small number. Coverage of potential participating populations (university student bodies) varies from country to country, although not all who serve do literacy work. In India, almost all universities (though not all of those universities' students) are involved in study service, with a total annual mobilization of about half a million students (not all directly involved in literacy, however). In Costa Rica, study service is compulsory for all students at the University of Costa Rica, and consideration is being given to making it obligatory for all university students in the country, as it already is in Mozambique. In Tanzania most if not all institutions of post-secondary education offer opportunities for study service, with teaching in primary school or literacy being a prerequisite for teacher certification.

The citing of study-service operations is both pervasive and selective. It is pervasive in the sense that, in general, students are posted individually or in groups in villages, cities, enterprises and organizations scattered throughout the territories of most of the countries reported on in the UNESCO document. Posting is, however, also selective to the extent that there are not enough students to meet manpower needs for literacy work or other activities; they are sent where they can be most productive. India has instituted a kind of twinning scheme under which each hundred-person unit of students is linked to a given village, poor quarter or other locality on a long-term basis (3,000 villages having been chosen for this purpose) so as to sure continuity through 'sustained and meaningful' (UNESCO, 1984:46) reciprocal contracts. By definition, sponsors of study service are institutions of higher education. In all cases, however, the universities act in concert with other bodies.

In none of these cases do students receive pay during periods of service. In countries reporting on this question, transport, board, lodging, and pocket-money are made available. Combined with a degree of compulsion, how does this low material return affect the morale of servicemen and women and, more generally, the spirit in which their work is carried out? In Costa Rica, all parties concerned (including the students themselves) take part in systematic evaluations, which 'have been very critical . . .' (UNESCO, 1984:23) Nevertheless, the evaluations have also shown that 'all the participants consider the experience to be of great educational value and beneficial for students and the community alike? While information is not available on students' attitudes there, Egypt reports that 'the communities who receive the service of the students, as well as the national community, consider the contribution of the students to be necessary and positive, particularly those programs concerning the fight against illiteracy... (UNESCO, 1984:34) At the very least, there would appear not to be a strong and/or widespread unwillingness among students taking part in these schemes, although enthusiasm does not seem to be their keynote, either.

In summary, participation of young people in the provision of literacy under study-service schemes, as illustrative of the program pattern, has the following main features:
- it is found in a limited number of countries (less than four percent of UNESCO's member states);
- but it is relatively widespread in terms of potential populations actually mobilized since it is an optional or obligatory part of students' regular undergraduate studies (whence the notion of 'program' pattern), although not all those mobilized do literacy work;
- its activities tend to be pervasive since the criteria for posting of students and choosing of groups with whom they work are broadly inclusive rather than narrowly exclusive, but there is also an element of selectivity since available manpower cannot meet all major needs;
- the initiative for the activities lies with sponsoring universities, which seek the assistance of NGOs and particularly, governments (which tend to provide major or total funding);
- minimum age and education attainments are self-defining since programs focus almost exclusively on undergraduate students in their late teens or early 20s (in middle and upper socio-economic strata, at least in developing countries);
- intensity of involvement tends to be limited in terms of aggregate total length of service required (six weeks to six months being normal parameters inside the extremes of two weeks and eight months), while scheduling is generally full-time (with the notable exception of youth who study part-time only),
- youth participation in literacy through study-service tends to involve at least an element of compulsion and requires a degree of self-sacrifice (only subsistence provided); strong, widespread unwillingness seems absent, however.

THE CAMPAIGN PATTERN

'Campaign' is construed here to mean a large-scale literacy effort designed to make major inroads into illiteracy nationally within a prescribed period of time (several months to a few years). In this respect, H.S. Bhola's book *Campaigning for Literacy* (Bhola, 1984) is comprehensive.

The following systematic review of the data on the campaign pattern of youth participation in provision of literacy is expressed chiefly by the 1980 National Literacy Crusade in Nicaragua and its follow-up since then, in terms of the key variables outlined earlier in this article.

Firstly, the campaign approach to literacy involving youth participation, as defined above, is limited to Ethiopia, (Mammo,1984:5), Nicaragua, (Arnove, 1981) and Tanzania, (Mammo et al,1983), to which may be added China (where it is used in at least some provinces), and perhaps Burma, Turkey and Thailand (although information on youth participation is not precise in these cases). In any event, not more than half a dozen countries seem to be concerned in our ten-year time frame.

Within campaign countries, mobilization is massive. During the Nicaraguan Campaign (1980), more than 225,000 literates volunteered to do literacy work, out of a population of 717,000 aged ten and above, of whom some 50% were illiterate.(Cardenal & Millar, 1982) The brunt of actual teaching fell on some 100,000 volunteers, divided between about 35,000 who taught in towns and a further 65,000 who formed the Popular Literacy Army (PLA), which moved from city to country during the Campaign. Along with factory and office workers, housewives and other townspeople, the urban teaching mobilized 'high-school and university students who for health or family reasons could not leave the city. (Arnove, 1981:249) Among PLA members, the 'vast majority were high-school and university students (Cardenal & Millar, 1982:208); indeed, they were 'mostly high-school students . . ' (Arnove, 1982,248)

While comprising the majority of all literacy teachers, young people thus mobilized also accounted for a sizeable proportion of the potentially mobilizable youth population. On the whole, one can calculate that the numbers of youthful volunteers in the Popular Literacy Army were at least equivalent to just over 1/3 of the total secondary and university student population, and to rather more than 1/3 of high-school pupils. There was, in any event, extensive coverage of the large potential youth population that could have been mobilized.

Correlating with the Campaign's massive nature was its non-selective approach to sites and target populations. In principle, there was but one huge target group and site: the 50% of Nicaraguans aged ten and above, who, living in both urban and rural areas, were illiterate.

The Campaign — and youth's participation in it — was sponsored by the Government through a Co-ordinating Unit working within the Ministry of Education. The practical organization of the Campaign and of youth's participation was heavily dependent on the active involvement of a large number of governmental and non-governmental bodies, however. The Nicaraguan Educators Organization, for example, provided seasoned teachers who ensured technical support for the young volunteers, (Cardenal & Millar, 1982:207) while the national Scout movement gave them training in camping — of direct relevance for young townspeople who would be spending several months in impoverished rural areas for the first time in their lives. (Managua Ministry of Education, 1980:167) The Sandinista youth played the central role in youth mobilization.

To combat illiteracy among one-half of the country's young people and adults (50% of Nicaraguans over ten years old) the authorities felt their only recourse was to mobilize as many of the other — literate — half as possible. Hence the idea that the undifferentiated mass of literates, 'the people', should make the undifferentiated mass of illiterates, also 'the people', literate, (Managua, 1980:155) and the popular slogan *'En cada Nica un maestro'* in each Nicaraguan a teacher', (Arnove, 1981:281) To wage the struggle most intensively in the rural areas, where the percentage of illiterates was highest and the percentage of potential literacy workers correspondingly low, required the priority mobilization and temporary transfer of those urban dwellers without family or professional/economic responsibilities, i.e., the student population. Thus, the main criteria for selection were availability and willingness to serve (expressed in a lyrical literacy worker's oath)(Rothschuh & Tamez, 1983:79)two characteristics linked with youthfulness.

The minimum age required to volunteer was 14, (Nicaragua/Prague, 1983) and minors had to have authorization from parents or guardians to take part in the Campaign. (Torres, 1983:7) As we have seen above, the bulk of Popular Literacy Army teachers were university and secondary-school students, with the latter comprising at least a simple majority of PLA volunteers. Students also accounted for a good part of the less numerous town-based literacy workers. On the whole, young people were the majority of literacy volunteers, and within the 'youth' category there was a distinct skewing toward people of secondary-school age (14 to 18 years). Although no minimal education re-quirement for participation seems to have been made explicit, a complete primary education appears in practice to have been the threshold. Urban, belonging either to the 8% of university-aged young people actually studying, or more likely to the 14.7% of secondary-aged young people effectively in school, the typical young literacy workers were relatively privileged, in fact 'largely middle-class youth.' (Managua Ministry of Education, 1980:167)

This profile has changed since the conclusion of the Campaign itself and the beginning of post-literacy work. At first, the requirements to become a Popu-lar Teacher (leader of post-literacy work) were (a) to be at least 14 years of age, and (b) to have taken part as a literacy worker in the Campaign. (Arnove, 1981:257) Initially, then, the post-literacy workers were to have a profile identical to the Campaign volunteers — were, in fact, to be drawn from among the same people. This soon changed, however, since 'Nicaragua did not have enough teachers to carry on the tasks of adult education. (Managua Ministry of Education, 1980:183)

The invention mothered by necessity in this case was a new kind of leader of post-literacy work. In the absence of external staff, local communities them-selves began to provide para-professional Popular Teachers in large numbers. Some 144,000 people (equivalent to about 36% of the some 400,000 made literate during the 1980 Campaign) signed up in 1981 for continuing education courses 'animated', if not exactly taught in traditional terms, by some 25,000 Popular Teachers. (Managua Ministry of Education, 1980:182) Similar num-bers of learners and Popular Teachers seem still to be active. (Arrién, 1985) While being generally of local rural (rather than external urban) origin, an undetermined but apparently large number of the Popular Teachers are also young, very young indeed in some cases. Rosa Maria Torres states that 'the efficient and enthusiastic participation of young Co-ordinators and Promo-tors (of post-literacy Popular Basic Education) of 10 to 14 years of age, who go to school in the morning and look after the Popular Education Centres in the afternoon, quickly called into question the validity of the earlier "no younger than 14 years" requirement. (Torres, 1983:21,27)

Educationally, too, the profile changed, since the minimum required *de facto* is no longer a completed formal primary education. In 1981, 40% of the Popular Teachers had gone no farther than completing their own basic literacy learning, while 16% had finished a first post-literacy level and 32% had attended a few years of primary school. (Torres, 1983:22)

In terms of intensity, there have also been two phases in the participation of young people in literacy (and post-literacy) work in Nicaragua. The first began in November 1979 with part-time forming up and preparation of the Popular Literacy Army units and reached its peak between 23 March and 15 August 1980 (the 4¾ months that the Campaign officially lasted). During that period, the PLA worked more than full-time, since its members helped the rural people with their regular farming tasks during the day and usually taught them before or after the normal hours of labour. In towns, young and other participants gave two to three hours of instruction a day, Monday through Saturday, during the Campaign, thus equivalent to a ¼ to almost ½-time commitment. In the second, post-literacy, phase, the Popular Teachers' involvement has been less intensive, generally amounting to two sessions a week of about two hours each, (Torres, 1983:23) but no time limit has been set in terms of months (or years), since adult education is intended to be a continuing process.

To what degree was/is youth participation in literacy and post-literacy work in Nicaragua voluntary? In material terms, sacrifice was/is involved, since neither the Campaign workers nor the post-literacy Popular Teachers were/are paid, remuneration being limited to food, lodging, clothing, and equipment for the Campaign workers and teaching materials for the Popular Teachers. The spirit of Campaign mobilization was not without regimentation, judging by the military vocabulary used to describe the operation ('fronts', 'brigades', 'literacy militia', 'Popular Literacy Army', etc.) and by the fact that PLA members were uniformed (jeans and peasant shirts). Yet, according to Robert Arnove, 'no-one was officially required or compelled to teach' and many more volunteered than could actually be mobilized'. (Arnove, 1981:259) What regimentation existed was largely overshadowed by the enthusiasm of the youngsters (and the less young) involved in teaching and learning — a joyfulness all the more extraordinary since the country was in a virtual state of war during the Campaign (several young literacy workers were murdered by *contra* groups precisely because they were involved in mass education). In explaining the success of the Campaign, its Co-ordinator and one of his principal assistants have stated that 'by far the most critical factor was an intangible one — the spirit . . ! If joining the Campaign was not an exceptional action for a young person, then, neither was it the result of massive coercion resulting in indifference or unwillingness; it was encouraged volunteering.

THE PATTERNS COMPARED AND SOME CONCLUSIONS

The main responses of the three patterns just described concerning the set of key variables are summarized in the following table. It should be stressed that neither the presentation of this table nor the discussion of it that follows expresses a value judgment on the quality of participation of young people in the provision of literacy through the different patterns.

It is clear from the cases examined that the campaign pattern is — and is likely to remain — a largely unrepeatable exception, linked to radical changes in the orientation and distribution of wealth and power in the countries concerned. At the other extreme is the project pattern is — of limited practical interest as a global option since, faced with the dramatic increase in the number

Table: *The Patterns Compared*

	Project Pattern	*Programme Pattern*	*Campaign Pattern*
1. Presence in world	Relatively numerous (more than ¼ of UNESCO member states)	Limited number of countries (less than 4% of Unesco member states)	Very limited (a handful of countries : 3? 4?)
2. Percentage of potentially 'mobilizable' youth actually mobilized	Scratches surface	High percentage of limited 'mobilizable' populations actually mobilized; not all for literacy work	Massive mobilization of large potential 'mobilizable' population
3. Criteria for choice of sites and target groups	Limited and selective	Pervasive and inclusive (but also selective *de facto* since number of young people mobilized is limited compared to needs)	Very comprehensive: non-selective posting and undifferentiated target group
4. Nature of sponsor	NGOs (with some other NGO and *ad hoc* government co-operation)	Universities (with some NGO assistance and trend for government funding)	Ministry of Education (with systematic, multi-level and active co-operation of other government units and NGOs)
5. Minimum age and education requirements	Older teenagers and young adults with secondary level; *ipso facto* middle- or upper-class (especially in developing countries)	University graduates (late teens, early 20s); *ipso facto* middle- to upper-class (especially in developing countries)	a) Campaign: bulk in 14–18 age range with complete primary education; urban middle-class (university students also); b) Post-literacy; rural, lower-class, younger adolescent, incomplete primary education
6. Intensity of involvement	Relatively long aggregate length: 6 to 24 months, ¹/₂-time to time and ¹/₂.	Limited aggregate length: 6 weeks to 6 months; generally full-time (except for part-time students)	a) Campaign: medium aggregate length (4³/₄ months) (i) more than full-time for majority in rural areas, (ii) ¹/₄- to ¹/₂-time for minority in towns; b) Post-literacy: unlimited length, spare time (4 hours per week)
7. Nature of youth participation:	Strictly voluntary; self-sacrifice; voluntary spirit of committed minority	An element of compulsion; self-sacrifice; no strong widespread unwillingness	Encouraged volunteering (neigher compulsory nor exceptional); self-sacrifice; general enthusiasm

of illiterates now occurring and likely to continue to occur in the world, it can have little more than the symbolic — albeit certainly worthwhile — meaning of lighting a candle rather than cursing the dark.

Eliminating the campaign and project patterns as global options does not *ipso facto* prevent certain of their elements from being useful for (and transferable to) the remaining global option: the program pattern. More systematic than the project pattern, yet more realistic (in most socio-political settings) than the campaign pattern, the program pattern could be enriched, systematized, and generalized by incorporating elements of both.

The remainder of this chapter is, then, devoted to an attempt to identify (a) major drawbacks of the program pattern as analyzed above, and (b) which experience gained under the project and campaign patterns offer guidance for overcoming those drawbacks.

1. Like the campaign pattern, the program pattern (at least as expressed in study service) is found only in a small number of countries in the world. Unlike the campaign pattern, however, the program pattern is present in countries with a variety of socioeconomic systems and does not require revolutionary change as a precondition to its existence.

2. A second problem with the program pattern is that although a relatively high percentage of potentially 'mobilizable' youth populations are in fact mobilized where study service exists, the 'mobilizable' populations themselves tend to be small. This is linked in turn with the minimum age and educational attainment requirements.

3. Another drawback identified in the program pattern is that only a few of the study-service schemes examined do literacy work, and even then, literacy work is not always a central activity. Experience acquired in the campaign pattern suggests that educated young people may be uniquely suited to participate in the provision of that part of development with which they have relatively extensive personal experience: education, and more particularly, the 3 Rs.

4. Like the campaign pattern, the program pattern tends to be pervasive and inclusive as regards criteria for choice of sites and target groups for literacy. Like the project pattern, it nonetheless applies a certain selectivity — and is obliged to do so for lack of manpower to meet major needs (for literacy workers *inter alia*). It seems fair to assume that if its manpower pool can be broadened and deepened by mobilization of younger teenagers, the program pattern would become less selective, although seldom if ever achieving the almost totally non-selective posting and undifferentiated target groups that characterize the campaign pattern.

5. Project-pattern sponsoring bodies tend to work as non-governmental loners, with occasional co-operation from other NGOs and, more importantly, occasional *ad hoc* funding from governments. In contrast, a factor for the success of the program and more particularly the campaign patterns seems to be the degree to which they are able to involve large numbers of other bodies, governmental and non-governmental, in a kind of coalition focused on youth's participation in literacy.

6. Many more young people could be involved in literacy work without jeopardizing its quality if the minimum age and educational attainments requirements of the campaign pattern were applied to the program pattern.

Similarly, the program pattern might benefit from a re-examination of the geographical and socioeconomic backgrounds of the youth pool from which it recruits. To date, like the project pattern, the program pattern has tended to limit itself to middle- and upper-class youth mainly from urban areas.

7. Clear in the above table is the limited intensity of youth's participation in literacy under the program pattern, compared with both other patterns. Indeed, it appears improbable that an aggregate total youth involvement of a few weeks or very few months can make for very effective literacy work. With regard to the length of participation, then, the program pattern could probably be improved by extending the aggregate minimum requirement for involvement in literacy teaching to at least five or six months.

8. Finally, there is the all-important question of compulsion. Obligatory study service and stricty voluntary service both have their rationales and their staunch partisans. While not offering a definitive answer, this chapter's comparison of the three patterns suggests that if (a) the degree of compulsion present in study service does not automatically lead to widespread or strong unwillingness among young people, nevertheless (b) a voluntary approach does appear to correlate with serious commitment (project pattern, in which participation is an exception) or general enthusiasm (campaign pattern, where participation is more the norm). In most cases, and if only because of limited resources, attempts to enrich, systematize and generalize the program pattern of youth involvement in provision of literacy need not necessarily depend upon compulsion as a means of mobilization.

REFERENCES

This chapter is an adapted version of an article written by Arthur Gillette that originally appeared in the *International Review of Education* (UNESCO Institute for Education, Hamburg) No. XXXI. The views expressed are not necessarily of UNESCO.

Arnove, R. F. (1981). 'The Nicaraguan National Literacy Crusade of 1980', *Comparative Education Review.* 25, No.2.

Conversation with Juan B. Arrién (1985), Director General, Planning Office, Ministry of Education of Nicaragua, March.

See Atta Donkor, F. (1985) 'Ghana: Education for Development among Non-Literate Rural Inhabitants'. *New from CCIVS.* No. 1.

Bhola, H. S. (1984). *Campaigning for Literacy.* Paris: UNESCO.

Cardenal, F. and Miller, V. (1982). 'Nicaragua: Literacy and Revolution'. *Prospects.* 12, No. 2.

Volunteering in Literacy Work: A Guide to National and International Opportunities (1985). Paris; Co-ordinating Committee for International Voluntary Service.

La Educacion en el Primer Ano de la Revolucion Popular Sandinista (1980). Managua: Ministry of Education

Mammo, G. (1984). *The National Literacy Campaign in Ethopia; A Case Study.* Addis Ababa; National Literacy Campaign Office and Department of Adult Education, Ministry of Education. Paper for CODE/CIDA Seminar for Programme Planners, December.

Mammo, G.; Bayouh, G.; and Aberra, A. (1983). In Bhola, H. S., with Müller, J., and Dijkstra, P. (eds). *The Promise of Literacy: Campaigns, Programs and Projects.* Baden-Baden: Nomos Ver lagsgesellschaft.

Nicaragua: For the Eradication of Illiteracy (1983). Prague: International Union of Students, Undated.

Rothshuh, T. G. and Tamez, C. (eds.) (1983). *La Cruzada de Alfabetization de Nicaragua: su Organization Y Estratégias de Participation y Movilizacion.* Paris; UNESCO (ED-83/WS/62).

Torres, R. M. (1983). *De Alfabetizando a Maestro Popular; La Post-Alfabetizacion en Nicaragua.* Managua; Instituto de Investigaciones Económicas y Sociales and Coordinadora Regional de Investigaciones Económicas y Sociales.

Study Service; A Tool if Innovation in Higher Education (1984). Paris; UNESCO.